MW00579145

HORACE: ODES

BOOK II

A COMMENTARY ON
HORACE
Odes, BOOK II

BY

R. G. M. NISBET

AND

MARGARET HUBBARD

PAUL VI H.S. LIBRARY
10675 LEE HIGHWAY
FAIRFAX, VA 22030

CLARENDON PRESS · OXFORD

*This book has been printed digitally and produced in a standard specification
in order to ensure its continuing availability*

OXFORD
UNIVERSITY PRESS

Great Clarendon Street, Oxford OX2 6DP

Oxford University Press is a department of the University of Oxford.
It furthers the University's objective of excellence in research, scholarship,
and education by publishing worldwide in

Oxford New York

Auckland Bangkok Buenos Aires Cape Town Chennai
Dar es Salaam Delhi Hong Kong Istanbul Karachi Kolkata
Kuala Lumpur Madrid Melbourne Mexico City Mumbai Nairobi
São Paulo Shanghai Taipei Tokyo Toronto

Oxford is a registered trade mark of Oxford University Press
in the UK and in certain other countries

Published in the United States
by Oxford University Press Inc., New York

© R. G. M. Nisbet and Margaret Hubbard 1978

The moral rights of the author have been asserted

Database right Oxford University Press (maker)

Reprinted 2004

All rights reserved. No part of this publication may be reproduced,
stored in a retrieval system, or transmitted, in any form or by any means,
without the prior permission in writing of Oxford University Press,
or as expressly permitted by law, or under terms agreed with the appropriate
reprographics rights organization. Enquiries concerning reproduction
outside the scope of the above should be sent to the Rights Department,
Oxford University Press, at the address above

You must not circulate this book in any other binding or cover
And you must impose this same condition on any acquirer

ISBN 0-19-814771-6

PREFACE

$59.82

Recd 8/06

THIS volume follows the same lines as our commentary on the first book of Horace's *Odes* (Oxford, 1970). Once again we have tried to explain the literary tradition within which the poet wrote, and once again we have quoted a fair number of illustrative parallels. A few critics of the earlier book thought that we were denying Horace's originality, or even the merit of Latin literature in general; such misinterpretations of our position are not now worth refuting. We should add that though we are much interested in the conventions that apply to different types of poem, we deplore attempts at too schematic a classification. The student of Augustan poetry must try to divine underlying forms, but he should not go about his business in the mechanical spirit of a post-office sorter.

The second book of the *Odes* contains poems of the middle range, with an emphasis on personal relationships and practical ethics: the philosophers play a larger part than in the first book and the *lyrici* considerably less. We have tried to make the poet's friends come alive as real people, and to show how the subject-matter and tone of voice are adapted to suit the temperament of the individual. We have done more than in the first volume to suggest instances of word-play and the tension of balancing and contrasting elements. Previously we were inclined to assume that such things were either too obvious or too uncertain to be worth mentioning, but here we have been more forthcoming and perhaps less prudent.

Once again we owe much to our friends. As before, Sir Roger Mynors gave unfailing encouragement. We have been helped on various points by Mr. E. L. Bowie, Dr. J. Briscoe, Mr. M. Davies, Dr. J. G. W. Henderson, Dr. H. M. Hine, Mrs. M. C. Howatson, Professor H. D. Jocelyn, Professor I. G. Kidd, Miss J. H. Martindale, Professor D. Pingree, Mr. D. A. Russell, Professor G. J. Toomer, and Professor M. L. West. We have also benefited from discussions with pupils, both graduates and undergraduates; one eminent reviewer was surprised when we said this before, so we say it again. Our greatest debt is to our University and our two Colleges, which have provided a suitable environment for the study of Horace.

M. H.
R. G. M. N.

Oxford
November 1977

CONTENTS

BIBLIOGRAPHY

(A) EDITIONS OF THE ODES

We have included only the editions which we have found most useful. For fuller lists cf. Schanz–Hosius 2. 152, Lenchantin–Bo (cited below), vol. 1, pp. xlv ff., C. O. Brink, *Horace on Poetry: The Ars Poetica*, pp. 43 ff.

Lambinus, D.: Lyons, 1561.

Dacier, A.: Paris, 1681.

Bentley, R.: Cambridge 1711; ed. 3, Amsterdam, 1728 (reprinted 1869).

Mitscherlich, C. G.: vol. 1, Leipzig, 1800.

Peerlkamp, P. Hofman: ed. 2, Amsterdam, 1862.

Orelli, J. C., revised by J. G. Baiter and W. Hirschfelder: vol. 1, ed. 4, Berlin, 1866.

Kiessling, A.: vol. 1, ed. 2, Berlin, 1890.

Wickham, E. C.: vol. 1, ed. 3, Oxford, 1896.

Keller, O., and Holder, A. (text and parallel passages): vol. 1, ed. 2, Leipzig, 1899.

Müller, Lucian: 2 vols., St. Petersburg and Leipzig, 1900.

Shorey, P., and Laing, G. J.: ed. 2, Chicago, 1910 (reprinted Pittsburgh, 1960).

Wickham, E. C., revised by Garrod, H. W.: ed. 2, Oxford, 1912. Oxford Classical Texts.

Heinze, R.: vol. 1, Berlin, 1930 (ed. 7 of Kiessling); ed. 10, 1960, with bibliographical appendix by E. Burck.

Campbell, A. Y.: ed. 1, London, 1945: ed. 2, Liverpool, 1953.

Tescari, O.: ed. 3, Turin, 1948.

Lenchantin De Gubernatis, M., revised by Bo, D.: 3 vol. (bibliography, text, indexes), Turin, 1957–60.

Klingner, F. (text only): ed. 3, Leipzig, 1959.

Turolla, E. (text and bibliography): Turin, 1963.

(B) OTHER BOOKS CITED

This is not a full bibliography, but simply a list of the abbreviated titles used in the commentary; such references as 'André 123' may be elucidated here. We have not included periodicals, for which we follow the abbreviations of *L'Année philologique*. References to Latin texts follow the system of the index to the *Thesaurus linguae Latinae*;

Greek references can be interpreted, where necessary, from L.-S.-J.
A select bibliography is prefixed to the commentary on every ode;
the expressions 'op. cit.' and 'loc. cit.' normally point to those
bibliographies, not to this list. For further bibliographical information see Schanz–Hosius 2. 127 ff.; the editions cited above by Heinze–
Burck, Lenchantin–Bo, Turolla; K. Büchner, *JAW* 267, 1939; *Der
kleine Pauly* 2. 1224; and above all *L'Année philologique* and *Gnomon*.

Alexiou   M. Alexiou, *The Ritual Lament in Greek Tradition*,
                       Cambridge, 1974.

ALL   *Archiv für lateinische Lexikographie und Gram-
                       matik*, ed. E. Wölfflin, Leipzig, 1884–1909.

Allen·   W. S. Allen, *Vox Latina, A Guide to the Pro-
                       nunciation of Classical Latin*, Cambridge, 1965.

André   J. André, *Études sur les termes de couleur dans la
                       langue latine*, Paris, 1949.

Axelson   B. Axelson, *Unpoetische Wörter, ein Beitrag zur
                       Kenntnis der lateinischen Dichtersprache*, Lund,
                       1945.

Beazley, *ABV*   J. D. Beazley, *Attic Black-figure Vase-Painters*,
                       Oxford, 1956.

Beazley, *ARV²*   J. D. Beazley, *Attic Red-figure Vase-Painters*,
                       ed. 2, Oxford, 1963.

Bell   A. J. Bell, *The Latin Dual and Poetic Diction*,
                       London, 1923.

Blümner   H. Blümner, *Römische Privataltertümer*, Munich,
                       1911.

Blümner, *Technologie* H. Blümner, *Technologie und Terminologie der
                       Gewerbe und Künste bei Griechen und Römern*,
                       Leipzig, 1875–87 (vol. 1, ed. 2, 1912).

Boucher   J.-P. Boucher, *Études sur Properce: problèmes
                       d'inspiration et d'art*, Paris, 1965.

Bowersock   G. W. Bowersock, *Augustus and the Greek World*,
                       Oxford, 1965.

Bramble   J. C. Bramble, *Persius and the Programmatic
                       Satire*, Cambridge, 1974.

Bruchmann   C. F. H. Bruchmann, *Epitheta Deorum quae apud
                       poetas Graecos leguntur*, Leipzig, 1893 (sup-
                       plement in Roscher, vol. 7).

Brunt   P. A. Brunt, *Italian Manpower, 225 B.C.–A.D. 14*,
                       Oxford, 1971.

Bücheler, *Kl. Schr.* F. Bücheler, *Kleine Schriften*, Leipzig, 1915–
                       1930.

Buffière   F. Buffière, *Les Mythes d'Homère et la pensée
                       grecque*, Paris, 1956.

CAH	*The Cambridge Ancient History*, Cambridge, 1923– .
Cairns	F. Cairns, *Generic Composition in Greek and Roman Poetry*, Edinburgh, 1972.
Carter	J. B. Carter, *Epitheta Deorum quae apud poetas Latinos leguntur*, Leipzig, 1902 (supplement in Roscher, vol. 7).
CGL	*Corpus Glossariorum Latinorum*, ed. G. Goetz, Leipzig, 1888–1923.
Cichorius	C. Cichorius, *Römische Studien*, Berlin, 1922.
CIE	*Corpus Inscriptionum Etruscarum*, Leipzig, 1893– .
CIL	*Corpus Inscriptionum Latinarum*, Berlin, 1863– .
Commager	S. Commager, *The Odes of Horace: A Critical Study*, New Haven and London, 1962.
Cook	A. B. Cook, *Zeus, A Study in Ancient Religion*, Cambridge, 1914–40.
Corp. paroem. gr.	*Corpus paroemiographorum Graecorum*, ed. E. L. Leutsch and F. C. Schneidewin, Göttingen, 1839–51 (reprinted Hildesheim 1958).
Costa	C. D. N. Costa (ed.), *Horace*, London and Boston, 1973.
Curtius	E. R. Curtius, *European Literature and the Latin Middle Ages*, translated by Willard R. Trask, London, 1953.
D'Arcy Thompson, *Birds*	D'Arcy W. Thompson, *A Glossary of Greek Birds*, London and Oxford, 1936 (reprinted Hildesheim, 1966).
D'Arcy Thompson, *Fishes*	D'Arcy W. Thompson, *A Glossary of Greek Fishes*, London and Oxford, 1947.
Darnley Naylor	H. Darnley Naylor, *Horace, Odes and Epodes*, Cambridge, 1922.
Dieterich	A. Dieterich, *Nekyia, Beiträge zur Erklärung der neuentdeckten Petrusapokalypse*, ed. 2, Leipzig and Berlin, 1913 (reprinted 1969).
Dilke	O. A. W. Dilke, *The Roman Land Surveyors*, Newton Abbot, 1971.
Doblhofer	E. Doblhofer, *Die Augustuspanegyrik des Horaz in formalhistorischer Sicht*, Heidelberg, 1966.
Dodds	E. R. Dodds, *The Greeks and the Irrational*, Berkeley, 1951.
Dover	K. J. Dover, *Greek Popular Morality in the time of Plato and Aristotle*, Oxford, 1974.

D.–S. C. Daremberg and E. Saglio, *Dictionnaire des antiquités grecques et romaines d'après les textes et les monuments*, Paris, 1877–1919.

Earl D. C. Earl, *The Political Thought of Sallust*, Cambridge, 1961.

Esteve-Forriol J. Esteve-Forriol, *Die Trauer- und Trostgedichte in der römischen Literatur*, Diss. Munich, 1962.

FGrH *Die Fragmente der griechischen Historiker*, ed. F. Jacoby, Berlin–Leiden, 1923– .

Fraenkel E. Fraenkel, *Horace*, Oxford, 1957.

Fraenkel, *Kl. Beitr.* E. Fraenkel, *Kleine Beiträge zur klassischen Philologie*, Rome, 1964.

Fraenkel, *Plautinisches* E. Fraenkel, *Plautinisches im Plautus*, Berlin, 1922 (cf. *Elementi plautini in Plauto*, translated by F. Munari, Florence, 1960).

Friedrich G. Friedrich, *Q. Horatius Flaccus: Philologische Untersuchungen*, Leipzig, 1894.

Gatz B. Gatz, *Weltalter, goldene Zeit und sinnverwandte Vorstellungen*, Hildesheim, 1967.

Gerhard G. A. Gerhard, *Phoinix von Kolophon*, Leipzig and Berlin, 1909.

Gigante M. Gigante, *Ricerche filodemee*, Naples, 1969.

Gow–Page, *GP* *The Greek Anthology: The Garland of Philip and some contemporary epigrams*, ed. A. S. F. Gow and D. L. Page, Cambridge, 1968.

Gow–Page, *HE* *The Greek Anthology: Hellenistic Epigrams*, ed. A. S. F. Gow and D. L. Page, Cambridge, 1965.

Grassmann V. Grassmann, *Die erotischen Epoden des Horaz*, Munich, 1966.

Grimal P. Grimal, *Les Jardins romains*, ed. 2, Paris, 1969.

Hadot I. Hadot, *Seneca und die griechisch-römische Tradition der Seelenleitung*, Berlin, 1969.

Hand F. Hand, *Tursellinus seu de particulis Latinis commentarii*, Leipzig, 1829–45 (reprinted Amsterdam, 1969).

Head B. V. Head, *Historia Numorum: A Manual of Greek Numismatics*, ed. 2, Oxford, 1911.

Hehn V. Hehn, *Kulturpflanzen und Haustiere*, ed. 8, Berlin, 1911.

Henry J. Henry, *Aeneidea*, London, 1873–1892 (reprinted Hildesheim, 1969).

Heurgon J. Heurgon, *La Vie quotidienne chez les Étrusques* Paris, 1961.

Housman   *The Classical Papers of A. E. Housman: collected and edited by J. Diggle and F. R. D. Goodyear*, Cambridge, 1972.

H.-Sz.   J. B. Hofmann, *Lateinische Syntax und Stilistik*, neubearbeitet von A. Szantyr, Munich, 1965.

IG   *Inscriptiones Graecae*, ed. maior, Berlin, 1873–1939.

ILS   H. Dessau, *Inscriptiones Latinae selectae*, Berlin, 1892–1916.

inscr. Ital.   *Inscriptiones Italiae*, Rome, 1931– .

Irwin   E. Irwin, *Colour Terms in Greek Poetry*, Toronto, 1974.

Kaibel, *EG*   G. Kaibel, *Epigrammata Graeca ex lapidibus conlecta*, Berlin, 1878 (reprinted Hildesheim, 1965).

Kambylis   A. Kambylis, *Die Dichterweihe und ihre Symbolik*, Heidelberg, 1965.

Kassel   R. Kassel, *Untersuchungen zur griechischen und römischen Konsolationsliteratur*, Munich, 1958 (*Zetemata* 18).

K.-G.   R. Kühner and B. Gerth, *Ausführliche Grammatik der griechischen Sprache: Satzlehre*, ed. 3, Hanover, 1904 (reprinted 1955).

Kier   H. Kier, *De laudibus vitae rusticae*, Diss. Marburg, 1933.

Klingner, *Studien*   F. Klingner, *Studien zur griechischen und römischen Literatur*, Zürich and Stuttgart, 1964.

Kroll   W. Kroll, *Studien zum Verständnis der römischen Literatur*, Stuttgart, 1924 (reprinted Darmstadt, 1964).

K.-S.   R. Kühner and C. Stegmann, *Ausführliche Grammatik der lateinischen Sprache: Satzlehre*, ed. 3, revised by A. Thierfelder, Darmstadt, 1955.

Latte   K. Latte, *Römische Religionsgeschichte*, Munich, 1960.

Lattimore   R. Lattimore, *Themes in Greek and Latin Epitaphs*, Urbana, 1962 (= *Illinois Studies in Language and Literature* 28, 1942, 1–2).

Lilja   S. Lilja, *The Roman Elegists' Attitude to Women*, Helsinki, 1965.

L.-S.-J.   H. G. Liddell and R. Scott, *A Greek–English Lexicon*, ed. 9, revised by H. Stuart Jones, Oxford, 1940.

Löfstedt, *Peregrinatio*   E. Löfstedt, *Philologischer Kommentar zur Peregrinatio Aetheriae*, Uppsala, 1911.

Löfstedt, *Syntactica*   E. Löfstedt, *Syntactica: Studien und Beiträge zur historischen Syntax des Lateins*, Lund, vol. 1, ed. 2, 1956; vol. 2, 1933.

Malcovati, *ORF*²   H. Malcovati, *Oratorum Romanorum Fragmenta liberae rei publicae*, ed. 2, Turin, 1955.

McGann   M. J. McGann, *Studies in Horace's First Book of Epistles* (*Coll. Latomus* 100), Brussels, 1969.

Neue–Wagener   F. Neue and C. Wagener, *Formenlehre der lateinischen Sprache*, ed. 3, Berlin, 1892–1905.

Newman   J. K. Newman, *Augustus and the New Poetry* (*Coll. Latomus* 88), Brussels, 1967.

Nilsson, *GGR*   M. P. Nilsson, *Geschichte der griechischen Religion*, Munich, vol. 1³, 1967; vol. 2², 1961.

Nissen   H. Nissen, *Italische Landeskunde*, Berlin, vol. 1, 1883; vol. 2, 1902.

Nock   A. D. Nock, *Essays on Religion and the Ancient World*, ed. Z. Stewart, Oxford, 1972.

Norden, *Agnostos Theos*   E. Norden, *Agnostos Theos: Untersuchungen zur Formengeschichte religiöser Rede*, Berlin, 1913 (reprinted Darmstadt, 1956).

Norden, *Kl.Schr.*   E. Norden, *Kleine Schriften zum klassischen Altertum*, Berlin, 1966.

OED   *A New English Dictionary on Historical Principles*, Oxford, 1888– .

Oltramare   . A. Oltramare, *Les Origines de la diatribe romaine*, Geneva, 1926.

Onians   R. B. Onians, *The Origins of European Thought about the Body, the Mind, the Soul, the World, Time, and Fate*, ed. 2, Cambridge, 1954.

Oppermann   H. Oppermann (ed.), *Wege zu Horaz*, Darmstadt, 1972.

Otto   A. Otto, *Die Sprichwörter und sprichwörtlichen Redensarten der Römer*, Leipzig, 1890 (reprinted Hildesheim, 1962).

Otto, *Nachträge*   *Nachträge zu A. Otto, Sprichwörter . . .*, ed. R. Häussler, Darmstadt, 1968.

Ox. pap.   *The Oxyrhynchus Papyri*, London, 1898– .

Page, *EG*   D. L. Page (ed.), *Epigrammata Graeca*, Oxford, 1975.

Page, *Sappho and Alcaeus*   Denys Page, *Sappho and Alcaeus*, Oxford, 1955.

Pape–Benseler   W. Pape and G. F. Benseler, *Wörterbuch der griechischen Eigennamen*, Brunswick, ed. 3, 1911 (reprinted Graz, 1959).

Pasquali — G. Pasquali, *Orazio lirico*, Florence, 1920 (reprinted with additions by A. La Penna, 1964).

Peek, *GV* — W. Peek, *Griechische Vers-Inschriften I*, Berlin, 1955.

Péron — J. Péron, *Les Images maritimes de Pindare*, Paris, 1974.

PIR — *Prosopographia Imperii Romani*, ed. 1, Berlin, 1897–8.

PIR² — *Prosopographia Imperii Romani*, ed. 2, Berlin and Leipzig, 1933– .

Platner–Ashby — S. B. Platner and T. Ashby, *Topographical Dictionary of Ancient Rome*, Oxford, 1929.

Plüss — Th. Plüss, *Horazstudien*, Leipzig, 1882.

PMG — *Poetae Melici Graeci*, ed. D. L. Page, Oxford, 1962.

Pohlenz — M. Pohlenz, *Die Stoa*, ed. 3, Göttingen, 1964.

Powell — J. U. Powell, *Collectanea Alexandrina*, Oxford, 1925.

Quinn — K. Quinn, *Latin Explorations*, London, 1963.

RE — *Real-Encyclopädie der classischen Altertumswissenschaft*, Stuttgart, 1893– .

Ribbeck, *TRF³* — O. Ribbeck, *Tragicorum Romanorum Fragmenta*, ed. 3, Leipzig, 1897.

RLAC — *Reallexikon für Antike und Christentum*, Stuttgart, 1950– .

Rohde, *Psyche* — E. Rohde, *Psyche* (English translation), London, 1925.

Rohde, *Roman³* — E. Rohde, *Der griechische Roman und seine Vorläufer*, ed. 3, Leipzig, 1914 (reprinted Hildesheim, 1960).

Roscher — W. H. Roscher, *Ausführliches Lexikon der griechischen und römischen Mythologie*, Leipzig, 1884–1937 (reprinted Hildesheim, 1965–).

Ross — D. O. Ross, Jr., *Style and Tradition in Catullus*, Harvard, 1969.

Schanz–Hosius — M. Schanz and C. Hosius, *Geschichte der römischen Literatur*, Munich, vol. 2, ed. 4, 1935.

Segal — C. P. Segal, *Landscape in Ovid's Metamorphoses* (*Hermes Einzelschriften* 23), Wiesbaden, 1969.

Shackleton Bailey, *Propertiana* — D. R. Shackleton Bailey, *Propertiana*, Cambridge, 1956.

Silk — M. S. Silk, *Interaction in Poetic Imagery with special reference to early Greek poetry*, Cambridge, 1974.

Stemplinger   E. Stemplinger, *Das Plagiat in der griechischen Literatur*, Leipzig, 1912.

Stroh   W. Stroh, *Die römische Liebeselegie als werbende Dichtung*, Amsterdam, 1971.

Suerbaum   W. Suerbaum, *Untersuchungen zur Selbstdarstellung älterer römischer Dichter (Spudasmata 19)*, Hildesheim, 1968.

SVF   *Stoicorum Veterum Fragmenta*, ed. J. von Arnim, Leipzig, 1905 (reprinted Stuttgart, 1964).

Syme   R. Syme, *The Roman Revolution*, Oxford, 1939.

Syndikus   H. P. Syndikus, *Die Lyrik des Horaz: eine Interpretation der Oden*, Darmstadt, 1972–3.

Taillardat   J. Taillardat, *Les Images d'Aristophane: études de langue et de style*, Paris, 1962.

Thes.l.L.   *Thesaurus linguae Latinae*, Leipzig, 1900– .

Troxler-Keller   I. Troxler-Keller, *Die Dichterlandschaft des Horaz*, Heidelberg, 1964.

van Geytenbeek   A. C. ·van Geytenbeek, *Musonius Rufus and Greek Diatribe*, Assen, 1963.

Vian   F. Vian, *La Guerre des géants: le mythe avant l'époque hellénistique (Études et commentaires 11)*, Paris, 1952.

Vischer   R. Vischer, *Das einfache Leben*, Göttingen, 1965.

Wackernagel,   J. Wackernagel, *Vorlesungen über Syntax*, ed. 2,
Vorlesungen   Basle, 1926–8.

Wagenvoort   H. Wagenvoort, *Studies in Roman Literature, Culture and Religion*, Leiden, 1956.

Weinstock   S. Weinstock, *Divus Julius*, Oxford, 1971.

Wilamowitz,   U. von Wilamowitz-Moellendorff, *Hellenistische
Hellenistische*   Dichtung in der Zeit des Kallimachos*, ed. 2,
Dichtung   Berlin, 1924 (reprinted, 1962).

Wilamowitz, *Kl.*   U. von Wilamowitz-Moellendorff, *Kleine Schrif-
Schr.*   ten*, Berlin and Amsterdam, 1971.

Wilamowitz, *Sappho*   U. von Wilamowitz-Moellendorff, *Sappho und
und Simonides*   Simonides*, Berlin, 1913 (reprinted 1966).

Wilkinson   L. P. Wilkinson, *Horace and his Lyric Poetry*, ed. 2, Cambridge, 1951.

Wille   G. Wille, *Musica Romana*, Amsterdam, 1967.

Williams   G. Williams, *Tradition and Originality in Roman Poetry*, Oxford, 1968.

Wissowa   G. Wissowa, *Religion und Kultus der Römer*, ed. 2, Munich, 1912.

Wistrand   E. Wistrand, *Opera Selecta*, Stockholm, 1972.

Wölfflin   E. Wölfflin, *Ausgewählte Schriften*, Leipzig, 1933.

THE SECOND BOOK OF
HORACE'S *ODES*

THE first three books of Horace's *Odes* were issued together, apparently in the latter part of 23 B.C. (vol. i, pp. xxv ff.). Yet the second book, though part of a larger whole, has a coherence of its own in terms of subject-matter, tone of voice, and arrangement. The following pages briefly indicate some of these particular features, and should be regarded simply as supplementary to the introduction of the first volume.[1]

The characteristics of the book may first be suggested in a negative form. The only political poem in the full sense is the opening ode with its eulogy of Pollio's history and its denunciation of civil war; in the last stanza Horace announces an intention of reverting to lighter subjects, and though he obviously exaggerates the triviality of the rest of the book, he avoids thereafter grand themes and a grand manner except where some irony is intended. Licinius Murena's fall from favour is treated from a personal rather than a national standpoint (2. 10), criticisms of luxury are linked to Augustan ideals only by implication (in 2. 15 more than in 2. 18), allusions to contemporary wars are oblique (2. 12. 1 ff., pp. 184 ff.), detached (2. 2. 17 ff., 2. 7. 1 ff., 2. 11. 1 ff.), or even semi-humorous (2. 6. 1 ff., 2. 9. 17 ff.). There is little of the ostentatious imitation of Greek lyric poets that is such a feature of the first book (though one may note the 'motto' from Bacchylides at 2. 18. 1 ff.), and there are no narrative odes on mythological subjects such as Paris (1. 15) or Europa (3. 27). Instead of the metrical virtuosity of Book I (where the first nine odes are all in different metres), there is a striking preponderance of Alcaics (12 poems) and of Sapphics (6 poems), with other metres only in the twelfth and eighteenth odes (contrast the 15 Asclepiad-based poems of Book I and the 11 of Book III). None of the poems has more than ten stanzas (compared with 2 in Book I and 10 in Book III), and only 1 has less than six (compared with 24 in Book I and 13 in Book III); no fewer than 9 of the 20 poems have six stanzas (compared with 3 out of 38 in Book I and 2 out of 30 in Book III), and this *mediocritas* is typical of the book as a whole, though not always so easy to quantify.

[1] R. G. M. Nisbet and M. Hubbard, *A Commentary on Horace, Odes I*, Oxford, 1970, pp. xi ff.

On the more positive side 13 out of the 20 poems are directly addressed to living individuals, to say nothing of the neglected allusions to
Maecenas in the eighteenth ode (pp. 282 f.) ; the corresponding figures
are 10 out of 38 in Book I and 5 out of 30 in Book III. The distinction
between real and fictitious persons should never be disregarded in
Horace, and poems addressed to the former are naturally coloured by
the interests and ethos of the addressee. Many of the references must
now escape us, but others can be guessed at with more or less probability (see the commentary). Sallustius seems to have sympathized
with the Stoics (2) and Dellius perhaps with the Epicureans (3),
Licinius certainly with the Peripatetics (10, pp. 152 f.), Postumus was
a religious man and possibly even a *pontifex* (14), Maecenas a devotee
of astrology (17, p. 273). The tone of voice is austere to Pollio, though
developing excitement and passion (1), genial to Dellius (3) and
Valgius (9), reticent to Postumus (14), romantic or theatrical to
Maecenas (12, 17). A friend's characteristics are often a subject for
humour : for instance there are mild jokes on the name of Grosphus
(2. 16. 17 n.) and possibly of Sallustius Crispus (2. 2. 3 n.), Septimius
is teased for his restless ambition (6, p. 94), Valgius for his sentimental elegies (9, pp. 136 f.), Postumus for his excessive scrupulosity
(14), Grosphus for his admiring cows (16), Maecenas for the discrepancy between his public and private faces (2. 12. 10 n.), for his
eschatological fantasies (17), and apparently for his exotic palace
(18, p. 289). A tactful sympathy is also characteristic of such poems ;
Horace consoles the exiled Pompeius by exaggerating his own lack
of resolution (7), the dismissed Licinius by Peripatetic maxims and
hints of better things (10, p. 157), the hypochondriac Maecenas by
agreeably overdrawn protestations of affection (17, pp. 273 f.). Taken
as a whole the book gives a highly original expression of *amicitia*
in a manner that foreshadows the later *Epistles* (though indeed the
writing of the two collections may to some extent have overlapped).
Such *amicitia* might not often be friendship between equals in the
modern sense ; Horace rather exemplifies a feeling for the *decorum*
in a variety of personal relationships within the complicated structure of Roman society.

This feeling is part of a wider interest in conduct that is naturally
expressed in philosophic terms (so much more significant in Roman
than in Hellenistic poetry) ; we are moving in the area where Cicero
had applied Greek enlightenment to upper-class Roman society. As
has been seen, Horace tends to draw on the great systems according to the interests of his addressee, but in general an Epicurean
humanity dominates, though without an Epicurean dogmatism. His
lively illustrations may sometimes depend on popular *diatribae*[1] (to

[1] W. Kroll, *WS* 37, 1915, 223 ff.

use a word of more convenience than precision) ; certainly his use of prosaic medical metaphors gives a new direction to the traditional associations of the Sapphic stanza (2. 2. 13 ff.). Though such witty eclecticism could have no interest for the technicians of the schools, it is wrong to regard it simply as a novel form of poetic ornament. Like other serious men of his day, Horace must have thought that philosophy was about something.

The book also contains an important encomiastic element, directed for the most part at significant personalities of the second rank (Pollio and Maecenas are obvious exceptions). It is a commonplace of modern Pindaric scholarship that insufficient attention has been paid to the *laudandus*;[1] the same thing could be said of Horace to a certain extent, yet his encomia (except for the set-piece 2. 1) are usually much less obvious than those of his Greek predecessors. Though the gratitude of the addressees must sometimes have taken a material form, he is particularly careful not to emphasize this aspect : the ode to Sallustius implicitly eulogizes the great man's use of wealth, but does not acknowledge any personal interest (2) ; the odes to Maecenas say nothing of his munificence (12, 17), though elsewhere a declaration of content is clearly intended as a *eucharisticon* (18, p. 290). Usually Horace insinuates his compliments indirectly, as when he praises Dellius's *horti* (3) or Postumus's happy marriage (14) ; in dealing with individuals as with the regime he understood that too obvious flattery tends to be counter-productive. Above all his genial humour may emphasize the amiability of the recipient, who in spite of his distinction is unwilling to stand on his dignity (see especially 9, 12).

The *Odes* are rhetorical (if one may dare to use the word in an unprejudicial sense), that is to say they seem designed to influence attitudes and actions (vol. i, p. xxv) ; even when Horace talks to himself, he counsels rather than meditates (5, p. 77). This aspect is particularly conspicuous in the second book (note the headings in the manuscripts of the type *paraenetice*). A lyric poet like Pindar had not hesitated to give advice even to Hieron,[2] but his gravest admonitions may say no more than what the ruler himself wishes to hear (cf. the symbouleutic treatises of a later age, or such speeches as Cicero's *pro Marcello*). Horace was more conscious than Pindar of social inferiority, and though he follows the literary tradition by speaking as man to man, his actual candour can easily be exaggerated.[3] Sometimes the great man is encouraged to adopt a position that he holds already, or thinks that he holds ; when Sallustius is

---

[1] E. L. Bundy, *Univ. California Publ. Class. Phil.* 18, 1962, 1 ff.

[2] See, for example, *P.* 1. 92 ff., A. Köhnken, *Hermes* 98, 1970, 1 ff.

[3] As by N. W. De Witt on the 'parrhesiastic poems', *CPh* 30, 1935, 312 ff.

advised to be generous (2, p. 33), or Dellius to be resilient (3, p. 52), Horace's remarks are meant not as a criticism, as is often supposed, but as a form of encomium. Sometimes the advice seems to be intended semi-humorously, as when the sentimental elegist Valgius is urged to revert to patriotic poetry (9) and the self-consciously moral Quinctius to relax at a symposium (11, p. 167). It is only in the ode to Licinius Murena that Horace explicitly advises a prominent man to revise his conduct (10), but even there his professed paraenesis seems largely a commissioned deprecation to Augustus (p. 157); he would not have written thus to Murena in the days of his power, or to Pollio ever.

Because of the lack of political poems little is certain about the chronology of the second book. A date before Actium might be assigned to the ode to Pollio (1) and to the long *diatribe* on luxury (18), but in both cases the balance of the arguments could easily be tilted the other way (see pp. 10, 290 f.). The ode to Dellius (3) must be placed after Actium, when its hero returned from the East (p. 52), and the same is probably true of the ode to Pompeius (7, p. 107). If the poem on the fallen tree (13) imitates Virgil's 'Orpheus episode', that most naturally puts it after 29 (p. 201); it would carry with it 17, the astrological poem to Maecenas (this reverses the argument of vol. i, p. 244). The ode to Valgius (9) must have been written after January 27 B.C., when Octavian assumed the name of Augustus, and perhaps before the Cantabrian campaign of 26 (p. 138); this last is apparently alluded to in the *recusatio* to Maecenas (2. 12. 1 n.), and probably also in the poem to Septimius (6, p. 94), though the reference in the poem to Quinctius should possibly be assigned rather to 29 (11, p. 170). The love-poems are usually impossible to date, but in the ode to Xanthias Horace claims to be now forty (2. 4. 23 f.), an age that he reached in December 25. The ode to Licinius Murena should probably be assigned to 23 B.C., though not everybody would agree (pp. 156 f.). The last poem in the book (20) is also presumably late, as it seems designed for the publication of the collection.

At this point a difficulty must be faced and controversy encouraged. Some metrical divergences in Horace's Alcaics seem to suggest that though the first three books of odes were issued together, Book II occupies in some respects an intermediate position between Books I and III (see the tables in vol. i, pp. xlii f.); for a further argument add the note on *atque* and *ac* at 2. 19. 11. We attempted to explain the difference between Books I and II by assigning part of the former to the triumviral period (vol. i, pp. xxviii ff.); this still seems to be a plausible date for Horace's metrical experiments (the Cleopatra Ode in 30 B.C. was surely not the first), and indeed we should now be more strongly inclined to fit 1. 14 there on political grounds. But it is less easy to relate Book II to Book III, where the metrical discrepancies are at least as conspicuous: the reference to morality and public building in 3. 6 is naturally assigned to 28 B.C. or thereabouts, yet as has been seen, the datable poems of the second book seem largely to spread over the following years. The most striking metrical novelty in Book III lies in the great increase of lines of the type *fatalis incestusque iudex* (i.e. Alcaic enneasyllables ending with a disyllable that is itself preceded by a word longer than a disyllable); these number 5 per cent of the total enneasyllables in Book I, 5·8 per cent in II, 24·6 in III, 30·2 in IV. We are now inclined to think that the type is particularly favoured in the more high-flown and formal odes, and that it is not by itself a reliable criterion of date; thus of the three instances in Book I two are in grandiose contexts (1. 34. 11, 1. 37. 11), and the same is true of four of the five instances in Book II (2. 1. 31, 2. 1. 35, 2. 13. 19, 2. 14. 19, while 2. 20. 11 might be regarded as mock-grandiloquent). Similarly of the twenty-nine instances of the pattern in Book III, nine are in 3. 4, thirteen more in the other Roman Odes (excluding the second), six in 3. 29, but none in the slighter 3. 17, 3. 21, 3. 23. It is noteworthy how even a single poem may show different metrical characteristics in different parts; see 2. 13. 7 n. for the oddities in the impetuous first half of the ode on the tree.

The book contains 20 odes (a number of such collections have a decimal basis), and as usual is arranged with a measure of design.[1] The opening ode is a dedication to Pollio, the most eminent of Horace's addressees, and the concluding stanza points to the rest of the book (2. 1. 37 n.); the last poem (20) is correspondingly addressed to Maecenas (who was honoured by the opening ode of the first book), and its character as a *sphragis* (p. 335) shows that it was also designed for its position (cf. 3. 30). The last poem of the first half (10) is addressed to Licinius Murena, who was certainly Maecenas's brother-in-law (pp. 152 f.); further symmetry would be obtained if the Quinctius of poem 11 were Pollio's brother-in-law (p. 168). In the first half of the book Alcaics and Sapphics alternate (cf. the alternation of dialogues and monologues in the bucolics of Virgil and Calpurnius, and of hendecasyllables and distichs in *Priapea* 1–14); if 1 and 10 are excluded, then 2–9 break up into pairs of poems with contrasting metres and more or less similar topics. Thus 2 and 3 recommend different philosophies to Sallustius and Dellius, both public men of the second rank (the juxtaposition of a Sallustius with

---

[1] Cf. especially vol. i, pp. xxiii f., W. Port, *Philologus* 81, 1926, 299 f., W. Ludwig, *Hermes* 85, 1957, 336 ff.; for bibliography see F.-H. Mutschler, *RhM* 117, 1974, 132 f., and for other Augustan authors V. Buchheit, *Studien zur Corpus Priapeorum*, 1962, p. 45 n. 3.

Pollio may also be deliberate); in 4 and 5 Horace advises Xanthias and himself on romanticized love-affairs; 6 and 7 are poems about comradeship and quietism that begin with *mecum* and end with *amici(o)*; 8 and 9 treat of love again in the elegiac manner, though the resemblance here is not close (some scholars go too far in seeing a pointed contrast between infidelity and excessive devotion). Port and Ludwig (opp. citt.) wish to regard 10 and 11 as another semi-philosophical pair, but the former seems too serious and the latter not philosophical enough; they think that the opening poem (on Pollio's history) is balanced by 12 (where Maecenas is incidentally invited to write a prose work on Augustus), but this is to split the book at a quite unconvincing place.

The second half of the book yields no correspondingly clear principle of arrangement (though all the odd-numbered poems continue to be written in Alcaics). 19 and 20 might be described in the vaguest sense as mythological fantasies, but it is implausible to regard them as both poems about Horace's poetry (this aspect of Bacchus is not underlined), or to compare the carefully delineated Bacchus of 19 with the unmentioned Apollo of 20. 17 and 18 both deal with death and with Maecenas (p. 289), and set the patron's grandeur against the poet's simplicity, but one cannot pretend that they make an obvious pair. 15 bears no relation whatever to 16, but perhaps some to 18 (both are *diatribae* against luxury); 16 and 17 would then have to go together (Port), but it seems unimportant that both end with a comparison between Horace and a richer friend. 13 and 14 can be combined more realistically as they are both Alcaic poems dealing with the underworld, but there is no significant connection between 11 and 12 (even if both encourage a busy man to think of pleasure rather than politics). It will be evident from the above that there are great dangers in too subtle an analysis of the arrangement of the book. The organization is most apparent in the first half, particularly in the formal aspect of metre; otherwise Horace may have noticed some superficial resemblances, which may or may not now be divined, but even then he was likely to have been left with a few poems that did not fit any scheme precisely. After all, he was not composing a cycle of odes, but in ancient terminology 'arranging a garland'.

1. MOTVM EX METELLO

[J. André, *La Vie et l'œuvre d'Asinius Pollion*, 1949; A. B. Bosworth, *Historia* 21, 1972, 441 ff.; Fraenkel 234 ff.; E. Gabba, *Appiano e la storia delle guerre civili*, 1956; P. Jal, *La Guerre civile à Rome*, 1963; E. Kornemann, *Die historische Schriftstellerei des C. Asinius Pollio*, *JKPh* Supp. 22, 1896, 555 ff.; C. W. Mendell, *YCIS* 1, 1928, 195 ff.; Plüss 127 ff.; O. Seeck, *WS* 24, 1902, 499 ff.; P. E. Sonnenburg, *RhM* 59, 1904, 506 ff.]

1–8. *Your theme is the civil war between Pompey and Caesar, a hazardous undertaking, as the ashes are still smouldering.* 9–16. *Lay aside tragedy for the moment, Pollio, you who are distinguished alike as orator, statesman, and soldier.* 17–28. *Already I can visualize the battles, and the subjugation of everything but Cato's spirit, when Carthage and Jugurtha were avenged at Thapsus.* 29–40. *The slaughter has extended over the whole world alike by land and sea—but such dirges are unsuited to my sportive Muse.*

The opening ode of the second book is appropriately addressed to C. Asinius Pollio, cos. 40 B.C., statesman, historian, and patron of letters. He was born in 76–5 of an old Italian family from Teate Marrucinorum (Chieti); his grandfather had played a prominent part against Rome in the Social War. He served on Caesar's staff in the invasion of Italy in 49 (6 n.), in Sicily against Cato (App. *civ.* 2. 40. 162, J. André, *REL* 25, 1947, 124 ff.), in Africa with Curio, at Pharsalus in 48, in the Thapsus campaign of 46 (Cic. *Att.* 12. 2. 1, Plut. *Caes.* 52. 6), at Munda in 45, the year of his praetorship; Caesar does not mention him in his *Bellum Civile*, but his subsequent promotion points at least to his political capacity. At the Ides of March in 44 he was governor of Hispania Ulterior, but though he protested his loyalty to the Republic (Cic. *epist.* 10. 31–3) he joined Antony before Plancus (App. *civ.* 3. 97. 399, Vell. 2. 63. 3), sacrificing his father-in-law in the proscriptions (p. 168); the historical tradition has no doubt been influenced by his own self-esteem (Bosworth, op. cit.), yet one may recognize a consistent search for compromise (Syme 180 f., M. Gelzer, *Chiron* 2, 1972, 297 ff.). In 41 he controlled Cisalpina in Antony's interest, perhaps as proconsul, but his manœuvres during the Perusine War seem half-hearted, and as consul in 40 he was one of the architects of the Treaty of Brundisium between Antony and Octavian. In 39 B.C. he waged a campaign against the Balkan Parthini (16 n.) for which he earned a triumph, but his political and military ambitions were now fulfilled. He declined to serve against Antony at Actium in view of his former relationship (Vell. 2. 86. 3

'discrimini vestro me subtraham et ero praeda victoris') ; but in spite of his ostentatious independence on minor issues his general support of the Augustan settlement should not be doubted (Bosworth, op. cit.). He lived till 4 A.D. 'nervosae vivacitatis haud parvum exemplum' (Val. Max. 8. 13. 4). See further *RE* 2. 1589 ff., *PIR²* A 1241, André, op. cit.

Pollio's literary interests also show a remarkable versatility. Already as a young man he was a friend of Catullus (12. 6 ff.) and Calvus (Sen. *contr.* 7. 4. 7), and the recipient of a famous *propempticon* by Cinna (56 B.C.), while in the turmoil of 43 he refers Cicero to Cornelius Gallus for a copy of his own tragedy (*epist.* 10. 32. 5). In Cisalpina he befriended the young Virgil, who in turn paid tribute to his political and military achievements (*ecl.* 4. 13 'te duce', 8. 6 ff., cf. below, 12 n.). He devoted the spoils of his Balkan victories to founding a national library (significantly in the Atrium Libertatis), which seems to have been intended as a literary centre on the Alexandrian model. He had already begun to write tragedies which were praised by Virgil (cf. *ecl.* 3. 86 for *nova carmina* rewarded by a bull, 8. 10), and later by Horace himself (9 n.) ; they were ignored by later critics, and may have been designed for reading rather than performance (for such plays cf. O. Zwierlein, *Die Rezitationsdramen Senecas*, 1966, pp. 158 ff.). Pollio seems in fact to have extended the practice of recitation by issuing a general invitation to his supporters; cf. Sen. *contr.* 4 praef. 2 'Pollio Asinius numquam admissa multitudine declamavit; nec illi ambitio in studiis defuit; primus enim omnium Romanorum advocatis hominibus scripta sua recitavit', A. Dalzell, *Hermathena* 86, 1955, 20 ff. Pollio's declamations (here explicitly distinguished from his recitations) are often cited by the elder Seneca, whose family he had known in Corduba (*contr.* 4 praef. 2–4, M. T. Griffin, *Seneca*, 1976, pp. 31 f.). Much more important were his speeches, which won him the repute of a major orator; later taste found them austere and rugged (13 n.).

But probably Pollio's supreme achievement was his lost *Historiae* (Syme 4 ff.), the subject of Horace's ode. His central theme was the civil war that began in 49 B.C. (Suidas 4. 185. 10 περὶ τοῦ ἐμφυλίου τῆς Ῥώμης πολέμου ὃν ἐπολέμησαν Καῖσάρ τε καὶ Πομπήιος), but he traced its origins back to 60 when Pompey and Caesar formed their original compact (1 n.). He went down to the death of Cicero in 43 (Sen. *suas.* 6. 24) and presumably the battle of Philippi in the following year. Some think that he continued to the death of Sextus Pompeius in 35, but in that case Appian would have known more about Pollio's victories in 39 (cf. E. Badian, *CR* N.S. 8, 1958, 161 f.). Others put the terminus at the defeat of Antony in 31–30, but in view of Pollio's neutrality that course would certainly have been full of hazard.

Horace's ode reflects the tone and substance of the *Historiae*

(Kornemann, Seeck, Sonnenburg, opp. citt.), and particularly of the proem, which he surely had read. Historians often began with a succinct declaration of intent emphasizing the importance and sensationalism of their subject (Lucian, *hist. conscr.* 53–4) and the complication of their work; cf. Sall. *Jug.* 5. 1 'bellum scripturus sum quod populus Romanus cum Jugurtha . . . gessit, primum quia magnum et atrox variaque victoria fuit', Tac. *hist.* 1. 2. 1 (possibly influenced by Pollio) 'opus aggredior opimum casibus, atrox proeliis, discors seditionibus, ipsa etiam pace saevum', below, 1 n. Most of Horace's ideas in the first two stanzas and some of his words are likely to be derived from Pollio ; see notes on 1 *motum, ex Metello consule, civicum,* 2 *causas, vitia, modos,* 3 *Fortunae,* 4 *amicitias,* 6 *plenum opus aleae,* 7 *tractas.* Certainly when the poet exaggerates the political danger of the undertaking (6) he would be guilty of unaccustomed indiscretion if the thought were original ; he must be echoing Pollio's own *captatio benevolentiae,* a feature natural in any preface (T. Janson, *Latin Prose Prefaces,* 1964, pp. 40 ff.).

Horace implies that Pollio has not yet issued his account of the civil war itself (17 *iam nunc*), but his description of a cavalry battle suggest that he may already have heard something on Pharsalus (19 n.). The vividness which he ascribes to Pollio is not incompatible with analytic power, and suits a historian who links Sallust and Tacitus ; certainly Pollio's gift for dramatic anecdote is well-established (Kornemann, op. cit., pp. 628 ff.). Horace's generous attitude towards Pompey (21 n.) and Cato (24 n.) can only reflect the impartiality of his model ; when the ode was being written Pollio cannot have reached Cato's death, but some of his outlook could have been revealed in his preface. The exclamations against civil war suit Pollio's professed opinions, at least after the event (ap. Cic. *epist.* 10. 31. 2 'itaque illud initium civilis belli saepe deflevi') ; such indignation would not have been out of place in a historical preface, and could have coloured similar outbursts in Virgil (*georg.* 1. 489 ff.), Horace (1. 35. 33 ff.), and Lucan (1. 8 ff., 7. 617 ff.). Some would go further and assign the tragedian Pollio to the so-called tragic school of historiography (for this cf. Plb. 2. 56. 7–12, B. L. Ullmann, *TAPhA* 73, 1942, 25 ff., C. O. Brink, *PCPhS* 6, 1960, 14 ff.). The label is a confusing one as most ancient historians described pitiful and fearful scenes without necessarily inventing as freely as Duris and Phylarchus ; cf. F. W. Walbank, *BICS* 2, 1955, 4 ff., *Historia* 9, 1960, 216 ff., *Polybius* (Sather Lectures), 1972, pp. 34 ff. Yet it remains probable that Horace is suggesting an affinity between Pollio's tragedies and his histories.

The date of Horace's ode cannot be determined with any certainty. When Sallust died in 35, Pollio took over his assistant Ateius

Capito, who gave him advice 'de ratione scribendi' (Suet. *gramm.* 10. 6) ; this would be an appropriate moment for the beginning of his work. When Horace is writing his ode the preface seems to have been recently published, presumably with a few books on the events of the fifties. Usually the ode is assigned to the years immediately following the defeat of Antony, and such a date well suits the likely progress of the *Historiae*; yet there are complications. In view of Pollio's conspicuous neutrality in 31–30, that was not the best time for a poet to court him; Horace's pessimistic reference to bloodstained seas, whether deriving from Pollio or not, could then only be interpreted as a comment on Actium. Again, when Horace says that the ashes are still smouldering, that might be unnecessarily tactless after the Augustan settlement (5 n.). One wonders whether a date about 34 could be possible, when a reference to naval warfare would naturally suggest Sextus Pompeius; the closely similar 1. 35 may also be assigned to the same period (vol. i, pp. xxviii f.), though that issue remains controversial. Nothing conclusive is shown by the metre, but the opening iambi at both 6 and 21 (admittedly a conjecture) tend to point to an earlier date (though two such openings are found in 1. 31 of 28 B.C.). The main difficulty about 34 B.C. is that it may not allow Pollio enough time to write anything significant; yet he need not have waited for Sallust's death, but might have begun at any date after his own retirement in 38. For a possible reminiscence of the *Georgics* ('published' in 29) see note on 29 *pinguior*; yet Horace might have been familiar with the passage earlier, and his imitation of Virgil is by no means proved. The last lines of the poem seem designed to suit the book as a whole, but as his collection neared completion Horace might have added a new stanza or given fresh significance to an old one (it certainly would be hard to believe that he was still lamenting the civil war in 23 B.C.).

From the formal point of view the ode is in part a dedication (P. White, *JRS* 64, 1974, 50 ff. with literature there cited); in an introductory poem the naming of the recipient is enough (cf. *epod.* I, *serm.* 1. 1, *epist.* 1. 1). The last stanza is programmatic in intention, and points to the abandonment for the rest of the book of grave political themes (37 n.). The poem as a whole is a laudation of Pollio as a historian : the first and second stanzas emphasize the interest and importance of his subject, the third and fourth suggest his qualifications as a tragedian and man of affairs, the fifth and sixth illustrate his work's realism and excitement, the seventh sets it in relation to his predecessor Sallust, the eighth and ninth show a mournful eloquence, by implication Pollio's, that Horace in the final stanza modestly disclaims for himself. Such praise of literary achievement could be paralleled in epigram (Call. *ep.* 27 on Aratus, Catull. 1 on

Nepos, 95 on Cinna), and most recently in Virgil's sixth and tenth
eclogues; for eulogy of a forthcoming work cf. Cic. *ac.* 1. 3 (a dedication) on Varro's *de lingua Latina*, Prop. 2. 34. 61 ff. (at the end of
a book) on Virgil's *Aeneid*. The ode's austere style, with its alliteration and absence of connectives, suggests as often the writer under
discussion (cf. also 6 n.); so perhaps does the variation of tone. The
prosaic period of the introduction (1–8) with its objective and political
vocabulary makes a marked contrast with the onomatopoeia and
ἐνάργεια of the battle-scene (17–20); this is followed by a rhetorical
outburst of indignation (29–36), which peters away into the usual
Horatian ironies (37 n.). But what makes the ode unique is its subject-
matter, which once again reflects the attitudes of Pollio himself.
In spite of all its splendour and vigour Horace's political poetry
sometimes seems unrelated to the real world; here for once he speaks
not simply as a panegyrist but with the judiciousness and authority
of a historian. Pollio had two great eclogues written in his honour:
Horace cannot match Virgil for charm and imagination, but the
rationality and controlled excitement of his ode were better calcu-
lated to suit the recipient.

Metre: Alcaic.

1. motum : a common euphemism for political convulsions (*Thes.
l.L.* 8. 1536. 84 ff.); Horace cannot yet say *bellum* (which comes in the
next line) as he is including the decade before the outbreak of war.
The austere understatement suits a historian and might be derived
from Pollio's own preface; cf. Augustus, *res gest.* 10. 2 (?), Sil. 1. 20
(of the Punic Wars) 'iamque adeo magni repetam primordia motus'.
For the definition of the theme in the opening words cf. *ars* 137,
West on Hes. *th.* 1, Sall. *hist.* fr. 1 'res populi Romani M. Lepido
Q. Catulo consulibus ac deinde militiae et domi gestas composui',
Virg. *Aen.* 1. 1 'arma virumque' (not 'ille ego'), Lucan 1. 1 'bella . . .
plus quam civilia'. Lucan's expression is strangely paralleled by
Tacitus's comment on Pollio's son 'tamquam . . . plus quam civilia
agitaret' (*ann.* 1. 12. 4); though the contexts are totally different,
it has been speculated that both writers might be alluding to a phrase
in Pollio's proem (Mendell, op. cit.).

ex Metello consule : by his prosaic statement of the *terminus a quo*
Horace again gives a hint of Pollio's historical manner (cf. Sall.
loc. cit., Tac. *hist.* 1. 1. 1). He may even be echoing the sub-title of
the *Historiae*, perhaps substituting *ex* for the more prosaic *a*. Cf.
Livy's *ab urbe condita*, the elder Pliny's *a fine Aufidi Bassi* (*nat.*
praef. 20, Plin. *epist.* 3. 5. 6), Tacitus's *ab excessu divi Augusti*,
Strabo's τὰ μετὰ Πολύβιον (11. 9. 3).

As Porphyrio says, Horace is referring to Q. Metellus Celer (*RE* 3. 1208 ff.), the consul of 60 B.C. and the husband of Cicero's enemy Clodia (probably Catullus's Lesbia). In Thucydidean manner Pollio recounted the antecedents of the war, in this case the pact between Pompey and Caesar in Metellus's consulship (Cic. *Att.* 2. 3. 3); Crassus did not join till the following year, and the historians who assign the 'triumvirate' to 60 B.C. may well have been misled by Pollio (R. Hanslik, *RhM* 98, 1955, 324 ff.). The alliance was viewed with foreboding by both Cato (Plut. *Caes.* 13. 3, *Pomp.* 47. 2 f.) and Cicero (*epist.* 6. 6. 4, *Phil.* 2. 24 'utinam, Cn. Pompei, cum C. Caesare societatem aut numquam coisses aut numquam diremisses'; cf. also Cael. *epist.* 8. 14. 2). Pollio's view that it was the true beginning of the war became canonical with later historians; cf. Vell. 2. 44. 1 'inita potentiae societas quae urbi orbique terrarum nec minus diverso cuique tempore ipsis exitiabilis fuit', Lucan 1. 84 f. 'tu causa malo-rum / facta tribus dominis communis, Roma', Plut. *Caes.* 13. 3 (below, 3 n.), Flor. *epit.* 4. 2.8. The theme is also hinted at by Virgil, *Aen.* 7. 317 (of Aeneas and Latinus) 'hac gener atque socer coeant mercede suorum'.

civicum : the adjective implies that citizens were fighting each other (1. 2. 21 n.). It is used as a grandiose equivalent of the normal *civilem* (imp. Claud. *ILS* 212. 1. 31 'in civili motu difficiliore') ; cf. Serv. *Aen.* 6. 772 (on *civili quercu*) '*civica* debuit dicere, sed mutavit ut e contra Horatius *motum ex Metello consule civicum*'. The tone is archaic (Porphyrio says *antiqua figura* and compares *hosticus*) ; it suits the language of a moralist or historian (3. 24. 26, Flor. *epit.* 3. 21. 5), perhaps of Pollio himself. The alliteration of the first line adds to the trenchancy, as does the juxtaposition of 'consul' and 'citizens'.

2. bellique causas : Hellenistic and Roman historians followed Thucy-dides in concerning themselves with causation; cf. 1. 16. 19 n., Plb. 3. 32. 6 (with Walbank 1. 358), Asellio, fr. 2 (on writing annals without recording motives) 'id fabulas pueris est narrare, non historias scribere', Cic. *de orat.* 2. 63, Quint. *inst.* 4. 2. 2, Tac. *hist.* 1. 4. 1 (the proem) 'ut non modo casus eventusque rerum qui plerumque for-tuiti sunt, sed ratio etiam causaeque noscantur', G. Avenarius, *Lukians Schrift zur Geschichtsschreibung*, 1956, pp. 116 f., A. Momi-gliano, *Secondo Contributo alla storia delli studi classici*, 1960, pp. 13 ff. For the origins of the Civil War cf. Liv. *epit.* 109, Lucan 1. 67–182, Petron. 119. 1–60, M. Pohlenz, *Causa Civilium Armorum*, *ΕΠΙΤΥΜΒΙΟΝ Heinrich Swoboda dargebracht*, 1927, pp. 201 ff. (= *Kl. Schr.* 2. 139 ff.), Jal, op. cit., pp. 360 ff., J. Brisset, *Les Idées politiques de Lucain*, 1964, pp. 35 ff., A. W. Lintott, *CQ* N.S. 21, 1971,

493 ff.; by his early starting-date Pollio tried to get behind the immediate occasion (cf. Herodotus, Thucydides, Polybius). He must have mentioned the alliance between Pompey and Caesar (cf. Plut. *Caes.* 13. 3, cited 3 n.), Caesar's lust for power (Plut. *Ant.* 6. 2–3, with a correction of superficial views), the character of the agents (Kornemann, op. cit., pp. 608 ff.), the moral decadence of the times (cf. Lucan 1. 160 ff.), the accident of Julia's death (Lucan 1. 111 ff., Plut. *Caes.* 23. 4, App. *civ.* 2. 19. 68).

vitia : 'evils' in the strong sense of the word; Fraenkel cites Thuc. 3. 82. 2 ἐνέπεσε πολλὰ καὶ χαλεπὰ κατὰ στάσιν ταῖς πόλεσι, γιγνόμενα μὲν καὶ αἰεὶ ἐσόμενα, ἕως ἂν ἡ αὐτὴ φύσις ἀνθρώπων ᾖ. Pollio seems to have engaged in pessimistic moralizing in the manner of Sallust or Tacitus; for similar views of the civil wars cf. 1. 35. 33 ff., Lucan 1 *passim*, Jal, op. cit., pp. 377 ff. (though *belli vitia* stresses the concomitants and not the antecedents of the conflict). Some compare Cic. *epist.* 7. 3. 2 'propter vitia multa quae ibi offendi quo veneram', Nep. *Att.* 16. 4 'sic enim omnia de studiis principum, vitiis ducum, mutationibus rei publicae perscripta sunt . . .'; but Horace is thinking of more than the blunders or even the character-faults of individual great men.

modos : something like *rationes*, the answers to the question 'how?' (whereas *causae* are the answers to the question 'why?'). Pollio described not just the events of the war (an anticlimax after *causas* and *vitia*) but their underlying relationships, not just what happened but the way it happened (Cic. *de orat.* 2. 63 'non solum quid actum aut dictum sit sed etiam quo modo'). Horace is using the terms of a historian, presumably Pollio, on the lines of the Greek τρόπος; cf. Plb. 2. 56. 13 οὐχ ὑποτιθεὶς αἰτίαν καὶ τρόπον τοῖς γινομένοις, Dion. Hal. *ant. Rom.* 5. 56. 1 ἀπαιτεῖ δ' ἕκαστος καὶ τὰς αἰτίας ἱστορῆσαι τῶν γινομένων καὶ τοὺς τρόπους τῶν πράξεων καὶ τὰς διανοίας τῶν πραξάντων.

3. ludumque Fortunae : for Fortune's sport cf. 3. 29. 50, Virg. *Aen.* 11. 427, Palladas, *anth. P.* 10. 80. 1 παίγνιόν ἐστι τύχης μερόπων βίος, Prato on [Sen.] *epig.* 24. 65. Naturally τύχη played an important part in Hellenistic historians and their Roman imitators; cf. especially F. W. Walbank, *Polybius*, vol. 1, pp. 16 ff., Cic. *epist.* 5. 12. 4 (to Lucceius) 'nihil est enim aptius ad delectationem lectoris quam temporum varietates fortunaeque vicissitudines', Liv. 21. 1. 2 (the proem to the decade) 'et adeo varia fortuna belli ancepsque Mars fuit ut propius periculum fuerint qui vicerunt'. Caesar notoriously owed much to Fortune, though he would not himself have equated her with the historians' capricious goddess (App. *civ.* 2. 88. 371, C. Brutscher, *MH* 15, 1958, 75 ff., Gabba, op. cit., pp. 125 ff., Weinstock 116 ff.). Pompey became a stock *exemplum* for the vicissitudes of

human life (Vell. 2. 53. 3, Lucan 8. 701 ff., Petron. 123 v. 244, Mayor on Juv. 10. 285 ff.).

gravisque . . . amicitias : Horace uses a discreet generalizing plural, but he means the particular alliance of Pompey and Caesar; cf. 1 n., Lucan 1. 86 'feralia foedera', 1. 87 'o male concordes', Plut. *Caes.* 13. 3. οὐ γὰρ ὡς οἱ πλεῖστοι νομίζουσιν ἡ Καίσαρος καὶ Πομπηίου διαφορὰ τοὺς ἐμφυλίους ἀπειργάσατο πολέμους ἀλλὰ μᾶλλον ἡ φιλία. 'Grievous friendships' is an oxymoron, as the adjective is naturally used of *inimicitiae* (*Thes.l.L.* 6. 2. 2298. 12 f.). The figure is helped by the use in political contexts of the word *amicitia*, commonly without any sharp distinction from its ordinary social sense (P. A. Brunt, *PCPhS* 11, 1965, 1 ff.).

4. arma, : *amicitias* and *arma* make an alliterative combination (cf. Wölfflin 253 ff.) ; as *principum* goes with both nouns, the more emphatic *gravis* does the same. There is an incision after *arma*, and a rolling period is then developed by the following clause; for participial cola cf. Fraenkel, *NGG*, 1933, 321 ff. = *Kl. Beitr.* 1. 95 ff. Editors put the break after *amicitias*, but this colometry impairs the contrast with *arma*; it also implies that the failure to expiate the civil war was an integral part of Pollio's theme instead of an incidental observation. The objects of *tractas* are arranged in four cola joined by -*que*, and this articulation is obscured if *et* is allowed to begin a fifth colon; each colon contains a genitive or the equivalent (*civicum, belli, Fortunae, principum*).

5. nondum expiatis : 'paene adhuc in manibus esse arma civilia' (Porph.). Some see a suggestion of fighting Parthians (1. 2. 29 n.) ; as Lucan makes a similar remark in his proem (1. 10 ff.), one could then look for a common source in Pollio. But in our passage one need not move beyond the immediate context : the history is hazardous because of the smouldering animosities of Roman *principes*, which may well have been exaggerated by Pollio himself.

uncta : cf. Sil. 9. 13 f. 'hostilique unguere . . . tela cruore'. Weapons were greased at the end of a campaign as a protection against rust (Porph. 'solent autem ungi arma cum post bellum transactum reponenda sunt') ; Horace bitterly suggests that old hatreds were actually preserved by the blood of the dead (contrast Plin. *nat.* 34. 146 'a ferro sanguis humanus se ulciscitur, contactum namque eo celerius robiginem trahit'). *uncta* hints at something unpleasant and messy; the verb can be used of smearing with poison (Virg. *Aen.* 9. 773), like χρίεσθαι. Bentley proposed *tincta*, objecting that blood would dry, but Lady Macbeth knew better; cf. also Amm. 23. 5. 19 'cuius in gladiis nondum nostrae propinquitatis exaruit cruor'.

cruoribus : the plural is poetic and grandiose; cf. Serv. *Aen.* 4. 687

'*cruores* usurpavit: nam nec *sanguines* dicimus numero plurali nec *cruores*', P. Maas *ALL* 12. 520. The usage may have originated with tragedy (Heinze), in imitation of Greek αἵματα (K.-G. 1. 15 f., Denniston on Eur. *El.* 1172). The Silver Age poets follow Virgil (*Thes.l.L.* 4. 1241. 65 ff.).

6. plenum opus aleae: Pollio's history is 'fraught with hazard' (could the English cliché be modelled on Horace?); there may be a tension between the weighty *plenum* and the flighty *alea*, which a Roman would connect with dice-throws (for another oxymoron cf. Ov. *ars* 1. 376 'alea grandis'). For the risks of contemporary history cf. Plin. *epist.* 5. 8. 12 'graves offensae, levis gratia'; here Horace must be echoing Pollio (p. 9). The 'accusative in apposition to the sentence' is a construction favoured by historians (K.-S. 1. 247 f.), and the use of *opus* suggests preface-style; cf. Mela 1. 1 'orbis situm dicere aggredior, impeditum opus et facundiae minime capax'. Yet in spite of the declaration of candour, the issues of 49 were in fact largely dead.

War was proverbially a gamble (Aesch. *sept.* 414 ἔργον δ' ἐν κύβοις Ἄρης κρινεῖ, ps.-Eur. *Rhes.* 183, Lucan 6. 7, Otto 12 f., *Thes.l.L.* 1. 1522. 15 ff.); Pollio seems to have suggested that the historian was running risks no less than the general. In particular he must have recalled Caesar's quotation from Menander at the crossing of the Rubicon, ἀνερρίφθω κύβος (Plut. *Caes.* 32. 6, *Pomp.* 60. 2, cf. Suet. *Jul.* 32 'iacta alea est', App. *civ.* 2. 35. 140). The source of this anecdote is obviously Pollio himself, who was present on the occasion (Plut. *Caes.* 32. 5); he is likely to have translated the phrase into Latin to maintain the stylistic unity of his work (cf. E. Hohl, *Hermes* 80, 1952, 246 ff.).

7. tractas: Horace makes it clear for the first time that the grandiloquent theme is not his own but someone else's; the word could have come from Pollio's preface (cf. Quint. *inst.* 1 pr. 21 'tractabimus'). As it means literally 'handle' it suits *arma*, underlines the unpleasantness of *uncta*, and makes a formal contrast with *incedis*.

incedis per ignis . . . : it was proverbially dangerous to walk through or over fire; cf. Ar. *Lys.* 133 f. κἄν με χρῇ, διὰ τοῦ πυρὸς / ἐθέλω βαδίζειν, Suidas 2. 291. 22 ἐν πυρὶ βέβηκας· τοῦτο ἐπιλέγειν χρὴ ἐν τοῖς ἐν ἐπισφαλέσι καὶ ἐπικινδύνοις πράγμασιν ἐμφιλοχωρεῖν ἐθέλουσι (otherwise *corp. paroem. gr.* 1. 239), *prov.* 6. 28 'Can one go upon hot coals, and his feet not be burned?', Otto 171. Horace combines an allusion to another well-known saying, πῦρ ὑπὸ τῇ σποδιῇ (Call. *ep.* 44. 2, cf. Gow–Page's note on *HE* 1081 f.). This properly referred to the sparks of a dormant love, but Horace *suo more* re-applies the phrase to give the idea of 'crossing a minefield' (where it is clear that there is danger, but not clear exactly where). For more or less similar expressions cf. Prop. 1. 5. 5 'ignotos vestigia ferre per ignis', Sen. *contr.* 1 praef. 22 'necesse me est per spinosum locum ambulantem suspensos pedes ponere', Paul. Nol. *epist.* 34. 9 'per ignes doloso cineri suppositos ambulamus' (clearly alluding to our passage).

What exactly is the image? Callimachus is thinking of a domestic fire, which was kept in at night by banking ash over the embers; but such a metaphor is incompatible with *incedis*. It seems simplest to think of the smouldering remains of a conflagration; cf. Pollio, Cic. *epist.* 10. 33. 5 'res enim cogit huic tanto incendio succurrere omnis' (*incendium* is often used thus by Cicero), Flor. *epit.* 4. 2. 53 'acrius multo atque vehementius Thessalici incendii cineres recaluerunt'. Some commentators refer to the aftermath of a volcanic eruption; cf. Macaulay, *History of England*, ch. 6 'When the historian of this troubled reign turns to Ireland his task becomes peculiarly difficult and delicate. His steps—to borrow the fine image used on a similar occasion by a Roman poet—are on the thin crust of ashes beneath which the lava is still glowing.' But eruptions were less common than conflagrations, and the Greeks talked of walking on fire without thinking of volcanoes (this is the crucial argument). Alternatively some have thought of ritual fire-walking as practised by the Hirpi of Soracte (cf. Str. 5. 2. 9, *RE* 8. 1933 f., Pease on Cic. *div.* 1. 30, H. Musurillo, *TAPhA* 94, 1963, 172 ff.); but the ash in this situation could hardly be called *dolosus* as the danger was obvious.

8. suppositos : the word has a hint of treachery, and so balances *doloso*.

9. severae Musa tragoediae : for Pollio's tragedies (of which not even a title survives) cf. *serm.* 1. 10. 42 f. 'Pollio regum / facta canit pede ter percusso' (presumably he wrote like Seneca in iambic trimeters rather than in senarii), Virg. *ecl.* 8. 10 [below, 12 n.]. *severae* refers to the conventional σεμνότης of tragedy (Pl. *Gorg.* 502 a–b), but may have particularly suited Pollio's style; cf. Tac. *dial.* 21. 7 'Pacuvium certe et Accium non solum tragoediis sed etiam orationibus suis expressit'. No particular Muse need be thought of (1. 24. 3 n.).

10. desit theatris : presumably Horace is referring to literary recitations, with which Pollio's name was associated (p. 8); for *theatrum* in such contexts cf. *epist.* 1. 19. 41 f. 'spissis indigna theatris / scripta pudet recitare', Petron. 90. 5, Tac. *dial.* 10. 5 (with Gudeman's note), Gell. 18. 5. 2, Apul. *flor.* 16 (of an open-air recital by Philemon at Athens). At the date of the poem there was only one stone theatre in Rome, but even if *theatra* here has the more comprehensive meaning of 'places for recitation', it keeps its normal association with

tragoediae (for the alliteration cf. 1. 7. 4 'Thessala Tempe', Allen 26 f.).
Alternatively Horace might be suggesting (with obvious exaggeration) that the fame of Pollio's tragedies extended outside the city. In
theory plural *theatra* can mean *spectacula* or *ludi* (2. 17. 26 n.); however, it seems better here to think of particular haunts now deserted
by the Muses (cf. Juv. 7. 6 'migraret in atria Clio').

Horace tells Pollio to do what he is manifestly doing already. He
begins as if he were recommending a holiday from weighty tasks
(cf. 1. 26. 3 n., 3. 8. 28 'linque severa', 3. 29. 25 ff., *epist.* 1. 5. 8, Mart.
4. 14. 6 'paulum seposita severitate'); it then transpires that he is
recommending something still more onerous. *desit* is more tactful
than a simple *absit*: the tragic Muse will be missed. It is suggested
that Pollio is the only tragic poet in the place, that the public duty
of historiography must take precedence, but that the great work is
simply an interruption to his true vocation.

· **ubi publicas res ordinaris** : for *ordinare* of the chronographer cf.
Nep. *Att.* 18. 1, Suet. *gramm.* 17. 4. The word need not imply mere
narrative history; συντάττειν is used of higher things (Dion. Hal. *ant.*
4. 7. 1). *publicas res* may seem a strange way of describing the facts of
history, but Horace is pointedly using a phrase properly applicable
to the statesman ('when you have set in order the affairs of the
nation'). Both *publicas res* and *ordinare* are unpoetical expressions
(Axelson 101) that catch the political tone of Pollio's writing.

11. grande munus : 'your sublime role'. *grande* is a term of literary
critics, particularly applicable to tragedy; cf. *ars* 80 'grandesque
coturni', Ov. *am.* 3. 1. 70, *Thes.l.L.* 6. 2. 2185. 52 ff. *munus* is a solemn
word for the poet's function in society; cf. *ars* 306 'munus et officium,
nil scribens ipse, docebo' (with Brink's note). Horace's words imply
that history is not a *grande munus* in the same sense as tragedy; as
a poet himself he professes to believe that poetry is the supreme art-
form.

12. Cecropio . . . coturno : the buskin is the traditional symbol of
tragedy (Ar. *ran.* 47, Bömer on Ov. *fast.* 5. 348); the tragedian is here
represented as a tragic actor (Ov. *am.* 2. 18. 18 'coturnato vate'), much
as the love-poet is a lover and the bucolic poet a goat-herd (cf. below,
18 n.). *Cecropio* is an appropriately grandiloquent equivalent of the
intractable *Atheniensi* (cf. 4. 12. 6, Call. *h.* 3. 227 Κεκροπίηθεν, Catull.
64. 172, etc.). Horace is surely echoing Virgil's compliment to
Pollio, *ecl.* 8. 10 'sola Sophocleo tua carmina digna coturno'. Recently
this line has been referred to Octavian's abortive *Ajax* (Suet. *Aug.*
85. 2, G. Bowersock, *HSCPh* 75, 1971, 73 ff., E. A. Schmidt, *Zur
Chronologie der Eklogen Vergils*, *SHAW* 1974, 6. Abh., 15 ff.); but
it is hard to believe that at the very time when Horace was singling

out Pollio's tragedies for praise (*serm.* 1. 10. 42 f.) Virgil chose to offer his old patron so unnecessary an insult.

At first sight the instrumental *Cecropio . . . coturno* appears overemphatic, but Horace is simply drawing a contrast between history and tragedy. One might be tempted to see a distinction between dramatic performances in the future and recited plays in the past; but the parallel *coturno* in Virgil (which refers to past plays) makes this implausible. D. Heinsius proposed *Cecropii . . . coturni*; this gives admirable sense, but the corruption is unlikely. N. Heinsius proposed *Cecropios . . . coturnos* (the singular would be better); *munus* in the sense of 'show' could appropriately be applied to history (cf. Cael. ap. Cic. *epist.* 8. 14. 4 for the *spectaculum* of civil war), but *repetes* does not go well with 'the buskin'.

13. insigne . . . : marks of the panegyric style are the long period, the postponed proper name (1. 4. 14 n.), the vocative in apposition (cf. 1. 10. 1 n. for hymns), and the sequence of 'deeds in peace and war' (Menander rhet. 3. 372 Sp., Doblhofer 22 ff.). The encomium is relevant to Horace's central theme: Pollio's position as a public man qualifies him to write history (cf. Syme 5).

maestis praesidium reis : Pollio was regarded as one of the greatest of all Roman orators after Cicero (Quint. *inst.* 10. 1. 113, Tac. *dial.* 25. 3). The titles of nine speeches are known (Malcovati, *ORF²*, pp. 516 ff., André, op. cit., pp. 67 ff.); in true Republican tradition eight of these are defences. Pollio's archaic manner was characterized by such epithets as 'strictum . . . et asperum' (Sen. *contr.* 4 praef. 3), 'salebrosa et exsiliens' (Sen. *epist.* 100. 7), 'durus et siccus' (Tac. *dial.* 21. 7).

maestis refers to the ostentatious misery of the accused (Mayor on Juv. 15. 135, Dover 195); for similarly conventional adjectives cf. 4. 1. 14 'et pro sollicitis non tacitus reis', Ov. *am.* 1. 10. 39 'miseros', *ars* 1. 460 'trepidos'. For the prosaic *praesidium* cf. 1. 1. 2 n., Corn. Sev. *carm.* fr. 13. 12 (on Cicero) 'unica sollicitis quondam tutela salusque'.

14. consulenti : understand *te*; normally the consul consulted the senate, but here the senate as a whole consulted Pollio. The paradox is supported by the use of *praesidium*; normally the senate provided protection for others (Cic. *dom.* 55), but here it is protected by Pollio (so Cic. *Sest.* 144 'Milonem . . . praesidium curiae'). It seems less pointed to interpret *consulenti* as *consilianti* or 'deliberating' (Sall. *Cat.* 52. 21, Virg. *Aen.* 11. 335). Pollio retained his authority in the senate till his old age, and when his grandson broke his leg in the *lusus Troiae* he made such effective protests that Augustus abandoned the institution (Suet. *Aug.* 43. 2).

Pollio : effectively enclosed by *consulenti curiae*, as suits his affectation of Republicanism. For the scansion of the name as a dactyl cf. *serm.* 1. 10. 42 and 85; Virgil elides the last syllable.

15. cui laurus . . . : 'for whom the bay produced everlasting adornments'; cf. Virg. *ecl.* 8. 13 for Pollio's *victrices . . . laurus. parere* is often used of acquiring or procuring honour, usually but not exclusively in the passive ([Virg.] *catal.* 9. 58 'ipsa sibi egregium facta decus parient'); but Horace also suggests the literal agricultural meaning 'to bring forth' (Ov. *rem.* 176 'ut sua quod peperit vix ferat arbor onus'). Similarly *honores* is both abstract glory and visible garlands (1. 17. 16 n.), and *aeternos* is not just 'everlasting' but 'evergreen' (Ov. *met.* 1. 565 'tu quoque perpetuos semper gere frondis honores'). There may also be a tension between *aeternos* and *peperit*; philosophers did not believe that what was born could be immortal (cf. the paradox in Dom. Mars. *epig. Bob.* 39. 2 'sive hominem peperi femina sive deum'). Horace seems to be suggesting that the *triumphator*'s garland sprouted miraculously, like the spear flung by Romulus from the Aventine to the Palatine (Ov. *met.* 15. 560 ff., Serv. *Aen.* 3. 46) or the sprig of bay carried by the white hen that the eagle dropped in Livia's lap (Plin. *nat.* 15. 136 f., Dio 48. 52. 3). It may be relevant that Pollio used the war-booty to build Rome's first national library (Plin. *nat.* 35. 10): for evergreen literature cf. Lucr. 1. 118 'perenni fronde coronam', Cic. *leg.* 1. 1 'nullius enim agricolae cultu stirps tam diuturna quam poetae versu seminari potest'.

16. Delmatico . . . triumpho : it is perhaps simplest to interpret 'at the Dalmatian triumph', when Pollio dedicated his garland of bay. An ablative of instrument with *peperit* does not seem quite coherent (*laurus* and *triumpho* are different aspects of the same thing); yet for similar 'disjunctiveness' in other Latin poets cf. 2. 3. 12 n.

Pollio triumphed over the Parthini on 25 October 39 or 38 B.C. (*inscr. Ital.* 13. 1. 86 f., 342 f., 568); though the campaign was a short one (Dio 48. 41. 7), the earlier date is by no means proved. The Parthini occupied the hinterland of Dyrrachium, well inside Antony's share of the empire; the boundary laid down by the treaty of Brundisium was at Scodra (Skutari), forty miles to the north (App. *civ.* 5. 65. 274, Dio 48. 28. 4). Hence it is argued that Pollio was proconsul of Macedonia (R. Syme, *CQ* 31, 1937, 39 ff.); in that case Horace's *Delmatico*, which should properly apply to Illyricum, is used loosely, as sometimes happens (op. cit., p. 42), for the area farther south.

Yet Horace may have had good reasons for associating Pollio with Dalmatia. In describing other campaigns against the Delmatae (in the strict sense of the term) Florus (normally based on Livy) comments 'hos . . . Asinius Pollio gregibus armis agris multaverat' (*epit.* 4. 12. 11, cf. Hier. *chron.* 170 b 'Asinius Pollio . . . qui de Dalmatis triumpharat'). More reliable is the dedication of Virgil's eighth eclogue, which is surely addressed to Pollio (12 n.) : 'tu mihi seu magni superas iam saxa Timavi / sive oram Illyrici legis aequoris, en erit umquam / ille dies mihi cum liceat tua dicere facta?' (6 ff.) ; these lines seem to look forward to Pollio's home-coming up the Adriatic (note 6 *iam* and 13 *victrices . . . laurus*). Operations in this area were a natural development of Pollio's recent career : in 41–40 his power-base had been in Cisalpina and round Ravenna, and in 40 B.C. he won over Domitius, then operating in the Adriatic, to Antony's cause (Vell. 2. 76. 2, App. *civ.* 5. 50. 212). Then again, there is a story that Pollio captured Salonae, near Split, on the Dalmatian coast (Porphyrio as well as Servius), and named his son Saloninus in celebration (ps.-Acro, Serv. *ecl.* 4. 1) ; Syme has called in question the very existence of this child (op. cit., pp. 44 ff.), yet it is agreed that the name 'Saloninus' was borne by Pollio's grandson (Tac. *ann.* 3. 75. 1). Syme derives 'Saloninus' from the *gentilicium* 'Salonius', pointing out that the adjective from 'Salonae' should properly be 'Salonitanus' ; yet Pollio might have been influenced by an existing Roman name, and at least in the third century A.D. 'Saloninus' is well attested at Salonae (J. J. Wilkes, *Dalmatia*, 1969, p. 334 n. 1). Pollio's Latin was sometimes non-classical, and if the MSS. may be trusted he used the form *Hirtinus* for *Hirtianus* at Cic. *epist.* 10. 33. 4 (cf. J. H. Schmalz, *Über den Sprachgebrauch des Asinius Pollio*, 1890, p. 11).

It is not clear how to reconcile these references to Dalmatia with Pollio's operations against the Parthini. One theory is that in the calmer political conditions of 39 he acted for both Octavian and Antony in clearing up the whole Adriatic coast (cf. J. André, *REL* 25, 1947, 142 ff.). Alternatively, it has been suggested that in spite of his previous allegiance Pollio governed Illyricum in 39 as Octavian's man, and that he operated from there against the Parthini (Bosworth, op. cit., pp. 462 ff.) ; but if he used his own seven legions, this substantial change in the balance of power should have been recorded somewhere. The knot could even be cut by positing that Illyricum was assigned to Octavian not at Brindisium in 40 (as the sources state) but at Tarentum in 37 ; Octavian's own campaigns in Illyricum begin in 35. But however we explain the difficulties, there seem to be too many coincidences if Pollio had nothing to do with Dalmatia.

17. iam nunc . . . : the mention of Pollio's military achievements leads naturally to his descriptions of war. Horace anticipates the thrills to come in the battle-scenes ; cf. Cic. *epist.* 5. 12. 2 (on Lucceius's hoped-for monograph) 'cerno iam animo quanto omnia uberiora atque ornatiora futura sint', Virg. *georg.* 3. 22 f. (on his projected celebration of Octavian) 'iam nunc sollemnis ducere pompas / ad delubra iuvat caesosque videre iuvencos'. His language suggests a seer's predictions of coming battles; cf. I. 15. 27 n. (on prophetic presents), Virg. *Aen.* 6. 87 (the raving Sibyl) 'et Thybrim multo spumantem sanguine cerno', Lucan 7. 292 (Caesar's forebodings before Pharsalus) 'videor fluvios spectare cruoris', Petron. 121 vv. 111 f. Yet Horace is not foreseeing an actual battle but Pollio's vivid reconstruction of past events. Such realism (ἐνάργεια) was commended by rhetorical theorists, particularly in historians; cf. Quint. *inst.* 8. 3. 61–71, 9. 2. 40–43, Lucian, *conscr. hist.* 51 τοιοῦτο δή τι καὶ τὸ τοῦ συγγραφέως ἔργον, εἰς καλὸν διαθέσθαι τὰ πεπραγμένα καὶ εἰς δύναμιν ἐναργέστατα ἐπιδεῖξαι αὐτά. καὶ ὅταν τις ἀκροώμενος οἴηται μετὰ ταῦτα ὁρᾶν τὰ λεγόμενα . . . τότε δὴ τότε ἀπηκρίβωται . . . τὸ ἔργον, G. Avenarius, op. cit. [2 n.], pp. 130 ff., P. Scheller, *De Hellenistica historiae conscribendae arte,* Diss. Leipzig, 1911, pp. 57 ff., Kroll 299 f., Williams 668 ff.

minaci murmure cornuum : for the onomatopoeic alliteration cf. Cic. *Arat.* 71, Lucr. 1. 68 f., 1. 276; for *murmur* in such contexts cf. *Thes.l.L.* 8. 1676. 10 ff. (the word can be applied to noises as loud as the roar of thunder or of an angry schoolmaster, cf. Mart. 9. 68. 4). Other accounts of Pharsalus mention the bugle-calls (Lucan 7. 475 ff., Plut. *Pomp.* 70. 1, App. *civ.* 2. 78. 326) ; Pollio might be the common source though the feature is conventional (Cic. *Marc.* 9 'sed tamen eius modi res nescio quo modo etiam cum leguntur, obstrepi clamore militum videntur et tubarum sono', P.-J. Miniconi, *Étude des thèmes guerriers de la poésie épique gréco-romaine,* 1951, p. 166). For bugles and similar instruments cf. Wille 75 ff. ; for the formal balance of *cornuum* and *litui* cf. 1. 1. 23 n., Lucan 7. 476 f., Sen. *Thy.* 574 f.

18. perstringis auris : Pollio is portrayed as a bugler on the principle that the writer does what he describes (*serm.* 1. 10. 36 'turgidus Alpinus iugulat dum Memnona', 2. 5. 41, Virg. *ecl.* 6. 46, 6. 62 f., 9. 19 f., Ov. *trist.* 2. 439). The verb suggests a blow that causes shock rather than injury (*per-* means 'along', not 'through'). With *auris* it describes a noise that makes the head reel (Sil. 15. 459), or by way of metaphor a jarring remark (Tac. *dial.* 27. 4). With other objects it is used of a grazing wound (Virg. *Aen.* 10. 344), a stinging rebuke (Cic. *Sest.* 14 etc.), of 'touching on the raw' (Tac. *ann.* 1. 13. 4 'suspicacem animum perstrinxere'), of nerve-racking terror (Val. Fl. 7. 81), of the pangs of first love (id. 7. 194).

19. fulgor : ancient armies sought to dazzle the beholder; cf. 1. 7. 19 n., Hom. *Il.* 11. 83, Plaut. *mil.* 1 ff., Prop. 4. 6. 26, Lucan 7. 214 f.,

Quint. *inst.* 10. 1. 30 'neque ego arma squalere situ ac rubigine velim, sed fulgorem in iis esse qui terreat, qualis est ferri quo mens simul visusque praestringitur', Miniconi, op. cit. [17 n.], pp. 164 f., *Thes.l.L.* 6. 1. 1516. 55 ff. In descriptions of the preliminaries of battle the assaults on eyes and ears are sometimes mentioned together (Lucan 6. 129 f., Tac. *ann.* 1. 68. 4).

fugacis : not proleptic; the horses are nervy but have not yet turned (as *voltus* shows). Such battle-scenes were favoured by the ancients in many genres (Cic. *orat.* 66, Menander rhet. 3. 373. 26 Sp. καὶ ἱππέων διασκευάσεις ἱππομαχίας), and elsewhere Horace is ironic (*serm.* 2. 1. 13 ff. 'neque enim quivis . . . / aut labentis equo describat vulnera Parthi'). Yet here he may be thinking particularly of Pharsalus, where a critical moment was the attack by Caesar's infantry on Pompey's non-Italian cavalry (Caes. *civ.* 3. 93. 6, Lucan 7. 525 ff., Plut. *Caes.* 45. 1, cf. below, 20 n.). *equos* could imply that the other side was using infantry, just as 1. 2. 39 *peditis* implies that the other side was using cavalry.

20. voltus : the realistic writer catches the decisive moment, as in a work of art (Virg. *Aen.* 8. 708 'laxos iam iamque immittere funes') ; Wilkinson 91 well compares the face of Darius on the Pompeian mosaic. Meineke called attention to the story that at Pharsalus Caesar ordered his men to strike at the Pompeians' faces (Plut. *Caes.* 45. 2, *Pomp.* 71. 5, App. *civ.* 2. 78. 328, Flor. *epit.* 4. 2. 50 'miles, faciem feri'). Such lively anecdotes are characteristic of Pollio (p. 9), who was present at the battle; Horace might have remembered his account, but if so he has developed it in a new way.

D. R. Shackleton Bailey suggests that *voltus* suits the faces of the terrorizing (1. 2. 40, 3. 3. 3) rather than the terror-stricken; he therefore suggests that the word is nominative and correlative with *fulgor* (*Proceedings of Leeds Philosophical Society, Lit. and Hist. Section*, vol. 10, part 3, p. 111). Yet it seems impossible to separate *equos* from *equitumque*; cf. Enn. *var.* 4 'equorum equitumque magister', Hom. *Il.* 21. 16 ἵππων τε καὶ ἀνδρῶν.

21. videre : the conjecture of Beroaldus and Bentley for *audire* of the MSS and ancient commentators (though it may be significant that Porphyrio on 17 paraphrases 'iam, inquit, videor mihi videre et audire ea quae historia refert') ; it is generally rejected by editors but supported by Shackleton Bailey, loc. cit. [20 n.]. *videor videre* is a common, though usually prosaic, *figura etymologica* that suits the austere manner of the poem (*trita sed eleganti sermone* says Bentley) ; cf. Plaut. *Curc.* 260 with Leo, Cic. *Lael.* 41 with Seyffert–Müller, Ov. *Pont.* 2. 4. 8 'et videor vultus mente videre tuos', Prud. *perist.* 2. 558, H. Haffter, *Untersuchungen zur altlateinischen Dichter-*

sprache (*Problemata* 10, 1934), pp. 39 ff., H.–Sz. 791 f. For the opening short syllable cf. 6 *periculosae*, vol. i, p. xl; the irregularity might have helped the corruption, together with palaeographic resemblance and a general impression that sounds were being talked about. For 'methinks I see' in similar contexts cf. 17 n., Plin. *paneg.* 17. 1 'videor iam cernere . . . triumphum . . .', Plut. *glor. Ath.* 349 c ὧν τὰς νίκας ὁρᾶν μοι δοκῶ προσερχομένας. For sounds followed by sights cf. Alpheus, *anth. P.* 9. 97. 1 f. (on the Iliad) Ἀνδρομάχης ἔτι θρῆνον ἀκούομεν, εἰσέτι Τροίην / δερκόμεθ' ἐκ βάθρων πᾶσαν ἐρειπόμενην.

If *audire* is to be defended one might try to understand *Pollionem de ducibus narrantem* (one of Porphyrio's explanations). This suits part of what Horace has been saying, namely that he can already imagine the stirring character of the forthcoming history (17 n.), but it fails to develop the further point that Pollio will actualize past battles. Fraenkel (236) says that *audire* takes up 18 *perstringis auris*, but the precise difficulty is that it fails to do so satisfactorily. Not only does a reference to sights come in between (19 *fulgor*), but after the bugles have assaulted our ears it is an anti-climax to understand *audire* of a recitation.

As an alternative Porphyrio referred *audire* to the speeches of the generals which were no doubt a feature of Pollio's work (cf. App. *civ.* 2. 72. 299 ff.). But *non indecoro pulvere sordidos* is an appeal to the eye rather than the ear, and the παρακελεύσεις took place before the generals were battle-stained. A further difficulty arises with 23 *et cuncta terrarum subacta*; now one has to translate *audire* as 'to hear of', a strange zeugma (Kiessling's interpretation, 'to hear Cato's last speech', is impossible).

magnos . . . duces: the discreet plural refers especially to Pompeius Magnus; this has the advantage of making *duces* balance 24 *Catonis*. It is true that *magnus* could be applied also to Caesar, emphasizing that he was just as good (cf. Catull. 11. 10 'Caesaris visens monumenta magni'); but though any general can be battle-stained (22 n.), the defeated suffer worse (cf. Lucan 8. 57 for Pompey in flight). In spite of his own part in the war, Pollio no doubt praised Pompey in his history (cf. App. *civ.* 2. 69. 287); in the same way Livy was called a *Pompeianus* by Augustus (Tac. *ann.* 4. 34. 3, Syme 317).

22. non indecoro pulvere: for the dust of the battlefield cf. 1. 6. 14 n., Hom. *Il.* 11. 151 f., Liv. 4. 33. 8, Miniconi, op. cit. [19 n.], p. 167. *non indecoro* makes an oxymoron with *sordidos*, which in other contexts might suggest not just dirt but disgrace. 'Honourable stains' were a commonplace in patriotic literature; cf. Xen. *Cyr.* 2. 4. 6 ἱδρῶτι καὶ σπουδῇ . . . κεκοσμημένος, Stat. *Theb.* 9. 710, Mart. 8. 65. 3, Plin. *paneg.* 13. 1 'imperatorium pulverem', Claud. 8. 532.

23. cuncta terrarum subacta : after Thapsus Caesar is reported to have been voted a statue with a globe under his feet (Dio 43. 14. 6, Weinstock 41 ff.). For the irrational partitive genitive with *cuncta* or *omnia* cf. K.–S. 1. 428 f., Shackleton Bailey, *Propertiana*, pp. 158 f. It belonged particularly to the historical style (Löfstedt, *Syntactica* 2. 294 n. 3), and seems to give a hint of Pollio's own manner; *cuncta* is a word favoured by historians (J. N. Adams, *BICS* 20, 1973, 129 ff.).

24. atrocem : the word is derived from *ater*, and is complimentary only by way of paradox; cf. Sil. 6. 378 'atrox illa fides' (of Regulus's grim devotion), 13. 369 'atrox virtus' (something of an oxymoron), Juv. 2. 11 f. 'hispida membra quidem et durae per bracchia saetae / promittunt atrocem animum' (of *tristes obsceni*). Pollio's own *ferocia* was notorious (Tac. *ann.* 1. 12. 4, cf. Dio 57. 2. 5, Bosworth, op. cit., pp. 441 ff.); though an old adversary of Cato in Sicily and Africa, he would have appreciated his intransigence.

animum Catonis : Cato's Stoic soul was unconquerable because he refused to live under Caesar; cf. Manil. 4. 87 'invicta devictum mente Catonem' (*mente* Bentley, *morte* codd.), Sen. *epist.* 71. 8, *epig.* 7 Prato 'invictum victis in partibus, omnia Caesar / vincere qui potuit, te, Cato, non potuit', Lucan 9. 18, Plut. *Cat. min.* 71. 1 μόνον ἀήττητον. The idealization of Cato was still permissible; cf. 1. 12. 35 n., Liv. fr. 55 'cuius gloriae neque profuit quisquam laudando nec vituperando nocuit'. Pollio praised other Republican leaders, even Brutus and Cassius (Tac. *ann.* 4. 34. 4), and Horace must have had clear evidence of his approval of Cato; cf. the attitude of his predecessor Sallust and of his imitator Appian (*civ.* 2. 99. 412).

25. Iuno : this stanza continues the theme of the Republican defeat in Africa; the allusion to Metellus Scipio (27 n.) balances those to Pompey (21 n.) and Cato. Tanit, the chief goddess of the Carthaginians, was identified by the Romans with Juno; cf. Virg. *Aen.* 1. 15 f. 'quam Iuno fertur terris magis omnibus unam / posthabita coluisse Samo', 1. 446, Pease on 4. 91, *RE* 4 A. 2178 ff. She continued to be worshipped in Africa until the Christian period, often under the title *Dea Caelestis* (*RE* 3. 1247 ff.).

deorum quisquis : English would say 'whoever of the *other* gods' (1. 10. 5 n., 2. 13. 9, K.–G. 2. 247). The comprehensive *quisquis* reflects the conventional blanket-clause of cult; cf. 1. 32. 15 n., *epod.* 5. 1 'at o deorum quidquid in caelo regit', Norden, *Agnostos Theos*, pp. 144 ff.

amicior : i.e. *quam Romanis*. Hera was hostile to the Trojans because of the judgement of Paris, and the story seemed to be given confirmation by the Carthaginian Wars. She was reconciled by varying accounts at the death of Turnus (*Aen.* 12. 807 ff.), the death of

Romulus (*carm.* 3. 3. 17 ff.), the second Punic War (Enn. ap. Serv. *Aen.* 1. 281). Consistency is not necessary with these legends, and here she remains implacable.

26. Afris : the name could include the Carthaginians (4. 4. 42 'dirus . . . Afer').

cesserat : gods were thought to leave a falling city; see Pearson on Soph. fr. 452, Hdt. 8. 41. 3, Austin on Virg. *Aen.* 2. 351, Lucan 7. 647 'transisse deos' (at Pharsalus), Joseph. *bell. Jud.* 6. 5. 3 (300) μεταβαίνομεν ἐντεῦθεν (cf. Tac. *hist.* 5. 13. 1), Sil. 2. 365 'et iam damnata cessit Carthagine Mavors', Plut. *Ant.* 75. 3 f. (Dionysus deserts Alexandria), Milton, *Nativity Ode* 'Peor and Baalim Forsake their temples dim', Housman, *Last Poems* 37. 7 'What God abandoned, these defended'.

There was a story in late antiquity that the Romans summoned Juno from Carthage by the rite of *evocatio*; cf. Serv. *Aen.* 12. 841 'constat bello Punico secundo exoratam Iunonem, tertio vero bello a Scipione sacris quibusdam etiam Romam esse translatam'. Macrobius preserves a *carmen* of the type used on the latter occasion (*sat.* 3. 9. 7, cf. Fraenkel 237 ff., A. Engelbrecht, *WS* 24, 1902, 478 ff.). However, the story is ignored by Virgil and other writers who might have been expected to use it (cf. E. Rawson, *JRS* 63, 1973, 168 ff.) ; it is regarded as a fiction by Wissowa (*RE* 6. 1152 f.) and by Latte (125 n. 2, 346 n. 4). Horace's words cannot be used to support it, as they imply that Juno remained hostile a century later.

impotens : 'powerless'; this, the primary meaning of the word, is not always recognized (cf. Catull. 8. 9 'nunc iam illa non volt: tu quoque impote⟨ns noli⟩'). 'In a fury' would be less obvious; and a pun is unlikely, as *rerum* and *sui* would have to be understood together.

27. victorum nepotes : Horace is thinking particularly of Q. Metellus Pius Scipio (*RE* 3. 1224 ff.), cos. 52 B.C., father-in-law of Pompey, the defeated commander at Thapsus in 46 (Cato deferred to his seniority); after the battle he committed suicide with the words 'imperator se bene habet' (Liv. *epit.* 114, Sen. *epist.* 24. 9 f.). By blood he was a Scipio, and though not directly descended from Aemilianus, the relationship was pointed out during as well as after the Thapsus campaign (Sen. loc. cit., Lucan 6. 788 f. 'deplorat Libycis perituram Scipio terris / infaustam subolem', Suet. *Jul.* 59, Dio 42. 57. 5). It cannot have escaped notice that his death took place a hundred years after the fall of Carthage; cf. Lucan 6. 309 ff. 'nec . . . Poenorumque umbras placasset sanguine fuso / Scipio'.

Scipio was also the grandson (by adoption), a *nepos* this time in the literal sense, of Q. Metellus Numidicus, cos. 109 B.C., who took

such a conspicuous part in the Jugurthine War; though ultimately
superseded by Marius he is given considerable credit by Sallust and
more by others (Vell. 2. 11. 2). With the last word of the stanza
Horace gives the topic an unexpected and sardonic twist: Scipio's
army must be sacrificed to the shades not just of the redoubtable
Carthaginians but of the barbaric Jugurtha (who was of special
interest to Pollio because of Sallust's recent monograph). It is now
seen that *Afris* suits Jugurtha at least as well as Carthage, and *tellure*
even better (Horace does not say *urbe*). Yet it would be wrong to
argue that Jugurtha is unequivocally the subject of the stanza;
the mention of Juno points more obviously to Carthage, and the
ambiguity is sustained up to and including *victorum nepotes rettulit
inferias*. For a less ingenious attempt to combine the two allusions
cf. Lucan 2. 90 f. (on Marius) 'nuda triumphati iacuit per regna
Iugurthae / et Poenos pressit cineres'.

28. rettulit inferias : human sacrifices were offered to dead warriors
in primitive religion (Hom. *Il.* 21. 26 ff., Virg. *Aen.* 10. 517 ff.), and
were particularly plausible in a Carthaginian context (cf. also Dido's
prayer for vengeance at Virg. *Aen.* 4. 622 ff.). Roman history records
dramatic executions that came perilously near sacrifice, as when
Gratidianus was killed at the tomb of Catulus (*RE* 14. 1827, Weinstock 398 f.). But often, as here, the reference is rhetorical; cf.
especially Lucan 1. 39 (of Thapsus) 'Poeni saturentur sanguine
manes', 4. 788 ff. 'excitet invisas dirae Carthaginis umbras / inferiis
Fortuna novis . . . ', 6. 310 f. [above, 27 n.], 10. 524. Lucan is not just
imitating Horace (who seems to complicate a familiar topic by
introducing Jugurtha), and Pollio has been suggested as a common source (H. Dahlmann, *RhM* 108, 1965, 142 ff.). He is unlikely
to have reached 46 B.C. at the time when Horace was writing,
but his indignant preface might have contained a similar observation.

29. quis non . . . : the slaughter of 46 leads to a more general denunciation of civil war down to the time of writing; such self-destruction
could gratify nobody but Rome's enemies, and not just the dead
Jugurtha but the real and menacing Parthians. The style is appropriately heightened: one may note the *polyptoton* of *quis*, the
anguished assonances (29, 33, 36), the concluding tricolon of 33–6
(reminiscent of the parallel 1. 35. 34 ff.), the *abundantia* and *variatio*
(particularly of words for 'blood', 'water', and 'Italian'). The passage
may be regarded as an instance of the figure *expolitio* (ἐξεργασία),
'cum in eodem loco manemus et aliud atque aliud dicere videmur'
(*rhet. Her.* 4. 54, R. Volkmann, *Die Rhetorik der Griechen und Römer*,
1885, pp. 257 f.).

Horace emphasizes the geographical extent of the conflict; cf. Sen. *suas.* 6. 6, Lucan 1. 5, 5. 266 f., 7. 870 ff., 8. 603 f., Flor. *epit.* 4. 2. 6 'commissum est intra Italiam, inde se in Galliam Hispaniamque deflexit reversumque ab occasu totis viribus in Epiro Thessaliaque consedit, hinc in Aegyptum subito transiluit, inde respexit Asiam, Africae incubuit, postremo in Hispaniam regyravit et ibi aliquando defecit', Jal, op. cit., pp. 278 ff. The point might well have been made by Pollio, whose own military service had been exceptionally wide-ranging (p. 7); Thucydides in his preface emphasizes the scale of his war (1. 1. 2).

Latino : cf. Lucan's proem (1. 9) 'gentibus invisis Latium praebere cruorem'; Lucan, like Horace (31 f.), is saying that the Civil War gave comfort to the Parthian enemy. Again it seems possible that Pollio's preface was the common source.

pinguior : 'fertilized' (cf. Colum. 2. 5. 2 'ut permixta humus praedicto alimento pinguescat'); *campus*, like 'field', suits both warfare and farming. Horace may be imitating Virg. *georg.* 1. 491 f. 'nec fuit indignum superis bis sanguine nostro / Emathiam et latos Haemi pinguescere campos' (where the verb suits the agricultural context). For the commonplace cf. further Plut. *Mar.* 21. 3 (on Aquae Sextiae) τὴν δὲ γῆν, τῶν νεκρῶν καταναλωθέντων ἐν αὐτῇ καὶ διὰ χειμῶνος ὄμβρων ἐπιπεσόντων, οὕτως ἐκλιπανθῆναι καὶ γενέσθαι διὰ βάθους περίπλεω τῆς σηπεδόνος ἐνδύσης ὥστε καρπῶν ὑπερβάλλον εἰς ὥρας πλῆθος ἐξενεγκεῖν, καὶ μαρτυρῆσαι τῷ Ἀρχιλόχῳ (292 W.) λέγοντι πιαίνεσθαι πρὸς τοῦ τοιούτου τὰς ἀρούρας, Aesch. *sept.* 587, Ov. *epist.* 1. 54, Petron. 120 v. 99, Sil. 3. 261 'uberior Rutulo nunc sanguine Thapsus', 14. 130, Stat. *Theb.* 7. 545 f., Shakespeare, *Richard II* 4. 1. 137 'The blood of English shall manure the ground'.

30. sepulcris ... testatur : Horace perhaps remembers Virg. *georg.* 1. 497 'grandiaque effossis mirabitur ossa sepulcris'; in fact the Caesarian dead at Pharsalus had a communal grave (App. *civ.* 2. 82. 348), while the Pompeians may have been left to rot (thus Lucan 7. 797 ff.). In panegyric a place is conventionally said to bear witness to a deed of valour (4. 4. 38 'testis Metaurum flumen', Enn. *var.* 8, Cic. *Manil.* 30, Catull. 64. 357, Tib. 1. 7. 9 f., Page, *EG* 456 ἀλκὴν δ' εὐδόκιμον Μαραθώνιον ἄλσος ἂν εἴποι, Eur. *Her.* 367 ff.); in particular a tomb might proclaim the message (cf. Anyte, *anth. P.* 7. 724. 3 f.). Here the war-graves give evidence of a crime; for the impiety of civil war cf. Jal, op. cit., pp. 391 ff. As *testari* implies observation there is a contrast with *auditum ... sonitum.*

31. Medis : cf. *epod.* 7. 9 f. 'sed ut secundum vota Parthorum sua / urbs haec periret dextera', 16. 11 f. In 41–40 B.C., in the aftermath of Philippi, the Parthians overran Syria and the south coast of Asia

Minor (vol. i, p. xxxii); though Horace began by talking of 48–46, his thought (perhaps following Pollio) must have been influenced by this major disaster, as well as by Antony's later failures. *Medis* is poetical for 'Parthians' as is *Hesperiae* for 'Italian' (1. 28. 26 n.); as the Medes are conventionally *Eoi*, the juxtaposition is pointed.

32. sonitum ruinae : the image is of a falling building, a common misfortune in Rome (Catull. 23. 9, Juv. 3. 7 f.). For political *ruinae* cf. 1. 2. 25 n., 3. 3. 8, 3. 5. 40. For *sonitum* cf. Sen. *dial.* 9. 11. 7 'saepe a latere ruentis aedificii fragor sonuit'; for the metaphor cf. *rhet. Her.* 4. 42 'fragor civitatis' (where the neologism is commented on), *Thes.l.L.* 6. 1. 1235. 82 ff.

33. qui gurges : after *campus* Horace passes to the sea by the conventional polarism (1. 6. 3 n.); cf. especially *epod.* 7. 3 f. 'parumne campis atque Neptuno super / fusumst Latini sanguinis'. Anybody writing after 36 B.C. must have thought primarily of the war against Sextus Pompeius (p. 10), even though there were naval operations in the earlier wars. *gurges* ('deep', cf. Henry 1. 368 ff.) makes a pair with the flowing *flumina*, just as *mare* with *ora* below; there is no significant distinction between *gurges* and *mare*, except that the latter is larger and harder to stain. Interrogative *qui* is used after *quis campus* for reasons of variety and perhaps euphony; the only other case in Horace is *epod.* 12. 7 'qui sudor', where s significantly follows (Löfstedt, *Syntactica* 2. 87 f.).

 flumina : the μάχη παραποτάμιος was common in ancient warfare, and blood-stained water became a gruesome cliché (de Jonge on Ov. *trist.* 4. 2. 42, R. Führer, *Formproblem-Untersuchungen zu den Reden in der frühgriechischen Lyrik*, 1967, pp. 128 f.). Cf. especially Lucan 7. 116 (on Pharsalus) 'sanguine Romano quam turbidus ibit Enipeus', 7. 700, 7. 789 f., 8. 33 f.; we cannot say whether this touch comes from Pollio or Lucan's own vivid imagination. For other battles near rivers cf. André, op. cit., p. 45; Seeck refers to the Egyptian campaign of 30, but the bloodshed then was insufficient to redden the Nile.

 lugubris : cf. 1. 21. 13 n., Hom. *Il.* 23. 86 ἀνδροκτασίης . . . λυγρῆς (the Latin adjective may have associations of the Greek λυγρός, cf. note on 1. 24. 3 *liquidam*). The line's repeated *u* sounds seem to give a sobbing tone (for such effects cf. Fraenkel 25 n.).

34. Dauniae : 'Apulian' is not simply a synecdoche for 'Italian'; Horace grieves for his countrymen in the dynasts' armies (cf. 1. 22. 13 f. 'militaris Daunias' with notes *ad loc.*). The name 'Daunia' was Greek rather than Italian (Str. 6. 3. 1), and strikes a note of grandeur;

it would have an extra dimension if it had been used by Ennius of
the land-battle of Cannae (cf. Sil. 12. 43 f. 'Dauni stagnantia regna /
sanguine', 12. 429). After *Latino* and the even more emotive *Dauniae*
the climax is reached at 36 with the emphatically placed *nostro*.

35. decoloravere: a true perfect to match *caret*; the stains are still
there. Ancient naval battles were fought at close quarters inshore,
and so here again blood-stained water is conventional. Cf. 2. 12. 3,
3. 6. 34, *orac.* 6 f. ap. Hdt. 8. 77, Aesch. *Pers.* 420, Timotheus 791.
31 ff., Manil. 4. 289, Sen. *clem.* 1. 11. 1 'post mare Actiacum Romano
cruore infectum', Lucan 3. 572 f. (Massilia), Sil. 14. 486, 556.

36. quae caret . . .: the emphatic alliteration picks up *-coloravere
caedes. ora* means 'shore' to balance *mare*, but it also suggests 'distant
clime'. For the emotional assonance *ora cruore* cf. Virg. *Aen.* 6. 314
'tendebantque manus ripae ulterioris amore', 1. 15. 20 n. The repeated weak caesura is very rare in the Alcaic decasyllable (only
1. 31. 16, 2. 13. 8), and perhaps is meant to suggest that the poet's
sorrow is getting out of control.

37. sed . . .: after his impassioned dirge Horace recalls himself to
the proper task of the lyric poet; cf. 3. 3. 69 ff. 'non hoc iocosae
conveniet lyrae. / quo, Musa, tendis? desine pervicax / referre sermones deorum et / magna modis tenuare parvis'. The 'quiet ending'
is found in the *Odes* (cf. 3. 5, 4. 2), just as in epic and tragedy; in
particular, laments should be brought under control before the end
of a poem (1. 24. 19 f.). Horace is also influenced by the passages
where Pindar recalls himself from a digression (Fraenkel 239, Thummer at *I.* vol. 1, pp. 123 ff. on 'Abbruchsformel'); but whereas Pindar
breaks off because he is straying from the encomium of his patron
(*I.* 6. 56, *N.* 3. 26 ff.), Horace is turning away from Pollio to himself.
This also is a form of flattery, and has affinities with *recusatio*; Horace
professes to be carried away by the pathos of Pollio's theme, but
suggests that such effects are beyond his own range.

Horace's stanza also derives some of its implication from its
position at the end of the first ode. He is saying in effect 'This is
the only serious political poem in the book, and from now I shall
treat of trivial themes'; the first of these propositions is less exaggerated than the second. Such declarations may be wrapped up in
different ways, particularly in opening poems: cf. *epod.* 14 'I am
trying to write *iambi* but love-elegy keeps breaking in', *carm.* 4. 1
'I can't help writing lyric after an interval, though I fear I am past
my best' (cf. E. Lefèvre, *RhM* 111, 1968, 166 ff.), Prop. 4. 1 'I meant
to write a book of aetiological poems, but I have included some of

the kind I know I can do', Stat. *silv.* 4. 7. 1 ff. 'I am leaving the wide open spaces (read *spatiata*) of the *Thebaid* for the more limited manœuvres of the Sapphic stanza'.

ne . . . : a final clause (cf. 2. 4. 1 n.); if it were a prohibition the asyndeton after 39 would be too abrupt.

Musa procax : 'wanton Muse' (contrasted with 9 'severae Musa tragoediae'); cf. Ov. *trist.* 2. 354 'Musa iocosa', Stat. *silv.* 1. 2. 7 'vultu petulans Elegea', 1. 5. 13 f. 'procax vittis hederisque, soluta / fronte, verecundo Clio mea ludit Etrusco'. Horace suggests that his Muse deals with light themes of love; for similar irony cf. 1. 6. 17 ff., 2. 12. 3, 3. 3. 69 ff. Some take *procax* as nominative and interpret 'brazenly rehandle' (cf. 3. 3. 70, cited on 37 *sed*); but it is artificial to separate *procax* from *Musa* and to dissociate it in meaning from *iocis* (which must have an erotic implication, especially when followed by *Dionaeo*). For the mention of the Muse in an introductory poem cf. 1. 1. 33 n., F. Cairns, *Mnemosyne* 22, 1969, 155 ff.

38. Ceae : Simonides of Ceos (cf. 4. 9. 7) was regarded as supreme in the pathetic style; cf. Catull. 38. 8 'maestius lacrimis Simonideis', *vita Aeschyli* 8, Dion. Hal. fr. 6. 2. 6 Us. τὸ οἰκτίζεσθαι μὴ μεγαλοπρεπῶς ἀλλὰ παθητικῶς, Quint. *inst.* 10. 1. 64 'praecipua tamen eius in commovenda miseratione virtus ut quidam in hac eum parte omnibus eiusdem operis auctoribus praeferant', Aristides, *orat.* 11. 127 D. ποῖος ταῦτα Σιμωνίδης θρηνήσει;

retractes : 'go over again what you have just handled in the last two stanzas'. Editors interpret 'what Simonides handled', but this lacks point; 'what Pollio handled' would suit 7 *tractas*, but involves the uncomplimentary imputation of *nenia* to the historian. *retractes* reinforces the idea of 'vain repetition' conveyed by *neniae* (see below); this is the decisive argument. The verb is used of a man who keeps on fingering a wound; cf. Cic. *Att.* 8. 9. 3 'sed haec omittamus ; augemus enim dolorem retractando', Ov. *trist.* 3. 11. 19 'et tamen est aliquis qui vulnera cruda retractet', 4. 4. 41 (for the scars of civil war cf. 1. 35. 33 'eheu cicatricum'). Peerlkamp saw the drift when he proposed *Cea retractes vulnera naenia*; but the implication of the verb need not be spelt out quite so literally.

munera : the rites paid to the dead (which in this case consist of lamentation). In funerary contexts there is not always a sharp distinction between this and the concrete sense of 'offerings'; but the former is better suited to the metaphorical *retractes*. Admittedly *munera* usually means 'gifts' in Horace, but for another apparent exception cf. 1. 18. 7 n.

neniae : the word here is used in its proper sense of θρῆνος or funeral-dirge (2. 20. 21, Cic. *leg.* 2. 62, Paul. Fest. 163 M. = 154–6 L.,

RE 16. 2. 2390 ff., Wille 65 ff.). Elsewhere in Horace it refers to a
magic spell (*epod.* 17. 29), a children's jingle (*epist.* 1. 1. 63), and
bed-time music (*carm.* 3. 28. 16). In all these places there is a suggestion of the repetitiousness characteristic of ancient laments (F.
Bücheler, *RhM* 37, 1882, 226 f. = *Kl. Schr.* 2. 432 f., Weinstock 352 ff.,
Alexiou 135 ff.), and this idea has particular force after the *abundantia* of the previous two stanzas. For laments for cities cf. 1. 7. 2 n.,
anth. P. 9. 101–3, 423, Aristides, *orat.* 18, Alexiou 83 ff.

39. mecum : emphatic and confiding, as to a friend or loved one; cf.
1. 32. 2 n.

Dionaeo : Dione in Homer was Aphrodite's mother, but was
identified with Aphrodite herself by Hellenistic and Roman poets;
cf. Theoc. 7. 116 (with Gow's note), Catull. 56. 6, Ov. *fast.* 5. 309 etc.
(cf. Bömer's note). The adjective was a learned substitute for the
metrically intractable *Venerius*; cf. Virg. *ecl.* 9. 47. The form *Dioneo*
is found in many MSS, but a feminine noun of the Greek first declension normally has an adjective in -*αιος* (Housman 2. 887 ff.).

sub antro : grottoes were associated with the Muses and poetry;
cf. 3. 4. 40 'Pierio . . . antro', Pind. *P.* 6. 49 ἐν μυχοῖσι Πιερίδων,
Catull. 61. 28, Prop. 2. 30 b. 26, 3. 1. 5, 3. 3. 14, Str. 9. 2. 25 τὸ τῶν
Λειβηθρίδων νυμφῶν ἄντρον, Stat. *silv.* 4. 5. 59 f. 'verecundo latentem /
barbiton ingemina sub antro', Juv. 7. 59 f., *Thes.l.L.* 2. 192. 8 ff.,
W. Berg, *Early Virgil*, 1974, pp. 116 ff. The scene also suits Venus;
cf. 1. 5. 3, Ov. *am.* 2. 18. 3 'ignava Veneris cessamus in umbra',
Segal 21.

40. quaere modos : writing poetry involves search and discovery
(εὕρεσις); cf. Lucr. 1. 143, Ellis on Catull. 116. 1, C. W. Macleod,
CQ N.S. 23, 1973, 305, R. Flower, *The Irish Tradition*, 1947, p. 24
(translating a ninth-century Irish poem) 'I and Pangur Bán my cat,
'Tis a like task we are at: Hunting mice is his delight, Hunting
words I sit all night'.

leviore plectro : the lightness of the plectrum (2. 13. 27 n.) suits
the lightness of the subject; cf. Ov. *met.* 10. 152 'nunc opus est
leviore lyra', Sen. *Ag.* 334, Stat. *silv.* 1. 4. 36 'tenuiore', *Theb.* 10. 446
'inferiore', Sidon. *carm.* 14. 27 'minore plectro'. Contrast 4. 2. 33
'maiore . . . plectro', Ov. *met.* 10. 150, *culex* 8 'graviore sono', Sen.
Ag. 338, Stat. *silv.* 1. 5. 1. In particular *leviore* makes an opposition
to the stern themes and style of Pollio (cf. D. West ap. Costa 31).

2. NVLLVS ARGENTO COLOR

[W. H. Alexander, *TAPhA* 74, 1943, 192 ff.; W. M. Calder III, *CPh* 56, 1961, 175 ff.; Commager 75 ff.; A. O. Hulton, *CPh* 56, 1961, 173 ff.; W. Kroll, *WS* 37, 1915, 224 f.; Pasquali 626 ff.]

1–8. *Silver underground has no lustre, Sallustius, who have set your face against unworked metal unless it is brightened by handling. Proculeius will live on by his generosity, carried forward on the wings of a posthumous reputation.* 9–16. *You can be king of a broader domain by subduing your avarice than by extending your territory; for a dropsy swells with self-indulgence unless the cause is removed.* 17–24. *Virtue, dissenting from the multitude, denies the felicity of Phraates: the true king looks at treasure without a backward glance.*

This ode is addressed to C. Sallustius Crispus (*RE* 1 A. 1955 f.), the historian's great-nephew and adopted son; it follows the poem to Pollio, Sallust's literary successor, but the sequence would have more point if there were a personal connection as well. Sallustius, though not initially a supporter of the regime, was to succeed Maecenas as Augustus's most trusted minister, partly because he was content with equestrian rank (Sen. *clem.* 1. 10. 1, Tac. *ann.* 3. 30. 3 'incolumi Maecenate proximus, mox praecipuus cui secreta imperatorum inniterentur'); on the emperor's death he undertook the confidential elimination of Agrippa Postumus (*ann.* 1. 6. 3). He was the fortunate proprietor of the Horti Sallustiani between the Pincio and the Quirinale (E. Nash, *Pictorial Dictionary of Ancient Rome* 1, 1961, 491 ff., Grimal 129 ff.); Tacitus in his obituary (A.D. 20) records both his luxury and his energy (*ann.* 3. 30. 2–3 'diversus a veterum instituto per cultum et munditias copiaque et adfluentia luxu propior. suberat tamen vigor animi ingentibus negotiis par, eo acrior quo somnum et inertiam magis ostentabat'). It is important for Horace's poem that he was a generous patron of literature; Crinagoras in a grateful epigram says that he deserved more than the Tres Fortunae (near the Horti) to expend on his friends (*anth. Pl.* 40 = Gow–Page, *GP* 1975 ff.):

γείτονες οὐ τρισσαὶ μοῦνον Τύχαι ἔπρεπον εἶναι,
    Κρίσπε, βαθυπλούτου σῆς ἕνεκεν κραδίης,
ἀλλὰ καὶ αἱ πάντων πᾶσαι· τί γὰρ ἀνδρὶ τοσῷδε
    ἀρκέσει εἰς ἑτάρων μυρίον εὐσοΐην;
νῦν δέ σε καὶ τούτων κρέσσων ἐπὶ μεῖζον ἀέξοι
    Καῖσαρ· τίς κείνου χωρὶς ἄρηρε Τύχη;

It had been a time-honoured custom of the Greek poets to praise their patrons for munificence; a suggestion may be implicit that their eulogists are appropriate beneficiaries, especially when something is added about posthumous glory. See Pind. *P.* 1. 92 ff. μὴ δολωθῇς, ὦ φίλε, κέρδεσιν ἐντραπέλοις· ὀπιθόμβροτον αὔχημα δόξας / οἶον ἀποιχομένων ἀνδρῶν δίαιταν μανύει / καὶ λογίοις καὶ ἀοιδοῖς. οὐ φθίνει Κροίσου φιλόφρων ἀρετά, *N.* 1. 31 f. οὐκ ἔραμαι πολὺν ἐν μεγάρῳ πλοῦτον κατακρύψαις ἔχειν, / ἀλλ' ἐόντων εὖ τε παθεῖν καὶ ἀκοῦσαι φίλοις ἐξαρκέων, *I.* 1. 67 f., Bacch. 3. 13 f. (on Hiero) οἶδε πυργωθέντα πλοῦτον μὴ μελαμφαρέϊ κρύπτειν σκότῳ. Theocritus in his *Charites* develops the same ideas much more blatantly (16. 22 ff., 29 ff.):

> Δαιμόνιοι, τί δὲ κέρδος ὁ μυρίος ἔνδοθι χρυσὸς
> κείμενος; οὐχ ἅδε πλούτου φρονέουσιν ὄνασις,
> ἀλλὰ τὸ μὲν ψυχᾷ, τὸ δέ πού τινι δοῦναι ἀοιδῶν . . .
> Μοισάων δὲ μάλιστα τίειν ἱεροὺς ὑποφήτας,
> ὄφρα καὶ εἰν Ἀΐδαο κεκρυμμένος ἐσθλὸς ἀκούσῃς . . .

He is equally candid in his encomium on Ptolemy (17. 106 f., 112 ff.):

> οὐ μὰν ἀχρεῖός γε δόμῳ ἐνὶ πίονι χρυσὸς
> μυρμάκων ἅτε πλοῦτος ἀεὶ κέχυται μογεόντων . . .
> οὐδὲ Διωνύσου τις ἀνὴρ ἱεροὺς κατ' ἀγῶνας
> ἵκετ' ἐπιστάμενος λιγυρὰν ἀναμέλψαι ἀοιδάν,
> ᾧ οὐ δωτίναν ἀντάξιον ὤπασε τέχνας.
> Μουσάων δ' ὑποφῆται ἀείδοντι Πτολεμαῖον
> ἀντ' εὐεργεσίης· τί δὲ κάλλιον ἀνδρί κεν εἴη
> ὀλβίῳ ἢ κλέος ἐσθλὸν ἐν ἀνθρώποισιν ἀρέσθαι;
> τοῦτο καὶ Ἀτρείδαισι μένει . . .

Horace makes use of such motifs in the first two stanzas of the ode, though his opening motto is derived from tragedy rather than lyric (1 n.). As the poem is a panegyric (*encomiastice* is the heading in one of the families of MSS), he assumes that Sallustius is already munificent (2 ff.); to see signs of criticism (Alexander and Calder, opp. citt.) goes against the conventions of both literature and society (above, pp. 3 f.). He gives an *exemplum* of generosity less legendary than Pindar's Croesus or Theocritus's Atreidae: by his mention of Proculeius (5 ff.) he gratifies another member of the imperial court, who may have had particular ties with Sallustius (the latter's natural father is unknown). Proculeius was also a patron of literature (5 n.), but Horace praises instead his Roman *pietas* to his brothers; he thus avoids any appearance of self-seeking, and introduces a moral note that coheres with the rest of the ode. In view of the literary antecedents of his opening theme and the known generosity to poets of both Sallustius and Proculeius, he is presumably

offering a return for subsidies received or expected; his reluctance
to say so directly makes a contrast with Theocritus and even
Pindar, but suits the aristocratic view of *beneficia*, which were
represented without conscious hypocrisy as reciprocal kindnesses
among friends (cf. Cic. *off.* 1. 56 'magna etiam illa communitas est
quae conficitur ex beneficiis ultro [et] citro datis acceptis' etc., A. R.
Hands, *Charities and Social Aid in Greece and Rome*, 1968, pp. 26 ff.).

Horace carries his delicacy so far that he presents the encomium
of a rich benefactor as a denunciation of materialism; it is convenient
for his case that meanness could be regarded as a particular aspect
of *avaritia* (9 n.). Already in the first eight lines there are hints of
moral philosophy, and from the third stanza this element dominates
the poem in a way that would have been impossible for classical
Greek lyric (Pasquali, loc. cit., Syndikus 1. 352 ff.); even the formula-
tions of later Greek epigram are half-hearted by comparison (Lucianus, *anth. P.* 10. 41. 1 πλοῦτος ὁ τῆς ψυχῆς πλοῦτος μόνος ἐστὶν ἀληθής).
It was an Epicurean view that wealth is attainable by the limitation
of desire (9 n.), but the prevailing attitudes are more characteristically
Stoic; even if some of Horace's aphorisms are commonplaces of
several schools, the conspicuous Stoicism of the last two stanzas
must be allowed to colour the poem as a whole. The value of riches
depends on their use (4 n.), posthumous fame is true immortality
(8 n.), avarice must be subdued and not merely modified (9 n.),
a personified Virtus teaches the correct use of language (19 nn.), the
only true king is the man who disdains wealth (9 n., 19 n., 21 n.).
The contrast with the following ode to Dellius is remarkable, but the
difference is not to be explained only by Horatian eclecticism (*epist.*
1. 1. 13 ff.); if the poet's practice elsewhere is a guide (cf. 2. 10,
pp. 152 f.), Sallustius himself is likely to have shown an interest in
Stoicism. Such a conclusion seems unwelcome because of Tacitus's
picture of ostentatious inertia (see above), but even he recognized
vigour; at the time of the ode Sallustius is still a young man with
forty-five years remaining of comfort and decline, and in the bracing
atmosphere of the twenties an aspiring courtier would make more
strenuous professions than Maecenas. Seneca did not find great wealth
incompatible with sincere Stoic convictions, and Sallustius's own
great-uncle, from whom he perhaps inherited his Pincian park, presented himself as a Sabine moralist with an admiration for Cato and
a horror of *avaritia* (for Stoic influences cf. Earl 6).

The ode to Sallustius is tightly organized in three blocks of two
stanzas; each is self-contained until the last pair, where the enjambement adds momentum to the climax. The argument proceeds by
paratactic statements and abrupt *exempla*; the illustrations blend
elements from lyric (7), philosophy, and the contemporary world.

The clipped *sententiae* suit the short stanzas (cf. 2. 10), and combine Stoic austerity (cf. Epictetus and Marcus Aurelius) with the pointedness of declamation; the density is remarkable even for Horace (cf. especially 2 ff., 13 ff., 17 ff.), and syntactical neologisms help the compression (6 *notus animi, 7 metuente solvi*). The style is deliberately 'unpoetical', but not therefore to be deplored (*pace* Axelson 112); the ugly description of dropsy is worlds away from Greek lyric (13 ff.), but reflects the plain-spoken parables of *diatribe*. The tone of the ode no less than its content suggests that in spite of his magnificence Sallustius affected the severity of his great-uncle (contrast the geniality of 2. 16); certainly he was no Maecenas as far as literature was concerned. When Horace invited the Muse to sport with lighter quill (2. 1. 37 ff.), we were not prepared for these Stoic Sapphics; once again he has surprised us with a brusque and dry but brilliantly concentrated and most original poem.

Metre: Sapphic.

1. **nullus argento color est**: it seems more pointed to refer this aphorism to silver in the mine (Housman cited below on 2) rather than to the miser's hoard (Porphyrio, Bentley, Heinze). It was a commonplace of moralists that precious metals were dirty in their natural state; cf. Sen. *epist*. 94. 58 'nihil est istis quamdiu mersa et involuta caeno suo iacent foedius, nihil obscurius', Plin. *nat*. 33. 95 (specifically of silver) 'nonnisi in puteis reperitur nullaque spe sui nascitur, nullis ut in auro luculentis scintillis', Tert. *cult. fem*. 1. 5. 1 'aurum et argentum, principes materiae cultus saecularis, ea sint necesse est unde sunt, terra scilicet', Cassiod. *epist*. 4. 34 'divitis auri vena similis est reliquae terrae si iaceat: usu crescit ad pretium'. Of course Horace's real subject is the correct use of wealth (cf. from a different standpoint Plut. *cup. div*. 528 a μηδενὸς ὁρῶντος μηδὲ προσβλέποντος τυφλὸς γίνεται καὶ ἀφεγγὴς ὁ πλοῦτος); but this in no way tells against an image from the mine. A comparison is being drawn between the lack of sparkle in unmined silver and the lack of attractiveness in unused wealth; such ingenious analogies were common in popular philosophy, notably in the extended similes of Plutarch's *Moralia*.

The question is complicated by an apparent allusion to the Greek tragic line οὐκ ἔστ' ἐν ἄντροις λευκός, ὦ ξέν', ἄργυρος (*trag. adesp*. 389 N.); unfortunately the drift of this line is itself uncertain, and we cannot be sure that Horace would represent it accurately. It is cited by Plutarch as the sort of thing a man of spirit would say to an importunate guest (*vit. pud*. 533 a), presumably 'there is no glittering silver in my humble home'; Heinze suggested that the poet was

referring to the caves of Philoctetes and that the resemblance to
Horace was fortuitous. But in spite of the important evidence of
Plutarch, the word-order suggests that λευκός is predicative ('silver
is not white in caverns'); in that case the similarity of Horace's
maxim is surely deliberate. The tragedian may be making a general
remark about unmined silver, with the same metaphorical point as
Horace's; for the use of ἄντροις cf. Cic. *nat. deor.* 2. 151 'nos e terrae
cavernis ferrum elicimus'. A reference to buried treasure seems less
likely, as people do not normally hoard their money in caves; yet
ἄντροις may have been so regarded by Claudian 1. 42 f. (perhaps influenced by his interpretation of Horace) 'hic non divitias nigrantibus
abdidit antris / nec tenebris damnavit opes'.

It is also worth mentioning that Sallustius owned copper-mines
near the Val D'Aosta (Plin. *nat.* 34. 3 'proximum bonitate fuit Sallu-
stianum in Ceutronum Alpino tractu'); cf. also *CIL* 5. 6821 (from the
same neighbourhood) 'C. Sallustio Crispi L.'. There is no evidence
that he owned silver-mines, but a poet might not trouble about the
difference.

color : the word can be used of a brightness as relatively colourless
as that of silver; cf. Ov. *epist.* 21. 219, Sen. *Ag.* 861 'lucis ignotae
metuens colorem', Plin. *nat.* 33. 58 'colore qui clarior in argento est
(quam in auro) . . . magisque diei similis est'. Horace's proposition
has a scientific air (Lucr. 2. 737 f. 'nullus enim color est omnino
materiai / corporibus'), but he turns out to be thinking of more than
a lack of secondary qualities in the dark.

avaris : the earth is niggardly because it is reluctant to yield its
minerals. The adjective also hints obliquely at the human miserliness
that is rejected in the next clause; for such an interaction between
an image and the true subject cf. 2. 9. 2 n.

2. abdito terris : cf. 3. 3. 49 ff. 'aurum inrepertum et sic melius
situm / cum terra celat spernere fortior / quam cogere humanos in
usus'; though Horace here suggests the opposite attitude, the inconsistency need cause no concern (cf. Aesch. *Prom.* 500 ff. ἔνερθε
δὲ χθονὸς / κεκρυμμέν' ἀνθρώποισιν ὠφελήματα, / χαλκὸν σίδηρον ἄργυ-
ρον χρυσόν τε). *abdito* suits a mine just as well as a hoard; cf. Cic.
nat. deor. 2. 98 'reconditas' (with Pease's note), 2. 151 'nos aeris
argenti auri venas penitus abditas invenimus', *laus Pis.* 225 f.
'abdita quid prodest generosi vena metalli / si cultore caret?',
Sen. *epist.* 94. 57. Plural *terris* might seem to suggest the mine,
but would not be incompatible with the hoard; cf. *serm.* 1. 8. 42 f.
'utque lupi barbam variae cum dente colubrae / abdiderint furtim
terris'.

inimice lamnae . . . : 'who have set your face against sheet-metal, unless it shines with judicious use'; if the text is right, the conditional clause must be taken closely with the vocative (Bentley). The earliest editors understood 'nullus argento abdito color est nisi splendeat usu'; Lambinus complained that this was as fatuous as saying 'no ugly woman is attractive unless she is beautiful'. But the incoherence is mitigated by the change to the subjunctive at *splendeat*, which could suggest that the hypothesis is not too obvious ('there is no sparkle in unmined silver—unless of course it should gain lustre from use'); the real objection to such a theory is that the lavish Sallustius cannot be called *inimice lamnae* without the qualification of the *nisi* clause. Lambinus himself emended to *abditae*, regarding the vocative as *avaris / abditae terris inimice lamnae / Crispe Sallusti*; but the parenthesis begins at an awkward place, is impossibly top-heavy, and interrupts the main proposition for too long.

Doubts may still be felt about the text (see especially Housman I. I = *JPh* 10, 1882, 187 and I. 96 f. = *JPh* 17, 1888, 309 f., A. Y. Campbell's edition, 1953, pp. 42 ff.); but some at least of the objections raised seem to lack substance. Housman thought that *inimice* and its train of dependants overbalanced the sentence; but the construction is admirably paralleled by 2. 3. 4 ff. 'moriture Delli, / seu . . .' (the protasis continues for four lines), Catull. 11. 1 ff. 'Furi et Aureli, comites Catulli (sc. *futuri*), / sive in extremos penetrabit Indos' (the protasis continues for ten further lines). The offending phrase is itself supported by Sil. 13. 723 'auro Curium non unquam cernit amicum'; or if it is objected that *inimicus* goes better with *auro* (cf. φιλόχρυσος) than with the over-specific *lamnae*, one may point to Cic. *epist.* 9. 23 'exspecta igitur hospitem cum minime edacem, tum inimicum cenis sumptuosis'. Indeed it could be argued that *inimicus* has a semi-philosophic nuance that suits the tone of the poem; though ancient moralists did not normally preach a total rejection of wealth, the reasonableness of the expression is preserved by the qualification *nisi temperato splendeat usu*. It is admittedly unusual that Horace should commend Sallustius for already following his improving maxim (it weakens the illusion of paraenesis if the point is acknowledged so explicitly); but one can hardly say that such tact to a patron is impossible (cf. perhaps Pind. *I. 2. 12* ἐσσὶ γὰρ ὦν σοφός).

Housman raised another objection to Bentley's construction: he maintained that 'unmined silver has no lustre' is not an argument against avarice, seeing that the avaricious 'do not propose to leave silver in the *mine*'. He therefore wished in lines 2–4 to interpose an indicative proposition against *hoarding*, in order to provide a connection with the instance of liberality in the second stanza. But this formulation may involve too literal an interpretation of the deliberately ambiguous opening maxim: though the nominal theme at that stage is the mine and not the hoard, the point of the semi-proverbial phrase is to recommend liberality rather than the extraction of minerals. It remains true that the case of Proculeius directly illustrates neither the opening maxim (which is negative in form) nor the description of Sallustius (which is not a generalization). But one must allow for some measure of ellipse in Horace's clipped argumentation (cf. 13 n.): from the opening maxim there can be derived the proposition 'silver when used does glitter' (even if *nisi splendeat usu* must be attached primarily to *inimice*).

Housman himself proposed *minimusque* or more plausibly *minuitque* (literally 'the lustre diminishes for sheet-metal'). He pointed to the common misreading of downstrokes (cf. 1. 35. 24?, *Thes.l.L.* 7. 1. 1623. 73 ff.), as well as to other confusions of *c* and *qu* in Horace's MSS. He cited the very striking parallel at Prud. *c. Symm.* 2. 754 f. 'candor perit argenti si defuit usus, / et fuscata situ corrumpit vena colorem'; in this apparent reminiscence of Horace, *perit* corresponds exactly to *minuit*. As he himself admitted, other classical instances of intransitive *minuere* are confined to the present participle (*Thes.l.L.* 8. 1039. 53 ff.), but one could meet this point by suggesting an imitation of φθίνει. It might be added that *minuit* suits the imagery of the poem with its series of paradoxical contrasts between increase and decrease: the shine of silver is impaired by saving and enhanced by moderate wear, by reducing his wealth Proculeius extends his fame (Horace might have recalled Pindar's οὐ φθίνει Κροίσου φιλόφρων / ἀρετά, cited above, p. 33), one can rule a broader domain by restricting one's avarice than by expanding one's territory (9 ff.), the desire for more is a swelling dropsy whose repletion seems deprivation (13 f.). But though from this point of view *minuitque* seems very attractive, it is not clear that a decisive argument has been found against *inimice*.

lamnae : sheet-metal, i.e. unminted silver ('ingots' gives the right drift though they are chunkier); cf. Sen. *ben.* 7. 10. 1 'lamnas utriusque materiae ad quam cupiditas nostra caligat', Ulp. *dig.* 34. 2. 27. 6 'argentum factum recte quis ita definierit, quod neque in massa neque in lamna neque in signato . . . insit', Blümner, *Technologie* 4. 230, 308. The word is sometimes used of actual cash (cf. Petron. 57. 4, 57. 6, 58. 8), but the usage seems too colloquial for Horace; there is more point in a reference to uncoined and therefore unusable metal. It remains true that *lamnae* has a contemptuous note, perhaps reinforced by the syncope (though the form is also attested at Val. Fl. 1. 123). The word cannot refer to unworked ore (in spite of Porphyrio's ambiguous 'pro rudi et infabricata materia').

3. Crispe Sallusti : see above, p. 32; for the inversion of *nomen* and *cognomen*, already attested in Republican Latin, cf. Ogilvie on Liv. 4. 23. 1, Gudeman on Tac. *dial.* 1. 1, H.–Sz. 410. Here there might be a verbal point in the emphasis on *Crispe*, which properly means 'crinkly' of hair; the word might make a contrast with *lamnae* either because sheets of silver are smooth, or because *lamna* could also mean 'a razor' at least in late Latin (cf. Sidon. *epist.* 8. 9. 5, vers. 24 f., *Thes.l.L.* 7. 2. 906. 57 ff.). For similar emphasis cf. 2. 9. 19 n., *epist.* 1. 8. 1 'Celso . . . Albinovano' (with perhaps a hint at the man's loftiness); the point is only worth considering here if *inimice* is retained above.

temperato : a philosophical word (2. 3. 3 n.): Sallustius is munificent without being profligate (cf. Stat. *silv.* 2. 2. 152 f. 'docta fruendi / temperies', 2. 3. 70 f. 'idem auri facilis contemptor et optimus idem / promere divitias opibusque immittere lucem'). This word puts the emphasis on the moral situation, whereas the opening line referred primarily to metal. But just as *avaris* pointed forward to human behaviour, so *temperato* can be referred also to silver, which should be rubbed neither too little nor too much.

4. splendeat : the verb suggests both the literal sparkle of the metal (stronger than 1 *color*) and the metaphorical lustre that is derived from benefactions; cf. Boeth. *cons. phil.* 2. 5 'atqui haec effundendo magis quam coacervando melius nitent'. The subjunctive may be meant to suggest that the hypothesis is not too obvious (see above on *inimice lamnae*), or perhaps rather it is an instance of virtual *oratio obliqua*, indicating Sallustius's own attitude (cf. Alexander, loc. cit.). Note how swiftly Horace has moved from unmined *argentum* to unworked *lamna* to usable plate or money.

usu : it was a commonplace paradox that metal is kept bright by handling but discoloured with disuse; cf. Soph. fr. 864 P. = 780 N. λάμπει γὰρ ἐν χρείαισιν ὥσπερ εὐγενὴς / χαλκός, Theoc. 16. 17 (on silver money) οὐδέ κεν ἰὸν ἀποτρίψας τινὶ δοίη, Ov. *am.* 1. 8. 51 'aera nitent usu', Apul. *flor.* 17. 79, Sidon. *epist.* 8. 7. 1, Cassiod. loc. cit. (above on 1 *color*). Horace's noun suits not just literal handling but the right employment of money, a favourite theme of the Stoics, who regarded riches as 'indifferent'; cf. *serm.* 1. 1. 73 'nescis quo valeat nummus, quem praebeat usum?', *SVF* 3. 117 πλούτῳ δὲ καὶ ὑγιείᾳ ἔστιν εὖ καὶ κακῶς χρῆσθαι (so 119, 122–3), Cebes 39. 4, Norden on Virg. *Aen.* 6. 608–17, M. T. Griffin, *Seneca*, 1976, pp. 295 ff.

5. vivet extento . . . aevo : Horace has precedent for an *exemplum* in his Greek prototypes (p. 33), and he honours friends elsewhere who are not the main subject of a poem (1. 24. 10 ff., 1. 36. 7, *epist.* 1. 3. 9 ff., 1. 12. 22 ff., cf. Virg. *ecl.* 6). The emphatic verb refers as often to

survival in the minds of men (Cic. *amic.* 102, Tib. 1. 4. 65, Ov. *met.*
15. 879 etc.); by a similar paradox great poems are said to live
(4. 9. 11, *epist.* 1. 19. 2, Call. *ep.* 2. 5). There is a minor variant *vivit*
here and a better attested *agit* below (Porphyrio 'per quam semper
volat', 7 'quasi fama illum agit pinna sua'); but Proculeius cannot
be said to 'live' in this metaphorical sense until his death, and he
seems to have been literally alive in 23–22 B.C. (see Tacitus, cited in
next note). For fame as a prolongation of life cf. Virg. *Aen.* 10. 468
'famam extendere factis', Stat. *Theb.* 4. 33, Sil. 9. 375 f., Plin. *epist.*
5. 8. 1, Symm. *epist.* 10. 12. 4.

Proculeius : Porphyrio comments 'Proculeius eques Romanus,
amicus Augusti, carissimae pietatis erga fratres suos Scipionem et
Murenam fuit, adeo ut bona sua cum his aequis partibus diviserit
quia illi bello civili erant spoliati'; this Murena was the alleged conspirator (Dio 54. 3. 5, below, p. 152), who was the brother-in-law of
Maecenas. In place of *Scipionem* (Porph. and ps.-Acro) Torrentius
proposed *Caepionem* (Murena's associate in the conspiracy), but
when Dio says that Proculeius interceded for Murena (loc. cit.) he
does not mention Caepio; as Caepio's father owned an estate at the
time of the conspiracy (Macr. *sat.* 1. 11. 21), the son might not have
needed Proculeius's subsidies. Horace presumably knew Proculeius
because of his relationship to Maecenas, but the reference to his
fratres would naturally have been deleted if the book had been published after the conspiracy (below, p. 156).

Proculeius himself enjoyed high favour with the Princeps (Dio
54. 3. 5), and was entrusted by him with the most delicate missions :
he was invited to kill his leader following a defeat by Sextus Pompeius
(Plin. *nat.* 7. 148), he played a skilful part in the capture of Cleopatra
(Dio 51. 11. 4, Plut. *Ant.* 78–9, cf. Shakespeare, *Antony and Cleopatra*),
he was even considered by Augustus as an unpolitical son-in-law
(Tac. *ann.* 4. 40. 6), presumably after the death of Marcellus. He
makes a good pair with Sallustius as an equestrian courtier and a
generous benefactor ; cf. Rutil. Lup. 1. 5 (on his liberality to his son),
Juv. 7. 94 f. 'quis tibi Maecenas, quis nunc erit aut Proculeius / aut
Fabius?' Pliny records his distinctive suicide (*nat.* 36. 183 'exemplum inlustre C. Proculeium Augusti Caesaris familiaritate subnixum
in stomachi dolore gypso poto conscivisse sibi mortem') ; this sounds
like an old man's despair, and was presumably a long way ahead.
See further *RE* 23. 1. 72 ff.

6. notus . . . animi paterni : the mannered genitive adds compression
and distinction ; cf. 4. 13. 21 f. 'notaque et artium / gratarum facies',
Prop. 1. 16. 2 (earlier than the Horatian passages) 'ianua Tarpeiae
nota pudicitiae' (see H. Tränkle, *Die Sprachkunst des Properz*,

Hermes Einzelschriften 15, 1960, 68 f.), Stat. *Theb.* 2. 274, Sil. 15. 270, 17. 147. The construction is easier because *notus* is a participle (cf. similar genitives with *admirandus, laudandus, venerandus*), but it is also found with *clarus* (Plin. *nat.* 37. 8) and many other adjectives (K.–S. 1. 443 ff., H.–Sz. 79). There can be no question in our passage of taking *notus* with *vivet* and dissociating it from the genitive; *vivet notus* is much weaker than absolute *vivet* (Bentley).

in fratres : for similar expressions cf. 4. 4. 27 f. 'paternus / in pueros animus Nerones', Cic. *S. Rosc.* 46 'qui animus patrius in liberos esset'. The noun balances *paterni*, as brothers proverbially quarrel (Thyestes, Polynices, Romulus) ; cf. Hes. *op.* 184, Lucr. 3. 72, Virg. *georg.* 2. 496, Bömer on Ov. *met.* 1. 145, Liv. 40. 8. 11, Tac. *ann.* 13. 17. 1, D. Vessey, *Statius and the Thebaid*, 1973, pp. 62 f.

7. aget : 'will carry forward' (cf. 'extento . . . aevo') ; the wings of fame here suggest wide-ranging movement (below, p. 333, Claud. 1. 34 'illum Fama vehit trans aequora'). Horace is saying more than 'carry' (Mart. 10. 3. 10 'quos rumor alba gemmeus vehit penna') or 'carry up' (Prop. 3. 1. 9 'quo me Fama levat terra sublimis', Stat. *silv.* 2. 7. 108, Pind. *I.* 1. 64 f. πτερύγεσσιν ἀερθέντ' ἀγλααῖς Πιερίδων).

metuente solvi : 'that disdains to droop'. *metuere* can be used where there is a fastidious hesitation rather than a real fear; cf. 3. 11. 10 'metuitque tangi' ('refuses to be touched'), 4. 5. 20 'culpari metuit fides' ('honour shuns reproach'), *serm.* 2. 5. 65 'metuentis reddere soldum' ('unwilling to pay up' in an ironic sense), Virg. *georg.* 1. 246 'Arctos Oceani metuentes aequore tingui' (= Aratus 48 ἄρκτοι . . . πεφυλαγμέναι 'Ωκεανοῖο), *Thes.l.L.* 8. 905. 30 ff. It should be noted further that these parallels go beyond mental hesitation towards overt refusal (cf. 2. 14. 16 n.) ; this tendency is accentuated in our passage, which suggests an undrooping wing. Horace's expression is admittedly an odd way of describing confident resolution, but there may be an element of paradox in his formulation : the man of true worth aims to be remembered and is shy only of failure. There is less edge in Sanadon's *renuente* (for the corruption cf. Housman, *Manil.* 1, p. xlix), while A. Y. Campbell's *nequeunte* is dull.

solvi means 'to droop', like a bird's wings (cf. Pind. *P.* 1. 6 ὠκεῖαν πτέρυγ' ἀμφοτέρωθεν χαλάξαις) ; contrast Hom. *Od.* 2. 149 τιταινομένω πτερύγεσσιν. By implication the wings of Proculeius's fame will be extended no less than his life (*solvi* balances 5 *extento*). Some see a reference to the melting wax of Icarus (4. 2. 2 ff.), but that illustration is too particular and too ill-omened.

8. fama superstes : for the phrase cf. Ov. *trist.* 3. 7. 50, Boeth. *cons.* 2 carm. 7. 17, *Thes.l.L.* 6. 1. 225. 26 f. ; here *fama* is Proculeius's own reputation, and must be distinguished from winged Rumour (Pease

on Virg. *Aen.* 4. 173, *RE* 6. 1977 ff.). The adjective is semi-legal: post-humous glory is a substitute for heirs. The thought is both Roman and Stoic; cf. Sen. *epist.* 102. 3 (= *SVF* 3. 100) 'id quod nostris placet, claritatem quae post mortem contingit bonum esse'. At a purely formal level *super-* seems to reinforce the loftiness of *pinna*, and *-stes* to be contrasted with the movement of *aget*.

9. **latius regnes** : for *late regnare* cf. 1. 12. 57 n., *Thes.l.L.* 7. 2. 1021. 67 f.; here the emphatic adverb balances 5 *extento*. The wise man is king by the Stoic paradox because of his self-control and inner security (21 n.); cf. especially Sen. *epist.* 113. 30 'o quam magnis homines tenentur erroribus qui ius dominandi trans maria cupiunt permittere (? promittere) felicissimosque se iudicant si multas milite provincias obtinent et novas veteribus adiungunt, ignari quod sit illud ingens parque dis regnum: imperare sibi maximum imperium est'. Here the notion is blended with the more typically Epicurean view that riches are achieved by limiting desire; cf. Democritus 284 ἢν μὴ πολλῶν ἐπιθυμέῃς, τὰ ὀλίγα τοι πολλὰ δόξει· σμικρὰ γὰρ ὄρεξις πενίην ἰσοσθενέα πλούτῳ ποιέει, Epicurus, fr. 135 εἰ βούλει πλούσιον Πυθοκλέα ποιῆσαι, μὴ χρημάτων προστίθει τῆς δὲ ἐπιθυμίας ἀφαίρει, sent. *Vat.* 25 πλοῦτος δὲ μὴ ὁριζόμενος μεγάλη ἐστὶ πενία, 44 ὁ σοφὸς εἰς τὰ ἀναγκαῖα συγκλεισθεὶς μᾶλλον ἐπίσταται μεταδιδόναι ἢ μεταλαμβάνειν. τηλικοῦτον αὐταρκείας εὗρε θησαυρόν, Manil. 4. 6 with Housman's note, Publil. E. 8 'effugere cupiditatem regnum est vincere', Claud. 3. 196 ff., Pasquali 631 ff. Horace's mention of territorial ownership gives the commonplace a characteristically Roman emphasis.

Horace is not suggesting that Sallustius is avaricious but quite the reverse; as often in *diatribe*, the second person can refer to the world at large rather than the direct recipient (below, p. 290). The mood of the verb helps the generalization ('one can reign'); cf. S. A. Handford, *The Latin Subjunctive*, 1947, pp. 107 ff. There is an easy slide from *domando* to the more hypothetical protasis *iungas*; for the same sort of progression cf. 3. 16. 39 ff. 'contracto melius parva cupidine / vectigalia porrigam / quam si Mygdoniis regnum Alyattei / campis continuem'.

avidum domando spiritum : the view that the passions should be subdued is characteristically Stoic (*SVF* 3. 443 ff.). Horace is re-ferring not to the desires in general (ἐπιθυμίαι), but to avarice in particular. He has glided from the notion of meanness (of which Sal-lustius is obviously innocent) to that of acquisitiveness, from which he dissociates his rich friend by this subtle transition.

The metaphor comes from taming animals (though it also suits subjugation by kings); cf. 1. 16. 22 n., Cic. *rep.* 2. 67 'at vero ea quae latet in animis hominum . . . non unam aut facilem ad subigendum

frenat et domat, si quando id efficit, quod perraro potest', Headlam–
Thomson on Aesch. *Eum.* 476, *Chald. orac.* 113 des Places (p. 52
Kroll) χρὴ δὲ χαλινῶσαι ψυχὴν βροτὸν ὄντα νοητόν, Boeth. *cons.* 3 *carm.*
5. 2. The physical nature of the verb makes a contrast with *spiritum*,
while the implied element of restriction makes a contrast with *latius*.
For the ablative of the gerund in gnomic statements cf. 2. 10. 2 f.,
4. 11. 30; the slightly archaic construction emphasizes the object
more clearly than the prosaic *spiritu domando* (K.–S. 1. 735 f.,
H.–Sz. 373).

10. **Libyam** ... : *latifundia* were often described in hyperboles; for
overseas instances cf. 3. 16. 41 f. [above, 9 n.], Sen. *contr. exc.* 5.
5. 2 [below, p. 241], Sen. *epist.* 89. 20 'hoc quoque parum est nisi
latifundis vestris maria cinxistis, nisi trans Hadriam et Ionium
Aegaeumque vester vilicus regnat . . .', 90. 39, Petron. 48. 3, Plin.
nat. 18. 35, Claud. 3. 196 ff. 'teneas utrumque licebit / Oceanum . . .
numquam dives eris' (following 194 f. 'populi servire coacti / plenaque
privato succumbunt oppida regno'), Pasquali 629 ff. As in several
of the above parallels, the large land-owner is here seen as a kind of
king (cf. 12 *serviat*); thus Horace can draw a contrast with the true
kingship of the wise man. L. Müller thought that he meant a literal
kingdom, but the target is Roman plutocracy rather than people
like Juba (who in 25 B.C. was given a new domain in Mauretania).
On the other hand Horace is unlikely to be alluding to African properties that Sallustius might have inherited from his great-uncle (*procos. Africa Nova*, 46–5); so hyperbolical a reminder of the historian's
malversations would be unnecessarily indiscreet.

11. **Gadibus** : the place is mentioned because of its proverbial remoteness (2. 6. 1 n.), which suits the fantastic hyperbole. Bücheler
suspected an allusion to Spanish mines, continuing the image of
1 f. (*RhM* 37, 1882, 227 f. = *Kl. Schr.* 2. 433); such a view might
seem to be supported by Sen. *Thy.* 353 ff. (on the indifference to
wealth of the true 'king') 'non quidquid fodit Occidens / aut unda
Tagus aurea / claro devehit alveo, / non quidquid Libycis terit /
fervens area messibus'. But in the absence of anything more specific,
the reader naturally understands Horace to refer to *latifundia*.

iungas : the word is sometimes used of joining up territories (cf.
Lucan 1. 167, Petron. 77. 3, Plin. *epist.* 3. 19. 2); here it makes a formal antithesis with *remotis* (literally 'taken away'). There also
seems to be a verbal play on 'breaking in' (*domando*) and 'yoking' (cf.
Cic. *Arat.* fr. 18. 3 'iunctum domitumque iuvencum'). The series of
verbs produces a sort of chiasmus (*regnes, domando, iungas, serviat*).

uterque Poenus : not only had there been extensive Carthaginian
settlement in southern Spain, but many of the inhabitants seem still

to have been regarded as Punic; cf. Str. 3. 4. 5–6, Sen. *dial.* 12. 7. 2,
Plin. *nat.* 3. 8 'oram eam in universum originis Poenorum existi-
mavit M. Agrippa', Mela 2. 96, Bücheler, loc. cit. [on *Gadibus*].
Gades (Gadir) had particularly strong Phoenician associations; cf.
Porph. ad loc. 'quia Carthaginem sicut Gadem Poeni condiderunt',
Cic. *Balb.* 32 'ignosco tibi si neque Poenorum iura calles . . .', *RE*
7. 454. *uterque* is used allusively in the celebration of far-flung em-
pires (Virg. *georg.* 3. 33 'utroque ab litore gentes', *Aen.* 7. 100 f.) ; here
it makes a contrast with *uni*.

13. crescit . . . : Horace justifies the previous stanza in the form of
an abrupt analogy: the full argument would have run 'for avarice
grows with what it feeds on just as a dropsy swells . . .'. *latius* is
opposed by *crescit* (the good and bad kinds of growth), *avidum
domando* by *indulgens sibi* (likewise describing the means), *spiritum*
by 16 *corpore*. In the same way *sitim* and *causa morbi* correspond to
elements implicit in the moral situation (see notes below) ; on the
other hand the analogy takes on a life of its own, and 15 *venis* has
no correlative.

   crescit suits both the disease (Ser. Samm. 493 f. 'acerbus / crescit
hydrops') and the love of money; cf. 3. 16. 17 'crescentem sequitur
cura pecuniam / maiorumque fames', Juv. 14. 139 'crescit amor
nummi quantum ipsa pecunia crevit'. The insatiability of avarice
is a commonplace of moralists; cf. *epist.* 1. 2. 56 'semper avarus eget',
Solon 13. 71 ff. W., Arist. *pol.* 1267ᵇ4 ff. ἄπειρος γὰρ ἡ τῆς ἐπιθυμίας
φύσις ἧς πρὸς τὴν ἀναπλήρωσιν οἱ πολλοὶ ζῶσιν, Gow on Theoc. 16. 65,
Sall. *Cat.* 11. 3 'semper infinita insatiabilis est, neque copia neque
inopia minuitur', Mayor on Juv. loc. cit., Otto 50 f., Oltramare 288.

   dirus : the adjective suits deadly diseases and destructive emotions
(Lucr. 4. 1046, 1090). There seems also to be a hint that avarice mul-
tiplies like the dread hydra of legend (*epist.* 2. 10 'diram qui contudit
hydram') ; cf. ps.-Sall. *epist.* 2. 8. 4 'avaritia belua fera immanis in-
toleranda est'. The alliteration of *s* in this sentence (noted by Wilkinson 138) would suit the hissing of a serpent.

   hydrops : according to ancient doctors dropsy was caused by self-
indulgence, resulted in thirst (*epist.* 2. 2. 146, but untrue), got worse
through drinking, could be relieved by abstinence and exercise
(*epist.* 1. 2. 34 'si noles sanus, curres hydropicus'), and was difficult
to cure (Ov. *Pont.* 1. 3. 24) ; cf. especially Cels. 3. 21. 2 'facilius in
servis quam in liberis tollitur quia cum desideret famem sitim mille
alia taedia longamque patientiam, promptius iis succurritur qui
facile coguntur quam quibus inutilis libertas est . . . 4 inter initia
tamen non difficilis curatio est si imperata sunt corpori sitis requies
inedia : at si malum inveteravit non nisi magna mole discutitur'. The

disease was used as an analogy for avarice, probably first in Cynic *diatribe*, though it was taken over by Cyrenaics, Stoics, and others; cf. Diogenes ap. Stob. 3. 10. 45, p. 419 Hense ὡμοίου τοὺς φιλαργύρους τοῖς ὑδρωπικοῖς· ἐκείνους μὲν γὰρ πλήρεις ὄντας ὑγροῦ ἐπιθυμεῖν πότου (the attribution is likely to be fictitious), Teles, περὶ πενίας καὶ πλούτου, p. 39 Hense καὶ εἴ τις βούλεται ἢ αὐτὸς ἐνδείας καὶ σπάνεως ἀπολυθῆναι ἢ ἄλλον ἀπολῦσαι, μὴ χρήματα αὐτῷ ζητείτω. ὅμοιον γάρ, φησὶν ὁ Βίων, ὡς εἴ τις τὸν ὑδρωπικὸν βουλόμενος παῦσαι τοῦ δίψους, τὸν μὲν ὕδρωπα μὴ θεραπεύοι, κρήνας δὲ καὶ ποταμοὺς αὐτῷ παρασκευάζοι, anon. ap. Stob. 4. 31. 84, p. 762 Hense, *gnom. Vat.* 434 Sternbach, Plb. 13. 2. 2 (cited below on 14 *causa morbi*), Lucil. 764 'aquam te in animo habere intercutem', Ov. *fast.* 1. 215 f. 'sic quibus intumuit suffusa venter ab unda / quo plus sunt potae plus sitiuntur aquae', Sen. *dial.* 12. 11. 3, Longinus 3. 4, Prud. *perist.* 2. 237 ff., *Thes.l.L.* 6. 3. 3137. 80 ff., F. J. E. Raby, *A History of Secular Latin Poetry in the Middle Ages*[2] 2, 1957, 209 'quanto plus adcumulant tanto plus marcescunt, / sunt velut hydropici, quorum membra crescunt: / cum plus bibunt sitiunt, magis exarescunt; / sic avari miseri numquam requiescunt', Dante, *inf.* 30. 52, *OED* s.v. 'dropsy', 'hydroptic' etc. For more general references to avarice as a disease cf. Headlam–Thomson on Aesch. *Ag.* 990–2 (health and wealth), Epicurus, fr. 471, *SVF* 3. 421–30, Galen 5. 51 K., Oltramare 287. Medical analogies were employed particularly by Cynics and Stoics; cf. Gerhard 11 f., H. Lackenbacher, *WS* 55, 1937, 130 ff. (on Persius), Hadot 13 ff., 142 ff., Bramble 35 f.

14. sitim : the word is significantly a common metaphor for *cupiditas*; cf. *epist.* 1. 18. 23 'argenti sitis importuna', Lucr. 3. 1084, Cic. *parad.* 6.

pellas : *pellit*, the reading of the MSS, seems very difficult. *hydrops* refers here to the disease of dropsy, not to the dropsical patient (as sometimes in Greek); this is shown by *dirus*. But it is not for the disease to drive out the thirst but for the instructed sufferer (i.e. the moral agent); cf. the medical use of *expellere* at *epist.* 2. 2. 137 'expulit helleboro morbum bilemque meraco', *Thes.l.L.* 5. 2. 1635. 34 ff. Peerlkamp proposed *pellas* (cf. 9 *regnes*); by a common corruption the ending has been assimilated to that of *crescit* (cf. 1. 8. 6 n., 1. 23. 1), perhaps because of an impression that *hydrops* refers to the patient. O. Peil (ap. L. Müller) proposed *pellis*; the sequence of tenses is not a serious objection, and the indicative in isolation could have a potential implication (= *pellere potes*), but such an explanation is unsatisfactory after *crescit*, which is of a different category. No doubt *pellis* is a marginally easier change than *pellas*, but it is dangerous to tamper with a text without being certain that the result gives satisfactory Latin.

causa morbi : the Stoics called spiritual sicknesses νοσήματα (SVF
3. 421 ff., cf. Cic. *Tusc.* 4. 23) ; but *morbi* here refers rather to particular manifestations of avarice (in metaphorical terms to symptoms
like *sitis*). The underlying moral condition is represented by *causa*
(for a similar metaphor cf. Lucr. 3. 1070 'morbi quia causam non
tenet aeger'). Presumably 13 *hydrops* is the disease rather than the
symptom; the word is picked up by *aquosus languor* (15 f.), and that
phrase is co-ordinate with *causa* (not *morbi*). The moralist, like the
doctor, aims to treat the causes rather than the symptoms; cf. Plb.
13. 2. 2 οὐκ εἰδὼς ὅτι καθάπερ ἐπὶ τῶν ὑδρωπικῶν οὐδέποτε ποιεῖ παῦλαν
οὐδὲ κόρον τῆς ἐπιθυμίας ἡ τῶν ἔξωθεν ὑγρῶν παράθεσις, ἐὰν μὴ τὴν
ἐν αὐτῷ τῷ σώματι διάθεσιν ὑγιάσῃ τις, τὸν αὐτὸν τρόπον οὐδὲ τὴν πρὸς
τὸ πλεῖον ἐπιθυμίαν οἵόν τε κορέσαι μὴ οὐ τὴν ἐν τῇ ψυχῇ κακίαν λόγῳ
τινὶ διορθωσάμενον, Sen. *epist.* 94. 6 'idem tibi de omnibus vitiis dico:
ipsa removenda sunt, non praecipiendum quod fieri illis manentibus
non potest. nisi opiniones falsas quibus laboramus expuleris, nec
avarus quomodo pecunia utendum sit exaudiet, nec timidus quomodo periculosa contemnat'.

15. venis : the veins are associated with the pulse (Pers. 3. 107) and
hence with fever (3. 91). They are mentioned naturally after *sitim*
as they were sometimes regarded as vehicles for liquids; cf. *serm.*
2. 4. 25, Virg. *ecl.* 6. 15, *georg.* 3. 482 f. 'sed ubi ignea venis / omnibus
acta sitis', Onians 42 f.

aquosus . . . languor : 'the watery sickness' picks up 13 *hydrops*;
cf. Prud. *cath.* 8. 62 f. 'et aquosus albis / umor in venis dominetur'.
aquosus is used unpoetically in medical contexts (Macr. *sat.* 7. 4. 22
'quod in eo aquosum est venae in vesicam refundunt', *Thes.l.L.*
2. 381. 71 ff.), but here it points to the Greek name rather than to the
visible symptoms. That justifies the apparent incompatibility of *languor*; of course there is deliberate point in the unexpected *iunctura*
(capped by Ser. Samm. 512 'frangit vires languoris aquosi'). *languor*
as often is a euphemism for illness, but also suggests the lassitude of
dropsy (Cels. 3. 24. 6).

albo corpore : ablative with *fugerit*. Horace is referring to λευκο-
φλεγματία (Cels. 3. 21. 2), the kind of dropsy that affected not just
the stomach but the whole body. *albo* suggests a sickly pallor; cf.
epod. 7. 15, *serm.* 2. 2. 21, Pers. 3. 98 'albo ventre lavatur', Sulpicia,
sat. 36 'ingluvie albus'. If the suggestion is right that *hydrops* has
a hint of the hydra (n. on 13 *dirus*), *albo* would cohere with the image;
cf. Call. fr. 194. 2 λευκὸς ὡς ὕδρου γαστήρ (a hydra is a glorified water-
snake), Plin. *nat.* 30. 21 '(enhydris) serpens masculus et albus'.

17. Cyri solio : the 'throne of Cyrus' picks up the idea of kingship
(9), which in the last two stanzas becomes the dominating theme

(21 n.); for the grandiloquent phrase cf. Plut. *Alex.* 30. 7 μηδεὶς ἄλλος ἀνθρώπων καθίσειεν εἰς τὸν Κύρου θρόνον πλὴν Ἀλεξάνδρου, Milton, *P.R.* 3. 33. Cyrus the Great was the founder of the Persian Achaemenid dynasty from which the Parthian Arsacids claimed descent. He was also a traditional *exemplum* of the good king (R. Höistad, *Cynic Hero and Cynic King*, 1948, pp. 73 ff., *RE* Suppl. 4. 1163 f.); the theme was given undeserved popularity by Xenophon's extremely influential *Cyropaedeia* (cf. Cic. *Q.f.* 1. 1. 23), and was used among others by the Stoic Panaetius (fr. 117 van Straaten = Cic. *off.* 2. 16). When ps.-Acro seems to say that Phraates was educated by Brahmins, his source surely referred to Cyrus's upbringing; such an accretion to the legend could have been made after the conquests of Alexander increased the interest in Indian sages.

Prahaten : the spelling of the paradosis should be retained, though the Monumentum Ancyranum has *Phrates* and *Φραάτης* (cf. *epist.* 1. 12. 27); Greek *ph* was represented by Latin *p* till the beginning of the first century (cf. *Poeni*). Phraates IV of Parthia experienced two revolts by Tiridates (vol. i, p. xxxii), the first about the time of Actium (Dio 51. 18. 2–3); Horace can hardly mean this, as the Romans had other preoccupations at the time (the resemblances of the ode to the *Satires* are not close enough to impose an early date). The second rebellion took place in 26, when Tiridates struck his own tetradrachms (March–May); cf. *British Museum Coins, Parthia*, 1903, p. 135 (with plate 23. 8 and 9), D. Sellwood, *Introduction to the Coinage of Parthia*, 1971, pp. 167 f. But Phraates soon regained his throne with the help of 'Scythians' from the north-east of his kingdom (cf. 1. 26. 5, W. W. Tarn, *Greeks in Bactria and India*, 1951, p. 306); Tiridates fled to Augustus in Spain (Justin 42. 5. 6), i.e. in 26–25 B.C.

The ode may therefore be assigned to about 25 B.C., shortly after the king's restoration. The rebellion had been supported, perhaps contrived, by Augustus, who saw that there were subtler ways of solving the Eastern question than Antony's long march through the Armenian mountains. Horace here seeks consolation in philosophy for the final fiasco; for an equally lofty attitude to political discomfiture cf. Cic. *Pis.* 42–3 'tantam virtutis vim esse voluerunt ut non posset esse umquam vir bonus non beatus. quae est igitur poena, quod supplicium? id mea sententia quod accidere nemini potest nisi nocenti . . .', 95 'equidem, ut paulo ante dixi, non eadem supplicia esse in hominibus existimo quae fortasse plerique . . .', 98 'mihi cui semper ita persuasum fuerit non eventis sed factis cuiusque fortunam ponderari'.

18. dissidens plebi : Stoics like other moralists expressed an aristocratic contempt for the crowd; cf. *epist.* 1. 1. 70 ff., Bramble 154 f.

By his refusal to run for magistracies Sallustius may have professed a disregard for the popular suffrage, though his real reasons could have been unpopularity or a preference for working behind the scenes. *plebi* makes a contrast with Cyrus and Phraates above; the word emphasizes the vulgarity of the delusion, *populum* (19) its extent. As *dissidens* means 'sitting apart' it makes a verbal point after *solio*; as it is used of political dissensions it also suits *plebi*.

beatorum : the synaloepha (vol. i, p. xliv) perhaps suits the super-fluity of the so-called 'beati', who are axed by the crisp *ex-* that follows. *beatus* properly described spiritual felicity, but was popu-larly used of the materially prosperous; Horace repeatedly exploits the ambiguities of the word (cf. especially *serm*. 1. 3. 142 'privatusque magis vivam te rege beatus'). Traditionally the Persian king was the supreme instance of the *beatus* (3. 9. 4, Pl. *apol*. 40 d, *Euthyd*. 274 a), but the philosophers dissented from the general view; cf. Pl. *Gorg*. 470 e δῆλον δὴ ὦ Σώκρατες ὅτι οὐδὲ τὸν μέγαν βασιλέα γιγνώσκειν φήσεις εὐδαίμονα ὄντα (see 472 a for the popular misapprehensions on the subject), Xen. *mem*. 4. 4. 6, Arist. *soph. el.* 173ᵃ26 τοῖς δὲ πολλοῖς ἄδοξον τὸ βασιλέα μὴ εὐδαιμονεῖν, Dio Chrys. 3. 1, 3. 29, 4. 25 (a bad man cannot be a real king) οὐδ᾽ ἂν πάντες φῶσιν Ἕλληνες καὶ βάρβαροι καὶ πολλὰ διαδήματα καὶ σκῆπτρα καὶ τιάρας προσάψωσιν αὐτῷ. Horace modernizes the topic by transferring it from Persia to Parthia.

19. eximit Virtus : the personification (προσωποποιία) of *virtus* (the Stoic ἀρετή), is here derived from moralizing discourse; cf. Cic. *fin*. 2. 65 'clamat virtus (Regulum) beatiorem fuisse quam potantem in rosa Thorium' (an anti-Epicurean passage), Pers. 5. 132 ff. (the ad-monitions of Avarice and Luxury). The verb (which is contrasted with *redditum*) has a dry and technical note that suits the political context; cf. Nep. *Att*. 10. 4, Sen. *dial*. 6. 3. 3 'eximes te numero vivorum', *Thes.l.L*. 5. 2. 1499. 8 ff., Milton, *Sonnet to Mr. H. Lawes* 5 'Thy worth and skill exempts thee from the throng'.

falsis . . . vocibus : cf. Cic. *carm*. fr. 3. 8 (*de cons*.) 'falsis Graiorum vocibus errant' (on the planets). The Stoics with their characteristic interest in language claimed that in their paradoxes they were giving words their 'true' meaning; cf. Diog. Laert. 7. 122 οὐ μόνον δ᾽ ἐλευθέρους εἶναι τοὺς σοφούς, ἀλλὰ καὶ βασιλέας, τῆς βασιλείας οὔσης ἀρχῆς ἀνυπευθύνου, ἥτις περὶ μόνους ἂν τοὺς σοφοὺς συσταίη, καθά φησι Χρύσιππος ἐν τῷ Περὶ τοῦ κυρίως κεχρῆσθαι Ζήνωνα τοῖς ὀνόμασιν (*SVF* 3. 617). Such points could be made more plausibly about the am-biguous *beatus*; cf. 4. 9. 45 f. 'non possidentem multa vocaveris / recte beatum', Sen. *epist*. 45. 9 'beatum non eum esse quem vulgus appellat'. Editors quote Sall. *Cat*. 52. 11 'nos vera vocabula rerum amisimus' (echoing Thuc. 3. 82. 4); but Horace is talking of a more fundamental misuse of language. *dedocet* (ἀποδιδάσκει) suggests a reversal of the usual moral διδαχή; philosophers sometimes grow ironic on the advantages of unlearning (cf. Pl. *Phaed.* 96 c, Diog. Laert. 6. 7 on Antisthenes, Cic. *fin.* 1. 20).

21. regnum : for the Stoic paradox that only the wise man is king cf. *SVF* 1. 216 (Zeno) οὔτε κωλύεται οὔτε κωλύει, οὔτε βιάζεται ὑπό τινος οὔτ᾽ αὐτὸς βιάζει τινα, οὔτε δεσπόζει οὔτε δεσπόζεται . . . εὐδαίμων δέ ἐστιν μάλιστα καὶ εὐτυχὴς . . . βασιλικός τε καὶ στρατηγικός, more extremely Chrysippus, loc. cit. [above, 19 n.]. For later references, sometimes derisive, cf. 4. 9. 39 ff. 'consulque non unius anni . . .' (a Republican version of the paradox), *serm.* 1. 3. 124 f. 'si dives qui sapiens est, / et sutor bonus et solus formosus et est rex . . .' (with Lejay's note), Lucil. 1226 'formonsus dives liber rex solus' (with Marx's note), Varro, *Men.* 245, Cic. *Mur.* 61, *fin.* 3. 75 'rectius enim appellabitur rex quam Tarquinius qui nec se nec suos regere potuit', Sen. *Thy.* 348 ff., Claud. 8. 261 ff., van Geytenbeek 127 ff.

diadema : the headband of Eastern kings (associated with Cyrus by Xen. *Cyr.* 8. 3. 13) which after Alexander became the symbol of royalty for the Greeks and Romans; cf. H.-W. Ritter, *Diadem und Königsherrschaft* (*Vestigia* 7), 1965, 6 ff., *RE* 5. 303 ff., Weinstock 333 ff. The triumphs of virtue were traditionally compared with the victor's garland; cf. *epist.* 1. 1. 49 f. 'quis . . . / magna coronari contemnat Olympia?', Dio Chrys. 9. 12 f. (on Diogenes), *2 Tim.* 4. 8 ὁ τῆς δικαιοσύνης στέφανος, but Clem. Alex. *paed.* 2. 8. 74 τὸ διάδημα τῆς δικαιοσύνης. When Horace was studying moral philosophy at Athens in 44, perhaps his preceptors contrasted the crown of virtue with the diadem that Antony had recently offered Julius Caesar.

tutum : cf. Solon 15. 2 ff. W. οὐ διαμείψομεθα / τῆς ἀρετῆς τὸν πλοῦτον, ἐπεὶ τὸ μὲν ἔμπεδον αἰεί, / χρήματα δ᾽ ἀνθρώπων ἄλλοτε ἄλλος ἔχει, Soph. fr. 194 P. = 195 N. ἀρετῆς βέβαιαι δ᾽ εἰσὶν αἱ κτήσεις μόνης. On the other hand the head that wears a literal diadem is uneasy (as Damocles found out and perhaps Phraates soon will); cf. Sen. *Thy.* 599 ff. 'ille qui donat diadema fronti / . . . anxius sceptrum tenet'.

22. deferens uni : the prize is bestowed rather than scrambled for; cf. *epist.* 1. 1. 49 ff. (the garland of virtue can be won *sine pulvere*). In Parthian coinage a goddess proffers the king a diadem or similar symbol (cf. 1. 34. 14 ff., *British Museum Coins, Parthia*, pl. 18. 15–17, pl. 19. 9); in our passage the coronation is performed not by Fortuna but Virtus. *uni* suggests the *solus sapiens rex* of the Stoic paradox.

propriamque laurum : with the diadem of the Great King is juxtaposed the bay not of the athlete but of the *triumphator*. The adjective means that the prize is a permanent possession (whereas real garlands wither); cf. *serm.* 2. 6. 5 'propria haec mihi munera faxis',

epist. 2. 2. 172, Cic. *p. red. in sen.* 9 'perenne ac proprium', Virg. *ecl.*
7. 31, Non. 573–5 L. = 361–2 M. 'proprium rursum significat per-
petuum'. It was a Stoic doctrine that virtue cannot be lost (*SVF*
I. 569 ἀναπόβλητος).

23. quisquis : at first sight the generalizing pronoun seems incompatible with *uni* (hence Cunningham's *si quis*) ; but Horace is talking
not of an individual but of a class (though this is less obvious in
the dative). From the proposition 'only the wise man is king' he has
inferred 'all wise men are kings' ; as a result he has allowed a more
liberal interpretation to the Stoic dogma.

oculo inretorto : the story of Solon's indifference to Croesus's
treasure-chamber (Hdt. I. 30. 1–3, I. 86. 5) was naturally elaborated
in discourses on wealth and wisdom, felicity and kingship; cf. Diod.
Sic. 9. 27. 2 καὶ ὁ Σόλων τὴν αὐτὴν ἀπόκρισιν ποιησάμενος ἐδίδασκεν ὡς
οὐ τοὺς πλεῖστα κεκτημένους ἀλλὰ τοὺς πλείστου ἀξίαν τὴν φρόνησιν
ἡγουμένους νομιστέον πλουσιωτάτους· ἡ δὲ φρόνησις οὐδενὶ τῶν ἄλλων
ἀντίρροπος οὖσα μόνους ποιεῖ τοὺς αὐτὴν περὶ πολλοῦ ποιουμένους μέγιστον
καὶ βεβαιότατον ἔχειν πλοῦτον (cf. Horace's *propriam*). In our passage
such an allusion follows naturally after the mention of Cyrus, who
was contrasted with Croesus by Xenophon and others (*Cyr.* 8. 2.
15 ff., E. Lefèvre, *Hermes* 99, 1971, 283 ff.).

oculo inretorto seems to mean 'without a backward glance';
the adjective is a coinage of Horace's own. For the thought cf.
Xen. *Cyr.* 8. 1. 42 μηδὲ μεταστρεφόμενοι ἐπὶ θέαν μηδενὸς ὡς οὐδὲν
θαυμάζοντες, Pl. *leg.* 9. 854 c τὰς δὲ τῶν κακῶν ξυνουσίας φεῦγε ἀμετα-
στρεπτί, Lucian, *pisc.* 46 προθεὶς χρυσίον καὶ δόξαν καὶ ἡδονήν, ὃν μὲν
ἂν αὐτῶν ἴδῃς ὑπερορῶντα καὶ μηδαμῶς ἑλκόμενον πρὸς τὴν ὄψιν, οὗτος
ἔστω ὁ τῷ θάλλῳ στεφόμενος. At first sight Horace's phrase seems
nonsensical (one cannot simultaneously gaze at something and refrain from a second glance), but we are meant to think of ἀμετα-
στρεπτί, which has less temporal implication than the Latin word. The
oxymoron must be deliberate ; L. Müller's *spernit* is more logical but
much less pointed.

Because of the illogicality Lambinus explained that the good man
gazes at riches without batting an eyelid; cf. *epist.* 1. 6. 3 ff., Plut.
comp. Dem. et Cic. 3. 6 πρὸς δωρέας βασιλέων ... ἀντιβλέψαι Δημο-
σθένης οὐκ ἂν ἐτόλμησεν, Synes. *de regno* 27 (= 30 D.) ὡς οὐκ εἰκός γε
αὐτὸν διαράμενον βλοσυροῖς ὀφθαλμοῖς ἀντιβλέψαι χρυσίῳ. This does
not suit *retorquere oculos*, which naturally implies not 'turn away
from' (*avertere*) but 'turn back to'; cf. Cic. *Cat.* 2. 2 'retorquet oculos
profecto saepe ad hanc urbem', ps.-Quint. *decl. mai.* 8. 8 'omnium
tamen in se retorquet oculos'. Porphyrio explains 'hoc est oculo
non invidenti' (cf. *serm.* 2. 5. 53 'limis', *epist.* 1. 14. 37 'obliquo oculo',

Call. fr. 1. 38 λοξῷ, Marx on Lucil. 704, Bömer on Ov. *met.* 2. 787,
E. M. Steuart, *CR* 38, 1924, 157 f.) ; but *retorto oculo* describes a backward look rather than a sidelong squint.

24. acervos : in a *diatribe* on avarice, 'heaps' naturally refers to
money ; for other instances of absolute *acervus* cf. Bell 220 f., *Thes.l.L.*
1. 375. 25 ff. (though usually a genitive can be supplied from the immediate context). The word may also convey associations of Stoicism
as it was used of the logical problem of the *sorites* ; cf. *epist.* 2. 1. 47,
Cic. *ac.* 2. 49, Pers. 6. 80 'inventus, Chrysippe, tui finitor acervi' (the
last line of the Stoic satirist), *Thes.l.L.* 1. 376. 50 ff. The reference to
stored treasure links the end of the poem with the beginning ('ring-
composition').

3. AEQVAM MEMENTO

[Commager 283 ff.; H. Juhnke, *Monumentum Chiloniense (Festschrift Burck)*,
1975, pp. 359 ff.; Wilkinson 37, 128 f.; Williams 112 f.; G. Witke, *CPh* 61,
1966, 250 ff.; A. J. Woodman, *AJPh* 91, 1970, 165 ff.]

*1–8. Maintain equanimity in hard times, Dellius, no less than
moderation in good; you will die whether you live in perpetual gloom
or enjoy your wine on feast-days in a secluded meadow. 9–16. The
hospitable trees and bustling brook are at your service; here is the place
for a party while there is time. 17–28. You must resign your properties
to an heir; rich and poor alike are blood-sacrifices to Hades; when our
lot comes up, all must sail into everlasting exile.*

Like the recipients of some other Horatian odes, Q. Dellius had
a career full of incident. He first emerged under Dolabella, Cicero's
unsavoury son-in-law, who was proconsul of Syria in 43 ; he then
transferred his allegiance to Cassius (Vell. 2. 84. 2, Sen. *suas.* 1. 7),
by some accounts securing a welcome by offering to murder his
former commander ; he next joined Antony, probably after Philippi,
and served with him in the East for ten years. His talents were
diplomatic rather than military : he brought Cleopatra to the Cydnus
in 41 B.C. (Plut. *Ant.* 25. 2 f.), he organized the restoration of Herod
in 40 (Joseph. *ant. Iud.* 14. 394), he ensnared Artaxes of Armenia in
34. He wrote the history of Antony's Parthian war, no doubt an
important source for Plutarch's biography (Str. 11. 13. 3, Plut. *Ant.*
59. 4 Δέλλιος ὁ ἱστορικός). His tastes attracted scandal : he was said
to have written *epistulae lascivae* to Cleopatra (Sen. loc. cit.), he
was thought ready to procure for Antony Herod's handsome young

kinsman Aristobulus (Joseph. *ant. Iud.* 15. 25 ff.), he was even described by an enemy as Antony's παιδικά (Dio 49. 39. 2). Shortly
before Actium he deserted again (Vell. 2. 84. 2 'exempli sui tenax'),
and thereafter obtained high favour with Augustus (Sen. *clem.*
1. 10. 1), though scarcely further employment. Messalla Corvinus
described him in a famous phrase as the circus-rider of civil war, 'de-
sultorem bellorum civilium' (Sen. *suas.* 1. 7); yet in a competition
for power where clear lines of principle were lacking, even the high-
minded author of the epigram was permitted to change sides twice.
See further *RE* 4. 2447 f., Schanz–Hosius 2. 327 f.

It must be asked how the personality of Dellius is related to the
poem. Horace is not urging a melancholy man to cheerfulness (in
spite of 5 'seu maestus omni tempore vixeris'); his paraeneses in-
culcate virtues that he represents his patrons as possessing. Nor is he
pressing the middle way on a vacillating temperament (thus Woodman, loc. cit.); in his political circus-act Dellius must have prided
himself on his inner balance and resilience. Rather the poet is recommending hedonism to a hedonist, the smooth and witty favourite
of the Alexandrian court, the rich proprietor of riverside *horti* (18),
who is known from other sources to have enjoyed his Falernian (8 n.).
The panegyrist makes such characteristics respectable by relating
them to the humane principles of Greek thought (5 ff.): death is
inevitable whether Dellius lives in perpetual gloom (this part of the
disjunction is drily stated in an extreme form) or takes a day off
occasionally to enjoy the peace of the countryside (the moderation
and colouring and sheer length of the clause indicate the poet's
sympathy). Horace prefixes to these reflections a more general admonition (1–4), which in spite of its imperatival form fulfils the
same purpose as an opening *sententia* (as at 1. 22. 1 ff., 1. 27. 1 f.).
Here he draws on abundant philosophical literature περὶ εὐθυμίας to
recommend equanimity in adversity and moderation in prosperity
(see 1 n.); the emphasis must be on the first clause (cf. 2 n.), as
nothing in the rest of the poem suggests that Dellius should restrain
his exuberance. Roman statesmen liked to think of themselves as
burdened by grave preoccupations (1. 7. 17 f.), but though Dellius
may have found life in Augustan Rome boring after the excitements
of Alexandria, nothing in his particular circumstances justifies talk
of *res arduae*. Horace seems to have taken over a bracing ethical
commonplace and used it unexpectedly to recommend enjoyment
to his supple and pleasure-loving friend.

In the third stanza the poem moves from generalizations to the
description of a particular parkland (9 n.). No doubt Horace is thinking of Dellius's own *horti*, but he paints the traditional landscape of
the *locus amoenus* with its trees and brook (9 n., 10 n., 12 n.); cf. Hom.

Od. 5. 63 ff. (Calypso's grotto), 7. 112 ff. (Alcinous's garden), Sappho 2. 5 ff., Pl. *Phaedr.* 230 b–c, G. Schönbeck, *Der Locus Amoenus von Homer bis Horaz*, Diss. Heidelberg, 1962, pp. 21 ff., Bömer on Ov. *fast.* 2. 315, Grimal 293 ff., Vischer 129 f., Curtius 195 ff., L. Arbusow, *Colores Rhetorici*, 1963, pp. 72 ff., 111 ff. In the fourth stanza, with another abrupt development, Horace uses the poet's prerogative to issue directions for a symposium; though *al fresco* festivities belong to the literary tradition (vol. i, pp. 215 f.), here too he is idealizing a possible Roman situation (for such entertainments cf. Cic. *off.* 3. 58, *Att.* 4. 5. 4 'de via recta in hortos', Mayor on Juv. 1. 75). But as so often in ancient literature the symposium is both an alleviation and a reminder of human mortality. The theme of death (already fore-shadowed by 4 *moriture*) is developed in the last section of the poem (17–28); the three stanzas provide a more than balancing epode to the two previous groups of two stanzas.

This melancholy element is reminiscent of the ode to Postumus (2. 14), which has much in common with our poem. In both death is inevitable whatever one does (3. 4. ff., 14. 5 ff.); the most prized properties must be left behind (3. 17 f., 14. 21); the river of the under-world must be crossed (3. 27 f., 14. 9 ff.) by all who live on earth (3. 23, 14. 10), whether great or small (3. 21 ff., 14. 11 f.). In both poems the Greek commonplaces are given an aristocratic Roman setting: the scene is staged among parkland trees (3. 9 ff., 14. 22), and the stored wealth falls to an expectant *heres* (3. 20, 14. 25). Certain formal elements are also similar: both odes have seven stanzas, *cedes . . . cedes* (3. 17 ff.) corresponds to *frustra . . . frustra* (14. 13 ff.), the blessings to be abandoned form a tricolon (3. 17 f., 14. 21 f.). On the other hand the Dellius ode shifts from gay to grave, whereas the tone of the Postumus ode is more uniformly melancholy: here Falernian is for present enjoyment, there Caecuban is for future waste. The more circuitous progression of thought in the Dellius ode might suggest that it was written later, but it must be remem-bered that the subtle and complex 1. 4 'solvitur acris hiems' precedes the monotone of 4. 7 'diffugere nives'. Firmer evidence is provided by the word *domus*, which appears in a similar context in both poems unqualified by any adjective (3. 17, 14. 21); as the latter passage is derived from Lucretius, who also mentions the *domus* (2. 14. 22 n.), there is a strong presumption that it should be given priority. But it is impossible to assign an absolute date to our poem; the most one can say is that it must have been written after Dellius's return from the East about 30 B.C.

The imagery of the Dellius ode is at least as brilliant as that of its more famous counterpart. The hospitable trees and scuttling brook are sketched with an economy and evocativeness that make

a favourable contrast with the lush descriptions of Hellenistic literature (cf. Troxler-Keller 84 ff.). There follow the red roses of the
symposium, the black threads of the Parcae, the villa plashed by the
yellow Tiber, the high-reared tower of wealth. The symposiast under
the pine-tree becomes a blood-sacrifice to Orcus, a beast in the herd
of shades, a lot that will suddenly fall from an impersonally shaken
urn, a passenger on Charon's wherry exiled from his park for ever.
After the strongly imagined sketches of the last stanzas we can begin
to suspect a serious interpretation of the first line: the cruel circumstances are those of human mortality in general (4 *moriture*), and
even a successful hedonist like Dellius will need all his equanimity
to endure them.

Metre: Alcaic.

1. aequam . . . : it was a traditional piece of wisdom that triumph
and disaster should be treated with equal indifference. The topic
is already found in Archilochus (128 W.): θυμέ, θύμ' ἀμηχάνοισι
κήδεσιν κυκώμενε, / . . . μήτε νικέων ἀμφάδην ἀγάλλεο, / μηδὲ νικηθεὶς ἐν
οἴκῳ καταπεσὼν ὀδύρεο, / ἀλλὰ χαρτοῖσίν τε χαῖρε καὶ κακοῖσιν ἀσχάλα /
μὴ λίην, γίνωσκε δ' οἷος ῥυσμὸς ἀνθρώπους ἔχει. For other early poetical
instances cf. Theognis 319 f., 441 ff., 591 ff., Eur. fr. 963 N., *IA* 920 f.
Philosophers of different schools affirmed the same doctrine; they
were no doubt influenced by the Democritean theory of εὐθυμίη
(fr. 3), which lay behind works by Panaetius (cf. fr. 45 van Straaten,
Pohlenz 1. 206 f., 2. 102), by the Augustan Athenodorus Calvus
(McGann 19 ff.), by Seneca (*de tranquillitate animi*, cf. Hadot 135 ff.),
and by Plutarch (cf. W. C. Helmbold, Loeb *Moralia*, vol. 6, pp.
163 ff.). See especially Epicurus, fr. 488 ἡ ταπεινὴ ψυχὴ τοῖς μὲν
εὐημερήμασιν ἐχαυνώθη, ταῖς δὲ συμφοραῖς καθῃρέθη, Aristo Chius
(Stoic), fr. 396 = *SVF* 1. 89. 20 f. οὕτως ὁ μὲν πεπαιδευμένος καὶ ἐν
πλούτῳ καὶ ἐν πενίᾳ οὐ ταράττεται, ὁ δ' ἀπαίδευτος ἐν ἀμφοῖν, Aristo
Ceus (Peripatetic), fr. 13 II Wehrli, Cic. *Tusc.* 4. 66, *off.* 1. 90 'nam ut
adversas res, sic secundas inmoderate ferre levitatis est, praeclaraque
est aequabilitas in omni vita et idem semper vultus eademque frons,
ut de Socrate itemque de C. Laelio accepimus', Sen. *epist.* 66. 6, 78. 29,
Plut. *tranq. anim.* 467 b. Such equanimity could be regarded as a
characteristic virtue of the Romans; cf. App. *praef.* 11. 43 οὔτε ταῖς
εὐπραγίαις ἐπαιρόμενοι μέχρι βεβαίως ἐκράτησαν οὔτε συστελλόμενοι
ταῖς συμφοραῖς. For other parallels cf. Lucil. 698 ff. (expressing dis-
agreement with Archilochus), Hor. *carm.* 2. 10. 21 ff., *epist.* 1. 10. 30 f.
'quem res plus nimio delectavere secundae, / mutatae quatient',
Liban. *epist.* 557. 5 (= 10. 523. 4 ff. F.), Quint. Smyrn. 14. 202 f.,
Paul. Sil. *anth. P.* 10. 74. 1 f.

aequam . . . mentem : a poetical variant (*Thes.l.L.* 1. 1037. 17 ff.) for the common *aequum animum* (*epist.* 1. 11. 30, 1. 18. 112, Plaut. *rud.* 402 'ergo animus aequos optimum est aerumnae condimentum'); the latter perhaps originated with the adverbial *aequo animo*. Such expressions do not seem to be derived from Greek; the nearest equivalent is εὐθυμία, 'cheerful resignation' (*CGL 2.* 317. 23 = 'aequanimitas').

memento . . . servare : in appearance a grave allocution; cf. 1. 7. 17, 3. 29. 32, Epicharmus, fr. 250 νᾶφε καὶ μέμνασ' ἀπιστεῖν. But as often Horace's injunction insinuates a tactful encomium: Dellius is not being taught a lesson he does not know or urged to a virtue he does not possess. The assonance with *mentem* gives unity to the aphorism.

rebus in arduis : a euphemism for adversity: times cannot be really bad for the good man. There is a characteristic verbal contrast between the 'even' mind and 'uphill' circumstances.

2. non secus ac bonis : instead of *in* of the manuscripts Bentley read *ac* (found in two manuscripts by Lambinus); for a discussion see C. O. Brink, *PCPhS* 17, 1971, 17 ff. If *in* is accepted the clause might be taken as coordinate with its predecessor ('equally in good fortune remember to keep your mind free from exaltation'); but this throws too much weight on the theme of modesty as opposed to cheerfulness (this argument also rules out Schütz's *nec secus*). It is also difficult to take *non secus . . . temperatam* as a subordinate parenthesis ('which in the same way has been restrained from exaltation in prosperity'); no other instance has been adduced of such a use of *non secus*. Even if one defends the paradosis as a novel Horatian brachylogy, the repetition of *in* seems otiose in so brachylogical a poet; admittedly at *epod.* 11. 4 the manuscripts offer 'mollibus in pueris aut in puellis urere', but there Bentley plausibly conjectured *aut pueris*. If Horace had omitted *in* in the second member (K.–S. 1. 580 f., Brink, loc. cit., p. 18), the word might well have been interpolated; in this case *ac* could have been squeezed out to restore the metre.

As an alternative to *ac* Housman proposed *ut* (1. 133 f. = *CR* 4, 1890, 341). He cited 3. 25. 8 ff. 'non secus . . . stupet Euhias / . . . ut mihi . . . / mirari libet' (but the hyperbaton is there considerable), Ov. *met.* 15. 180 'non secus ut flumen' (ut *h*: ac *cett.*), Virg. *georg.* 2. 277 ff. (but there *non setius* probably refers backwards). Housman pointed out that *ut* is easier palaeographically than *ac*, but the corruption is probably to be explained as interpolation rather than misreading.

3. insolenti . . . laetitia : archaic Greek poets warn against the hybris generated by prosperity (Solon 6. 3 f. W. τίκτει γὰρ κόρος ὕβριν, ὅταν πολὺς ὄλβος ἔπηται / ἀνθρώποις ὁπόσοις μὴ νόος ἄρτιος ᾖ, Theognis 153 f., echoed by many successors); but Horace's treatment owes more to Hellenistic moral philosophy. The Peripatetic Aristo of Ceos wrote a treatise Περὶ τοῦ κουφίζειν ὑπερηφανίας, which is in part preserved in Philodemus's Περὶ κακιῶν (fr. 13 Wehrli); for a Latin therapy see Cic. *Tusc.* 4. 65 ff. The lessons were already familiar in second-century Rome; cf. Cato, *or.* fr. 163 'scio solere plerisque hominibus rebus secundis atque prolixis atque prosperis animum excellere atque super-biam atque ferociam augescere atque crescere . . . secundae res laetitia transvorsum trudere solent a recte consulendo atque intel-legendo', Aemilianus ap. Cic. *off.* 1. 90.

Horace's language is based on the vocabulary selected by Cicero to translate the Stoic doctrine of the passions in *Tusc.* 3 and 4. *laetitia* represents the irrational ἡδονή of Stoic doctrine, as opposed to the rational χαρά (Cicero's *gaudium*); cf. *Tusc.* 3. 24 'voluptas gestiens, id est praeter modum elata laetitia', 4. 11–13. *insolentius* is used of self-assertive ostentation in the same context (4. 20). *temperatam* describes the regulation of the passions enjoined by the philosophers (cf. 4. 22 'temperantia sedat appetitiones', 4. 30).

4. moriture : the attributive use of the future participle was alien to the spoken language (except for *futurus*), but because of its brevity was cultivated in the Silver Age (H.–Sz. 390), notably in the metrically convenient vocative. In our passage the participle represents the apodosis of the following conditional clause (cf. 2. 2. 2 *inimice* n.); note the tension with 5 *vixeris*.

5. seu . . . : for the thought cf. Plaut. *Bacch.* 1193 ff., Antiphanes, *anth. P.* 11. 168. 3 ff. κοῦτε πιών, οὔτ᾽ ἄνθος ἐπὶ κροτάφοις ἀναδήσας, / οὐ μύρον, οὐ γλαφυρὸν γνούς ποτ᾽ ἐρωμένιον, / τεθνήξῃ, πλουτοῦσαν ἀφεὶς μεγάλην διαθήκην, / ἐκ πολλῶν ὀβολὸν μοῦνον ἐνεγκάμενος, Julianus, ibid. 7. 33.

6. in remoto gramine : grass is particularly prized in Mediterranean countries, and hence appears as a conventional resting-place in the *amoenus locus*; it presupposes the shade and stream of the rest of the picture. Cf. *epod.* 2. 24, *epist.* 1. 14. 35, Pl. *Phaedr.* 230 b πάντων δὲ κομψότατον τὸ τῆς πόας, ὅτι ἐν ἠρέμα προσάντει ἱκανὴ πέφυκε κατακλινέντι τὴν κεφαλὴν παγκάλως ἔχειν, Theoc. 5. 31 ff. ἄδιον ᾀσῇ / τεῖδ᾽ ὑπὸ τὰν κότινον καὶ τάλσεα ταῦτα καθίξας. / ψυχρὸν ὕδωρ τουτεὶ καταλείβεται· ὧδε πεφύκει / ποία, χά στιβὰς ἅδε, *Anacreontea* 30. 1 ff. [below, p. 169], Lucr. 2. 29 f. 'in gramine molli / propter aquae rivum sub ramis arboris altae', Milton, *P.L.* 4. 325 ff.

remoto means not just 'distant' but 'withdrawn from the bustle of the world', according to the precepts of the Epicureans among

others; cf. *serm.* 2. 1. 71 f. 'ubi se a vulgo et scaena in secreta re-
morant / virtus Scipiadae et mitis sapientia Laeli', 2. 6. 16 'ubi me
in montis et in arcem ex urbe removi' (less philosophically, Cic.
Verr. 5. 80, *epist.* 7. 20. 2 'remoto salubri amoeno loco'). A word like
prato would combine more conventionally with the participle, but
gramine is more vivid.

per dies festos : the person who enjoys himself on holidays is the
type of the temperate and contented man ; the motif seems to have
belonged to the treatises Περὶ εὐθυμίας. Cf. Democritus, fr. 230 βίος
ἀνεόρταστος μακρὴ ὁδὸς ἀπανδόκευτος, 232 τῶν ἡδέων τὰ σπανιώτατα
γινόμενα μάλιστα τέρπει, Epicurus, *epist.* 3. 131 τὸ συνεθίζειν οὖν ἐν
ταῖς ἁπλαῖς καὶ οὐ πολυτελέσι διαίταις . . . τοῖς πολυτελέσιν ἐκ διαλειμ-
μάτων προσερχομένους κρεῖττον ἡμᾶς διατίθησι. The point is particularly
emphasized in Roman writers with their strong feeling for the calendar and for the difference between *otium* and *negotium*; cf. *serm.*
2. 2. 82 ff., Cic. *de orat.* 2. 22 'repuerascere' (the whole dialogue is
characteristically set *ludorum Romanorum diebus*), Lucr. 2. 23 'interdum', Sen. *dial.* 9. 17. 4 ff.

per is distributive ('as feast-days come round') ; cf. 2. 14. 15 'per
autumnos', 3. 22. 6 'per exactos . . . annos', *carm. saec.* 21, *epist.*
2. 1. 147, Suet. *Vesp.* 19. 1 'dabat sicut Saturnalibus viris apophoreta,
ita per Kal. Mart. feminis'. Some editors interpret 'throughout the
holidays' (2. 9. 6 'mensis per omnis'), but such carousing would be
excessive (it is unnatural to apply *per dies festos* only to the reclining
and not to the drinking). Horace is rather drawing a contrast between
continual gloom (*omni tempore*) and the discriminating enjoyment
commended by the philosophers.

7. reclinatum : cf. above on 6 *in remoto gramine*, 1. 1. 22 n., Eur.
Hipp. 210 f. ὑπό τ' αἰγείροις ἔν τε κομήτῃ / λειμῶνι κλιθεῖσ' ἀναπαυσαί-
μαν, Antiphilus, *anth. P.* 9. 71. 5, Mart. 9. 90. 1 'in gramine florido
reclinis', Milton, *P.L.* 4. 333 f. 'sidelong as they sat recline On the
soft downy bank damasked with flowers', Kier 35 ff.

bearis : Horace uses this word in a serious context at 4. 8. 29 'caelo
Musa beat' (a semi-religious archaism) and elsewhere more collo-
quially (*epist.* 1. 18. 75, 2. 2. 121) ; it does not occur (except adjectival
beatus) in any other classical author. It is found originally in Plautus
and Terence and reappears, perhaps as a self-conscious archaism,
in Marcus Aurelius (ap. Fronto, p. 68 van den Hout = p. 75 N.)
and Apuleius (*apol.* 37 'beasti' in the sense of 'Thank you'). The
active form of the verb suits the Horatian view that felicity is self-
engendered rather than due to divine grace (2. 16. 1 n.).

8. interiore nota : *nota* is used of the *titulus* of a wine and hence of
the type itself ; cf. *serm.* 1. 10. 24, Cic. *Brut.* 287 (for the metaphorical

de meliore nota cf. Catull. 68. 28, Curius ap. Cic. *epist.* 7. 29. 1).
Naturally the older wines were in the interior part of the cellar
(Porph.); cf. 3. 28. 2 'reconditum'. *interiore* makes a verbal contrast
with *remoto*, conceivably also with *nota* (which suggests something on
the outside).

Falerni : cf. 1. 20. 9 n. Dellius missed his Falernian at Alexandria :
cf. Plut. *Ant.* 59. 4 προσέκρουσε δὲ Κλεοπάτρᾳ παρὰ δεῖπνον εἰπὼν αὐτοῖς
μὲν ὀξίνην ἐγχεῖσθαι, Σάρμεντον δὲ πίνειν ἐν ᾽Ρώμῃ Φαλερῖνον.

9. quo : 'to what purpose?'; for the alternation with 11 *quid* cf. Ov.
met. 13. 516 f. 'quo ferrea resto / quidve moror?' After a general
reference to 'secluded lawns' in the second stanza, Horace in the
third pictures himself and Dellius as already situated in a particular
locus amoenus; for such abrupt scene-setting cf. 1. 19. 13 ff., 2. 11.
13 f. 'cur non sub alta vel platano vel hac / pinu iacentes...?'
(where *hac* makes the point explicit). In the fourth stanza a simpler
poet might have continued, 'Surely, in order that we may enjoy
ourselves', but to answer one's own question like this seems somewhat naive (metrical elaboration protected Horace, unlike hexameter
poets, from having such answers foisted on him by interpolators).
Instead he moves direction again by ordering preparations for the
symposium; already in the third stanza *hospitalem* has provided
a hint that an entertainment is appropriate.

The elliptical character of the transitions has caused doubts
about the text (cf. especially C. O. Brink, *PCPhS* 17, 1971, 19 f.). For
quo Lambinus read *qua* (which he found in some manuscripts), and
was followed by Bentley among others. This involves accepting
Fea's *et* for *quid* in 11, where Lambinus's *qua* gives an unlikely cor-
reption; M. Haupt once proposed *ramisque et* (*Opuscula* 1. 91 f.), but
-*que* cannot be put at the end of a clause to pair it with its successor.
No doubt *qua* and *et* provide a smoother run than the transmitted
reading; but the latter gives an impression first of immediacy and
then of urgency that suits the dramatic aspect of Horace's lyric.

pinus : most probably *Pinus pinea* L., the stone or parasol pine,
a common shade tree on the coasts of Italy anywhere south of
Ravenna (A. Mitchell, *A Field Guide to the Trees of Britain and
Northern Europe*, 1974, pp. 170 f.). For its presence in idyllic landscapes cf. 2. 11. 13 f., Theoc. 1. 1 f. (its mention in the opening line is
significant) ἁδύ τι τὸ ψιθύρισμα καὶ ἁ πίτυς, αἰπόλε, τήνα, / ἁ ποτὶ ταῖς
παγαῖσι μελίσδεται, 5. 49, Ov. *ars* 3. 692, Hehn[8] 301 ff., Grimal, index
s.v. Pin, D.–S. 3. 291. Virgil praised it as a garden tree (*ecl.* 7. 65),
Horace had one at his villa (3. 22. 5), Ovid in exile fondly remembered
the pines of his own suburban *horti* (*Pont.* 1. 8. 43 f.).

ingens : cf. 2. 10. 9 f. 'saepius ventis agitatur ingens / pinus' (referring specifically to height) ; *Pinus pinea* can grow to eighty feet, which is quite high by Italian standards. One looks for a contrast with the size of the white poplar, to match the implied contrast of their colours; but the poplar is conventionally a tall tree (*epod.* 2. 10 'altas maritat populos', Phaedr. 3. 17. 4), as is confirmed here by the twining of the branches. Lambinus (on *epod.* 2. 10) considered *altaque populus* in our passage; but the repetition of a word for size would be feeble. Perhaps *ingens* refers not only to height but to bulk as well (cf. Virg. *georg.* 2. 489 'ingenti ramorum protegat umbra'). The dense spread of the pine's branches (which with *Pinus pinea* is considerable) may be contrasted with the more tenuous and open texture of the white poplar (though it does not taper like the Lombardy poplar).

albaque populus : the λεύκη or white poplar (*Populus alba* L., A. Mitchell, op. cit., pp. 176 f., 181) ; cf. 1. 7. 23 n., Virg. *ecl.* 9. 41 f. 'hic candida populus antro / imminet', Tib. 1. 4. 30. It loves growing by water (Theophr. *hist. plant.* 4. 8. 1), and according to Pliny was the only tree whose leaves rustled against each other (*nat.* 16. 91) ; both characteristics made it suitable for a pleasure garden. Whether ancient poets speak of the white poplar (λεύκη) or the black (αἴγειρος), their readers should try to forget the now ubiquitous Lombardy.

The mountain pine and black poplar are conjoined by Homer (*Il.* 13. 389 f. = 16. 482 f.). The two trees are portrayed together in wall-painting (cf. M. Rostovtzeff, *MDAI(R)*, 1911, p. 6, O. Elia, *Pitture murali e musaici nel Museo Nazionale di Napoli*, 1932, fig. 36).

10. umbram hospitalem : for the idea of 'hospitable covert' (Milton, *P.R.* 2. 262) cf. Pl. *Phaedr.* 230 b νὴ τὴν Ἥραν, καλή γε ἡ καταγωγή (on the scene quoted above, 6 n.), 259 a (οἱ τέττιγες) ἡγούμενοι ἀνδράποδ' ἄττα σφίσιν ἐλθόντα εἰς τὸ καταγώγιον ὥσπερ προβάτια μεσημβριάζοντα περὶ τὴν κρήνην εὕδειν, Anacreontea 18. 17, Plut. *Lucull.* 42. 1 Μουσῶν τι καταγώγιον. The topic moves from Greek prose to Roman poetry ; cf. Virg. *georg.* 4. 23 f. '(apes) vicina invitet decedere ripa calori, / obviaque hospitiis teneat frondentibus arbos', 4. 109, Ov. *met.* 10. 555 f.

consociare amant : cf. Ach. Tat. 1. 15. 2 ἔβαλλον οἱ κλάδοι, συνέπιπτον ἀλλήλοις ἄλλος ἐπ' ἄλλον, αἱ γείτονες τῶν πετάλων περιπλοκαί, τῶν φύλλων περιβολαί, τῶν καρπῶν συμπλοκαί. τοιαύτη τις ἦν ὁμιλία τῶν φυτῶν, Longus 4. 2 ἐν μετεώρῳ δὲ οἱ κλάδοι συνέπιπτον ἀλλήλοις καὶ ἐπήλλαττον τὰς κόμας. amant means 'are glad', not simply 'are accustomed' (φιλοῦσι) ; the construction with the infinitive is found several times in Horace and later poets (*Thes.l.L.* 1. 1956. 35 ff.). Some scholars see a suggestion that the trees are making love (Wilkinson, loc. cit.), and hence perhaps an oblique invitation to do likewise; but the emphasis is on the kindliness of the welcome, and Dellius's symposium seems more elderly.

11. **ramis** : the word is curiously emphatic at the end of a clause and beginning of a line (so Darnley Naylor 213). Presumably it makes a contrast with *rivo* (note the alliteration) ; it might be going too far to understand a hint of *obliquis*. The pause at *ramis* is not a strong one ; the question-mark in modern punctuation makes it hard to show this clearly.

obliquo : 'swerving'; when a brook is held up by an obstacle (as is perhaps suggested by *laborat*), it gets away by changing direction. The epithet is found elsewhere of rivers, like σκολιός; cf. Ov. *met.* 9. 18 'cursibus obliquis inter tua regna fluentem', *epist.* 6. 87 'illa refrenat aquas obliquaque flumina sistit' (Medea halts the streams in spite of their propensity to shoot off at an unexpected angle). It has been suggested that in our passage *obliquo* means 'downhill' (D. A. Kidd, *CR* 63, 1949, 7 f.) ; but this is not supported by the parallels, and does not suit *laborat trepidare*, which implies an element of difficulty (see further H. J. Rose and G. H. Poyser, *CR* 64, 1950, 12 f.).

12. **lympha** : the word is poetical (used by Ovid only in the *Metamorphoses*). The Romans rightly or wrongly connected it with νύμφη, which is occasionally found for 'water' (Antigonus, *anth. P.* 9. 406. 3, Antiphanes, ibid. 9. 258, Plut. *sept. sap.* 147 f) ; cf. *serm.* 1. 5. 97 f. 'lymphis iratis', Bömer on Ov. *met.* 3. 451. Cool streams and springs are a constant element in the *amoenus locus*; cf. *ars* 17 'et properantis aquae per amoenos ambitus agros', Sappho 2. 5 f. ἐν δ' ὕδωρ ψῦχρον κελάδει δι' ὔσδων / μαλίνων, Pl. *Phaedr.* 230 b ἥ τε αὖ πηγὴ χαριεστάτη ὑπὸ τῆς πλατάνου ῥεῖ μάλα ψυχροῦ ὕδατος, ὥστε γε τῷ ποδὶ τεκμήρασθαι, Theoc. 1. 7 f., Moschus 1(5). 12 f., *culex* 148 ff., Bömer on Ov. *met.* 3. 31, above, pp. 52 f. and 6 n. The mania for water gardens attached to the villas of Roman magnates put a constant strain on public supplies (cf. Prop. 3. 2. 12 'non operosa rigat Marcius antra liquor') ; the diversion of water *ad hortorum usus* was combated with no more than temporary success by Caelius, Agrippa, and Frontinus (cf. Cic. *epist.* 8. 6. 4, Frontin. *aq.* 2. 75 ff.).

fugax : cf. Prud. *cath.* 5. 116 'fonticulis . . . fugacibus', Virg. *georg.* 4. 19, Manil. 4. 417, *Thes.l.L.* 6. 1. 1474. 69 ff., 1482. 70 ff. The word is appropriate to a stream that has just got clear of an obstacle (Sen. *nat.* 6. 17. 2 'prona cum ipsis quae obiacebant fugit'). It also suits an escaping nymph (*lympha*).

trepidare : of quick and agitated movement; cf. *epist.* 1. 10. 21 'quae (aqua) per pronum trepidat cum murmure rivum', Auson. *Mos.* 29, Tennyson, *The Brook* 'And make a sudden sally'. The word makes a pointed contrast with *laborat* ('is at pains to scurry'), and is significantly placed in the swifter decasyllable. Horace seems to be personifying the stream as a bustling servant, just as the trees are genial hosts; cf. 4. 11. 9 ff. 'cuncta festinat manus, huc et illuc / cursitant mixtae pueris puellae, / sordidum flammae trepidant rotantes / vertice fumum', *pap. Genev. inv.* 271 οὐρανός μοι στέγη, γῆ πᾶσα στρῶμα, ποταμοὶ πάντες διάκονοι, ὗλαι τράπεζα (cf. *MH* 16, 1959, 83). There seems also to be a contrast between the fretting of the brook and the calm of mind suitable to philosophic gentlemen.

rivo : the instrumental ablative is almost a synonym for the nominative *lympha*; if anything, one would have expected the stream to be the subject and the water the instrument. This figure is common in Latin poetry, and was given by Postgate the convenient label of 'disjunctiveness'; for instances see Housman on Manil. 1. 539, Shackleton Bailey, *Propertiana*, pp. 33 ff. Note the onomatopoeia of the *l*'s and *r*'s.

13. huc . . . : for the connexion of thought cf. above on 9 *quo*. Wine, perfume, and flowers are often associated by Horace as symbols of the symposium (1. 4. 9 f., 1. 36. 15 f., 2. 7. 6 ff., 20 ff., 2. 11. 14 ff., 3. 14. 17 f., 3. 29. 2 ff.). See also Alcaeus 362 [at 2. 11. 18 n.], *Anacreontea* 7. 5 ff., *sap. Sol.* 2. 7 (disapprovingly) οἴνου πολυτελοῦς καὶ μύρων πλησθῶμεν, καὶ μὴ παροδευσάτω ἡμᾶς ἄνθος ἀέρος· στεψώμεθα ῥόδων κάλυξιν πρὶν ἢ μαρανθῆναι, Juv. 9. 128, 11. 122 (with Mayor's note).

nimium brevis : for *brevis* cf. 1. 36. 16 'breve lilium', Mart. 1. 43. 6. For the rose's ephemeral life cf. *corp. paroem. gr.* 1. 304. 14 ff. ῥόδον παρελθὼν μηκέτι ζήτει πάλιν· ἐπὶ τῶν μεταμελουμένων περί τι καὶ μὴ δυναμένων τι ἀνύσαι, Theoc. 27. 9 f. with Gow's note, Prop. 4. 5. 61 f., anon. *anth. P.* 11. 53, Philostratus, *epist.* 55 (34), *ros. nasc.* 33 ff., *anth. Lat.* 84. 9. The theme continues in authors of the sixteenth and seventeenth centuries; cf. Ronsard, *Ode à Cassandre, Amours,* 1553, p. 266 'Mignonne, allon voir si la rose Qui ce matin avoit declose Sa robe de pourpre au soleil, A point perdu, cette vesprée, Les plis de sa robe pourprée, Et son teint au vostre pareil', Spenser, *F.Q.* 2. 12. 74 'Loe see soone after, how she fades, and falles away', Waller, *Goe Lovely Rose,* Herrick, *Hesperides* 'Gather ye Rosebuds while ye may'. The development of the rose since the eighteenth century has made the topic obsolete.

14. flores amoenae . . . rosae : cf. 3. 15. 15 'flos purpureus rosae', 3. 29. 3, 4. 10. 4, *Cypria* fr. 3. 4 Kinkel ῥόδου . . . ἄνθει καλῷ. amoena is regularly applied to the rose; cf. *carm. epig.* 967. 1 'ut rosa amoena homini est quom primo tempore floret', Apul. *met.* 4. 2. 5, 11. 13. 2, *Thes.l.L.* 1. 1963. 73 f. There is a poorly attested variant *amoenos,* which involves taking *brevis* as genitive; cf. Ov. *trist.* 5. 2. 23 'quot amoenos Ostia flores' (for the reading see Housman 3. 924 f. = *CQ*

10, 1916, 137). The interlaced word-order is more characteristic of Horace; yet cf. 1. 31. 3 f. 'non opimae / Sardiniae segetes feracis'.

ferre iube : as often in sympotic poetry the identity of the assistant is left vague; cf. 2. 11. 18 n.

15. dum . . . : for the motif 'while ye may' cf. 2. 11. 16 n., Juv. 3. 27 'dum superest Lachesi quod torqueat'. It is naturally associated with the theme of *aequanimitas*; cf. Sen. *Herc. f.* 174 ff. 'novit paucos / secura quies, qui velocis / memores aevi tempora numquam / reditura tenent. dum fata sinunt, / vivite laeti'.

res . . . : the 'tricolon crescendo' (1. 21. 1 n.) balances *vina, unguenta, nimium . . . rosae. res* means not 'wealth' but 'circumstances'; cf. *serm.* 2. 1. 18 'cum res ipsa feret', Ter. *ad.* 855 ff. 'numquam ita quisquam bene subducta ratione ad vitam fuit, / quin res, aetas, usus, semper aliquid adportet novi, / aliquid moneat', Afran. *com.* 140 'res tempus locus simul otium hortabatur', Cic. *Cael.* 77 'iam aetas omnia, iam res, iam dies mitigarit'. *aetas* here is 'time' rather than 'youth' (Dellius was not a Thaliarchus).

sororum : a sinister euphemism for the three Parcae who spin the fates of men (Roscher 2. 3095, 3099).

16. fila : indicating the destined length of life; cf. *epod.* 13. 15 f., Virg. *Aen.* 10. 814 f., Ov. *am.* 1. 3. 17 'quos dederint annos mihi fila sororum', Stat. *Theb.* 1. 632 f., Milton, *Lycidas* 76 'And slits the thin-spun life'. The threads are here black because Horace is thinking of death (Mart. 4. 73. 4, 6. 58. 7 f., Auson. 401. 45 νήματα πορφύρεα, translating our phrase), elsewhere if a man's luck is bad (Ov. *Ib.* 244, *trist.* 4. 1. 64, 5. 13. 24); for other colours cf. *RE* 15. 2482. In our passage *atra* makes a contrast with the red roses above (also mentioned at the end of a line).

17. cedes : the verb has a legal flavour, being used in such expressions as *cedere bonis, cedere possessione* (*Thes.l.L.* 3. 725. 35 ff.); it therefore balances *heres* at the end of the stanza (cf. Ov. *epist.* 9. 110 with Palmer's note). For the commonplace that property must be vacated at death cf. 2. 14. 21 n.

coemptis saltibus : the *saltus* are upland pastures and woods, such as Horace elsewhere deplores; cf. *epist.* 2. 2. 177 ff. 'quid vici prosunt aut horrea? quidve Calabris / saltibus adiecti Lucani, si metit Orcus / grandia cum parvis?' *coemere* ('to buy up') suits an element of acquisitiveness; cf. 1. 29. 13, Cic. *Verr.* 4. 8 'mercatorem . . . in provinciam misimus, omnia qui signa, tabulas pictas, omne argentum, aurum, ebur, gemmas coemeret', Suet. *vit. Verg.*, p. 2 Hardie (on the poet's father) 'egregieque substantiae silvis coemendis et apibus curandis auxisse reculam'.

domo : a town house (as in the parallel 2. 14. 21), contiguous with neither the *latus fundus* nor the *villa suburbana*. 💙

18. villaque : the right bank of the Tiber was fringed with the villas and *horti* of the great ; for the next century cf. Plin. *nat.* 3. 54 'pluribus prope solus quam ceteri in omnibus terris amnes accolitur adspiciturque villis'. Sophisticated Romans like Dellius bathed and boated there ; cf. vol. i, p. 113 (citing Cic. *Cael.* 36), Prop. 1. 14. 1 ff. 'tu licet abiectus Tiberina molliter unda / Lesbia Mentoreo vina bibas opere, / et modo tam celeres mireris currere lintres, / et modo tam tardas funibus ire ratis'. See further Grimal 108 ff., 136 ff., 162 ; there is a map on p. 114.

flavus . . . lavit : the adjective was perhaps used by Ennius of the Tiber (1. 2. 13 n.). *lavere* 'to lave' (*epod.* 16. 28, *Thes.l.L.* 7. 2. 1047. 82 ff.) is likewise more poetical than *lavare* (in Horace only as a deponent in the sense 'take a bath'). The alliteration of *l* and *v* suggests rippling water (note also *villa*).

19. exstructis . . . divitiis : 'wealth built up to a towering height' (as opposed to the horizontal *coemptis*) ; cf. Bacch. 3. 13 πυργωθέντα πλοῦτον (for another resemblance see above, p. 33), *com. pall. inc.* 56 'cur rem dilapidas quam meus (miser *codd.*) exstruxit labor?' Others think of the less imaginative metaphor of the rich man's 'pile' ; cf. 2. 2. 23 f. 'ingentis . . . acervos', *serm.* 1. 1. 44 'constructus acervus' (the prefix makes an important difference), *epist.* 1. 2. 47, Epicurus, fr. 480 ἐξ ἐργασίας θηριώδους οὐσίας μὲν πλῆθος σωρεύεται, βίος δὲ ταλαίπωρος συνίσταται. It is wrong to take the phrase to refer directly either to tall villas (3. 29. 10, Sen. *epist.* 89. 21) or to villas built out into the sea (so ps.-Acro, A. R. Anderson, *CPh* 10, 1915, 456) ; both interpretations give too much emphasis to the villa at the expense of the other possessions, while the second gives to *altum* too specialized a sense for the context.

20. heres : cf. 2. 14. 25 n.

21. divesne . . . : the adjective picks up *divitiis* from the previous line ; for the polarism 'rich and poor' in contexts refering to death cf. 2. 14. 11 n. Cunningham and Peerlkamp inserted *et* after *prisco* to balance *pauper et infima de gente* ; postponed *et* is found elsewhere in the *Odes* (1. 29. 14, 1. 31. 10, 3. 4. 70), but it is clumsy when the first member consists of a single word (*divesne*). In fact *dives* is virtually substantival and the line makes a single complex ('a rich man of ancient lineage') ; Horace is suggesting (what may not have been true of Dellius) that wealth guarantees a respectable pedigree.

Inacho : the earliest king of Argos (*RE* 9. 1218 f.), and therefore typifying immemorial antiquity (3. 19. 1 f., Sen. *Thy.* 337, *schol.*

Ven. Ar. *pax* 530 τὰ ἐν τῷ Ἰνάχῳ περὶ τοῦ ἀρχαίου βίου). His son Phoroneus is described as the father of mortals (cf. *Phoronis,* fr. 1 Kinkel, Acusilaus, *FGrH* 2 F 23, Pl. *Tim.* 22 a) ; the genealogists put eighteen generations between him and Hercules (Apollod. 2. 1 ff.). Inachus's descendants were said to have colonized Italy (Soph. fr. 270 P. = 248 N.) ; among the many places assigned an Argive origin were Ardea (Virg. *Aen.* 7. 371 f.), Tibur (see Bömer on Ov. *fast.* 4. 71 ff.), Falerii, and Caere (Dion. Hal. *ant. Rom.* 1. 20; even more wide-ranging 1. 21). It would give an extra point if Dellius came from such a town, but in view of the proverbial character of Inachus the suggestion can only be tentative.

22. nil interest an : the monosyllable before the caesura is relatively rare in Alcaic hendecasyllables (vol. i, p. xli). Sometimes it is preceded by an elision (as at 2. 13. 2 'quicumque primum et'), sometimes by another monosyllable (as at 1. 9. 2 'Soracte nec iam') ; greater freedom is shown in the fourth book. The only parallels left are 3. 5. 33 'qui perfidis se credidit hostibus' (where *se* is enclitic) and 3. 21. 10 'sermonibus te neglegit horridus' ; in our line the irregularity is mitigated because *inter* can almost be detached from *est*.

23. sub divo moreris : 'sub caelo agas ac per hoc vivas' (Porphyrio). Horace is imitating old poetical expressions contrasting life with the underworld; cf. Hom. *Il.* 4. 44, 5. 267 ὅσσοι ἔασιν ὑπ' ἠῶ τ' ἠέλιόν τε (with Gow on Theoc. 16. 5), Aesch. *Eum.* 373 f. δόξαι δ' ἀνδρῶν καὶ μάλ' ὑπ' αἰθέρι σεμναὶ / τακόμεναι κατὰ γᾶς μινύθουσιν ἄτιμοι, Virg. *Aen.* 1. 546 f., 3. 339, 6. 436 f. In our passage the point is underlined by the contrast between *divo* and *Orci* ; note also the use of *moror* for a man's temporary sojourn on earth (2. 20. 3 n.). Some interpret Horace's phrase as 'live unhoused' (applied only to the poor and lowly, with a colourless *sis* understood in the first clause) ; this suits the meaning of *sub divo* elsewhere (3. 2. 5, *Thes.l.L.* 5. 1. 1642. 65 ff., 73 ff., 1658. 32 ff.), but the material cited above argues against it. Moreover the first interpretation gives a pointed contrast with 27 f. 'aeternum exsilium' ; it is also paralleled by the grandiloquent periphrasis in the similar Postumus ode 'quicumque terrae munere vescimur' (2. 14. 10).

24. victima : the word keeps its implication of an animal sacrifice; cf. Cic. *Flacc.* 95 'quam potestis P. Lentulo . . . mactare victimam gratiorem quam si L. Flacci sanguine illius nefarium in vos omnis odium saturaveritis?' For other comparisons (expressed in the more languid form of the simile) cf. Hom. *Od.* 11. 411 ὡς τίς τε κατέκτανε βοῦν ἐπὶ φάτνῃ, Thuc. 2. 51. 4 ὥσπερ τὰ πρόβατα, Lucr. 6. 1237, Palladas, *anth. P.* 10. 85. 1 f. καὶ τρεφόμεσθα / ὡς ἀγέλη χοίρων σφαζομένων ἀλόγως. For the implication 'destined victim' cf. 3. 23. 9, Gray, *Ode on a Distant Prospect of Eton College*, 'the little victims play'.

nil miserantis : for the inexorability of the underworld gods cf. 1. 24. 17 n., 2. 14. 6.

25. omnes eodem . . . : cf. 1. 28. 15 n. *eodem* is euphemistic for 'to the Underworld'.

cogimur : like *compello, cogo* suggests the image of the herd of the dead (1. 24. 16 n., 18 n., 2. 14. 9 n., 2. 18. 38 n., *Thes.l.L.* 3. 1520. 82 ff.). The verb might be thought to pick up *victima* (just as 21 *divesne* picks up 20 *divitiis*); but in this series of quickly changing images it is probably more effective to keep each element distinct.

26. versatur : the lots are shaken to determine our order of death; cf. 3. 1. 14 ff., Stat. *silv.* 2. 1. 219. One should distinguish the places where the urn is used in underworld trials (Virg. *Aen.* 6. 432, Prop. 4. 11. 19); yet the legal association of the word provides a bridge to *exsilium*.

serius ocius : cf. Archinus (?) ap. Clem. *strom.* 6. 2. 22. 4 πᾶσι μὲν ἀνθρώποις ὀφείλεται ἀποθανεῖν ἢ πρότερον ἢ εἰς ὕστερον, Prop. 2. 28. 58 'longius aut propius mors sua quemque manet', Ov. *met.* 10. 32 f. 'omnia debemur vobis paulumque morati / serius aut citius sedem properamus ad unam'. Such pairs of contrasting words (often with asyndeton) go back to early Latin, and are found alike in formal and colloquial contexts. In Latin the emphasis if anything falls on the second element; contrast English 'sooner or later'. For similar expressions cf. J. Marouzeau, *Traité de stylistique*, ed. 5, 1970, pp. 277 ff., K.–S. 2. 149 ff., H.–Sz. 829 ff.

27. sors exitura : cf. Hom. *Il.* 3. 325, 7. 182, Cic. *Att.* 1. 19. 3 'cum de consularibus mea prima sors exisset', *Thes.l.L.* 5. 2. 1358. 31 ff.; distinguish the shaking from the drawing of lots (Pease on Cic. *div.* 2. 86). *urna* should be taken with *exitura* as well as with *versatur*; there is a contrast with *impositura cumbae* below. The postponement of the subject *sors exitura* till the end of the clause suits the sudden emergence of the lot (Wilkinson 37). The unusual word-break after the fourth syllable of the line is made easier by the elision (vol. i, p. xli, n. 1); perhaps the rhythm suggests the spilling of the lot after the monotonous shuffling of *serius ocius*.

in aeternum exsilium : for the synaloepha cf. 3. 29. 35 f.; the elisions seem to give a sombre touch. The noun carried a strong emotional content for the Roman political and property-owning classes (the ancients derived it from *ex solo*). Christians used the metaphor of the exclusion of the damned from blessedness (Aug. *c. Jul.* 3. 3. 9, p. 706 'in aeternum exulare a regno dei', Dante, *Inf.*

23. 126, *Purg.* 21. 18 'eterno esilio') or of the state of the soul before the resurrection (Tert. *resurr.* 17. 2). ·

28. cumbae : the word is particularly used of Charon's boat (Norden on Virg. *Aen.* 6. 413 f., *Thes.l.L.* 4. 1588. 11 ff.). For the thought that all must embark cf. Prop. 3. 18. 24 'scandenda est torvi publica cumba senis', *epiced. Drusi* 357 f. 'fata manent omnes, omnes exspectat avarus / portitor et turbae vix satis una ratis', Palladas, *anth. P.* 10. 65. 5 f. ἀλλ' ἅμα πάντες / εἰς ἕνα τὸν κατὰ γῆς ὅρμον ἀπερχόμεθα. Perhaps it is not over-fanciful to see a contrast with Dellius's riverside residence, where boating must have been one of the principal attractions.

4. NE SIT ANCILLAE

[F. Cairns, *QUCC* 24, 1977, 121 ff.; Pasquali 489 ff.; F. Wilhelm, *RhM* 61, 1906, 91 f.]

1–12. Do not be ashamed of loving a slave-girl, Xanthias; so did Achilles, Ajax, and Agamemnon. 13–20. Phyllis must surely be a king's daughter; so unmercenary a character comes of no common stock. 21–4. I can admire her beauties with detachment as I am now forty.

It was a convention of Hellenistic epigram, as of ancient society itself, that friends might be cross-examined, teased, and patronized about their love-affairs. Callimachus makes appropriate deductions from a young man's sighs or from other suspicious behaviour; cf. *ep.* 43. 5 f. ὤπτηται μέγα δή τι· μὰ δαίμονας οὐκ ἀπὸ ῥυσμοῦ / εἰκάζω, φωρὸς δ' ἴχνια φὼρ ἔμαθον, 30. 5 f. ἔγνων· Εὐξίθεός σε συνήρπασε, καὶ σὺ γὰρ ἐλθὼν / τὸν καλόν, ὦ μόχθηρ', ἔβλεπες ἀμφοτέροις. When the bucolic Bucaeus reveals his girl-friend's identity he is greeted with mockery by his more sophisticated companion (Theoc. 10. 17 εὗρε θεὸς τὸν ἀλιτρόν· ἔχεις πάλαι ὧν ἐπεθύμεις). A refusal to name the lady could create the worst possible impression; cf. Catull. 6. 1 ff. 'Flavi, delicias tuas Catullo, / ni sint illepidae atque inelegantes, / velles dicere nec tacere posses. / verum nescioquid febriculosi / scorti diligis: hoc pudet fateri'. Horace himself in an epode blurts his secrets at a symposium (11. 8 ff.) and in an ode extracts a damaging admission from a young acquaintance (1. 27. 18 f. 'a miser, / quanta laborabas Charybdi'). Propertius mocks Ponticus for having succumbed to a slave-girl (1. 9. 4 'et tibi nunc quaevis imperat empta modo'); with his superior experience he can divine other people's loves (5 ff.), and insists on a confession (33 f.). For these and similar cross-examinations cf. F. Leo, *Ausgewählte Kl. Schr.* 2. 146 ff., F. Jacoby, *RhM* 69, 1914, 393 ff. (= *Kl. philol. Schr.* 2. 216 ff.), F. Cairns, op. cit. and *Hermes* 98, 1970, 38 ff.

Horace's ode shows the same situation and the same avuncular banter, but things have now gone a little further: Xanthias has admitted to loving a slave-girl. In real life such attachments were regarded with equanimity, and attested even of eminent persons (W. L. Westermann, *The Slave Systems of Greek and Roman Antiquity*, 1955, p. 74). There is no incompatibility between the ode and contemporary ideology: Augustus himself was concerned with sexual morality only so far as it seemed to affect the national interest (H. Last, *CAH* 10. 443 ff.). Of course a married man would incur his wife's displeasure if he showed signs of becoming an *ancillariolus* (Sen. *ben.* 1. 9. 4, Mart. 12. 58. 1), and Stoic moralists considered such connections disgraceful for men no less than women (Musonius 12, p. 66 Hense, van Geytenbeek 76); but even Quintilian is ready to give arguments on both sides of the question (*inst.* 5. 11. 34–5). When Horace advises a social climber not to seduce his patron's slaves, he is only concerned because the great man may want them for himself (*epist.* 1. 18. 72 ff.).

But for Horace's poem the literary antecedents are more important than the sociological facts. Captive Troades were familiar from Greek Tragedy, and kidnapped princesses from New Comedy (14 n.); enslavement to a slave was a paradox of erotic poetry (6 n.). At a more realistic level Philodemus proclaimed the advantages of low-class women (*serm.* 1. 2. 121, cf. vol. i, p. 370); our ode is influenced by several of his epigrams (3 *niveo* n., 23 n., 24 n.), and particularly by *anth. P.* 5. 132 (cf. A. H. Griffiths, *BICS* 17, 1970, 36 f., G. Giangrande, *Maia* 25, 1973, 65 f.):

> ὦ ποδός, ὦ κνήμης, ὦ τῶν (ἀπόλωλα δικαίως)
> μηρῶν, ὦ γλουτῶν, ὦ κτενός, ὦ λαγόνων,
> ὦ μαστῶν, ὠμοῖν, ὦ τοῦ ῥαδινοῖο τραχήλου,
> ὦ χειλῶν (χειρῶν cod.), ὦ τῶν (μαίνομαι) ὀμματίων,
> ὦ κατατεχνοτάτου κινήματος, ὦ περιάλλων
> γλωττισμῶν, ὦ τῶν (θῦέ με) φωναρίων.
> εἰ δ' Ὀπικὴ καὶ Φλῶρα καὶ οὐκ ᾄδουσα τὰ Σαπφοῦς,
> καὶ Περσεὺς Ἰνδῆς ἠράσατ' Ἀνδρομέδης.

For similar justifications of slave-loves cf. Rufinus, *anth. P.* 5. 18. 1 ff. μᾶλλον τῶν σοβαρῶν τὰς δουλίδας ἐκλεγόμεσθα / οἱ μὴ τοῖς σπαταλοῖς κλέμμασι τερπόμενοι / . . . μιμοῦμαι Πύρρον τὸν Ἀχιλλέος ὃς προέκρινεν / Ἑρμιόνης ἀλόχου τὴν λάτριν Ἀνδρομάχην (presumably echoing a Hellenistic source), Ov. *am.* 2. 8. 11 f. (to Cypassis) 'Thessalus ancillae

facie Briseidos arsit, / serva Mycenaeo Phoebas amata duci' (*Thes-*
salus and *arsit* suggest direct borrowing from our poem), Dio Chrys.
15. 5 οὐ πολλοὶ Ἀθηναίων συγγίγνονται θεραπαίναις αὐτῶν, οἱ μέν τινες
κρύφα, οἱ δὲ καὶ φανερῶς; οὐ γὰρ δήπου βελτίους εἰσὶ πάντες τοῦ ῾Ηρα-
κλέους, ὃς οὐδὲ τῇ ᾿Ιαρδάνου δούλῃ συγγενέσθαι ἀπηξίωσεν (the commonplace has now flowed from epigram to prose rhetoric). For the topic
cf. also Curt. 8. 4. 26 (Alexander and Roxane) 'Achillem quoque, a
quo genus ipse deduceret, cum captiva coisse'.

But though the subject-matter of Horace's ode is traditional, the
treatment is new; where others are sensuous or cynical, he prefers
upper-class Roman banter, rather as in the ode to Iccius (1. 29). He
professes to take seriously his young friend's infatuation, and keeps
up the heroic parallels in the best romantic tradition (2 *prius* n.);
yet there is something implausible about a slave-girl's snowy complexion, and something disquieting about prototypes like Tecmessa (6 n.) and Cassandra. The pointed style is also individual:
words are artfully placed to set each other off (see for instance the
notes on 2 *insolentem*, 3 *niveo*, 6 *captivae*, 10 *Thessalo*, 12 *Grais*, 14
Phyllidis), and the concentrated paradoxes of 10 ff. suggest Roman
declamation rather than Hellenistic epigram. In the second half of
the poem Horace proceeds from consolation to congratulation,
achieving a dramatic movement within his restricted compass; he
protests that Phyllis is a king's daughter with an unmercenary
nature, quite different from the *scortum* usually revealed by such
cross-examinations (Cairns, op. cit.). With the last stanza the lady's
charms are listed in the manner of erotic literature, but Horace's dry
and discreet catalogue makes an ostentatious contrast with the
febrile exclamations of Philodemus. He explains with a final twist
that at the advanced age of forty he is too old to have any personal
interest; the *renuntiatio amoris* is itself a traditional motif (23 n.,
vol. i, p. 72, Cairns 79 ff.), but whereas his predecessors had been
self-pitying or at best resigned, Horace's modest excuses are not here
intended to be convincing. He has not only done something new
with the commonplaces but has added an individual tone of voice.

Metre: Sapphic.

1. ne . . . : a final clause, not a prohibition. The purpose is not that
of Briseis but of the poet himself ('in case . . . , let me tell you');
cf. H.-Sz. 535, C. O. Brink, *PCPhS* 15, 1969, 4 ff.

ancillae : the word is prosaic; here it is given emphasis (cf. *serva*
below) by being placed before *amor* with *tibi* intervening.

pudori : cf. 1. 27. 15 f. 'non erubescendis adurit / ignibus', Catull.
6. 5 'hoc pudet fateri' (both from cross-examinations of friends in

love). The disgrace need not be great; cf. Plaut. *Epid.* 107 f. 'idne pudet te, quia captivam genere prognatam bono / in praeda es mercatus? quis erit, vitio qui id vortat tibi?'

2. Xanthia Phoceu : *Xanthia* implies fair hair, unsuited to servile associations, but corresponding to that of Phyllis (14 n.) and perhaps also of Achilles below (cf. Hom. *Il.* 1. 197); the Greek proper name detaches the comment from any identifiable situation. Some MSS oddly head the poem 'ad Xanthiam iatraliptam', and a connection has been suspected (*RE* 9 A. 1334) with the wrestling-trainer mentioned by Plato, *Meno* 94 c. It is perhaps conceivable that an ancient prosopographer traced some masseur who took his professional name from the famous trainer, but Horace's elegant hero could have nothing to do with such a person.

The mention of Xanthias's community suggests sympotic literature rather than Roman society (1. 27. 10 n.). Perhaps Horace associated Phocis with Delphi and the Pythian Apollo; in that case there might be a hint of the god's fair hair. Or perhaps he conflated Phocis with Phocaea (cf. Lucan 3. 697 where *Phoceus* means 'from the Phocaean Massilia'); there might then be a formal contrast between Xanthias's fair hair and black-skinned seals (for the seals of Phocaea cf. *RE* 20. 444, Head 587 f.). But of course the name need have no special significance.

prius : 'ere now'; for this usage in the citation of precedents cf. Catull. 51. 15 f. 'otium reges prius et beatas / perdidit urbes', Prop. 2. 28. 7, Meleager, *anth. P.* 5. 172. 5 ἤδη γὰρ καὶ πρόσθεν, *Anacreontea* 8. 13 ἐμαίνετο πρὶν Αἴας, Petron. 139. 2. At first sight there are attractions in combining *prius* with *insolentem* and interpreting 'though formerly arrogant', but in a parody of heroic *exempla* the former use of *prius* has more point. Alternatively one might consider 'formerly disdainful to women' (cf. Prop. 1. 1. 2 'contactum nullis ante cupidinibus', Agathias, *anth. P.* 5. 299. 8 ὁ πρὶν ἀεροιπότης ἤριπον ἐξαπίνης, Paul. Sil. ibid. 5. 300. 3), or 'formerly inexperienced' (cf. 1. 5. 8 'emirabitur insolens'); but *insolentem* when applied to Achilles naturally refers to general arrogance (*ars* 122), and ought to make a social contrast with the juxtaposed *serva* (cf. 6 'captivae dominum', 7 f. 'triumpho . . . rapta').

The appeal to precedents (*exempla*, παραδείγματα) was a favourite form of ancient argumentation (1. 12. 37 n., H. Canter, *AJPh* 54, 1933, 201 ff.); three was the maximum number in Homer, and the optimum for the rhetoricians (Plin. *epist.* 2. 20. 9 'sufficiunt duo fabulae, an scholastica lege tertiam poscis?'). The manœuvre was frivolously extended to erotic literature; cf. especially pp. 67 f., Theognis 1345 f. παιδοφιλεῖν δέ τι τερπνόν, ἐπεί ποτε καὶ Γανυμήδους / ἤρατο

καὶ Κρονίδης, Theoc. 8. 59 f. with Gow's parallels, 13. 5 f. ἀλλά καί
Ἀμφιτρύωνος ὁ χαλκεοκάρδιος υἱός / . . . ἤρατο παιδός, Philodemus,
anth. P. 5. 123. 6, Boucher 248 ff. For other mock-grandiloquent comparisons with Achilles cf. 1. 8. 13 ff., Plaut. mil. 1287 ff. 'verum quom
multos multa admisse acceperim / inhonesta propter amorem atque
aliena a bonis: / mitto iam ut occidi Achilles civis passus est'.

3. serva Briseis : in the first book of the Iliad Briseis is a status-
symbol, not an object of affection; the furthest Homer goes is
at 9. 336 ἄλοχον θυμαρέα, 342 f. ὡς καὶ ἐγὼ τὴν / ἐκ θυμοῦ φίλεον
δουρικτητήν περ ἐοῦσαν. Later writers romanticized the theme; cf.
epist. 1. 2. 13 'hunc (Peliden) amor, ira quidem communiter urit
utrumque', Prop. 2. 8. 29 ff., Ov. am. 1. 9. 33 'ardet in abducta
Briseide magnus Achilles', 2. 8. 11 [above, pp. 67 f.], epist. 3 (with H.
Jacobson, Ovid's Heroides, 1974, pp. 18 ff.), Plut. aud. poet. 33 a, Ach.
Tat. 1. 8. 5, Quint. Smyrn. 3. 551 ff., E. Rohde, Roman³, pp. 109 f.
serva is prosaic and realistic; servus and serva are avoided by epic
poets (Axelson 58), but Horace wishes to associate Briseis with his
friend's ancilla.

   niveo colore : the detail is not in Homer (though note Il. 1. 184
καλλιπάρηον), but presumably goes back to a Hellenistic poet (Pasquali, loc. cit.) ; cf. Prop. 2. 9. 10, Ov. ars 3. 189 'pulla decet niveas;
Briseida pulla decebat', Dares 13 'Briseida formosam, alta statura,
candidam, capillo flavo et molli, superciliis iunctis, oculis venustis,
corpore aequali, blandam affabilem verecundam animo simplici piam'
(cf. below flavae, fidelem, lucro aversam), Malalas, chronographia,
p. 101 Dindorf ἦν μακρή, λευκή . . . σύνοφρυς (clearly derived from
the same source as Dares). In our poem niveo is pointed after serva,
as one expects slaves to have a dusky complexion (Cic. Pis. 1 'color
iste servilis'). In love a dark skin sometimes needed apology, though
there was no colour-bar ; cf. Asclepiades, anth. P. 5. 210. 3 εἰ δὲ μέλαινα,
τί τοῦτο; καὶ ἄνθρακες, Meleager, ibid. 12. 165, Philodemus, ibid.
5. 121. 1 f. μικκὴ καὶ μελανεῦσα Φιλαίνιον, ἀλλὰ σελίνων / οὐλοτέρη καὶ
μνοῦ χρῶτα τερεινοτέρη, Lucr. 4. 1160 'nigra melichrus est' (see Gow
on Theoc. 10. 27), Virg. ecl. 2. 15 ff., 10. 38 f., Ov. ars 2. 643 f., rem.
327, epist. 15. 35 f. 'candida si non sum, placuit Cepheia Perseo /
Andromede patriae fusca colore suae', Mart. 4. 62, 7. 13, 7. 29. 8 'nota
tamen Marsi fusca Melainis erat', Strato, anth. P. 12. 5, 12. 244.

4. movit : the word has point when applied to the unrelenting Achilles
and the immovable Ajax (Hom. Il. 11. 558 ff., 17. 746 ff., Acc. trag.
158 'pervico Aiax animo atque advorsabili').

5. Telamone natum : the grandiloquent phrase (1. 12. 50 n.) gives
the dignity of the Homeric Τελαμώνιος as well as distinguishing the

greater Ajax from the son of Oileus. The well-informed reader is also reminded without waste of words that Telamon himself loved the captive Hesione (Roscher 1. 2592 ff.).

6. **captivae dominum** : the juxtaposition underlines the paradox of enslavement to a slave; cf. 1. 33. 14 n., Sen. *Ag.* 175 'amore captae captus', Val. Fl. 2. 146. *captivae* balances 3 *serva* just as *forma* balances *colore*; the variation of the cases is characteristic.

Tecmessae : the scansion *Těcmessae* has a hint of Greek tragedy, where κμ does not automatically lengthen. Tecmessa was famous from the *Aias* of Sophocles, where she is an estimable wife and mother; she perhaps appeared in the *Armorum Iudicium* of Pacuvius and Accius, and was the subject of a play by Caesar Vopiscus (Ribbeck, *TRF³*, pp. 263 f.). She was by no means a romantic heroine; cf. Ov. *ars* 3. 517 ff. 'odimus et maestas; Tecmessam diligat Aiax, / nos, hilarem populum, femina laeta capit. / numquam ego te, Andromache, nec te, Tecmessa, rogarem / ut mea de vobis altera amica foret. / credere vix videor, cum cogar credere partu, / vos ego cum vestris concubuisse viris'.

7. **arsit Atrides** . . . : Horace rhetorically varies the pattern of *movit Achillem*, and at the same time makes the expression stronger. For Agamemnon's passion for Cassandra cf. Eur. *Tro.* 255 ἔρως ἐτόξευσ' αὐτὸν ἐνθέου κόρης, Ov. *am.* 1. 9. 37 f. 'summa ducum Atrides visa Priameide fertur / Maenadis effusis obstupuisse comis', 2. 8. 12 [above, p. 68], Sen. *Ag.* 189. The parallels suggest that *triumpho* refers to the victory at Troy, not the return to Argos. The former interpretation also gives more point to *arsit*: Agamemnon himself went on fire in the city that he burned (for similar puns cf. *epod.* 14. 13 f., Dioscorides, *anth. P.* 5. 138. 2, Lucr. 1. 473 ff.).

8. **virgine rapta** : for the ablative after *ardere* cf. 3. 9. 6, *epod.* 14. 9, Ov. *am.* 2. 8. 11. *rapta* means 'dragged off into captivity' (cf. Hom. *Il.* 22. 62 ἑλκηθείσας τε θύγατρας); there is a climax after *ancillae*, *serva*, *captivae*.

9. **barbarae postquam** . . . : the stanza was deleted by Peerlkamp, but Horace is piling up the heroic detail. The trailing temporal clause is a mannerism of high poetry; cf. Hom. *Od.* 1. 2 ἐπεὶ Τροίης ἱερὸν πτολίεθρον ἔπερσε, Pind. *O.* 1. 26 f., *P.* 4. 122 f. *postquam* suggests the austerity of annalistic epic (Enn. *ann.* 149, Virg. *Aen.* 3. 1) and *Thessalo victore* the formality of a military historian (for ablative absolute in this style cf. E. Fraenkel, *Plautinisches*, pp. 236 ff. = *Elementi*, pp. 228 ff., 428 f.).

In Homer the Trojans are not barbarians though their Carian allies are described as βαρβαροφώνων (*Il.* 2. 867). Later ages saw the war in pan-Hellenic terms; cf. *epist.* 1. 2. 7 'Graecia barbariae lento collisa duello' (again in epic style), Hdt. 1. 3, Isoc. 4. 159, Cic. *off.* 3. 99, G. K. Galinsky, *Aeneas, Sicily, and Rome*, 1969, p. 98 n. 94. Sometimes the word suggested Oriental magnificence (Enn. *scaen.* 94 V. = 89 J. 'ope barbarica', Austin on Virg. *Aen.* 2. 504), sometimes a note of moral disapproval (schol. Ven. B. *Il.* 6. 450 on Hector and Andromache μιμεῖται δὲ καὶ βαρβάρων φιλογύναιον ἦθος οἳ περὶ πλείστου ποιοῦνται τὰς γυναῖκας); cf. Buffière 354 ff.

10. Thessalo : Achilles, as in the parallel at Ov. *am.* 2. 8. 11 [p. 67]; for his part in the victory which he did not see cf. 4. 6. 3 f., Pind. *I.* 8. 51 f. The word is contrasted not only with *barbarae* but with *Hector* (note the position in the line); as Porphyrio says, this shows that Horace is not referring to Neoptolemus.

ademptus Hector : for the euphemism cf. 2. 9. 10 'Mysten ademptum'; in our passage the verb also suits the literal reduction of a load. The meaning is 'the removal of Hector'; for the *ab urbe condita* construction cf. 1. 37. 13 n., H.-Sz. 393 f. Yet the personal Latin idiom provides a typical Horatian paradox: Hector's self-sacrifice was a betrayal of the city, and he influenced events most decisively by his disappearance from the scene.

11. fessis : for the war-weariness of the Greeks cf. Hom. *Il.* 2. 134 ff., Catull. 64. 366, Virg. *Aen.* 2. 109.

leviora tolli : Horace is characteristically combining allusions to Hom. *Il.* 24. 243 f. (Priam on Hector) ῥηίτεροι γὰρ μᾶλλον Ἀχαιοῖσιν δὴ ἔσεσθε / κείνου τεθνηῶτος ἐναιρέμεν and 22. 287 f. (Hector to Achilles) καί κεν ἐλαφρότερος (*levior*) πόλεμος Τρώεσσι γένοιτο / σεῖο καταφθιμένοιο. *tollere* means not only 'to destroy' but also 'to lift' (Horace may have thus interpreted ἐναιρέμεν); hence the word goes well with *leviora* (cf. D. West ap. Costa 41). Troy's dependence on Hector became a poetical commonplace; cf. anon. *anth. P.* 7. 139. 1 Ἕκτορι μὲν Τροίη συγκάτθανεν, Virg. *Aen.* 9. 155, Arbronius Silo ap. Sen. *suas.* 2. 19, Housman on Manil. 2. 3, Sen. *Ag.* 211, Drac. *Romul.* 9. 64 f.

12. Grais : the word is pointedly juxtaposed with *Pergama*, and together with *barbarae* frames the stanza. This is the heroic form, the only one used by Virgil (though he has *Graecia*). *Graecus* had prosaic and even unflattering associations; it is used by Horace twice in the *Odes*, at 1. 20. 2 (of a Greek jar) and 3. 24. 57 (disparagingly of a hoop). See further A. Ernout, *Philologica* III, 1965, pp. 87 f., Austin on Virg. *Aen.* 2. 148.

13. nescias : *nescio an* and *haud scio an* often introduce a tentative affirmative ('I am inclined to think'); cf. K.–S. 2. 521 ff. *nescias* is not easy to parallel; A. Y. Campbell comments 'the second person, by a natural and notorious figure of speech, is playful for "you may say *nescio an*"'. The subjunctive causes no difficulty as it is found even with the first person (Löfstedt, *Syntactica* 2. 133). Of course there is irony in Horace's reassurances: an upper-class Roman would expect to know for certain all about his fiancée's background.

generum : 'a prospective son-in-law' (*Thes.l.L.* 6. 2. 1771. 68 ff.); it is not necessary to interpret *decorent* as *decoraturi sint. gener* is occasionally used of extra-marital associations, but here Horace is humorously assuming that marriage is contemplated (which would be impossible of course with a slave). The praises of the bride's parentage and character conform to the traditional pattern of *epithalamia* (Menander rhet. 3. 403. 7 ff. and 18 ff. Sp.).

beati : cf. Soph. *Ai.* 487 ff. (Tecmessa speaks) ἐγὼ δ' ἐλευθέρου μὲν ἐξέφυν πατρός, / εἴπερ τινὸς σθένοντος ἐν πλούτῳ Φρυγῶν· / νῦν δ' εἰμὶ δούλη.

14. Phyllidis : the name occupies the same place in the second half of the poem as *Xanthia* in the first. *Phyllidis* suggests dark green leaves, and makes a colour contrast with *flavae*. The girl's blonde hair suits Xanthias better than her own name or servile status.

decorent : the word is emphatic after the caesura and makes a contrast with I *sit pudori*. Horace implausibly suggests that far from being a disgrace Phyllis's parents may turn out a social asset.

15. regium . . . genus : in Greek tragedy captive women belonged to princely families, and in New Comedy an exotic foreign origin was sometimes claimed; cf. Menander, *Carch.* 35 f. θυγατὴρ Ἀμίλκου τοῦ στρατηγοῦ, δραπέτα / Καρχηδονίων ἐμή 'στι μήτηρ, Plaut. *Truc.* 530 ff. 'adduxi ancillas tibi eccas ex Suria duas / . . . sed istae reginae domi / suae fuere ambae, verum earum patriam ego excidi manu'. See also 3. 27. 25, Petron. 57. 4 'eques Romanus es; et ego regis filius', Stat. *silv.* 2. 6. 98 ff., Pasquali 495 'quale donna di piacere moderna non vanta se stessa figlia di buona famiglia decaduta?'

certe : it seems best to interpret as *profecto*, 'I'm sure'; the affirmation is stronger than in *nescias an*, and leads up to the confidence of *crede* in the next stanza. It is true that after an expression for 'perhaps' one might wish to interpret *certe* as *saltem*, 'at all events' (Hand 2. 23 f.); but this is here inappropriate as *regium* is stronger than *beati*.

16. maeret : for the grief of captive women cf. for instance Soph. *Tr.* 325 ff., Ap. Rhod. 4. 35 ff., Enn. *scaen.* 92 V. = 87 J. 'o pater, o patria, o Priami domus', Ov. *ars* 3. 517 [6 n.].

iniquos : when applied to gods this naturally means 'unpropitious' (1. 2. 47 n.); even household gods could be regarded as potentially hostile (3. 23. 19 'mollivit aversos penates', 1. 35. 24 n.). Horace may be saying in effect *regium est genus et regii penates, quorum iniqui-tatem maeret* (for the *ab urbe condita* construction cf. 10 n.). *iniquos* does not suit *genus*, but a zeugma is perhaps possible; her lineage now does her no good either. To get round the awkwardness some editors put a comma after *genus* and interpret 'her lineage is royal'; but *genus* and *penates* make a natural pair (Prop. 1. 22. 1), and *regium* must colour the whole couplet if coherence is to be preserved (note 13 *beati*, 15 *regium*, balanced in two negative clauses by 17 *scelesta*, 20 *pudenda*). As an alternative one might consider taking *iniquos* as 'superior to her present condition' (cf. *epod.* 11. 18 'desinet imparibus certare summotus pudor' of giving up the unequal struggle); ad-mittedly this would be an unparalleled meaning of the Latin word, and there is no obvious Greek equivalent that might have encouraged Horace to try a poetical *calque.*

17. scelesta : a conventional insult like πονηρός.

18. dilectam : *diligere* is sometimes used in a passionate sense (Ov. *met.* 5. 395, Sen. *Ag.* 186), but here humorously suggests a stable affection. The verb keeps some of its primary meaning of 'to single out' (cf. 2. 10. 6); the variant *delectam* suggests the slave-market too brutally, and is uneconomical when combined with *de.*

sic fidelem : not 'so loyal' (of degree) but 'loyal as she obviously is' (with a movement of the hand). With a twinkle in his eye Horace puts the most favourable construction on the situation. There is added humour in the idea that disinterestedness in a slave-girl can only be explained by exalted birth.

19. lucro aversam : probably *lucro* is ablative, representing the prosaic *a lucro* (cf. *serm.* 2. 3. 107 'aversus mercaturis'); the dative has a different nuance at Quint. *inst.* 7. 1. 11, Tac. *ann.* 1. 66. 1, etc. The avarice of courtesans was a well-worked theme in comedy and elegy; cf. Plaut. *Truc.* 22 ff., Tib. 2. 4. 14 with K. F. Smith's parallels, Prop. 3. 13. 1 ff., Ov. *am.* 1. 8, 1. 10, *anth. P.* 5. 29–34, Alciphron 3. 14, Aristaenetus 1. 14, Lilja 143 ff., A. Day, *The Origin of Latin Love-Elegy*, 1938, pp. 93 ff., *RLAC* 3. 1165 ff. But there were striking ex-ceptions, at least in fiction; cf. Antiphanes, fr. 212, Plaut. *Most.* 204 f., Prop. 3. 15. 6, *RLAC* 3. 1173 ff.

20. pudenda : the word picks up 1 *pudori*; cf. also Suet. *Vit.* 2. 2 'sive pudendis parentibus atque avis'. Horace is thinking of inherited nobility of character (cf. *nasci*) rather than of maternal training (Juv. 6. 239 f., Lucian, *dial. mer.* 6). For the idea that fine people must have fine parents cf. Hom. *Od.* 4. 64, 611 αἵματός εἰς ἀγαθοῖο, φίλον τέκος, οἵ᾽ ἀγορεύεις, *h. Aphr.* 132, Virg. *Aen.* 1. 606, M. Marcovich, *GRBS* 16, 1975, 8, Dover 91 f.

21. bracchia . . . : for catalogues of charms cf. Philodemus, *anth. P.* 5. 132 (Horace's model, cf. p. 67), *serm.* 1. 2. 92 'o crus, o bracchia' (alluding to the same poem), Ov. *am.* 1. 5. 19 ff. 'quos umeros, quales vidi tetigique lacertos! / forma papillarum quam fuit apta premi! / quam castigato planus sub pectore venter! / quantum et quale latus! quam iuvenale femur!', *met.* 1. 497 ff., Petron. 126. 15–17, Rufinus, *anth. P.* 5. 48, Dioscorides, ibid. 5. 56, Maxim. *eleg.* 5. 23 ff., Aristaenetus 1. 1. (the motif is humorously reversed at Catull. 43. 1 ff. 'salve nec minimo puella naso . . . , *moret.* 33 ff.). For physiognomic lists see further Rohde, *Roman*[3], pp. 160 ff., J. Fürst, *Philologus* 61, 1902, 427 ff., G. Misener, *CPh* 19, 1924, 97 ff. (especially 122 f.), E. C. Evans, *TAPhA* 72, 1941, 96 ff. and *Transactions of American Philosophical Society* 59, 1969, 5 ff.

teretesque : 'rounded'; cf. Paul. Fest. 362 M. = 499 L. 'rotundus in longitudine', Serv. *Aen.* 6. 207. The adjective is used of the neck (Cic. *Arat.* fr. 9. 5 T., Lucr. 1. 35), of arms (Catull. 61. 174), of fingers (Ov. *ars* 1. 622), of the *membra* in general (Suet. *Jul.* 45). It is generally applicable to *surae* and need imply no exceptional attractiveness; cf. Ov. *met.* 11. 80 'aspicit in teretes lignum succedere suras' (the metamorphosis of the disagreeable matrons who killed Orpheus), Lact. *opif.* 13. 5 'teretibus suris clementer exstantibus sensimque tenuatis' (on the forethought shown by the Deity in the construction of the human body). It remains true that a short-skirted *ancilla* had conspicuous legs; contrast *serm.* 1. 2. 94 f. 'matronae praeter faciem nil cernere possis, / cetera, ni Catia est, demissa veste tegentis'.

22. integer : 'untouched' (the word is akin to *intactus*), 'heart-whole'; cf. 3. 7. 22 'voces audit adhuc integer' (where there is the same hint of virtue unimpaired). Caution was desirable in praising a bride; cf. Menander rhet. 3. 404. 11 f. Sp. τῆς παρθένου φυλάξῃ διὰ τὰς ἀντιπιπτούσας διαβολὰς κάλλος ἐκφράζειν. Horace humorously suggests that in spite of Phyllis's remarkable fidelity Xanthias may regard him as a rival.

laudo : to a learned reader there might be an ambiguous suggestion of the Greek ἐπαινῶ, 'no thank you'; cf. Virg. *georg.* 2. 412 f. 'laudato ingentia rura : / exiguum colito'.

fuge suspicari : for *fuge* = *noli* cf. 1. 9. 13 n.; for *suspicari* of sexual jealousy cf. 1. 17. 25 n. One must understand *eum* as antecedent to *cuius* (2. 16. 13 n.); for *suspicari* with a personal object cf. Plaut. *asin.* 888 f., Apul. *met.* 10. 24. 2. Heinze regards *fuge suspicari* as parenthetic, but then one might have expected a subjunctive *trepidarit*

with a causal nuance. It is best to see two balancing clauses with
a chiastic pattern; the relative clause is now not an inorganic appen-
dage but an effective climax (age might seem the best guarantee of
Horace's honourable intentions).

23. **trepidavit** : 'has hustled'; the word suggests fret as well as speed.
In view of the other reminiscences of Philodemus in this poem (p. 67),
Horace may be recalling *anth. P.* 5. 112. 3 f. ἐρρίφθω· πολιὴ γὰρ ἐπείγεται
ἀντὶ μελαίνης / θρὶξ ἤδη, συνετῆς ἄγγελος ἡλικίης (in an epigram re-
nouncing love). The construction with the infinitive is a poeticism;
cf. Virg. *Aen.* 9. 114 'ne trepidate meas, Teucri, defendere navis'.

aetas : Horace's own life; he can speak of it impersonally as he has
no control over its speed. Villeneuve interprets 'time' as at 1. 11. 8,
2. 3. 15, 2. 5. 14 (i.e. he takes *cuius* only with *lustrum*); *claudere* suits
an unsympathetic external power that has locked up with officious
punctuality. Janus, the god of the opening year, was associated
with doors and keys (Suid. 1. 2. 604 on Januarius οἱ δὲ πλάττουσιν
αὐτὸν ἐν τῇ δεξιᾷ χειρὶ κλεῖδα κατέχοντα, Roscher 2. 1. 36 ff., Bömer
on Ov. *fast.* 1. 125); for late imperial instances of Aeon with a key cf.
Roscher 1. 1. 195, Nilsson, *GGR* 2². 498 f. On the other hand *trepidavit*
suits the fret of living rather than the gliding of the years (2. 14. 2);
and most important, in a calculation of the poet's age one expects
aetas to refer to his individual life (see next note).

24. **claudere lustrum** : a *lustrum* was a censorial *quinquennium* (*RE*
13. 2040 ff.); therefore Horace is now over forty. He is imitating
Philodemus, *anth. P.* 11. 41. 1 ἑπτὰ τριηκόντεσσιν ἐπέρχονται λυκάβαντες;
the mannered learning of the archaic λυκάβαντες is represented in
a Roman context by the solemn reference to lustres (for similar cal-
culations by poets cf. Call. fr. 1. 6 τῶν δ' ἐτέων ἡ δεκὰς οὐκ ὀλίγη,
A. Cameron, *Porphyrius the Charioteer*, 1973, pp. 65 f.). *lustrum
condere* was an expression for a rite at the conclusion of a census
(R. M. Ogilvie, *JRS* 51, 1961, 31 ff.), and Bentley considered *condere*
here; but the technicality would be too precise for a reference to
Horace's own life. *claudere* suits the end of a period of time (*Thes.l.L.*
3. 1309. 3 ff.); contrast *aperire* (ibid. 2. 215. 61 ff.).

For statements in a poem about the author's age cf. *epist.* 1. 20.
26 ff. 'forte meum si quis te percontabitur aevum / me quater un-
denos sciat implevisse Decembris / conlegam Lepidum quo dixit
Lollius anno' (duxit *codd.*), *carm.* 4. 1. 6 'circa lustra decem', Asclepiades, *anth. P.* 12. 46. 1 οὐκ εἴμ' οὐδ' ἐτέων δύο κείκοσι καὶ κοπιῶ
ζῶν, Enn. *ann.* p. 67 (= Gell. 17. 21. 43, citing Varro) 'eumque cum
septimum et sexagesimum annum haberet, duodecimum annalem
scripsisse idque ipsum Ennium in eodem libro dicere' (a controversial
passage), Ov. *trist.* 4. 10. 95 ff., *Ib.* 1 f., Suerbaum 115 ff., 322 f. Most

of these instances come from the beginnings or ends of books; so too Philodemus's epigram cited above seems to be his *coronis* (*anth. P.* II. 41. 7). As Horace was forty in December 25, he must have written our poem shortly before publication in 23; but he reserved the places of honour for grander declarations.

5. NONDVM SVBACTA

[K. Büchner, *JAW* 267, 1939, 134; Commager 253 f.; J. B. Leishman, *The Art of Marvell's Poetry*, 1966, pp. 165 ff. (on English imitations); Oppermann 352 ff.; K. J. Reckford, *Horace*, 1969, pp. 103 ff.]

1–9. *She is not yet ready for breaking in, but is still capering with the bull-calves. 9–16. Do not thirst for sour grapes, for soon the vintage-time will bring maturity; your losses will be her gains, and Lalage will be the pursuer,* (17–24) *dearer than coy Pholoe, pale Chloris, and Gyges with his girlish looks.*

The primary problem of this poem was already posed by the pseudo-Acronian scholia: 'incertum est quem adloquatur hac ode, utrum amicorum aliquem an semet ipsum'. The view that Horace is talking to himself was preferred by Kiessling, Heinze, and Housman (3. 1087 = *CR* 37, 1923, 104), but others complain of the resulting obscurity. Yet a private paraenesis without a named recipient would be at least as unusual, and if the subject-matter was too discreditable for an eminent friend, a Xanthias or Thaliarchus could easily have been invented. At the beginning of the ode the girl is not named either, and this suits the idea that one has interrupted private musings; cf. Menander, *Sicyon.* 397 ff., *frag. Grenfellianum* 3 ff. (Powell, p. 177) ὀδύνη μ' ἔχει / ὅταν ἀναμνησθῶ / ὡς κατεφίλει 'πιβούλως μέλλων / με καταλιμπάνειν . . . , Ter. *eun.* 49 'exclusit; revocat; redeam? non si me obsecret' (for such self-questionings in general cf. W. Schadewaldt, *Monolog und Selbstgespräch*, 1926, Williams 461 ff.). In particular Horace seems to be influenced by the soliloquizing scazons of Catullus 8 (below, p. 79); when he says 'dilecta quantum non Pholoe fugax' (17), the confident assertion suggests that no less than Catullus he is talking about himself. The addressee of the ode has an interest in boys as well as girls (20 ff.), just like the poet or his persona (4. 1. 29 ff., *epod.* 11. 4, *serm.* 2. 3. 325 'mille puellarum, puerorum mille furores'). Above all, he is described as middle-aged and past his best (14); a tactful ironist like Horace says this kind of thing about himself, not about even his imaginary friends.

It was taken for granted in antiquity, even by the most serious writers, that the sexual instincts of men and beasts are essentially the same (*h. Aphr.* 3 ff., Aesch. *cho.* 599 ff., Soph. fr. 941. 9 ff. P. = 855. 9 ff. N., Eur. *Hipp.* 1274 ff., Lucr. 1. 19, Sen. *Phaedr.* 331 ff.). In a male-dominated world the consequences of this view were applied particularly to women, at least in the more sensuous forms of poetry. Girls are portrayed as skittish young animals frisking in green fields; the poet sees himself sometimes as the male animal, but more often as the trainer. Horace elsewhere compares Chloe to a fawn (1. 23) and Lyde to a filly 'quae velut latis equa trima campis / ludit exsultim metuitque tangi, / nuptiarum expers et adhuc protervo / cruda marito' (3. 11. 9 ff.); for other such references to horses cf. V. Buchheit, *Studien zum Corpus Priapeorum*, 1962, p. 104. The prototype for such passages may be found in a fragment of Anacreon (417), fortunately preserved in pseudo-Heraclitus's work on allegory (*quaest. Hom.* 5):

πῶλε Θρηκίη, τί δή με λοξὸν ὄμμασι βλέπουσα
νηλέως φεύγεις, δοκεῖς δέ μ' οὐδὲν εἰδέναι σοφόν;
ἴσθι τοι, καλῶς μὲν ἄν τοι τὸν χαλινὸν ἐμβάλοιμι,
ἡνίας δ' ἔχων στρέφοιμί σ' ἀμφὶ τέρματα δρόμου·
νῦν δὲ λειμῶνάς τε βόσκεαι κοῦφά τε σκιρτῶσα παίζεις,
δεξιὸν γὰρ ἱπποπείρην οὐκ ἔχεις ἐπαμβάτην   (cf. Silk 126).

Our poem takes from Anacreon the idea of talking about a girl in a series of sustained animal metaphors (for some particular imitations see 6 *campos*, 8 *ludere*, 9 *praegestientis*), but whereas the *double entendre* in the original is characteristically elegant and discreet, Horace seems to rush into love-poetry like a bull in a china-shop. The Romans were no doubt often brutal in their sexual habits (cf. Nock 1. 480), and Horace had a talent for sustained impropriety (*epist.* 1. 20. 1 ff.), but his crudity here needs some explanation; after all he is purporting to show his restraint towards the girl.

Perhaps a clue is provided by the opening words of the second section, 'tolle cupidinem / immitis uvae'; as well as introducing a contrasting and more 'poetical' series of images, Horace seems in part to be recalling the fable of 'sour grapes' (10 n.). That is to say, he now hints that the real reason for his surprising *continentia* is that the girl is not to be had; the ode begins to emerge as an adaptation of a common type, the poem of virulent reproaches addressed to a disdainful woman. But whereas the frustrated lover usually complains 'she does not love me but one day will be old and sorry', here Horace remoulds the pattern to say 'one day she will be mature and willing' (Cairns 86). It is illuminating to make a comparison

with Catullus's scazons of renunciation, though there the components
are more conventionally distributed (8. 9 ff.) :

> nunc iam illa non volt: tu quoque impotens noli,
> nec quae fugit sectare, nec miser vive . . .
> —at tu dolebis cum rogaberis nulla.
> scelesta, vae te, quae tibi manet vita ?
> quis nunc te adibit ? cui videberis bella ?

Horace like Catullus soliloquizes about his beloved, resigns himself
to her unattainability, predicts the changes that time will bring (in
his case favourable), and draws a Sapphic contrast between flight
and pursuit (13 n.) ; similarly the opening words of his next section
'dilecta quantum' (17) seem to be reminiscent of Catullus 8. 5 'amata
nobis quantum amabitur nulla'.

At this point another problem arises. Horace professes to prefer
the animal vitality of Lalage to three more fugitive and enigmatic
beauties : why then does he go on about them for the last two stanzas?
('nunc per ineptum Gygae praeconium Lalages obliviscimur' Peerlkamp). The poem's dying fall may partly be explained by formal and
artistic reasons ; so too the change from a major to a minor key. The
romantic and evocative descriptions (18 ff., 23 f.) make a piquant
contrast with the clear-cut equivocations of the opening stanzas ;
we have proceeded from the iambic to the elegiac mood, in the
manner of the *Epodes*. The symmetry of the love-affairs, and their
sexual indifference, evoke the artificial, amoral world of Hellenistic
poetry (Theoc. 2. 44 f., Call. *ep.* 25, Virg. *ecl.* 10. 37, Grassmann 122).
At the same time Horace seems to suggest the indecisive yearnings
of the unfulfilled lover, so different from the ultra-realistic directness
of the opening stanza ; similarly elsewhere he first renounces love,
and then dreams of a fugitive and evanescent Ligurinus (4. 1. 33 ff.).
He may even be hinting at one of the consolations of the rejected
suitor, that there are almost as good fish in the sea as ever came out
of it (Hom. *Od.* 21. 251, Theoc. 11. 76, Lucr. 4. 1173, Virg. *ecl.* 2. 73,
Mart. 1. 68. 8, Macedonius, *anth. P.* 5. 245. 7 f.). Such an analysis may
seem over-complex, but the same strands seem to be found at the
conclusion of the eleventh epode (23 ff.) :

> nunc gloriantis quamlibet mulierculam
> > vincere mollitie amor Lycisci me tenet,
> unde expedire non amicorum queant
> > libera consilia nec contumeliae graves,
> sed alius ardor aut puellae candidae
> > aut teretis pueri longam renodantis comam.

In spite of its brutal opening the poem turns out to have subtlety as well as ingenuity, though not indeed the supreme Horatian virtues of humanity and sense.

Metre: Alcaic.

1. **nondum**: the word is naturally used of untrained cattle (Hom. *Il.* 10. 293 ἀδμήτην ἦν οὔπω ὑπὸ ζυγὸν ἤγαγεν ἀνήρ) and of girls without sexual experience (Hes. *op.* 521 οὔπω ἔργα ἰδυῖα πολυχρύσου Ἀφροδίτης, Sil. 13. 829). Here in its emphatic position it sums up the message of the poem; Horace must have remembered Philodemus, *anth. P.* 5. 124. 1 ff. οὔπω σοι καλύκων γυμνὸν θέρος, οὐδὲ μελαίνει / βότρυς ὁ παρθενίους πρωτοβολῶν χάριτας / . . . φεύγωμεν, δυσέρωτες, ἕως βέλος οὐκ ἐπὶ νευρῇ· / μάντις ἐγὼ μεγάλης αὐτίκα πυρκαϊῆς. *nondum* is picked up by 2 *nondum* and 3 *nec*; the ode proceeds by a series of tricola (6 n., 10 n., 20 n.). The girl must be thought of as very young, as the age even for legal marriage was 12 (Dio 54. 16. 7); see further E. Eyben, 'Antiquity's view of puberty', *Latomus* 31, 1972, 677 ff.

subacta: the verb is properly applied to the breaking-in of animals; for the process with ploughing-cattle cf. Virg. *georg.* 3. 163 ff., Colum. 6. 2 (no doubt relatively humane), K. D. White, *Roman Farming*, 1970, pp. 280 ff. Often it is used metaphorically, sometimes with a sexual implication (cf. *carm. pop.* ap. Suet. *Caes.* 49. 4 'Gallias Caesar subegit, Nicomedes Caesarem', *epig. Bob.* 24. 2); for the same pun as in our poem cf. Lucil. 1041 ff. 'anne ego te †acuam atque animosam / Tessalam ut indomitam frenis subigamque domemque? / — "tune iugo iungas me? anne et succedere aratro / invitam et glebas subigas proscindere ferro?"' So in Greek (but less crudely) Hom. *Il.* 18. 432 ἀνδρὶ δάμασσεν (cf. δάμαρ, ἀδάμαστος, ἀδμής).

ferre iugum: in this clause the girl, but not the man, is thought of as 'bearing the yoke'; cf. Plaut. *Curc.* 50 ff. 'iamne ea fert iugum? / — tam a me pudica est quasi soror mea sit, nisi / si est osculando quippiam impudicior', Catull. 68. 118 'indomitam ferre iugum docuit', Stat. *silv.* 1. 2. 164 f., Call. *ep.* 45. 3 ἦλθεν ὁ βοῦς ὑπ' ἄροτρον ἑκούσιος (of a καλὸς παῖς). Elsewhere the two partners bear the yoke together (cf. 3 *aequare*), either in joint subjection to Venus (1. 33. 11 n., *h. Aphr.* 3) or in loyal *coniugium* with each other. By way of paradox the man may even be broken in by the woman (Ov. *epist.* 6. 97).

valet: 'has the strength to'. The subject is not mentioned; this suits a soliloquy (above, p. 77), and makes easy the double reference to the heifer and the girl.

2. **cervice**: the word is found repeatedly in contexts referring to yokes; for a metaphorical usage cf. Sen. *dial.* 6. 1. 3 'subactis iam cervicibus omnium et ad Seianianum iugum adactis indomitus'.

In our passage there seems also to be a gynaecological significance; cf. Cels. 4. 1. 12 'vulvae cervicem', Gal. *de usu part.* 14. 3 = 4. 146 K. τῶν ὑστερῶν αὐχήν (*pars vaginalis* L.–S.–J.), Clem. *paed.* 2. 10. 92. 3. If that is so, *iugum* supplies an obvious *double entendre*; when Horace embarks on an extended pun, every word ought to tell.

munia : the word ('obligations') would be humorously formal for ploughing by an animal; it is used with mock-seriousness by Grattius of a hunting-dog (*cyn.* 260) and by the elder Pliny of bees (*nat.* 11. 29). For the metaphor here cf. ps.-Acro 'obsequia lege debita, quod vult intellegi de inplendo uxoris officio', Dacier 'c'est un mot honnête, pour exprimer les plus tendres caresses de l'amour'. For 'marital duties' cf. Prop. 2. 22A. 24, 2. 25. 39, Ov. *am.* 1. 10. 46, 3. 7. 24, *ars* 2. 688 'officium faciat nulla puella mihi', *Thes.l.L.* 8. 1667. 11 ff. (*munera*).

comparis : a yoke-fellow, one of a paired team. Sometimes as here the word suggests the compatibility of human mates; cf. Lucr. 4. 1255 f. 'inventast illis quoque compar / natura ut possent gnatis munire senectam', Catull. 68. 126, Ov. *am.* 3. 5. 38. In popular language, notably in inscriptions, *compar* meant no more than *coniunx* (*Thes.l.L.* 3. 2004. 79 ff.).

3. aequare : yoke-mates had to be evenly matched, and the idea is readily transferred to human relationships (1. 33. 11 n., 1. 35. 28 n.). But here the reference is less to height than to 'keeping in step' (cf. Virg. *georg.* 3. 169 'iunge pares et coge gradum conferre iuvencos'); for the implication cf. Lucr. 4. 1195 f., Ov. *ars* 2. 725 f. 'sed neque tu dominam velis maioribus usus / desere [desine *codd. pler.*], nec cursus anteat illa tuos', *rem.* 413.

tauri : here, as often, a symbol of virility; cf. Aesch. *Ag.* 245 ἀταύρωτος, Ar. *Lys.* 217, Petron. 25. 6 'posse taurum tollere qui vitulum sustulerit', Cook 1. 634, Taillardat 71 f.

ruentis in venerem : the verb is used of animals running amok (cf. *epist.* 2. 2. 75 'hac lutulenta ruit sus'); for more metaphorical stampedes cf. Virg. *georg.* 3. 244 'in furias ignemque ruunt', Manil. 3. 654 f. 'tum pecudum volucrumque genus per pabula laeta / in venerem partumque ruit', Nemes. *ecl.* 2. 3. Here Horace is crudely literal; cf. Arist. *hist. anim.* 575ᵃ13 f. βοῦς δὲ πληροῖ μὲν ὁ ἄρρην ἐκ μιᾶς ὀχείας, βαίνει δὲ σφοδρῶς ὥστε συγκάμπτεσθαι τὴν βοῦν, Don. *hec.* 503 [below, 15 n.].

4. tolerare pondus : cf. Arist. *hist. anim.* 540ᵃ5 f. οὔτε τοὺς ἄρρενας ἐλάφους αἱ θηλεῖαι ὑπομένουσιν, εἰ μὴ ὀλιγάκις, οὔτε τοὺς ταύρους αἱ βόες, Plin. *nat.* 10. 174 'taurorum cervorumque feminae vim non tolerant; ea de causa ingrediuntur in coitu'. So of human lovers Maxim. *eleg.* 5. 34 'non tolerant pondus subdita membra tuum'.

5. circa ... est animus : cf. Ter. *eun.* 816 'iamdudum animus est in
patinis', Ar. *pax* 669 ὁ νοῦς γὰρ ἡμῶν ἦν τότ' ἐν τοῖς σκύτεσιν. Often
such phrases suggest that the mind and body are in different places
(*epist.* 1. 12. 13, Ar. *Ach.* 398 ὁ νοῦς μὲν ἔξω συλλέγων ἐπύλλια, Lyco-
phronides, *PMG* 844. 3 f., Plaut. *Pseud.* 34, K. F. Smith on Tib. 4.
8. 7 = 3. 14. 7) ; but in our passage that is ruled out by *fluviis* ...
solantis (6 f.). *circa* still has a considerable local element (1. 18. 2 n.),
but this is often attenuated ; cf. Tac. *dial.* 3. 4 'omne tempus circa
Medeam ... consumas' (with Gudeman's note), Sulp. Sev. *Mart.*
2. 4 'animus ... circa monasteria ... semper intentus', Thuc. 7. 31. 3
ὄντι δ' αὐτῷ περὶ ταῦτα, *Thes.l.L.* 3. 1090. 17 ff.

virentis : the word suits grassy fields, but also suggests the sap of
youth (1. 9. 17 n.).

6. campos : for the comparison of young girls with heifers in a field
cf. *h.Dem.* 174 f. αἱ δ' ὥστ' ἢ ἔλαφοι ἢ πόρτιες ἤαρος ὥρῃ / ἄλλοντ' ἂν
λειμῶνα ... For meadows as a symbol of virginity cf. Anacreon
417. 5 [above, p. 78], Eur. *Hipp.* 73 f. σοὶ τόνδε πλεκτὸν στέφανον ἐξ
ἀκηράτου / λειμῶνος, ὦ δέσποινα, κοσμήσας φέρω, Moschus 2. 63 with
Bühler's note (abduction scenes in meadows), C. M. Bowra, *Greek
Lyric Poetry*, 1961, pp. 260 ff. But a *campus* was broad enough to
wander in with freedom (cf. 3. 11. 9), and Horace is thinking of
something less secluded than Euripides (cf. 7 *aestum*) ; for meadows
with erotic associations cf. Anacreon 346 fr. 1. 7 ff. τὰς ὑακινθίνας
ἀρούρας / ἵνα Κύπρις ἐκ λεπάδνων / ... κατέδησεν ἵππους, J. M. Bremer,
Mnemosyne 28, 1975, 268 ff.

iuvencae : the word primarily means 'a heifer', but in the present
context can readily be understood of a girl; cf. 2. 8. 21 'iuvencis'
with note (of youths), Ov. *epist.* 5. 117 'Graia iuvenca' (Cassandra's
oracular description of Helen). The usage was not standard till the
Christian period when *iuvencula* and *iuvenculus* were used almost as
diminutives of *iuvenis* (without the point of our passage) ; cf. Porph.
on 2. 8. 21 'iuvenci ergo non tantum boves dicuntur sed et homines,
quamvis in usu sit ut non nisi per deminutionem iuvenculos dicamus'.
Names for young animals are often applied to girls ; cf. δάμαλις (1.
36. 13 n.), μόσχος, πόρτις, πῶλος, Βοίδιον, Vitula.

nunc ... , nunc ... : the second and third members of another
tricolon (1 n.). The adolescent girl's moods change as unpredictably
as the young animal's (cf. Catull. 2. 5 ff.).

fluviis : for the conventional picture of animals and rivers cf.
3. 29. 21 f., Hom. *Il.* 6. 508, Lucr. 2. 362 ff., Virg. *georg.* 3. 143. Sometimes pure streams suggest virginity in symbolical landscapes ; cf.
Ibycus 286. 1 ff. ἦρι μὲν αἵ τε Κυδώνιαι / μηλίδες ἀρδόμεναι ῥοᾶν / ἐκ
ποταμῶν, ἵνα Παρθένων / κῆπος ἀκήρατος, Eur. *Hipp.* 78 Αἰδὼς δὲ

ποταμίαισι κηπεύει δρόσοις, Segal 23 ff. In our passage, if the pun
is to be sustained, *fluviis* ought to be applicable also to the girl;
the word is occasionally used like *flumina* of liquids in general.
Cold baths were favoured by moralists (Ar. *nub.* 837 with Dover's
note, R. Ginouvès, *Balaneutikè*, 1962, pp. 135 f., 217), and were
particularly fashionable in Augustan Rome; perhaps douches of
aqua frigida were prescribed for the pangs of adolescence.

7. solantis : applicable both to literal and metaphorical heat; for
the former cf. Claud. 17. 196 'ille vel Aethiopum pluviis solabitur
aestus', for the latter cf. Catull. 2. 7 'et solaciolum sui doloris', Virg.
ecl. 6. 46 'Pasiphaen nivei solatur amore iuvenci', Nemes. *ecl.* 2. 27
'solamen amoris'. The verb is used quite naturally with non-personal
objects; cf. further Cic. *Mil.* 97 'esse hanc unam quae brevitatem
vitae posteritatis memoria consolaretur', Virg. *georg.* 1. 159 'con-
cussaque famem . . . solabere quercu', *Aen.* 1. 239 with Austin's
note, *Thes.l.L.* 4. 480. 48 ff. παραμυθεῖσθαι has a similar range of
meanings; cf. Dio Chrys. 1. 9 ᾄδουσιν ἡσυχῇ τὸ ἔργον παραμυθούμενοι
(so Virg. *georg.* 1. 293 'cantu solata laborem'), Alciphron 1. 1. 2 πῦρ
ἀνάψαντες τὸ πικρὸν τοῦ κρυμοῦ παρεμυθούμεθα.

aestum : the animal seeks relief from the noonday sun (Virg. *Aen.*
7. 495 'ripaque aestus viridante levaret'), the girl from her feverish
emotions (Nemes. *ecl.* 2. 14 f. 'flammati pectoris aestus / . . . parant
relevare'). The two kinds of *aestus* go together in bucolic poetry
(Virg. *ecl.* 2. 8 ff.); for similar puns cf. Ov. *am.* 3. 2. 39, 3. 5. 35 f., *ars*
3. 697, *met.* 7. 815, Marvell, *Damon the Mower* 17 ff. 'This heat the
Sun could never raise . . .'. *gravis* suits both senses; cf. Catull. 68.
62 'cum gravis exustos aestus hiulcat agros', 2. 8 'ut tum gravis
acquiescat ardor'.

8. ludere : the verb suits alike the lively young animal (Lucr. 1. 261,
2. 320) and the skittish girl (3. 11. 10, 3. 15. 12 'lascivae similem ludere
capreae', 4. 13. 4); Horace is imitating Anacreon's παίζεις (above,
p. 78). The *vituli* are younger than the *iuvenci* of 2. 8. 21 (who are
now ready for mating); cf. Varro, *rust.* 2. 5. 6 'prima (aetas) vitulo-
rum, secunda iuvencorum'.

salicto : the osier-clump on the river-bank (*udo*) provides leaves
for the heifer; cf. Lucr. 2. 361 ff. (of a mother-cow) 'nec tenerae
salices atque herbae rore vigentes / fluminaque illa queunt . . . /
oblectare animum', Virg. *georg.* 3. 175 'vescas salicum frondes' (for
the *pubi indomitae* of cattle), *RE* 8 A. 1. 589. A dense *salictum* might
also give cover to a flirtatious or amorous girl; cf. Virg. *ecl.* 3. 65 'et
fugit ad salices et se cupit ante videri', 10. 40 'mecum inter salices
lenta sub vite iaceret'. But nothing else in the poem suggests that
Lalage is in a real meadow; the fresh shoots of the *salictum* seem

to have a symbolical significance. It may be relevant that the willow, and in particular the *agnus castus*, had associations with virginity (H. Rahner, *Zeitschr. f. kathol. Theol.* 56, 1932, 231 ff.) ; cf. Plin. *nat.* 24. 59 'Graeci lygon vocant alias agnon, quoniam matronae Thesmophoriis Atheniensium castitatem custodientes his foliis cubitus sibi sternunt', Hier. *in Zach.* 3. 14 (*PL* 25. 1537) 'usumque ligni nomen quod Graece dicitur ἄγνος indicat castitatem' (see L.–S.–J. s.v.), Methodius of Philippi, *symp.* 4. 3. 99 ἐν τύπῳ γὰρ τῆς παρθενίας τὴν ἰτέαν πανταχοῦ παραλαμβάνουσιν αἱ θεῖαι γραφαί.

9. **praegestientis** : *gestire* suggests a physical movement (cf. *gestus*), and suits the friskiness of a restive animal or the excitability of an emotional girl; Horace is imitating Anacreon's σκιρτῶσα (above, p. 78). For the rare compound cf. Catull. 64. 145 f. 'quis dum aliquid cupiens animus praegestit apisci, / nil metuunt iurare, nihil promittere parcunt', Cic. *Cael.* 67 'praegestit animus iam videre'; as both these parallels refer to lively expectation, the prefix is not intensive (Prisc. *gramm.* 3. 50) but temporal (so also Catull. 46. 7 'iam mens praetrepidans avet vagari'). However, our passage does not mean 'is agog to play in the future' (she is already capering with the *vituli*), but 'is exulting to play precociously'; for the infinitive cf. *ars* 159 'gestit paribus conludere'.

tolle cupidinem : Horace's self-exhortations are humorously inflated; cf. 1. 27. 2 f., *epod.* 16. 39 'muliebrem tollite luctum', *epist.* 1. 12. 3. *cupido* would be a grandiose word for a longing for grapes; clearly it is chosen because of its erotic sense.

10. **immitis uvae** : properly *uva* seems to be a collective word for the bunch (βότρυς), while *racemus* refers to the single grape (ῥάξ) ; but the distinction is often blurred. For the vine as an erotic symbol cf. Ibycus 286. 4 ff. αἵ τ' οἰνανθίδες / αὐξόμεναι σκιεροῖσιν ὑφ' ἕρνεσιν / οἰναρέοις θαλέθοισιν (in his κῆπος ἀκήρατος, cf. above, 6 n.), Catull. 62. 54 f. (the vine and the elm), Ov. *met.* 14. 661 ff. Presumably grapes were associated with breasts (cf. Virg. *georg.* 2. 102 'tumidis bumaste racemis') ; for apples with a similar implication cf. ps.-Theoc. 27. 50 μᾶλα . . . χνοάοντα with Gow's note, Aristaenetus 1. 3, 2. 7, B. O. Foster, *HSCPh* 10, 1899, 52 ff., A. R. Littlewood, ibid. 72, 1968, 157. The change of metaphor from *iuvenca* to *uva* seems to be traditional; cf. 3. 11. 11 f. 'protervo / cruda marito', Theoc. 11. 21 μόσχω γαυροτέρα, φιαρωτέρα ὄμφακος ὠμᾶς, Catull. 17. 15 f. 'et puella tenellulo delicatior haedo, / adservanda nigerrimis diligentius uvis'.

immitis means 'unripe' of the grape-cluster (*mitis* refers primarily to mellow fruit). The adjective is also used here to suggest an immature girl: cf. Ar. fr. 610 ὀξυγλύκειάν τἄρα κοκκιεῖς ῥόαν (Kock comments 'nondum maturae puellae vim paras' and compares our passage), Varro, *Men.* II 'virginis acerbae', Honestus, *anth. P.* 5. 20. 3 f. εἴη μήτ' ὄμφαξ μήτ' ἀσταφίς, ἡ δὲ πέπειρος / ἐς Κύπριδος θαλάμους †ὥρια καλλοσύνη†, anon. ibid. 5. 304, Aristaenetus 2. 7 Σικελὸς ὀμφακίζει . . . παρατρυγῶν παιδισκάριον. For other such expressions in similar contexts cf. Archil. *Supp. Lyr. Graec.* (ed. Page) 478 Νεοβούλη[ν μὲν ὦν / ἄ]λλος ἀνὴρ ἐχέτω· αἰαῖ πέπειρα . . . , Alcaeus 119. 9 ff., Ar. fr. 141 ὦ πρεσβῦτα πότερα φιλεῖς τὰς δρυπεπεῖς ἑταίρας / ἢ σὺ τὰς ὑποπαρθένους ἀλμάδας ὡς ἐλάας στιφρᾶς, Theoc. 27. 9 f. with Gow's note, Epigonus, *anth. P.* 9. 261, Taillardat 50.

Horace seems also to be recalling the proverbial 'sour grapes' (thus Dillenburger); cf. Aesop 15 ὄμφακές εἰσιν. οὕτω καὶ τῶν ἀνθρώπων ἔνιοι τῶν πραγμάτων ἐφικέσθαι μὴ δυνάμενοι δι' ἀσθένειαν τοὺς καιροὺς αἰτιῶνται, Phaedr. 4. 3. 4 'nondum matura es; nolo acerbam sumere', Babr. 19. 8 ὄμφαξ ὁ βότρυς, οὐ πέπειρος ὡς ᾤμην. Similarly the applepickers in Sappho's *epithalamium* (105a. 3) οὐκ ἐδύναντ' ἐπίκεσθαι (cf. Aesop, loc. cit.); but whereas Sappho is straightforwardly eulogistic, Horace is affecting more complicated emotions (above, p. 78). It should be noted that on this interpretation *immitis* is given yet another implication: the adjective is used elsewhere of a girl who rebuffs her suitor (I. 33. 2 n.).

iam tibi: *iam* means 'presently' (cf. I. 4. 16); grapes can mature very rapidly, as do girls in southern climates. The adverb is repeated with anaphora in 13 and 15; the ensuing tricolon balances the one based on *nondum* in the first stanza (there is also a contrast with *nunc . . . nunc* in the second stanza). *tibi* is not simply an ethic dative ('soon you will see'); it describes a positive advantage (*dativus commodi*), as is shown by 13 'iam te sequetur'.

lividos: the dull bluish-grey colour of lead, bruises, or plums (André 171 ff.), here used of grapes beginning to turn; cf. Prop. 4. 2. 13 'prima mihi variat liventibus uva racemis', Juv. 2. 81 'uvaque conspecta livorem ducit ab uva'.

11. Autumnus: for the personification cf. *epod.* 2. 17 ff., Ov. *met.* 2. 27 ff. (with Bömer), 15. 209 ff., *fast.* 4. 897 (with Bömer), G. M. A. Hanfmann, *The Season Sarcophagus in Dumbarton Oaks*, 1951. The word is less autumnal than some uses of 'autumn', but as in Keats's ode suggests the season when fruits ripen and are picked. Such ideas are readily mentioned in erotic contexts; cf. Sappho 105a (see next note), Pind. *I.* 2. 4 f. Ἀφροδίτας / . . . ἀδίσταν ὀπώραν, fr. 123. 1 ἐρώτων δρέπεσθαι, Ar. *pax* 1339 τρυγήσομεν αὐτήν, Macedonius, *anth. P.* 5. 227. 5, anon. (17 cent.) ap. Leishman, op. cit., p. 170 'Autumn will shortly come and greet her, Making her taste and colour sweeter; Her ripeness then will soon be such As she will fall even with a touch'.

12. purpureo . . . colore : the phrase should be taken partly with *distinguet* (which suits embellishing marks); the lush scene is described in a single elaborate colon that extends from *iam tibi* to *colore* (for equally appropriate *abundantia* cf. 1. 17. 14 ff. on the cornucopia, 2. 11. 13 ff.). It would be less effective to understand a comma after *racemos*; the mottled appearance of the grapes is represented not simply by *distinguet* and *varius* but by the fact that two different colour-words (*lividos* and *purpureo*) form part of the same complex. For similar imagery in erotic contexts cf. Sappho 105a. 1 οἷον τὸ γλυκύμαλον ἐρεύθεται ἄκρῳ ἐπ' ὕσδῳ, Chaeremon fr. 12 N. πολλὴν ὀπώραν Κύπριδος εἰσορᾶν παρῆν / ἄκραισι περκάζουσαν οἰνάνθαις †χρόνου, Philodemus, *anth. P.* 5. 124. 1 f. [above, 1 n.]. For the association of *purpureus* with the complexion of youth cf. Phrynichus, fr. 13 N. [cited on 2. 9. 16], Virg. *Aen.* 1. 590 f. 'lumenque iuventae / purpureum', Philippus, *anth. P.* 11. 36. 1 f. παρειαῖς / οἰνωπαῖς. However, A. Y. Campbell comments 'designat poeta virginis adultae mammas venis variegatas' (1945 edition), and this explanation might suit the imagery of *racemos* (cf. n. on 10 *immitis uvae*); cf. Ov. *met.* 3. 482 ff. (when Narcissus beats his breast) 'pectora traxerunt roseum percussa ruborem / non aliter quam poma solent quae candida parte / parte rubent, aut ut variis solet uva racemis / ducere purpureum nondum matura colorem' (an evident imitation of our passage), Ar. *eccl.* 901 ff. τὸ τρυφερὸν γὰρ ἐμπέφυκε / τοῖς ἀπαλοῖσι μηροῖς / κἀπὶ τοῖς μήλοις ἐπαν/θεῖ (where Σ^R wrongly comments ταῖς παρειαῖς).

varius : the word (like ποικίλος) describes lively variegation of colour (cf. Austin on Virg. *Aen.* 4. 202); it is therefore strong enough for its late and somewhat isolated position. It is a *vox propria* of the grape, applied to the moment when it begins to become *livida*; cf. Cato, *agr.* 33. 4 'ubi uva varia fieri coeperit', 73, Ov. *met.* 3. 484 (cited above), Drac. *Romul.* 11. 17, schol. Juv. 2. 81 'hoc ex proverbio sumitur *uva uvam videndo varia fit*'. *varius* and *purpureo* are pointedly juxtaposed and cannot be entirely separated; if they say different things, that simply increases the variegated effect of this subtly elaborated passage. For other such shimmering scenes cf. Hes. *scut.* 399 ὅτ' ὄμφακες αἰόλλονται, Virg. *ecl.* 9. 49 'duceret apricis in collibus uva colorem', Aristaenetus 1. 3, Nonnus 12. 304 ff. ὧν ὁ μὲν ἡμιτέλεστος ἐὰς ὠδῖνας ἀέξων, / αἰόλα πορφύρων, ἑτερόχροϊ φαίνετο καρπῷ, / ὃς δὲ φαληριόων ἐπεπαίνετο σύγχροος ἀφρῷ . . . (there is surely a Hellenistic prototype behind all those mottled clusters).

13. iam te sequetur : a clear imitation of one of the most famous lines in ancient love-poetry, Sappho 1. 21 καὶ γὰρ αἰ φεύγει, ταχέως διώξει (vol. i, pp. 369 f.). At this stage the heifer is still felt to be the nominal subject of the sentence, and it is implausible to think of a revival of the stock-breeding metaphor only at 15 f. 'proterva fronte'. Therefore it is worth pointing out that cows, like Pasiphae, are sometimes mentioned as taking the sexual initiative; cf. Arist. *hist. anim.* 572ª31 αἱ δὲ βόες ταυρῶσιν, Plin. *nat.* 8. 177 'conceptio uno initu peragitur, quae si forte pererravit, xx post diem marem femina repetit'.

currit: the present must be preferred to the variant *curret*, as Horace is propounding a general maxim. Similar expressions are used of time (Sen. *Herc. f.* 178 ff., Palladas, *anth. P.* 10. 81. 4 ὁ δὲ χρόνος τρέχει), of life (*Anacreontea* 30 B. τρόχος ἅρματος γὰρ οἷα / βίοτος τρέχει κυλισθείς, Juv. 9. 126 ff. 'festinat enim decurrere [velox / flosculus angustae miseraeque brevissima] vitae / portio'), and of youth (Theognis 986 οὐδ' ἵππων ὁρμὴ γίνεται ὠκυτέρη, Theoc. 27. 8, Alcaeus, *anth. P.* 12. 29. 1 f. Πρώταρχος καλός ἐστι, καὶ οὐ θέλει· ἀλλὰ θελήσει / ὕστερον· ἡ δ' ὥρη λαμπάδ' ἔχουσα τρέχει). In our passage Horace must mean 'time' (cf. 2. 4. 23 n.), but he varies the common-place to suggest that to the very young the flight of the years can bring advantages. Some interpret *aetas* of Lalage's present im-maturity or future adolescence; but the girl's age cannot subtract years from Horace. Nor can the word refer to a period of human life in general (e.g. 'youth'); any such term that is applicable to one party is inapplicable to the other.

ferox: the years stampede as uncontrollably as wild horses; cf. Ov. *fast.* 6. 772 'fugiunt freno non remorante dies'. The adjective is naturally used of mettlesome animals; cf. Plaut. *Men.* 863 (of horses) 'indomitos ferocis', Virg. *Aen.* 4. 135, Henry 1. 587 f. Orelli thought that Horace was referring to the *indomita aetas* of young girls like Lalage, but *aetas* cannot mean this or any other time of life (see previous note); moreover on this hypothesis Lalage's *ferocia* when untamed would not make a clear enough contrast with her *proterva frons* a little later. Cruquius and Wakefield suggested the transposition of *ferox* and 17 *fugax*, and their conjecture has been approved by Housman 1. 143 and by C. O. Brink, *PCPhS* 17, 1971, 22 f. But though *fugax* suits time elsewhere (2. 14. 1 n.), it is less appropriate here: Horace is emphasizing what the years will bring Lalage, not what they will take away from himself. *ferox* in 17 would also cause difficulties (see note ad loc.).

14. illi quos tibi dempserit adponet annos: for similar observations in a simpler form cf. *ars* 175 f. 'multa ferunt anni venientes com-moda secum, / multa recedentes adimunt', Soph. *Tr.* 547 f. ὁρῶ γὰρ ἥβην τὴν μὲν ἕρπουσαν πρόσω, / τὴν δὲ φθίνουσαν (Deianeira on Iole and herself). Here Horace is saying something more pointed: the lapse of time ought to be the same for everybody, yet the self-same years are gain to the young girl and loss to the middle-aged man (so Heinze). It is true that *annos* has a suggestion of the Sophoclean ἥβη (Porph. 'mira conceptio in eo quod est *illi annos adponet quos tibi dempserit*, sed annos hic pro viribus ac flore aetatis accipe', Manil. 5. 269 'Virginis hoc anni poscunt', Petron. 81. 4, 119. 20); on the other hand to translate 'youth' rather than 'years' would blunt Horace's paradox. Bentley considered *quot* for *quos*; this again weakens the epigram by making the years equivalent rather than identical. He himself favoured *quod* ... *annus* (cf. 2. 16. 31 f. 'et mihi forsan tibi quod negarit / porriget hora'); once more this sacrifices point for clarity, and a nominative *annus* ('one day soon') seems somewhat superfluous after *aetas*.

Bentley complained that Horace's statement seems to imply the curtailment of the man's life; cf. Prop. 4. 11. 95 'quod mihi detractum est vestros accedat ad annos', Ov. *met.* 7. 168 'deme meis annis et demptos adde parenti'. In a sense he is right; we are being given a witty new application of the commonplace by which people like Alcestis offer themselves for another (cf. further Stat. *silv.* 5. 1. 177 f. with Vollmer's note). It may be added that *apponere* has a ring of the balance-sheet; cf. 1. 9. 14 f., Pers. 2. 1 f. 'hunc, Macrine, diem numera meliore lapillo / qui tibi labentis apponit candidus annos'. To indicate the double aspect of time, whose giving is in a sense a taking, Persius characteristically replaces Horace's paradox by another, 'labentis apponit'; for another application of the same *sententia* cf. Sen. *dial.* 6. 21. 6 'illi ipsi qui adiciebantur adulescentiae anni vitae detrahebantur'.

15. **proterva fronte petet**: another series of puns. *fronte* suits both Lalage's future effrontery and the forehead of cattle. *proterva* describes Lalage's oncoming behaviour (1. 19. 7); but the word was naturally applied to aggressive male animals (cf. Plaut. *Truc.* 257 'quis illic est qui tam proterve nostras aedis arietat?', Don. *hec.* 503 'protervus est qui dum alius obvius est proterit, quod faciunt et tauri appetitu coitus feminarum in quas calent'). *petet* (the future is obviously necessary) is used of sexual overtures (1. 33. 13 n.) as the equivalent of Sappho's διώξει (13 n.), but it also implies the butting of horns; cf. Virg. *ecl.* 3. 87 'iam cornu petat et pedibus qui spargat harenam', Serv. *georg.* 4. 10 '*haedique petulci*. lascivi, exultantes. et petulci dicti ab appetendo, unde et meretrices petulcas vocamus'.

16. **Lalage**: Horace at last makes explicit what has been clear all along, that he is talking about a girl. The name suggests youthful twittering (1. 22. 10 n.); λαλεῖν and its derivatives are often used in love-poetry (Meleager, *anth. P.* 5. 148. 1, 5. 149. 1, 5. 171. 2, etc.).

maritum : 'mate' rather than 'husband' (which would be too formal); the word is applicable to animals (1. 17. 7 n., 3. 11. 12). Though the mate is unspecified, *te* must be implied; only thus is balance sustained with 10 *iam tibi* and 13 *iam te* (in the first two members of the tricolon).

17. dilecta quantum : again one must understand *a te* (see previous note); Porphyrio wrongly comments 'dilecta generaliter accipe: a quocumque qui eam viderit dilecta' (so Mitscherlich, Orelli). For similar comparisons by lovers cf. Hom. *Il.* 14. 315 ff. (Zeus to Hera), Catull. 8. 5 (above, p. 79). In spite of Catullus, Horace means 'quae tum diligetur' rather than 'quae nunc diligitur'; the immature Lalage does not make a strong enough contrast with the other beauties. There should be a comma after *maritum* but not after *dilecta*; the participial clause forms a new colon (2. 1. 4 n.).

Pholoe fugax : the name is normally used of reluctant girls (1. 33. 7 n.) ; for a high-spirited Pholoe (as here in conjunction with Chloris) cf. 3. 15. 7 ff. 'non si quid Pholoen satis, / et te, Chlori, decet: filia rectius / expugnat iuvenum domos' (but in that poem both parties are behaving out of character). For *fuga* and *fugax* 'de puellis captationem virorum effugientibus' cf. Bömer on Ov. *met.* 1. 530, 1. 541; in our passage the adjective gives a clear contrast with 16 *petet* (cf. Sappho's φεύγει, above, 13 n.), and also balances 15 *proterva* (cf. the paradox at *epist.* 1. 7. 27 'inter vina fugam Cinarae maerere protervae'). On the other hand Cruquius's *ferox* (13 n.) would provide no contrast if it meant *proterva*; and if it meant *indomita* the contrast would not be clear enough.

18. Chloris : the name here suggests pallor rather than the sap of youth; the surviving daughter of Niobe was called Chloris because terror made her pale for life (Paus. 2. 21. 9). This interpretation suits the white arms and the clear moonlight below, and provides a good contrast with the *purpureus color* of the future Lalage (12 n.).

albo sic umero nitens : the *umerus* extends farther than the English shoulder, and the word is more poetical (cf. 1. 21. 12). *albo* suggests a dull whiteness, and makes an oxymoron with *nitens* (André 27); cf. Serv. *georg.* 3. 82 'aliud est candidum esse, id est quadam nitenti luce perfusum, aliud album, quod pallori constat esse vicinum'. The adjective is not normally used of female beauty ('pro candido' says Porphyrio unsubtly); here it suggests that the girl had the pallid glitter of the moon (Ov. *am.* 1. 8. 35 'erubuit. decet alba quidem pudor ora . . .'). The juxtaposition with *Chloris* is pointed; χλωρός is yellower than *albus* but both colours suit the moonlight, and the conflation is characteristic of Roman poetry (cf. 12 n.).

19. pura : the moon is 'clear' when the sky is cloudless; cf. 1. 34. 7, 3. 29. 45, Ov. *epist.* 17 (18). 71 'radiis argentea puris', K. F. Smith on Tib. 1. 9. 36, Pind. *P.* 6. 14 φάει . . . ἐν καθαρῷ. Applied to the girl the adjective suggests unimpaired beauty (cf. 3. 19. 26 'puro te similem, Telephe, Vespero'); her shoulder is like a marble statue (cf. 1. 19. 6 'splendentis Pario marmore purius', with note ad loc.). *pura* also suits the chastity of the virgin moon, and hints that Chloris is passionless compared with the future Lalage.

nocturno : the use of the adjective is more poetical than an adverbial 'by night' (cf. 2. 13. 7). At the same time its position between *pura* and *renidet* is evocative; the undimmed brightness of the moon is contrasted with the normal attributes of night.

renidet luna : the simile goes back to Sappho 96. 9 ff. (comparing a girl to the moon that outshines the stars) : φάος δ᾽ ἐπί/σχει θάλασσαν ἐπ᾽ ἀλμύραν / ἴσως καὶ πολυανθέμοις ἀρούραις. Later poets characteristically concentrated on the reflected light; cf. Val. Fl. 3. 558 f. (on Hylas leaning over the pool) 'stagna vaga sic luce micant ubi Cynthia caelo / prospicit', Nonnus 5. 487 f. (on Artemis bathing) φαίης δ᾽ ὡς παρὰ χεῦμα παλίμπορον Ὠκεανοῖο / ἑσπερίη σελάγιζε δι᾽ ὕδατος ὄμπνια Μήνη, 38. 122 ff. (on Clymene swimming), Shakespeare, *Venus and Adonis* 492 'Shone like the moon in water seen by night'. For other encomiastic references to the moon cf. 1. 12. 48 n., Rohde, *Roman*[3], p. 163, H. Usener, *Kleine Schriften* 4, 1913, 10 f.

Horace, like Sappho, is referring to the moon in the sky rather than to the moonlight in the water; the sentence is bound together more effectively if *nocturno . . . mari* is a dative rather than a local ablative (as most commentators assume). It is true that *renidere* normally describes reflected light (2. 18. 1 f., Virg. *georg.* 2. 282 'aere renidenti'); but here Horace uses the verb in an evocative way to suggest the reciprocal action of moon and sea (for the opposite process cf. Lucr. 2. 325 f. 'fulgor ibi ad caelum se tollit totaque circum / aere renidescit tellus'). *pura* suits the moon's clear outline (and the girl's white shoulder) better than a shimmering reflection; Chloris is like Tennyson's Maud, 'Passionless pale cold face star-sweet on a gloom profound' (3. 4). For a more debatable point see the next note.

20. Cnidiusve Gyges : the most prudent interpretation is to take *Gyges* as coordinate with 17 *Pholoe* and 18 *Chloris*; Pholoe is characterized by a word, Chloris by a couple of lines, but Gyges by a whole stanza (for the expanding tricolon cf. 1. 21. 1 n.). Yet the colometry causes difficulty: *-ve* marks a very slight transition compared with *non Chloris albo*, and at this late stage in the stanza *Cnidiusve Gyges* seems the end of the old colon and not the beginning of the new.

If this is so, Chloris by a paradoxical climax is compared not just to the moon but to another human beauty.

The obvious objection is that the nocturnal sea has nothing to do with Gyges, but perhaps Horace has undermined his uncharacteristic poeticism by yet another play on words: the moon glints to the sea and Gyges to his male lover (*nocturno* coheres with both interpretations). *mas-maris* is rare in poetry (1.21.10), but suits the animal tone of the ode (cf. Ov. *am.* 2. 6. 56 'oscula dat cupido blanda columba mari'); of course there would be some oddity in Horace's choice of words, but this is sometimes unavoidable in a pun. At *serm.* 2. 8. 14 f. 'procedit fuscus Hydaspes / Caecuba vina ferens, Alcon Chium maris expers' Housman referred *maris expers* to Alcon and interpreted 'emasculate' (2. 861 f. = *CQ* 7, 1913, 27 f.); 'unsalted' must be at least part of the meaning (cf. Lejay ad loc. for the evidence for Chian wine), but a syntactical ambiguity seems worth considering (though such things in Latin are rare). Persius imitated this passage at 6. 38 f. 'postquam sapere urbi / cum pipere et palmis venit nostrum hoc maris expers'; here again Housman interpreted *eviratum*, but a pun on *insulsum* would preserve the oxymoron with *sapere*. At *carm.* 1. 5. 15 f. we supported Zielinski's conjecture 'suspendisse potenti / vestimenta maris deae' (*deo* MSS, editors, reviewers); perhaps it might be further speculated that in this punning poem *potenti maris* bears the secondary sense of 'dominating the male sex, τοῦ ἄρρενος' (thus tentatively Quinn 194 n. 2). Such an interpretation would explain the odd hyperbaton, which has the effect of calling attention to *maris*; if there is a witty point in the word's juxtaposition with *deae*, then the dislocation is justified.

Gyges was a lover in 3. 7. 5, perhaps also in a lost work of Ovid (Porphyrio naively comments 'de huius pueri pulchritudine etiam Ovidius locutus est'). The name may have been used by Hellenistic poets to evoke the voluptuous associations of Lydia (1. 8. 1 n.); *Cnidius* specifies the boy's city in the common Greek way (1. 27. 10 n.). Horace no doubt associates Cnidos with Aphrodite, and perhaps in particular with the famous statue of Praxiteles (1. 30. 1 n.). Such an interpretation would suit the colometry offered above: the marble-like glitter of Gyges is being compared to the white shoulder of Chloris.

21. si puellarum insereres choro : 'if you set him in a ring of girls'; Horace is alluding to the disguise of Achilles on Scyros (1. 8. 13 n.). *inserere* suggests the twining of a flower in a circular garland (*serta*); cf. Plin. *nat.* 20. 247 'inseritur coronis'.

22. mire : to be taken with *falleret*; for the hyperbaton cf. 2. 12. 15 f. 'bene . . . fidum'. The adverb pulls against the juxtaposed *sagacis*

(just as *falleret* does more obviously). Here it is a strong word
('miraculously'); perhaps Horace recalled the invisibility of King
Gyges in Plato's story (*rep.* 359–60). Some join *mire* with *sagacis*,
but a conversational θαυμασίως ὡς would be superfluous padding.
They compare *serm.* 2. 3. 27 f. '"et miror morbi purgatum te illius".
—"atqui / emovit veterem mire novus"'; but there in fact *mire*
strengthens the verb, just as in our passage.

   sagacis . . . hospites : 'suaviter hic hospites pro ignotis dicit, hoc
est qui ipsum puerum non nossent' (Porphyrio); in particular the
word recalls the visit of Odysseus and Diomedes to Scyros (cf. *Stat.
Ach.* 1. 844 'hospitii'). *sagacis* suggests the keen scent of a bloodhound
or the perspicacity of Odysseus, who was not in fact deceived by the
disguise of Achilles; cf. Philostr. Jun. *imag.* 1. 5 σοφὸς ὢν 'Οδυσσεὺς
καὶ ἱκανὸς τῶν ἀδήλων θηρατής.

23. discrimen obscurum : 'the obscuring of the distinction'; for
the emphasis on the adjective cf. 2. 4. 10 n. (on the *ab urbe condita*
construction). Yet the Latin usage makes possible characteristically
Horatian paradoxes (loc. cit.): *discrimen* (which implies fine observation) not only points in the opposite direction from its verb
fallit but makes a striking oxymoron with *obscurum*. Our passage is
imitated by Stat. *Ach.* 1. 336 f. 'fallitque tuentes / ambiguus tenuique
latens discrimine sexus'.

   solutis crinibus : characteristic of the *delicatus puer*; cf. 1. 29. 8 n.,
epod. 11. 28 [above, p. 79]. The ablative is instrumental with *obscurum*; cf. Ov. *met.* 14. 57 f. 'obscurum verborum ambage novorum /
. . . carmen'. Horace seems to be punning on the shadowing effect
of long hair; cf. Ov. *met.* 13. 845 'humerosque ut lucus obumbrat',
Archil. 31 W. ἡ δέ οἱ κόμη / ὤμους κατεσκίαζε καὶ μετάφρενα (Synesius,
laudatio calvitii, p. 211 Terz., comments in quoting the passage
οὐκοῦν ἅπαντες οἴονταί τε καὶ λέγουσιν αὐτοφυὲς εἶναι σκιάδειον τὴν
κόμην). The play on words is increased by the fact that *discrimen*
can mean 'a parting of the hair' (*Thes.l.L.* 5. 1. 1356. 19 ff.).

24. ambiguoque vultu : *ambiguus* can refer either to the uncertainty
of somebody's sex or to sexual ambivalence itself; cf. Ov. *met.* 4.
279 f. 'nec loquor ut quondam naturae iure novato / ambiguus fuerit
modo vir modo femina Sithon', Lucian, *dial. deor.* 3 (23). 1 ὁ δὲ
θῆλυς καὶ ἡμίανδρος καὶ ἀμφίβολος τὴν ὄψιν· οὐκ ἂν διακρίναις (cf. *discrimen*) εἴτ' ἔφηβός ἐστιν εἴτε καὶ παρθένος, anon. *anth. P.* 9. 783. 4
(with Auson. 100. 4 [p. 349 P.]). For similar uncertainties cf. Anacreon
360. 1 ὦ παῖ παρθένιον βλέπων, Stat. *silv.* 2. 6. 39 'dubiae . . . formae'
(with Vollmer's note), *Ach.* 1. 744, Juv. 15. 137 'ora puellares faciunt
incerta capilli' (with Mayor's note). In our passage *ambiguo* (like
obscurum) seems to be in formal opposition to *solutis*, which suggests

the λύσις or unravelling of a problem: cf. Quint. *inst.* 7. 2. 49 'solvet ambiguitatem'. The ambiguity of Horace's language is subtly chosen to match his subject.

6. SEPTIMI GADIS

[F. Klingner, *Philologus* 90, 1935, 285 ff. (= *Studien*, pp. 314 ff.) ; W. Ludwig, *WS* N.F. 4, 1970, 101 ff.; R. Philippson, *RhM* 69, 1914, 735 ff.; Plüss 140 ff.; C. Segal, *Philologus* 113, 1969, 235 ff.; H. Swinburne, *Travels in the Two Sicilies*, ed. 2, 1790 ; Troxler-Keller 119 ff.; P. Wuilleumier, *Tarente des origines à la conquête romaine*, 1939 = *Bibl. des écoles françaises d'Athènes et de Rome* 148]

1-8. Septimius, you would go with me to fight the Cantabrians, but I wish to spend my declining years at Tibur, as I have had enough of arduous expeditions. 9-20. If that proves impossible I shall sally forth for Tarentum with its rich produce and mild climate. 21-4. You too must hearken to the call, and share my felicity till the day I die.

Septimius is described by Porphyrio as an *eques Romanus* who was a *commilito* of Horace; the latter statement is probably a bad guess, based on 8 *militiae* and the supposed analogy of Pompeius in the next poem. Horace may have been considerably older, as he confidently expects to predecease his friend (22 ff.); when he recommends him to the young Tiberius, perhaps about 21 B.C. (*epist.* 1. 9), he is hardly speaking of a middle-aged contemporary. He describes Septimius in the epistle as *fortem . . . bonumque* (1. 9. 13); the compliment is conventional, yet *fortem* suggests the more active virtues. The ambitious young man did well in the imperial household, and was promoted in due course to the inner circle; the success of his career is shown by Augustus's letter to Horace 'tui qualem habeam memoriam poteris ex Septimio quoque nostro audire; nam incidit ut illo coram fieret a me tui mentio' (Suet. *vit. Hor.* 30 ff. Rostagni).

In the first stanza of the ode Septimius is ready to face the rebellious Cantabrians; this strongly suggests that they were under arms at the time of writing. They were temporarily subdued by Statilius Taurus in 29 B.C. or soon after (Dio 51. 20. 5) ; they were defeated again by Augustus in 26, and when he fell ill, by his legates in 25, when the temple of Janus was closed (vol. i, p. xxxi); they gave more trouble in 24, after Augustus's return to Rome, but it would have been tactless to underline this new outbreak. A date about 29 would suit Horace's reference to war-weariness (8 n.), and the following ode to Pompeius, which has a general resemblance to our poem (Ludwig, op. cit.), seems to belong to that time. On the other hand a later date is supported by affinities in the *Epistles* (1. 7. 45 associating Tibur and Tarentum, 1. 9 recommending Septimius to Tiberius), and *senectae* (6) becomes more realistic as Horace approaches forty (25 B.C.). Horace's immediate model had talked of visiting the scenes of Caesar's conquests (Catull. 11. 10 'Caesaris visens monumenta magni'), and a hint at Augustus's campaigns might be a deft form of imitation; the reference to the enemy's recalcitrance need not have been indiscreet as it simply underlines the resolution of the Princeps. Finally it may be mentioned that Horace shows similar weariness in 3. 14, a poem certainly datable to 24 B.C.

Some suppose that Septimius has exhorted Horace to join him in the Cantabrian campaign, and that the poet is gracefully expressing his excuses (A. Rostagni, *AAT* 70, 1934–5, 28 ff. and on Suet. *vit. Hor.* 30). It is suggested that Augustus was in Spain when he invited Horace to become his secretary (ibid. 20 ff. 'nunc occupatissimus et infirmus Horatium nostrum a te cupio abducere'), and that when the poet pleaded ill-health (ibid. 29 'si per valetudinem tuam fieri posset'), the Princeps took on Septimius instead (ibid. 30 ff., cited above). But if the Cantabrian War had been the immediate occasion of the poem, the accompanying references to Gades and the Syrtes would blur the issue; and if Septimius had joined Augustus's entourage as early as 25, it might be superfluous for the less enterprising Horace to recommend him to Tiberius in 21. It seems more likely that Horace has brought up to date a commonplace from Catullus on distant journeys (1 n.), and that to tease his pushing young friend he assumes that he wants to join Augustus in the Spanish mountains.

Horace explains that he himself is incapable of such an Odyssey, as he has grown weary in the service of his country; he will live out his life at Tibur, the fashionable hill-resort only eighteen miles from Rome. If the fates block his path (as sometimes happens to epic heroes) he will make do with Tarentum, which of course was even more sequestered and relaxing than the cool heights of Tibur. The humour is best illustrated by the fifteenth epistle where Horace renounces the warm baths of Baiae, not from any unexpected asceticism but because he is enticed by the more luscious flesh-pots of the South (*epist.* 1. 15. 24 'pinguis ut inde domum possim Phaeaxque reverti'). The adjectives used of Tarentum by the poets are particularly revealing: *serm.* 2. 4. 34 'molle Tarentum' (cf. Macr. *sat.* 3. 18. 13), *epist.* 1. 7. 45 'imbelle', Virg. *georg.* 2. 197 'saturi', Juv. 6. 297 'coronatum et petulans madidumque Tarentum', Sidon. *carm.* 5. 430 'uncta'. The area was regarded as a land of wine (19 n.) and honey

(14 n.), of milky water (10 n.) and fertile greenery (*epist.* 1. 16. 11, Tullius, *anth. Lat.* 873a. 5 'vitis oliva seges surgunt tellure feraci'), where the atmosphere was conspicuously leisured and Greek; cf. Theopompus, *FGrH* 115 F 233 λέγουσι δὲ καί τινα τοιοῦτον λόγον οἱ Ταραντῖνοι, τοὺς μὲν ἄλλους ἀνθρώπους διὰ τὸ φιλοπονεῖσθαι καὶ περὶ τὰς ἐργασίας διατρίβειν παρασκευάζεσθαι ζῆν, αὑτοὺς δὲ διὰ τὰς συνουσίας καὶ τὰς ἡδονὰς οὐ μέλλειν ἀλλ' ἤδη βιῶναι, Sen. *dial.* 9. 2. 13, Plut. *Pyrrh.* 13. 4, Wuilleumier, op. cit., pp. 233 ff., Bowersock 80 f. No place could be more suitable for a poet (Gell. 13. 2. 1 says that Pacuvius retired there), or for an Epicurean; cf. Cic. *fam.* 7. 12. 1 (to Trebatius in Gaul) 'indicavit mihi Pansa meus Epicureum te esse factum. o castra praeclara! quid tu fecisses si te Tarentum et non Samarobrivam misissem?'

Horace's mellow and harmonious description of Tarentum seems delightfully adapted to his subject, but it is written within an idealizing literary tradition. The panegyric of real or imaginary places was a long-established theme of poets, later categorized by the rhetoricians (vol. i, p. 92, E. Kienzle, *Der Lobpreis von Städten und Ländern in der älteren griechischen Dichtung*, Diss. Basel, 1936); for praises of Italy cf. Varro, *rust.* 1. 2. 3 ff., Virg. *georg.* 2. 136 ff., Str. 6. 4. 1, Dion. Hal. *ant. Rom.* 1. 36 ff. In accordance with this tradition Horace gives Tarentum a γένος or lineage by mentioning its Spartan oecist; cf. Menander rhet. 3. 353. 4 Sp., Kienzle, op. cit., pp. 65 f. He describes the trees and the produce, the river and the sheep; cf. Menander 3. 387. 11 ff. ἐρεῖς δὲ καὶ περὶ ποταμῶν . . . καὶ πεδίων καὶ σπερμάτων καὶ δένδρων . . . ὅτι τούτων οὐδενός ἐστιν ἐνδεής, F. Wilhelm, *RhM* 77, 1928, 410 f., Kienzle, op. cit., pp. 39 ff., 45 f., 54 ff., 59. He recommends the equable climate, the εὐκρασία τῶν ὡρῶν, a concept going back to the Ionian ethnographers (Hdt. 3. 106. 1) that was applied particularly to the Golden Age (Gatz 229) and to Italy; cf. Str. 6. 4. 1, Dion. Hal. *ant. Rom.* 1. 37. 5 ἀέρα κεκραμένον ταῖς ὥραις συμμέτρως, Menander 348. 1 ff. ('exaggerate spring and minimize winter', cf. 17 n.), 383. 17 f., 387. 10, Kienzle, op. cit., pp. 15 ff., 27 f., 53, Goethe, *Mignon* 3 'Ein sanfter Wind vom blauen Himmel weht' (though his waterfall and dragon are too Romantic for Horace). Structurally, too, the passage conforms to type. The suggestion that Tarentum is only a δεύτερος πλοῦς belongs to a stereotyped pattern (Virg. *georg.* 2. 483 ff. 'sin has ne possim naturae accedere partis / . . . flumina amem silvasque inglorius'); the circuitous approach suggests the priamel of encomia (1. 7. 1 n.), though Tibur is not rejected in a critical spirit. The comparison with other favoured regions is another convention of panegyric (Mart. 12. 63 on Corduba, Menander rhet. 3. 383. 18 f. καὶ συγκρινεῖς τούτων ἕκαστον), and the whimsical personification of products had found recent precedent in the *Georgics*

(see on 15 *decedunt*); but instead of saying that different areas produce different things (*serm.* 2. 4. 31 ff., Virg. *georg.* 2. 109, Plin. *nat.*
9. 169), Horace applies to Tarentum what Varro had said of Italy,
that it produces everything best (*rust.* 1. 2. 6, Prop. 3. 22. 18 'natura
hic posuit quidquid ubique fuit', Dion. Hal. *ant. Rom.* 1. 36. 3).
The anaphora of *ille* (13, 21) is also natural in encomia (cf. 1. 21. 13 n.
for hymns), and relative *ubi* in encomia of places. Finally at 22 *ibi
tu* Horace rounds off his description by coming back to his friend
and himself; for a similar movement cf. Sappho 2. 5 (to Aphrodite)
ἐν δ' ὕδωρ ... 9 ἐν δὲ λείμων ... 13 ἔνθα δὴ σὺ (cited by C. Gallavotti,
Parola del Passato 1, 1946, 120).

    The tone of the last stanza has caused perplexity: why does
Horace end so serene a poem by dwelling on his own funeral? Yet
phrases like 'till the end of my days' are natural enough even when
the writer is thinking of the happiness of life; cf. Pind. *I.* 7. 40 ff.
ὅ τι τερπνὸν ἐφάμερον διώκων / ἕκαλος ἔπειμι γῆρας ἔς τε τὸν μόρσιμον /
αἰῶνα, D. C. Young, *Pindar Isthmian 7, Myth and Exempla*, 1971,
pp. 12 ff., 40 f. 'Till death us do part' is common in declarations of
love and friendship; cf. 3. 9. 24 'tecum vivere amem, tecum obeam
libens', Tib. 1. 1. 60 'te teneam moriens deficiente manu', Ov. *am.*
1. 3. 18 f. 'tecum quos dederint annos mihi fila sororum / vivere con-
tingat teque dolente mori'. With his world-weary pose Horace affects
to believe that his demise is not too far distant, and that the more
energetic Septimius will survive him (cf. 2. 17. 6 n.). But his words
are not morbid or sentimental like those of the elegists, nor yet are
they a straight-faced recommendation to live and die well (thus
Segal, loc. cit.); rather their dry formality keeps up the mock-
dignity that has gone before (22 n., 23 n.). The poem ends as it
began with the theme of friendship (so the neighbouring 2. 7); *vatis*
is a grand word (1. 1. 35 n.), but the intimate *amici* tugs incongruously
in the opposite direction (cf. *epist.* 1. 7. 11 'ad mare descendet vates
tuus'). One is encouraged to believe that the bard is not taking
himself too seriously, and that this supremely attractive poem retains its charm and humour to the last.

Metre: Sapphic.

1. **Gadis**: Cadiz lay at the ends of the earth, and a journey there,
though natural for Hercules, could not be contemplated by an
ordinary man; cf. 2. 2. 10 f. 'remotis Gadibus', Pind. *N.* 4. 69 Γαδείρων
τὸ πρὸς ζόφον οὐ περατόν, 3. 20 ff., *O.* 3. 43 ff. (with Péron 72 ff.),
corp. paroem. gr. 2. 661 τὰ γὰρ Γαδείρων οὐ περατά· ἐπὶ τῶν πορρωτάτω
καὶ ἀδυνάτων (with Leutsch's note), Juv. 10. 1 (with Mayor's note),
Otto, *Nachträge*, p. 167. Cicero uses the name humorously, like Tim-

buctoo, of an incredibly distant foreign town (*dom.* 80). In our passage the implication is mock-heroic.

aditure mecum : for *adire* of dangerous expeditions cf. Caes. *Gall.* 3. 7. 1 'quod eas quoque nationes adire . . . volebat', *Thes.l.L.* 1. 622. 49 ff. For the use of the future participle cf. 2. 3. 4 n. Here the nuance is 'who are ready to go'; a real journey is not being considered.

To declare one's willingness to share arduous journeys was a conventional sign of devotion (1. 22. 5 n.), formalized in the military oath (2. 17. 10 n.). The ends of the earth are often mentioned in such contexts; cf. Prop. 1. 6. 3 f. (the Rhipaean mountains), Ov. *am.* 2. 16. 21 (the Syrtes, as here), Stat. *silv.* 3. 5. 19 ff., 5. 1. 127 ff., Mart. 10. 13 (20). 7 f. (Gaetulia), Claud. 5. 241 (Libya). Elsewhere Horace uses the commonplace seriously (*epod.* 1. 11 ff.), but in our passage he imitates and compresses the deliberately fantastic hyperboles of Catull. 11. 1 ff. (which determined his choice of metre): 'Furi et Aureli, comites Catulli, / sive in extremos penetrabit Indos / litus ut longe resonante Eoa / tunditur unda . . .'.

2. indoctum . . . : the Cantabrians are like animals that have not been broken in (cf. 3. 3. 14 f., Stat. *silv.* 5. 2. 33 f. 'indocilemque fero servire Neroni / Armeniam'); for the application of the image to Spain cf. Flor. *epit.* 2. 17. 8 'impatientes iugi', Justin 44. 5. 8. As the word also means 'uneducated', it balances *barbaras* below. Similarly *nostra* balances *mecum*; though it means *Romana*, it gives a hint of more personal vainglory.

et : for Sapphic lines ending in *et* cf. vol. i, p. xliv. Here the repetition of the phenomenon in successive lines seems to suggest restless scurrying; contrast the placid cola of the second and third stanzas, and the flowing enjambements of the fourth and fifth.

3. barbaras Syrtes : the shoals and sandbanks on the Libyan coast; for their swirling tides cf. 1. 22. 5 n. The adjective refers to the savagery of the natives; cf. *dirae* 53, Lucan 9. 439 ff. 'Nasamon, gens dura . . . qui proxima ponto / nudus rura tenet, quem mundi barbara damnis / Syrtis alit', 10. 477, Pease on Virg. *Aen.* 4. 41, *RE* 16. 1777.

Maura . . . unda : the adjective keeps up the idea of *barbaras* (1. 22. 2 n.), but it seems to suit the Atlantic better than the central Mediterranean (cf. Juv. 10. 148 f. 'Africa Mauro / percussa Oceano'). Perhaps Horace is showing a poet's disregard for geography (cf. 2. 20. 15); he might have included a commonplace incompatible with the Syrtes under the influence of Catull. loc. cit. [1 n.] 'Eoā / tunditur undā' (referring to outer ocean in the other direction). Yet there was an ancient view that floods in the Syrtes were caused by distant surges in the Tyrrhenian and Aegean seas; cf. E. Wistrand, *Eranos* 43, 1945, 35, citing Val. Fl. 4. 711 ff. (as emended by him), Avien. *orb. terr.* 156 ff., Dion. *perieg.* 103 ff. Such theories went back to the researches of Posidonius at Gades; cf. frr. 214–20 Edelstein and Kidd, especially fr. 219. 15 'dicunt enim moveri exteriorem Oceanum ad lunae ambitum, compati vero interius mare', *RE* Supp. 7. 213 ff., M. Laffranque, *Poseidonius d'Apamée,* 1964, pp. 184 ff.

5. **Tibur** : the familiar and refreshing resort is emphatically contrasted with the distant Gades and the hot Syrtes. Horace distinguishes Tibur from his own rustic Sabinum, 15 miles further on (cf. 3. 4. 21 ff.). At some stage he acquired a house at Tibur (1. 7. 13 n.), but there is no evidence for this as early as the time of *Odes* I–III.

Argeo positum colono : after *Tibur* one should think of Tiburnus rather than his brother Catillus (1. 7. 13 n.). He is called Argive as a grandson of Amphiaraus (3. 16. 11 f. 'auguris Argivi', *RE* 1. 1889 f.). Many Italian towns had legendary κτίσεις which had been collected by Cato (Dion. Hal. *ant. Rom.* 1. 11. 1) and most recently by Varro (in the tradition of Alexandrian scholarship); cf. 1. 18. 2, 2. 3. 21 n., 3. 17. 6 ff., *epod.* 1. 29 f., *serm.* 1. 5. 92. The heroic allusion here suits the pretence that going to Tibur is a glorious enterprise.

Argeo makes a reassuring contrast with 3 *barbaras,* and the Greek form (rather than *Argivo*) increases the dignity of the periphrasis; cf. Ov. *am.* 3. 6. 46 'Tiburis Argei', Mart. 4. 57. 3, *ILS* 3098 (from Tibur) 'Iunoni Argeiae C. Blandus procos.'. The dative of agent is also grandiloquent (cf. 11 n.); later parallels with *colono* suggest a prototype in epic (*paneg. in Mess.* 139 'Theraeo tellus obsessa colono', Petron. 5. 10, Claud. 5. 40). *colono* is not just ἄποικος or 'colonizer' but more grandly οἰκιστής or 'founder'; it also gives an impression of settled cultivation to offset the wastes of the first stanza (cf. Segal, loc. cit.) and the military service of line 8. *positum* means 'founded' (Pease on Virg. *Aen.* 4. 212), but also suggests a contrast with *Syrtes* and *aestuat;* Horace craves for stability and *terra firma.*

6. **meae . . . senectae** : the case is dative rather than genitive; the phrase balances 7 *lasso. meae* is emphatic (like 13 *mihi*) ; other people can go where they like. *sedes* suggests a settled abode; Horace will wander no more. For an imitation cf. Mart. 4. 25. 7 'vos eritis nostrae requies portusque senectae'.

7. **sit modus** : 'let there be a limit' (1. 16. 1 n., Plaut. *merc.* 652 'quis modus tibi exsilio tandem eveniet, qui finis fugae?') ; this interpretation is strongly supported by Julius Polyaenus, *anth. P.* 9. 7. 5 f. ἤδη μοι ξενίης εἶναι πέρας, ἐν δέ με πάτρῃ / ζώειν τῶν δολιχῶν παυσάμενον καμάτων, Tac. *ann.* 2. 14. 4 (see note on *maris* below). Many

editors regard *Tibur* as still the subject, and this admittedly gives a more direct antecedent to 9 *unde*, but the alleged parallels refer to a more physical ending: cf. *serm.* 1. 5. 104 'Brundisium longae finis chartaeque viaeque', Avien. *orb. terr.* 100 'hic modus est orbis Gadir locus', *ora* 341 f. 'hic Herculanae stant columnae quas modum / utriusque haberi continentis legimus', *Thes.l.L.* 8. 1261. 72 ff. Peerlkamp proposed *domus*, which is accepted by Heinze; the collocation with *sedes* is attested elsewhere (Catull. 68. 34 f., Ov. *met.* 1. 574), but the tautology does not suit Horace's economical style. *modus* fits the unadventurous mood of the poem, and makes a good contrast with the ends of the earth; *domus* is flat by comparison.

lasso : Horace is boasting in the manner of Odysseus κακὰ πολλὰ πέπονθα / κύμασι καὶ πολέμῳ (Hom. *Od.* 17. 284 f.) ; exertions of campaigning are a commonplace (*serm.* 1. 1. 5, Dover 163 f.). Perhaps he is even imitating some phrase of Alcaeus (A. Platt, *JPh* 21, 1892, 46, L. Alfonsi, *Aegyptus* 24, 1944, 113 ff.) ; cf. 50. 1 τὰς πόλλα παθοίσας κεφάλας, *carm.* 2. 13. 27 f. (referring to Alcaeus) 'dura navis, / dura fugae mala, dura belli'. Yet the heroics are undercut a little by the everyday *lassus*, found only here in the *Odes* (cf. Axelson 29 f., Austin on Virg. *Aen.* 2. 739) ; contrast 2. 7. 18 'fessum'.

maris : corresponds to *unda*, just as *viarum* to *Gadis aditure*, and *militiae* to *Cantabrum* (the order is characteristically varied). For the collocation with *viarum* cf. *epist.* 1. 11. 6 'odio maris atque viarum', Ov. *trist.* 5. 4. 2 'lassaque facta mari lassaque facta via', Tac. *ann.* 2. 14. 4 'si taedio viarum ac maris finem cupiant'. These passages suggest that the genitives should be taken at least partly with *lasso*, which otherwise would be less well integrated in the sentence; for this construction with *fessus* cf. Virg. *Aen.* 1. 178 'rerum', Stat. *Theb.* 3. 395 'bellique viaeque', *Thes.l.L.* 6. 1. 611. 6 ff. But probably the genitives should be understood with *modus* as well ; due measure is needed in sailing the immeasurable sea (1. 28. 1 n.).

viarum : in similar contexts this refers to the long marches of the Roman legionary (K. F. Smith on Tib. 1. 1. 26). Here one should think rather of journeys by the *comes* of Maecenas (cf. *serm.* 1. 5, *epist.* 1. 17. 52 ff.).

8. militiaeque : Horace had fought at Philippi in 42 B.C. at the age of 22 ; if this was his only *militia*, how could he talk of war-weariness some sixteen years later? It seems likely that he joined Maecenas in the campaign against Sex. Pompeius (2. 17. 20 n.). He may also have been present at Actium (Wistrand 289 ff. = *Horace's Ninth Epode*, 1958, R. Hanslik, *Serta Philologica Aenipontana*, 1962, pp. 335 ff.). In the first epode he announces his intention of accompanying Maecenas, and the declaration would be strangely prominent if the

arrangements were cancelled; the emphasis on Liburnian galleys in the first line might even suggest that the poem was written after the battle. Similarly the ninth epode professes to be a running commentary on Actium, which is more natural for an observer on the spot; when Horace says 'when shall I drink at Maecenas's house?', there is some suggestion that he is far from Rome. Finally one may point to *epist.* 1. 20. 23 'me primis urbis belli placuisse domique'; it is hard to believe that *belli* suggests only the tyrannicide Brutus (cf. 2. 7. 1 n.).

9. **Parcae** . . . **iniquae** : here the goddesses of destiny, not of death. For *iniquus* of deities cf. 1. 2. 47 n., 2. 4. 16; here the epithet is not conventional but predicative ('cruelly'). *prohibent* suggests that Horace has not yet settled in Tibur, and may be diverted by malevolent powers in true epic fashion; cf. Hom. *Od.* 1. 75 (Poseidon) πλάζει δ' ἀπὸ πατρίδος αἴης, Virg. *Aen.* 1. 31 (Juno) 'arcebat longe Latio'. There is no thought of ill-health; rather Horace is making a joke about the shortness of the expedition, and contriving a lead-in to the mention of Tarentum.

10. **dulce** : with *ovibus* the word means *gratum* (the jacketed sheep were naturally thirsty), but it has also associations (like γλυκύ) of fresh, 'sweet' water (Austin on Virg. *Aen.* 1. 167). The river and fields make a peaceful contrast with the sea and mountain-dwellers of the first stanza.

pellitis : Horace gives an unheroic picture of the leather-jacketed *Graecum pecus* of Tarentum (Colum. 7. 4. 1). Cf. Varro, *rust.* 2. 2. 18 'ovibus pellitis quae propter lanae bonitatem ut sunt Tarentinae et Atticae pellibus integuntur ne lana inquinetur', 2. 11. 7, Colum. 7. 2. 3, 7. 4. 5 'saepius detegenda et refrigeranda est', Plin. *nat.* 8. 189 'ovium summa genera duo, tectum et colonicum, illud mollius, hoc in pascuo delicatius, quippe non tectum rubis vexatur'. The custom was introduced from Greece; cf. Diog. Laert. 6. 41, Blümner, *Technologie* 1.² 99 f., M. Rostovtzeff, *A Large Estate in Egypt in the Third Century B.C.* (*Wisconsin Studies in Social Science and History* 6), 1922, p. 180, L.–S.–J. s.v. ὑποδίφθερος. For the famous Tarentine wool see further Calp. *ecl.* 2. 69, Petron. 38. 2, Swinburne, op. cit., pp. 48 ff., Wuilleumier, op. cit., pp. 217.

Galaesi flumen : for the genitive ('stream of Galaesus') cf. 3. 13. 1, Virg. *Aen.* 1. 247 'urbem Patavi', H.–Sz. 62 f.; the matter-of-fact apposition ('River Galaesus') seems to have been avoided by the poets (Hall on Claud. *rapt.* 3. 332). The area was a famous beauty-spot near Tarentum; cf. Virg. *georg.* 4. 126 'qua niger umectat flaventia culta Galaesus' (probably the origin of the commonplace, cf. Ludwig, op. cit.), Prop. 2. 34. 67 f. 'tu canis umbrosi subter pineta

Galaesi / Thyrsin et attritis Daphnin harundinibus', Stat. *silv.* 2. 2. 111, Claud. 1. 260, Sidon. *carm.* 24. 59. The stream was particularly connected with the famous Tarentine sheep (Stat. *silv.* 3. 3. 93, Mart. 8. 28. 3 f.). The very name may have suggested fertility and whiteness because of its association with γάλα.

The Galaesus should probably be placed at the east end of the Mare Piccolo, in the neighbourhood either of the Cervaro in the NE (Swinburne, op. cit. 2. 46 ff., cf. his map at 2. 58), or of the Canale d'Ajedda half-way down (T. J. Dunbabin, *CQ* 41, 1947, 93 f.). Polybius puts the stream forty stades from Tarentum (8. 33. 8), and the reading is supported by Livy's *quinque milia* (25. 11. 8); this suits the Canale d'Ajedda as well as making strategic sense (Dunbabin, loc. cit.). The Galaesus is often identified with the Citrezze or Giadrezze, which flows into the north side of the Mare Piccolo about two miles from the city; cf. F. Lenormant, *La Grande-Grèce, paysage et histoire* I, 1881, 19 ff., George Gissing, *By the Ionian Sea*, 1901, ch. 5. There is a church of Sta Maria di Galeso in the neighbourhood, and the railway-station of Taranto Galese; but no medieval evidence is cited for the name, and the location does not suit Polybius. These streams are all small, especially the Citrezze, and not particularly beautiful; deforestation must have changed the landscape of the whole area. See further C. Knapp and others, *Classical Weekly* 20, 1926–7, 91 ff., 121, 136 f., and 21, 1927–8, 190 f.

11. **regnata** : the passive of *regno* and the dative of agent are alike Grecizing and grandiloquent; cf. 3. 29. 27 f. 'regnata Cyro / Bactra', Virg. *Aen.* 3. 14, 6. 793 f., Stat. *Theb.* 1. 334, K.–S. 1. 102. The phrase formally balances line 5; Tarentum has as glorious an origin as Tibur. For the Tarentine monarchy cf. Wuilleumier, op. cit., p. 176.

petam : the word strikes a grandiose note, as if Horace were proposing a heroic enterprise (cf. *epod.* 16. 42). The tense is therefore a resolute future rather than the subjunctive; cf. 2. 17. 10 'ibimus'.

Laconi . . . Phalantho : the leader of the Partheniae who was said to have founded the Spartan colony about 708 B.C.; cf. 3. 5. 56 'Lacedaemonium Tarentum', Wuilleumier, op. cit., pp. 33 ff. It is relevant that φάλανθος meant 'balding', perhaps also 'grey-haired' (F. Bücheler, *RhM* 37, 1882, 229 = *Kl. Schr.* 2. 434); cf. *anecdota Graeca*, ed. Bekker, 1. 171 φάλανθος, ὁ ἀναφαλανθίας, ὁ οὐδέπω μὲν φαλακρός, ὑπὸ δὲ τῆς οὐλότητος τῶν τριχῶν τὸ μέτωπον μεῖζον ἀναφαίνων, 3. 1096 Κερκυραίων . . . φάλανθος φαλακρός, Suidas 4. 694 φάλανθοι φαλακροί· ἄνθος γὰρ ἡ λευκὴ θρίξ, Hesychius φάλανθον· πολιόν . . . οἱ δὲ φαλακρόν (cf. W. Deecke, *RhM* 37, 1882, 374 f. for the Messapian Balakras). One might even see a formal contrast with *pellitis* (*Ph* makes alliteration with *p*, cf. 2. 1. 10 n.). The name adds a touch of

humour after the heroics of *regnata*; the world-weary Horace, with
his grey and receding hair (2. 11. 15 n., *epist*. 1. 7. 25 f. 'reddes . . .
nigros angusta fronte capillos') could go to no better place than
the realm of Phalanthus the Bald. With similar mock-heroics Callimachus called himself Battiades, 'scion of the stutterer' (*ep*. 35. 1).

14. angulus: the word suggests remoteness and inconspicuousness
rather than snugness; cf. *epist*. 1. 14. 23 'angulus iste feret piper et
tus ocius uva', Prop. 4. 9. 65 f. (Hercules speaks) 'angulus hic mundi
nunc me mea fata trahentem / accipit', Hier. *vir. ill*. praef. 'in hoc
terrarum angulo' (Bethlehem), *Thes.l.L*. 2. 57. 60 ff. So in Greek
Marc. Aur. 3. 10 μικρὸν δὲ τὸ τῆς γῆς γωνίδιον ὅπου ζῇ (see Dodds on
Pl. *Gorg*. 485 d 7 for a somewhat different usage).

ridet: the personification is more strongly felt than with *arridere*.
Elsewhere the verb is used of bright weather (Enn. *ann*. 457 f.,
Lucr. 5. 1395), glittering water (Lucr. 1. 8, Catull. 31. 14), the abode
of the gods (Lucr. 3. 22), a house filled with flowers (Catull. 64. 284)
or silver (*carm*. 4. 11. 6); cf. J. Svennung, *Catulls Bildersprache*,
1945, pp. 139 f., and for γελᾶν West on Hes. *th*. 40. For the lengthening
of *-et* before a vowel cf. 2. 13. 16 n.

Hymetto: after the Spartan oecist comes the Athenian mountain
(cf. 2. 18. 3–7); Tarentum combines the best of Greece and Italy. For
the honey of Attica in general and Hymettus in particular cf. *serm*.
2. 2. 15, Erucius, *anth. P*. 7. 36. 4, Theon, *rhet*. 2. 113. 32 f. Sp. (in a discussion of rhetorical σύγκρισις) ἐπειδὴ πέφυκε τὸ κάλλιστον μέλι ἐν
τῇ Ἀττικῇ γίνεσθαι, Otto 169 (with *Nachträge*, pp. 106, 172), Frazer
on Paus. 1. 32. 1, *RE* 9. 138, 15. 1. 367 f. For Tarentine honey cf.
3. 16. 33, 4. 2. 27 'apis Matinae' (cf. 1. 28. 3 n.), Varro ap. Macr. *sat*.
3. 16. 12 'ad victum optima fert ager Campanus frumentum, Falernus
vinum, Casinas oleum, Tusculanus ficum, mel Tarentinus'; Virgil's
'old man of Tarentum' (*georg*. 4. 125 ff.) was a bee-keeper. The
compendious comparison is normal (K.–S. 2. 566 f., H.–Sz. 826); yet
it encourages the fancy that Tarentine honey stands up to a mountain, and that a single olive takes on all Venafrum.

15. decedunt: simple *cedere* is commonly used in such comparisons,
which show a truly Roman class-consciousness; cf. *serm*. 2. 4. 70
'Picenis cedunt pomis Tiburtia', Mart. 7. 28. 3 f., 12. 31. 3, *Thes.l.L*.
3. 729. 69 ff., Curtius 162 ff. *decedere* is livelier as it suggests ὑπεκ-
χωρεῖν, 'to give place'; the personification seems to be suggested by
Virg. *georg*. 2. 97 f. 'firmissima vina / Tmolius adsurgit quibus et rex
ipse Phanaeus' (these marks of deference are combined at Cic.
senec. 63 'salutari appeti decedi assurgi'). There may even be humour
in the idea of unyielding honey. *certat* gives a contrasting note of
aggressiveness, and suggests a *certamen* or ἀγών (cf. Virg. *georg*. 2.

138, Stat. *silv.* 2. 7. 29 'provocas trapetis'); one recalls the contest
between the olive-tree and the bay at Call. fr. 194.

16. **Venafro** : a town in the valley of the Volturno, here balancing the
Greek *Hymetto*. It was particularly famous for its olive-groves (hence
viridi); cf. *serm.* 2. 4. 69, 2. 8. 45, Cato, *agr.* 146. 1, Varro, *rust.* 1. 2. 6
'quod oleum (conferam) Venafro?', Str. 5. 3. 10, Plin. *nat.* 15. 8 'principatum in hoc quoque bono optinuit Italia e toto orbe, maxime agro
Venafrano...', Juv. 5. 86, *RE* 8 A. 670. For Tarentine oil cf. Nissen,
2. 2. 862, Wuilleumier, op. cit., pp. 213 f.; it is still a staple product
of the area. The olive is naturally mentioned in encomia of landscapes; cf. Soph. *O.C.* 694 ff., V. Buchheit, *Der Anspruch des Dichters
in Vergils Georgika*, 1972, pp. 49 f.

17. **ver ubi longum** ... : a paradox, as Mediterranean springs are
short; the point is exaggerated when Virgil gives Italy the attributes
of the Golden Age (*georg.* 2. 149 'hic ver adsiduum'). Mild winters
were a conventional topic in the encomia of places; cf. *epist.* 1. 10. 15
'est ubi plus tepeant hiemes?', Pers. 6. 6 f., Stat. *silv.* 1. 2. 157, Auson.
298. 10 (p. 153 P.), Menander rhet. 3. 348. 5 f. Sp. μᾶλλον γὰρ ἐλάττους
καὶ ἀσθενεστέρας ἐπαινετέον (cf. above, p. 95). As *bruma* is derived
from *brevima* (cf. Varro, *ling.* 6. 8), there seems to be a verbal contrast
with *longum* (so perhaps Lucan 10. 299 on the Nile 'aliena crescere
bruma'). For the climate of Tarentum with its southern exposure
and sheltering hills cf. Sen. *dial.* 9. 2. 13 'hiberna caeli mitioris',
Wuilleumier, op. cit., p. 4.

18. **Iuppiter** : not just an impersonal weather-god (1. 22. 20 n.) but
a benevolent patron (*praebet* means *largitur* and not just *reddit*).
Jupiter had an important place in Tarentine cult, and his bronze
colossus in the agora must have been familiar to every visitor (Str.
6. 3. 1).

    amicus : cf. Stat. *silv.* 2. 2. 4 f. (a clear imitation of our passage)
'qua Bromio dilectus ager, collisque per altos / uritur et prelis non
invidet uva Falernis', 3. 5. 102 'caraque non molli iuga Surrentina
Lyaeo', 4. 8. 8 f., Sil. 12. 526 f. 'Allifanus Iaccho / haud inamatus
ager', Mart. 4. 44. 3 'haec iuga quam Nysae colles plus Bacchus
amavit', 12. 98. 3. *amicus* is supported by a *testimonium* (Serv.
Aen. 3. 553); if right it must mean 'dear to' in the sense of 'under the
protection of' (cf. 1. 26. 1 'Musis amicus' with note ad loc., F. Dirl-
meier, *Philologus* 90, 1935, 68 ff. = *Ausgewählte Schriften*, 1970,
pp. 92 ff.). Aulon need feel no envy as it has friends in high places;
this keeps up the social imagery of *decedunt* and *certat*. Theoretically
one might interpret *amicus* as active in the sense of 'well-disposed
towards' (Colum. 3. 11. 8 'vineis amicus etiam silex'); but this goes

against the imitations cited above, weakens the point of *invidet*, and destroys the parallel between the patronage of Bacchus and of Jupiter.

Heinsius conjectured *amictus* ('vine-clad'); cf. *epist.* 1. 16. 3 'amicta vitibus ulmo', Flor. *epit.* 1. 11. 5 'amicti vitibus montes' (*amici* is a variant), *Thes.l.L.* 1. 1891. 55 ff. (for *vestire* of vegetation cf. Pease on Cic. *nat. deor.* 2. 98, Hosius on Auson. *Mos.* 157). This is open to the same objections as the active sense of *amicus*, and if *Baccho* stands simply for 'the vine' there is a serious anti-climax after the personal *Iuppiter*. A. Y. Campbell proposed *amatus*, a very interesting conjecture; this is closer to the parallels than *amicus*, suits *invidet* equally well (lovers are as jealous as courtiers), and *fertili* ('prolific') perhaps a little better. It also avoids the anticipation of 24 *amici*, though Horace can be surprisingly indifferent to such repetitions (1. 29. 16 n.). But the main difficulty can be explained if we assume that Horace or his imitators gave *amicus* here a slight erotic implication; cf. Prop. 1. 18. 20 'fagus et Arcadio pinus amica deo'.

Aulon : a Greek word for a valley, often used as a place-name; for the Tarentine Aulon cf. Mart. 13. 125. 1 'nobilis et lanis et felix vitibus Aulon'. The name has been thought to lie behind Monte Melone, some ten miles east of the city (cf. *RE* 4 A. 2303); see also H. Swinburne, op. cit. 2. 89 'Horace's Amicus Aulon, which critics have transported to every hill within ten miles of Taranto . . . seems to have been about six miles from the present town to the east, at a part of the coast where a well-watered valley, full of orange and other fruit-trees, is sheltered from every rude blast by an amphitheatre of low eminences, most happily adapted to the growth of the vine'. But this is only a guess.

19. fertili : cf. Prop. 4. 6. 76 'Bacche, soles Phoebo fertilis esse tuo', Ov. *met.* 5. 642 'dea fertilis' (of Ceres), Nicarchus, *anth. P.* 6. 31. 1 εὐκάρπῳ Διονύσῳ. Bentley approved *fertilis* (with Serv. loc. cit.); this led him to suggest *apricus* for *amicus*, but the conjunction of two nominative adjectives is most implausible.

Baccho : Dionysus was the principal god of the region, and the city was famous for its heavy drinking (Wuilleumier, op. cit. pp. 496 ff., 232 f.). For the local wines cf. Plin. *nat.* 14. 69, Athen. 1. 27 c πάντες ἁπαλοί, οὐ πλῆξιν οὐ τόνον ἔχοντες, ἡδεῖς, εὐστόμαχοι. The allusion to the vintage of autumn balances the references to spring.

20. invidet : 'invidet enim tantum qui inferior est' (Porph.). For the personification cf. Val. Fl. 2. 607, Stat. *Theb.* 7. 274 f., *silv.* 1. 2. 150 f., 2. 2. 5.

21. ille . . . **locus** : not Aulon (Orelli) but the *ager Tarentinus* in general; the anaphora (p. 96) binds together the encomium. *mecum* echoes the first line by the principle of ring-composition (vol. i, p. 263); so *amici* below corresponds to the first word, *Septimi*.

beatae . . . **arces** : the acropolis of Tarentum stood on the peninsula (now an island) between the Mare Piccolo and the Mare Grande (Wuilleumier, op. cit., pp. 239 ff., *RE* 4 A. 2304); cf. Virg. *georg.* 4. 125 'sub Oebaliae . . . turribus arcis', Sil. 12. 435. Yet the plural suggests 'towers' in a vaguer and more poetical sense; cf. *epod.* 7. 6 (of Carthage), Lucan 3. 340, Pease on Virg. *Aen.* 4. 234. Horace also suggests a refuge (cf. *arceo*) from the cares and follies of the world; cf. *serm.* 2. 6. 16 ff. 'ergo ubi me in montes et in arcem ex urbe removi / . . . nec mala me ambitio perdit', Empedocles 4. 8 σοφίης ἐπ' ἄκροισι θοάζειν, Ar. *nub.* 1024 καλλίπυργον σοφίαν, Lucr. 2. 8 'edita doctrina sapientum templa serena', *ciris* 14, Sen. *epist.* 82. 5, Stat. *silv.* 2. 2. 131 f. 'tu celsa mentis ab arce / despicis errantis', Claud. 17. 6, Aug. *beat. vit.* 2. 10 'arcem philosophiae', Boeth. *cons. phil.* 1. 3. 44 ff. 'nostra quidem dux copias suas in arcem contrahit', A. Alfonsi, *RSF* 4, 1949, 207 ff. (however, at Cic. *Hortens.* fr. 115 Grilli, which he also quotes, the correct reading is *artibus*). This interpretation is supported by *beatae*, which would otherwise be too spiritual; cf. Virg. *catal.* 5. 8 'nos ad beatos vela mittimus portus'. ·

22. postulant : a humorously imperious word for so agreeable an invitation; it is incongruous that the energetic Septimius should be summoned to such a place. The word is correlative with 23 *debita* (Don. Ter. *Andr.* 422 '*postulamus* iure'). This suggests that the following clause likewise is not over-serious.

23. debita . . . **lacrima** : when cremation was complete it was customary to sprinkle the ashes with wine or water (Blümner 501, Onians 277 ff.); cf. Petron. 65. 11 'sed tamen suaviter fuit, etiam si coacti sumus dimidias potiones supra ossucula eius effundere'. Tears were substituted by the poets; cf. Eur. *Or.* 1239 δακρύοις κατασπένδω σε, Theoc. 23. 38 ἐπισπείσας δὲ τὸ δάκρυ, Gow–Page on *HE* 4285, Prop. 2. 1. 77, Bömer on Ov. *fast.* 3. 560, Citroni on Mart. 1. 88. 6. The conjunction of *lacrima favillam* creates a realistic image of water sizzling on ash. Yet the phrase is saved from offensiveness by its formality; *debita* suits funerary contexts, and the poetical singular (cf. δάκρυ) is dry and uneffusive. As an austere and classical poet Horace asks no more than the tribute of a tear.

7. O SAEPE MECVM

[K. Büchner, *Studien zur römischen Literatur* 1, 1964, 51 ff.; E. Burck, *DAU* 1. 2, 1951, 49 ff. (= *Vom Menschenbild in der römischen Literatur*, 1966, pp. 157 ff.); N. E. Collinge, *The Structure of Horace's Odes*, 1961, pp. 128 ff.; Fraenkel 9 ff.; Lessing, *Rettungen des Horaz, Sämmtliche Schriften*, ed. Lachmann, 4, 1854, pp. 29 ff.; K. Meister, *EPMHNEIA, Festschrift Otto Regenbogen*, 1952, pp. 127 ff.; F. Stella Maranca, *Iapigia* 6, 1935, 263 ff.; Th. Zielinski, *Raccolta di scritti in onore di Felice Ramorino*, 1927, pp. 603 ff.]

1–8. *You have been restored unexpectedly to Italy, Pompeius, with whom I shared the perils of civil war and the pleasures of the symposium.* 9–16. *I shared with you the rout at Philippi, when the brave were broken and the aggressive laid low; but while I was snatched away from the battlefield, you were sucked back by the waves of war.* 17–28. *So find rest and forgetfulness under my bay-tree. Renew the pleasures of the symposium; I mean to riot like a Bacchanal at the restoration of my friend.*

The poet is here celebrating the return after many years of an old comrade of the Philippi campaign called Pompeius (5 n.). Horace had joined Brutus in the summer of 44 B.C. at a time when he was studying at Athens (*epist.* 2. 2. 46 'dura sed emovere loco me tempora grato'); Romans of good family studying Greek philosophy in such a city naturally favoured the Republican cause (cf. Plut. *Brut.* 24. 2), but we cannot tell whether Pompeius was one of them. In the following year there was fighting at Dyrrachium, in Thrace, and in Lycia, but our poem's talk of repeated perils is humorously exaggerated (1 n.). The carefree symposia of the second stanza belong to this period rather than to Athens: Asia had much to offer young officers who wished to alleviate the tedium of military service (Cic. *Mur.* 12 'et si habet Asia suspicionem luxuriae quandam, non Asiam numquam vidisse sed in Asia continenter vixisse laudandum est', Sall. *Cat.* 11. 5–6, Liv. 39. 6. 5). In spite of the ironic mask of his middle age, the young Horace had the tact and force to be admitted to Brutus's Asian headquarters (*serm.* 1. 7. 18 f.) and to be promoted *tribunus militum*; it is sometimes suggested that Brutus was in difficulty over appointments, but there must have been plenty of officer-material on the Republican side. But in so aristocratic a milieu some naturally despised the upstart (*serm.* 1. 6. 46 ff.), and one can detect in our poem traces of Horace's resentment (11 f.).

In September 42 Brutus and Cassius recrossed the Hellespont to confront the forces of Antony and Octavian at Philippi, where the via Egnatia passed between the mountains and the sea. Here in October and November two great battles took place that ended with the suicide of the two leaders and the final destruction of the Roman Republic. Horace had no obligation to suffer further for a hopeless cause: he escaped the battlefield, we do not know how (13), and though his property was lost he himself was allowed to return to Rome (*epist.* 2. 2. 49 ff. 'unde simul primum me dimisere Philippi, / decisis humilem pennis inopemque paterni / et laris et fundi . . .'). His friend Pompeius was swept back by the tides of war (15 f.); presumably he joined Murcus and Ahenobarbus, who had won a great victory in the Adriatic, and ultimately Sextus Pompeius (Vell. 2. 72. 4, Dio 47. 49. 4), to whose family he may have owed his very name. After the defeat of Sextus in 36, he may have joined Antony in the East, like others of the defeated party (cf. Syme 232); this date is an inappropriate setting for our poem, which implies that Pompeius has been further afield than the western Mediterranean (4 'Italoque caelo', cf. Syndikus 1. 381 n. 6). Probably he was recalled after Actium, perhaps in the amnesty of 30 (Vell. 2. 86. 2, Dio 53. 16. 1); this seems to be hinted at by Horace's word *oblivioso* (21 n.).

The ode may be compared with other addresses of welcome and speeches on arrival, a traditional category that can be recognized in ancient literature from the time of Homer (Cairns 21); cf. especially Hom. *Od.* 16. 23 ff. (Eumaeus greets Telemachus), Alcaeus 350 ἦλθες ἐκ περάτων γᾶς . . . (welcoming Antimenidas from Eastern wars), Aesch. *Ag.* 503 ff. (the herald arrives in Argos), Catull. 9 (greeting Veranius), 31 (home-coming to Sirmio), Hor. *carm.* 1. 36 (greeting Numida), Ov. *am.* 2. 11. 43 ff., Sen. *Ag.* 392a ff., Stat. *silv.* 3. 2. 127 ff., Mart. 8. 45, 11. 36, Juv. 12. In the third century A.D. Menander rhetor gave an account of the 'epibaterion' (3. 377 ff. Sp.), a term which he used to include the speeches both of the welcomer and the welcomed (cf. Cairns 18 ff.); though he is giving instruction in prose epideixis, particularly in honour of rulers (cf. *carm.* 3. 14, 4. 5), his analytic technique may be extended to the more private sorts of poem (see the valuable list of commonplaces in Cairns 22 ff.). Conventional topics in our ode are the dangers of the past (1 ff., 9 ff., Cairns 22 § 8), the incredulity of the speaker (3 n.), the hint of divine intervention (3 n.), restoration to the Penates (4 n.), the suggestion of distant climes (4 n.), the friend's special relationship with the poet (5 n.), his shared activities (6 n.), his sacrifice *ex voto* (17 n.), his length of absence and weariness (18 n.), the celebratory symposium (21 ff., cf. vol. i, pp. 401 f.). Of course some of these features are almost inevitable in any poem of this kind, but here as always the recurring elements are more stereotyped in ancient than in modern literature.

The ode contains other reminiscences of Greek poetry, though their extent is very problematical. Horace's escape from the battlefield in a mist is Homeric (13 n.), and the fall of his comrades is likewise depicted in epic terms (11 n.). The loss of his shield, as described in the third stanza, is certainly modelled on Archilochus (10 n.), and perhaps also his rescue by Mercury (13 f.); cf. the mutilated account of a battle on the *Monumentum Archilochi* (fr. 51. IV A Diehl = 106 Lasserre = 95 W.):

δ᾽ ἐπὶ στρατηγ[
νῦν ἐεργμένω[
πῆ μ᾽ ἔσωσ᾽ Ἑρμ[ῆς
ἀλκίμω[

The supplement Ἑρμῆς is due to Zielinski, loc. cit.; the M is read without a dot by Hiller von Gaertringen, *IG* xii Suppl., p. 213 (though at *NGG* N.F. 1, 1934, 49 he had read Δ), and it is implicitly endorsed by Lasserre after an independent inspection (cf. his Budé edition, pp. lxxxii f.). It may be significant that the Sapae, who are mentioned in the inscription shortly before the passage quoted, are to be identified with the Saioi, who were fighting Archilochus when he lost his shield; cf. Str. 12. 3. 20, G. M. Kirkwood, *Early Greek Monody*, 1974, pp. 219 f. The inscription continues (96 W.):

ὅτι δὲ Γλαῦκ[ος - - - ἀπῆρεν εἰς Θά]σον μάχῃ κρατησ[άντων - - -] δηλοῖ ὁ ποιητὴ[ς ἐν τούτοις·

Γλαῦκε, τίς σε θεῶν νό]ον
καὶ φρένας τρέψ[ας
γῆς ἐπιμνήσαιο τ[ῆσδε
δει]νὰ τολμήσας με . [
]αν εἷλες αἰχμῆι καὶ [

Here Archilochus is reproaching Glaucus for forgetting his country; perhaps, like Horace, he is drawing a contrast between his own escape and his friend's prolonged absence (Zielinski, op. cit.). In that case Horace's 'o saepe mecum' might be derived from a heroic δεινὰ τολμήσας μεθ᾽ ἡμέων (*suppl.* Friedländer). But even if Horace has imitated Archilochus in some respects, his symposia are likely to owe more to Alcaeus; cf. the notes on 5 *mero fregi*, 21 *oblivioso*, 22 *exple*, 23 *udo . . . apio*, 24 *deproperare*, 28 *dulce . . . furere*. If Alcaeus's welcome to Antimenidas (350) had survived as a whole, some analogies might be apparent.

Horace's poem is a masterpiece of tact. He thanks Octavian obliquely for his friend's restoration (3 n.) without any of the obvious flattery that Cicero had employed in similar circumstances (*Marc.* 4 ff.). He speaks of the disastrous battle with praiseworthy reticence (10 *sensi*), and of his escape by an indirect literary allusion (10 n.); by playing down his own military qualities he consoles Pompeius, who has been on the losing side once again, and at the same time

keeps himself right with the victor (cf. *epist.* 2. 2. 47 f. 'arma /
Caesaris Augusti non responsura lacertis'). He sympathizes good-
humouredly with his friend's war-weariness (18), and invites him to
forget past disasters by renewing past symposia (21 ff.); the conventional celebration is described with warmth as well as liveliness.
Yet in spite of all its charm the poem to some extent offends.
Philippi was the most savage conflict of two violent decades (Dio
47. 39. 1), with 24,000 dead on the first day alone (Plut. *Brut.* 45. 1);
yet Horace treats Brutus, who had raised him up, with disrespectful
irony (2 n.), and his fallen *comites* with Homeric bluntness (12 n.).
He cannot be blamed for abandoning the certainties of his youth,
and no doubt felt that he had made a foolish mistake; but it is disconcerting to find him describing so terrible an experience with discreet jokes and elegant allusions. The whimsicality of his treatment
may be attributed not just to the frivolity that covers hurt but to
political discretion. Yet after all, he could have said nothing.

Metre: Alcaic.

1. o . . . deducte : the interjection is grandiloquent; so also the
vocative participle and the postponement (with hyperbaton) of
Pompei. Cf. 3. 21. 1 ff. 'o nata mecum consule Manlio / . . . pia testa',
epod. 17. 46, *epist.* 1. 1. 1 ff., Catull. 36. 11 'nunc o caeruleo creata
ponto', Arnold, *Scholar Gipsy* 'O born in days when wits were fresh
and clear', G. P. Goold, *HSCPh* 69, 1965, 32. The idiom is probably
sacral in origin; cf. Soph. *OT* 200 ff. ὦ τᾶν πυρφόρων / ἀστραπᾶν
κράτη νέμων / ὦ Ζεῦ πάτερ, Eur. *Cycl.* 353 f., Norden, *Agnostos Theos,*
pp. 166 ff.

mecum : this word also strikes a heroic note and suggests the
shared dangers of the ἑταῖρος or Kamerad; cf. 1. 7. 30 f. 'o fortes
peioraque passi / mecum saepe viri', 2. 6. 1 'Septimi, Gadis aditure
mecum' (see note), possibly Archilochus 96 W. [above, p. 108], Ar.
vesp. 236 f. ἥβης ἐκείνης ἡνίκ᾽ ἐν Βυζαντίῳ ξυνῆμεν / φρουροῦντ᾽ ἐγώ τε
καὶ σύ, Prop. 1. 6. 1, Lucan 1. 299 f., Stat. *silv.* 5. 1. 127, Tennyson,
Ulysses 46 'Souls that have toiled, and wrought, and thought with
me'.

tempus in ultimum : *tempus* refers as often to a dangerous moment
(καιρός), *ultimum* (cf. *extremus,* ἔσχατος) to a supreme crisis (D. W.
Packard, *Concordance to Livy,* 1968, 4. 1237). In our passage, after
saepe, the adjective seems deliberately over-drawn.

2. Bruto militiae duce : the ablative absolute is characteristic of
military narrative (2. 4. 9 n.); by this detached construction Horace
avoids a direct assertion that Brutus was responsible for the repeated

crises. Yet the *figura etymologica* with *deducte* seems to imply reproach; the participle, which need mean no more than a colourless 'brought', now begins to suggest incompetent manœuvres (cf. *bell. Alex.* 7. 1 'ut ad extremum periculi omnes deducti viderentur'). An unsympathetic reader might even be conscious that *brutus* means 'stupid' (for the pun cf. Cic. *Att.* 6. 1. 25, 14. 14. 2, Plut. *Caes.* 61. 5), but here at least any gibe lies under the surface.

3. quis te . . . : the question expresses surprise rather than a desire for knowledge (Serv. *Aen.* 1. 615 'admirantis . . . est, non interrogantis'). Incredulity was conventional in such situations (Hom. *Od.* 16. 23 f. = 17. 41 f., 24. 401, Aesch. *Ag.* 506 f., Catull. 9. 3 'venistine domum ad tuos penates?', 31. 5, Sen. *Ag.* 393a); it is sometimes linked with the theme of supernatural deliverance (Hom. *Od.* 23. 258, 24. 401 θεοὶ δέ σε ἤγαγον αὐτοί). In our poem Horace seems to be thinking of Octavian, who is contrasted with the juxtaposed Brutus; by adopting so enigmatic a formula he performs his *gratiae* unofficiously, and at the same time suggests the superhuman qualities of the merciful ruler (Cic. *Marc.* 8 'simillimum deo iudico').

redonavit : the rare verb suggests gracious concession like *condonare* or sometimes *donare* (Lucan 7. 850); cf. 3. 3. 33 'Marti redonabo', *ILS* 6349 'redonatori viae populi', *hist. Apoll.* 10, Greg. Tur. *Franc.* 6. 8 'quem homo reddere noluit, Dominus suo munere redonabit' (note the difference from the objective *reddere*). *dis patriis* is dative (cf. Tac. *ann.* 14. 12. 3 'sedibus patriis reddidit'); the concession is being made not to a mere human intercessor but to the Penates themselves. This explanation involves a slight zeugma with *caelo*, but if the nouns were ablative the compliment would be less tactful.

Quiritem : balancing *militiae* in sense; for the antithesis cf. 3. 3. 57 'bellicosis . . . Quiritibus' (an oxymoron), Lucan 5. 358, Suet. *Jul.* 70, *hist. Aug.* 18. 52. 3. But the proleptic *Quiritem* says something more official than *civem* (cf. Mommsen, *Staatsrecht* 3, 1887, 5 f.); Pompeius must have suffered a *capitis deminutio* and been restored to full citizen rights (cf. Meister, op. cit., pp. 129 f.). The singular is an archaism (Fest. 254 M. = 304 L. 'Quiris leto datus'), used here as a grandiloquent affectation; cf. Porph. ad loc. 'adtende singulari numero dictum, quod non facile apud veteres invenias' (i.e. in classical authors), anon. *gramm.* 5. 588. 21 f. 'Quirites singularem numerum non habet. quamquam Maecenas dixit Quiritem; sed non recipitur', Neue–Wagener 1. 659.

4. dis patriis : the Penates; cf. *serm.* 2. 5. 4 f. 'patriosque penates / adspicere' (of Ulysses), Plaut. *merc.* 834 'di penates meum parentum', Augustus, *res gest.* app. 2 [θεῶν π]ατρίων ('deum Penatium' in the Latin version), Weinstock 226 n. 1. Such gods are naturally men-

tioned in poems of home-coming; cf. Aesch. *Ag.* 519, 810, Catull. 9. 3
[above, 3 n.], 31. 9 'venimus larem ad nostrum', Sen. *Ag.* 392a,
Juv. 12. 89 f. Here they are the Penates of the commonwealth as
a whole (as *Quiritem* suggests) rather than simply of Pompeius's own
house; cf. Cic. *dom.* 144 (with R. G. Nisbet's note), *ILS* 4616a 'dis
reducibus patriis Suetrius Sabinus leg. Aug. pr. pr. fec.'. See further
RE 18. 4. 2242 f., Wissowa 163, *Thes.l.L.* 5. 1. 908. 38 ff.

Italoque caelo : *caelum* in the sense of 'clime' is particularly used
of changes of scene (*epist.* 1. 11. 27 'caelum non animum mutant
qui trans mare currunt', Sil. 10. 419). Horace implies that Pompeius
has come from far off, presumably the East (above, p. 107); this suits
the conventions of the poem of homecoming (1. 36. 4, Alcaeus 350. 1).
caelo also suggests that Italy is climatically attractive (Varro, *rust.*
1. 2. 4, cf. above, p. 95); in conjunction with *dis* the word has hints
of paradise. There is something a little pointed in applying nationality
to the universal sky (cf. 2. 16. 19 n.); for a similar attitude cf. Rupert
Brooke, *The Soldier*, 'breathing English air', 'blest by suns of home',
'under an English heaven'.

5. Pompei : the reading of cod. R (Vaticanus Reginae 1703), supported by the title in one family of MSS and by Porphyrio on 15
(though not on 1); the bulk of the tradition offers the non-existent
Pompi or the unmetrical *Pompili*. For the diphthong cf. Prisc.
gramm. 2. 304. 25 (comparing *epist.* 1. 7. 91 'Vultei'). Horace's friend
is given the cognomen 'Varus' by ps.-Acro and the title in one family
of manuscripts; he must certainly be distinguished from the prosperous Pompeius Grosphus of 2. 16.

  prime : not 'earliest' but 'dearest' (ps.-Acro 'praecipue, id est
cuius amor ante omnes sit'); cf. Ov. *trist.* 1. 5. 1 'o mihi post nullos
umquam memorande sodales', 4. 5. 1, Mart. 1. 15. 1. Exaggerations
of friendship are a conventional element in the poem of welcome; cf.
Catull. 9. 1 f. 'Verani, omnibus e meis amicis / antistans mihi milibus
trecentis', Cairns 22 § 3. There need be no invidious comparison with
later friends, as the context clearly refers to the drinking-companions
of Horace's *militia*.

6. cum quo . . . : the words echo 1 *mecum*, but Horace's reminiscences now seem to parody the heroic theme (already *sodalium*
implies the symposium rather than the battlefield). *morantem* would
suit a straggling enemy, but here suggests the impatience of the
reveller. *saepe* repeats the grandiloquence of the opening line, but
now the true parallel is Call. *ep.* 2. 2 f. ἐμνήσθην δ' ὁσσάκις ἀμφότεροι /
ἥλιον ἐν λέσχῃ κατεδύσαμεν (for the theme of shared activities in the
address of welcome Cairns cites 1. 36. 7 ff., Ar. *av.* 678 f.; for similar
remarks in the *propempticon* cf. vol. i, p. 43). *fregi* evokes the boastful

soldier with his talk of breakthroughs (cf. 11 'cum fracta virtus'), but here the word is used idiomatically of the working day (see below).

mero fregi : for the verb cf. 1. 1. 20 'partem solido demere de die' (with note ad loc.); the Romans also talked of *intercisi dies, subseciva tempora*, and *diem diffindere* (in the sense of 'to adjourn a case'). Porphyrio suggests that Horace began carousing at midday, but *morantem* implies a later start. It was thought reprehensible to dine and drink during the working day; cf. *serm.* 2. 8. 3, Plaut. *asin.* 825 f., Ter. *ad.* 965 'scortum adducere, adparare de die convivium', Catull. 47. 5 f. 'vos convivia lauta sumptuose / de die facitis' (with Fordyce's note), Cic. *Att.* 9. 1. 3 (with Shackleton Bailey's note). But much might be excused to young officers on active service, and Horace's impatience had lyric precedent (Alcaeus 346. 1 πώνωμεν· τί τὰ λύχν' ὀμμένομεν;).

mero refers to the unmixed wine of a carousal (1. 18. 8 n.). The word is unexpectedly juxtaposed with *fregi*; even though the verb is used metaphorically, a liquid does not seem hard enough to be an appropriate instrument. As he plays the boastful soldier Horace is perhaps parodying the achievement of Hannibal: cf. Juv. 10. 153 'montem rumpit aceto' (with Mayor's note).

7. coronatus . . . : perhaps the garland of the drinker is implicitly contrasted with the decoration of the soldier. *nitentis* refers not just to the sleekness and spruceness of youth but to the hair-oil of the symposium (1. 4. 9 n.).

8. malobathro : an exotic spice, used as an unguent, deodorant, flavouring, medicine, or soporific. The name is derived from the Sanskrit *tamāla pattra*, 'the leaf of the tamala'; the Greeks regarded *ta-* as the neuter plural article, and so produced a singular μαλάβαθρον (E. Schwyzer, *NJA* 49, 1922, 458 ff.). The epithet 'Syrian' might refer to something from farther East (2. 11. 16 n.); yet Pliny mentions a Syrian species of *malobathrum* (*nat.* 12. 129), even though he says that the better sort came from India. See further Schwyzer, loc. cit., *RE* 14. 818 ff., 16. 2. 1709, *Thes.l.L.* 8. 205. 70 ff., J. I. Miller, *The Spice Trade of the Roman Empire*, 1969, pp. 74 ff.

9. Philippos . . . sensi : after the pleasures of the symposium Horace turns to the horrors of the battle, here hinted at with meaningful reticence (cf. 3. 4. 26 'Philippis versa acies retro'). For the abbreviated use of the place-name cf. Tac. *hist.* 3. 49. 1 'post Cremonam', Flor. *epit.* 2. 8. 13, S. Lilliedahl, *Florusstudien*, (*LUA* 24, 1928), pp. 48 ff., H.–Sz. 827. For the sinister sense of *sentire* cf. 3. 27. 22, 4. 4. 25, 4. 6. 3, Prop. 2. 10. 18, Ov. *epist.* 9. 46 with Palmer's note (similarly 1. 15. 27 'nosces').

10. **relicta** : some commentators are puzzled by Horace's candour: to abandon one's shield was a supreme disgrace, and the ῥίψασπις was an object of contempt in Athenian comedy and oratory. See especially Ar. *nub.* 353 with Dover's note, Pl. *leg.* 944 c, Diod. Sic. 15. 87. 6 (on the death of Epaminondas at Mantinea) πρῶτον μὲν γὰρ τὸν ὑπασπιστὴν προσκαλεσάμενος ἐπηρώτησεν εἰ διασέσωκε τὴν ἀσπίδα. τοῦ δὲ φήσαντος καὶ θέντος αὐτὴν πρὸ τῆς ὀράσεως πάλιν ἐπηρώτησε πότεροι νενικήκασιν (so Cic. *fin.* 2. 97), Sext. Emp. *Pyrrh.* 3. 216 ἀλλὰ καὶ ὁ δειλὸς καὶ ὁ ῥίψασπις ἀνὴρ κολάζεται παρὰ πολλοῖς νόμῳ· διὸ καὶ ἡ τὴν ἀσπίδα τῷ παιδὶ ἐπὶ πόλεμον ἐξίοντι διδοῦσα Λάκαινα σὺ ἔφη τέκνον, ἢ ταύταν ἢ ἐπὶ ταύταν (he goes on to criticize Archilochus for the poem cited below). These attitudes are still found in the Roman period: cf. *epist.* 1. 16. 67 'perdidit arma, locum virtutis deseruit', Plaut. *trin.* 1034 'scuta iacere, fugereque hostis', Plb. 6. 37. 11, Cic. *de orat.* 2. 294 'ut non modo non abiecto sed ne reiecto quidem scuto fugere videar', Dion. Hal. *ant. Rom.* 9. 53. 4, Tac. *Germ.* 6. 4 'scutum reliquisse praecipuum flagitium'.

On the other hand several Greek poets mentioned the loss of a shield with self-conscious insouciance. Archilochus claimed to have left his behind when fighting the Thracians: ἀσπίδι μὲν Σαΐων τις ἀγάλλεται, ἢν παρὰ θάμνῳ, / ἔντος ἀμώμητον, κάλλιπον οὐκ ἐθέλων· / αὐτὸς δ' ἐξεσάωσα· τί μοι μέλει ἀσπὶς ἐκείνη; / ἐρρέτω· ἐξαῦτις κτήσομαι οὐ κακίω (5 W.). Alcaeus wrote a poem on the loss of his shield at Sigeum; cf. 428 (a) Ἄλκαος σάος . . . , Hdt. 5. 95. 1 αὐτὸς μὲν φεύγων ἐκφεύγει, τὰ δέ οἱ ὅπλα ἴσχουσι Ἀθηναῖοι, Page, *Sappho and Alcaeus*, p. 153. Finally an obscure fragment of Anacreon seems to have mentioned a similar misadventure: ἀσπίδα ῥίψας ποταμοῦ καλλιρόου παρ' ὄχθας (381 (b) = 85 Gentili).

In view of these passages Horace must be making use of a poetical topic (cf. Lessing, Fraenkel) that may have been fictional even with some of his Greek predecessors. A literary poet fighting near the Thracian coast would have remembered that this was where Archilochus had lost his shield (just as bookish subalterns at Gallipoli knew the Homeric place-names); similarly Cicero at Delos recalls Archilochus's ἄκρα Γυρέων (105. 2 W., Cic. *Att.* 5. 12. 1). Thasos, with its many Archilochean associations, is conspicuous from the ridge between Philippi and the sea (as Mr. E. L. Bowie points out to us), and some of the Republican remnants surrendered there after the battle. Horace's euphemistic *relicta*, though quite natural in itself (Liv. 25. 18. 14 'parma atque equo relicto'), is clearly modelled on Archilochus's κάλλιπον. It may be admitted that Roman officers did on occasion carry shields (A. Ruppersberg, *Philologus* 68, 1909, 523 ff.), and that their loss was possible in any rout. But Horace's literal experiences are quite irrelevant; for the purposes of the poem he is no more autobiographical than in the following stanza, where he claims to have been rescued by Mercury.

non bene : Horace is suggesting the bald understatements of military men; the ablative absolute is another mark of the style (cf. 2). He does not imitate the defiant nonchalance of Archilochus, but on the other hand he is not making a serious admission of dishonour; for his motives cf. above, p. 108.

parmula : a circular round shield, smaller than the *clipeus*, particularly used by cavalry and light-armed troops (D.-S. 1. 2. 1256, RE 18. 4. 1539 ff.). The type was now obsolete (Fest. 238 M. = 274 L. 'quarum usum sustulit C. Marius, datis in vicem earum Bruttianis') ; this fact helps to remove Horace's account from the world of real campaigning. The soldiers' diminutive could be emotionally neutral, but in our passage suits the deprecatory tone ('poor old shield').

11. fracta virtus : cf. Val. Max. 7. 5. 3 'cuius virtutem iniuriae non fregerunt, sed acuerunt', *Thes.l.L.* 6. 1. 1246. 79 ff. There is a paradox in Horace's words : one does not expect *virtus* to break. He is clearly alluding to Brutus's unbending Stoicism; cf. Porph. ad loc. 'quia virtute se Cassius et Brutus praecipue iactabant', Vell. 2. 72. 2, Plut. *Brut.* 46. 3, 50. 5, 52. 5, App. *civ.* 4. 129. 544. One remembers particularly his moment of truth at Philippi when he quoted a tragic poet before committing suicide : ὦ τλῆμον ἀρετή, λόγος ἄρ' ἦσθ', ἐγὼ δέ σε / ὡς ἔργον ἤσκουν· σὺ δ' ἄρ' ἐδούλευες τύχῃ (Dio 47. 49. 2 = *trag. adesp.* 374 N.). But Horace's allusion is not so specific here, though he refers elsewhere to the tragic line (*epist.* 1. 6. 31 'virtutem verba putas', 1. 17. 41).

minaces : Horace seems to be thinking of the aggressiveness of Brutus's army (cf. App. *civ.* 4. 124. 520). The adjective is somewhat uncomplimentary, and makes a contrast with the downfall of the next line (cf. 2. 12. 11 f.). Yet it would be too unfriendly to interpret 'idle boasters'(Hom. *Il.* 7. 96 ὤμοι ἀπειλητῆρες), or to emphasize that these aristocrats were overbearing to their own side.

12. turpe solum : Porphyrio hesitates about the meaning: 'aut cruore foedatum . . . aut nomen est loco adverbii positum' (so ps.-Acro 'aut cruentum aut quo prostrati turpiter precarentur'). In its most literal sense the adjective refers to dirt (Ov. *trist.* 1. 3. 93 f. 'foedatis pulvere turpi / crinibus'); battlefields were dusty places (1. 15. 20 n., 2. 1. 22). But there must also be a suggestion of humiliation: *turpe* sets off *virtus* as *solum* the towering *minaces* (for the use of the adjective for the adverb cf. Prudentius cited below). Bentley regarded *turpe* as an exclamation (cf. Sil. 2. 231 f. 'vel si cunctos metus acer in urbem, / heu deforme! rapit'); but such an artificiality is impossible in a language without punctuation.

tetigere mento : the epic phrase refers to death on the battlefield; the decisive parallels are Sil. 15. 380 'labensque impresso signavit gramina mento' (of the heroic death of Marcellus), Prud. *perist.* 1. 49 'tunc et ense caesa virtus triste percussit solum' (a clear imitation of our passage by a poet steeped in Horace). For similar expressions cf. Hom. *Il.* 2. 418 πρηνέες ἐν κονίῃσιν ὀδὰξ λαζοίατο γαῖαν, *Od.* 22. 94 χθόνα δ' ἤλασε παντὶ μετώπῳ, Eur. *Phoen.* 1423, Virg. *Aen.* 10. 349 'fronte ferit terram', 10. 489 'terram . . . petit ore cruento', 11. 418 'ore momordit', Sen. *Oed.* 480 'ore deiecto petiere terram', *Herc. f.* 895 f. 'adverso Lycus / terram cecidit ore', Sil. 5. 526 f.

Many commentators (including ps.-Acro, Heinze, Syndikus) understand Horace to refer to prostration before the conqueror; cf. Curt. 8. 5. 22 'unum ex iis mento contingentem humum per ludibrium coepit hortari ut vehementius id quateret ad terram', Mart. 10. 72. 5 ff., Plut. *Aem. Paul.* 26. 9, Amm. 18. 8. 5, L. R. Taylor, *Divinity of the Roman Emperor*, 1931, pp. 256 ff. and *JHS* 47, 1927, 53 ff. Such Eastern humiliations were inappropriate for Roman gentlemen, but it might be argued that Horace is describing the attitude of a suppliant either metaphorically or with rhetorical exaggeration; cf. Caes. *civ.* 3. 98. 2 (after Pharsalus) 'passisque palmis proiecti ad terram flentes ab eo salutem petiverunt'. Yet *solum tetigere* (like *fracta virtus*) naturally describes the battle rather than the ensuing capitulation; the next stanza draws a contrast between the death in action of the Republican leaders and the escape of Horace and Pompeius. A forthright reference to 'biting the dust' suits the Homeric tone of the passage (cf. the rescue in the next stanza).

mento : cf. Sil. loc. cit.; that passage suggests that there is nothing ridiculous in *mento* here. Aristocratic officers naturally hold their chins up, particularly when they are described as *minaces* (the words seem to be etymologically connected).

13. Mercurius : 'iucunde autem a Mercurio se sublatum de illa caede dicit significans clam et quasi furto quodam se inde fugisse' (Porphyrio). Horace is imitating the epic scenes where a hero is whisked away from the battlefield by a god; cf. Hom. *Il.* 3. 380 f., 5. 344 f., 11. 751 f., 20. 321 ff., 443 f. τὸν δ' ἐξήρπαξεν Ἀπόλλων, / ῥεῖα μάλ' ὥς τε θεός, ἐκάλυψε δ' ἄρ' ἠέρι πολλῇ (cf. Lucil. 231, Hor. *serm.* 1. 9. 78), 'Phalaris' to Stesichorus, *epist.* 92, p. 435 Hercher καὶ οὐκ ἂν ἐκφύγοις ὅλως τὰς ἐμὰς χεῖρας, οὐδ' ἂν εἰ θεῶν σέ τις καθ' ὑμᾶς τοὺς ποιητὰς ἀιστώσειεν, Liv. 4. 28. 4 'an deum aliquem protecturum vos rapturumque hinc putatis?', Val. Fl. 6. 745 ff., Sil. 9. 484 f., *Il. lat.* 308 f., 464 f.

Mercury makes no such dramatic rescues in the epic poets, but for an apparent imitation of Archilochus cf. above, p. 108. As διάκτορος he was naturally good at escorting people unobserved (1. 10. 16 *fefellit* with note ad loc.), and must have been traditionally associated with escapes from danger; cf. Alciphron 3. 36. 4 ἐγὼ δὲ, ᾗ ποδῶν εἶχον ᾠχόμην, καὶ σῴζομαι οὐχ ὑπὸ τοῦ τῆς Ἀτλαντίδος Μαίας παιδὸς ψυχαγωγηθείς. He was also an unpretentious god of poetry, and Horace may even have regarded him in some sense as his special protector (2. 17. 29 n., vol. i, pp. 127 f.).

celer : Horace emphazises once more the speed of his flight (9 'celerem fugam'), but here the conventional epithet gives an impression of detachment. For parallels cf. Hes. *op.* 85, *h. Dem.* 407, Eur. *Hel.* 243 ὠκύπουν (in a context where Hermes snatches up Helen), Alexander Aetolus 3. 11 Powell, Carter 68 f., Bömer on Ov. *met.* 2. 838.

14. denso . . . aere : for such disguises cf. Bömer on Ov. *met.* 2. 790. Here *aere* means 'mist' in the Homeric sense of ἀήρ (*Il.* 3. 381, 20. 444, 21. 597); cf. Virg. *Aen.* 1. 411, Val. Fl. 5. 400. But as the word normally means 'air', it is also in formal tension with 12 *solum* and 16 *unda*.

paventem : Horace lays no claim to the *virtus* of the leadership; again the disparaging word is designed to console Pompeius, who (it is hinted) showed greater resolution. But Horace's fright should not be taken too seriously, as it is caused by the aerial journey rather than the battle; cf. 4. 4. 8 f. (of an eaglet) 'insolitos docuere nisus / venti paventem'.

sustulit : 'lifted up' and not simply 'removed' (in spite of *per hostis*); cf. Hom. *Il.* 20. 325 Αἰνείαν δ' ἔσσευεν ἀπὸ χθονὸς ὑψόσ' ἀείρας, Virg. *Aen.* 10. 664, Val. Fl. 6. 747 f., Sil. 9. 485 'sublatum', 1. 2. 48 n.

15. resorbens : for the verb cf. Lucr. 6. 695 'aestumque resorbet', Virg. *Aen.* 11. 627, Tac. *Agr.* 10. 6, Plin. *epist.* 60. 20. 9. The prefix is contrasted with that of *sustulit* and there is onomatopoeia after *rursus*. For the metaphor cf. 1. 14. 2, Eur. *Heracleidae* 427 ff. ὦ τέκν', ἔοιγμεν ναυτίλοισιν οἵτινες / χειμῶνος ἐκφυγόντες ἄγριον μένος / ἐς χεῖρα γῇ συνῆψαν, εἶτα χερσόθεν / πνοαῖσιν ἠλάθησαν ἐς πόντον πάλιν.

16. unda : cf. *epist.* 2. 2. 47 'civilisque rudem belli tulit aestus in arma' (of Horace joining Brutus). Here as there the water is metaphorical (as is shown by *rursus*); yet the image would have an extra dimension if Horace's friend took part in the naval campaign of Sextus Pompeius. For the wave of war cf. Tyrtaeus 12. 22 W., Aesch. *sept.* 64 with Tucker's note, Soph. *Ant.* 670, Lucr. 5. 1435 'belli . . . aestus', *Thes.l.L.* 6. 1. 947. 54 ff., Péron 259 ff.

fretis tulit aestuosis : 'swept along seething straits' (ablative). A *fretum* is a narrow channel that naturally *fervet* (Varro, *ling.* 7. 22);

it helps Horace's purpose that *aestus* can be used of human emotions while *fretum* suits metaphorical *angustiae*.

tulit corresponds to *sustulit* as *in bellum* to *per hostis* and *fretis aestuosis* to *denso aere*; the resemblance between the two verbs is not accidental, but emphasizes that both Horace and Pompeius were carried by forces beyond their control (cf. Cic. *de orat.* 3. 145, *Brut.* 282, Liv. 4. 33. 11, 21. 49. 2 'tres in fretum avertit aestus', Quint. *inst.* 6. 2. 6 'aestu fertur'). Some obtain a contrast by regarding *rursus . . . tulit* as the equivalent of *rettulit*; but *rursus* must be taken with *resorbens* (both halves of the stanza break neatly into two cola).

17. ergo : after two groups of two stanzas to set out the antecedent circumstances, Horace now draws the necessary consequences in a crowning group of three stanzas (for the pattern 2+2+3 cf. for example 2. 3). *ergo* points the sequence of thought with an explicitness unusual in the *Odes*; it marks the change from the past to the present, from description to exhortation, from δέσις to λύσις. A similar form of construction is often found in epigrams; note in particular Catullus's use of *quare* (1. 8, 12. 10, 39. 9, 44. 16, 69. 9, 114. 5).

obligatam : cf. Cic. *leg.* 2. 41 'sponsio qua obligamur deo'; the enallage for *obligatus* is characteristic of high poetry. *redde*, the *vox propria*, is pointedly juxtaposed.

Iovi : offerings *ex voto* are naturally mentioned in the poem of home-coming (1. 36. 1 ff., Cairns 22), and Jupiter *conservator* (σωτήρ) or *redux* is an obvious recipient; cf. Ov. *epist.* 13. 50, Juv. 12. 5 f. 'quatit hostia funem / Tarpeio servata Iovi', 12. 89, *ILS* 2219 'pro salute et reditu d. n. imp. Caesaris ... Domitius Bassus ... templum Iovis reducis ... exornavit'. It has been suggested that Horace here (as at 3 *quis*) is hinting at Octavian (cf. Wilkinson 33 f.); but in such situations sacrifices to the celestial Jupiter are stereotyped, and the sacral word *dapem* (particularly grandiose in the singular) seems to confirm that *Iovi* is used in its normal sense (cf. Cato, *agr.* 132. 2 'Iuppiter dapalis, macte istace dape pollucenda esto', *RE* 10. 1132).

18. longaque fessum militia : the poem of home-coming naturally refers to weariness and the length of absence; cf. Aesch. *Ag.* 504 f., Catull. 31. 8 f. 'peregrino / labore fessi', Sen. *Ag.* 393a. In the previous ode Horace describes himself as *lassus* after military service (2. 6. 7 n.), but here he characteristically applies to Pompeius the grander *fessus*.

latus depone : for similar phrases cf. Lucr. 1. 258, Bömer on Ov. *met.* 2. 865. The verb suggests the unloading of burdens (cf. Catullus's home-coming poem, 31. 8 'cum mens onus reponit'), perhaps even the laying down of arms (Cic. *Phil.* 5. 3 'arma deponat', *Thes.l.L.* 5. 1. 576. 50 ff.).

19. sub lauru mea : *mea* is given emphasis by the unusual rhythm (see next note), and balances *tibi* below; as in old days 'you and I' is once more appropriate. Horace seems also to be drawing a contrast with 18 *militia*; in spite of his misadventures he has achieved a *laurus* of his own (F. Bücheler *RhM* 37, 1882, 229 = *Kl. Schr.* 2. 435). The bay was normally associated with the *triumphator*, but was claimed by Horace for the poet (3. 30. 15 f., 4. 2. 9, cf. Kambylis 175 f., Suerbaum 310 f.). Horace uses the fourth declension for the bay-tree, the second for the garland (3. 4. 19, 3. 30. 16), but the grammarians authorize no general conclusions (Serv. *ecl.* 2. 54, Neue–Wagener 1. 761 ff.).

Horace is giving a symposium in honour of Pompeius's return; for such entertainments in life and literature cf. vol. i, pp. 401 f., Cairns 23. The setting seems to be the garden of a town-house; this is also suggested by the modest singular *lauru*. As the bay-tree is symbolic, one need not ask whether Horace's house is likely to have boasted such an amenity; for the lack of realism in descriptions of symposia cf. vol. i, p. 116 (on 1. 9) and p. 244 (on 1. 20). Some set the scene at the Sabinum, but that was too remote to occur to an ancient reader.

nec : the only place where Horace ends an Alcaic enneasyllable with a monosyllabic word. The slumping of the rhythm seems to hint at weariness, and need not be the mark of a particularly early date.

20. parce cadis tibi destinatis : the verb is entirely appropriate in the context (cf. 3. 28. 7), but might have a special point when addressed to a soldier ('give no quarter to your fated victims'). Horace tactfully pretends that the wine has been ear-marked for Pompeius; cf. vol. i, p. 244 (on 1. 20), 3. 29. 4 'pressa tuis balanus capillis', Hom. *Od.* 2. 350 ff. (Eurycleia kept choice wine in the hope of Odysseus's return). *destino* is a word of fastening (Caes. *Gall.* 3. 14. 6, *Thes.l.L.* 5. 1. 755. 51 ff., Onians 333); so there may be a correspondence with *obligatam* (Onians 439) at the beginning of the stanza.

21. oblivioso ... Massico : the second stanza of the final section echoes the second stanza of the first: Horace revives the delights of his youthful symposia, wine, garlands, and perfume (cf. 2. 11. 14 ff.). But now the wine is of reassuring Italian vintage (cf. 1. 37. 5); in the East the *malobathrum* was worthier of an adjective. For *oblivioso* cf. 1. 18. 4 n., Alcaeus 346. 3 οἶνον ... λαθικάδεον, Pl. *leg.* 666 b δυσθυμίας λήθη; here the word suits a demobilized soldier, particularly in a

time of amnesty (cf. Cic. *Phil.* 1. 1 'Graecum etiam verbum usurpavi
... atque omnem memoriam discordiarum oblivione sempiterna
delendam censui'). For the transferred epithet Shorey compares
Shakespeare's 'drowsy syrup', Milton's 'oblivious pool', Tennyson's
'forgetful shore'.

levia : *leve* applied to metal-ware properly means 'without chasing
or relief'; cf. Juv. 14. 62 'hic leve argentum, vasa aspera tergeat alter',
Non. 244 M. = 366 L., F. Drexel, *MDAI(R)* 36/7, 1921/2, pp. 43 ff.
(a similar use of λεῖος), *Thes.l.L.* 2. 809. 10 ff. (*asper*), *RE* 6 A. 1750 ff.,
Mayor on Juv. 1. 76. Embossed silver was naturally more luxurious
(Cic. *Verr.* 4. 52); Horace might therefore in part be disclaiming
ostentation (cf. the simple wreaths below). But in the present context *leve* suggests in particular the sheen of burnished metal; cf.
1. 2. 38 'galeaeque leves', Virg. *Aen.* 5. 558, 7. 626, perhaps 5. 91.
Descriptions of symposia sometimes refer to the preparation of the
silver in honour of the occasion; cf. 4. 11. 6, *epist.* 1. 5. 7 'iamdudum
splendet focus et tibi munda supellex', 1. 5. 23 f., Plaut. *Pseud.* 162.
More indirectly the idea of smoothness suits the mood of the stanza
with its bland wine and soothing oil, while the alliteration of *oblivioso* and *levia* may suggest to some readers the plash of liquids (cf.
2. 3. 18).

22. ciboria : the first syllable is short in Nicander (cited below), and
in the absence of other evidence should be regarded as short here (cf.
vol. i, p. xl). The *ciborium* is properly the cup-shaped seed-box of
the *colocasium* or 'Egyptian bean' (in reality a gigantic water-lily
ten feet high, 'Nelumpium speciosum'); for this plant cf. Theophr.
hist. plant. 4. 8. 7 f., Nicander, *georg.* fr. 81. 1 ff. (with Gow's note),
Virg. *ecl.* 4. 20, W. T. Thiselton-Dyer, *JPh* 34, 1918, 299 ff., *RE* 13.
1518 ff. *ciboria* were used for drinking from, and the name was also
applied to man-made cups of the same tapering shape; cf. Porph.
ad loc., Str. 17. 1. 15, Athen. 11. 477 e, *Thes.l.L.* 3. 1038. 39 ff., D.–S.
1. 2. 1171, W. Hilgers, *Lateinische Gefässnamen*, 1969, p. 146. The word
came to be used in the Christian Church either for a canopy over the
altar or for a chalice-shaped vessel containing the sacramental bread
(no doubt associations with *cibus* played a part).

The *ciborium* cup, like the *colocasium* plant, was particularly
associated with Egypt; cf. Athen. loc. cit., Hesych. 2. 475 Αἰγύπτιον
ὄνομα ἐπὶ ποτηρίου. Bücheler used this fact to argue that Pompeius
served with Antony in Egypt (*RhM* 37, 1882, 229 = *Kl. Schr.* 2. 435),
a conclusion plausible enough on other grounds (above, p. 107); but
the allusion here seems tactless, and Horace has no reason to possess
specifically Egyptian ware. No doubt the use of the artificial *ciborium*
was diffused over the Greek East; the foreign vessel is a souvenir

of the shared symposia of the past, and here pointedly contrasted with the juxtaposed *Massico*.

exple : 'fill full' (Alcaeus 346. 5 πλήαις κὰκ κεφάλας). The word is contrasted with *funde* (Alcaeus 50. 1 χέε μοι μύρον, 362. 3 f., Pl. *resp.* 398 a); the idea of abundance is conveyed in the first case by *ex-*, in the second by *capacibus*. With *ciboria* and *de conchis* the two verbs form a chiasmus.

23. conchis : shell-shaped vessels, here in the form of a Triton's horn (Bühler on Moschus, *Europa* 124), as *funde* suggests; elsewhere the word is used of flat basins (like scallops). For 'shells' of unguents cf. Mart. 3. 82. 27, Juv. 6. 303 f. 'cum perfusa mero spumant unguenta Falerno, / cum bibitur concha' (unexpected behaviour). There might be a contrast with the smooth *ciboria* above; real shells were rough (Virg. *georg.* 2. 348 'squalentis . . . conchas') and metal *conchae* could have artificial fluting (Sidon. *epist.* 4. 8. 4 'cavatur striaturis' of a basin). For shell-shaped vessels of various sorts cf. *serm.* 1. 3. 14 'concha salis' (there a real shell), D.–S. 1. 2. 1431, *Thes.l.L.* 4. 28. 48 ff., Headlam on Herodas 1. 79, Hilgers, op. cit. [22 n.], pp. 50, 151 ff.

quis : 'quis interrogative, sed cum quodam hortamento dicitur' (Porph.); cf. 2. 11. 18 n.

udo . . . apio : for celery garlands cf. 1. 36. 16 n.; add ps.-Acro on 4. 11. 3 'Alcaeus frequenter se dicit apio coronari' (436). Porphyrio comments 'udo autem apio pro viridi, vel quod in aqua nascatur'; for the latter cf. Hom. *Il.* 2. 776, Theoc. 13. 40 ff., Nicander, *ther.* 597, Virg. *georg.* 4. 121 (hence the various rivers called Selinus). In our passage the adjective suggests the moist coolness of the garland (ps.-Acro 'corona enim apii ebrietatem dicitur prohibere', cf. Athen. 15. 675 d); it continues the theme of refreshing liquids.

24. deproperare : for this rare old word cf. Plaut. *Cas.* 745, *Poen.* 321; for the accusative cf. Sil. 2. 265, *cod. Iust.* 8. 10. 14. 2 (so 3. 24. 62 'properet', *epist.* 1. 2. 61 'festinat', cf. σπεύδειν). The grandiose compound is characteristic of Horace (1. 5. 8 n.), and makes a piquant contrast with the lightness of his theme. The celery is thought of as ready to hand (4. 11. 2 f. 'est in horto, / Phylli, nectendis apium coronis') ; for improvised garlands at a symposium cf. 1. 38. 5, and for other signs of haste 2. 11. 13 ff. The poet's urgency is reflected by the short sentences (cf. 1. 11. 6 ff., 3. 19, Alcaeus 346), the breathless enjambements (cf. 1. 35. 33 ff., 2. 16. 17 ff.), and the repeated questions (cf. 2. 11. 18 ff.).

25. curatve myrto : like celery, myrtle suggests a simple wreath (1. 38. 5 n.); as the plant was dry (Theophr. *caus. plant.* 6. 18. 8) it

makes a contrast with the moist celery above, and as it was associated with Venus (*RE* 16. 1. 1180 f.) it leads naturally to the next
sentence. For the mannered word-order cf. 2. 19. 28 n.; as with *deproperare*, the grand language is interestingly at variance with the
theme (cf. 2. 11. 23 f.).

arbitrum . . . bibendi: cf. Macr. *sat.* 2. 8. 5 'arbitris et magistris
conviviorum'. He was 'appointed by Venus' because the *iactus
Venerius* was the best throw on the dice; cf. 1. 4. 18 n., Plut. *Cat. min.*
6. 1 ἐν δὲ τοῖς δείπνοις ἐκληροῦτο περὶ τῶν μερίδων· εἰ δὲ ἀπολάχοι,
πρῶτον αἴρειν τῶν φίλων κελευόντων, ἔλεγε μὴ καλῶς ἔχειν ἀκούσης τῆς
Ἀφροδίτης.

27. Edonis: a Thracian tribe whose king Lycurgus was driven mad
by Dionysus (cf. Aesch. 'Ηδωνοί, frr. 69 ff. Mette). Their women-folk
are represented as Maenads (Prop. 1. 3. 5, Ov. *met.* 11. 69), so the
name goes well with *bacchabor*; Horace is not simply referring to
the hard drinking of the Thracians (1. 27. 2 n.). There may also be
another allusion to the Philippi area.

recepto: the participle is emphatic, and warmer than 'received';
it suggests that Pompeius has been handed over to his friends'
welcoming arms (cf. 4. 2. 47 f. 'recepto / Caesare felix', Virg. *Aen.*
9. 262).

28. dulce . . . furere: 'aut ebrium esse aut certe saltare' (ps.-
Acro). For the commonplace cf. 3. 19. 18 'insanire iuvat', 4. 12. 28
'dulce est desipere in loco', *epist.* 1. 5. 15 'patiarque vel inconsultus
haberi' (the more restrained expression suits the genre and the
recipient), *Anacreontea* 8. 3 θέλω θέλω μανῆναι, 11. 12, *PMG, carm.
conv.* 902. 2 σύν μοι μαινομένῳ μαίνεο, Menander, fr. 354. 2 καὶ συμ-
μανῆναι δ' ἔνια δεῖ, Callias, fr. 20 Kock, Sen. *dial.* 9. 17. 10 'sive Graeco
poetae credimus, aliquando et insanire iucundum est', R. Renehan,
CR N.S. 13, 1963, 131 f. Seneca's words may refer to Menander (*aliquando* corresponds to ἔνια), or may come from a lost Greek poem
(R. Renehan, *RhM* 112, 1969, 187 f. suggests Alcaeus's welcome to
Antimenidas). There is a paradox in Horace's *dulce* as insanity is
usually distressing; cf. 3. 4. 5 f. 'amabilis insania', *Anacreontea* 51. 14
χαριέντως δὲ μανῆναι.

amico: the word links the last line of the ode with the first;
cf. 'vatis amici' at the end of 2. 6, a poem that shows other resemblances. Pompeius is not now just a *comes* or *sodalis*, but is given the
more serious name of friend.

8. VLLA SI IVRIS

[E. Burck, *Gymnasium* 67, 1960, 170 ff. = *Vom Menschenbild in der römischen Literatur*, 1966, pp. 183 ff.; E. Castorina, *La Poesia d'Orazio*, 1965, pp. 185 ff.; Commager 148 ff.; Pasquali 477 ff.; H. F. Rebert, *CW* 22, 1929, 126 f.]

1–8. *If you had suffered in the slightest from your previous perjuries I should believe you, Barine; but you come out more beautiful than ever.* 9–16. *It is a positive advantage to violate the most extravagant oaths; Venus and her retinue simply laugh.* 17–24. *What is more, young men continue to be enslaved; you bring dread to mothers, fathers, and wives.*

It was an age-old dictum of Greek popular wisdom that lovers' oaths might be broken with impunity. The exemption had been granted by Zeus himself when he lied to Hera about Io: cf. Hes. fr. 124 ἐκ τοῦ δ' ὅρκον ἔθηκεν ἀποίνιμον ἀνθρώποισι / νοσφιδίων ἔργων περὶ Κύπριδος (ἀποίνιμον Schneidewin: ἀμείνονα codd.). The ἀφροδίσιος ὅρκος was a familiar commonplace from the time of Plato; cf. *symp.* 183 b (with Bury's note), *Phileb.* 65 c, Cornutus, *nat. deor.* 24, Aristaenetus 2. 20, *corp. paroem. gr.* 1. 221 ἀφροδίσιος ὅρκος οὐκ ἐμποίνιμος (apparently an iambic trimeter from which γάρ has been omitted). Callimachus applied the aphorism to a concrete situation, which he sketched with characteristic precision and economy (*ep.* 25):

> ὤμοσε Καλλίγνωτος Ἰωνίδι μήποτ' ἐκείνης
> ἕξειν μήτε φίλον κρέσσονα μήτε φίλην.
> ὤμοσεν· ἀλλὰ λέγουσιν ἀληθέα τοὺς ἐν ἔρωτι
> ὅρκους μὴ δύνειν οὔατ' ἐς ἀθανάτων.
> νῦν δ' ὁ μὲν ἀρσενικῷ θέρεται πυρί, τῆς δὲ ταλαίνης
> νύμφης ὡς Μεγαρέων οὐ λόγος οὐδ' ἀριθμός

(for a possible allusion by Horace cf. 22 n.). Often the original form of the commonplace is adapted to make the woman the deceiver; cf. Dioscorides, *anth. P.* 5. 52 ὅρκον κοινὸν Ἔρωτ' ἀνεθήκαμεν· ὅρκος ὁ πιστὴν / Ἀρσινόης θέμενος Σωσιπάτρῳ φιλίην. / ἀλλ' ἡ μὲν ψευδής, κενὰ δ' ὅρκια, τῷ δ' ἐφυλάχθη / ἵμερος· ἡ δὲ θεῶν οὐ φανερὴ δύναμις. / θρήνους, ὦ Ὑμέναιε, παρὰ κλήισιν ἀύσαις / Ἀρσινόης, παστῷ μεμψάμενος προδότῃ. For other epigrams on the perjuries of men or girls cf. Asclepiades, *anth. P.* 5. 7, 5. 150, Meleager, ibid. 5. 8, 5. 175, 5. 184.

The stern Roman attitude to breaches of faith was reminiscent of archaic Greece (compare Catull. 30. 11 f. with Archilochus 173 W., Alcaeus 129. 21 ff., Hipponax 115. 15 f. W., Theognis 599 ff.), but their poets continued in the Hellenistic literary tradition. A Plautine *lena* uses a Latin pun to compare lovers' oaths with hotch-potch:

'similest ius iurandum amantum quasi ius confusicium' (*cist.* 472).
Later poets repeat the same cynicism (Tib. 1. 4. 23 f. 'gratia magna
Iovi; vetuit pater ipse valere / iurasset cupide quicquid ineptus
amor', 13 n.); Propertius by contrast heaps up hyperbolic reproaches (1. 15. 33 ff.), sometimes with a characteristic inversion of
the commonplace (2. 16. 47 ff., Cairns 137, M. Hubbard, *Propertius*,
1974, pp. 62 f.). In our poem Horace wittily exaggerates the traditional topic; instead of merely noting that treachery has no consequences, he describes with humorous exaggeration how Barine
thrives on her behaviour. Ovid develops and caps Horace's wit in
am. 3. 3 (cf. especially 13 f. 'perque suos illam nuper iurasse recordor /
perque meos oculos, et doluere mei'); elsewhere he happily recalls the
divine Hesiodic precedent (*ars* 1. 635 f. 'per Styga Iunoni falsum
iurare solebat / Iuppiter; exemplo nunc favet ille suo'). For further
details see Pasquali, loc. cit., Otto 17 f.

Porphyrio comments on the opening line of our poem 'scaenicum
principium. intellegendum enim aliquos sermones praecessisse
quibus Varine haec noctem sui iure iurando interposito repromiserit;
dein postquam fefellerit, tum in haec verba hunc erupisse'. The plot
is skilfully conveyed by a speech that seems part of a larger situation;
for other instances of the same technique cf. 1. 27 (significantly based
on epigram) and the one-sided altercations of elegy (often similarly
based). Yet the poem is not really convincing as an address to somebody who is actually present (the half-admiring reproaches could
serve no imaginable purpose); rather Horace is talking about
Barine at long range in the second person (for this type of dramatic
monologue cf. Quinn 90 ff., who cites 4. 13 as an example). Barine
herself is a literary caricature, at once the romantic mistress of
Roman elegy who swears undying loyalty to an individual and the
popular courtesan of Greek epigram with a swarm of lovers on her
doorstep (19 n.). Horace is mocking the vivid nocturnes of epigram
(9 ff.) and the intensity of love-poetry (Syndikus 1. 390 ff., a discussion which, however, overstates the seriousness of Roman elegy). In
particular his ode is like a skit on the reproaches of his own fifteenth
epode, and concentrates in a single pregnant colon (10 f.) the ex-
pansively described scene of that poem:

> nox erat et caelo fulgebat luna sereno
> inter minora sidera,
> cum tu magnorum numen laesura deorum
> in verba iurabas mea . . .   (1 ff.)

Now he adopts his mature and worldly pose of a man who can no
longer be hurt (cf. 1. 5); like the gods themselves he reacts not with
injured indignation but cynical amusement.

The humorous intention of the ode is shown by the exaggerated vehemence of the expostulations (cf. 2. 13. 1 ff.); the tone is set in the opening line with its happy coinage of *iuris perierati*. Each stanza breaks into three clauses that develop to a climax, and each outdoes its predecessor in extravagance (cf. 7 n., 9 *expedit*, 13 *ridet*, 17 *adde quod*, 21 n.). Each contains a fantastic hyperbole, the non-existent fleck on Barine's finger-nail (3 n.), her oaths by her own head, her mother's ashes, and the whole firmament (5 f., 9 ff.), Cupid's whetting of burning arrows on a bloody grindstone (15 f.), the swarming of the city's youth to the tyrant's maisonette (17 ff.), the dread of possessive mothers, parsimonious fathers, and neglected brides (21 ff.). Plays on words and pointed antitheses occur with a frequency unusual even for Horace: see notes on 5 *obligasti*, 6 *enitescis*, 7 *prodis*, 8 *publica cura*, 9 *expedit*, 10 *fallere*, 11 *signa*, 15 *ardentis* (the more obvious instances go some way towards supporting the others). The poem reaches a crescendo with the last stanza when Barine is hailed in a parodic hymn as a destroyer of marriage (21 n.); the pun on *aura* in the concluding line is worthy of the Ode to Pyrrha (1. 5). Horace has adopted a style and an attitude so effortlessly that it is easy to forget how much he has transmuted his raw materials.

Metre: Sapphic.

1. **ulla**: the adjective (emphasized by its separation from *poena*) suggests that even the slightest penalty would have satified the poet; the argument is hammered home by *umquam, dente, uno, ungui*. These words are conspicuously placed at the beginnings and ends of lines (*ulla* being balanced by *umquam* and *dente* by *ungui*). The short, unperiodic Sapphic stanza lends itself to such pointing, though the hyperbaton between *ulla* and *umquam* also suits spoken expostulations.

iuris tibi perierati: the expression is less general than *periurii* (which might mean 'perjury' rather than 'a perjury'), and also more emphatic (note the *figura etymologica*). It is a sardonic imitation of *ius iurandum*, with a change from the now inappropriate gerundive to the perfect participle; it is not a technicality (ps.-Acro's *ius iuratum* lacks corroboration), but it has a technical air (cf. *res amotae, laesa maiestas*, etc.). The form *perierati* is supported independently in the codex Bernensis of Horace and in good MSS. of Diomedes (*gramm.* 1. 524. 4), who cites the line for another purpose; it should perhaps be preferred as underlining the parody of *ius iurandum* and the oxymoron with *iuris*. For other instances of *perierare* (as opposed to *periurare* and *peierare*) cf. H. Usener, *JKPh* 91, 1865, 226 f. (= *Kl. Schr.* 2. 66 ff.); he points out that the etymology of *peierare* tended to be forgotten, until finally it was connected with *peius*.

tibi should be taken both with *iuris perierati* (to which it is attached by the word-order) and with *nocuisset* (which needs a supplement) ; the change in syntactical category would not have obtruded itself on an ancient. Barine is conspicuous alike for her perjuries and her exemption from punishment.

2. **poena** : an allusion to ἀποίνιμος in Hesiod (as emended) and ἐμποίνιμος in the Greek proverb (above, p. 122).

Barine : a girl from Bari is *Barina* in Latin (cf. *Tarentina*), though the hybrid form *BAPINΩN* is attested on the coinage (Head 45). Therefore *Barine* seems to be used as the name of the girl (cf. *CIL* 6. 32522 b *Barinus*) rather than a description of her origin (1. 27. 10 n.) ; the word would retain its associations with the free-and-easy South, and the Greek termination suits a freedwoman. It might conceivably be relevant that the βαρῖνος was a kind of carp (Arist. *hist. anim.* 538ª15, D'Arcy Thompson, *Fishes*, p. 24) : see perhaps Arist. *hist. anim.* 568ᵇ26 ff. κυπρῖνος δὲ καὶ βάλερος (v.l. βαλῖνος) καὶ οἱ ἄλλοι πάντες ὡς εἰπεῖν ὠθοῦνται μὲν εἰς τὰ βραχέα πρὸς τὸν τόκον, μιᾷ δὲ θηλείᾳ πολλάκις ἀκολουθοῦσιν ἄρρενες καὶ τρισκαίδεκα καὶ τεσσαρεσκαίδεκα.

There is a well-supported variant *Varine*, found also in Porphyrio's text (cf. *CIL* 9. 4739 'Varinus', F. Bücheler, *RhM* 37, 1882, 229 f. = *Kl. Schr.* 2. 435 f.) ; but neither the name nor the hybrid form has any point. One side of the tradition heads the poem *Iullae* (or *Iuliae*) *Barinae* ; but this name seems simply to be derived from the opening word *ulla*.

umquam : the adverb economically insinuates that Barine's perjuries have been numerous.

3. **dente . . . nigro** : 'uglier by a black tooth' (ablative of measure of difference) ; the noun cannot be collective (thus Heinze) as Horace is emphasizing the slightness of the possible blemish (1 n.). For the concern of beautiful girls about such disfigurements cf. Ov. *ars* 3. 279 f. 'si niger aut ingens aut non erit ordine natus / dens tibi, ridendo maxima damna feres'; bad teeth were a literary hall-mark of decayed courtesans (4. 13. 10 f., *epod.* 8. 3, Caecil. *com.* 268, Prop. 4. 5. 68). For the idea that disfigurement might be a punishment for perjury cf. Ov. *am.* 3. 3. 1 ff. 'esse deos i crede : fidem iurata fefellit, / et facies illi quae fuit ante manet . . .' (so of diseases in general Juv. 13. 230 f.).

uno . . . ungui : white specks on the finger-nail were regarded as a consequence of lying; cf. [Alex. Aphr.] *probl.* p. 14 Us. διὰ τί ἐν τοῖς ἐπὶ τῶν ποδῶν ὄνυξι τὰ λευκὰ σημεῖα οὐκ ἐγγίγνεται ὥσπερ ἐπὶ τοῖς τῶν χειρῶν, ἃ καλοῦσιν οἱ μὲν ἐραστὰς οἱ δὲ ψεύδη (cited by H. Usener, *RhM* 24, 1869, 342 = *Kl. Schr.* 2. 230 f.). Usener testifies to the belief in German nurseries, and Dacier comments 'j'ai vû beaucoup de gens qui appelloient vulgairement *mensonges* ces petits marques blanches ou noirs qui paroissent quelquefois sur les ongles'; these marks are still called 'bugie' in Italy. For similar superstitions in ancient and modern times about spots on the tongue or nose cf. Theoc. 9. 30 μηκέτ' ἐπὶ γλώσσας ἄκρας ὀλοφυγγόνα φύσω (Gow cites the scholia and Photius), 12. 23 f. ἐγὼ δέ σε τὸν καλὸν αἰνέων / ψεύδεα ῥινὸς ὕπερθεν ἀραιῆς οὐκ ἀναφύσω, Usener, loc. cit.

In view of this evidence *albo* should be understood from *nigro* above (Usener conjectured *albo* for *uno*, but that is too unsubtle). *uno* should probably be taken only with *ungui*, not ἀπὸ κοινοῦ with *dente*; it seems awkward to combine the ἀπὸ κοινοῦ construction with an implicit antithesis (*uno dente nigro vel uno albo ungui*). Horace is proceeding from a black tooth to an even more trivial blemish, so that *uno* is appropriately attached to the latter; for the unimportance of the finger-nail cf. *epist.* 1. 1. 104, Lucr. 6. 947, Sen. *nat.* 6. 2. 5. Alternatively one could understand *nigro ungui* of a discoloured nail (at Ov. *ars* 3. 276 *scaber unguis* precedes *niger dens* in the list of physical blemishes); but the superstition about white specks was widely diffused (as is shown by the popular names), and as they are harder to explain than black bruises they could be regarded as a punishment for perjury.

4. turpior : the adjective is appropriately juxtaposed not with *dente* (which is qualified by *nigro*) but with *ungui* (where the blemish is not explicitly stated); balance is thus achieved.

5. crederem : understand *tibi nunc iuranti*, not *deos vindices esse periurii* (ps.-Acro's alternative explanation on the lines of Ov. *am.* 3. 3. 1). After the vehement tricolon of the first stanza, the apodosis is stated in a single contemptuous word, which derives emphasis from coming first in the stanza and being followed by a pause.

simul : Barine had a treacherous intention even in the moment of swearing (hence *perfidum*); therefore one would have expected the gods to take immediate revenge.

obligasti . . . votis caput : Barine 'bound her head by vows' (in the sense of *devotionibus*), i.e. she promised it as a forfeit if she was speaking false. For a curse on the eyes in a similar situation cf. Prop. 1. 15. 35 ff.; for *devotio capitis* in general cf. Cic. *dom.* 145, Pease on Virg. *Aen.* 4. 357. For metaphorical *obligare* cf. 2. 7. 17 n., Onians 324 ff. (on δεῖν etc.); in conjunction with *caput* the verb retains a hint of its literal force (cf. Plaut. *Epid.* 369 'ibi leno sceleratum caput suom inprudens adligabit'). *votis* is ablative, not dative (Kiessling); cf. Ulp. *dig.* 50. 12. 2 pr. 'si quis rem aliquam voverit, voto obligatur'.

6. enitescis : the verb has a hint of light as well as beauty (cf. Virg. *Aen.* 4. 150 'tantum egregio decus enitet ore'); Horace is giving new life to the metaphor of *nitor* (1. 19. 5), *nitere* (1. 5. 13), and *nitidus* (in the last two the image is progressively weakened). *enitescere* is intractable in hexameters and elegiacs except for the perfect *enituit* (derived from *enitere*); but vigorous inchoatives of this kind are often found in early and late Latin. In a purely formal sense *enitescis* balances *obligasti*, which literally suggests blindfolding (Sen. *dial.* 5. 11. 4 'obligatis oculis'); the verbs that end lines 5–7 show a progression in their prefixes (*ob-*, *e-*, *pro-*) that makes a contrast with the carefully contrived anticlimax of the previous stanza (*poena, dente, ungui*).

7. pulchrior : the comparative answers to 4 *turpior*, just as *multo* to *uno*. Note the alliteration with *perfidum* above and *publica* below (all first words in the line); the adjectives are thus set off against one another.

    prodis : at first sight the verb seems to mean 'turn out' (*exis*, ἀποβαίνεις); this is suggested by *simul* (which prepares us for a new development), by *enitescis* (the inchoative verb leads to the final upshot), and by the appositional *publica cura*. But *publica* points also to 'sally forth' in a literal sense, of a famous beauty making her promenade; cf. Tib. 1. 9. 70 'Tyrio prodeat apta sinu', Prop. 1. 2. 1 'quid iuvat ornato procedere, vita, capillo?' (with Shackleton Bailey, *Propertiana*, p. 8), 2. 25. 43, Ov. *ars* 3. 131 (with Brandt), Lucian, *dial. mer.* 6. 2 ὁρᾷς οἷα πρόεισι, Apul. *met.* 4. 29. 4 (of Psyche) 'in matutino progressu'. Perhaps both interpretations can be heard simultaneously ('come out'); for similar ambiguity cf. Pers. *prol.* 3 'ut repente sic poeta prodirem' ('emerge').

8. publica cura : *cura* (μέλημα) in a personal sense suggests the language of the love-poets; cf. Virg. *ecl.* 10. 22 'tua cura Lycoris', *Thes.l.L.* 4. 1475. 42 ff. In our passage sentiment is undermined by *publica* (δημοσία) with its hint of promiscuity; cf. Meleager, *anth. P.* 5. 175. 7 ἔρρε, γύναι πάγκοινε, Sen. *epist.* 88. 37 'an Sappho publica fuerit', Juv. 10. 312. *publica cura* is a witty phrase as it belongs to the political world and suggests that Barine causes a national crisis; for another play on the noun's ambiguity cf. 1. 14. 18 n.

9. expedit : the verb marks a contrast with 2 *nocuisset*; such perjuries are positively advantageous. One need not understand *tibi*, though Barine's conduct is obviously still the theme (cf. 13 *hoc*); for the slightly more general formulation cf. Sedley's translation 'Thus Heaven and Earth seem to declare They pardon Falsehood in the Fair'. Kiessling suggested a formal antithesis between *obligasti* ('tied up') and *expedit* ('sets free'); this gives a characteristically Horatian pun, though it is blurred for the modern reader by the previous point at 6 *enitescis*.

matris cineres : for such oaths cf. Prop. 2. 20. 15 ' ossa tibi iuro per matris et ossa parentis', Ov. *epist*. 3. 103, 8. 119, Sen. *contr*. 7 praef. 7 'per patris cineres qui inconditi sunt'; similarly the violation of a parent's ashes was particularly horrible (*ars* 471). A man would have sworn by his father's ashes (Propertius is eccentric to mention both parents); a courtesan naturally concentrates on her mother, who may be the only parent she knows (cf. Lucian's *dial. mer.*).

opertos : for the euphemism cf. Tac. *ann*. 15. 28. 2 'operire reliquias malae pugnae', Auson. 198. 18 'cineres opertos'; so more normally Stat. *Theb*. 5. 329 'cineres iurare sepultos'. The participle cannot imply that the buried dead are ineffective avengers; that would not cohere with the mention of the deathless gods (11 f.), and would anticipate the climax at 13 *ridet hoc* (cf. Pasquali 485). Rather Horace suggests the sinister power of the Di Manes, which might have been expected to deter Barine; admittedly the choice of participle may have been influenced by a desire for epigrammatic point (see below on 10 *fallere* and 11 *signa*).

10. fallere : a common formula in oaths was *si sciens fallo*; here the witnessing gods as well as the injured party are said to be deceived (Liv. 2. 45. 13 'consulem Romanum miles semel in acie fefellit: deos numquam fallet', Virg. *Aen*. 6. 324). The verb literally means 'to escape notice', λανθάνειν, a word that is naturally used in accusations of treachery (Theognis 599, Meleager, *anth. P*. 5. 184. 1 ἔγνων, οὔ μ' ἔλαθες, Strato, ibid. 12. 237. 3). This association gives point to the collocation with *opertos*; it is as if Barine escapes the notice of what is itself hidden.

toto ... cum caelo : a common combination (Bömer on Ov. *met*. 1. 71), but here *toto* is emphasized by the extent of the hyperbaton. The comprehensiveness is derisive ('sky and all'); cf. Catull. 79. 2 'te cum tota gente, Catulle, tua'. In conjunction with *divos* below the noun also suggests 'heaven'.

taciturna : the silence of night is transferred to the stars (Pease on Cic. *nat*. 2. 104, p. 804). In our passage the effect is sinister rather than reassuring (see above on the balancing *opertos*); cf. Lucr. 5. 1190 'noctis signa severa'. *taciturna* is more personal than *tacita* (1. 31. 8 n.), and suggests that the stars are paradoxically silent witnesses (Aesch. *Pers*. 819 ἄφωνα σημανοῦσιν, Eur. *Hipp*. 1076 ἀφώνους μάρτυρας); so Philodemus in a different context calls the lamp τὸν σιγῶντα ... συνίστορα τῶν ἀλαλήτων (*anth. P*. 5. 4. 1).

11. signa : for swearing by the stars cf. Virg. *Aen*. 4. 519 f. with

Pease's note, 9. 429; like the all-seeing sun by day, they make good witnesses in cloudless Mediterranean skies (Prop. 2. 9. 41, Juv. 8. 149 f. 'sed sidera testes / intendunt oculos', Plut. *conv. sap.* 161 f). They provide a serene background to lovers' passions (*epod.* 15. 2, Catull. 7. 7 f.), and receive their confidences and protests (Bion, fr. 11, *frag. Grenfellianum* 11, p. 177 Powell, Meleager, *anth. P.* 5. 191, Marcus Argentarius, ibid. 5. 16). As *signa* suggests conspicuousness there seems to be a contrast with *opertos* above (Heinze).

gelidaque . . . morte carentis: an appropriately grandiloquent equivalent for the *deos immortalis* of oaths, whose deathlessness made them good avengers; for the use of *carens* to represent a privative cf. 1. 28. 1, 1. 31. 20, 3. 24. 17, 3. 26. 10, 3. 27. 39. *morte carentis* balances *cineres opertos* at the beginning of the stanza; *di manes* and *di superi* are naturally combined as θεοὶ ὅρκιοι. Death is conventionally chill (Pease on Virg. *Aen.* 4. 385); the adjective here is mock-solemn and even sinister, like *opertos* and *taciturna* in their different ways.

13. ridet . . . Venus ipsa: Venus is a patroness of lovers and presumably one of the deities invoked (Lygd. 6. 48, Paul. Sil. *anth. P.* 5. 279. 5), yet she shows remarkable insouciance (Ov. *am.* 1. 8. 85 f., 2. 8. 19 f.). For her characteristic smile cf. 1. 2. 33 n., 3. 27. 67; the emphatic opening verb (cf. 5 *crederem*, 9 *expedit*) shows the simplicity and directness of her response. Normally it is Jupiter who is amused; cf. Ov. *ars* 1. 633 'Iuppiter ex alto periuria ridet amantum', Lygd. 6. 49 f., Shakespeare, *Romeo and Juliet* 2. 1. 134 f. 'At lovers' perjuries, They say, Jove laughs'.

inquam: the verb marks both a repetition and a climax (cf. *ipsa*); for a similar movement cf. Cic. *Verr.* 2. 1. 90, *fin.* 2. 69.

14. simplices Nymphae: the guilelessness of the Nymphs is set against the duplicity (1. 6. 7 n.) of Venus δολοπλόκος and Barine herself (for *simplicitas* as a quality cf. O. Hiltbrunner, *Latina Graeca*, 1958, pp. 15 ff.). Yet even they show no reaction but amusement; editors compare Virg. *ecl.* 3. 9 'sed faciles Nymphae risere', but there the adjective seems to mean 'easy-going'. The nymphs are mentioned here as regular members of Venus's retinue (1. 4. 6, 1. 30. 6).

ferus et Cupido: cf. Bion, fr. 9. 1, Meleager, *anth. P.* 5. 177. 1 κηρύσσω τὸν Ἔρωτα τὸν ἄγριον, 5. 178. 6, Bruchmann 111; the Latin epithet is significantly used of Mars (cf. Meleager, *anth. P.* 5. 180. 1 βροτολοιγὸς Ἔρως). Yet even Cupid is moved to laughter; *simplices* and *ferus* suggest in opposite ways that the amusement is out of character.

15. semper: to be taken with *acuens*, not *ardentis*; the adverb is used like αἰέν of a god's standing activity (cf. 1. 32. 10, 1. 35. 17).

After calling attention to the ambiguity Porphyrio comments 'eleganti autem conceptione de amore dicitur et *ardentis sagittas* et *semper acuens* et *cruenta cote*'.

ardentis : love conventionally burns (Pease on Virg. *Aen.* 4. 2), and Cupid's darts are fiery missiles; cf. Moschus 1. 29 τὰ γὰρ πυρὶ πάντα βέβαπται, Meleager, *anth. P.* 5. 180. 1 πυρίπνοα, 12. 48, Oppian, *cyneg.* 2. 422, Musaeus 41 (with Kost), Hier. *epist.* 54. 7 'ardentes diaboli sagittae ieiuniorum et vigiliarum frigore restinguendae sunt'. In Horace's context the adjective also suggests the sparks generated by friction with the whetstone; cf. Tac. *ann.* 15. 54. 1 'asperari saxo et in mucronem ardescere iussit'. The fires of love match the chill of death (at much the same place in the previous stanza); and as *ardentis* can mean 'ardent', it picks up *ferus* at a formal level.

16. cote : for the use of the whetstone by Cupids cf. Philodemus, *anth. P.* 5. 124. 3 ἀλλ' ἤδη θοὰ τόξα νέοι θήγουσιν Ἔρωτες. The scene is illustrated in Correggio's 'Danae'.

cruenta : cf. Aesch. *Eum.* 859 αἱματηρὰς θηγάνας; the phrase goes one better than the αἱματόφυρτα βέλη of epigram (Meleager, *anth. P.* 5. 180. 8). Dacier suggested that the blood is a substitute for the oil or water that were usually used as cooling agents; Mitscherlich comments on such theories 'nollem vero eo progressos esse viros doctos ut quaererent quonam sanguine eos ista perfusa cogitari deberet; e qua nodosa atque anxia quaestione mirum ni Horatius si ei obiecta foret, risu se expediturus fuisset'. Horace might even be playing with a verbal reminiscence of λίθον ὀκριόεντα (the phrase is later used of a pumice-stone by Paul. Sil. *anth. P.* 6. 65. 5), though he is not likely to have seriously confused the adjective with (ὀ)κρυόεντα or to have connected the latter with *cruenta*.

17. adde quod : not only do the gods condone Barine's perjuries but young men learn nothing from them. For *adde quod* cf. *serm.* 1. 2. 83, 2. 7. 78, 2. 7. 111, *epist.* 1. 18. 52, Acc. *trag.* 209; the argumentative transition is unsuited to epic, but is used freely by Lucretius and Ovid (Horace may have remembered Lucr. 4. 1121 f. 'adde quod absumunt viris pereuntque labore, / adde quod alterius sub nutu degitur aetas'). In our passage *adde* seems formally to balance *crescit*.

pubes : ἥβη (1. 25. 17), perhaps here with an idea of military re-cruits. These adolescents are to be Barine's future victims (as is shown by *tibi crescit*); the word cannot therefore be a comprehensive term that includes the *priores* below.

tibi crescit : 'are reared up for you'; for parallels to the phrase cf. Caes. Bass. *gramm.* 6. 256 'tibi nascitur omne pecus, tibi crescit haedus' (the manuscripts have *herba*, but *haedus* is read by Mar.

Victorin. ibid. 125 and Terent. Maur. 1915, ibid. 382), Sen. *Herc. f.*
870 f. 'tibi (morti) crescit omne / et quod occasus videt et quod ortus',
schol. Juv. 9. 133 'multos inberbes habes tibi crescentes' (Housman
plausibly supposed that the scholiast is wrongly paraphrasing a lost
line, but his own supplement is unconvincing). *tibi crescit* may be
a phrase applied to sacrificial victims (in which case it will foreshadow
the ritual pattern of the last stanza); the anaphora of *tibi* in the
line cited by the metricians suits a sacral interpretation. The Latin
victima sometimes suggests future doom rather than present suffering
(2. 3. 24 n.).

18. servitus: abstract for *servi*, like *servitium*. For the slavery of
love cf. 1. 33. 14 n.

†crescit† **nova**: the repetition of *crescit* is more difficult than editors
realize. In the previous line the word meant that each individual adolescent is growing up to be Barine's victim. The second *crescit* (combined with *nova*) implies that a new class of lovers comes into being
to supplement the old (=*succrescit*); cf. ps.-Acro ad loc. 'id est
semper adiunguntur tibi novi', Plin. *epist.* 2. 8. 3 'nam veteribus
negotiis nova accrescunt'. One might try to defend the inelegance of
the repetition by suggesting a flavour of archaic religious *carmina*
(see Fraenkel 443 n. 5 on 4. 5. 17 f. 'tutus bos etenim rura perambu-
lat, / nutrit rura Ceres'); but even in that passage, where the text is
also hard to believe, the meaning of *rura* does not change direction.

Instead of this second *crescit* one looks for a word that makes a
middle term between *tibi crescit* (of the adolescents) and *nec relinquunt* (of the old lovers). Perhaps *haeret* would suit (the spelling
eret might have helped the corruption); the verb could suggest close
embraces (*epod.* 15. 6 'lentis adhaerens bracchiis'), obsessive devotion
(*serm.* 2. 3. 261 f. 'haeret / invisis foribus', Plaut. *Epid.* 191 'nam ego
illum audivi in amorem haerere apud nescioquam fidicinam', Cic.
Cael. 67 'haereant iaceant deserviant'), servile attentiveness (Ov. *am.*
3. 11. 17 'lateri patienter adhaesi'), the catching of a fly in a web or
a fish on a hook. On this assumption three categories are mentioned,
the adolescent *pubes* who are growing up, the new recruits who are
just being enslaved, and the *priores* who cannot get away; this
arrangement suits the general pattern of the poem, where three more
or less balancing clauses are found in every stanza.

In place of *crescit* Lehrs proposed *ut sit* (*quae sit* would have been
better); but a subordinate clause reduces the emphasis and destroys the tricolon. L. Müller proposed *pubes ubi crescit omnis /
servitus crescit nova*; this is open to the same objections, and also
loses the convincingly paralleled *tibi crescit*. A. Y. Campbell proposed
pubes tibi gestit omnis servitus scisci nova; as well as losing *tibi crescit*

and the tricolon, this involves the false assumption that *scisci nova* with the dative can mean *adscisci*. One might try *gestit* in the second clause ('the new slaves are agog with anticipation'); but the verb does not seem to tie up sufficiently with Barine (nothing can be readily understood to correspond with 17 *tibi* or 19 *dominae*).

nec priores : the climax : even those who have been deceived before (7 *iuvenum*) persist in their devotion. One should understand *servi* to balance *servitus nova*. The third colon is bound more directly to the second than the second to the first (cf. 3 *vel*, 11 *que*) ; hence the pattern A, B, *nec* C.

19. impiae... dominae : cf. 1. 33. 14 n., 2. 12. 13 n. Barine is described as *impiae* because she breaks faith with gods and men ; the emphatic adjective reinforces 1 *perierati* and 6 *perfidum*.

tectum... relinquunt : the young men are like real slaves who cannot leave the house without permission. Barine is a *domina* in respect of her admirers, not her property ; so her apartment is called not a *domus* but less emotively a *tectum*. For her swarm of lovers cf. Pl. (?) *anth. P.* 6. 1. 1 f. ἥ ποτ' ἐραστῶν / ἑσμὸν ἐπὶ προθύροις Λαῒς ἔχουσα νέων, Prop. 2. 6. 1 f.

20. saepe minati : the compressed use of the deponent participle (= *quamquam minati sunt*) belongs to mannered poetry. For the spasmodic resolutions of the obsessional lover cf. *epod.* 11. 19 ff., *serm.* 2. 3. 262 ff. 'nec nunc, cum me vocet ultro, / accedam? an potius mediter finire dolores? / exclusit; revocat. redeam? non si obsecret' (echoing Ter. *eun.* 46 ff.), Plaut. *asin.* 156 ff., Tib. 2. 6. 13 f. (with K. F. Smith's note), Pers. 5. 171 ff. (on the lover's loss of *libertas*), Paul. Sil. *anth. P.* 5. 254. 1 ff., 5. 256. 5 f. (the theme obviously comes from New Comedy).

21. te... te... tua : the anaphora of the pronoun suggests the language of a hymn (1. 10. 9 n.), and follows on well from *tibi crescit* above (17 n.). E. Ensor, *Hermathena* 12, 1903, 108 ff., plausibly sees a parody of Catull. 61. 51 ff. (to Hymen) 'te suis tremulus parens / invocat, tibi virgines / zonula soluunt sinus, / te timens cupida novos / captat aure maritus'; Horace keeps the tricolon and the anaphora of his model, and seems to echo the concluding cadence *aure maritus*, but he wittily transfers the anxiety from the young husband to the old fathers and the newly married *virgines*. Barine is an imperious goddess who bestows not joy and family concord (like Hymen), but misery and disunity ; instead of bringing the bridegroom to his bride she lures him off course and delays his return.

suis... iuvencis : their adolescent sons (cf. 2. 5. 6 n.); the expression suggests the protracted solicitude of the mothers and the clumsy precocity of the lads. The emphatic possessive (significantly juxtaposed with *te*) underlines the mothers' possessiveness (for this theme in Anacreon and others cf. vol. i, p. 274); but Pasquali was unrealistic to suppose that the sons were contemplating marriage with Barine (487 f.). Kiessling thought that mothers feared for their daughters, fathers for their sons, and wives for their husbands; but the plight of the brides is not obvious till the next line.

metuunt: the verb suits dread of a deity; cf. 1. 35. 9 ff. (the hymn to Fortune) 'te . . . metuunt tyranni', *Thes.l.L.* 8. 905. 4 ff.

22. senes parci : 'suaviter vero et ex rei natura mater pudori filii, pater senex patrimonio suo timet' (Mitscherlich). The situation was derived from Comedy as well as life; cf. *serm.* 1. 4. 48 ff., Plaut. *merc.* 46 ff., Ter. *heaut.* 99 ff., Lucr. 4. 1129 'et bene parta patrum fiunt anademata mitrae', Prop. 2. 23. 17 f. 'nec poscet garrula quod te / astrictus ploret saepe dedisse pater', *RLAC* 3. 1163, H.-W. Rissom, *Vater- und Sohnmotive in der römischen Komödie*, Diss. Kiel, 1971, pp. 224 ff.

miseraeque nuper virgines nuptae : normally one expects brides to be happy; Horace is perhaps adapting ταλαίνης νύμφης in the Callimachean prototype (also at the end of the poem), though there the situation is different (above, p. 122). *nuper* is bound to *nuptae* by the assonance; the phrase equals the normal *novae nuptae*. *virgines* is seldom used imprecisely, and when it is there is usually a special point. Horace's oxymoron is deliberate (cf. Ov. *epist.* 6. 133 'adultera virgo'): the girls have not been married for long (cf. 3. 11. 35 of Hypermestra), and because of Barine their new status is largely nominal.

23. tua ne retardet . . . : the clause applies only to the last subject; cf. 1. 35. 13 (also a hymn). For the proleptic accusative ('I know thee who thou art') cf. 1. 17. 24 ff., K.-S. 2. 578 ff., H.-Sz. 471 f. Horace avoids too blunt a description of infidelity: *tua aura* implies that Barine's attraction is automatic, *retardet* that it is only temporary (like Calypso's). (*re*)*tardare* is natural of winds (Cic. *Att.* 6. 8. 4).

24. aura : in conjunction with *retardet* one thinks first of a breeze in the sea of love (cf. 1. 5. 16 n., Eur. *IA* 69, *trag. adesp.* 187 N. δισσὰ πνεύματα πνεῖς, "Ερως, A. La Penna, *Maia* 4, 1951, 202 ff.); paradoxically Barine's *aura* attracts men rather than speeding them on their way (cf. Prop. 2. 27. 15 'si modo clamantis revocaverit aura puellae'). The word also has a hint of 'emanation', 'influence', 'aura'; cf. 1. 5. 11 f. 'aurae fallacis' (where there is a play on both senses of the word), Virg. *Aen.* 6. 204 'auri . . . aura refulsit' (Servius

glosses *splendor* and cites our passage), Plin. *nat.* 32. 7 (the electric ray), Claud. *carm. min.* 29. 38 f. (on magnetism) 'ferrumque maritat / aura tenax', Onians 73 f. In particular Horace is conveying a suggestion of smell, not of perfume (ps.-Acro) but of a female animal in heat (as is shown by *iuvencis*); for ancient candour in this matter cf. Virg. *georg.* 3. 250 f. 'nonne vides ut tota tremor pertemptet equorum / corpora, si tantum notas odor attulit auras?', Oppian, *hal.* 4. 113 f. (wrasses in the mating season) οἱ δ' ὑπ' ἔρωτος / αὔρῃ θελγόμενοι φιλοτησίῃ ἀμφαγέρονται, vulg. *Ier.* 1. 2. 24 'onager assuetus in solitudine, in desiderio animae suae attraxit ventum amoris sui', Claud. 10. 289 f. (*epithalamium* for Honorius) 'nobilis haud aliter sonipes quem primus amoris / sollicitavit odor'. It is no argument to say that such an interpretation is incompatible with *retardet*; Horace is using *aura* in several senses simultaneously (Bell 390).

maritos: newly-married men (balancing *nuptae*); the normal Latin for husband is *vir*. The word suits the imagery as it can be used also of animals (1. 17. 7 n., 2. 5. 16).

9. NON SEMPER IMBRES

[W. S. Anderson, *CSCA* 1, 1968, 35 ff.; F. Bücheler, *RhM* 37, 1882, 230 f. = *Kl. Schr.* 2. 436; Esteve-Forriol 32 ff.; P. Murgatroyd, *Mnemosyne* 28, 1975, 69 ff.; Pasquali 257 ff.; Quinn 158 ff.; Williams 671 ff.]

1–8. Bad weather does not last for ever, Valgius, either in Italy or on the Eastern frontier. 9–17. But you pester Mystes with your tears night and morning, though Antilochus and Troilus were not always wept for by their aged parents. 17–24. Cease your laments and let us celebrate together Augustus's victories on the Eastern frontier.

C. Valgius Rufus had been a close friend of Horace's for a good many years. Already in the *Satires* he appears in the inner circle of critics who are distinguished from more remote grandees like Pollio and Messalla (1. 10. 81 ff.):

> Plotius et Varius, Maecenas Vergiliusque,
> Valgius et probet haec Octavius optimus atque
> Fuscus, et haec utinam Viscorum laudet uterque.

He was a man of varied aptitudes who translated the rhetorical handbook of his teacher Apollodorus (Quint. *inst.* 3. 1. 18) and also wrote on grammatical and philological questions (G. Funaioli, *Grammaticae Romanae Fragmenta*, 1907, pp. 482 ff.). The elder Pliny mentions an unfinished monograph on herbal medicine and drily cites its fulsome dedication to Augustus (*nat.* 25. 4 'post eum unus inlustrium temptavit C. Valgius eruditione spectatus imperfecto volumine ad divum Augustum, inchoata etiam praefatione religiosa ut omnibus malis humanis illius potissimum principis semper mederetur maiestas'). Valgius attained a suffect consulship in 12 B.C. (hence Porphyrio's imprecise comment 'Valgium consularem amicum suum solatur') ; its relatively belated date suggests that he was a distinguished member of the cultural establishment rather than a leading man of affairs.

In particular, Valgius was a poet, and here again his versatility was remarkable. The anonymous panegyrist on Messalla thought him capable of political eulogy (179 f. 'est tibi qui possit magnis se accingere rebus / Valgius; aeterno propior non alter Homero') ; though such suggestions were conventional in *recusatio* (1. 6. 1 *Vario* n.), the comparison with Homer would be pointless if he had not sometimes attempted the grander manner. One of the fragments strikes a rustic note (5 Morel 'sed nos ante casam tepidi mulgaria lactis / et sinum bimi cessamus ponere Bacchi?') ; two others seem to come from an elegiac *iter* (3 and 4) ; we have part of an epigram of a satirical cast (1 'situ rugosa, rutunda / margarita') ; Seneca mentions a work on Etna, which may have been a didactic poem (*epist.* 51. 1). It is more significant for our ode that Valgius spoke admiringly of the neoteric Cinna: cf. fr. 2. 1 ff. 'Codrusque ille canit quali tu voce canebas / atque solet numeros dicere, Cinna, tuos, / dulcior ut numquam Pylio profluxerit ore / Nestoris aut docto pectore Demodoci'. In our poem Horace makes it plain that he wrote sentimental elegy (9 'flebilibus modis'), some of it apparently on the dead Mystes (see below). For further details on Valgius see Schanz–Hosius 2. 172 ff., *RE* 8 A. 1. 272 ff., H. Bardon, *La Littérature latine inconnue* 2, 1956, pp. 19 ff., A. Rostagni, *Studi in onore di Luigi Castiglioni* 2. 809 f.

In the first two stanzas Horace declares that the fury of the elements does not last for ever; he is making the common analogy with the vicissitudes of human happiness (1 n.). He cleverly uses a number of words that hint at grief as well as the weather (the more obvious metaphors support the others as at 2. 14. 1 ff.) ; see notes on 1 *imbres, nubibus, hispidos*, 2 *manant*, 3 *vexant, inaequales*, 5 *stat glacies iners*, 7 *laborant*, 8 *viduantur*. Such ambiguities seem to be derived from sympotic poetry; cf. *epod.* 13. 1 'horrida tempestas caelum contraxit' (with its hint of *contrahere frontem*), 5 'obducta solvatur fronte senectus' (a clear reference to clouded skies), 18 'deformis aegrimoniae' (the adjective evokes the bleakness of winter), *carm.* 1. 7. 15 f. 'albus ut obscuro deterget nubila caelo / saepe Notus' (with a suggestion of wiping away tears), Wilkinson 126 ff., G. Nussbaum,

Latomus 24, 1965, 133 ff. So in a more general way the storms outside Alcaeus's symposium are associated with human cares, the
rivulets on Sipylus suggest Niobe's grief, the frost on the doorstep
suits the lover's reception; similarly Orpheus mourns Eurydice in
a cold climate (Virg. *georg.* 4. 517 ff., cf. below, 8 n.). For a modern
elaboration of Horace's symbolism cf. Housman, *A Shropshire Lad*
31. 1 ff.:

> On Wenlock Edge the wood's in trouble;
>   His forest fleece the Wrekin heaves;
> The gale, it plies the saplings double,
>   And thick on Severn snow the leaves . . .
> The gale, it plies the saplings double,
>   It blows so hard, 'twill soon be gone;
> Today the Roman and his trouble
>   Are ashes under Uricon.

In the central section of the poem (9–17) Horace complains that
unlike bad weather Valgius's laments for Mystes are never-ending.
Roman gentlemen of the highest probity showed a humane sorrow
on the deaths of slave-boys (Cic. *Att.* 1. 12. 4, Plin. *epist.* 8. 16. 1 ff.,
8. 19); Statius provides two tasteless specimens of *solacia* for such
occasions (*silv.* 2. 1, 2. 6, cf. vol. i, pp. 280 f.). Sometimes these
lamentations must have passed the boundary between the sentimental and the erotic (see Gell. 19. 12 for the grief of Herodes
Atticus); Valgius's elegies, Horace implies, were of the latter kind,
as was natural in the genre. Mystes is unlikely to have been a real
person, as that would make the ode far too heartless (cf. Quinn
and Anderson, opp. citt.); he was presumably a fiction of Valgius's
own, or even a type-figure ascribed to him by Horace (cf. 1. 33. 2 n.
for the Glycera imputed to Tibullus). Quinn and especially Anderson
argue that Mystes is not dead but has left Valgius for a rival; this
interpretation cannot be finally disproved, but it blunts the wit of
the fourth stanza (cf. 10 *ademptum* n.). It should also be noted that
Horace's lines on Hesperus closely resemble a fragment of Cinna (10
nec tibi n.); as Valgius declared himself an admirer of Cinna (above,
p. 135), his elegies are likely to have been Horace's immediate source
(the emotionalism suits). Cinna seems to have been describing
Zmyrna's myrrh-like tears at the time of her metamorphosis (cf.
Ov. *met.* 10. 500 ff.); if Valgius took over this tragic motif he was
surely talking of death rather than mere desertion (Virgil made a
similar use of Cinna's theme in describing the lament of Orpheus,
cf. 10 n.).

    Horace on the other hand is parodying Valgius's sentimentality;
for his rejection of the conventions of love-elegy cf. vol. i, p. 370,
Quinn 154 ff., B. Otis, *TAPhA* 76, 1945, 177 ff. His ode imitates the

form of a *consolatio* (vol. i, p. 280, Esteve-Forriol, loc. cit.), not the whole of an epicedion in all its rhetorical amplitude (Esteve-Forriol 126 ff.), but the final *suasio* to the bereaved (1. 24. 1 n.); it should be seen as such even by those who think that Mystes is still alive. For comparison with the weather in similar writings cf. ps.-Plut. *cons. Apoll.* 103 b ὥσπερ ... ἐν θαλάττῃ εὐδίαι τε καὶ χειμῶνες, οὕτω καὶ ἐν τῷ βίῳ πολλαὶ καὶ ποικίλαι περιστάσεις; Horace's elaborate imagery is particularly suited to a neoteric who may have found pathetic fallacies congenial. Valgius's continuous lamentation is presented as something contrary to nature (cf. ps.-Plut. ibid. 114 f τὸ γὰρ δὴ ἀτελεύτητον νομίζειν τὸ πένθος ἀνοίας ἐστὶν ἐσχάτης); in particular the verb *urges* (9 n.) suits the idea that the dead do not like excessive grief (Menander rhet. 3. 414. 21 Sp. μέμφεται τοῖς θρηνοῦσι, Esteve-Forriol 150). Then follow the traditional mythological *exempla* (Hom. *Il.* 24. 602 καὶ γάρ τ' ἠΰκομος Νιόβη, Esteve-Forriol 154 ff., Kassel 70 ff.), but a mischievous ambiguity becomes apparent (see notes on 13–16): Antilochus and Troilus were not just brave warriors but καλοὶ παῖδες (just like Mystes), Nestor and Priam were paradigms not just for suffering but for debility (unlike Valgius). Finally at 17 ff. comes the climax of a consolation, the adjuration to weep no more (for similar injunctions cf. 2. 20. 23 n.). In the spirit of the genre Horace suggests alternative occupations (cf. Stat. *silv.* 2. 6. 95 'ubi nota reis facundia raptis?'); he maliciously proposes that Valgius should join him in writing about the settlement of the Eastern frontier.

Eastern geography in fact plays a dominating part in the poem: the first stanza contains *exempla* from Armenia and the Caspian, the last two refer to Augustus's *nova tropaea* from Mount Niphates (19 n., 20 n.), and the humiliations of the Euphrates and the Geloni. The poets had already exaggerated Octavian's military achievement in the settlement of the East in 30 B.C.: cf. *serm.* 2. 5. 62 'iuvenis Parthis horrendus', Virg. *georg.* 1. 509 'hinc movet Euphrates, illinc Germania bellum', 2. 171 f., 4. 560 f. 'Caesar dum magnus ad altum / fulminat Euphraten bello', Syme 300 f. In particular Virgil's two accounts of the triumphs of 29 show a considerable resemblance to our poem:

> addam urbes Asiae domitas pulsumque *Niphaten*
> fidentemque fuga Parthum versisque sagittis
> et duo rapta manu diverso ex hoste *tropaea*.
>
> *(georg.* 3. 30 ff.)
>
> hic Lelegas Carasque sagittiferosque *Gelonos*
> finxerat: *Euphrates* ibat iam mollior undis ...
> indomitique Dahae, et pontem indignatus Araxes.
>
> *(Aen.* 8. 725 ff.)

Horace may have been influenced not only by Virgil but by the actual pageantry of 29, when the rivers and mountains of the East were commemorated in the triumphal procession (20 n., 21 n.).

But though Horace's language is similar to Virgil's, he may have a slightly different historical perspective: in view of the use of the name Augustus (assumed in January 27) it seems awkward to understand the *nova tropaea* as simply those of 29. It may be argued that Valgius had actually embarked on a commemoration of the Eastern settlement, and that in this sense it was still topical; a point in favour of this suggestion is the association of Valgius's name with Armenia (4 f.) at the beginning of the poem (i.e. before any explicit military reference). About 31 B.C., the time of the *Panegyricus in Messallam*, he was being mentioned as a promising writer of political epic (above, p. 135); as he seems to have belonged to Messalla's own circle, he might have been particularly interested in Eastern frontier policy. Yet at a time when political events were moving so rapidly, Valgius's supposed poem seems an insufficient justification for *nova* (particularly as the word is combined with *Augusti*); and one's doubts are increased by the parallel passage at Prop. 2. 10. 13 f. (written about the time of the Arabian expedition in 26 B.C.) 'iam negat Euphrates equitem post terga tueri / Parthorum et Crassos se tenuisse dolet'. Perhaps Horace is conflating the triumph of 29 with the rebellion of Tiridates (2. 2. 17 n.), which may already have begun in 27 B.C.; Augustus characteristically seems to have been behind this indirect aggression (2. 2. 17 n.), and early successes could have been represented as Roman victories. If Horace wrote the ode soon after the beginning of the Parthian rebellion, his words would readily be associated with it; on the other hand if he wrote it after Augustus's Spanish campaign of 26, it might seem tactless to concentrate on the Eastern front.

But whatever the date of the poem, Horace's real concern is not with the Niphates and the Geloni, but with literature and with friendship. He underlines an amusing inconsistency in Valgius's poetic style, teases him for the preciosity of his elegies, and professes an unconvincing enthusiasm for more invigorating themes. He thus pays a compliment to the regime, without committing himself to more extended eulogies and without any loss of intimacy and charm; Valgius was a practised courtier, but here he has been outmanœuvred in the most amiable possible way. With its delicate irony and subtle allusiveness the ode is one of Horace's most harmonious and amusing poems; it marks a high point of Augustan urbanity, and makes us think with affection both of the author and of the recipient.

Metre: Alcaic (the free use of enjambement between stanzas is noteworthy).

1. **non semper** . . . : the vicissitudes of human happiness are often compared with the weather; this may bring the consolation that sunny days are round the corner. Cf. 1. 7. 15 ff., 2. 10. 15 f., Pind. *P.* 5. 10 f. εὐδίαν ὃς (Κάστωρ) μετὰ χειμέριον ὄμβρον τεὰν / καταιθύσσει μάκαιραν ἑστίαν, Eur. *HF* 101 f. κάμνουσι γάρ τοι καὶ βροτῶν αἱ συμφοραί, / καὶ πνεύματ' ἀνέμων οὐκ ἀεὶ ῥώμην ἔχει, fr. 330. 6 f. N. οὕτω δὲ θνητῶν σπέρμα τῶν μὲν εὐτυχεῖ / λαμπρᾷ γαλήνῃ, τῶν δὲ συννέφει πάλιν, com. fr. adesp. 118. 4 K., Theoc. 4. 41 ff. θαρσεῖν χρή, φίλε Βάττε· τάχ' αὔριον ἔσσετ' ἄμεινον. / ἐλπίδες ἐν ζωοῖσιν, ἀνέλπιστοι δὲ θανόντες, / χὠ Ζεὺς ἄλλοκα μὲν πέλει αἴθριος, ἄλλοκα δ' ὔει, Acc. *trag.* 260 'splendet saepe, ast idem nimbis interdum nigret' (with the opposite emphasis), Ov. *fast.* 1. 495 f. 'nec fera tempestas toto tamen horret in anno, / et tibi, crede mihi, tempora veris erunt' (with Bömer's note), *trist.* 2. 142, 5. 8. 31 f., *Pont.* 4. 4. 1 f. 'nulla dies adeo est australibus umida nimbis / non intermissis ut fluat imber aquis', Sen. *epist.* 107. 8 f. 'nubilo serena succedunt; turbantur maria cum quieverunt; flant in vicem venti . . . ad hanc legem animus noster aptandus est', ps.-Plut. *cons. Apoll.* 103 b (above, p. 137), Ronsard, *Amours*, 1552, p. 74, 1553, p. 247, Herrick, *Hesperides, Good precepts, or counsell* 7 f., Housman, *Last Poems* 18. 16 f., Otto 113, *Nachträge*, pp. 154 f.

imbres : the word can be used sentimentally of tears; cf. Catull. 68. 56, Ov. *ars* 1. 532, *trist.* 1. 3. 18, Asclepiades, *anth. P.* 5. 145. 3 κάτομβρα γὰρ ὄμματ' ἐρώντων, 5 ἐμὸν ὑετόν.

nubibus : for the rare ablative of separation with *manare* cf. 1. 17. 16 n., Stat. *Theb.* 6. 423 'nec Oleniis manant tot cornibus imbres' (he perhaps misunderstands the contruction at *carm.* 1. 17. 16). The word suits the idea of the 'clouded brow' (see *epod.* 13. 5, cited above, p. 135) ; cf. *epist.* 1. 18. 94 'deme supercilio nubem', Hom. *Il.* 17. 591 τὸν δ' ἄχεος νεφέλη ἐκάλυψε μέλαινα, Cic. *Pis.* 20 'frontis tuae nubeculam' (with Nisbet's note), Stat. *silv.* 1. 3. 109 'detertus pectora nube' (with Vollmer's note and Housman 2. 637 f. = *CR* 20, 1906, 37 f.), Pease on Virg. *Aen.* 4. 477. There is therefore no attraction in Campbell's *stirpibus* (cf. Prud. *perist.* 11. 120 'stirpibus hirtus ager').

hispidos . . . agros : 'the unkempt countryside' (*hispidos* is the reading of the manuscripts, the scholiasts, and Diom. *gramm.* 1. 524). The adjective primarily means 'bristling' (like *hirtus* and *horridus*) or 'rough' (Plin. *nat.* 9. 9 'squamis . . . hispido corpore'), and hence is applied to uncultivated wastes; cf. Sil. 12. 395 f. 'hispida tellus . . . Calabri', Stat. *Theb.* 6. 256 f. 'hispida circum / stant iuga', Macr. *sat.* 5. 1. 19 'silvis et rupibus hispida', Cassiod. *in psalm.* 131. 6, p. 949 b Migne '(campi) facti sunt . . . ex hispidis nitidi' (this antithesis is important). If the text is sound Horace is presumably describing the scruffiness of a wintry landscape, whose rough and jagged outlines are unclothed by greenery (cf. Plin. *nat.* 22. 17 'aspectu hispidas' of plants, *Thes.l.L.* 6. 3. 2833. 19 ff.); one must forget the attractions that weeds and wilderness have for later poets and painters (see note on 2. 10. 15 'informis hiemes'). Williams, loc. cit., refers *hispidos* to weather-beaten cornfields, but the adjective hardly suggests so specific a picture: *agros* when followed by *mare* and *oris* naturally means 'countryside' in general, and in Mediterranean lands winter rather than harvest-time is the typical rainy season. The adjective may seem a little vague for Horace's purpose (winter is not men- tioned), but it seems to have been chosen for its ambiguity (see below on *manant*): as Bücheler pointed out (loc. cit.), it suggests the un- trimmed appearance of a dishevelled human being, and therefore of a mourner. The point could of course have been more obviously con- veyed by *horridos*, but that would lack the onomatopoeia of *hispidos*. For the use of the word in watery contexts cf. Apul. *met.* 4. 31. 6 'Portunus caerulis barbis hispidus', Claud. *rapt. Pros.* 1. 70 f. 'glacieque nivali / hispidus' (of Boreas's icicles).

It is an obvious objection to *hispidos* that one looks for a proper name to correspond to *Caspium, Armeniis, Gargani.* Yet Horace often begins an ode with a general maxim (Williams, loc. cit.), which might even have translated a familiar quotation from a lost Greek poem; such a *sententia* could well be followed by particular *exempla* from the Caspian, Armenia, and Gargano. Williams seems wrong however to give the opening maxim a particular reference to Italy (balancing Gargano below); Horace does not say 'yonder fields' as if he were looking out from a symposium, but couches his remark in a com- pletely general form.

The most interesting conjecture that has been proposed is *Histri- cos* (mentioned by Orelli). The name usually described Istria, the hinterland of Trieste, not a particularly wet part of the world; but the ancients connected this area with the Danube (Ister) more closely than fact allows (Hipparchus ap. Str. 1. 3. 15, Nepos ap. Plin. *nat.* 3. 127 f., Mela 2. 16, 2. 63, J. O. Thomson, *History of Ancient Geography*, 1948, pp. 48, 141, 197). The Danube basin has much of its rainfall in the summer, which seems strange to Mediterranean peoples; cf. Hdt. 4. 50. 3 ὄμβροι πολλοί τε καὶ λάβροι. Indeed the very name *Danubius* (a corruption of *Danuvius*) may be due to an association with clouds; cf. Joh. Lyd. *magist.* 3. 32 οὕτω δὲ αὐτὸν οἱ Θρᾷκες ἐκάλεσαν διότι ἐπὶ τὰ πρὸς ἄρκτον ὄρη καὶ θρασκίαν ἄνεμον συννεφὴς ὁ ἀὴρ ἐκ τῆς ὑποκειμένης τῶν ὑγρῶν ἀμετρίας σχεδὸν διὰ παντὸς ἀποτελούμενος αἴτιος αὐτοῖς συνεχοῦς ἐπομβρίας ἀποτελεῖσθαι νομίζε- ται, Δανούβιον δὲ τὸν νεφελοφόρον ἐκεῖνοι καλοῦσι πατρίως, O. Keller, *Lateinische Volksetymologie und Verwandtes*, 1891, pp. 8 f. It could be argued in favour of this conjecture that the Danube had been the scene of important military operations by Crassus in 29 (*CAH* 10.

117 f.). Yet when all is said and done *hispidos* remains the most attractive reading because it supports the ambiguity of the passage.

2. manant: 'ooze' is not a natural word for rain; at Stat. *Theb.* 6. 423 (cited above on 1 *nubibus*) it conveys a learned allusion to the horn of plenty (*carm.* 1. 17. 15 'manabit'). Horace must have used it here because it is a *vox propria* for tears; cf. 4. 1. 34, *epist.* 1. 17. 59, *Thes.l.L.* 8. 320. 29 ff. For the use in a poetic image of terms more appropriate to the literal subject cf. D. West, *The Imagery and Poetry of Lucretius*, 1969, pp. 43 ff. ('transfusion of terms'), Silk, *passim*.

Caspium: the storms of the Caspian are known to the geographers; cf. Mela 3. 38 'omne atrox saevum sine portibus, procellis undique expositum', Dionys. *perieg.* 706, 721, Avien. *orb. terr.* 84 f. 'hic prolapsus aquae, boreali fusus ab alto / terga procelloso turgescit Caspia fluctu', 891, Prisc. *perieg.* 683, *RE* 10. 2286. See further *Encyclopaedia Britannica*[11] 5. 454 'The prevalent winds of the Caspian blow from the south-east, usually between October and March, and from the north and north-west, commonly between July and September. They sometimes continue for days together with great violence, rendering navigation dangerous, and driving the sea-water up over the shores' (cf. Curt. 6. 4. 19). However the Caspian does not provide a conventional literary *exemplum*, and in extant classical poetry is not mentioned till the Augustan age; cf. Prop. 2. 30. 20, Virg. *Aen.* 6. 798 f. 'huius (Augusti) in adventum iam nunc et Caspia regna / responsis horrent divum et Maeotia tellus'. The Romans were taking an interest in Armenia at the time (4 n.), and the poets naturally exaggerated the geographical extent of their involvement. Perhaps they were assimilating Augustus's exploits to those of Alexander (cf. Norden, *RhM* 54, 1899, 468 ff. = *Kl. Schr.*, pp. 424 f., on Virg. *Aen.* 6. 791 ff.); graphic accounts of Caspian storms seem to derive from romantic Hellenistic biographers rather than intelligence work by contemporary strategists (cf. Str. 11. 7. 4 προσεδοξάσθη δὲ καὶ περὶ τῆς θαλάττης ταύτης πολλὰ ψευδῆ διὰ τὴν Ἀλεξάνδρου φιλοτιμίαν, W. W. Tarn, *Alexander the Great*, 1948, 2. 5 ff., J. R. Hamilton, *CQ* N.S. 21, 1971, 106 ff.).

3. vexant: the verb is used of the action of the winds on ships, clouds, or the sea; cf. Lucr. 1. 274 f. 'montis . . . supremos / silvifragis vexat flabris', 1. 279. It originally described a violent movement (the word is a stronger cognate of *vehere*), though later it was applied to milder forms of harassment; cf. Gell. 2. 6. 5 'nam qui fertur et rapsatur atque huc atque illuc distrahitur is vexari proprie dicitur' (defending Virg. *ecl.* 6. 76 'Dulichias vexasse rates'). It suits Horace's analogy that the word is also used of mental upheavals.

inaequales : 'irregular'; the squalls are all the more dangerous because they suddenly change their pace and direction (I. 3. 13 n.). The combination with *usque* may be a little pointed; cf. Arist. *poet.* 1454ᵃ27 f. ὁμαλῶς ἀνώμαλον. The adjective also suits gusts of emotion; cf. Aesch. *Ag.* 219 φρενὸς πνέων δυσσεβῆ τροπαίαν (with Fraenkel's note), Sen. *dial.* 3. 17. 5 'affectus cito cadit, aequalis est ratio', Péron 170 ff. Some interpret 'roughening the water's surface'; this is less obvious, less specific (being true of the mildest breeze), and admits no clear metaphorical application.

4. **Armeniis in oris** : the snows of the country had harassed Xenophon (*anab.* 4. 4. 8 ff., 4. 5. 1 ff.), Lucullus (Plut. *Lucull.* 32), and most recently Antony (Dio 49. 31. 1) ; see further Str. 11. 5. 6 (tobogganing on Mount Masius), 11. 14. 4. But though Claudian has a passing reference to Armenian snows (5. 29), the poets in general concentrate on the frosty Caucasus, which is further to the north, and which they anyway often identify with the mythical Rhipaean mountains. Horace's choice of *exemplum* is presumably influenced by a Roman preoccupation with the area (cf. 20 *Niphaten*), which looked forward to the settlement of 20 B.C. (*CAH* 10. 254 ff.).

5. **amice** : the word is appropriate in affectionate expostulation; cf. 2. 14. 6 n., Pind. *P.* 1. 92, Soph. *El.* 916 f. ἀλλ', ὦ φίλη, θάρσυνε. τοῖς αὐτοῖσί τοι / οὐχ αὐτὸς αἰεὶ δαιμόνων παραστατεῖ, Theoc. 4. 41 φίλε Βάττε. In particular the declaration of friendship suits the sympathy desirable in a *consolatio* (cf. vol. i, pp. 280 f.).

stat glacies iners : cf. Lucan 5. 436 'sic stat iners Scythicas astringens Bosporus undas', Asclepiadius, *anth. Lat.* 541. 2, Pope, *Temple of Fame* 56 'impassive ice'; so more generally of the inactivity of winter 4. 7. 12 'bruma . . . iners' (cf. 1. 22. 17 n.). There is a contrast between the torpid ice and the gusts of the Caspian; cf. 3. 4. 45 f. 'qui terram inertem, qui mare temperat / ventosum'. Horace seems to be hinting at the numbness and listlessness of bereavement; cf. κρυερός, παχνοῦσθαι, Ov. *epist.* 10. 44 'torpuerant molles ante dolore genae'.

6. **mensis per omnis**: Horace rings the changes on expressions for 'always'; here he suggests that the bad weather continues through all seasons. Ever since Homer phrases like ἤματα πάντα were common ; cf. West on Hes. *th.* 305, Landgraf on Cic. *S. Rosc.* 154 'omnibus horis'. In our passage the phrase is to be taken also with the next clause, which would otherwise lack a temporal expression.

Aquilonibus : cf. Ap. Rhod. 2. 1100 αὐτὰρ ὅγ' ἡμάτιος μὲν ἐν οὔρεσι φύλλ' ἐτίνασσεν, Varro At. 6 'frigidus et silvis Aquilo decussit honorem', Virg. *georg.* 2. 404, Boeth. *cons.* 1 poet. 5. 19 f. For metaphorical

parallels cf. Sappho 47 Ἔρος δ' ἐτίναξέ μοι / φρένας, ὡς ἄνεμος κὰτ
ὄρος δρύσιν ἐμπέτων, Ibycus 286. 9 ff. Θρηίκιος Βορέας / ἀίσσων παρὰ
Κύπριδος ἀζαλέ/αις μανίαισιν ἐρεμνὸς ἀθαμβὴς / ἐγκρατέως πεδόθεν
λαφύσσει (West: φυλάσσει cod.) / ἡμετέρας φρένας, Hor. epod. 11. 5 f.
'hic tertius December ex quo destiti / Inachia furere silvis honorem
decutit' (where the bleak image reflects the speaker's desolation),
carm. 3. 17. 9 ff. 'cras foliis nemus...' (where as usual in sympotic
verse the storm symbolizes the troubles of the world), Virg. Aen.
4. 441 ff.

7. **querqueta Gargani**: an onomatopoeic effect seems to be intended.
Gargano is the mountain spur that projects into the Adriatic north
of Foggia (RE 7. 755 f.), perhaps mentioned by Horace for reasons
of Apulian patriotism, though Venusia is nowhere near; for the
characteristic addition of an Italian place-name cf. 1. 21. 6 n. In
antiquity the area was remote and little-mentioned, but in the
Norman and Swabian periods the shrine of St. Michael became a
famous curative centre of pilgrimage; he displaced Calchas and the
physician Podalirius (Lycophron 1047 ff., Str. 6. 3. 9), but his own
fortune is now diminished by the more up-to-date cult of the neighbouring Padre Pio. For the woods cf. epist. 2. 1. 202 'Garganum
mugire putes nemus aut mare Tuscum', Sil. 4. 560 f., 8. 628 f.; now-
adays the national Foresta Umbra once more covers a substantial
part of Gargano (cf. Enciclopedia Italiana 16. 388).

laborant: the trees strain in the wind, a different picture from the
snow-covered branches of 1. 9. 3. The verb also suggests human suffering; so more explicitly Housman's 'the wood's in trouble' (above,
p. 136).

8. **viduantur orni**: for the manna ash in a similar context cf. 1. 9.
12 n. Once again there is a suggestion of human bereavement; cf.
Virg. georg. 4. 518 'arvaque Rhipaeis numquam viduata pruinis'
(where there is a contrast with the bereaved Orpheus).

9. **tu**: the emphatic pronoun points a reproach (2. 18. 17, 3. 29. 25).
Valgius is compared to his disadvantage with the weather of the first
stanza, as is underlined by the repetition of semper.

urges: the lamentations of the bereaved were thought to disturb
the peace of the dead; cf. Prop. 4. 11. 1 'desine, Paulle, meum lacrimis
urgere sepulchrum', Tib. 1. 1. 67, carm. epig. 963. 12, 965. 7 f. 'quid
lacrimis opus est, Rusticelli carissime coniunx, / extinctos cineres
sollicitare meos?', 995. 19 f., 1198. 11 f., Stat. silv. 2. 6. 96 'quid
caram crucias tam saevis luctibus umbram?', Rohde, Psyche, ch. 5,
n. 49. The word may maliciously suggest the solicitations of a lover
(1. 5. 2 n.); Valgius gives Mystes no peace even after he has lost him.

flebilibus modis : the adjective must primarily mean 'tearful' to sustain the contrast with the rain; cf. Cic. *Tusc.* 1. 106 'pressis et flebilibus modis', Sen. *Herc. O.* 1090 f., *epist.* 88. 9, Auson. 184. 2, E. Löfstedt, *Vermischte Studien*, 1936, pp. 84 ff. But there also seems to be an underlying hint (not of course serious) that Valgius wrote pitiable poetry; for similar ambiguities about literary sentimentality cf. 1. 33. 2 f. 'neu miserabiles / decantes elegos', Pers. 1. 34 'Phyllidas, Hypsipylas, vatum et plorabile siquid'.

10. Mysten : the name is found in real life, borne by people with religious parents (Pape–Benseler 2. 967). Though not attested in the fragments of Valgius, it suits the view of love as an initiation (common in sentimental as well as satirical writers); cf. Ar. *Lys.* 832, Meleager, *anth. P.* 5. 191. 7 f. Κύπρι, σοὶ Μελέαγρος, ὁ μύστης / σῶν κώμων, Cic. *Att.* 1. 18. 3 'M. Luculli uxorem Memmius suis sacris initiavit', Prop. 2. 6. 31 f. 'a gemat . . . qui protulit . . . / orgia (Ruhnken: iurgia *codd.*) sub tacita condita laetitia', Petron. 140. 5, K. Kost on *Musaios, Hero and Leander* 145, H. H. O. Chalk, *JHS* 80, 1960, 43 f.

ademptum : this is naturally taken as a euphemism for death, as is shown by the lamentations of 10–12 and the *exempla* of 13–17. The wit of the next stanza consists precisely in the fact that though the assumed grief of Valgius outdoes that of Nestor and Priam, his relation to Mystes is far other than theirs to Antilochus and Troilus. This is blurred if the cause of Valgius's grief is simply that Mystes has deserted him. See also above, p. 136.

nec tibi . . . : the germ of this theme can already be found in Hom. *Il.* 23. 109 μυρομένοισι δὲ τοῖσι φάνη ῥοδοδάκτυλος Ἠώς (cf. the conflation of two Homeric lines in ps.-Plut. *cons. Apoll.* 114 e μυρομένοισι δὲ τοῖσι μέλας ἐπὶ ἕσπερος ἦλθε). But the mention of both sunset and dawn is an affectation of neoteric and elegiac lament; cf. Cinna, fr. 6 'te matutinus flentem conspexit Eous, / te [Hollis: et *codd.*] flentem paulo post vidit Hesperus idem' (for Valgius's admiration for Cinna see above, p. 135), Virg. *georg.* 4. 466 'te veniente die, te decedente canebat'. Horace goes further than his models by mentioning the evening before the morning; he thus suggests that Valgius lamented all night (so too Tasso, *Ger. lib.* 12. 90 'Lei nel partir, lei nel tornar del sole, Chiama con voce stanca, e prega e plora', Tennyson, *Mariana*, Alexiou 93).

Vespero : Horace knew that the Evening and Morning Stars are one and the same (the planet Venus), as he shows below by the paradoxical *fugiente solem*. The identification was made early in the East; among the Greeks it was assigned by some to Pythagoras, and Ibycus (who also lived in Samos) is said to have mentioned it (331). It was popularized in an influential erotic epigram attributed to Plato (*anth. P.* 7. 670 ἀστὴρ πρὶν μὲν ἔλαμπες ἐνὶ ζωοῖσιν ἑῷος, / νῦν δὲ θανὼν λάμπεις ἕσπερος ἐν φθιμένοις); for later developments cf. Call. fr. 291. 3 ἑσπέριον φιλέουσιν, ἀτὰρ στυγέουσιν ἑῷον, Meleager, *anth. P.* 5. 172. 1 ff., 12. 114, Catull. 62. 34 f. 'nocte latent fures, quos idem saepe revertens, / Hespere, mutato comprendis nomine Eous', Cinna (above, *nec tibi* n.), *ciris* 352, Sen. *Phaedr.* 750 ff., *ros. nasc.* 45 f. The topic was given added currency in romantic writing by the importance of Hesperus in the epithalamium and by its identification with Phaethon, the beloved of Aphrodite (Eratosthenes, *cataster.*, pp. 196 f. Robert, Wilamowitz, *Hermes* 18, 1883, 417 ff. = *Kl. Schr.* 1. 131 ff., *Hellenistische Dichtung* 2. 279, J. Diggle, *Euripides: Phaethon*, 1970, pp. 10 ff.); it is called the star of Aphrodite from the Hellenistic age (*RE* 20. 1. 653, 8 A. 1. 888). For Hesper-Phosphor see further Pfeiffer on Call. loc. cit., Pease on Cic. *nat. deor.* 2. 53, Roscher 1. 2. 2603 f., 3. 2. 2519 ff., *RE* 8. 1251 ff.

11. surgente : the evening star does not rise over the horizon, but becomes visible as the sunlight fades; for similar expressions cf. Catull. 62. 1 f. 'Vesper Olympo / exspectata diu iam tandem lumina tollit', Virg. *ecl.* 6. 86, 8. 30 'tibi deserit Hesperus Oetam' with Heyne's note, 10. 77, *culex* 203, Sen. *apocol.* 4. 26 'aut qualis surgit redeuntibus Hesperus astris', Serv. *Aen.* 2. 801 'secundum persuasionem eorum qui circa montes habitant; illinc enim oriri vel occidere putantur sidera unde videri vel incipiunt vel desinunt', A. Le Bœuffle, *REL* 40, 1962, 120 ff., D. A. Kidd, *Latomus* 33, 1974, 24 f.

decedunt amores : for a similar movement of thought cf. Ibycus 286. 6 f. ἐμοὶ δ' ἔρος / οὐδεμίαν κατάκοιτος ὥραν (cf. 6 *Aquilonibus* n. for another parallel from the same poem). The verb suits astronomical settings, especially when juxtaposed with *surgente*; cf. *epist.* 1. 6. 3 f. 'solem et stellas et decedentia certis / tempora momentis', *ecl.* 2. 67 f. 'sol crescentes decedens duplicat umbras. / me tamen urit amor. quis enim modus adsit amori?', *georg.* 4. 466 'te decedente canebat' (the passage must have been in Horace's mind), *Thes.l.L.* 5. 1. 122. 30 ff. Plural *amores* is more sentimental than *amor*; it may even have been the title of a book of Valgius's poems.

12. rapidum . . . solem : the adjective by origin means *qui rapit*; it it is applicable to tearing rivers or the scorching sun (Shackleton Bailey, *Propertiana*, p. 317). In juxtaposition with *fugiente* the emphasis must primarily be on speed (Mediterranean sunrises are sudden); cf. Virg. *georg.* 1. 424 'solem ad rapidum lunasque sequentis', 2. 321 f. But the two meanings of the word cannot be too sharply divided, as the sun in its career tears up everything in its path (cf. the use of *rapere, corripere* with *viam*).

fugiente : cf. 3. 21. 24 'dum rediens fugat astra Phoebus', *Thes.l.L.*
6. 1. 1493. 14 ff., 1501. 15 ff., Bömer on Ov. *met.* 2. 114. There is a
similar astronomical use of φεύγειν (Hes. *op.* 620, Eur. *Ion* 84) and
διώκειν (ibid. 1158).

13. **ter aevo functus** : the Homeric Nestor is said to have seen three
generations; cf. Hom. *Il.* 1. 250 ff. with van Leeuwen's note, 9. 57 f.
(Diomede might be his youngest son), *Od.* 3. 245, Cic. *senec.* 31
'tertiam iam aetatem hominum videbat', Plut. *Cato mai.* 15. 5
Σερουίου Γάλβα κατηγόρησεν ἐνενήκοντα γεγονὼς ἔτη. κινδυνεύει γάρ,
ὡς ὁ Νέστωρ, εἰς τριγονίαν τῷ βίῳ καὶ ταῖς πράξεσι κατελθεῖν. Latin
writers sometimes seem to extend his age to three human lives or
three centuries (perhaps because of the ambiguity of *saeculum*);
cf. Laev. *carm.* fr. 9 'trisaeclisenex', Prop. 2. 13. 46, *paneg. in Mess.*
50 f., Ov. *met.* 12. 187 f., Manil. 1. 764 f., Juv. 10. 248 f., *RE* 17. 1. 119.
Horace somewhat satirically follows this tradition; he seems to be
combining expressions like (*de*)*functus aevo* (cf. 2. 18. 38 f. 'functum
. . . laboribus') and *ter functus consulatu*. The epic allusion may seem
a compliment to a Homerizing poet like Valgius, but Nestor was
an *exemplum* not only of extreme old age but of sexual decrepitude
(cf. Juv. 6. 326, below, 15 n.).

amabilem : the word is found five times in the *Odes* and twice elsewhere in Horace; it is seldom used by other poets (Axelson 102 f.).
On the surface it suggests the amiable qualities of the dead Antilochus, but it is amusingly chosen because it is capable of erotic
implications. Lambinus suggested that it represents the Greek
ἀγαπητός (or 'late-born'); his idea would be worth considering as
a secondary meaning if it could be shown that this adjective was
applied to Antilochus.

14. **ploravit** : *plorare* (whence French *pleurer*) is less grandiose than
flere (below, 17), but suits the stylistic level of elegy (cf. Grassmann
102 f.).

omnis . . . annos : the phrase goes even further than *mensis per
omnis* (6) ; this time the hyperbaton adds emphasis to *omnis*.

Antilochum : in the *Iliad* Antilochus is a brave young hero, the
slayer of a large number of Trojans and the victor in the chariot
race in Book 23. The *Aethiopis* also told how he sacrificed his life
to save his father from Memnon (Proclus, *chrest.* p. 106 Allen, cf.
also pp. 126 f., Pind. *P.* 6. 36 βόασε παῖδα ὅν). He is used as an *exemplum* in consolation by Dio Chrys. 29. 20 (a funeral oration for
the young boxer Melancomas) ἔτι δὲ τῶν παλαιῶν τοὺς ἐξοχωτάτους
ἀκούομεν οὐδένα αὐτῶν ἐπὶ πολὺ ἐλθόντα τοῦ βίου, Πάτροκλόν τε καὶ
Ἀντίλοχον . . .
But legend gave Antilochus a less heroic role, which is here

maliciously hinted at by Horace: already in Homer he was closely associated with Achilles (*Il.* 17. 652 ff., 18. 1 ff., *Od.* 11. 467 f., 24. 15 f., 24. 76 ff.), and later writers developed the erotic possibilities of the situation. Cf. Philostr. *imag.* 2. 7. 1 τὸν Ἀχιλλέα ἐρᾶν τοῦ Ἀντιλόχου πεφώρακας οἶμαι παρ' Ὁμήρῳ; below he gives Antilochus the attributes of a παῖς καλός (2. 7. 5 ἡβάσκει μὲν ὑπήνης πρόσω . . .). Such a sentimentalized Antilochus provides an excellent counterpart both to Mystes and to Troilus (see below).

15. impubem parentes : for laments on early death cf. Pease on Cic. *nat. deor.* 2. 72, 3. 80, Virg. *Aen.* 4. 68, Esteve-Forriol 138, E. Griessmair, *Das Motiv der Mors immatura in den griechischen metrischen Grabinschriften,* 1966, Lattimore 184 ff. For *impubem* cf. Q. Smyrn. 4. 431 f. ἔτ' ἄχνοον εἰσέτι νύμφης / νηῗδα; in view of Troilus's reputation as a καλὸς παῖς (see below), there may be a malicious irony in the suggestion that he had not yet reached the age of sexual experience. Similarly Horace underlines that the mourners were parents and sisters; Priam like Nestor might have been too decrepit an *exemplum* for Valgius's comfort (cf. Mart. 11. 60. 3 f. 'ulcus habet Priami quod tendere possit alutam, / quodque senem Pelian [Pylium?] non sinat esse senem', Juv. 6. 325 f. 'quibus incendi iam frigidus aevo / Laomedontiades et Nestoris hirnea possit').

16. Troilon : Troilus was the youngest son of Priam and Hecuba, and was killed by Achilles; he was regarded by Aristarchus as a full-grown warrior (schol. on *Il.* 24. 257 ἱππιοχάρμης), but normally appears both in art and literature as a boy or youth (Roscher 5. 1215 f., 1223 ff.). See especially Ibycus 282. 41 ff. τῷ δ' ἄρα Τρωΐλον / ὡσεὶ χρυσὸν ὀρει/χάλκῳ τρὶς ἄπεφθον ἤδη / Τρῶες Δαναοί τ' ἐρόεσσαν / μορφὰν μάλ' ἐΐσκον ὅμοιον, Phrynichus, fr. 13 N. λάμπει δ' ἐπὶ πορφυρέαις παρῇσι φῶς ἔρωτος (cf. Soph. fr. 619 P. = 562 N., with Pearson's discussion, pp. 253 ff.), Lycophron 307 ff., Q. Smyrn. 4. 425 ff. (comparison to a flower), Serv. *Aen.* 1. 474 'et veritas quidem hoc habet: Troili amore Achillem ductum palumbes ei quibus ille delectabatur obiecisse; quas cum vellet tenere, captus ab Achille in eius amplexibus periit. sed hoc quasi indignum heroo carmine mutavit poeta'. In the same area of ideas we may also note Strato, *anth. P.* 12. 191. 4 (on a boy with a new beard) ἐχθὲς Τρωῒλος ὤν, πῶς ἐγένου Πρίαμος;

Troilus appears as an *exemplum* in consolation for *mors immatura* in Callimachus (fr. 491 μεῖον ἐδάκρυσεν Τρωῒλος ἢ Πρίαμος, a line cited in Cic. *Tusc.* 1. 93 and ps.-Plut. *cons. Apoll.* 113 e). Pasquali (259 f.) conjectures that Callimachus's fragment comes from an epicedion for a beautiful youth, but the hypothesis is rejected by Pfeiffer (*CQ* 37, 1943, 32 n. 51 = *Ausgewählte Schriften,* 1960, p. 146

n. 51). It is more relevant to our passage that Statius compares to Troilus the lost *delicatus* of Flavius Ursus (*silv.* 2. 6. 30 ff.).

17. flevere semper : *semper* rounds off the series of temporal expressions. It balances 9 *semper* at the beginning of the middle section of the poem; in the same way *flevere* picks up 9 *flebilibus*.

desine . . . : for this motif in *consolatio* cf. p. 137. *tandem* sounds a note of impatience; for the same movement as in our poem cf. I. 23. I 'vitas' (corresponding to *urges*), 9 'atqui' (corresponding to *at*), II f. 'tandem desine matrem / tempestiva sequi viro'. The genitive *querellarum* is a grandiose Graecism, appropriate to a mannered writer like Valgius; cf. Virg. *Aen.* 10. 441 'desistere pugnae', Sil. 10. 84 'desinit irae', Löfstedt, *Syntactica* 2. 417, H.–Sz. 83.

mollium . . . querellarum : the adjective suggests both the effeminacy of continual lamentation (*epod.* 16. 39, Archilochus 13. 10 W. γυναικεῖον πένθος) and sentimentality of style (cf. Hermesianax 7. 36 Powell μαλακοῦ πνεῦμα τὸ πενταμέτρου of Mimnermus, *serm.* I. 10. 44 'molle atque facetum' of the *Eclogues*); it may even hint indirectly at the *mollities* of Valgius's purported relationship with Mystes. *querellae*, whether expostulations or laments, are usually shrill; so there may be an oxymoron here in calling them 'soft'.

18. potius . . . cantemus : for the suggestion of alternative outlets in *consolatio* cf. above, p. 137. *potius nova* makes a contrast with *desine*, and the vigorous *cantemus* with the whining *querellarum*. The first person verb indicates the speaker's pretended sympathy (cf. 2. 16. 17 n.); this too is appropriate to the type of writing.

19. Augusti . . . Caesaris : a topical compliment to Octavian's new name (for the date cf. above, p. 138). Though the *cognomen* is sometimes placed before the *nomen* (2. 2. 3 n.), the effect here is to bring out the adjectival force of *Augusti* (cf. Virg. *Aen.* 6. 792, 8. 678, Liv. 4. 20. 7, 28. 12. 12, R. Syme, *Historia* 7, 1958, 183) ; otherwise Horace would be taking up a lot of space to say very little.

tropaea : the word properly describes arches and similar monuments, but is used here as often less concretely of victories. *nova tropaea* and *rigidum Niphaten* must belong to a single colon; it offends both rhythm and common-sense to join the latter phrase to *volvere vertices* below (whether the Niphates was a mountain or a frozen river, it could not roll eddies). It is therefore natural to assume that the *tropaea* were won at Niphates ; otherwise there is not enough to indicate that Niphates was conquered no less than the Euphrates and Geloni in the next stanza. In these circumstances it is difficult to see a reference either to Augustus's Cantabrian campaign of 26/5 or to Terentius Varro's Alpine victories of 25 (thus vol. i, p. xxxii) ;

in any event it would have been tactless to treat the former as less important than Eastern questions (worth only half a colon against two and a half), and unintelligible to hint at the latter in the context of greater achievements.

20. **rigidum** : the adjective suits the stark outline of a mountain, especially when covered in snow; cf. Ov. *met.* 4. 527, 8. 797 'rigidique cacumine montis', 11. 150. It also suggests the obduracy of an enemy (cf. Virgil's *pulsum*, cited above, p. 137); there is a contrast with 17 *mollium*. Those who think that Niphates is a river refer *rigidum* to ice (Ov. *trist.* 3. 10. 48, Claud. *rapt. Pros.* 2. 65 f. 'rigentem... Tanain'), and can thus see a contrast with the eddies of the Euphrates; but then the adjective gives no suggestion of obduracy, and the contrast with *mollium* becomes purely formal.

Niphaten : a mountain range in central Armenia, according to the geographers and some of the poets; cf. Str. 11. 12. 4, *RE* 17. 1. 706 f., C. Müller on Ptol. *geog.* 5. 12. 1. The word must have conveyed associations of νιφάς, 'snow'; cf. Steph. Byz. 477, who also quotes from Pisander the epithet εὐσκόπελος (not in Kinkel). The name had recently been given currency by Virgil (above, p. 137); presumably the mountain was portrayed in the triumph of 29 as a symbol of Armenia (for such representations cf. Ov. *Pont.* 2. 1. 39, *epiced. Drusi* 313, Tac. *ann.* 2. 41. 2 'simulacra montium fluminum proeliorum', *RE* 7 A. 1. 503). It may have been chosen for that purpose because of associations with Alexander the Great (see below); similarly the claim to have bridged the Araxes (Virg. *Aen.* 8. 728) seems to have been a conscious imitation of Alexander (Serv. auct. ad loc.; cf. Curt. 5. 5. 3 f.).

Later poets usually regard Niphates as a river (possibly because of a misunderstanding of our own passage and of Virgil, loc. cit.); cf. Lucan 3. 245 'volventem saxa Niphaten', Sil. 13. 765 f. (of Alexander) 'qui . . . Pellaeo ponte Niphaten / astrinxit', Juv. 6. 409 ff., Claud. 7. 72 (but cf. *rapt. Pros.* 3. 263 'arduus . . . Niphates'). Plutarch seems to use the name of the upper Tigris; see *Alex.* 31. 5 (a romancing account of the site of Gaugamela) τὸ . . . πεδίον τὸ μεταξὺ τοῦ Νιφάτου καὶ τῶν ὀρῶν τῶν Γορδυαίων (cf. Arrian, *anab.* 3. 7. 7 ἐν ἀριστερᾷ μὲν ἔχων τὰ Γορδυαίων ὄρη, ἐν δεξιᾷ δὲ αὐτὸν τὸν Τίγρητα, Curt. 4. 10. 8); it should be noted that by some definitions the Tigris rose in the area of Mount Niphates (Str. loc. cit.), and the name could have been extended to the river. Some argue that Virgil's *pulsum . . . Niphaten* suggests a river flowing backwards; but the participle is equally applicable to the dislodgement of an immovable mountain (cf. Horace's *rigidum*). The rhetorical conventions of χωρογραφία in encomium favour the conjunction of a mountain with a river and a plain; cf. *epist.* 2. 1. 252 f. 'terrarumque situs et flumina dicere et arces / montibus impositas', Menander rhet. 3. 373. 17 ff. Sp. διαγράψεις καὶ φύσεις καὶ θέσεις χωρίων ἐν οἷς οἱ πόλεμοι, καὶ ποταμῶν δὲ καὶ λιμένων καὶ ὀρῶν καὶ πεδίων, Doblhofer 69 ff., 98 f.

21. Medumque flumen: the Euphrates (Call. *h. Ap.* 108 Ἀσσυρίου ποταμοῖο); at one time it was called the Medos (ps.-Plut. *fluv.* 20. 1 = *geogr. Graec. min.* 2. 659). Rivers were centres of a country's communications, and if boats could be denied to the other side made powerful defensive lines; hence they were sometimes portrayed in triumphal processions (20 n.).

additum: Porphyrio explains 'id est, ad numerum gentium victarum accessisse'; cf. 3. 5. 3 f. 'adiectis Britannis / imperio' (*adiungere* is often so used). There is something unusual and pointed in combining the word not with *imperio Romano* but with *victis gentibus*; cf. Ov. *ars* 1. 177 f. 'parat Caesar domito quod defuit orbi / addere' (an important parallel). E. Ensor objects that the Euphrates was not annexed, and interprets 'set over to guard' (*Hermathena* 12, 1903, 106); cf. 3. 4. 78 f. 'nequitiae additus / custos', Plaut. *aul.* 556 'quem quondam Ioni Iuno custodem addidit', Lucil. 469, Stat. *Theb.* 4. 426. But it is awkward to think of the river as acting on the Roman side and simultaneously humbled in defeat.

22. minores volvere vertices: for similar humiliations cf. Virg. *Aen.* 8. 726 ff. (above, p. 137), Prop. 2. 1. 31 f. 'attractus in urbem / septem captivis debilis ibat aquis', 3. 4. 4, 4. 3. 35, Ov. *ars* 1. 223 f., *fast.* 1. 286, *trist.* 4. 2. 41 f., Lucan 5. 268, Petron. 123. 241 f., *carm. epig.* 895. 4, Tac. *ann.* 1. 79. 4 'quin ipsum Tiberim nolle prorsus accolis fluviis orbatum minore gloria fluere', Flor. *epit.* 3. 10. 9 'nec Rhenus ergo inmunis; nec enim fas erat ut liber esset receptator hostium atque defensor', F. Christ, *Die römische Weltherrschaft in der antiken Dichtung* (*Tüb. Beitr.* 31), 1938, pp. 47 ff. The noun refers literally to the river's eddies (the Homeric δῖναι), but there also seems to be a pun on 'diminished heads' (cf. Quinn 161); contrast 3. 16. 19 'late conspicuum tollere verticem'. The alliteration of *v* and *r* suits swirling water; for the former cf. 2. 3. 18. *minores* makes a formal contrast with *additum* above.

23. intraque praescriptum: there is a hint of the discipline of the ring where horses and their riders were trained; cf. Cic. *de orat.* 3. 70 'ex ingenti quodam oratorem inmensoque campo in exiguum sane gyrum compellitis', *off.* 1. 90 (= Panaetius, fr. 12 van Straaten) 'ut equos propter crebras contentiones proeliorum ferocitate exultantes domitoribus tradere soleant ut iis facilioribus possint uti, sic homines secundis rebus ecfrenatos sibique praefidentis tamquam in gyrum rationis et doctrinae duci oportere', Prop. 3. 3. 21 'cur tua praescriptos evecta est pagina gyros?'

Gelonos : this Scythian tribe appears from Hdt. 4. 108 f. (perhaps derived from Aristeas) to Amm. 31. 2. 14 (*RE* 7. 1014 ff.). They are mentioned on several other occasions in Augustan poetry without any precision (2. 20. 19, 3. 4. 35, Virg. *georg.* 2. 115, 3. 461, *Aen.* 8. 725) ; Horace is here in harmony with Virgil's account of the triumphs of 29 (above, p. 137). The Geloni suit this ode not just as a remote north-eastern tribe (cf. 2 *Caspium*, 4 *Armeniis*) but because their very name must have suggested *gelu* to a Roman reader (cf. 5 *glacies*, 20 *Niphaten*).

24. exiguis equitare campis : *exiguis* picks up *minores* and makes alliteration with *equitare*. There is something of an oxymoron : plains are naturally *lati* (3. 11. 9) and *equitare* suggests aggressive prancing (1. 2. 51 n.).

10. RECTIVS VIVES

[K. M. T. Atkinson, *Historia* 9, 1960, 440 ff.; R. Hanslik, *RhM* 96, 1953, 282 ff.; S. Jameson, *Historia* 18, 1969, 204 ff.; W. C. McDermott, *TAPhA* 72, 1941, 255 ff.; D. Stockton, *Historia* 14, 1965, 18 ff.; M. Swan, *HSCPh* 71, 1966, 235 ff.; D. West ap. Costa 47 ff.]

1–12. *You will follow the right course, Licinius, if you neither push out to sea too persistently nor hug the shore too close. The man who chooses the golden mean avoids the squalor of a hovel, the unpopularity of a palace. Height is a danger to trees and buildings and mountains.* 13–28. *A heart that is prepared for anything hopes in adversity and fears in prosperity; just as the seasons change, so the vicissitudes of life; misfortune does not last, and cruel Apollo sometimes relaxes. In difficult straits you should show spirit, but when the wind is too favourable you must shorten sail.*

'ad Licinium Murenam: optimum esse medium vitae statum': thus the superscription in Klingner's Ψ group of manuscripts (β in Wickham–Garrod). At once a crucial question is posed: is Horace's Licinius somebody otherwise unknown (Heinze, Atkinson), or is he to be identified with the Murena who was Maecenas's brother-in-law? This Murena engaged in angry debate with Augustus at the trial of Primus for unauthorized warfare in Thrace: when Horace advises Licinius to shorten sail (22 ff.), should this be connected with

Murena's notorious candour (Dio 54. 3. 4 ἀκράτῳ καὶ κατακορεῖ τῇ παρρησίᾳ πρὸς πάντας ὁμοίως ἐχρῆτο)? Soon afterwards Murena was accused of involvement in Caepio's conspiracy, and put to death after attempting to escape (Dio 54. 3. 5). There is a notorious chronological problem about the dating of these events (23 or 22 B.C.?), and it must be asked whether Horace's poem contributes to a solution.

Maecenas's brother-in-law is described by many names (RE 5 A. 706 f.), Licinius Murena (Dio 54. 3. 3), L. Murena (Vell. 2. 91. 2), Terentius Varro (Strabo), Varro (Seneca, Tacitus), Varro Murena (Suetonius). The conflated name 'Varro Murena' was borne by an aedile by 44 B.C. (ILS 6075 with Cic. Phil. 13. 26, cf. Cic. epist. 13. 22. 1), presumably the conspirator's father; he was probably a Licinius Murena adopted by a Terentius Varro (RE 5 A. 705 f., S. Treggiari, Phoenix 27, 1973, 255 f.), which is why Maecenas's wife, the conspirator's sister, is called Terentia. But the conspirator may also have called himself 'Licinius Murena', the form used by Dio (cf. Stockton, op. cit., p. 40); as has been mentioned, a Horatian superscription independently gives the same form of name, though without further identifying the person concerned (for these superscriptions, which go back to antiquity, cf. F. Klingner, Hermes 70, 1935, 262 f. = Studien, pp. 468 f.). So there is nothing in Horace's vocative Licini to preclude the view that the eminent subject of the ode (9 ff.) is Maecenas's brother-in-law.

Horace makes other possible allusions to the same person. In the Satires he mentions a Murena who gave his party hospitality at Formiae (1. 5. 38); this man may have been a relative of his patron (cf. Cic. epist. 16. 12. 6 for an A. Varro in the same neighbourhood, perhaps the conspirator's father). Elsewhere the poet praises Proculeius for helping his impoverished brothers (carm. 2. 2. 5 ff.); Maecenas's Murena was one of them (Dio 54. 3. 5). The augur Murena who is celebrated in the symposium of carm. 3. 19 might also be the Licinius of our poem; thus Horace speaks of the same man both as Aristius and Fuscus (vol. i, pp. 261 f.). Yet all this falls short of proof, and it is time for a disregarded piece of evidence to be thrown into the scales. Strabo records how the philosopher Athenaeus of Seleuceia (in Cilicia) was involved in Murena's fall (14. 5. 4): εἶτ᾽ ἐμπεσὼν εἰς τὴν Μουρήνα φιλίαν ἐκείνῳ συνεάλω φεύγων, φωραθείσης τῆς κατὰ Καίσαρος τοῦ Σεβαστοῦ συσταθείσης ἐπιβουλῆς· ἀναίτιος δὲ φανεὶς ἀφείθη ὑπὸ Καίσαρος. The story of the joint escape suggests that he was a 'domestic chaplain' in Murena's household (like Philodemus in Piso's and Diodotus in Cicero's). The significant thing is that Athenaeus was one of the leading Peripatetics of the day (Str. loc. cit. ἄνδρες ἀξιόλογοι τῶν ἐκ τοῦ περιπάτου φιλοσόφων Ἀθήναιός τε καὶ

Ξέναρχος). Horace's ode is a commendation of the middle way, and the *mediocritas* which he enjoins was a Peripatetic watchword (5 n.). As Horace delights to allude to the tastes of his addressees, it would be a strange coincidence if the Licinius of the ode were somebody other than Athenaeüs's patron.

The date of Murena's downfall is a much more intractable problem. Dio, the only narrative source (54. 3), assigns the trial of Primus and the ensuing conspiracy to 22 B.C. The trouble is caused by the entry in the Capitoline Fasti for the beginning of 23 B.C. (*inscr. Ital.* 13. 1. 59 and tab. xxxviii, frr. xlii–xliii):

> A. T[erentius A. f. — n. Var]ro Murena
> [14 or 15 letters] est. in e(ius) l(ocum) f(actus) e(st)
> Cn. Calpurn]ius Cn. f. Cn. n. Pis[o

The consulship of this Murena is omitted by the other Fasti, which treat Calpurnius Piso as *consul ordinarius* with Augustus; hence many moderns identify the consul with the conspirator, put the date of the conspiracy in 23 rather than Dio's 22, and posit that Murena was driven from office and omitted from most Fasti (Stockton, Jameson, opp. citt.). The difference of *praenomen* does not cause an insuperable difficulty: *L.* in Velleius may be a corruption for *Licinius*, or Varro Murena may have had two *praenomina* (Treggiari, op. cit., p. 256 suggests that he was born before his father's adoption). The lacuna in the inscription presents an annoying problem; *in mag. damnatus* is constitutionally impossible (he would have to demit office first), and *magistratu motus* (Hanslik) lacks satisfactory parallels. Alternatively it has been suggested that the Murena of the inscription died or was condemned while still consul-designate; in such cases an entry sometimes appears in the Capitoline Fasti but is omitted elsewhere (Swan, op. cit.).

The year 23 was marked by a notable series of events that may throw light on our problem. During the consulship of Augustus and Piso the Princeps fell seriously ill (Dio 53. 30. 1); on any realistic view of human nature, speculation and intrigue must have been rife. Augustus's build-up of Marcellus (1. 12. 46 n.), the son of his sister Octavia, had alarmed senatorial sentiment; when he had given him his daughter and the aedileship in preference to his stepson Tiberius, the empress Livia must have been grievously mortified. Maecenas may have looked with favour on the young man's hopes (he could expect nothing from the disapproving eyes of Agrippa and Livia), and Murena may also have had points of contact. The Athenaeus Mechanicus who dedicated a work on artillery to one Marcellus (ed. R. Schneider, *Abh. Gött. Wiss.* 12. 5, 1912) seems to have been Murena's Peripatetic friend (Cichorius 271 ff., F. Lammert, *RhM* 87, 1938, 333);

among the philosophers he cites in his preface are Aristotle and the
Peripatetic Strato (fr. 14 Wehrli). Vitruvius, who uses Athenaeus's
work (Lammert, loc. cit.) belonged to the same cultured circle (1
praef. 2 to Augustus 'per sororis commendationem') ; he may even
have had connections with Formiae (*RE* 14. 966, more speculatively
9 A. 437 f.), where the Murenae had a villa (at Vitr. 2. 8. 9 'aedilitatem
Varronis et Murenae' McDermott, op. cit., p. 258, deletes *et*). Another
member of the group was the Stoic Athenodorus Calvus, who like
Athenaeus came from Cilicia (Cichorius 279 ff., Bowersock 32 ff.,
39 f., *RE* Suppl. 5. 47 ff.) ; he is a significant source for Horace in the
Epistles (McGann 26 ff.).

Augustus unexpectedly recovered and quickly resolved the
anxieties of the senate. At the end of June 23 he gave up his annual
consulship, thereby releasing places for the ambitious; his successor,
Sestius, was a former Republican, as indeed was his colleague Piso.
He based his regime instead on the so-called *tribunicia potestas*,
which gave him as much real power but could be represented as
a retreat. He pleased loyalists so much at the trial of Primus that
he was given the additional right to convene the senate as often as he
pleased (Dio 54. 3. 3, H. F. Pelham, *Essays on Roman History*, 1911,
pp. 77 f.) ; as the consul had this right without restriction, this implies
that the new constitution preceded the trial of Primus, and *a fortiori* that Murena lost his office to Piso considerably earlier than
the conspiracy (cf. J. P. V. D. Balsdon, *Gnomon* 33, 1961, 395). In the
summer of 23 Augustus also acquired *maius imperium* even in the
senatorial provinces; this looks like an attempt to resolve some of
the constitutional uncertainties that had been revealed by Primus's
operations (Stockton, op. cit., p. 29). But the point may have less
significance for the chronology than is sometimes supposed. Perhaps
Primus committed his alleged offence in the first half of 23 but was
tried after his return in 22 ; though the rules about *imperium* had
been changed in the interval, the senate, under the delusion that
it had won over-all concessions, may still have insisted that war
could not be waged in its provinces without its own consent.

The new constitution must be seen as a decisive defeat for Marcellus and his associates. Agrippa had proved more than a match
for his youthful rival (cf. Vell. 2. 93. 1), and when he was given
Augustus's ring from his sick-bed, it was a clear indication that he
was regarded as the heir (Dio 53. 30. 2, P. Sattler, *Augustus und der
Senat*, 1960, p. 67). Soon afterwards he was dispatched to the East
with Augustus's full confidence (Syme 342), perhaps to secure the
legions in Syria, where Murena's brother may have been legate (cf.
Jameson, op. cit., p. 219). The triumph of the senatorial party was
complete when Marcellus died towards the end of 23 (for the time of

year cf. Jameson, op. cit., pp. 214 ff., Swan, op. cit., p. 242). The grief
and jealousy of his mother Octavia knew no bounds (Sen. *dial.* 6. 2.
3–5), in spite of a consolation from Athenodorus Calvus (Plut. *Public.*
17. 5, Cichorius 281 f.). The young man had been treated by Anto-
nius Musa, Augustus's own doctor and an eminent pharmacologist
(Galen 13. 463 K.); it is hardly surprising that the scandal-mongers
suspected Livia (Dio 53. 33. 4).

The events of 22 suit the changed balance of power (if Dio's
chronology may for the moment be accepted). When Primus was
tried for his disregard of the senate's assumed prerogatives he alleged instructions from Augustus (Dio 54. 3. 2), but the Princeps
denied the charge, perhaps as part of his renewed understanding
with the senate. The accused man next pleaded directions from
Marcellus (which he had no legal authority to give); if Marcellus
had still been alive (as is believed by those who reject Dio's chronology), he would surely have been repudiated a second time (cf.
Hanslik, op. cit., p. 285). Primus's counsel Murena was naturally
indignant at the treatment of his client (perhaps he saw a parallel to
his own betrayal the previous year), and he expressed himself with
Republican candour. Soon afterwards he was accused of having
conspired with Fannius Caepio to assassinate Augustus (Suet. *Aug.*
19. 1, 56. 4); the two men were convicted *in absentia*, and killed after
a dramatic attempt at escape (Macr. *sat.* 1. 11. 21). Athenaeus, who
had joined their flight, was generously acquitted (Str. 14. 5. 4),
and returned to Cilicia with the words ἥκω νεκρῶν κευθμῶνα καί
σκότου πύλας / λιπών (Eur. *Hec.* 1 f., Bowersock 35). Maecenas had
early news of the discovery of the plot, and in his terrible dilemma
betrayed the secret to his wife Terentia (Suet. *Aug.* 66. 3); predic-
tably she informed her brother, who may have gone into hiding at
this point. Though Augustus was astute enough to foresee this
outcome (he must have hoped for a tactful suicide rather than
another state trial), he could not overlook the indiscretion of his increasingly embarrassing minister. Maecenas lost the substance if not
the semblance of imperial favour (cf. Tac. *ann.* 3. 30. 3–4)—to the
great detriment of humane letters; the lightning had indeed hit the
mountain-tops.

The first three books of Horace's odes seem to have been given to
the world in the consulship of Sestius, that is to say in the second
half of 23 (vol. i, p. xxxvi); before the constitutional crisis was resolved he had not even the authority of a consul-designate, and the
prominence given to him in 1. 4 would have seemed inappropriate.
It must now be considered how the date of 'publication' suits various hypotheses. (1) Suppose the ode was written before 23 B.C. and
contained simply a string of conventional aphorisms. It would be

a strange coincidence if Horace warned Murena about the perils of
success before he had become consul, and consoled him for misfortune before he was removed from office, only to see his words
miraculously fulfilled before or after the publication of the poem.
(2) This coincidence is diminished but not removed if the recipient
of the ode (i.e. Maecenas's brother-in-law) is a different person from
the consul of 23. In that case Horace writes about the dangers of the
mountain-tops to a man who has not reached the summit (but soon
meets with disaster), and he publishes his poem within a year of the
condemnation or sudden death of a man of similar name who had
attained the consulship. (3) Suppose that the conspiracy is assigned
to 23 (in spite of Dio) and that Murena's dismissal is part of a single
sequence of events. Horace must write the ode in the short period
when Murena is out of favour for insulting Augustus, but has not
yet been accused of treason; this is an inappropriate moment for
warnings against the perils of timidity (3 f.). Then in the second
half of the year he 'publishes' his ode, in spite of the spectacular
scandal that in the meantime has killed Murena, put Athenaeus in
jeopardy, and blighted the political career of Maecenas; in the same
book he praises Proculeius in an expendable stanza for cherishing
his brother Murena (2. 2. 5 ff.), who *ex hypothesi* has just been detected
in conspiracy against Augustus. And Dio in recounting the crisis
misses one of the most sensational facts of all, that Murena was
consul ordinarius when the trouble began.

(4) It seems much more likely that Murena's downfall should be
put in two distinct stages (Hanslik, op. cit.). He may have been
driven from office early in 23, perhaps for showing too great officious-
ness in Marcellus's interest at a time when Augustus's health was
already precarious (there were previous illnesses in 25 and 24); or
he might have been pressed to abandon his prospects while still
consul-designate (cf. Swan, op. cit.). Horace consoles him for his
disappointment, but further catastrophe comes in 22, too late for
changes in the *Odes* but in time for the municipal *Fasti*. It is an
objection to this theory that Murena is described as a good man
apart from his conspiracy (Vell. 2. 91. 2), but perhaps he was removed for being more royalist than the king. It is another difficulty that Velleius puts the death of Marcellus about the time
of the conspiracy (2. 93, Jameson, op. cit., pp. 223 f.), but perhaps
the second stage of Murena's downfall dragged on from the end
of 23 to the spring of 22. It is interestingly suggested that the
extra *Feriae Latinae* of October 23 are in celebration of Murena's
destruction (*inscr. Ital.* 13. 1. 151, Dio 54. 3. 8, Jameson, op. cit.,
pp. 225 f.), but if significance is attached to the publication of
the *Odes* the time-scheme then becomes uncomfortably tight. When

Dio assigns the dedication of Jupiter Tonans to 22 (54. 4. 2), he is thought to have made another mistake for 23, seeing that Augustus left Rome before the consular elections in 22 and dedicated the temple on 1 September (Jameson, op. cit., pp. 226 f.); but the argument is uncertain owing to the electoral confusions of the period (Dio 54. 6. 1–2).

Horace's ode is skilfully adapted to an intermediate stage in his friend's downfall. If Murena were still consul it would be absurd to talk of present misfortunes (17 'si male nunc') and an impropriety to offer good advice, but after his removal from office greater liberties become possible. In his paraeneses Horace normally advised his patrons to do what they are doing already; here he is able to avoid offence by citing Murena's own Peripatetic maxims. The appeal to the experience of humanity lessens the humiliation of the individual; it was also a consolation for Murena to be reminded that he had reached the summit. At the same time there is a trace of *deprecatio* to the Princeps, appropriately wrapped up in third-person allegory: Jove brings back fair weather (for similar allusions to Augustus cf. *epist.* 1. 19. 43 'Iovis auribus', Ov. *met.* 15. 871 'Iovis ira'), and Apollo sometimes prefers the lyre to the bow. Like his divine patron, Augustus sometimes relaxed over poetry (3. 4. 37 ff.); by his graceful and unservile acknowledgement of Murena's fault, Horace is not only offering him a tactful hint (no doubt at Maecenas's suggestion) but putting in a plea for forgiveness.

From the formal point of view Horace's organizational skill is a match for his subtlety in personal relationships. The ode is concerned with the mean between two extremes (as suits the Peripatetic recipient); the topic lends itself to a series of antitheses, which are sustained throughout the poem. The first stanza contains a paraenesis about extremes of conduct; at this stage recklessness is stressed no more than timidity. The second stanza turns to extremes of wealth and life-style (still represented as a matter of personal decision); here by a chiastic arrangement the more flamboyant course is given the emphatic position at the end. The third stanza proceeds from wealth to power (for the sequence cf. 2. 16. 9 n.); this time the three parallel clauses point in the same direction and put the emphasis entirely on a fall from greatness (to suit Licinius's own situation). It should further be observed that the poet has now glided from extremes of conduct to extremes of fortune; 7 f. *invidenda . . . aula* marks the transition from the envy of men to that of the gods.

The second half of the poem begins with a new paraenesis (13 ff.), this time tactfully put in a general form; as extremes of fortune are still the subject, the paraenesis develops into a consolation (15–20). The poet explains that good and bad fortune can easily change: in

the first two sentences (13–17) he holds the balance fairly evenly
between the two possibilities (except that his chiasmus ends with
the more favourable), but in the next two (17–20) he concentrates
entirely on a change from bad to good (thus reversing the pattern of 9–12). He has now resumed his series of antitheses: two
longer sentences come on the outside (13–15, 18–20), two shorter
ones in the middle (West, loc. cit., pp. 48 f.). In the last stanza he
once more addresses Licinius (which he has not done since the beginning of the poem); he also returns to the navigational metaphor
of the opening lines (though weather imagery of different sorts is
found in the central stanzas). Now he combines the themes of conduct and fortune: one should adjust one's actions to counterbalance
the prevailing conditions (for moral weighting cf. Arist. *Nic. eth.*
1109ᵃ30 διὸ δεῖ τὸν στοχαζόμενον τοῦ μέσου πρῶτον μὲν ἀποχωρεῖν τοῦ
μᾶλλον ἐναντίου, Sen. *epist.* 13. 12 'vitio vitium repelle, spe metum
tempera'). This time the warning against pride is put in the emphatic
last position (the opposite order from lines 1–4, and yet another
instance of ring-composition); thus Horace not only gives Licinius
appropriate advice but insinuates that all is not lost. The poem's
dense argument and intricate structure perhaps suit an address to
a would-be Peripatetic; certainly the short and usually self-contained
Sapphic stanza lends itself to clipped aphorisms (cf. 2. 2). But the
imagery is poetic rather than philosophic: the dead metaphors of
rocks and wind are reactivated by ingenious accumulation. And
though Horace's reasoned maxims may seem at first sight to lack
universal appeal (contrast 2. 16), in fact he is applying his tact as
well as his intelligence to a very real human predicament. It is easy
to understand why the ode was a particular favourite with educated
men of affairs in the seventeenth century.

Metre: Sapphic.

1. rectius vives : cf. *epist.* 1. 6. 29 'vis recte vivere', 1. 16. 17, Cic.
Tusc. 5. 12, etc.; the phrase suits a man of Murena's philosophical
interests. *recte* suggests a straight course (Lucr. 6. 28, C. M. Bowra,
Pindar, 1964, pp. 252 f., Bramble 118 n. 1); it therefore coheres with
the nautical image that follows. The implication of the comparison
is simply 'than if you pursue extremes'; there is no overt criticism
of Licinius's present behaviour. The formal future suits the senten-
tiousness of the admonition.

   neque . . . : the voyage of life was a natural metaphor to the
nautical Greeks (cf. Pl. *leg.* 803 b, C. Bonner, *H. Theol. Rev.* 34, 1941,
49 ff., H. Rahner, *Greek Myths and Christian Mystery*, English translation, 1963, pp. 328 ff.); in particular the story of Scylla and Charyb-

dis was given moral applications, especially in late antiquity (Otto 82). For a striking parallel to Horace's expression cf. Lollius Bassus, *anth. P.* 10. 102 μήτε με χείματι πόντος ἄγοι θρασύς, οὐδὲ γαλήνης / ἀργῆς ἠσπασάμην τὴν πολυνηνεμίην. / αἱ μεσότητες ἄρισται· ὅπη δέ γε πρήξιες ἀνδρῶν, / καὶ πάλι μέτρον ἐγὼ τάρκιον ἠσπασάμην. / τοῦτ' ἀγάπα, φίλε Λάμπι, κακὰς δ' ἔχθαιρε θυέλλας· / εἰσί τινες πρηεῖς καὶ βιότου ζέφυροι. Bassus, who wrote on the death of Germanicus in 19 A.D. (*anth. P.* 7. 391), seems to be imitating Horace rather than relying on a common source (cf. Pasquali 205 f.) ; μεσότητες is unusually philosophical to have been originated by a Greek poet (curiously in this respect the Roman poets were more enterprising), and Horace's *mediocritas* suits Licinius so well (above, pp. 152 f.) that it is likely to be independent. For less close parallels cf. further Prop. 3. 3. 23 f. 'alter remus aquas, alter tibi radat harenas: / tutus eris', Ov. *met.* 2. 137 'medio tutissimus ibis' (with Bömer's note), Sen. *Herc. O.* 694 ff. 'stringat tenuis litora puppis / nec magna meas aura phaselos / iubeat medium scindere pontum: / transit tutos Fortuna sinus / medioque rates quaerit in alto, / quarum feriunt sipara nubes', *Ag.* 103 ff., *Oed.* 882 ff.

altum . . . : 'the high seas', contrasted with *litus* (so Virg. *Aen.* 5. 163 f.) ; the word also suggests the idea of political height (cf. the third stanza). *urgendo* is stronger than *premendo* below; though applicable to literal force, it is· not quite natural with *altum*, and better suits Murena's uncompromising perseverance. With careful tact Horace advises against ambition only when it is too persistent (*semper*) ; the word is balanced by *nimium* below.

2. procellas . . . horrescis : political storms are common in Latin; cf. also *ars* 28 'serpit humi tutus nimium timidusque procellae' (of the unenterprising poet). In our passage the verb is edged, as the sea and cornfields literally 'shiver at the storm' ; for the same point cf. Virg. *Aen.* 12. 453, Ov. *am.* 2. 11. 25 'cum ventos horret iniquos', *fast.* 2. 147 (see also 2. 13. 15 n.).

3. premendo : cf. Ov. *ars* 1. 40 'haec erit admissa meta premenda rota' (where *terenda* is a variant). As *premere* can almost mean 'to smooth down', there may be a slight verbal point in the collocation with *iniquum*.

4. litus : for the metaphor cf. Theognis 575 f., 855 f., Péron 309 ff. It may be significant that the fish *murena* (or murry) was caught when it came to the shore; cf. Arist. *hist. anim.* 543ª28 f. ἐξέρχονται δὲ ταῦτα εἰς τὸ ξηρόν, καὶ λαμβάνονται πολλάκις, Plin. *nat.* 9. 76, 32. 14 'ob id sibilo a piscatoribus tamquam a serpentibus evocari et capi' (it was believed to mate on land with snakes), Nicander, *ther.* 825 f.

with Gow's note, D'Arcy Thompson, *Fishes*, p. 163, *RE* 16. 1. 653 f. One might be tempted to suspect a characteristically Roman allusion to Licinius's *cognomen*, which an ancestor had derived from his fishponds (Colum. 8. 16. 5 'velut ante devictarum gentium Numantinus et Isauricus, ita Sergius Orata et Licinius Muraena captorum piscium laetabantur vocabulis'). The objection to such a theory is not so much the obscurity of the information (for it is widely attested) as a feeling that the occasion is inappropriate for such frivolities; yet the ancient attitude to puns on names was very different from our own, and the seriousness of Murena's predicament at this stage should not be exaggerated.

iniquum : a litotes for 'hostile' or 'dangerous'. The word also suggests the literal unevenness of shallow waters (for *litus* in this sense cf. 2. 18. 21 n.); the same ambiguity is found at Virg. *Aen.* 10. 303 'inflicta vadi dorso dum pendet iniquo'.

5. auream : the adjective implies outstanding value; cf. 4. 2. 22 f. 'moresque aureos', Lucr. 3. 12 'aurea dicta', Aug. *civ.* 18. 18 'Apuleius in libris quos asini aurei titulo inscripsit'. It is naturally used by lovers (1. 5. 9 n.) and by moralists (Pl. *leg.* 645 a τὴν τοῦ λογισμοῦ ἀγωγὴν χρυσῆν καὶ ἱεράν, Lucian, *Men.* 4 χρυσοῦν . . . βίον); on both counts it suits *diligit*. In our passage the adjective makes a brilliant oxymoron with *mediocritas* (which sometimes has an implication of mediocrity); it is contrasted alike with *obsoleti* and with the literal glitter of the rich man's *aula* (D. West, loc. cit., p. 49). Horace's phrase is repeated by Ausonius (419. 28), and the 'Golden Mean' is attested in English from 1587 (*Oxford Dictionary of Proverbs*³, 1970, p. 317).

mediocritatem : moderation was a persistent ideal of poets; cf. Hes. *op.* 694, Theognis 220, 331, Phocylides 12 D. πολλὰ μέσοισιν ἄριστα· μέσος θέλω ἐν πόλει εἶναι, Pind. *P.* 11. 52 f. τῶν γὰρ ἀνὰ πόλιν εὑρίσκων τὰ μέσα μακροτέρῳ / ὄλβῳ τεθαλότα μέμφομ' αἶσαν τυραννίδων, Aesch. *Eum.* 529 with Groeneboom, *trag. adesp.* 547. 3 ff. N. οὐδ' ἀσφαλὲς πᾶν ὕψος ἐν θνητῷ γένει / . . . ἡ δὲ μεσότης ἐν πᾶσιν ἀσφαλεστέρα . . . , Palladas, *anth. P.* 10. 51. 5 f. ἡ μεσότης γὰρ ἄριστον, ἐπεὶ τὰ μὲν ἄκρα πέφυκεν / κινδύνους ἐπάγειν, ἔσχατα δ' ὕβριν ἔχει. As Murena was nominally a Peripatetic (above, pp. 152 f.), Horace is alluding particularly to the Aristotelian doctrine that excellence lies within an intermediate range on a scale (not necessarily the half-way mark); cf. *Nic. eth.* 1106ᵃ27 ff., W. F. R. Hardie, *Aristotle's Ethical Theory*, 1968, pp. 129 ff. For Latin references cf. *serm.* 1. 1. 106 f. 'est modus in rebus, sunt certi denique fines / quos ultra citraque nequit consistere rectum', *epist.* 1. 18. 9 'virtus est medium vitiorum et utrimque reductum', Cic. *Mur.* 63, *Brut.* 149 'cum omnis virtus sit . . . mediocritas', *Tusc.* 3. 22, *off.* 1. 89 'mediocritatem illam . . . quae est inter nimium et parum, quae placet Peripateticis et recte placet' (at *Tim.* 23 he invents and rejects the rendering *medietas*).

6. diligit : the word suggests the philosopher's choice (προαίρεσις) more than the English 'love'.

tutus : Bentley took with *diligit*; this would give the adjective the common meaning of 'careful' or 'playing safe' (*serm.* 2. 1. 20 'recalcitrat undique tutus', Brink on *ars* 28, Shackleton Bailey, *Propertiana*, pp. 86 f.). But it is much better to punctuate after *diligit* and to refer *tutus* to the objective security of an established home; cf. *trag. adesp.* (cited on 5) ἀσφαλεστέρα, Sen. *Herc. f.* 199 f. 'humilique loco sed certa sedet / sordida parvae fortuna domus', *Herc. O.* 675 f. In that case *tutus* formally balances *sobrius*, though the function of the two adjectives is different: the former expresses the result of freedom from poverty, the latter the condition of freedom from envy. It is no objection to this punctuation that *caret* is second word in the first clause and first word in the second; for this pattern cf. *ciris* 391 f., Juv. 6. 585 f.

caret : 'avoids'; the verb is sometimes more positive than 'lacks' (cf. 2. 14. 13 n.).

obsoleti : 'dilapidated'; the word goes well with *sordibus* (cf. *epod.* 17. 46, Cic. *Sest.* 60).

7. invidenda : the ancients took it for granted that grand houses aroused envy; cf. 3. 1. 45 'invidendis postibus', Mart. *spect.* 2. 3. For the advantages of the middle way cf. Arist. *pol.* 1295ᵇ30 f. (on the μέσοι or middle classes) οὔτε γὰρ αὐτοὶ τῶν ἀλλοτρίων ὥσπερ οἱ πένητες ἐπιθυμοῦσιν οὔτε τῆς τούτων ἕτεροι, Sotades fr. 10. 1 f. Powell ὁ πένης ἐλεεῖται, ὁ δὲ πλούσιος φθονεῖται, / ὁ μέσως δὲ βίος κεκραμένος δίκαιός ἐστιν, *anth. Lat.* 276.

8. sobrius : pointedly juxtaposed with *aula*, the last place to expect *sobrietas*. The word may have suggested σώφρων in meaning as well as sound (cf. *CGL* 3. 332. 60). The mention of a palace leads naturally from the dangers of wealth to the dangers of power (9 ff.).

9. saepius . . . : the illustrations of the perils of greatness go back to Hdt. 7. 10 ε (the speech of Artabanus to Xerxes) ὁρᾷς τὰ ὑπερέχοντα ζῷα ὡς κεραυνοῖ ὁ θεὸς οὐδὲ ἐᾷ φαντάζεσθαι, τὰ δὲ σμικρὰ οὐδέν μιν κνίζει· ὁρᾷς δὲ ὡς ἐς οἰκήματα τὰ μέγιστα αἰεὶ καὶ δένδρεα τὰ τοιαῦτα ἀποσκήπτει τὰ βέλεα. φιλέει γὰρ ὁ θεὸς τὰ ὑπερέχοντα πάντα κολούειν. The theme becomes a commonplace; cf. especially Lucr. 5. 1131 f. 'invidia quoniam, ceu fulmine, summa vaporant / plerumque et quae sunt aliis magis edita cumque' (for lightning cf. 1. 2. 3 n.), Lucr. 6. 421 f., Maecen. ap. Sen. *epist.* 19. 9 'ipsa enim altitudo attonat

summa', Liv. 45. 35. 5 'intacta invidia media sunt: ad summa ferme
tendit', Ov. *rem.* 369 f. 'summa petit livor: perflant altissima
venti; summa petunt dextra fulmina missa Iovis', Sen. *Ag.* 92 ff.,
Phaedr. 1125 ff., *Oed.* 8, *Octavia* 897 f. 'quatiunt altas saepe procellae /
aut evertit Fortuna domos', Vollmer on Stat. *silv.* 2. 7. 90, Otto 148,
Nachträge, p. 165. A variation is the story of beheading the tall stalks
(Hdt. 5. 92 ζ. 2, Liv. 1. 54. 6, Ov. *fast.* 2. 705 ff.); for the contrast
between the stubborn oak and the pliant reed cf. Soph. *Ant.* 712 ff.,
Aesop 101 Chambry (= 71 Hausrath), Lucianus, *anth. P.* 10. 122. 5 f.
οὐ θρύον οὐ μαλάχην ἄνεμός ποτε, τὰς δὲ μεγίστας / ἢ δρύας ἢ πλατά-
νους οἶδε χάμαι κατάγειν, Babrius 36, Avian. *fab.* 16, Macr. *sat.* 7. 8. 6,
E. Grawi, *Die Fabel vom Baum und dem Schilfrohr in der Weltlitera-
tur*, Diss. Rostock, 1911.

    saevius was a conjecture for *saepius* in the Rouen edition of 1701;
for the confusion of *v* and *p* in Horace cf. Housman 1. 102 = *JPh* 17,
1888, 316 (who looks with favour on *saevius* here). It seems in fact
to have been an ancient variant (C. O. Brink, *PCPhS* 17, 1971, 23 ff.);
cf. the imitations by Fronto 209 N. (= 199 van den Hout) 'sed profecto sicut arborum altissimas vehementius ventis quati videmus, ita
virtutes maximas invidia criminosius insectatur', Isid. *synon.* 2. 89
'alta arbor a ventis fortius agitatur et rami eius citius in ruina con-
fringuntur, excelsae turres graviore casu procumbunt, altissimi
montes crebris fulminibus feriuntur'. On the other hand cf. Porphyrio on 11 'et hic et in superiore *saepius* per zeugma accipiendum,
ut sit *saepius feriunt*'; though somewhat overstated, this note shows
that *saepius* was also an ancient reading.

    It is argued that *saevius* is necessary in order to give a proper
balance to *graviore* in the next line; it could be suggested on the
other hand that the absence of a corresponding comparative in the
third clause (lightning either hits or misses) tells against a strong
word like *saevius* here (contrast the references to height, *ingens . . .
celsae . . . summos*, which appear in all three clauses). The adjective
saevus can be used of winds even in informal contexts (Cic. *Att.* 5. 12. 1
'saevo vento'), but the personification suits the adverb less well; and
agitatur does not seem quite strong enough to be combined with it.
By comparison *saepius* may seem banal to some, but words like
πολλάκις are often found in gnomic statements; in the passages cited
above note αἰεί (Hdt.), *plerumque* (Lucr., cf. 1. 34. 7 n., Cic. *div.* 2. 45
'quid cum in altissimos montis, quod plerumque fit'), *ferme* (Liv.),
saepe (*Octavia*).

10. graviore casu : cf. *trag. adesp.* 547. 11 N. ὄγκου δὲ μεγάλου πτῶμα
γίγνεται μέγα, Liv. 30. 30. 23, Lucian, *Charon* 14 ἐπαιρέσθωσαν ὡς ἂν
ἀφ' ὑψηλοτέρου ἀλγεινότερον καταπεσούμενοι, Juv. 10. 105 ff. 'numerosa

parabat / excelsae turris tabulata unde altior esset / casus et impulsae praeceps immane ruinae', Hosius on *Octavia* 377 ff., 896, A. Cameron, *Claudian*, 1970, p. 331 n. 1. Before engineering became a science, *ruinae* were commoner (already a topic at Catull. 23. 9) ; the ancient buildings that have survived were good ones. For the grandiloquent *figura etymologica* with *decidunt* cf. Lucr. 1. 741 'et graviter magni magno cecidere ibi casu'. The alliteration with *celsae* reinforces the epigram (so below 'feriuntque . . . fulgura').

12. fulgura : some have wished to read *fulmina*, the proper word for the bolt as opposed to the flash ; cf. Sen. *Ag.* 96, *Phaedr.* 1132 (both imitations). But Horace's text is supported by two of the three *testimonia* in Jerome (*epist.* 60. 16, 108. 18), and *fulgur* can bear the required meaning (*Thes.l.L.* 6. 1. 1519. 79 ff.).

13. infestis : probably with the passive meaning 'exposed to danger', 'insecure'. The interpretation 'hostile' is admittedly closer to *adversis* (the normal opposite of *secundis*), and it suits the weather imagery of the poem ; on the other hand *sortem* suggests that Horace is thinking of the victim rather than of the storm. For the dative cf. Sall. *Cat.* 40. 2 'quem exitum tantis malis sperarent', *Thes.l.L.* 5. 1. 741. 38 ff. ; for the dative with *metuere* cf. 2. 8. 21, *Thes.l.L.* 8. 904. 38 ff. Ablatives ('in times of trouble', etc.) would bind the sentence much less effectively.

metuit secundis : for this kind of contrast cf. 2. 3. 1 n. Compare Asinius Pollio's comment on Cicero (Sen. *suas.* 6. 24) 'utinam moderatius secundas res et fortius adversas ferre potuisset ; namque utraeque cum evenerant ei, mutari eas non posse rebatur', Sen. *nat. 3 praef.* 8 'in melius adversa, in deterius optata flectuntur'.

14. alteram : with the second member the adjective is euphemistic for *malam*; cf. Pind. *P.* 3. 34, Soph. *Phil.* 503, Dem. 22. 12 ἀγάθ' ἢ θάτερα, ἵνα μηδὲν εἴπω φλαῦρον.

bene praeparatum : to be prepared for trouble (προφυλάξασθαι) was the advice of many philosophers, especially Stoics; cf. Diog. Laert. 6. 63 (on Diogenes the Cynic) ἐρωτηθεὶς τί αὐτῷ περιγέγονεν ἐκ φιλοσοφίας ἔφη Εἰ καὶ μηδὲν ἄλλο, τὸ γοῦν πρὸς πᾶσαν τύχην παρεσκευάσθαι, Ter. *Phorm.* 241 ff. 'quam ob rem omnis, quom secundae res sunt maxume, tum maxume / meditari secum oportet quo pacto advorsam aerumnam ferant, / pericla damna exilia ; peregre rediens semper cogitet / aut fili peccatum aut uxori' mortem aut morbum filiae : / communia esse haec, fieri posse, ut ne quid animo sit novom; / quidquid praeter spem eveniat, omne id deputare esse in lucro', Cic. *Tusc.* 3. 28 ff., *off.* 1. 81 'illud etiam ingeni magni est, praecipere cogitatione futura et aliquanto ante constituere quid accidere possit in

utramque partem, . . . nec committere ut aliquando dicendum sit
"non putaram"', Virg. *Aen.* 6. 103 ff. 'non ulla laborum, / o virgo,
nova mi facies inopinave surgit; / omnia praecepi atque animo
mecum ante peregi' (with Norden's note), Sen. *epist.* 18. 6, 77. 3–5,
78. 29, 91. 8, 107. 4, *dial.* 7. 8. 3, *Phaedr.* 994, ps.-Plut. *cons. Apoll.*
103 f, 112 d, Housman, *More Poems* 6 'So I was ready When trouble
came'. The opposite case was put by the Epicureans: cf. Cic. *Tusc.*
3. 32 'nam neque vetustate minui mala neque fieri praemeditata
leviora, stultamque etiam esse meditationem futuri mali aut fortasse
ne futuri quidem; satis esse odiosum malum omne cum venisset
. . .'. See further Pohlenz 2. 82, P. Rabbow, *Seelenführung*, 1954,
pp. 160 ff., Kassel 66 ff., 87 f., C. C. Grollios, *Seneca's ad Marciam:
Tradition and Originality*, Athens, 1956, pp. 48 ff., Otto, *Nachträge*,
p. 203.

15. pectus : the syntactical break after the second syllable is attested
elsewhere in Horace's Sapphics only at 1. 2. 49 and 2. 16. 18. But the
pause need not be long, as the ode here begins to gather momentum;
cf. the enjambement at the end of the stanza.

informis : Southerners are depressed by the dreariness of wintry
landscapes, whether because of snow or the lack of vegetation. Cf.
Virg. *georg.* 3. 354 'aggeribus niveis informis (terra)' (Serv. ad loc.
'nivis superfusione carens varietate formarum'), Sen. *Herc. O.* 384
'deforme solis aspicis truncis nemus', *apocol.* 2. 1, Sil. 3. 489, Juv.
4. 58, Claud. *carm. min.* 39. 3, Lucian, *Sat.* 9 τὰ δένδρα ξηρὰ καὶ γυμνὰ
καὶ ἄφυλλα καὶ οἱ λειμῶνες ἄμορφοι. At *epod.* 13. 18 'deformis aegrimoniae' the adjective helps to sustain the weather imagery of the
poem.

reducit : such words are readily used of the cycles of nature; cf.
3. 29. 20 'referente', Virg. *georg.* 1. 249. For the comparison of changing
weather with human vicissitudes cf. 2. 9. 1 n.

17. submovet : perhaps like a lictor 'moving on' a crowd (cf. 2. 16.
10). For a similar personification cf. Soph. *Ai.* 670 f. τοῦτο μὲν
νιφοστιβεῖς / χειμῶνες ἐκχωροῦσιν εὐκάρπῳ θέρει.

olim : 'one day'; cf. Theoc. 4. 41 τάχ' αὔριον ἔσσετ' ἄμεινον, Tib.
2. 6. 19 f. (with K. F. Smith's note). *quondam* below means 'sometimes', like ποτε in maxims.

18. citharae : Bentley preferred the genitive to the variant *cithara*;
cf. 2. 1. 9 'Musa tragoediae', Eur. *Hyps.* fr. 64. 101 Bond μοῦσαν . . .
κιθάρας Ἀσιάδος. He argued that *musam* refers to the music and not
to an external mythological personage: 'non enim hoc vult Horatius,
Apollinem nescioquam ex novem sororibus tacentem vel dormientem
cithara sua suscitare' (it is no objection to this view that *musam*

balances *Apollo*). The music is latent in the lyre itself, and does not have to be evoked out of the air; in these circumstances it is awkward to say 'awakens with the lyre'. Heinze argues that *cithara* makes a sharper contrast with *arcum*, but *citharae* could also be emphatic; it perhaps even suggests that the κλαγγή of the two instruments alternates.

19. suscitat: the lyre when played is like a sleeper awakened; cf. Pind. *N.* 10. 21 ἀλλ' ὅμως εὔχορδον ἔγειρε λύραν, *I.* 8. 3 with Thummer's note, Eur. *Hipp.* 1135 μοῦσα . . . ἄυπνος, Cratinus 222. 1 K., Ar. *ran.* 370, Lucr. 2. 412 f. 'musaea mele, per chordas organici quae / mobilibus digitis expergefacta figurant', Gray, *Progress of Poesy* 1 'Awake, Aeolian lyre, awake'. For *tacentem* cf. Call. *h.* 2. 12 σιωπηλὴν κίθαριν.

neque semper: as so often in Horace there is an alternation of positive and negative propositions. *semper* not only balances 18 *quondam* but echoes 2 *semper*; it is the disregard of *mediocritas* that is criticized.

arcum: even Apollo the destroyer (3. 4. 60, 4. 6. 1 ff.) sometimes assumes a more kindly aspect; cf. 1. 21. 11 n. (the juxtaposition of the god's two stringed instruments), *carm. saec.* 33 'condito mitis placidusque telo' (Serv. *Aen.* 3. 138 'contra si citharam teneat, mitis est'), *h. Ap.* 6 ff., Prop. 4. 6. 69, *laus Pis.* 142 f., *eleg. in Maecen.* 1. 51 f., Sen. *Ag.* 326 ff. 'arcus victor pace relata, / Phoebe, relaxa / . . . resonetque manu pulsa citata / vocale chelys'. For an apparent reference to Augustus see above, p. 157; this gives a good sequence of thought after 'non si male nunc, et olim / sic erit'. The image of the taut bowstring normally occurs in exhortations to relax, and Horace may be hinting indirectly that this is the best course for everybody; cf. Hdt. 2. 173. 3 (King Amasis defends himself for following business with pleasure) τὰ τόξα οἱ ἐκτημένοι, ἐπεὰν μὲν δέωνται χρᾶσθαι, ἐντανύουσι, ἐπεὰν δὲ χρήσωνται, ἐκλύουσι. εἰ γὰρ δὴ τὸν πάντα χρόνον ἐντεταμένα εἴη, ἐκραγείη ἄν, ὥστε ἐς τὸ δέον οὐκ ἂν ἔχοιεν αὐτοῖσι χρᾶσθαι. οὕτω δὴ καὶ ἀνθρώπου κατάστασις· εἰ ἐθέλοι κατεσπουδάσθαι αἰεὶ (*semper*) μηδὲ ἐς παιγνίην τὸ μέρος ἑωυτὸν ἀνιέναι, λάθοι ἂν ἤτοι μανεὶς ἢ ὅ γε ἀπόπληκτος γενόμενος. τὰ ἐγὼ ἐπιστάμενος μέρος ἑκατέρῳ νέμω (cf. Arist. *Nic. eth.* 1176b32 ff.), Ov. *epist.* 4. 91 'arcus et arma tuae tibi sunt imitanda Dianae: / si numquam cesses tendere, mollis erit', Phaedr. 3. 14. 10, Stat. *silv.* 4. 4. 30 ff., Dio Chrys. fr. 5 von Arnim καὶ τόξον καὶ λύρα καὶ ἄνθρωπος ἀκμάζει δι' ἀναπαύσεως, gnom. *Vat.* 17 Sternbach, Otto 36, K. Praechter, *Hermes* 47, 1912, 471 ff. (suggesting that the theme was found in such treatises as Athenodorus περὶ σπουδῆς καὶ παιδιᾶς).

21. rebus angustis: 'dire straits' (Petron. 61. 9 'in angustiis amici apparent'), not simply 'straitened circumstances'. The adjective suits the nautical imagery, but it may also have suggested constriction (cf. *ango*) and even anguish (*angor*) more forcibly than English 'narrow'.

animosus : combined with *fortis* by Cicero and others (*Thes.l.L.* 2. 88. 41 ff.). The word suits the imagery of the sentence as it suggests wind (cf. Virg. *georg.* 2. 441 'animosi euri', *Aen.* 1. 57 with Austin's note) ; for the association of wind and pride cf. Onians 170, Péron 170 f. The idea of spiritual inflation makes a contrast with *angustis*.

atque : the only case in the *Odes* of *atque* at the end of a line ; 3. 11. 18 *eius atque* is surely corrupt (*exeatque* Bentley). Perhaps the onward sweep of the lines suggests impetuosity (cf. 2. 6. 2 n.) ; in the same way the alliteration of *a* may convey some special implication (a defiant breath or a persistent wind?).

22. adpare : 'show yourself'; Murena's resolution is to appear in his demeanour. For the use with an adjective cf. *Thes.l.L.* 2. 266. 10 ff.

23. contrahes : the future picks up 1 *vives*. When the wind was too strong the ancients lowered the yard (ὑφίεσθαι) or shortened sail (συστέλλειν); cf. L. Casson, *Ships and Seamanship in the Ancient World*, 1971, pp. 275 ff. The nautical Greeks used sailing metaphors for 'letting oneself go' or 'pulling in one's horns' in speech or behaviour; cf. Pind. *P.* 1. 91 f. ἐξίει δ᾽ ὥσπερ κυβερνάτας ἀνὴρ / ἱστίον ἀνεμόεν, *I.* 2. 39 f. (with Péron 52 ff.), Eur. *Med.* 524 (with Page), Ar. *ran.* 997 ff., 1220 f. (with Taillardat 183 ff.). So Cic. *Att.* 1. 16. 2 'contraxi vela' (*Thes.l.L.* 4. 759. 17 ff.), Prop. 3. 9. 30, Ov. *trist.* 3. 4. 32, Sen. *epist.* 19. 9 'hic te exitus manet nisi iam contrahes vela, nisi quod ille sero voluit, terram leges' (*ille* is Maecenas, and Seneca may have remembered that our ode was about his brother-in-law), *anth. Lat.* 407. 7, Otto, *Nachträge*, p. 223.

secundo : a following wind (*sequendo*), ἵκμενος οὖρος. The adjective picks up 13 *secundis*, and is paradoxically modified by *nimium* (which balances the contrary excess of line 3) ; cf. Sen. *Thy.* 615 f., *Ag.* 90 f. 'vela secundis inflata notis / ventos nimium timuere suos' (*nimium* with *suos*), Soph. *OT* 1314 f. νέφος . . . δυσούριστον.

24. turgida : for the bellying sail of prosperity cf. *epist.* 2. 2. 201 'non agimur tumidis velis aquilone secundo'. The word carries a suggestion of puffed-out pride (Sil. 2. 28 'tumefactaque corda secundis').

11. QVID BELLICOSVS CANTABER

[F. Bücheler, *RhM* 37, 1882, 231 ff. = *Kl. Schr.* 2. 437 ff.; Plüss 151 ff.; F. A. Sullivan, *CPh* 57, 1962, 167 ff.]

1–12. *Do not worry, Quinctius, about far-off enemies or the few requisites of our short lives. Youth and beauty vanish and change, so do not weary yourself with long-term schemes.* 13–24. *Better to drink in this shady pleasance with roses and spikenard for our greying hair. Bring water quickly, boy, from the convenient brook—and an exclusive whore of exquisite simplicity.*

The recipient of this poem is presumably the Quinctius of *epist.* 1. 16; for friends commemorated in epistles as well as odes one may compare Maecenas (*epist.* 1. 1, etc.), Albius Tibullus (1. 4), Manlius Torquatus (1. 5), Septimius (1. 9), Aristius Fuscus (1. 10), Iccius and Grosphus (1. 12). In the epistle Quinctius is spoken to with some warmth (1. 16. 16 'incolumem tibi me praestant Septembribus horis'). It is no matter for surprise that Horace explains to him the layout of his Sabine estate; few of his grander friends could have visited him there, and for literary purposes he might describe even a place that was known to his correspondent. It emerges from the epistle that Quinctius was prosperous and well known (1. 16. 18 'iactamus iampridem omnis te Roma beatum'); this suits the ode's references to long-term scheming and elegant *horti*. If the Stoic tendencies of the epistle seems inconsistent with the Epicureanism of the ode, perhaps Horace is teasing Quinctius for self-conscious righteousness and devotion to business.

Both the ancient and modern commentators have assumed from line 2 of the ode that Hirpinus is Quinctius's *cognomen* (for the word-order cf. 2. 2. 3 n.). In fact Horace is alluding to his sophisticated friend's association with the backwoodsmen of central Italy (cf. Catull. 12. 1 'Marrucine Asini', where *Marrucine* is surely not a *cognomen*). If the emphatic *Hirpine* is taken as geographical it neatly sets off *Hadria* ('the Scythians will have water to cross before they get to you'). Commentators do not observe that about 85 B.C. a certain C. Quinctius C. f. Valgus was patron of Aeclanum, one of the leading towns of the Hirpini (*ILS* 5318); for other mentions of the name cf. *ILS* 5627 (*duovir quinquennalis* at Pompeii), *ILS* 5636, *carm. epig.* 12 (sets up monument at Casinum), *RE* 24. 1103 f. The patron of Aeclanum is to be identified with the Valgus who was father-in-law of Rullus (Cic. *leg. agr.* 3. 3, H. Dessau, *Hermes* 18, 1883, 620 f.); the latter appears as 'Valgius' in many authorities (e.g. *RE* 24. 1104, 8 A. 271), but in fact the manuscript reading *uulgi* (a genitive) is at

least as compatible with 'Valgus'. Cicero reveals that this person
acquired much land during the Sullan proscriptions (*leg. agr.* 2. 69);
see especially 3. 8 'tui soceri fundus Hirpinus ... sive ager Hirpinus
(totum enim possidet)', 3. 14 'eos fundos quos in agro Casinati opti-
mos fructuosissimosque continuavit' (cf. the Casinum inscription
cited above), E. T. Salmon, *Samnium and the Samnites*, 1967, p. 390.
One is strongly impelled to regard Horace's friend (not mentioned in
Dessau's article) as a descendant, perhaps a grandson, of the Sullan
carpet-bagger.

Another more speculative identification may be hazarded. Our
poem introduces the second half of the book, a position elsewhere of
some prominence (cf. 1. 20 and 3. 16 to Maecenas, the central 4. 8
to the political Censorinus); what has Quinctius done to deserve this
distinction? Now Pollio's father-in-law was a Quinctius of unknown
antecedents who was prosperous enough to be proscribed in the
triumviral period (App. *civ.* 4. 12. 46, R. Syme, *Historia* 4, 1955, 68). If
he belonged to one of the new families that made good in central
Italy after the Social War, his daughter would have made an attractive match for an ambitious member of the defeated Marrucine
aristocracy. In that case Horace's friend might be Pollio's brother-
in-law; the first and eleventh poems of the book would balance one
another in the same way as the twentieth (to Maecenas) and the
tenth (to Maecenas's brother-in-law).

The ode breaks naturally into two sections of three stanzas each.
The first half is a paraenesis couched in a fairly general manner:
Quinctius is urged not to worry about things distant in space or
time. In the second half Horace turns to positive recommendations;
it emerges that the adjurations are set in *horti* (presumably his
friend's as in the Dellius Ode), and here the poet recommends an
immediate symposium. In contrast with the leisured reflections of
the first part, the increasingly urgent tone suggests that there is not
much time to lose (13 *cur non?*, 16 *dum licet*, 18 *quis puer ocius?*,
22 *dic age*, 23 *maturet*). The two halves of the poem are linked by
cross-references that connect the general aphorisms with the particular situation; cf. 3 f. *remittas quaerere* . . . 18 *curas*, 6 *arida* . . .
17 *uncti*, 7 *amores* . . . 21 *scortum*, 8 *canitie* . . . 15 *canos*, 9 *floribus*
. . . 14 *rosa*.

Many of the features of Horace's ode have obvious precedents in
Greek lyric or epigram. It was a common theme to describe arrangements for a symposium, with the poet himself giving instructions
to the servants (vol. i, pp. 402, 421 f.). The traditional concomitants
of Greek and Roman parties are all included, wine, perfume, flowers,
and music (2. 3. 13 f., vol. i, p. 402, J. Griffin, *JRS* 66, 1976, 87 ff.); the
customary girl is given literary associations by her Greek name, ivory

lyre (22 n.), and Spartan hair-style. The scene is set out of doors in
an agreeable *amoenus locus*, with the conventional shade and water
(above, pp. 52 f.). The poet represents himself as grey-haired (15 n.)
and somewhat elderly; there are sententious observations on the
passing of youth, the brevity of happiness (16 n.), the consolations of
wine. Horace's themes are particularly common in the *Anacreontea*;
one may compare 7 and especially 30: ἐπὶ μυρσίναις τερείναις / ἐπὶ
λωτίναις τε ποίαις / στορέσας θέλω προπίνειν. / . . . τί σε δεῖ λίθον
μυρίζειν; / τί δὲ γῇ χέειν μάταια; / ἐμὲ μᾶλλον, ὡς ἔτι ζῶ, / μύρισον,
ῥόδοις δὲ κρᾶτα / πύκασον, κάλει δ' ἑταίρην. / πρὶν ἐκεῖσε δεῖ μ' ἀπελθεῖν /
ὑπὸ νερτέρων χορείας / σκεδάσαι θέλω μερίμνας. Here as in our poem we
have open-air repose with wine, perfume, roses, and a girl; here too
we have the *dum licet* motif, the uncertainty of the future, and the
dissipation of cares.

But though Horace's themes are so conventional, he handles them
suo more in an original way. The *Anacreontea* were simple in metre
and naïve in style, but the ode is complex and varied. The idealized
Greek scene is harmonized with a realistic Roman element: the
successful Quinctius is plausibly represented as combining worldly
anxieties with suburban *horti* and a cellar of vintage wine. The incompatible blessings of luxury and simplicity (both belonging to the
tradition) are here juxtaposed with sophisticated humour (cf. perhaps Philodemus, *anth. P.* 11. 34 for a similar ambivalence). The
natural pleasance implies enviable prosperity (13 ff.) and life's modest
needs include the perfumes of the east (16), yet the vintage wine is
allayed by the running brook (19 f.) and even the exotic Lyde wears
an uncomplicated bun (23 f.). In the same way the style of the poem
sometimes affects informality (13 *cur non, vel hac*, 14 *sic temere*, 17
potamus, 18 *ocius*, 23 *maturet*), sometimes grandeur (14 f. *rosa odorati*,
17 n. *dissipat Euhius*); the girl's seclusion is belied by the plain
speaking of *scortum* (21), and her simple hair-style is elaborated with
exquisite involutions (23 n.). The ode has a true Horatian charm that
humorously relates the relaxation of a Roman gentleman to the
hedonism of Greek poetry, and it is hard to believe that even Peerlkamp could have denied its authenticity.

Metre: Alcaic.

1. **Cantaber . . . Scythes**: this most peaceful of odes begins on a
menacing note with foreign enemies in the West and the East.
The Cantabri in N. Spain were notoriously warlike (Str. 3. 3. 8,
Sil. 3. 326 ff.), while the savagery of the Scythians was proverbial
alike in Greek and in Latin (Curt. 4. 6. 3 'Scytharum bellicosissima
gente'). For the use of the singular in military contexts cf. 1. 19. 12 n.

There were Cantabrian wars in 29 B.C., 26/5, and 24 (above, p. 93, vol. i, p. xxxi); the Scythian threat is mentioned in odes of diverse date (vol. i, p. xxxiv). 27/6 B.C. might seem a suitable moment for our poem, when the Cantabrians are giving serious trouble and the Scythians have not yet sent their peace mission of 25 B.C. (Oros. 6. 21. 19). But it could be argued in favour of 29 that Horace is not likely to urge indifference when Augustus is campaigning in the Spanish mountains (26 B.C.).

2. Hadria divisus obiecto: after the threatening *bellicosus* Horace proceeds to reassurance. For natural barriers cf. Cic. *Pis.* 81 'non Alpium vallum contra ascensum transgressionemque Gallorum, non Rheni fossam . . . Germanorum immanissimis gentibus obicio et oppono' (with Nisbet's note), Juv. 10. 152, Flor. *epit.* 3. 4. 1 'Thraces . . . in Hadriaticum mare usque venerunt, eoque fine retenti quasi interveniente natura contorta in ipsas aquas tela miserunt'. Of course the Scythians were kept away by much more than the Adriatic, but the understatement simply emphasizes the absurdity of such anxieties.

One must understand with *Cantaber* 'separated by the Pyrenees and Alps'; for the brachylogy cf. *serm.* 2. 2. 11 ff. 'seu pila velox / . . . seu te discus agit, pete cedentem aera disco', *epist.* 1. 3. 23 ff. The construction is not analogous with that of *bellicosus* above, which is naturally taken ἀπὸ κοινοῦ with both *Cantaber* and *Scythes*. There is no objection to giving the Scythian both an adjective and a participle (in an emphatic new clause); for the colometry cf. 2. 1. 3 ff. 'gravisque / principum amicitias et arma, / nondum expiatis uncta cruoribus' (see note ad loc.). Peerlkamp thought of referring *divisus* to Quinctius, but the word better suits the distant nation (cf. Virg. *Aen.* 3. 383); if the clause is so taken it balances *poscentis . . . pauca* below (cf. 4 n.).

3. remittas quaerere: for the commonplace cf. vol. i, p. 135 and 1. 26. 3 n. In similar contexts Horace uses *mittere* (1. 38. 3 n.), *omittere* (3. 29. 11, *epist.* 1. 18. 79), *fugere* (2. 4. 22 n.); *remittere* suggests the slackening of tension ('forbear') rather than the complete abandonment of concern. For the infinitive cf. Ter. *Andr.* 827, Sall. *Jug.* 52. 5.

4. nec trepides in usum: the weight of the argument is on this clause: 'just as your worry about the Scythians is groundless (because the distances are vast), so too your agitation about your daily bread (for our human needs are small)'. For *usum* cf. Lucr. 6. 9 f. 'ad victum quae flagitat usus / omnia iam ferme mortalibus esse parata', Liv. 26. 43. 7 'quae belli usus poscunt suppeditentur' (see Housman on Manil. 4. 8). *trepides* refers as usual not to fear and trembling but to bustling and excitement (cf. 2. 3. 12, 3. 29. 32); this provides enough of a prospective element to justify *in*.

5. **poscentis aevi pauca** : 'of a life-span that requires but little'. Horace is not only making the philosophical point that men's needs are few (1. 31. 17 n.); by his use of *aevi* rather than *vitae* he is emphasizing that the main reason for this is life's shortness. He is referring to the allotted span of mankind in general, not just Quinctius's or his own; at this point in the poem the aphorisms are couched in a universal form. *aevi* does not connote 'old age' (as contrasted with *iuventas* below); rather it comprises both *iuventas* and *canitie*. The 'few needs' include those of the present, which are described in the second half of the ode with a humorous blend of hedonism and moderation.

fugit retro . . . : this sentence picks up and justifies *nec trepides . . . pauca* (a colon should be printed after *pauca*); a man's total needs are few because youth is short and the appetite for pleasure diminishes. Then in the third stanza the mutability of beauty and the pointlessness of long views are treated in reverse order, thus completing a chiasmus.

For Horace's commonplace cf. 2. 5. 13 n., 2. 14. 1 n. The past seems to be running away as a landscape recedes from a moving ship (Virg. *Aen.* 3. 72 'provehimur portu terraeque urbesque recedunt'). *retro* means 'into the distance' (cf. Virg. *Aen.* 3. 496 'arva . . . semper cedentia retro'); Horace is adopting the common ancient posture of facing the past rather than the future (cf. πρόσθε as opposed to ὄπισθε). Some interpret rather 'behind our backs', i.e. 'in the past' (cf. 3. 29. 46 'quodcumque retro est'), but this does not seem so natural with a verb of motion like *fugit*.

6. **levis iuventas** : the general maxim is an indirect exhortation to enjoyment while something of youth remains (1. 9. 16 n.). It is true that Horace and Quinctius are now middle-aged (15 *canos*), but in Latin usage *iuventus* and *senectus* often adjoin each other. The adjectives are distributed with characteristic economy: youth is smooth-faced and sleek, age is wrinkled (2. 14. 3, Theoc. 29. 28) and dried-up (1. 25. 19 n., Plut. *an sen. ger. resp.* 789 c ἀζαλέῳ γήρᾳ, Irwin 37 f.).

7. **pellente . . . amores** : cf. Eur. fr. 23. 1 N. ἀλλ' ἢ τὸ γῆρας τὴν Κύπριν χαίρειν ἐᾷ, Pl. *resp.* 329 a–c, Cic. *senec.* 47. *pellente* balances the conventional *fugit* above. Heinze sees a military metaphor, but *lascivos* suggests rather a reference to driving off animals. For *pellere* of banishing sleep cf. Colum. 10. 69, Sil. 7. 300.

8. facilemque somnum : for the adjective cf. 3. 21. 4, Ov. *epist.* 11. 29. The phrase balances *lascivos amores*: desire may be refractory for the young, but sleep is accommodating. For the slumbers of the carefree cf. 2. 16. 15 n.; for the insomnia of the elderly cf. Stat. *Theb.* 1. 433 f. 'magnis cui sobria curis / pendebat somno iam deteriore senectus'. Nock (2. 711) remarks 'under the Empire we seem to see an increased appreciation of the blessings of sleep'. One cannot compare the incidence of insomnia in different periods, but some talk about it more; cf. especially Sen. *dial.* 1. 3. 10 (on Maecenas), *Herc. f.* 1065 ff., Stat. *silv.* 5. 4, Mayor on Juv. 3. 235, Fronto 227 ff. Naber = 216 ff. van den Hout (the fable of Sleep), Waszink on Tert. *an.* 43. 7.

9. floribus . . . vernis : in Mediterranean countries particularly the brief bloom of spring flowers is compared with human life and beauty. Cf. Mimnermus 2. 1 f. ἡμεῖς δ' οἷά τε φύλλα φύει πολυάνθεμος ὥρη / ἔαρος (developing Hom. *Il.* 6. 146), ps.-Theoc. 23. 28 f. καὶ τὸ ῥόδον καλόν ἐστι, καὶ ὁ χρόνος αὐτὸ μαραίνει· / καὶ τὸ ἴον καλόν ἐστιν ἐν εἴαρι, καὶ ταχὺ γηρᾷ, Tib. 1. 4. 29 (with K. F. Smith's abundant parallels), *ros. nasc.* 35 f., Plin. *nat.* 21. 2 'flores vero odoresque in diem gignit (natura), magna ut palam est admonitione hominum quae spectatissime floreant celerrime marcescere'.

    honor : 'grace', 'bloom', χάρις; cf. Val. Fl. 6. 492 ff. 'lilia . . . quis vita brevis totusque parumper / floret honor'.

10. luna : for the phases of the moon cf. Plin. *nat.* 2. 41 ff., Pease on Cic. *nat. deor.* 2. 50. Here they are a reminder of human vicissitudes; cf. Soph. fr. 871 P. = 787 N. ἀλλ' οὑμὸς αἰεὶ πότμος ἐν πυκνῷ θεοῦ / τροχῷ κυκλεῖται καὶ μεταλλάσσει φύσιν, / ὥσπερ σελήνης ὄψις εὐφρόνας δύο / στῆναι δύναιτ' ἂν οὔποτ' ἐν μορφῇ μίᾳ, / ἀλλ' ἐξ ἀδήλου πρῶτον ἔρχεται νέα / πρόσωπα καλλύνουσα καὶ πληρουμένη, / χὤταν περ αὐτῆς εὐπρεπεστάτη φανῇ / πάλιν διαρρεῖ κἀπὶ μηδὲν ἔρχεται, Ov. *met.* 15. 196 ff., Spenser, *F.Q.* 7. 7. 50. Some compare also 4. 7. 13 'damna tamen celeres reparant caelestia lunae' (cf. Fraenkel, *MH* 22, 1965, 66 ff.); but as *caelestia* and *celeres* show, that line refers to the changes of weather brought about by the passage of time.

    rubens : the moon conventionally blushes (Prop. 1. 10. 8, Orient. *comm.* 1. 116), for instance before a storm, or an eclipse, or as a sign of embarrassment (Virg. *georg.* 1. 431, Ov. *met.* 4. 332, Lejay on Hor. *serm.* 1. 8. 35, André 337 f.). In our passage the word seems to hint at the bloom of youth (2. 5. 12 n.); similarly *honor* is applicable to people as well as flowers, *nitet* reminds us of human *nitor* (1. 5. 13, 1. 19. 5), and the personified *voltu* is preferred to the scientific *facie* (cf. Sen. *Phaedr.* 747 'exerit vultus rubicunda Phoebe', Virg. *georg.* 4. 232 'os . . . honestum'). For such 'interaction' in the use of imagery cf. 2. 9. 2 n.

11. **aeternis . . . consiliis**: 'deliberations that look to the infinite future'. The schemes of a worldly man seem to be based on the assumption that he will live for ever; cf. 2. 16. 17 n., Sen. *dial.* 6. 11. 5 'immortalia aeterna volutat animo et in nepotes pronepotesque disponit, cum interim longe conantem eum mors opprimit'. For the use of *aeternis* cf. 1. 4. 15 'spem longam' with note ad loc., *corp. paroem. gr.* 2. 228 μακρὰς ἐλπίδας μισῶ, Gigante 100. The adjective (= *aeviternis*) appears to pick up 5 *aevi* (for the balance of these clauses see note on 5 *fugit*), but the relation, though apparently pointed, must be purely formal: when *aeternis* (following *semper* and *uno*) is contrasted with the phases of the moon, it must mean 'eternal' rather than 'life-long' (*pace* Kiessling, who cites *epist.* 1. 10. 41 'serviet aeternum').

minorem . . .: ἥττονα, *imparem* (cf. *serm.* 2. 3. 310). *consiliis* is ablative of comparison with *minorem* and of instrument with *fatigas*; the double construction is characteristically Horatian (cf. 2. 6. 7, 2. 14. 15 f.). For *animum fatigare* cf. *Thes.l.L.* 6. 1. 347. 54 ff. (with a hint in our passage at the mortal soul of the Epicureans); so also Plin. *epist.* 9. 3. 2 (of those who do not *immortalitatem suam cogitare*) 'nec brevem vitam caducis laboribus fatigare'.

13. **sub alta vel platano vel hac pinu iacentes**: it is a convention of pastoral to suggest alternative places for repose (Theoc. 1. 21, Virg. *ecl.* 5. 5 f., Calp. 1. 8, 6. 66, Nemes. *ecl.* 1. 30 f.). Horace's word-order is affectedly casual and suggests the search for a suitable place: the tree is to be tall at any rate, perhaps a plane or better *this* pine (for the vivid deictic pronoun cf. 2. 3. 13, 2. 14. 22). The shady plane-tree is a regular feature of the *locus amoenus*; cf. Hom. *Il.* 2. 307, Pl. *Phaedr.* 229 a–b (the prototype for much of this sort of scene-painting) ὁρᾷς οὖν ἐκείνην τὴν ὑψηλοτάτην πλάτανον; . . . ἐκεῖ σκιά τ᾽ ἐστὶν καὶ πνεῦμα μέτριον, καὶ πόα καθίζεσθαι ἢ ἂν βουλώμεθα κατακλινῆναι, 230 b ἥτε γὰρ πλάτανος αὕτη μάλ᾽ ἀμφιλαφής τε καὶ ὑψηλή . . . [see above, 2. 3. 6 n.], Calp. 4. 2 'sub hac platano quam garrulus adstrepit umor', Ach. Tat. 1. 2. 3. For planes in Roman *horti* cf. 2. 15. 4 n., for pines cf. 2. 3. 9 n.; for *iacentes* cf. 2. 3. 7 n.

14. **sic temere**: the phrase is modelled on Greek οὕτως εἰκῇ, 'without more ado', 'just anyhow'; cf. Pl. *Hipparch.* 225 b–c μή μοι οὕτως εἰκῇ . . . ἀλλὰ προσέχων τὸν νοῦν ἀπόκριναι, *Gorg.* 506 d with Dodds's note, Sen. *Phaedr.* 394 'sic temere iactae colla perfundant comae' (suggested by our passage, as is shown by 393 'odore . . . Assyrio'). *sic* is a deictic word that balances *hac*; it implies 'as you see us', 'as we are'. *temere* (= *inconsulto*) suggests an informality that is contrasted with the long-term *consilia* above; cf. Eur. *Ba.* 685 f. πρὸς πέδῳ κάρα /

εἰκῇ βαλοῦσαι σωφρόνως, Ov. *am.* 1. 14. 21 f. 'ut Thracia Bacche / cum temere in viridi gramine lassa iacet'.

Sometimes *sic* can have a similar implication without another adverb; cf. Ter. *Andr.* 175 'mirabar hoc si sic abiret' (Don. '*sic* pro *leviter et neglegenter*, quod Graeci οὗτω dicunt'), Cic. *Att.* 14. 1. 1, *Thes.l.L.* 1. 69. 75 ff. For this usage in Greek cf. Dodds on Pl. *Gorg.* 503 d, *ev. Joh.* 4. 6 ὁ οὖν ᾽Ιησοῦς κεκοπιακὼς ἐκ τῆς ὁδοιπορίας ἐκαθέζετο οὕτως ἐπὶ τῇ πηγῇ, L.–S.–J. s.v. οὕτως IV. Yet some of the Latin instances cited have different nuances; cf. *serm.* 1. 2. 106 '(leporem) positum sic tangere nolit' ('placed in front of your eyes', representing Call. *ep.* 31. 4 τῇ, τόδε βέβληται θηρίον), *epist.* 1. 13. 12 f. 'sic positum servabis onus ne forte sub ala / fasciculum portes librorum' (*sic* points to *ne* as at *ars* 151 f.).

    rosa . . . odorati : not perfume but garlands (for the singular cf. 1. 5. 1 n.) ; Horace suggests that the flowers are to be had for the picking in Quinctius's *horti*. He thus maintains his affectation of simplicity (somewhat belied by the artificiality of the language) ; cf. Epictet. 1. 19. 29 ἀλλὰ χρυσοῦν στέφανον φορήσω. — εἰ ἅπαξ ἐπιθυμεῖς στεφάνου, ῥόδινον λαβὼν περίθου· ὄψει γὰρ κομψότερον. For roses at the symposium cf. further 1. 36. 15 n., 1. 38. 4 n., *Anacreontea* 41. 1 f. στεφάνους μὲν κροτάφοισιν / ῥοδίνους συναρμόσαντες, 42, Bömer on Ov. *fast.* 5. 336, Hehn 251 ff.

    Probably *canos capillos* should be taken with *uncti* as well as with *odorati*; the interlaced word-order is appropriately exquisite, and it is desirable that both clauses should contain a suggestion of sobriety as well as of hedonism (*canos* in a sense balances 14 *sic temere*, 20 *lympha*, 21 *devium*, 23 *incomptum*). There seems also to be a contrast between the delicate scent of local rose-petals and the thick smear of exotic nard (cf. Call. fr. 110. 77 f. πολλὰ πέπωκα / λιτά, γυναικείων δ᾽ οὐκ ἀπέλαυσα μύρων).

15. canos : the adjective picks up 8 *canitie* and makes a colour contrast with 14 *rosa*. For the white-haired hedonist cf. Alcaeus 50 κὰτ τὰς πόλλα παθοίσας κεφάλας . . . χέε μοι μύρον / καὶ κὰτ τῶ πολίω στήθεος, Anacreon 395. 1 ff. πολιοὶ μὲν ἡμῖν ἤδη / κρόταφοι κάρη τε λευκόν, / χαρίεσσα δ᾽ οὐκέθ᾽ ἤβη / πάρα, γηραλέοι δ᾽ ὀδόντες, 358. 7, 379 a, *Anacreontea* 1, 6, 37, 45, 50, 51, Dio 46. 18. 3 (Fufius Calenus's invective against Cicero) τίς δ᾽ οὐκ ὀσφραίνεται τῶν πολιῶν σου τῶν κατεκτενισμένων; Horace's suggestion of elderliness is an ironic exaggeration, but it helps the humour that he was prematurely grey; cf. *epod.* 17. 23 (when he was perhaps little more than thirty), *carm.* 3. 14. 25, *epist.* 1. 7. 26, 1. 20. 24.

16. dum licet : Horace's intricate complex (14 n.) is disrupted by this more conversational reminder : roses wither, and so does life itself

(cf. 9 ff.). For 'while ye may' as a poetical motif cf. 1. 9. 16 n.,
1. 9. 17 n.; add Lejay on *serm.* 2. 6. 96, Prop. 1. 19. 25, Ov. *ars* 3. 61,
Sen. *Phaedr.* 774.

Assyriaque nardo : there is a contrast with 6 ff. *arida . . . canitie.*
The noun is found in all three genders; the feminine (supported
by the great bulk of the paradosis and explicitly by Porphyrio)
properly belongs to the plant (cf. 3. 29. 4 'pressa tuis balanus capillis').
Thus *nardo uncti* closely balances *rosa odorati.*

Assyria is grandiose for *Syria.* The place-names were in origin the
same, and though they came to have specialized functions, they
were often interchanged, particularly in the adjectival form (Th.
Nöldeke, *Hermes* 5, 1871, 443 ff.). 'Syrian' was a conventional epithet
of perfume in general (cf. 2. 7. 8, Theoc. 15. 114 with Gow's parallels,
Meleager, *anth. P.* 4. 1. 43, Philodemus, ibid. 11. 34. 2, Prop. 1. 2. 3,
Athen. 15. 689 a) ; for the use of *Assyrius* in such contexts cf. Catull.
68. 144, Virg. *ecl.* 4. 25, Tib. 1. 3. 7.

For Syrian nard cf. Dioscorides, *mat. med.* 1. 7. 1 νάρδου ἐστὶ γένη
δύο· ἡ μὲν γάρ τις καλεῖται 'Ινδική, ἡ δὲ Συριακή· οὐχ ὅτι ἐν Συρίᾳ
εὑρίσκεται, ἀλλ' ὅτι τοῦ ὄρους ἐν ᾧ γεννᾶται τὸ μὲν πρὸς Συρίαν τέτραπται
τὸ δὲ πρὸς 'Ινδούς, Plin. *nat.* 12. 45 (he distinguishes Syrian nard from
Indian, Gallic, and Cretan). The explanation of Dioscorides seems
implausible, though J. I. Miller identifies a special sort of spikenard
on the West of the Hindu Kush (*The Spice Trade of the Roman Empire*, 1969, pp. 88 f.) ; Syria's place on the trade routes seems enough
to associate it with a particular product (cf. ibid. pp. 91, 119 ff.). Certainly there is nothing to be said for Bücheler's view (op. cit.) that
Syrian nard was comparatively ordinary; this is contradicted by
Pliny, loc. cit. 'in nostro orbe proxime laudatur Syriacum', and the
exotic form *Assyria* increases the impression of luxury.

17. potamus : the verb suggests deep drinking (1. 20. 1 n., Isid. *diff.*
1. 74 'bibere naturae est, potare luxuriae') ; it is a more drastic word
than *bibere*, and is on the whole used by the epic poets only for
special effects. Similarly *uncti*, while not unpoetical, is more physical
and less rarefied than *odorati.*

dissipat Euhius . . . : this maxim on the power of wine (vol. i,
p. 228) should be seen as a crisp Callimachean parenthesis, perhaps
best represented not by brackets (which have too subordinating an
effect) but by dashes; such an interpretation prevents interruption
to the series of questions and allows 17 *potamus* to be picked up by
pocula. For the scattering of cares cf. 1. 18. 4 n.; the motif is characteristic of early Greek poetry rather than the Alexandrians, for whom
it is too trite (G. Giangrande in *L'Épigramme grecque* [*Fondation
Hardt, Entretiens* 14], pp. 171 f.). *dissipat* is a natural word for

scattering cares (Sen. *dial.* 9. 7. 3, *carm. epig.* 1504 A. 6), but in conjunction with *Euhius* may have a witty edge: the god of the Bacchae usually scatters dismembered bodies (Arnob. *nat.* 5. 19. 'caprorum reclamantium viscera cruentatis oribus dissipatis', *Thes.l.L.* 5. 1. 1488. 12 ff.).

18. edaces : cf. 1. 18. 4 n., Hom. *Il.* 6. 202 ὃν θυμὸν κατέδων, Catull. 66. 23, Cic. *fin.* 1. 51 'sollicitudines quibus eorum animi noctes diesque exeduntur'. In our passage the word makes a formal contrast with *potamus*.

quis puer : *puer* is commonly used in addresses to slaves (cf. vol. i, p. 421), but here underlines the contrast between the briskness of the boy and the elderliness of the reclining drinkers. Instructions to slaves are sometimes put in an indefinite form; cf. Alcaeus 362. 2 περθέτω πλέκταις ὑπαθύμιδάς τις, Pind. *N.* 9. 50, Aesch. *Ag.* 944 f. (with Headlam–Thomson on 935), Pearson on Soph. fr. 593. 4, Eur. *Ba.* 346, Plaut. *Epid.* 398 f., Ter. *ad.* 634. For interrogatives cf. 2. 7. 23 ff., Eur. *Hel.* 435 τίς ἂν πυλωρὸς ἐκ δόμων μόλοι;, 892, *Ba.* 1257 f., *Cycl.* 502, Ar. *Lys.* 1086 (with van Leeuwen's note), Asclepiades, *anth. P.* 5. 181. 3 f., Claud. 10. 128 f. The usage suggests the impatience of everyday speech, but it was also undesirable in the higher styles of literature for servants to be mentioned by name (contrast *serm.* 2. 7. 2).

ocius : the use of the adverb belongs to the spoken language, being particularly common in comedy; cf. *serm.* 2. 7. 34 'nemon oleum feret ocius?', 2. 7. 117, Ter. *heaut.* 832, Pers. 3. 7 f. 'ocius adsit / huc aliquis', Juv. 14. 252. θᾶσσον is similarly used; cf. Hom. *Od.* 20. 153 f. (Eurycleia prepares for the feast) ταὶ δὲ μεθ' ὕδωρ / ἔρχεσθε κρήνηνδε, καὶ οἴσετε θᾶσσον ἰοῦσαι. In our passage the note of urgency suits the idea of extinguishing a fire.

19. restinguet : the ancients normally diluted their wine, except for ritual purposes (1. 19. 15 n.) and in love-toasts (Gow–Page, *HE* 1063 f.). Hence it was a convention of sympotic verse to ask the servant to bring both wine and water; cf. Anacreon 356 a, 396. 1 φέρ' ὕδωρ, φέρ' οἶνον, ὦ παῖ, Lygd. 6. 57 f. Yet though conventional, in our passage the request seems to underline the moderation of Horace's festivities.

ardentis : pointedly juxtaposed with *restinguet*. For fiery wine cf. Eur. *Alc.* 758 f., Meleager, *anth. P.* 9. 331. 3 f. τοὔνεκα σὺν Νύμφαις Βρόμιος φίλος· ἢν δέ νιν εἴργῃς / μίσγεσθαι, δέξῃ πῦρ ἔτι καιόμενον, Ov. *ars* 1. 244, Mart. 9. 73. 5, Juv. 10. 27.

20. praetereunte lympha : a stream is a conventional feature of the symposium *al fresco* (2. 3. 11 f., 1. 1. 22 n.), so we can make no inferences about the layout of Quinctius's *horti*. The water lies ready

to hand, and so suits the element of simplicity in the poem; contrast the luxurious Falernian. The instrumental ablative (participle as well as noun) is placed with pointed emphasis at the end of the sentence; the impatient *quis puer ocius?* would have led us to expect an order for wine rather than for water.

21. quis . . . : for the distribution of orders to slaves cf. *serm.* 2. 2. 67 'dum munia didit', Plaut. *Pseud.* 161 ff., Juv. 14. 60 ff. For the invitation to Lyde cf. 3. 14. 21 (below on 23), *serm.* 1. 2. 122, Alcaeus 368 κέλομαί τινα τὸν χαρίεντα Μένωνα κάλεσσαι / αἰ χρῆ συμποσίας ἔτ' ὄνασιν ἔμοιγε γένεσθαι, Asclepiades, *anth. P.* 5. 185. 6 καὶ Τρυφέραν ταχέως ἐν παρόδῳ κάλεσον, Automedon, ibid. 11. 29. 1, *Anacreontea* 30. 15 (above, p. 169). See further Marcus Argentarius, *anth. P.* 7. 403. 1 f. Ψύλλος ὁ τὰς ποθινὰς ἐπιμισθίδας αἰὲν ἑταίρας / πέμπων ἐς τὰ νέων ἡδέα συμπόσια.

·**devium scortum :** Porphyrio rightly comments 'belle devium scortum Lyden ait quae corpore quidem quaestum faciat sed non publice prostet'; in Quinctius's exclusive suburban *horti* such girls had to be sent for. The adjective makes an oxymoron with *scortum*, which implies public access; the blend of the cheap and the exquisite fits the mood of the poem. *devium* also suits *eliciet*, which implies difficulty; cf. Claud. 18. 82 f. 'ille vel aerata Danaen in turre latentem / eliceret'. It is relevant that *elicere* is a word from irrigation (cf. Virg. *georg.* 1. 108 f. 'undam elicit' with Serv. auct., *Thes.l.L.* 5. 2. 367. 79 ff.); this suggests a contrast between the available stream and the girl who is hard to get.

scortum is arrestingly unpoetical and anti-Romantic; it is not used, for instance, by the elegiac poets (except for Sulpicia ap. Tib. 3. 16. 4). On the other hand it is in no way vulgar or obscene; it is found often not only in Comedy but in Cicero's speeches, and even at *senec.* 50. And it can be used, at least humorously or informally, of girls with some claim to sophistication; cf. Catull. 10. 3 f. 'scortillum . . . / non sane illepidum neque invenustum'. It should be noted that *devium scortum* is in apposition to the emphatic *Lyden* and not *vice versa* (for the mannered word-order cf. 1. 3. 20 'infames scopulos Acroceraunia' with note ad loc.); that is to say, there is not even the slightest of pauses after *domo*.

22. Lyden : cf. 3. 11. 7, 3. 28. 3. The name is exotic (cf. 1. 8. 1 n. on Lydia), and was borne by the hetaera of Antimachus (Athen. 13. 597 a). Its Greek and poetical associations make a paradoxical contrast with the previous *scortum*.

eburna . . . cum lyra : again an exotic touch; for such decoration cf. *PMG* 900. 1 εἴθε λύρα καλὴ γενοίμην ἐλεφαντίνη, Ar. *av.* 218 f., *RE*

5. 2362. For courtesans with musical interests, sometimes implausible, cf. 1. 17. 19 n., 3. 14. 21, 3. 28. 9 ff., 4. 11. 34 ff.

dic age : the urgent phrase belongs to the spoken language (*serm.* 2. 7. 92), but is compatible with a higher style (3. 4. 1).

23. maturet : the intransitive use is somewhat colloquial (cf. *Thes.l.L.* 8. 497. 32 ff.) ; the word does not govern *nodum*, as Lyde cannot use the lyre as a comb. For the poet's impatience cf. 3. 14. 21 'properet', *serm.* 1. 2. 122 'neque cunctetur', Asclepiades, *anth. P.* 5. 185. 6 ταχέως, Philodemus, ibid. 5. 46. 8 εὐθὺ θέλω.

incomptum Lacaenae more comae religata nodum : this is the reading of one side of the tradition; *comam* and *comas* are also well attested. The admittedly mannered *nodum* can be analysed as a Greek internal accusative (Hdt. 4. 175. 1 λόφους κείρονται), or *religata* may be felt as a sort of middle voice (Thuc. 1. 6. 3 κρωβύλον ἀναδούμενοι τῶν ἐν κεφαλῇ τριχῶν). 'Spartan hair' is a characteristic Horatian hypallage like 1. 31. 9 'Calena falce', 3. 6. 38 'Sabellis ligonibus'. Lyde is compared to Spartan hair by a sort of compendious comparison (2. 6. 14 n.) ; though this construction normally takes the form κόμαι Χαρίτεσσιν ὅμοιαι, sometimes it is the main member that is abbreviated (Cic. *Pis.* 20 'quem ego civem . . . cum deorum immortalium laude coniungo', *Tusc.* 5. 73 'huic . . . non multum differenti a iudicio ferarum'). *incomptum . . . nodum* is unparalleled, but the *nodus* was undeniably simple (24 n.). It is a point in favour of this interpretation that 'Lacaenae / more comae' makes a more convincing unit than 'Lacaenae / more' (which has an unusual break after the trochee).

It will be argued on the other hand that *comam* or *comas* is needed to give *religata* a clear enough specification ; but the corresponding ἀναδεδεμένη (which is suggested by the Graecizing syntax) is so naturally used of hair that it does not require such an accusative. If *comam* or *comas* is accepted one would have to interpret 'with her hair bound up into an uncombed knot' (ἀκτένιστον τὰς τρίχας κρωβύλον ἀναδεδεμένη) ; but the combination of a retained accusative *comam* and an internal accusative *nodum* seems too intricate even for this passage. Some editors favour 'in comptum . . . comam religata nodum' (cf. Ov. *met.* 3. 169 f. 'capillos / colligit in nodum') ; but where the emphasis is on haste and simplicity it is implausible to interpret *incomptum* as two words (cf. also Ap. Rhod. 3. 50 ἀψήκτους δὲ χεροῖν ἀνεδήσατο χαίτας). Nor can one easily say with Kiessling that *comptum Lacaenae more* means virtually 'unadorned' ; *Lacaenae more* seems to belong not just to *comptum* but to the whole clause. Torrentius proposed 'incomptam . . . comam religata nodo' (cf. Bentley ad loc., C. O. Brink, *PCPhS* 17, 1971, 25 ff., Syndikus) ; the conjecture derives support from the parallel 3. 14. 21 f. 'dic et argutae properet Neaerae / murreum nodo cohibere crinem'. But *nodo* at the end of the stanza seems strangely isolated when unsupported by an earlier adjective; the emphatic *praetereunte lympha* above is not really similar. If *nodum* is kept, the elaborate symmetry of the sentence is at variance with the simplicity it describes, a contradiction that is paralleled elsewhere in the poem (above, p. 169).

Lacaenae : the adjective makes a contrast with the exotic *Lyden* (cf. Alcman 1. 67 f.). For the simplicity of the Spartan hair-style cf. Prop. 3. 14. 28 'est neque odoratae cura molesta comae'. There seems to be nothing in literature or art to connect the *nodus* particularly with Sparta; yet it was associated with outdoor girls (24 n.), and that for Horace would be enough. Brink, loc. cit. (who follows the reading of Torrentius and Bentley) suggests that the Spartan analogy applies only to *incomptam*; yet this makes *nodo* all the more isolated.

24. nodo : a knot or bun of hair; cf. 3. 14. 22 (cited above), Ov. *met.* 8. 319 (Atalanta) 'crinis erat simplex, nodum collectus in unum', Sen. *Phaedr.* 401 f. (Amazons), Stat. *Theb.* 2. 238 (on Diana) with Mulder's note. See further *RE* 7. 2126, D.-S. I. 2. 1360 f., Dorothy B. Thompson, *Troy, The Terracotta Figurines of the Hellenistic Period,* 1963, pp. 40 ff.

12. NOLIS LONGA FERAE

[G. Davis, *Philologus* 119, 1975, 70 ff.; Fraenkel 219 ff.; B. R. Morris and R. D. Williams, *Philological Quarterly* (Iowa) 42, 1963, 145 ff.; G. Williams 299 ff. and *JRS* 52, 1962, 35 ff.; W. Wimmel, *Kallimachos in Rom, Hermes Einzelschriften, Heft* 16, 1960]

1–12. *Martial themes of history or mythology are unsuitable for lyric poetry, and it will be better that you yourself, Maecenas, should record Augustus's conquests.* 13–20. *I was meant to celebrate my lady Licymnia with her loyal heart and graceful accomplishments.* 21–8. *Would you accept all the wealth of the Orient for a curl of Licymnia's hair, when she leans across to receive kisses—or to snatch them?*

This poem belongs to the type conveniently known as *recusatio*, where the poet rejects heroic subjects in favour of more modest themes (vol. i, pp. 81 ff.). In his famous prototype Callimachus had written a manifesto against the pretentious matter and inflated

manner of neo-epic, and had named kings and heroes as unsuitable
subjects (fr. 1. 3 ff.) :

εἵνεκε]ν οὐχ ἓν ἄεισμα διηνεκὲς ἢ βασιλή[ων
πρήξι]ας ἐν πολλαῖς ἤνυσα χιλιάσιν
ἢ προτέρ]ους ἥρωας, ἔπος δ' ἐπὶ τυτθὸν ἐλ[ίσσω . . .

As instances of rejected topics Horace mentions the Numantine
War, which had featured in a Lucilian *recusatio* (1 n.), and the first
two Punic Wars, central subjects of the epics of Naevius and Ennius;
at the same time by hinting at contemporary campaigns against
the Cantabrians and Sextus Pompeius (1 n., 2 n.), he pays the indirect
compliments that played an important part in Roman *recusatio*.
Similarly in the second stanza he refuses to write about Centaurs
and Giants, who had perhaps been repudiated by Callimachus in
a similar context (7 n.) ; once more he seems to be pointing to Augustus's enemies, who may have been alluded to in mythological guise
in the public monuments of his own day (5 n., 6 n., 9 n.). In the third
stanza, again within the tradition of the *recusatio* (10 n.), he mentions
an alternative writer who might honour Augustus more effectively;
his reference to kings is based on the Callimachean prototype, but
is given contemporary relevance (12 n.).

The conventions of the *recusatio* are developed in the fourth
stanza, which is the centre of the poem in function as well as in
position (for more or less similar structures cf. L. A. Moritz, *CQ* 18,
1968, 116 ff., Williams 122 f.). To contrast his own limited abilities
with those of others Horace uses emphatic *me* with anaphora (for
parallels cf. 1. 6. 5 n., 1. 6. 13 n.) ; and he chooses the Muse as his
counsellor (1. 6. 10 n.), just as Callimachus had claimed Apollo (fr.
1. 22). But at this point a crucial problem presents itself: 'me dulcis
dominae Musa Licymniae / cantus ... voluit dicere' (13 ff.). In the
recusatio the theme of love is often set against that of war (cf. 1. 6.
17 f., *Anacreontea* 23, 26 A σὺ μὲν λέγεις τὰ Θήβης, / ὁ δ' αὖ Φρυγῶν
ἀυτάς· / ἐγὼ δ' ἐμὰς ἁλώσεις, Prop. 1. 7. 1 ff., Ov. *am.* 2. 18. 12) ; on
that basis one expects Licymnia to be Horace's own mistress, a view
that seems to be confirmed by *fulgentis oculos, fidum pectus, mutuis
amoribus*. Yet ps.-Acro (on *serm.* 1. 2. 64) identifies the lady with
Terentia, Maecenas's temperamental wife (*RE* 5 A. 716); the two
names are metrically equivalent, and since Bentley editors have
cited similar pseudonyms (Lesbia for Clodia, Lycoris for Cytheris,
Delia for Plania, Cynthia for Hostia, Perilla for Metella, cf. Apul.
apol. 10). They assume that *dominae* should be understood as
either *uxoris tuae* or *patronae meae* (cf. Mart. 12. 31. 7 'munera sunt
dominae') ; the former is totally impossible after *me*, the latter is at
least Latin, but goes against the conventions of the *recusatio*. On

the other hand if Licymnia is Horace's love, one can even explain 21 ff. 'num tu . . . Phrygiae . . . opes / permutare velis crine Licymniae?'; after what has gone before, these words are naturally interpreted 'if *you* were as lucky as I am, would *you* . . . ?' Perhaps Horace is talking of his own mistress throughout, and the ambiguity of *num tu* has deceived ps.-Acro and his modern successors; cf. Nisbet ap. G. Williams, *JRS* 52, 1962, 36 n. 13, Morris–R. D. Williams, op. cit., Davis, op. cit.

This interpretation may not be the whole truth, but the difficulties are not always accurately defined. It is objected that a mere *hetaera* could not dance at Diana's festival (17 ff.); but the occasion was a popular one (20 n.), and Propertius invites Cynthia to do exactly the same (2. 28. 60 'munera Dianae debita redde choros'). It is said that *nec . . . dedecuit* is meant to forestall the criticism that a great lady is demeaning herself; in fact the suggestion seems to be that an older woman can dance with as much style as the young girls (17 n.). Yet it remains strange that Horace should have given himself a mistress whose artistic and other accomplishments are so ill-suited to his normal *persona*; a wish to outdo Propertius at his own game might be the reason (see below), but a feeling lingers that this extended self-congratulation is oddly out of line with the expected ironies of the Horatian *recusatio* (cf. 1. 6. 20 'non praeter solitum leves'). At the most literal level Horace must be talking of his own lady, but in an ode that contains a considerable element of ingenious allegory (see notes on the first two stanzas) ps.-Acro's identification, though stated too unequivocally, might fairly represent yet another double-meaning; such an interpretation would rest on firmer ground if we could only be sure that a contemporary would connect 'Licymnia' and 'Licin(n)ia', and that he would associate the latter name with Terentia (13 n.). If this theory is correct, Horace is cleverly exploiting the ambiguity of 13 *dominae* (both *amicae* and *patronae*) and 21 *num tu* (both emphatic and unstressed); when he says to Maecenas 'would *you* exchange Licymnia's lock for the treasures of the East?' he means him to see that the question is less fanciful than it pretends.

An obvious objection to any such theory is the strong Roman sense of propriety: would a leading citizen have allowed even oblique comments to be made about his wife in this way? Some of the difficulty rests on a misunderstanding: Licymnia's dancing is displayed on a religious occasion (19 n.), and commentators do wrong to compare her with Sempronia, the dissolute aristocratic lady described by Sallust (*Cat.* 25. 2 'litteris Graecis Latinis docta, psallere saltare elegantius quam necesse est probae . . . 5 posse versus facere, iocum movere, sermone uti vel modesto vel molli vel procaci; prorsus multae facetiae multusque lepos inerat'). It is true that the elegists' mistresses sometimes show similar talents; cf. Prop. 1. 2. 27 ff., 1. 4. 13, 2. 3. 17 ff. 'quod posito formose saltat Iaccho / ... par Aganippeae ludere docta lyrae' (see the whole context), Lilja 133 ff. But Propertius, like Horace himself, owes less to the musical dancing-girls of Greek epigram than to a more innocent poetical tradition; cf. Theoc. 18. 35 f. (Helen's *epithalamium*) οὐ μὰν οὐδὲ λύραν τις ἐπίσταται ὧδε κροτῆσαι, / Ἄρτεμιν ἀείδοισα καὶ εὐρύστερνον Ἀθάναν, Peek, GV 1925 (= Kaibel, EG 560). 5 f. (an early imperial epitaph from Campania) Μοῦσα δὲ καὶ σοφίαν καὶ πάκτιδα τὰν φιλέραστον (δωρήσατο) / συμφωνίαν ἐρατοῖς μειξαμένα μέλεσιν. As far as artistic accomplishments go, Horace has not demeaned Licymnia: Propertius has rather idealized Cynthia.

But if Licymnia really conceals Terentia, other aspects of Horace's portrait are more indiscreet. Even the reference to flashing eyes seems a little too personal (14 n.), but the faithful heart of the same stanza may redress the balance; on the other hand the amorous scene at the end of the poem has unavoidable associations with erotic epigram. Poetic convention may be a substantial excuse (Williams, *JRS*, loc. cit.): the Greek pseudonym takes the ode out of the realm of literal description. Williams further suggests that it was written for Maecenas's wedding, when greater freedom of speech might be permitted (*Tradition and Originality*, loc. cit.); but there are no traces of the familiar style and topics of the epithalamium (Hesperus does not leave Oeta here), and the marriage may well have taken place in the triumviral period (cf. *serm*. 1. 5. 38 [above, p. 152], Suet. *Aug*. 69. 2), that is to say before the date of the ode (see below). Perhaps a more promising line of defence would be the unconventional personality of Maecenas himself: he seems to have tolerated *epod*. 14. 9 f. 'non aliter Samio dicunt arsisse Bathyllo / Anacreonta Teium' (where there must surely be an oblique allusion to his actor-friend of the same name). Matrons, it is true, were usually treated with more respect, but Maecenas's salon may have combined the licence of old Etruria with that of fashionable Rome; cf. Theopompus, *FGrH* 115 F 204 εἰσάγουσι παρ' αὐτοὺς οἱ διάκονοι τῶν λύχνων ἔτι καιομένων ὁτὲ μὲν ἑταίρας, ὁτὲ δὲ παῖδας πάνυ καλούς, ὁτὲ δὲ καὶ γυναῖκας (see the whole context), Heurgon 98 ff. with pl. 15 (the tomb of the Triclinium at Tarquinia).

For a parallel with Horace's ode one may compare the opening elegy of Propertius's second book, where the poet professes to sing of love because he is incapable of grander themes. To illustrate his point he gives a summary catalogue of stories from mythology; like Horace he includes the battle of the Gods and Giants, and later returns to the same topic (below, 7 n.). Again like Horace he lists

Roman wars, some from earlier history (cf. 21 'animos Carthaginis altae'), some from his own day (27 ff.):

> nam quotiens Mutinam aut civilia busta Philippos
>   aut canerem Siculae classica bella fugae,
> eversosque focos antiquae gentis Etruscae,
>   et Ptolomaeei litora capta Phari,
> aut canerem Aegyptum et Nilum, cum attractus in urbem
>   septem captivis debilis ibat aquis,
> aut regum auratis circumdata colla catenis,
>   Actiaque in Sacra currere rostra Via . . .

The last couplet shows a striking parallel with lines 11 f. of our poem 'ductaque per vias / regum colla minacium': both poets are clearly alluding to Octavian's triumphs in 29 B.C.

It is fairly clear that Propertius should be given the priority; see W. Wili, *Festschrift E. Tièche*, 1947, pp. 186 ff., Wimmel, loc. cit., D. Flach, *Das literarische Verhältnis von Horaz und Properz*, Diss. Marburg, 1967, pp. 58 ff. (for the opposite view cf. J.-H. Kühn, *Hermes* 89, 1961, 104 ff.). The latest historical allusion in Propertius's whole second book is his forecast of the Arabian expedition of 26–25 (2. 10. 16); as well as hinting at this (24 n.), Horace's ode seems to refer to the Cantabrian campaigns of the same years (1 n.). Propertius mentions civil war with self-conscious independence (an indication of a relatively early date), but Horace humours Maecenas with innocuous banter. Propertius's mythological and historical illustrations are abundant, while Horace makes only a selection; the former spells out the reference to the necks of kings, the latter is content with a hint. Propertius's allusions to contemporary campaigns are clear and explicit, whereas Horace's are tentative and oblique (those who doubt the double meaning should note the parallel with the elegy). In Propertius the theme of the poet's love is dominant (as suits the programmatic poem to a book of elegies), but here again Horace is playing a more complicated game. In a few deft sentences he conjures up another Cynthia with flashing eyes and a faithful heart, graceful accomplishments and passionate kisses; and he leaves it to the initiated to suspect that he is talking about Maecenas's love rather than his own. The ode is pointedly shorter than the diffuse elegy and at first sight seems comparatively colourless, but it shows, if nothing else, true Horatian ingenuity.

Metre: Second Asclepiad (as in the earlier and less sophisticated *recusatio*, 1. 6).

1. **nolis**: Horace begins his reasoned apology with a courteous potential subjunctive. Such a second person is often generalizing ('one

would hesitate'), and so to some extent here; it is only at 9 *tu*
that Maecenas is clearly identified.

bella Numantiae : a characteristic Horatian adaptation of the
prosaic *bellum Numantinum*; cf. 4. 5. 27 f. 'ferae / bellum . . .
Hiberiae', Tac. *ann.* 1. 3. 7 'bella civium' (with Goodyear's note),
Löfstedt, *Syntactica* 1². 123. Numantia was a Celtiberian town near
the upper Douro which fought repeated wars against Rome in the
second century B.C. The greatest of these lasted ten years, twenty
by Strabo's reckoning (3. 4. 13), and ended in 133 with the destruction
of the city by Scipio Aemilianus. The long campaign was waged with
true Spanish ferocity, and the Romans were horrified by the canni-
balism and mass suicide of the defeated (Flor. *epit.* 2. 18. 15). See
further App. *Ib.* 76. 322–98. 427, A. Schulten, *Numantia*, 1914–31 and
RE 17. 1254, H. Simon, *Roms Kriege in Spanien*, 1962, pp. 143 ff.,
A. E. Astin, *Scipio Aemilianus*, 1967, pp. 147 ff.

It must be asked why the *bellum Numantinum* is given the most
prominent place among Rome's many great wars. It is perhaps significant that Polybius wrote a prose monograph on the subject (Cic.
epist. 5. 12. 2, *RE* 21. 2. 1474), but no doubt Horace is particularly
thinking of the *recusatio* of Lucilius who was himself a participant
(620 f.) : 'hunc laborem sumas laudem qui tibi ac fructum ferat / . . .
percrepa pugnam Popili, facta Corneli cane'. Here an imaginary
interlocutor is urging the satirist to celebrate the final victory of
his aristocratic friend, Scipio (Marx ad loc., J. Christes, *Der frühe
Lucilius*, 1971, pp. 72 ff.; the speech is assigned to Lucilius himself
by C. Cichorius, *Untersuchungen zu Lucilius*, 1908, pp. 114 ff.).
Horace must have been familiar with this passage as he imitates it
elsewhere: cf. *serm.* 2. 1. 10 ff. 'aude / Caesaris invicti res dicere,
multa laborum / praemia laturus'.

It is also likely to be relevant that in 26–25 B.C. Augustus fought
the Cantabri in the north of Spain (vol. i, p. xxxi, R. Syme in *Legio
VII Gemina*, Leon, 1970, pp. 79 ff.); the area was little more than
100 miles from Numantia, a negligible distance to mapless poets in
Rome. The legendary Numantine ferocity (1 *ferae*) was repeated
in Augustus's campaign; cf. Str. 3. 4. 17 for similar tales of suicide.
If Horace wrote the ode while Augustus was in Spain or soon after,
he must have seen the analogy with Scipio's mountain campaign,
the triumphant end of a protracted war; the propitious *exemplum*
would have occurred to senatorial panegyrists. Indeed, the fit is so
perfect that it can be used as a positive argument for such a dating
(cf. 24 n. on the Arabian expedition); we are almost driven there in
any event as the ode seems to have been written after Propertius's
elegy celebrating the triumphs of 29 (above, p. 183; the argument is
not simply circular).

2. **durum** : the only reading with authority; ps.-Acro interprets 'qui summa difficultate victus sit' (cf. 4. 14. 50 'duraeque tellus audit Hiberiae'). The adjective corresponds to *longa* and makes a contrast with 3 *mollibus*; it is a strong argument that the stanza as a whole is wittily pointed (see note on 4 *modis*, and for illuminating analogies on 19 *ludentem*). One might also compare Cic. *senec.* 10 (on Fabius) 'Hannibalem iuveniliter exsultantem patientia sua molliebat'; Cicero might be alluding to some word in Ennius, whose famous lines on Fabius are quoted in the same context.

dirum has negligible manuscript support but at first sight seems attractive. The adjective was conventionally applied to Hannibal, whose invasion had left a scar on the folk-memory of Italy (N. Horsfall, *Philologus* 117, 1973, 138; one could add a reference to Carthaginian infanticide); cf. 3. 6. 36 'Hannibalemque dirum' (*v.l.* 'durum'), 4. 4. 42 'dirus . . . Afer', Quint. *inst.* 8. 2. 9 'proprie dictum, id est quo nihil inveniri possit significantius, ut (dixit) . . . Horatius acrem tibiam Hannibalemque dirum', Sil. 16. 622, Juv. 7. 161 'miserum dirus caput Hannibal implet', Sidon. *carm.* 7. 129 f. In view of the distribution of the epithet it may go back to Ennius, in which case it would have a particular application here. The corruption is an easy one; cf. perhaps *serm.* 1. 2. 40 where the MSS. offer 'dura inter saepe pericla' (*CR* N.S. 16, 1966, 327, Diggle and Goodyear on Coripp. *Ioh.* 6. 355). But though the adjective would balance *ferae*, it destroys the convincing contrast with *mollibus*; perhaps the best theme for patriotic poetry was not the Roman defeat by Hannibal but the later counter-offensive.

Hannibalem : naturally given prominence as a central theme of Ennius's epic; Propertius mentions Carthage in his parallel elegy (above, p. 183). With typical *variatio* Horace moves from a city (*Numantiae*) to a general to a battle-ground (*Siculum mare*).

It is argued above and below that *bella Numantiae* and *Siculum mare* hint indirectly at more recent conflicts; if complete symmetry were to be maintained, *Hannibalem* would also have to suggest a contemporary, presumably the African Cleopatra (at *epod.* 9. 23 ff. Octavian after Actium is compared with Marius and Africanus). The analogy is much less obvious than the other two; it should be remembered that ancient poets sometimes indulged in ὑπόνοια without committing themselves to systematic allegory (cf. the *Eclogues*). If all the terms of the second stanza were ambiguous (see below), it would be difficult to resist a similar conclusion for *Hannibalem*; but even there no precise equivalent is offered for *Lapithas*.

Siculum mare : Horace is going further and further back in time; now he is alluding to the great naval battles of the First Punic War at Mylae (260 B.C.) and the Aegatian Islands (241 B.C.), which must have been celebrated by Naevius in his *Bellum Punicum*. There is a clear parallel with Octavian's naval war against Sextus Pompeius, which was an obvious subject for patriotic poetry: Cornelius Severus wrote on the matter (Quint. *inst.* 10. 1. 89, Schanz–Hosius 2. 268 f.), and the theme is expressly mentioned by Propertius in the elegy that Horace is here imitating (above, p. 183). Maecenas and Horace seem both to have participated (2. 6. 8 n., 2. 17. 20 n.), and the former at least may have been in the ships at Mylae (36 B.C.) when Agrippa repeated the famous victory; cf. *eleg. in Maecen.* 1. 41 f. 'illum piscosi viderunt saxa Pelori / ignibus hostilis reddere ligna ratis'. Panegyrists of Octavian could not possibly have forgotten the historical associations of these waters.

3. **Poeno purpureum sanguine** : for such descriptions of naval warfare cf. 2. 1. 35 n. Horace deliberately depicts the scene of horror with the incongruous softness that he deprecates: *purpureum* when combined with *mollibus* would normally suggest luxury, but here it is followed by *sanguine*. The sea was picturesquely described as 'purple' (Hom. *Il.* 16. 391, Cic. *ac.* 2. 105, André 100 f.), but here the colour is produced by blood (Hom. *Il.* 17. 361, Plin. *nat.* 9. 135, Sil. 4. 168, André 97). Horace is also playing on the associations of the Phoenicians with purple (cf. 3. 6. 34 'infecit aequor sanguine Punico', André 88 ff.) ; though *Punicus* and *Poenus* normally refer to Carthage rather than Tyre, yet cf. *epod.* 9. 27 'punico / lugubre mutavit sagum', Prop. 4. 3. 51 'Poenis . . . ostris'.

   mollibus : cf. 1. 6. 10 'imbellisque lyrae' (with note ad loc.); Horace may be influenced by Prop. 2. 1. 41 'duro . . . versu' (below, 7 n.). *mollis* particularly suits love-poetry; cf. Hermesianax 7. 36 Powell [2. 9. 17 n.], Prop. 1. 7. 19, *culex* 35 (*mollia carmina* as opposed to themes of Lapiths and Giants), Ov. *trist.* 2. 307 with Owen's note. For Horace's pretence of triviality cf. 1. 6. 9 ff., 2. 1. 37 ff., 3. 3. 69 f.

4. **aptari** : the word is used of accommodating a style or theme to an appropriate medium; cf. *epist.* 1. 3. 12 f. 'fidibusne Latinis / Thebanos aptare modos studet auspice Musa?', Sidon. *epist.* 9. 15. 1 vers. 29 f. 'si lyrae poeticae / Latiare carmen aptet absque Dorico'. Horace seems to be conveying some of the musical associations of ἁρμόζειν (though that refers primarily to the stringing of the lyre); cf. Prop. 3. 3. 35 f. 'haec carmina nervis / aptat'. For the characteristic ancient belief that the metre should reflect the subject cf. *ars* 73 f., Ov. *am.* 1. 1. 2, *rem.* 381 f.

   citharae : here exclusively the instrument of lyric; contrast *Anacreontea* 2. 1. δότε μοι λύρην 'Ομήρου, Prop. 2. 10. 10 'nunc aliam citharam me mea Musa docet'. For the contrast of epic and lyric cf. Quint. *inst.* 10. 1. 62 'Stesichorum ... epici carminis onera lyra sustinentem' (a paradoxical remark).

modis : this word for music or poetry suggests the idea of limitation ('measures'); there is thus a verbal contrast with *longa* in the first clause. As has been seen, *durum* in the second clause (2 n.) is in opposition to *mollibus*. It is desirable that the same balance should be sustained in the third clause; presumably as the sea is immeasurable (1. 28. 1 n., 2. 6. 7, Lucan 5. 182 'modus Oceani') it cannot be fitted to the measures of the *cithara* (whereas epic poetry is compared to the ocean at 4. 15. 3, Call. *h.* 2. 106, Prop. 3. 9. 3 and 35). Horace's epigram is helped by the *ab urbe condita* construction of 'Siculum mare purpureum' ('the reddening of the Sicilian sea'); the Latin form of words implies that the sea itself is confined to a narrow space (for a similar use of the construction cf. 2. 4. 10 n.).

5. saevos Lapithas : for the battle of the Lapiths and Centaurs at Hippodamia's wedding cf. Roscher 2. 1. 1035 ff.; for its appearance in *recusationes* see below, 7 n. In fifth-century art it was one of the subjects of the pediment at Olympia and the metopes of the Parthenon; it also appeared on the shoes of Pheidias's Parthenos (Plin. *nat.* 36. 18) as well as in an earlier painting by Micon in the Theseum (Paus. 1. 17. 2). Continuous accounts in literature are surprisingly few; a certain Melesandrus of Miletus wrote a poem on the subject (Ael. *var. hist.* 11. 2), and a Hellenistic model may lie behind Ovid's lively story (*met.* 12. 210–530). Horace simply gives a dry summary of this as of other rejected topics; such catalogues are characteristic of Hellenistic poetry, which preferred allusion to narration (Boucher 300 ff.), and in particular of the *recusatio*, which aimed at the brevity of *praeteritio* (cf. 1. 6. 5 ff.).

When the Lapiths are mentioned alongside a Centaur, one may expect them to stand for civilization against barbarism (as in fifth-century art). On the other hand they are sometimes described as barbarians themselves (Virg. *Aen.* 7. 304 f. 'Mars perdere gentem / immanem Lapithum valuit'), and their king Pirithous is a defeated sinner in Horace's fourth Roman ode (3. 4. 79 f., cf. Ov. *met.* 8. 612 f.). In our passage *saevos*, which can hardly be taken as complimentary, points to the latter interpretation; if the Lapiths are regarded as savage creatures they are on all fours not only with Hylaeus but with the giants of line 7.

nimium mero : for the drunkenness of the Centaurs at Hippodamia's wedding cf. 1. 18. 8 n. *nimium* describes excessive behaviour (cf. Aeschin. 2. 41 πολὺς ἦν τοῖς ἐπαίνοις καὶ ἐπαχθής); the dry euphemism suggests the language of a historian (cf. Sall. *hist.* 2. 53, etc.). The nuance seems to be 'outrageous with wine' (cf. Tac. *hist.*

4. 23. 2 'praeferoces initio et rebus secundis nimii'). Some interpret
'excessive in his drinking' (cf. Tac. *hist.* 1. 35. 1 'nimii verbis', 4. 80. 3,
ann. 13. 13. 2), but this balances *saevos* less well; lyric poets could
write about drunken centaurs but not about aggressive ones.

6. **Hylaeum** : a centaur; the name means 'wild man of the woods'.
He appears on the sixth-century François Vase as a participant in
the battle with the Lapiths (Beazley, *ABV*, p. 76); for an illustration
cf. P. E. Arias, *A History of Greek Vase Painting*, 1962, pl. 43. For
literary references cf. Virg. *georg.* 2. 456 f. 'Rhoetumque Pholumque /
et magno Hylaeum Lapithis cratere minantem', Ov. *met.* 12. 378
(Hyles), Stat. *Theb.* 6. 538 f. He is associated elsewhere with the
Atalanta legend (Prop. 1. 1. 13, *RE* 9. 109).

In view of the apparent political allusions above and below (see
notes on 1, 2, 7) it may be possible to see another one here (Dacier).
The epithet *nimium mero* is well suited to Antony (1. 37. 12 n.), and
when Octavian's propagandists attacked the self-indulgence of the
Alexandrian court they could well have included a reference to
licentious centaurs; for such invective cf. Cic. *Pis.* 22 'quod quidem
istius in illis rei publicae luctibus quasi aliquod Lapitharum aut
Centaurorum convivium ferebatur, in quo nemo potest dicere utrum
iste plus biberit [an vomuerit] an effuderit'. It might even be relevant
that Antony had been a *magister* of the Luperci, and jokes about his
savage dress could have become part of the literary tradition (note
the pun at Cic. *Phil.* 2. 111 'tuum hominis simplicis pectus vidimus')
When Propertius describes Antony's ships at Actium as 'Centaurica
saxa minantis' (4. 6. 49), he may be thinking of barbaric violence as
well as of missiles; in Virgil's boat-race (*Aen.* 5. 121 f.) the Centaurus
is significantly sailed by the reckless Sergestus, the ancestor of Sergius Catilina (on the other hand the Centaurus of 10. 195 ff. dis-
charges *saxa* but has no evil associations).

domitosque : an appropriately heroic word for 'laid low'; cf. 3. 4.
72, Ov. *trist.* 2. 333, Pind. *N.* 7. 90 (of Heracles) Γίγαντας ὃς ἐδάμασας.
As the verb is primarily used of taming animals it is well suited to
Hercules. Cunningham proposed *domitosve*, but for *-que* after a
negative cf. *epod.* 16. 6 ff., *serm.* 2. 6. 19, H.–Sz. 500, Austin on Virg.
Aen. 2. 37.

Herculea manu : the use of the adjective instead of the genitive
is a grandiose touch that suits the epic context; cf. 1. 3. 36
'Herculeus labor', Löfstedt, *Syntactica* 1². 107 ff. There was an oracle
that the giants could only be destroyed if the gods were helped
by a mortal; Hercules was summoned to the rescue and killed
Alcyoneus and Porphyrion among others (West on Hes. *th.* 954,
Vian 193 ff.). There were also legends that on separate occasions

he killed the Lapiths (Roscher 2. 2. 1862 f.) and Hylaeus among other Centaurs (Virg. *Aen.* 8. 293 f. 'tu nubigenas, invicte, bimembris / Hylaeumque Pholumque manu . . . mactas'). Yet it seems wrong to take *domitos Herculea manu* ἀπὸ κοινοῦ with all three accusatives; *domitos* balances *saevos* and *nimium*, and the Lapiths are naturally connected here with the Centauromachy rather than with their later destruction.

If the context contains an element of allegory (see especially the next note), Hercules naturally represents Augustus: both were portrayed as benefactors of humanity who rid the world of monsters and were rewarded with semi-divine honours (3. 3. 9 ff., 4. 5. 36, *epist.* 2. 1. 10 ff., V. Buchheit, *Vergil über die Sendung Roms*, 1963, pp. 116 ff.). The comparison must have been made particularly during Augustus's absence in the far West, that is to say at the very time when the ode was probably written; cf. 3. 14. 1 'Herculis ritu' (on the triumphal approach in 24 B.C.). Virgil's account of the ceremonies at the Ara Maxima (*Aen.* 8. 184 ff.) seems in part to reflect the same occasion; for other historical allusions in that passage cf. D. L. Drew, *The Allegory of the Aeneid*, 1927, pp. 7 ff., G. Binder, *Aeneas und Augustus*, 1971, pp. 145 ff.

7. **Telluris iuvenes** : the giants were born from earth, γηγενεῖς (Hes. *th.* 184 f. with West's note, *RE* Suppl. 3. 660); cf. Naev. *bell. Pun.* 19. 3 M. 'Runcus ac Purpureus, filii Terras'. *iuvenes* means 'young warriors' (Heinze); cf. 3. 4. 50 'fidens iuventus horrida bracchiis'. Some interpret simply 'sons' as at 4. 5. 9 'ut mater iuvenem'; but there *mater* defines the relationship. Elsewhere *iuvenis* is used of a son with an offhand detachment inappropriate to our passage (Juv. 8. 262, 10. 310, 14. 121).

The attack of the Giants on the Gods was a long-established poetical theme (*RE* Suppl. 3. 656 ff., Vian, *passim*). Already Xenophanes rejects the story on moral grounds as unsuitable for the symposium: cf. 1. 21 f. οὔ τι μάχας διέπειν Τιτήνων οὐδὲ Γιγάντων / οὐδὲ ⟨ ⟩ Κενταύρων, πλάσματα τῶν προτέρων. One would conjecture that a Hellenistic poet, perhaps Callimachus, adapted these lines to a manifesto on neo-epic, which may in turn have influenced the Roman poets; Horace and the *culex* (see below) both mention Centaurs as well as Giants, a feature that might be derived from Xenophanes through a Hellenistic intermediary. For instances of the topic in *recusationes* cf. Prop. 2. 1. 19 f. 'non ego Titanas canerem, non Ossan Olympo / inpositam, ut caeli Pelion esset iter', 39 ff. 'sed neque Phlegraeos Iovis Enceladique tumultus / intonet angusto pectore Callimachus, / nec mea conveniunt duro praecordia versu / Caesaris in Phrygios condere nomen avos' (*intonet* comes from Call. fr. 1. 20

βροντᾶν), 3. 9. 47 f. 'te duce vel Iovis arma canam caeloque minantem /
Coeum et Phlegraeis Oromedonta iugis', Ov. *am.* 2. 1. 11 ff., *trist.*
2. 333 f. 'at si me iubeas domitos Iovis igne gigantas / dicere, conantem debilitabit opus' (for the erroneous assumption that Ovid really
intended such a poem cf. Owen's commentary, pp. 66 ff.), *culex* 26 ff.
'tibi namque canit non pagina bellum / triste Iovis ponitque ⟨. . .⟩ /
Phlegra, Giganteo sparsa est quae sanguine tellus, / nec Centaureos
Lapithas compellit in enses'. For other references to the pretentious-
ness of such themes (piling Pelion on Ossa) cf. Ar. *av.* 824 f. τὸ
Φλέγρας πεδίον, ἵν' οἱ θεοὶ τοὺς γηγενεῖς / ἀλαζονευόμενοι καθυπερηκόν-
τισαν, Ov. *met.* 10. 150 f., Philostr. *vit. soph.* 518 οὕτω τι μεγαλοφωνίας
ἐπὶ μεῖζον ἤλασεν ὥστε καὶ Γιγαντίαν ξυνθεῖναι.

If the reader is on the alert for contemporary parallels (cf. 1 n.,
2 n.), it is not difficult to see analogies with Horace's Giants (V.
Buchheit, *Hermes* 94, 1966, 94 ff. and *Der Anspruch des Dichters in
Vergils Georgika*, 1972, p. 143). Pindar had used Typhos to symbolize
the barbarians defeated by the Deinomenids at Himera and Cumae
(*P.* 1. 15 ff.), and his Porphyrion seems to suggest the arrogance of
Athenian imperialism (*P.* 8. 12); the gigantomachies of the Parthenon metopes and the shield of Pheidias's Parthenos represented
the repulse of the Persian invaders, that of the Great Altar at Pergamum the victory of Attalus I over the Galatians (about 240 B.C.).
Similarly the monsters of Horace's fourth Roman Ode stand for the
anarchic forces that Augustus had overthrown (3. 4. 69 ff., Fraenkel
278 ff.); for allegorical gigantomachies in later Latin literature cf.
Lucan 1. 35 f., Mart. 8. 49 (50). 1 ff. In our passage one might think
of the tyrannicides (Dacier), who had rebelled impiously against
a future god and been defeated within a hundred miles of Phlegra
(Pallene), the traditional scene of the Gigantomachy; the very
name 'Brutus' suggests a son of Tellus (cf. 1. 34. 9 'bruta tellus' with
note ad loc.), and Horace might even have remembered the original
Brutus who achieved *imperium* after kissing Mother Earth (Liv.
1. 56. 12 'scilicet quod ea communis mater omnium mortalium esset').
Alternatively he might again be alluding to the Antonians; if we
knew more about contemporary public sculpture the reference would
be clearer. The Palatine temple of Apollo portrayed the defeat of
the 'Gauls' at Delphi in 278 B.C. (Prop. 2. 31. 13 'deiectos Parnasi
vertice Gallos'), and the god's overthrow of the clambering barbarians was presumably associated with a gigantomachy (Call. *h.*
4. 174 calls them ὀψίγονοι Τιτῆνες) no less than the victory of Attalus
(see above). It has been supposed that the temple of Jupiter Tonans,
dedicated in 22 B.C., had such a relief; cf. Buchheit, op. cit., p. 97,
citing Claud. 28. 44 f. 'iuvat infra tecta Tonantis / cernere Tarpeia
pendentes rupe Gigantas'. But Claudian may be referring to *colossi*

on the Capitoline (Plin. *nat.* 34. 39–43) rather than a frieze, which would be difficult to see from the Palatine; in any case *Tonantis* may refer to the principal temple of Jupiter Capitolinus (L. Jeep, *RhM 27*, 1872, 269 ff.).

unde : = *ex quibus* (1. 12. 17 n.); the archaic usage keeps up the heroic tone. The word is to be taken closely with *periculum*; cf. Cic. *Phil.* 7. 2 'a quo maius periculum quam ab ullis nationibus extimescendum est', Tac. *ann.* 1. 80. 2.

8. fulgens . . . domus : cf. 3. 3. 33 f. 'lucidas . . . sedes' (which suggests a more serene light), Hom. *Il.* 1. 532 αἰγλήεντος Ὀλύμπου. For *domus* applied to the gods (=δῶμα) cf. 1. 3. 29, *Thes.l.L.* 5. 1. 1978. 44 ff.; here *periculum contremuit* partly suggests the meaning 'household'.

contremuit : *contremisco* is a solemn old word (E. Skard, *Ennius und Sallustius*, 1933, pp. 64 ff.); for the transitive use cf. Virg. *Aen.* 3. 648 (*tremesco*), Sen. *epist.* 65. 24, *Thes.l.L.* 4. 775. 72 ff. For the terror caused to the gods by the rebel onslaught cf. 3. 4. 49 f. 'magnum illa terrorem intulerat Iovi / . . . iuventus'. The verb also hints at the literal shaking of Olympus; such a commotion was normally caused by the thunder of Jupiter (1. 34. 11 n., Enn. *ann.* 541 'contremuit templum magnum Iovis altitonantis').

9. Saturni : Cronos played no part in the legend of the Gigantomachia; from the time of Euripides this was often confused with the earlier Titanomachia (cf. 3. 4. 54 ff.), in which of course he fought on the same side as the Titans (West on Hes. *th.* 617–719). Horace may be suggesting an attempt to restore the *ancien régime* (Apollodorus 1. 6. 1 says that Earth bred the Giants to avenge the Titans, cf. *Telluris iuvenes*); the epithet *veteris* also helps us to interpret 'the house that had been Saturn's'. The poet would thus be combining references to both battles in the manner of Propertius (2. 1. 19 f., cited 7 n.).

If the allegorical undercurrent is to be sustained one looks for a secondary meaning; already Dacier suggested that the house of Saturn stands for Latium (cf. Virg. *Aen.* 8. 319 ff., Wissowa 206) but this does not suit *fulgens*. Perhaps one might rather propose the *aedes Saturni* (Platner–Ashby 463 f.); for the poetical use of *domus* for a temple cf. *Thes.l.L.* 5. 1. 1970. 18 ff. This building was the site of the Roman *aerarium*, and enemies in a civil war could plausibly be accused of having designs on temple treasuries (cf. Cic. *Phil.* 2. 93 for Antony and Ops, App. *civ.* 4. 73. 311 for Cassius at Rhodes). *fulgens* suits a glittering building (3. 3. 42 f. 'stet Capitolium / fulgens', *Thes.l.L.* 6. 1. 1509. 58 ff.); the word would have significance in or after 42 B.C., when the *aedes Saturni* was restored by Plancus (*ILS* 41 and 886). We need hardly inquire about the precise degree of glitter achieved by the time of Brutus's death ; Horace could have ignored the finer points of chronology (he was abroad at the time), or he might be thinking partly or mainly of Antony's threat in 31.

veteris : Cronos is called γέρων, παλαιγενής, παλαίτατος, πρεσβύτης (Bruchmann 166 f.) ; cf. also Virg. *Aen.* 7. 180 'Saturnusque senex', Carter 91. But *veteris* stresses his displacement rather than his age ; cf. Aesch. *Prom.* 96 (of Zeus) ὁ νέος ταγὸς μακάρων, 310, Timotheus 796. 3 f. νέος ὁ Ζεὺς βασιλεύει, / τὸ πάλαι δ᾽ ἦν Κρόνος ἄρχων.

tuque : the construction is difficult. Horace is saying ' Just as the Numantine War and Gigantomachia are unsuitable for lyric, so too the battles of Augustus, which it will be better that you should de-scribe in prose'. But instead of using *ut* and *ita* he makes the two clauses coordinate (for such *comparatio paratactica*, common in Pindar, see Fraenkel 220) ; and he adds emphasis as well as variety by making Maecenas the subject of the sentence instead of putting him in a subordinate clause. He also follows the diffident negative *nolis* with the confident positive *dices*; by this casual change of direction he makes his triumphant solution seem offhand and obvious.

Many commentators give -*que* an adversative implication, but the sentence is pointing in the same direction as its predecessor. Fraenkel takes the third and fourth stanzas together (with a comma at 12 *minacium*) ; he interprets 'and whilst you, Maecenas, may in prose record Caesar's triumphs, my Muse . . .'. But a first sentence lasting for five stanzas is too clumsy and complicated ; and it spoils a climax if the suggestion that Maecenas should write prose history is stowed away in what would be virtually a subordinate clause.

pedestribus : πεζός can be applied to verse unaccompanied by music (Soph. fr. 16 P. = 15 N. καὶ πεζὰ καὶ φορμικτά with Pearson's parallels), to prose (L.-S.-J. s.v., Quint. *inst.* 10. 1. 81 'prorsam orationem et quam pedestrem Graeci vocant'), or to uninflated verse (Call. fr. 112. 9 αὐτὰρ ἐγὼ Μουσέων πεζὸν ἔπειμι νομόν, cf. Pfeiffer's biblio-graphy ad loc.). In our passage *pedestribus* refers obviously to prose ; as the word has a military tone ('footslogging' rather than 'pedes-trian'), it balances 10 *proelia*. Elsewhere Horace uses *pedester* in Callimachean fashion of satire and comedy ; cf. *serm.* 2. 6. 17 'saturis Musaque pedestri' (a paradox), *ars* 95 'sermone pedestri'. See further Norden, *Kl. Schr.*, pp. 9 f. (with material on the contrasting theme of the Muses' chariot), *Antike Kunstprosa*, 1909, I. 33 n. 3, M. Puelma Piwonka, *Lucilius und Kallimachos*, 1949, pp. 327 ff., K. Thraede, *Studien zu Sprache und Stil des Prudentius* (*Hypomne-mata* 13), 1965, pp. 51 ff.

10. dices . . . melius : 'it will be more appropriate that you should write', not 'you will write with greater skill'; for the emphatic use of the adverb cf. 1. 2. 22 n., Brink on *ars* 40. Maecenas seems to have given some account of Octavian at Philippi (Plin. *nat.* 7. 148), but reminiscences are not history and one should not take Horace too seriously (Serv. *georg.* 2. 41 'Augusti Caesaris gesta descripsit' actually interprets our passage of a historical poem). Suggestions for alternative authors are offered in the *recusatio* without much regard for probability (1. 6. 1 n.); Horace is turning the tables on his patron, and does not expect a positive response. It would be wrong to see a gibe at Maecenas's bad verses, but there may be an oblique reminder that his tastes no less than Horace's were too artistic for military narrative.

proelia: after his tactful circumlocutions Horace comes to the point and indicates what he is declining to do. *proelia* were conventional in *recusatio*; cf. 1. 6. 17, 4. 15. 1, *serm.* 2. 1. 13 ff., *epist.* 2. 1. 254, Virg. *ecl.* 6. 3 'cum canerem reges et proelia', *georg.* 3. 46, Prop. 2. 1. 45, 3. 9. 38. The common source may be Virgil, but the wide diffusion of the topic suggests that Callimachus may have referred to battle in a similar context; however, at fr. 1. 4 [above, p. 180] Lobel's πρήξιας is the most plausible supplement (cf. Dioscorides, *anth. P.* 11. 195. 5).

11. ductaque . . . colla: at a triumph the defeated enemy rulers were marched through the streets of Rome; cf. 4. 2. 34 ff., *epod.* 7. 7 f. With pointed compression the participle is combined with *colla*, which economically suggests bonds; cf. Prop. 2. 1. 33 [above, p. 183], *Thes.l.L.* 3. 1662. 77 ff.

12. regum . . . minacium: Callimachus had referred to the deeds of kings in his famous prologue to the *Aetia* [above, p. 180]; for imitations in the Roman *recusatio* cf. Virg. *ecl.* 6. 3 [above, 10 n.], Prop. 3. 3. 3 'reges, Alba, tuos et regum facta tuorum', Wimmel, op. cit., pp. 78 ff. Horace makes the commonplace topical by hinting at the Eastern rulers paraded in the triumph of 29. *minacium* refers to the characteristic arrogance of these princes in the days of their power; cf. 4. 3. 8 'quod regum tumidas contuderit minas'. As the adjective suggests towering height, it makes a contrast with the humiliation implied by the juxtaposed *colla*; cf. 2. 7. 11 n., Ov. *trist.* 4. 2. 45 'collaque Romanae praebens animosa securi', *epiced. Drusi* 277 f.

13. dulcis: accusative plural, not genitive singular. In this eulogistic stanza *cantus* needs a sympathetic adjective no less than *oculos* and *pectus*.

dominae: for the ambiguity see above, pp. 180 f. For the use of the word as a synonym for *amica* cf. Lucil. 730, Tib. 1. 1. 46 with

K. F. Smith's note, *Thes.l.L.* 5. 1. 1938. 1 ff. The usage is not attested in comedy but belongs to the world of epigram and novel (Paul. Sil. *anth. P.* 5. 230. 8, Ach. Tat. 2. 4. 4). Originally it must have suggested the conceit of the *servitium amoris*; cf. 1. 33. 14 n., where however the references to Catullus should be deleted (L. P. Wilkinson, *CR* N.S. 20, 1970, 290).

Licymniae : the implications of the name are crucial for the meaning of the poem (pp. 180 ff.), but unfortunately are difficult to determine. If a covert allusion to Terentia is intended, there is probably a hint of Licinia, which was one of the *nomina* of her family (p. 152), though she herself does not seem to have used it; it is relevant that the spelling *Licinn-* is found in literary and epigraphic texts (Plut. *C. Gracch.* 38. 6, Javol. *dig.* 24. 3. 66 pr., *IG* 7. 110, 1777). Less plausibly one might point out that Licymna was the acropolis of Tiryns and *Licymnius* a poetical equivalent for *Tirynthius* (Stat. *Theb.* 4. 735); as no absurdity was too great for Roman philologists, the latter name might conceivably have been connected with the Terentii. Again, one might posit an imagined link with *lucumo*, the Etruscan word for a prince; among a range of similar names from Etruria cf. *CIE* 1. 3932 'luχumni' and *CIL* 11. 1788 (Volaterrae) 'Laucumnia Felicitas' (see *RE* 13. 1706 ff., W. Schulze, *Zur Geschichte lateinischer Eigennamen, AGG* N.F. 5, 1904, 179). One may quote in this connection Virg. *Aen.* 9. 545 ff. 'primaevus Helenor / Maeonio regi quem serva Licymnia furtim / sustulerat'; perhaps Virgil might be imitating Horace by connecting the Lydian king with an Etruscan-sounding name.

On the other hand if we dismiss all possible allusions to Terentia, Horace may simply be deriving the name from ὑμνεῖν (note the next word *cantus*); though this is a false etymology, it is sufficiently defended by the analogy of Polyhymnia (originally Polymnia, and nothing to do with singing). The first part of the name causes greater difficulty: a connection with λιγύς does not seem convincing. Th. Birt suggested that when γλυκύς was pronounced by Romans the initial γ tended to be dropped (*Horaz' Lieder, Studien zur Kritik und Auslegung*, 1926, pp. 101 f.); he compared *lac* for *glacte, liquiritia* for γλυκύριζα. This would give an admirable point with *dulcis* above; but even if this explanation is correct, a poet of Horace's ingenuity could have combined it with one of the other associations.

14. voluit dicere : for advice by the Muse in the *recusatio* cf. above, p. 180. The infinitive picks up 10 *dices*: for the verb's application to singing and serious poetry cf. 1. 21. 1 n., Löfstedt, *Peregrinatio*, pp. 282 ff.

lucidum fulgentis : for the mannered adverbial accusative cf. 1. 22.

23, 2. 19. 6, 3. 27. 67, K.–S. 1. 281, H.–Sz. 40. The verb (used by Plin. *nat.* 11. 151 of cats' eyes) helps to underline that Licymnia is in love; cf. Hom. *Il.* 3. 397 ὄμματα μαρμαίροντα (Aphrodite), Cic. *har. resp.* 38 'coniventis illos oculos abavi tui magis optandos fuisse quam hos flagrantis sororis' (Clodia). The repetition after 8 *fulgens* may be deliberate, though it does not seem particularly pointed to the modern reader: there is a general contrast in these stanzas (e.g. *dulcis* balances *saevos*), though details cannot be pressed.

15. bene : Horace now comes to the climax in his list of Licymnia's attributes. Porphyrio seems right to take *bene* with *fidum* (cf. *male fidus*); for the hyperbaton cf. 2. 5. 22 n., 4. 12. 7 f. 'quod male barbaras / regum est ulta libidines', *epist.* 1. 2. 50 'bene cogitat uti'. The word does not suit so well the objective relationship described by *mutuis*; certainly it must refer to Licymnia rather than to her lover (the emphasis is then in the wrong place). The adverb is one of quality ('properly') rather than degree (*valde* Porphyrio); the latter usage is too colloquial here, and would if anything have a weakening effect (Heinze).

mutuis . . . amoribus : the sentence is bound together most tightly if this is taken as dative with *fidum*; some see an ablative of quality, but the adjective is not qualitative enough. The interlaced word-order (*bene mutuis fidum . . . amoribus*) suits the reciprocity of the affection; cf. *carm. epig.* 959 b. 3 'fido fida viro veixsit'. But here *mutuis* must refer to both parties (see the parallels below), not simply to the man.

For other references to mutual love cf. 3. 9. 13, 4. 1. 30, *epod.* 15. 10, Catull. 45. 20 (Septimius and Acme) 'mutuis animis amant amantur', Tib. 1. 6. 14, Sulpicia ap. Tib. 3. 11. 6, [Virg.] *catal.* 4. 12. So too in Greek, Theoc. 12. 15 f. ἦ ῥα τότ' ἦσαν / χρύσειοι πάλιν ἄνδρες ὅτ' ἀντεφίλησ' ὁ φιληθείς, 18. 51 f., Bion fr. 12. However, the view of *fides* implied is characteristically Roman; cf. R. Reitzenstein, *SHAW* 3, 1912, 12. Abh. 9 ff., Ross 80 ff.

17. nec . . . dedecuit : the words are probably not just the equivalent of *decuit* but imply that Licymnia has overcome some obstacle; cf. 1. 38. 6 ff. 'neque te ministrum / dedecet myrtus neque me sub arta / vite bibentem' (the myrtle, simple though it is, graces you, and even at my age I can wear it with style), Ov. *am.* 1. 7. 12 (my lady's hair, though dishevelled, did not disgrace her), 3. 15. 4 (though I was born at Sulmo my love-poetry has done me credit). In our passage the handicap is presumably that of an older woman dancing with un-married girls; this conjunction could sometimes seem unsuitable (3. 15. 4 ff.), but to suggest an absence of impropriety here would be a very back-handed compliment. The tense of the verb seems to be a true perfect : Horace is referring to a recent occasion and in no way implies that Licymnia's dancing days are over.

ferre pedem : cf. Virg. *georg.* 1. 11 'ferte simul Faunique pedem . . .' (for the commoner *referre pedem* cf. Bömer on Ov. *met.* 2. 439), Eur. *El.* 859 θὲς ἐς χόρον, ὦ φίλα, ἴχνος. All three infinitives refer to activities on Diana's day (20 n.) ; otherwise the sentence is unbalanced. For sacred dancing cf. 4. 1. 25 ff., Liv. 27. 37. 13 'virgines sonum vocis pulsu pedum modulantes incesserunt', Wille 187 ff.

18. certare ioco : for the ablative cf. 4. 1. 31 'nec certare iuvat mero', *epist.* 1. 19. 11 ; there is something of an oxymoron in the juxtaposition of these two words. Horace seems to be referring to some sort of amoebaean raillery, perhaps appropriate to Diana of the Aventine (20 n.) ; cf. the *ioci veteres* sung by young girls against Mars (Ov. *fast.* 3. 695). At first sight one might suppose that nothing more is meant than informal merriment (for *certare* in non-competitive contexts cf. 1. 1. 8 n., Stat. *Theb.* 2. 244 'certant laetitia', *silv.* 1. 4. 13) ; yet one looks for a more organized activity to set alongside *ferre pedem* and *dare bracchia*. Horace cannot simply be referring to witticisms at parties (Sall. *Cat.* 25. 5 'posse versus facere, iocum movere') ; that would disrupt the sequence of the two clauses that refer to dancing.

dare bracchia : to stretch out the hands, whether in dancing or in boxing (Ov. *fast.* 2. 368), to ask mercy (Prop. 4. 3. 12) or to give help (Ov. *Pont.* 2. 6. 13), to embrace a lover (*carm.* 3. 9. 2 f.) or a ghost (Virg. *Aen.* 2. 792). One should distinguish expressions that refer to the clasping of hands (Prop. 3. 5. 20 'Musarumque choris implicuisse manus') or the linking of arms (Ov. *fast.* 6. 329, Stat. *Ach.* 1. 319 f. 'bracchia ludo / nectere'). Arm movements were very important in ancient dancing, but Horace is thinking of something less elaborate than the χειρονομία of a *pantomima*.

19. ludentem : used here of dancing (cf. 3. 15. 5 'inter ludere virgines', Virg. *ecl.* 6. 28) ; so Greek παίζειν (Hom. *Od.* 6. 106, etc.). The word balances *ioco* (cf. 2. 19. 25 f.) just as *bracchia* balances *pedem*; for similar structures cf. 4 n., 2. 15. 20 n.

nitidis : the adjective suggests the spotless finery appropriate to a religious festival. On Diana's day Roman women washed their hair (Plut. *quaest. Rom.* 287 f).

virginibus : for such choruses cf. 1. 21 (vol. i, pp. 253 f.), 4. 6. 31 ff., Catull. 34. In Greece, where girls were secluded, religious festivals offered a traditional opportunity for falling in love ; cf. Plut. *virt. mul.* 249 d οἱ δὲ μνηστῆρες ἐθεῶντο παιζούσας καὶ χορευούσας, Gow on Theoc. 2. 66, Headlam on Herodas 1. 56, Rohde, *Roman*[3], pp. 155 f., Gerald Brenan, *South from Granada*, 1957, ch. 19 'The only day in the year on which one could be sure of seeing them was the feast of

Corpus Christi, when they all came out and walked about in their new dresses' (*nitidis*). Though Horace is talking about an older woman in the emancipated world of Rome, he may be influenced by this common literary motif.

20. Dianae celebris die : Diana had a famous old temple on the Aventine, recently restored by L. Cornificius (*carm. saec.* 69, Suet. *Aug.* 29. 5, Wissowa 249 f., Latte 173, Platner–Ashby 149 f.); her festival was on 13 August (Afran. *com.* 141 'sanctum diem Dianae'). This was likewise the day of Fortuna Equestris, which might have had special importance for Maecenas, and also of Octavian's first triumph in 29 B.C.; but though the calendar was something real to the Romans, we cannot say whether these particular details would have seemed significant. For the archaic and appropriately grandiloquent scansion *Dīanae* cf. 1. 21. 1 n.

The adjective(= 'thronged') properly belongs to the temple; cf. Lucil. 992, Lucr. 5. 1166 f. 'delubra deum . . . festis celebrare diebus'. Here it is applied to the goddess herself (cf. Tib. 2. 1. 83, 3. 10. 23); the transference is perhaps easier because the temple could be known simply as *Dianae* (like St. Paul's). The Aventine Diana must have attracted numerous worshippers among the poorer classes; cf. Paul. Fest. 345 M. = 467 L. 'servorum dies festus erat Idibus Augusti quia eo die rex Tullius filius ancillae aedem Dianae dedicavit'.

21. num tu . . . : for the ambiguity cf. above, p. 181.

tenuit : the verb is used in heroic contexts of kingdoms, etc.; cf. 3. 17. 8, Virg. *Aen.* 7. 735, etc.

dives Achaemenes : the legendary founder of the Persian Achaemenid dynasty (Hdt. 3. 75. 1, *RE* 1. 199 ff.), here given the wealth of historical Eastern kings; cf. 3. 1. 44, *epod.* 13. 8. For the rejection of Eastern magnificence in romantic contexts cf. 3. 9. 4, Sappho 16. 17 ff. τᾶς κε βολλοίμην ἔρατόν τε βᾶμα / κἀμάρυχμα λάμπρον ἴδην προσώπω / ἢ τὰ Λύδων ἄρματα καὶ πανόπλοις / [πεσδομ]άχεντας, 132 ἔστι μοι κάλα πάις χρυσίοισιν ἀνθέμοισιν / ἐμφέρην ἔχοισα μόρφαν Κλέις ἀγαπάτα, / ἀντὶ τᾶς ἔγωὐδὲ Λυδίαν παῖσαν οὐδ' ἐράνναν . . . , Call. fr. 75. 43 ff. οὔ σε δοκέω τημοῦτος, Ἀκόντιε, νυκτὸς ἐκείνης / ἀντί κε τῇ μίτρῃς ἥψαο παρθενίης, / οὐ σφυρὸν Ἰφίκλειον ἐπιτρέχον ἀσταχύεσσιν / οὐδ' ἃ Κελαινίτης ἐκτεάτιστο Μίδης / δέξασθαι (imitated by Aristaenetus 1. 10), Theoc. 8. 53 μή μοι γᾶν Πέλοπος, μή μοι Κροίσεια τάλαντα / εἴη ἔχειν, Catull. 45. 21 f. [below, 24 n.], Prop. 1. 8. 33 ff., Tib. 2. 2. 15 f. For similar declarations in other contexts cf. 1. 38. 1 n., Tyrtaeus 12. 6 W. (οὐδ' εἰ) πλουτοίη δὲ Μιδέω καὶ Κινυρέω μάλιον (I should not admire a coward), Eur. *Herc.* 643 ff. μή μοι μήτ' Ἀσιήτιδος / τυραννίδος ὄλβος εἴη, / μὴ χρυσοῦ δώματα πλήρη / τᾶς ἥβας ἀντιλαβεῖν.

22. pinguis Phrygiae : for the semi-proverbial fertility of north-west Asia Minor cf. *epist*. 1. 3. 5, Cic. *Manil*. 14, Catull. 46. 5. But Horace is not thinking just of agricultural productivity, but of the wealth of Midas (cf. Tyrtaeus and Callimachus cited above, *RE* 15. 2. 1531).

Mygdonias : Hellenistic and Roman poets used the adjective to mean 'Phrygian'; cf. Moschus 2. 97 f. with Bühler's note, Paus. 10. 27. 1. Horace is alluding to Mygdon, the legendary king of Phrygia (the word thus balances *Achaemenes*); presumably he is also associating the Etruscan Maecenas with the wealth of Asian kings (so 3. 16. 41 f.). For the enallage cf. Catull. 61. 27 f. 'Thespiae / rupis Aonios specus', Norden on Virg. *Aen*. 6. 2. Horace heaps up the luxurious words to increase the impression of opulence (so 1. 17. 14 ff.); the alliteration of *p* (including *ph*) seems to serve the same effect.

23. permutare velis : the urbanity of 1 *nolis* is repeated. *permutare* means 'to take in exchange' (cf. 1. 17. 2 n.). The compound is not invariably prosaic (cf. Virg. *Aen*. 9. 307, Stat. *Theb*. 6. 329, etc.), but here at least has a hint of commerce (a *permutatio* was a bill of exchange); cf. 3. 1. 47 f. 'cur valle permutem Sabina / divitias operosiores', *epist*. 1. 7. 35 f. 'nec / otia divitiis Arabum liberrima muto'.

crine : the word probably bears its original sense of a lock or tress of hair (*ciris* 122, Plin. *nat*. 2. 178 'Berenices crinem', i.e. πλόκαμον). Singular *crinis* is often used collectively for all the hair (1. 32. 12, 3. 14. 22), but the other explanation suits the hyperbole better (cf. Stat. *Theb*. 9. 901 'hunc toto capies pro corpore crinem'). For this reason the word has been interpreted of a single hair, which one does not expect to be worth much (cf. Otto 279 on *pilus*); but such a use of *crinis* does not seem to be clearly paralleled.

Horace is describing the beauty of Licymnia's hair as she leans over to have her neck kissed (the comparison with *crine* continues in the last stanza). He is presumably thinking of golden locks (note the hint at Midas above); cf. Alcman 1. 51 ff. ἁ δὲ χαίτα / τᾶς ἐμᾶς ἀνεψιᾶς / Ἀγησιχόρας ἐπανθεῖ / χρυσὸς ὡς ἀκήρατος, Palladas, *anth. P.* 6. 60 ἀντὶ βοὸς χρυσέου τ' ἀναθήματος ῎Ισιδι τούσδε / θήκατο τοὺς λιπαροὺς Παμφίλιον πλοκάμους· / ἡ δὲ θεὸς τούτοις γάνυται πλέον ἤπερ Ἀπόλλων / χρυσῷ ὃν ἐκ Λυδῶν Κροῖσος ἔπεμψε θεῷ.

24. plenas aut Arabum domos : cf. 4. 12. 24 'plena dives ut in domo', Eur. *Herc*. 645 [above, 21 n.], fr. 328. 1 N. For the reputed wealth of the Arabs cf. 1. 29. 1 n., 3. 24. 1 f.; an ancient reader might have sensed a contrast between the 'full houses' of Arabia Felix (Virg. *georg*. 2. 115 'Eoasque domos Arabum') and the poor nomads of Arabia Deserta, ἡ ἐρῆμος Ἀραβία (*RE* 2. 345). Horace seems to be alluding by way of climax to Aelius Gallus's expedition in 26–25 B.C. (vol. i, p. xxxiv); for his apparent connection with Terentia cf.

pp. 223 f. It is an argument in favour of this view that Catullus 45. 22 'mavult quam Syrias Britanniasque' makes a similar topical allusion to Crassus and Caesar (for other resemblances between the two poems cf. 15 n., 25 n.).

25. cum : the variant *dum* is inferior; it implies that Licymnia is admired only as long as she bends her neck. One might say 'dum cervicem detorquet, oscula infigis', but one expects 'cum cervicem detorquet, pulcherrimam putas'.

detorquet . . . cervicem : Porphyrio comments 'magnifice depinxit fastidium mulieris avertentis se ab eo qui osculari se velit'. He is no doubt right about the *fastidium* (which makes a contrast with *flagrantia*), but *avertentis* should not be exaggerated: at this stage Licymnia gives passive consent, and it would be wrong to anticipate the feigned reluctance of the next clause. Kisses on the neck were highly acceptable in erotic writing; cf. Prop. 3. 8. 21, Lucian, *dial. mer.* 3. 2 ἀνακλάσας τὸν αὐχένα τῆς Θαΐδος ἐφίλησεν, Ach. Tat. 2. 4. 4 σὸν ἔργον ἤδη δέσποινάν τε καλεῖν καὶ φιλῆσαι τράχηλον, Alciphron 2. 7. 1, *Thes.l.L.* 3. 1660. 42 ff. Horace presumably remembers the kissing-scene in Catull. 45. 10 ff. 'at Acme leviter caput reflectens' (though the detail is different). The absence of a caesura after the sixth syllable is unusual, even if *de* is to some extent detachable (cf. 1. 18. 16); the rhythm may be designed to support the idea of a languid change of direction.

26. facili saevitia : an oxymoron: *facili* suggests compliance (1. 25. 5 n.), but *saevitia* the reverse (Prop. 1. 1. 10 'saevitiam durae contudit Iasidos'). For similar flirtations cf. 1. 9. 21 n., Tib. 1. 4. 53 ff., Ov. *ars* 1. 663 ff.

27. poscente magis : 'more than a girl who asks' (Rutgers ap. Macleane); for a close parallel to the construction cf. *epist.* 1. 17. 43 f. 'coram rege sua de paupertate tacentes / plus poscente ferent'. The verbs in the sentence describe five different attitudes of the girl to the man (*poscente* making a contrast with *negat*); for *oscula poscere* of the girl cf. Ov. *met.* 4. 334. The phrase is generally interpreted 'more than her suitor' (which is less close to the parallel from the *Epistles*); but anything that plays down the enthusiasm of the man also seems to detract from the attractiveness of the girl. Some interpret as an ablative absolute ('as the suitor becomes more insistent'); but the absence of a noun is unconvincing (in spite of K.–S. 1. 773), and to say that the man's urgency is increasing weakens the impact of the last line. On the other hand absolute *poscente* becomes quite superfluous if *magis* is taken with *gaudeat*, and in that case it is also difficult to supply *quam dare*.

gaudeat . . . occupet : '(she refuses kisses) only to exult when they
are snatched—and sometimes snatch them first herself'. We suggest
that the subjunctives are final, not essentially different from *epist.*
I. I. 12 'condo et compono quae mox depromere possim'. Such final
clauses sometimes have an ironic nuance, for instance in describing
peripeties ('only to' in English); cf. Tac. *ann.* II. 25. 5 'haud multo
post flagitia uxoris noscere ac punire adactus, ut deinde ardesceret
in nuptias incestas', R. G. Nisbet, 'Voluntas Fati in Latin Syntax',
AJPh 44, 1923, 27 ff. The present instance only seems difficult because of the extreme compression.

Editors generally understand the relative clauses to be adjectival,
with a causal nuance justifying *facili*. This makes sense for *gaudeat*,
but not for *occupet*. The kisses refused in 26 would be undesirably
conflated with the ones snatched in 28; the situation is different with
a final clause which clearly describes a later development. What is
most important, *occupet* is too emphatic to be put in a parenthesis.

The variant *occupat* has some authority; it seems also to be supported by ps.-Acro's comment 'artem meretriciam designat cum
velut irata aut negat amatori oscula aut interdum ultro expetit' (on
the other hand Porphyrio has *non occupet* in his note as well as his
lemma). The indicative is certainly much more satisfactory than
the conventional interpretation of *occupet*: see especially Bentley,
O. Keller, *Epilegomena zu Horaz*, 1879, pp. 154 f., C. O. Brink,
PCPhS 17, 1971, 27 f. Now the kisses are divided into three clearly
defined categories; cf. Tib. I. 4. 55 f. '(oscula) rapta dabit primo,
post afferet ipse roganti, / post etiam collo se implicuisse volet'.
The substitution of *interdum* for a third *aut* seems possible, though
it is difficult to find a perfect parallel: Brink quotes *serm.* 2. 2. 131 f.
'illum aut nequities aut vafri inscitia iuris, / postremum expellet
certe vivacior heres' (but there the third clause is different from its
predecessors as it describes something inevitable), Lucr. 6. 715 ff.
(where a single *aut* is not picked up because a long sentence ends in
anacoluthon), perhaps better Prop. 2. 22. 43 'aut si es dura, nega:
sin es non dura, venito' (where the retreat from *aut* to *sin* makes the
second clause less resolute). On the other hand the sentence is badly
balanced when the third clause is so much shorter than its predecessor (unless this emphasizes Licymnia's turn of speed); and it seems
better to have *eripi* and *rapere* in parallel clauses. It is also a little
awkward to understand *oscula* with *rapere occupat*; in the middle
clause *negat* would have *quae . . . eripi* as its object, and so *oscula*
would not need to be supplied there so explicitly.

eripi . . . rapere : the former verb implies real or feigned reluctance.
For the infinitive with *occupet* (= $\phi\theta\acute{a}\nu\eta$) cf. Plaut. *Stich.* 89 'ferre
advorsum homini occupemus osculum', Varro, *Men.* 145, Liv. I. 14. 4.

13. ILLE ET NEFASTO

[Fraenkel 166 ff.; F. Heidenhain, *ZG* 62, 1908, 225 ff.; F. Klingner, *Hermeneia, Festschrift Otto Regenbogen*, 1952, 119 ff. = *Studien*, pp. 325 ff.; R. Reitzenstein, *Hermes* 57, 1922, 357 ff.]

1–12. *It was an accursed evildoer, capable of every villainy, who planted the tree that nearly killed me.* 13–20. *The sailor is afraid of stormy waters, the soldier of enemy action, but the greatest dangers are unexpected.* 21–8. *I nearly found myself in the underworld, listening to the songs of Sappho and Alcaeus.* 29–40. *The shades are enthralled particularly by the political poems; even Cerberus is stilled, the damned forget their suffering, and Orion is diverted from the chase.*

Horace's escape from a falling tree is a familiar but puzzling episode. The historicity of the experience should not be doubted: it is associated in time with Maecenas's recovery from illness (2. 17. 25 ff., vol. i, pp. 243 f.), compared with the battle of Philippi as one of the crises of the poet's life (3. 4. 26 ff., cf. 2. 17. 20 n.), and assigned with circumstantial particularity to the first of March (3. 8. 1). The year is much more problematical (3. 8. 9 ff.):

> hic dies anno redeunte festus
> corticem adstrictum pice dimovebit
> amphorae fumum bibere institutae
> consule Tullo.

These Sapphics probably belong to 25 B.C. (vol. i, p. xxxiii), but *anno redeunte* need not imply a first anniversary; E. Ensor identified Tullus with the consul of 33 B.C. (not of 66 as generally supposed) and assigned the accident to that year (*CR* 16, 1902, 209 ff.). Horace's praise of Alcaeus in our poem suits a relatively early period, when he was most consciously modelling himself on the classical *lyrici* (vol. i, p. xxix, Fraenkel 167); there are also some metrical irregularities, which are not however sufficient to demonstrate a pre-Actium dating (7 n.). Nothing is proved by the reference to the Parthian dread of the Romans (18 f.); even when Antony was in charge, such patriotism would not come amiss (cf. perhaps vol. i, p. xxix, though the dating of 1. 35 remains controversial). It is more important that the ode has affinities with the νέκυια of the Fourth *Georgic*, and that the marvellous powers of Alcaeus seem to be modelled on those of Orpheus (see notes on 33 *stupens* and 36 *recreantur*); this suggests a date later than Actium, in spite of all the uncertainties about 'publication' in the ancient world. If that is so, another explanation must be sought for Tullus's wine in 3. 8: perhaps

it points to the acquisition of the Sabine farm in 33 (Kiessling), or as
the jar sounds an old one, Horace may mean the consul of 66, which
could even have been the date of Maecenas's birth.

Though Horace's misadventure was a real one, his account of it is
written within a literary tradition. Death from falling objects made
one of the innumerable possible topics of sepulchral epitaph, and
a satiric adaptation of the motif describes how a boy was killed
by the tomb of his step-mother (anon. *anth. P.* 9. 67). In a fanciful
epideictic epigram Martial tells how the swineherd Amyntas fell
to his death while collecting acorns; the offending tree is denounced
in terms similar to Horace's (II. 41. 5 f. 'triste nemus dirae vetuit
superesse rapinae / damnavitque rogis noxia ligna pater'). In the
same way dedicatory epigrams (or their literary imitations) could
be written on escapes from such accidents (cf. Bianor, *anth. P.* 9.
259); when Trimalchio is bruised by a falling acrobat, he calls for
his tablets and writes some verses (Petron. 55. 2 'non oportet hunc
casum sine inscriptione transire'). Similarly when a colonnade col-
lapsed near Regulus, the famous *delator*, Martial wrote two epigrams
on the situation (I. 12 with Citroni, I. 82); the first of these contains
the phrase *quam paene* which also occurs in our poem (21 n.). Reflections on the vicissitudes of fortune were conventional on such
occasions; for a parody of the motif cf. *serm.* 2. 8. 61 f. 'heu, Fortuna,
quis est crudelior in nos / te deus?' (of the *ruina* on Nasidienus's
dinner-table).

But though the starting-point of the ode belongs to the area of
epigram, Horace's treatment is far more complicated. In the first
three stanzas he goes back to the ἀρχὴ κακῶν (2 n.) and denounces
the planter of the tree with humorous exaggeration; the torrential
period is sustained by anaphora (1 ff., 11), enjambement (8 n.), and
balancing pairs of words (*nefasto, sacrilega; posuit, produxit; nepotum,
pagi; perniciem, opprobrium; parentis, hospitis; venena, nefas*).
Horace's σχετλιασμός is like an inversion of the μακαρισμός that a
tree-planter might reasonably expect; though not formally a curse
(it contains no *pereat*), it has much in common with the traditional
imprecations against 'first inventors' (2 n.). Mock-ferocious ἀραί were
in fact a minor category of literature (Cairns 93 ff., *RLAC* 7. 1214 f.);
one may refer to Callimachus's *Ibis* (frr. 381 f.), similar poems by
Euphorion (frr. 8–10 Powell, *RE* 6. 1. 1181) and Moero (fr. 4 Powell,
RE 15. 2512 f.), Tibullus 1. 5 (D. E. Oppenheim, *WS* 30, 1908, 146 ff.),
Propertius's elegy on the *lena* (4. 5), Ovid's *Ibis* (cf. La Penna's
edition, pp. xxxii ff.), and the anonymous *Dirae* in the *Appendix
Vergiliana*. Horace's own third and tenth epodes belong to the same
type; the former in particular resembles the opening of our poem
with its exaggerated references to poisoning and parricide (6 n.).

Another illuminating parallel is Ovid, *amores* 1. 12; the poet denounces certain writing-tablets ('inutile lignum') in terms reminiscent
of our ode (5 n., 11 n.). Ovid must be largely influenced by Horace,
but there may have been other literary antecedents of which we
know nothing.

The fourth and fifth stanzas of the ode show a remarkable change
of tone from the boisterous 'epodic' opening. Horace's idiosyncratic
experience leads him to moral generalizations in the manner of
ancient poetry (cf. 1. 22. 1 ff. for the reverse sequence); he is concerned not so much with death's inevitability (which is taken for
granted) as with the impossibility of foreseeing the form it will
actually take. He illuminates his theme by the types of the soldier
and sailor (common in *diatribe*), but he adds a contemporary note
by a reference to the Parthian wars. He encloses his two *exempla*
within two sombre *sententiae* (13 f., 19 f.), which go beyond popular
philosophy to classical Greek lyric; cf. especially Simonides 521:

> ἄνθρωπος ἐὼν μή ποτε φάσῃς ὅτι γίνεται,
> μηδ' ἄνδρα ἰδὼν ὄλβιον ὅσσον χρόνον ἔσσεται·
> ὠκεῖα γὰρ οὐδὲ τανυπτερύγου μυίας
> οὕτως ἁ μετάστασις.

Similar reflections, if not this actual passage, must have been found
in the dirge on the Scopadae, who perished in the *ruina* of their
banqueting-hall; cf. Favorinus, fr. 109 Barigazzi (after quoting the
first two lines) ἀλλὰ μηδὲ οἶκον. ὥσπερ ἀμέλει ὁ ποιητὴς διεξέρχεται τὴν
τῶν Σκοπαδῶν ἀθρόαν ἀπώλειαν. Simonides was said to have had
a narrow escape himself; cf. 510 (with Page's note), Call. fr. 64. 11 ff.
(with Pfeiffer's note), W. J. Oates, *The Influence of Simonides of
Ceos upon Horace*, Diss. Princeton, 1932, pp. 2 ff., J. H. Molyneux,
Phoenix 25, 1971, 197 ff. It is tempting to speculate that Horace
applied to his own mundane accident reflections from this famous
threnos; he might even have derived from the same source the idea
of a scene in the underworld. It is no argument against this view
that Simonides's personal involvement in the accident was probably
fictitious (cf. W. J. Slater, *Phoenix* 26, 1972, 232 ff.); by the scholarly
standards of antiquity a misreading of the poem must have been
possible, and where the scholiasts led, Horace would not hesitate to
follow.

In the second half of the poem Horace proceeds to a description
of the underworld that he has so nearly observed at first hand. Such
experiences, whether by *catabasis* or *necyomanteia*, had been part
of literature since the *Odyssey*; later legends were particularly associated with Heracles (Bacch. 5. 56 ff., Norden on Virg. *Aen*. 6. 309–
12, H. Lloyd-Jones, *Maia*, 19, 1967, 206 ff.), with Dionysus (2. 19.

29 n.), and with Orpheus (see the next paragraph). The paintings of Polygnotus and others helped to give vividness to the traditional stories; cf. Paus. 10. 28–31, Plaut. *capt.* 998 f., Pease on Cic. *nat. deor.* 2. 5. Philosophers wrote on τὰ ἐν Ἅιδου, notably Plato in his myths, Heracleides Ponticus, and the Peripatetic Dicaearchus; but Horace, unlike Virgil, shows no trace of this mystical side (even his sinners are relatively harmless). Less serious authors repeatedly satirized the theme, thus showing its popularity, for instance Aristophanes in his *Frogs* and lost *Gerytades*, Menippus in his νέκυια, Lucian in his *Menippus* and elsewhere (R. Helm, *Lukian und Menipp*, 1906, pp. 17 ff., J. Bompaire, *Lucien Écrivain*, 1958, pp. 365 ff.). In Roman poetry there were underworld scenes by Virgil in *georg.* 4 and *Aen.* 6, by Tibullus (1. 3. 57 ff.) and Propertius, in the post-Virgilian *culex*, by Seneca (*Herc.f.* 662 ff.), Silius (13. 400 ff.), and Statius (*Theb.* 8. 1 ff.). See further Rohde, *Psyche*, Norden on Virg. *Aen.* 6, Dieterich, *passim*, J. Kroll, *Gott und Hölle*, 1932 (*Studien der Bibliothek Warburg* 20), *RE* 10. 2359 ff., D. Vessey, *Statius and the Thebaid*, 1973, pp. 238 ff.

Horace borrows some features from the *Georgics* (33 n., 36 n.), but for chronological reasons is unlikely to have been influenced by the *Aeneid*; therefore the hint of Roman institutions in *iudicantem* and *descriptas* (23 n.) is all the more noteworthy. His most remarkable novelty is the singing of Sappho and Alcaeus; yet one of the traditional attractions of the after-life was the pleasure of meeting dead authors (Ar. *ran.*, Pl. *apol.* 41 a, Cic. *senec.* 83, Ael. *var. hist.* 13. 20). Music played a part in the pagan underworld no less than in the Christian heaven (*apoc.* 5. 8, 14. 2, 15. 2 f.); cf. Pind. fr. 129. 6 f. καὶ τοὶ μὲν ἵπποις γυμνασίοισί τε . . . τοὶ δὲ πεσσοῖς, / τοὶ δὲ φορμίγγεσσι τέρπονται, Ar. *ran.* 154, ps.-Pl. *Axioch.* 371 c–d (for the same motif in an 'Orphic' papyrus poem cf. R. Merkelbach, *MH* 8, 1951, 9). The epigrammatists allowed Anacreon to continue the pursuits of his life (ps.-Simonides, *anth. P.* 7. 25. 9 f. μολπῆς δ' οὐ λήγει μελιτερπέος, ἀλλ' ἔτ' ἐκεῖνον / βάρβιτον οὐδὲ θανὼν εὔνασεν εἰν Ἅιδῃ, cf. 7. 27. 1 f., 7. 30. 3 f.); in Lucian's Elysium he performs together with Homer and Stesichorus (*ver. hist.* 2. 15). But Horace seems to have been particularly influenced by the story of Orpheus, whose catabasis to Hades was the subject of lost Greek poems (cf. Kern, frr. 293–6, Dieterich 128 ff., Norden, *Kl. Schr.*, pp. 505 ff., C. M. Bowra, *CQ* N.S. 2, 1952, 113 ff. = *On Greek Margins*, 1970, pp. 213 ff.). He is described as charming Pluto by his singing (1. 24. 13 n., Hermesianax, fr. 7. 13 Powell, Damagetus, *anth. P.* 7. 9. 7 f., Sen. *Herc.f.* 569 ff.); like Alcaeus in our poem he stilled Cerberus (3. 11. 15 ff., Virg. *georg.* 4. 481 ff.), impressed the shades (ibid. 471 f., Ov. *met.* 10. 40 f.), and relieved the torments of the damned (3. 11. 21 ff., Virg. *georg.* 4. 484, Ov. *met.* 10. 41 ff.). The Roman poets follow their Greek models in describing the music of the underworld (Virg. *Aen.* 6. 657, Tib. 1. 3. 59 with K. F. Smith's note); for the presence of poets cf. Virg. *Aen.* 6. 645 (Orpheus), 6. 662 (with Norden's commentary, pp. 34 f.), 6. 667 (Musaeus), Ov. *am.* 3. 9. 61 ff. (Calvus, Catullus, Gallus), Sil. 13. 781 ff. (Homer), Stat. *silv.* 2. 7. 114 (Lucan), 5. 3. 24 ff. (Statius's father), Dante, *Inf.* 4. 83 ff. (including 'Orazio satiro'), *Purg.* 22. 100 ff.

But though different sections of the ode can be assigned to literary categories it is less easy to determine the intention of the whole. It is wrong to see the fall of the tree as a *Todeserlebnis* that gave a new direction to Horace's spiritual development; the unreasonable exaggerations of the poet's invective (1 ff.) do not encourage such portentous conclusions. Yet it might also be mistaken to regard the opening stanzas simply as a contrived personal lead-in to the main theme of the poem (Fraenkel 166 ff.); the accident must have been a significant one to set beside Maecenas's illness, and it is likely enough to have been the genuine starting-point for the poet's reflections on death. But what is the point of Horace's νέκυια? He is not suggesting that poets are under special protection, for even if he himself escaped death, clearly Sappho and Alcaeus did not. He is not promising poets a literal life in the underworld (Reitzenstein, op. cit.), for such superstitions formed no part of his intellectual system. His only overt pronouncement is a literary judgement in favour of Alcaeus's style (30 n.), in keeping with which he maintains a masculine and matter-of-fact note until the last four lines; the unsentimental realism about Sappho's *puellae populares* (25) and the grotesque portrayal of Cerberus's ears mark a reaction against the emotional power of Virgil's Orpheus episode. The ode may in fact be read largely in literary terms: Horace has delighted to move from truculent invective to serene harmonies while preserving structural coherence and the impression of an individual personality (cf. vol. i, p. xxiii). Yet the piquant contrasts extend beyond words to the realities of the poet's own situation; on the one hand he is a Sabine countryman quick to show anger at the brute object that has so nearly extinguished him, but he is also the conscious heir and imitator of Alcaeus's themes and style. It does not seem mere romantic subjectivism to sense an unspoken thought (cf. Heinze): if he escapes the meaningless accidents of fortune (cf. Milton, *Lycidas* 73 ff.), perhaps he himself may have the same capacity to enthral, to console, and to survive.

Metre: Alcaic (as suits the subject).

1. **nefasto . . . die**: Horace begins with a very Roman scrupulosity (Fraenkel, *Plautinisches*, p. 109 = *Elementi*, p. 103), but his language

is technically inaccurate. A *dies nefastus* (marked N on the calendar) was simply a day on which public business could not be transacted, and there were over a hundred of them. On the other hand a *dies religiosus* (not marked on the calendar) was bad for new undertakings; in this category were included the anniversaries of great defeats, as well as the days after the Kalends, Nones, and Ides (Wissowa 443 f.). Horace's imprecision was common even in senatorial circles; cf. Tac. *ann.* 14. 12. 1, Suet. *Tib.* 53. 2, Gell. 4. 9. 5 'quos multitudo imperitorum prave et perperam nefastos appellat'.

posuit : when the word is used of planting trees, it seems to emphasize their location or arrangement; cf. Virg. *ecl.* 1. 73 'pone ordine vitis', *georg.* 2. 278 (of the *quincunx*), Colum. 4. 1. 2. Here the tree seems to have been deliberately placed where it would cause most trouble.

2. quicumque : we suggest that the word should be enclosed by commas, and that *fuit* should be understood. For the omission of the verb cf. Virg. *Aen.* 1. 330 'sis felix nostrumque leves, quaecumque, laborem', Lucan 8. 642 f. 'sed, quisquis, in istud / a superis immisse caput' (see Housman), Ar. *ran.* 38 f. ὡς κενταυρικῶς / ἐνήλαθ᾽ ὅστις, Paus. 3. 8. 2 τὸ ἐπίγραμμα ἐποίησεν ὅστις δή. Editors interpret *quicumque primum posuit*, but this destroys the balance between *primum* and *pro-*; for the inelegance of the construction cf. Bentley's comment 'vah ut execraretur tam inficetam stribliginem si ad vivos redire posset Horatius'.

The contemptuous *quicumque* suits invective against an unknown originator; cf. Prop. 1. 17. 13 f. 'a pereat, quicunque rates et vela paravit / primus', Tib. 1. 4. 60, Ov. *met.* 15. 104. The parallel from Propertius, as well as many others, puts *primus* in the relative clause. But in those passages the main clause is occupied by a curse on an inventor; Horace's sentence is differently organized.

primum : the word is naturally used in references to inventors and other originators; cf. 1. 3. 12 n. Horace is parodying the topic of the ἀρχὴ κακῶν; cf. 1. 16. 18 n., Hom. *Il.* 1. 6. ἐξ οὗ δὴ τὰ πρῶτα διαστήτην ἐρίσαντε, 5. 62 f., 11. 604, *Od.* 8. 81, Hdt. 1. 5. 1, 5. 97. 3, Thuc. 2. 12. 3, Ar. *Ach.* 515 ff., Plb. 18. 39. 1, Virg. *Aen.* 2. 97. In particular he is going one better than the poets who traced a sequence of events back to the felling of trees; cf. Eur. *Med.* 1 ff. εἴθ᾽ ὤφελ᾽ Ἀργοῦς μὴ διαπτάσθαι σκάφος / Κόλχων ἐς αἶαν κυανέας Συμπληγάδας / μηδ᾽ ἐν νάπαισι Πηλίου πεσεῖν ποτε / τμηθεῖσα πεύκη, *Hec.* 630 ff. ἐμοὶ χρῆν πημονὰν γενέσθαι / Ἰδαίαν ὅτε πρῶτον (*primum*) ὕλαν / Ἀλέξανδρος εἰλατίναν / ἐτάμεθ᾽ ..., Enn. *scaen.* 248 f. V. = 210 f. J. 'neve inde navis inchoandi exordium / cepisset'. The Ennian passage (which unlike its Euripidean model started with the felling of the trees)

became a stock instance of the *argumentum longius repetitum* (Pease
on Cic. *nat. deor.* 3. 75); for an English analogy cf. *Oxford Dictionary
of English Proverbs*[3], 1970, p. 865 'For want of a nail the shoe is lost;
for want of a shoe the horse is lost; for want of a horse the rider is
lost'. Once it is seen that Horace's *primum* is wittily emphatic its
separation from *posuit* seems quite natural.

sacrilega manu : the hand that tended the tree had robbed a
church (cf. *serm.* 1. 3. 117 'qui nocturnus sacra divum legerit');
'wicked' or 'impious' is not specific enough to balance the crimes
below. *manu* suggests that the tree received personal attention (Cic.
senec. 59 'multae etiam istarum arborum mea manu sunt satae',
Virg. *georg.* 1. 199, 3. 176, 3. 395, Ov. *Pont.* 1. 8. 47 f. 'sunt ibi si vivunt
nostra quoque consita quondam / sed non et nostra poma legenda
manu'); with *sacrilega* it implies past thievery and present taint (cf.
epod. 3. 1 'impia manu', Liv. 29. 18. 8, Gregorius, *anth. P.* 8. 218. 4
χείρεσιν οὐχ ὁσίαις). The Greeks regarded a ἱερόσυλος as a major sinner,
and the Romans with their respect for property and religion were
at least as sensitive; see *RE* 1 A. 1678 ff., Mommsen, *Strafrecht*,
1899, pp. 760 ff., Mayor on Juv. 14. 261, I. Opelt, *Die lateinischen
Schimpfwörter*, 1965, s.v. *sacrilegus*, E. Mensching, *MH* 24, 1967, 26 ff.

3. produxit : 'brought you forward', i.e. 'tended'. The verb is used
of bringing up children; cf. Plaut. *asin.* 544 'audientem dicto, mater,
produxisti filiam', Mayor on Juv. 14. 228. One recalls how Virgil
personifies his young trees (*georg.* 2. 23).

arbos : Horace's odes tend to have addressees, even a ship or a
wine-jar (vol. i, p. xxiv); for invective against inanimate objects
cf. Ov. *am.* 1. 12, Opelt, op. cit. [2 n.], pp. 250 ff. The form *arbos* is not
only metrically necessary, but adds a note of archaic dignity.

nepotum : normally a tree-planter was a benefactor of posterity; cf.
Caecil. *com.* 210 'serit arbores quae saeclo prosint alteri' (approved
by Cicero, *Tusc.* 1. 31, *senec.* 24), Virg. *ecl.* 9. 50 'carpent tua poma
nepotes', *georg.* 2. 58, 2. 294.

4. opprobriumque pagi : 'to the disgrace of the parish' ('quasi ad
illius regionis infamiam pertineret' Porph.). In panegyric it is
natural to say that somebody brings blessings to his descendants
and credit to his city, but in ψόγος the situation is reversed (cf.
Prop. 3. 19. 19 f.). Some translate 'to be the disgrace of the parish'
(for personified *opprobrium* cf. 4. 12. 7, Catull. 28. 15), but this explanation is incompatible with *in*. Nor can one interpret 'for the
taunts of the parish'; then the phrase would not balance *nepotum
perniciem*.

Horace did not live in a village, but he belonged to a *pagus* (*RE*
18. 2. 2318 ff.), a more scattered rural area. Cf. *epist.* 1. 18. 104 f.

'me quotiens reficit gelidus Digentia rivus / quem Mandela bibit, rugosus frigore pagus'; here he mentions Mandela as part of his own community (not just as another place with the same water-supply), and by the formulaic *bibit* [2. 20. 20 n.] he identifies the community's unifying feature. The alliteration of *p* is noticeable in this stanza and may indicate contempt; cf. 'pah', ἀπέπτυσα, Ar. *nub.* 6 ἀπόλοιο δῆτ' ὦ πόλεμε πολλῶν οὕνεκα, Eur. *Hipp.* 22 f.

5. **illum et . . . :** for variations of this argument cf. Eur. fr. 328 N. ὅστις δόμους μὲν ἥδεται πληρουμένους / γαστρὸς δ' ἀφαιρῶν σῶμα δύστηνος κακοῖ / τοῦτον νομίζω κἂν θεῶν συλᾶν βρέτη, Ov. *am.* 1. 12. 15 f. 'illum etiam qui vos ex arbore vertit in usum / convincam puras non habuisse manus'.

parentis . . . sui : the pronoun adds emphasis ('his own father'). Parricide was particularly loathsome to the ancients with their strong patriarchal feelings; hence *parricida* (like the more moderate πατραλοίας) was a common term of abuse (Opelt, op. cit. [2 n.], s.v.).

6. **fregisse cervicem :** the crime is committed by the most monstrous method; cf. *epod.* 3. 1 f. 'parentis olim siquis impia manu / senile guttur fregerit', *epist.* 1. 16. 37, *Thes.l.L.* 3. 948. 77 ff. Singular *cervix*, though common in verse of all periods, is perhaps first attested in prose at Varro, *rust.* 2. 2. 3 (of a sheep's neck).

penetralia : the seat of the *penates* (Paul. Fest. 208 M. = 231 L., Pease on Cic. *nat. deor.* 2. 68); and the *penates* were *hospitales dei* (Cic. *Verr.* 4. 48).

7. **nocturno :** night adds to the horror, as in the case of Macbeth. The poets, with their dislike of adverbs, often use temporal adjectives instead (cf. νύχιος), sometimes with mock-grandiloquent effect; cf. 2. 5. 19, *serm.* 1. 3. 117 [2 n.], *ars* 269, Juv. 4. 108 'et matutino sudans Crispinus amomo'.

cruore : for hiatus at the end of the third line of an Alcaic stanza the only parallels are 11 f. *caducum / in*, 1. 16. 27 f. *amica / opprobriis* (probably an early poem); perhaps in the present case there is a fractional pause before the climax in *hospitis* (significantly the genitive is not sandwiched). A further oddity is the rhythm of 8 (*hospitis*; *ille venena Colcha*), where the strong pause after the dactyl is paralleled only at 1. 35. 36 (perhaps early), 1. 37. 12 (30 B.C.), 2. 17. 8 (also in a poem dealing with the tree); the amphibrach *venena* is paralleled at 1. 31. 16 (securely dated to 28 B.C.) and 2. 1. 36. There is another unusual hiatus after the short vowel at the end of line 8; however for hiatus after *m* at the end of an Alcaic stanza cf. 2. 9. 12, 2. 17. 4, 3. 5. 36 (though in all of those places the break is more pronounced). It is noteworthy that these irregularities are concentrated in the

impetuous first half of the poem; it would be unwise to use them as
a criterion for early dating.

8. hospitis : balancing 5 *parentis* (note the chiasmus). For guest-
murder cf. Plaut. *most.* 479 'hospes necavit hospitem', Bömer on
Ov. *met.* 1. 144, *Thes.l.L.* 6. 3. 3021. 8 ff., *RLAC* 8. 1088 f. Offences
against gods, parents, and guests (or two of the three) are often
mentioned together; cf. Dieterich 163 ff., Aesch. *Eum.* 269 ff. (with
G. Thomson's note on the Greek Commandments), Enn. *scaen.* 211
V. = 177 J. (with Jocelyn's note).

    Colcha : Colchis suggests Medea's sorceries; cf. *epod.* 17. 35,
Roscher 2. 2. 2486, *Thes.l.L. onom.* 2. 529. 80 ff. For the short form of
the adjective cf. Ap. Rhod. 4. 485 Κόλχον . . . στόλον, *Thes.l.L. onom.*
2. 529. 61 ff.; for similar instances cf. 1. 31. 12 n., Brink on *ars* 32,
Wackernagel, *Vorlesungen* 2. 58 ff. The variant *Colchica* is more
prosaic (*epod.* 5. 24, 17. 35); here it produces an incredible elision
at the end of the stanza.

9. quidquid . . . : for adjectival *quidquid* (rare in the neuter) cf. Plaut.
Men. 811 'quidquid tibi nomen est', Virg. *Aen.* 10. 493, *Aetna* 23,
Neue–Wagener 2. 511; for the omission of *aliud* cf. 2. 1. 25 n. The
word is particularly applicable to the comprehensive pharmacopoeia
of a witch; cf. Tib. 2. 4. 56 'quidquid et herbarum Thessala terra
gerit', Ov. *met.* 7. 224 ff., Sen. *Med.* 707 'quaecumque generat invius
saxis Eryx', *Herc. O.* 465 f., Housman, *A Shropshire Lad*, 62. 63 f. 'He
gathered all that springs to birth   From the many-venomed earth'.
Such hyperboles become particularly common in the Silver Age.

    concipitur nefas : *nefas* is concrete ('abomination'); cf. Virg. *Aen.*
10. 497, Lucan 6. 569, Claud. *carm. min.* 53. 4 'invisum genitura nefas'
(the Giants). *concipitur* means 'is engendered' (Conington translates
'is hatched') ; cf. Sen. *Med.* cited above, *Herc. f.* 30 'quidquid horridum
tellus creat'. There is a strong implication of nastiness; cf. Catull.
64. 155 'quod mare conceptum spumantibus exspuit undis?', Drac.
Romul. 10. 577 'male conceptis praegnatur terra venenis'. Editors
interpret 'whatever wrong is imagined' (cf. Ov. *met.* 10. 351 f. 'dum
corpore non es / passa nefas, animo ne concipe'); this is weakly
abstract after *venena*, does not suit the physical *tractavit* (unless by
an unnatural paradox), and deprives *usquam* of effective point (the
diversity of products is a familiar topic [above, p. 96], but the same
horrors can be imagined anywhere).

10. tractavit : stronger than the diffident *crediderim fregisse*; Horace
now treats his hypotheses as facts. The verb suggests messy handling
(*epod.* 3. 7 f. 'an malas / Canidia tractavit dapes?') ; ancient poisons
were slimier than the modern synthetics.

agro qui statuit meo : such a tree was not a growing organism but a wooden post, set up only to fall down again (*caducum* balances *statuit*); cf. Cic. *Pis.* 19 'qui tamquam truncus atque stipes, si stetisset modo, posset sustinere tamen titulum consulatus'. *meo* is contrasted with *te* below: 'what impertinence to erect *you* on *my* land!' Horace speaks with the pride of a proprietor (21 *domini*), as if the land had always been his; elsewhere he is more realistic (2. 14. 24 n.).

11. **te, triste lignum** : the emphatic pronoun (repeated with anaphora below) gives a mock-inflated effect that would normally be more appropriate to hymns and panegyrics (1. 10. 9 n., 2. 16. 33 ff.). In these circumstances *triste lignum* is naturally read as vocative, not accusative; perhaps so also *caducum* below, in spite of the oddity, as a parody of independent vocatives in cult (cf. 2. 19. 8 'parce, gravi metuende thyrso', with note ad loc.). The tree is treated as a lifeless log; cf. *serm.* 1. 8. 1 'inutile lignum', Lucil. 733 'ardum miserinum atque infelix lignum sabucum vocat', Ov. *am.* 1. 12. 7 'ite hinc difficiles, funebria ligna, tabellae'. Horace is thinking of the *infelix arbor*, properly a tree that did not bear fruit, hence one used for punishments (cf. Ov. *am.* 1. 12. 18) and generally sinister; cf. Cic. *Rab. perd.* 13 (citing an old formula) 'caput obnubito, arbori infelici suspendito', Catull. 36. 8 'infelicibus ustulanda lignis' (so Cic. *Mil.* 33), Plin. *nat.* 16. 108, Macr. *sat.* 3. 20. 2, J. André, *Hommages à Jean Bayet, Collection Latomus* 70, 1964, pp. 35 ff., *RE* 9. 1540 ff.

caducum : after eleven lines of vituperation Horace at last breaks the suspense and reveals why he is so angry. The adjective here means not 'falling' but 'with a propensity to fall' (as *statuit* shows); cf. Ov. *fast.* 5. 144, Plin. *nat.* 17. 121 'quibus tenuis aut caducus rimosusque cortex'. Perhaps Horace is hinting at *caduca auspicia*, the omens derived from falling objects (see Pease on Cic. *div.* 1. 19, p. 113); in that case the word suggests the same range of ideas as 1 *nefasto die.* It might even be relevant that *caducus* is used of property without an owner (*CGL* 5. 273. 64 'quae non habent dominum et cadere possunt'); that would give a play on words with *domini* below.

13. **quid quisque vitet ...** : cf. Simonides 521 (above, p. 203). The *sententia* also belongs to philosophy; cf. Sen. *epist.* 30. 16 (citing Epicurus, fr. 503 Usener) 'sed consideremus, inquit, tunc cum aliqua causa moriendi videtur accedere, quanto aliae propiores sint quae non timentur. hostis alicui mortem minabatur, hunc cruditas occupavit', 49. 11, *nat.* 6. 2. 5 'et ego timeam terras trementes quem crassior saliva suffocat?'

numquam ... satis cautum est : 'is never adequately provided for'; the impersonal passive suits the generalization (cf. 2. 16. 13).

cautum est suggests 'taking care' of every contingency (cf. Cic. *Verr.* 2. 1. 88 'semper enim existimasti . . . satis cautum tibi ad defensionem fore si . . .') ; the perfect is not gnomic but implies that complete cover is never achieved. *homini* is *dativus commodi* as much as 'dative of agent' ; the word would be feeble for the *Odes* if it meant simply 'one', and must be a reminder of mortal vicissitudes (cf. Simonides 521. 1, cited above, p. 203). It is plural in effect (cf. 1. 3. 35 'pennis non homini datis') ; hence there is no inconsistency with *quisque*, which is placed as often in the subordinate clause.

14. in horas : 'from one hour to the next'; cf. *serm.* 2. 7. 10, *ars* 160, Plin. *epist.* 3. 17. 3 'ipse valeo si valere est suspensum et anxium vivere, exspectantem in horas timentemque pro capite amicissimo quidquid accidere homini potest', Hand 3. 341 ff. For the thought that man cannot predict far ahead cf. 1. 11. 8 n., Theognis 159 f. οἶδε γὰρ οὐδεὶς / ἀνθρώπων ὅ τι νὺξ χἠμέρη ἀνδρὶ τελεῖ (with van Groningen's parallels), Pind. *O.* 12. 10 ff.

Bosphorum : the straits were dangerous to ancient shipping because of the twisting channel and the strength of the current; cf. 3. 4. 30, Plb. 4. 43–4, *RE* 3. 742 ff., A. E. Zimmern, *The Greek Commonwealth*, ed. 5, 1931, pp. 28 f.

15. Poenus : the adjective has been suspected, though not always for significant reasons. Porphyrio comments : 'Bosforum. fauces sunt Pontici maris, unde cum longissime Africa sit, quid ita Poenus navita eum perhorrescat? numquid ergo Bosforum pro quolibet freto posuit?' But Horace can hardly be thinking of Carthaginian sailors, who would not be thus singled out by a Roman after the fall of Carthage ; if the word is correct it must refer to the Phoenicians (cf. *epod.* 16. 59 'Sidonii . . . nautae'). *Poenus* in this sense is admittedly unparalleled, but the difficulty does not seem insuperable in a poet (cf. 2. 12. 3 n.).

It is further objected that the Phoenicians had no particular association with the Bosphorus, yet cf. Lucian, *Tox. 4* τοὺς Φοίνικας . . . οὐκ εἰς τὸν Πόντον . . . μόνον ἐσπλέοντας. They could be mentioned as typical sailors, just as the Parthians in the next stanza are typical warriors (R. Zimmermann, *PhW* 52, 1932, 814 f.). Lachmann proposed *Thynus* (accepted by Heinze) ; the Thyni inhabited the part of Asia Minor that lies east of the Bosphorus. But they were not typical sailors, and seem too unimportant to balance the Romans and Parthians of the next stanza. Their familiarity with the Bosphorus would breed contempt ; they could not regard it, like other peoples, as a unique hazard at the ends of the earth.

A more serious objection to *Poenus* was raised by Peerlkamp. The sailor shares a verb with the soldier of the next stanza; for the association of these typical βίοι cf. 1. 1. 15 ff., 2. 16. 1 ff., Norden, *Kl. Schr.*, p. 30, n. 70. But *miles* is not qualified by an adjective of nationality; therefore it is surprising to find *navita* thus qualified. Peerlkamp proposed *aestus*, Moser *portas* (reading *Bosphori* in both cases), Friedrich (76 ff.) *unum*. One might sooner try *prudens* (i.e. *providens*); cf. 16 *caeca*, 19 *improvisa*, 2. 10. 2 f. 'dum procellas / cautus horrescis' (see note ad loc. for the paradox of deliberate fears). But perhaps the paradosis can be defended by inferring *miles Italus* from *Italum* in 18; for patriotic reasons Horace might not wish to stress that Italian soldiers could be afraid.

perhorrescit : cf. Ov. *met.* 6. 704 'latumque perhorruit aequor'; the verb is stronger than *timet* below, especially in view of the intensive prefix. There may be a verbal point in the idea of shivering at the shivering waves; cf. 2. 10. 3 n., *epod.* 2. 6 'neque horret iratum mare'.

ultra : 'over and above' (cf. Hirt. *Gall.* 8. 39. 3 'nullum ultra periculum vererentur'); it may be admitted that in a context referring to straits one might expect the word to bear a local sense. But Horace cannot mean 'while passing the Bosphorus the seaman fears nothing on the far side'; *ultra* could not depend on *fata* in this way. Nor can he mean 'when he is on the far side of the Bosphorus the seaman fears nothing else'; it would be absurd to suggest that the dangerous Euxine could be sailed without qualms. We have tentatively considered *ultro*, 'gratuitously'; as fears normally come unbidden, there would be a conscious paradox in the idea of 'going out of one's way to be afraid'.

16. caeca : 'unseen'; the word is emphatic like *improvisa* below.

timet aliunde fata : the text has been suspected, mainly because of the unexpected scansion of *timēt*. The irregularity is mitigated, first because the offending syllable is *in arsi*, secondly because the vowel is sometimes long by nature in early Latin; cf. Plaut. *Poen.* 845 'proinde habet orationem quasi ipse sit frugi bonae', *merc.* 696, Lucr. 2. 27 'nec domus argento fulget auroque renidet', Nettleship's appendix to Conington's Virgil, vol. iii, pp. 472 f., R. G. Kent, *Mélanges Marouzeau*, 1948, pp. 303 ff., Austin on Virg. *Aen.* 1. 308. For similar phenomena in Horace cf. 1. 13. 6 'certa sede manet, umor et in genas', 2. 6. 14 'angulus ridet, ubi non Hymetto', 3. 16. 26 'quam si quidquid arat impiger Apulus'; though the break is stronger in those passages than in our own, one may also compare 1. 3. 36 'perrupit Acheronta', 3. 24. 5 'si figit adamantinos'. So even if there is no perfect parallel to our passage, the evidence taken as a whole seems to justify the irregularity.

Lachmann proposed *timetve* (on Lucr. 2. 27); the meaning would be 'neque caeca fata timet aut ultra aut aliunde' (for the ἀπὸ κοινοῦ construction cf. 2. 19. 28 n.). But this disjunction involves giving a local interpretation to *ultra* (Kiessling), which seems to be impossible (see note ad loc.); Müller's temporal interpretation ('afterwards') involves the same difficulties, besides being less natural in itself. On the other hand if *ultra* means simply 'over and above', then -*ve* becomes pointless.

17. sagittas et celerem fugam : an economical description of 'Parthian shots' (1. 19. 11 n., Prato on [Sen.] *epig*. 33. 2). Arrows and flight make a good pair, but the adjective belongs only to the latter. 'To fear flight' is a characteristic Horatian paradox (cf. Lucr. 3. 472 'sequitur ... fuga cervos'); to speak of hendiadys (*sagittas fugientium*) obscures the menace of the Parthian get-away.

18. catenas ... Italum robur : the Parthian fears that he will be led away in chains to meet his death in a Roman dungeon; this fate would affect only a few princes, yet cf. *carm. saec*. 53 f. 'manus potentis / Medus Albanasque timet securis' (a very significant parallel). *robur* was applied particularly to the Tullianum in Rome, and this does not seem to suit *Italum* (the difficulty is diminished rather than removed by taking the adjective ἀπὸ κοινοῦ with *catenas*). But the noun did not have to be a proper name (Plaut. *Curc*. 692 'in robusto carcere', Liv. 38. 59. 10); the phrase suggests oak-wood from Italian forests, and more indirectly hints that Rome's wars were now a co-operative effort. *robur* is a sinister euphemism with an implication of hardness; it thus balances *catenas* and makes a contrast with *sagittas* and *celerem fugam*.

Many editors refer *robur* to the Roman army and the qualities it displayed (Pollio ap. Cic. *epist*. 10. 33. 1); for the barbarian fear of Italian soldiers cf. 2. 20. 17 f. But after *catenas* it is confusing not to understand *robur* as 'dungeon'. It is an even greater difficulty that *catenas* would then refer not to death but to the enslavement of prisoners (1. 29. 5 n.); yet death is the subject under discussion (19 *leti*) and not other unexpected disasters (Friedrich 78 ff.). It would, however, be true to say that *robur Italum* is a cliché of the military historians to which Horace has pointedly given a new application.

19. improvisa : the word states an emphatic antithesis; the force that carries off nations is unexpected, and not the one they fear. For the commonplace cf. Pind. *N*. 7. 30 f. ἀλλὰ κοινὸν γὰρ ἔρχεται / κῦμ' Ἀΐδα, πέσε δ' ἀδόκητον ἐν καὶ δοκέοντι, Aesch. *Prom*. 680 ἀπροσδόκητος, *trag. adesp*. 127. 8 ἄφαντος, Archias, *anth. P*. 7. 213. 6 and 9. 111. 4 ἀπροϊδής, Lucr. 3. 959 'et nec opinanti mors ad caput adstitit ante', Philodemus, *de morte* 4. 37. 19 ff. (Gigante 79) τὸ τοίνυν συναρπάζεσθαι

θανάτου προσπίπτοντος ὡς ἀπροσδοκήτου τινὸς καὶ παραδόξου συναν-
τῶντος, ἡμεῖν μὲν οὐχί, γίνεται δὲ περὶ τοὺς πλείστους . . .

20. rapuit rapietque : the verb suits *vis* ('force') which implies impetus as well as power. ἁρπάζειν is similarly used of death (Call. *ep.*
2. 6, 41. 2). For the *polyptoton* cf. *ars* 70 (with Brink's note), H.–Sz.
708, Barrett on Eur. *Hipp.* 441 f.

gentis : cf. Sen. *Herc. f.* 557, 775 'cumba populorum capax'; so
Xerxes weeps that none of his army will live to be a hundred (Hdt.
7. 46. 2), and Servius Sulpicius consoles Cicero with the thought
that whole cities have been destroyed (*epist.* 4. 5. 4). Here the word
is particularly appropriate as Horace has been talking of Romans
and Parthians.

21. quam paene : cf. Mart. 1. 12. 6 (on Regulus's accident) 'heu quam
paene novum porticus ausa nefas', 6. 58. 3 f. 'o quam paene tibi
Stygias ego raptus ad undas / Elysiae vidi nubila fusca plagae'.
The collocation is found in a variety of styles, being used also by
Terence (*heaut.* 814), Ovid, Seneca, and Silius.

furvae : an old Latin word for black, particularly associated with
death (André 60, *Thes.l.L.* 6. 1. 1651. 30 ff.). Everything about Pro-
serpine was 'sable', her dress in particular; cf. anon. *anth. P.* 7. 352.
1 f. καὶ τὰ κελαινὰ / ὄμνυμεν ἀρρήτου δέμνια Περσεφόνης, Aesch. *cho.*
1049 φαιοχίτωνες (of the Furies), Eur. *Alc.* 843 f. ἄνακτα τὸν μελάμπεπλον νεκρῶν / Θάνατον, Irwin 173 ff.

regna Proserpinae : for the kingdom of the underworld cf. 3. 4. 46,
epod. 17. 2 'regna per Proserpinae', Virg. *Aen.* 6. 154, 269, 417,
8. 244 f., *culex* 273, J. Kroll, op. cit. [p. 204], p. 392 ; for the importance
of kings in Latin imagery cf. Fraenkel, *Plautinisches*, pp. 187 ff. =
Elementi, pp. 178 ff. For similar Greek expressions cf. Theognis 974
δώματα Περσεφόνης (so Pind. *O.* 14. 20 f. μελαντειχέα . . . δόμον /
Φερσεφόνας, *I.* 8. 55), Lucian, *Men.* 10 τοῦ Πλούτωνος τὰ βασίλεια
(palace). The *o* of *Proserpina* is normally long (cf. 1. 28. 20, *serm.*
2. 5. 110), but is also short in Seneca's imitation, 'vidisti Siculae
regna Proserpinae' (*Herc. f.* 548).

22. vidimus : the plural is modest, not pompous. *videre* is sometimes
used of an unpleasant experience (1. 2. 13 n., 1. 3. 19 n.). Yet in our
passage the dominating emotion seems to be curiosity rather than
horror.

Aeacum : the pious father of Peleus had originally no special function in the underworld, though he appears with a seat of honour
or as guardian of the gate (cf. Ar. *ran.* 464 ff.). Plato makes him
a judge alongside Minos and Rhadamanthys (*Gorg.* 524 a, *apol.* 41 a);
such judges were originally no more than arbitrators among the dead

(Hom. *Od.* 11. 568 ff., Virg. *Aen.* 8. 670 'his dantem iura Catonem', Ov. *met.* 13. 25 f.). By a later tradition, already known to Plato, they imposed punishments for misdeeds in life; and that is the implication here (contrast *sedes . . . piorum*). *iudicantem* sounds an official note; cf. Virg. *Aen.* 6. 432 'quaesitor Minos urnam movet', Prop. 4. 11. 19 'aut si quis posita iudex sedet Aeacus urna'. See further *RE* 1. 926, Rohde, *Psyche*, ch. 7, n. 13, Dodds on Pl. *Gorg.* loc. cit., R. Helm, *Lukian und Menipp*, 1906, pp. 31 ff.

23. sedesque : the word is often used of the abode of the dead (1. 10. 18, 3. 3. 34); so Greek ἕδραι (Eur. *Alc.* 125, Lycophron 445). Originally Elysium was placed above ground in the far West (Hom. *Od.* 4. 563 ff., Hes. *op.* 167 ff., cf. *epod.* 16. 41 f.), but in later eschatology it was a separate part of the underworld; cf. Rohde, *Psyche*, ch. 2, Roscher 6. 123 f.

descriptas : the MSS. offer *descriptas* or *discriptas* or *discretas*; the decision must be made on grounds of sense, not by splitting hairs about relative authority. *descriptas* means 'marked out', 'assigned', 'allocated' (like lands); cf. Tac. *ann.* 11. 19. 1 'natio Frisiorum . . . consedit apud agros a Corbulone descriptos'. The dead go where they are sent, saints and sinners alike; cf. 2. 18. 30 'rapacis Orci fine destinata', Cic. *rep.* 6. 13 'sic habeto, omnibus qui patriam conservarint adiuverint auxerint certum esse in caelo definitum locum', Virg. *Aen.* 6. 431 'nec vero hae sine sorte datae, sine iudice sedes' (*datae* is a formal 'assigned' rather than simply 'given'), Lucian, *Men.* 17 ἐπειδὰν γάρ, ὦ ἑταῖρε, ὁ Αἰακὸς ἀπομετρήσῃ ἑκάστῳ τὸν τόπον. The tone of *descriptas* may seem technical and prosaic, but it follows well on *iudicantem*.

discriptas would give the added idea of distribution (for the confusion with *describere* cf. Brink on *ars* 86). Bücheler thought that the different categories of *pii* were distributed in different places (*RhM* 13, 1858, 603 = *Kl. Schr.* 1. 139), but the notion is quite pointless in the context. One might try to see a contrast between the front *ordines* of the *pii* (προεδρία) and the standing-room for the *volgus* at the back (32); *discriptas* would then suggest individual reserved seats (as assigned to priests at Athens), a whimsical interpretation of *sedes piorum*. Similarly if Tacitus, loc. cit., had written *agros . . . discriptos*, this would imply that Corbulo had distributed land among individuals instead of making a collective award.

discretas may have been read by Porphyrio, who comments *separatas* (his lemma *descriptas* has no independent authority). The Blest are well described as separate either from the world of men or from the damned; cf. *epod.* 16. 63 'Iuppiter illa piae secrevit litora genti', Hes. *op.* 167 f. τοῖς δὲ δίχ' ἀνθρώπων βίοτον καὶ ἤθε' ὀπάσσας / Ζεὺς

Κρονίδης κατένασσε πατὴρ ἐς πείρατα γαίης, Virg. *Aen.* 6. 477 f., 8. 670
'secretosque pios', *culex* 374 f. 'quo, maxime Minos, / conscelerata pia
discernis vincula sede', Stat. *Theb.* 4. 524, Lact. *inst.* 7. 7. 13 'esse
inferos Zeno Stoicus docuit et sedes piorum ab inpiis esse discretas'.
discretas is more 'poetical' than *descriptas* and has found favour with
many scholars (cf. Brink on *ars*, p. 33). Yet the word seems to emphasize too much the separateness of the *pii* (we find at 32 that the
volgus is also listening to Alcaeus); it also lacks the official tone of
descriptas, and so balances *iudicantem* less well (see note above).

    piorum : the blessed dead; cf. 3. 4. 6, Cic. *Phil.* 14. 32 'piorum estis
sedem et locum consecuti', Virg. *Aen.* 5. 734, 8. 670, *carm. epig.* 1165. 1,
etc. The word represents the Greek εὐσεβῶν; cf. ps.-Pl. *Axioch.* 371 c,
Call. *ep.* 10. 4, Rohde, *Psyche*, ch. 14. 2 n. 133 (citing inscriptions).

24. Aeoliis fidibus : because Sappho and Alcaeus wrote in an
Aeolic dialect; cf. 3. 30. 13 'Aeolium carmen', 4. 3. 12, 4. 9. 12
'Aeoliae fidibus puellae', Prop. 2. 3. 19, Ov. *epist.* 15. 200, anon.
anth. P. 9. 184. 2 Σαπφοῦς τ' Αἰολίδες χάριτες, Gray, *Progress of Poesy*,
'Awake, Aeolian lyre, awake'. It may be relevant that Terpander,
the traditional inventor of the lyre, also came from Lesbos. Aeolia
was the land of Aeolus, the lord of the winds, so the name suits
musical 'airs' (see 2. 16. 38 *spiritum* n.); cf. Pind. *N.* 3. 79 Αἰολῆσιν
ἐν πνοαῖσιν αὐλῶν. There may also be a suggestion of varied notes;
cf. Soph. *ichn.* 319 αἰόλισμα τῆς λύρας (with Pearson).

    querentem : love-poems in antiquity are generally sad, and so
could be called *querellae* (2. 9. 18). Yet the word particularly suits
Sappho's reproaches; cf. 94 τεθνάκην δ' ἀδόλως θέλω . . . , 131 Ἄτθι,
σοὶ δ' ἔμεθεν μὲν ἀπήχθετο / φροντίσδην, ἐπὶ δ' Ἀνδρομέδαν πόσα. She
continues in death her preoccupations in life; cf. below, 39 n., Antip.
Sid. *anth. P.* 7. 30. 3 f. (on Anacreon). For the verb of sound after
vidimus (μετάληψις αἰσθήσεως) cf. 1. 14. 6 n.

25. Sappho : for her vogue cf. 4. 9. 10 ff., Str. 13. 2. 3, Laurea, *anth. P.*
7. 17 (with Gow–Page, *GP* 2, p. 462), E. Malcovati, *Athenaeum* N.S.
44, 1966, 3 ff., A. La Penna, *Maia* 24, 1972, 208 ff. Horace has clear
reservations (below, 30 n.), yet modern romantics are ready to find
an anticipation of their own approach; cf. Fraenkel 167 'By the
side of Alcaeus there appears in a moving attitude Sappho, whom
Horace was wise enough never to imitate, for the very reason that
he understood her so well and admired her so much'.

    popularibus : this can only mean 'from the same *populus*' (*civibus
suis* Porph.). One must ask why Horace wastes a word on such par-
ticularization; what would it matter if these girls were foreigners or
resident aliens? The answer must surely be that they were Lesbians
in more senses than one.

For a similar observation cf. *epist.* 1. 19. 28 'mascula Sappho'
where the *double entendre* is unmistakable (cf. *epod.* 5. 41), *pace*
Fraenkel 346 n. 3 'When Philipp Buttmann knew he was soon to die,
he felt it heavy on his conscience that he had done a grave injustice
to Horace by reading, with many others, the vulgar slander into
mascula . . .'. See also Ov. *epist.* 15. 19 'atque aliae centum quas non
sine crimine amavi', 15. 201, Max. Tyr. 18. 9, Suidas 4. 323. 7 πρὸς ἃς
καὶ διαβολὴν ἔσχεν αἰσχρᾶς φιλίας, RE 1 A. 2361 f., Page, *Sappho and
Alcaeus*, pp. 133 ff., G. Devereux, *CQ* N.S. 20, 1970, 17 ff., M. L. West,
Maia 22, 1970, 324 ff., M. Marcovich, *CQ* N.S. 22, 1972, 19 ff. Such
comments have been thought the fictions of a later age (Wilamowitz, *Sappho und Simonides*, 1913, pp. 17 ff., Kroll, *RE* 12. 2100 ff.),
but they are fully supported by the fragments.

26. et te : such apostrophe produces not only a metrically convenient
vocative but variety, emphasis, and an impression of emotional involvement; cf. Virg. *Aen.* 6. 14 ff. with Norden, 1. 555 with Austin,
H.–Sz. 836 f., Newman 46.

plenius : 'with more resonance'; cf. Cic. *de orat.* 1. 132, *Brut.* 289
'subsellia grandiorem et pleniorem vocem desiderant', Quint. *inst.*
11. 3. 15 'qualitas (vocis) magis varia. nam est . . . et plena et exilis'.
There is thus a qualitative contrast with the *exilitas* of Sappho's
querellae; note the change from the thin vowels of *fidibus querentem*
to the more open sounds of *plenius . . . plēctro* (for 'hidden quantity'
cf. Allen 65 ff.). La Penna points also to the rhetorical sense of
'copious', an idea that was associated with the 'scale' of the grand
style (op. cit., p. 209 n. 1, Gudeman on Tac. *dial.* 18. 4); but this
does not suit *sonantem* so well.

aureo . . . plectro : ablative of instrument with *sonantem* (to balance
24 *Aeoliis fidibus*), not of quality with *Alcaee* (in spite of 4. 2. 33
'maiore poeta plectro'). Apollo's plectrum was traditionally golden
(*h. Ap.* 185, Pind. *N.* 5. 24, Eur. *Her.* 351), like his lyre and other
accoutrements (Pind. *P.* 1. 1, Call. *h.* 2. 32 ff.); hence a golden plectrum was dedicated at Delphi by the Megarians (Plut. *Pyth. orac.*
402 a). Horace's adjective is therefore highly eulogistic; cf. Quint.
inst. 10. 1. 63 'Alcaeus in parte operis aureo plectro merito donatur'
(alluding to our passage). For plectra of gold, ivory, wood, horn, and
goat's hoofs cf. Headlam on Herodas 6. 51.

27. dura . . . : Horace is contrasting the toughness of Alcaeus's life
and poetry with the *mollities* of Sappho. No doubt he detects and
exaggerates a resemblance to the rigours of his own military career;
cf. 2. 6. 7 f. 'sit modus lasso maris et viarum / militiaeque' (with note
ad loc.).

navis : Alcaeus's best-known poems on ships were allegorical (6,

326, cf. vol. i, pp. 179 f.), but in our passage a purely political *navis* would not balance *fugae* and *belli*. There is nevertheless some attraction in supposing that Horace intends an allusion to the famous ship (a view perhaps supported by the singular *navis*), though for present purposes the allegory is not exploited. For Alcaeus's sufferings cf. 326. 5 χείμωνι μόχθεντες μεγάλῳ μάλα, but there also seems to be a suggestion of hard boards (Prop. 1. 8. 6 'in dura nave iacere potes?').

28. fugae : ' exile'; yet the word retains enough of its primary meaning to make an oxymoron with *dura* and an antithesis with *belli*. The scholiast on Alcaeus 114 mentions τὴν φυγὴν τὴν πρώτην when the defeated faction fled to Pyrrha (elsewhere on Lesbos); cf. further 130. 23 ff. ἔγ[ωγ' ἀ]πὺ τούτων ἀπελήλαμαι / φεύγων ἐσχατίαισ' ὡς δ' 'Ονυμακλέης / ἔνθα[δ'] οἶος ἐοίκησα λυκαιμίαις, Arist. *pol.* 1285ᵃ36 ff., Page, *Sappho and Alcaeus*, pp. 197 ff. The scholiast's words imply a later exile; this was presumably the time when Alcaeus went to Egypt, his brother Antimenidas to the East, and Sappho to Sicily (Page, op. cit., pp. 223 ff.).

dura belli : for the association of Alcaeus with war cf. 1. 32. 6 n. The phrase is the climax of the stanza; it is given additional emphasis by the relatively weak position of *mala* ('evils'), the common element of the last three clauses.

29. sacro ... silentio : εὐφημία is appropriate to a sacred occasion (cf. Call. *h.* 2. 17 εὐφημεῖτ' ἀίοντες ἐπ' Ἀπόλλωνος ἀοιδῇ, Synes. *h.* 1. 72 ff. with Terzaghi's note); similarly all nature was hushed at the magic songs of Orpheus (1. 12. 10 n.). Here the language of religion is transferred to poetry; cf. 3. 1. 2 'favete linguis', Prop. 4. 6. 1, Ar. *thesm.* 39 ff. For the grandiose plural *digna* (ἄξια) cf. 4. 11. 29, Virg. *Aen.* 6. 662 'Phoebo digna locuti' (on the *pii vates* of the underworld). The ablative depends solely on *digna*, not on *mirantur*; of course it is implied that the crowd is actually silent.

30. mirantur ... dicere : 'are enthralled that they say'; there is no suggestion that the shades are surprised by something unexpected. *dicere* is in tension with *silentio*.

sed magis ... : Horace is giving a dramatic form to a comparative judgement between Sappho and Alcaeus (La Penna, cited above, 25 n.). σύγκρισις was a common technique in rhetoric, biography, and literary criticism (cf. the *certamen Hesiodi et Homeri* and the ἀγών in the *Frogs* of Aristophanes); see F. Leo, *Die griechisch-römische Biographie* ..., 1901, pp. 149 ff., F. Focke, *Hermes* 58, 1923, 327 ff., H. Erbse, ibid. 84, 1956, 398 ff. A comparison of Sappho and Alcaeus was an obvious exercise; cf. Ov. *epist.* 15. 29 f. 'nec plus Alcaeus

consors patriaeque lyraeque / laudis habet quamvis grandius ille
sonet'. Horace is reacting against the tastes of the neoterics and
their Augustan successors (cf. La Penna, loc. cit.); at the same time
he is making a manifesto about his own poetry, which purported to
imitate the practical outlook and masculine style of Alcaeus.

31. exactos tyrannos : Melanchrus, the tyrant of Mitylene, was overthrown by Pittacus and the brothers of Alcaeus (Diog. Laert.
1. 74); Alcaeus himself may have been too young to participate
(75. 7 f., Page, *Sappho and Alcaeus*, pp. 151 f.). The next tyrant was
Myrsilus, who also seems to have been in exile at some stage; the
commentary at Alcaeus 305. i. 15 ff. refers to a certain Mnemon who
provided a boat for his return (Page, op. cit., pp. 180 f.).

32. densum umeris : the *volgus* of the dead has standing-room only,
as at a Roman *contio* (Cic. *Flacc.* 16, Varro, *Men.* 334, Mommsen,
Staatsrecht 3, 1887, 396). *densum* balances *bibit* (which can suggest
porosity); there is a conscious paradox in applying the adjective
to shades. *umeris* balances *aure*, and gives the idea of a ghostly
jostling; for the ablative cf. Ov. *met.* 14. 360 'densum trabibus
nemus', *Thes.l.L.* 5. 1. 546. 68 ff. The elision seems to increase the
impression of overcrowding.

bibit aure : 'cupidissime audit' (Porph.); this comment would be
superfluous with Bentley's conjecture *densum avida bibit aure*. The
Romans spoke of drinking words in (*epist.* 1. 2. 67, Plaut. *Persa* 170,
Prop. 3. 6. 8, *Thes.l.L.* 2. 1966. 35 ff., Onians 43); the unsophisticated metaphor seems less characteristic of Greek (though cf. κατα-
πίνειν). Similarly ears can be *bibulae, patulae, rimosae*; they *hauriunt*
(Pease on Virg. *Aen.* 4. 359), *sitiunt, devorant*, even *respuunt*; cf.
also *epist.* 1. 8. 16 'instillare', Lucil. 610 'per auris pectus inrigarier'.

volgus : so Sen. *Oed.* 598, Stat. *Theb.* 4. 478. The word suggests
the number of the shades (cf. Virg. *Aen.* 6. 309 ff., G. Thaniel,
Phoenix 25, 1971, 237 ff.), their unimportance (contrast 37 *Pelopis
parens*), and a Roman readiness to listen respectfully to political
harangues. *volgus* is contrasted with *tyrannos*.

33. quid mirum . . . : an *a fortiori* argument. *illis carminibus* refers
to Alcaeus (Porph.); the emphasis of the previous stanza lies not on
utrumque (a μέν clause) but on *sed magis . . .* For the ablative with
stupere cf. *serm.* 1. 4. 28.

stupens : for the power of music to hypnotize cf. Pind. *P.* 1. 6 ff.;
the effect was particularly remarkable in the case of Cerberus, who
could cause *stupor* in others (Ov. *met.* 10. 64 ff.). Horace's language is
suggested by the ἐπωδαί of Orpheus, particularly as described by
Virgil; cf. *georg.* 4. 481 ff. 'quin ipsae stupuere domus atque intima

leti / Tartara caeruleosque implexae crinibus anguis / Eumenides,
tenuitque inhians tria Cerberus ora, / atque Ixionii vento rota con-
stitit orbis' (immediately following the passage imitated at 2. 14. 9),
Ov. *met.* 10. 40 ff., Sen. *Herc. O.* 1061 ff. The hero of a catabasis had
to neutralize the guards; cf. 2. 19. 29 ff., 3. 11. 15 ff., Virg. *Aen.* 6.
417 ff. (Cerberus is doped), 8. 296, Lucian, *Men.* 10 ὁ δὲ Κέρβερος
ὑλάκτησε μέν τι καὶ παρεκίνησε, ταχὺ δέ μου κρούσαντος τὴν λύραν παραχρῆμα ἐκηλήθη ὑπὸ τοῦ μέλους, Synes. *h.* 8. 19 ff. (on Christ's descent),
J. Kroll, op. cit. [p. 204], pp. 375 ff. Horace develops Virgil's theme
further by attributing these magical powers not to a temporary
visitor but to a resident poet of the underworld.

34. demittit ... aures : for this sign of placability cf. Hom. *Od.* 17.
302 (Argos) οὔατα κάββαλεν ἄμφω, Hes. *th.* 771 [below, 2. 19. 30 n.],
Sen. *Herc. f.* 810, G. Thomson on Aesch. *Ag.* 1227–9. The ears are
black because Cerberus was a black dog (Tib. 1. 3. 71, Sen. *Herc. O.*
23), as suited the underworld (cf. 21 *furvae*). The emphasis is laid
on the adjective, which is separated considerably from the un-
emphatic *auris* (picking up 32 *aure*): the sinister appearance of
Cerberus underlines the *a fortiori* argument.

belua centiceps : Cerberus is assigned fifty heads by Hesiod (*th.*
312), but three is the normal number (2. 19. 31 n.); in art he is two-
or three-headed, which has obvious conveniences. For a hundred
heads cf. Pind. *fr.* 249 b ἑκατογκεφάλας, Sen. *apocol.* 13. 3 'Cerberus,
vel ut ait Horatius, belua centiceps' (with irony at the grandiloquent
and Graecizing compound). Similar expressions may sometimes refer
to snakes' heads ('propter multitudinem anguium' Porph.); cf. 3.
11. 17 f. 'centum ... angues', Apollod. 2. 5. 2, Cook 3. 1. 403, Roscher
2. 1. 1126 f., *RE* 11. 273 f. But in our passage Horace can only be
thinking of dogs' ears; the paratragic hyperbole is deliberately
grotesque, and designed for the rhetorical sense rather than the eye
(one may contrast the three heads in the more pictorial scene of
2. 19. 29 ff.).

35. capillis Eumenidum : for the Eumenides in the underworld cf.
Aesch. *Eum.* 267 ff., Virg. *Aen.* 6. 280, Prop. 4. 11. 22. For their
snakes cf. Virg. *georg.* 4. 482 f. [above, 33 n.], Aesch. *cho.* 1049 f.,
RE 7. 311, Suppl. 8. 124 f.

36. recreantur angues : the snakes of the Eumenides are aroused by
the warlike poems of Alcaeus (for such awakening cf. Aesch. *Eum.*
124 ff., Norden on Virg. *Aen.* 6, p. 214); here the verb makes a contrast with 33 *stupens*. In the *Georgics* the snakes are hypnotized no
less than Cerberus (4. 481 ff., cited 33 n.); but Horace, who is describing a more invigorating poet than Orpheus, seems to have

taken the opportunity of capping Virgil (again an indication that he is the imitator). Editors assume that both writers are saying the same thing, but they do not explain how *recreantur* comes to mean 'are lulled to rest'. The best one can think of is that the word might be a *calque sémantique* for παραψύχειν in the sense of 'to pacify' (Call. *h.* 6. 45 φᾶ δὲ παραψύχοισα κακὸν καὶ ἀναιδέα φῶτα); it would derive this extended sense because both verbs naturally mean 'to refresh' (1. 22. 18 'recreatur aura', 3. 4. 40 'Pierio recreatis antro', Soph. *ichn.* 317 παραψυκτήριον of music). But such an explanation makes the relation of *recreantur* and *stupens* very obscure: the words would be pulling in the same direction under the guise of a formal antithesis.

37. quin : suggested by Virg. *georg.* 4. 481 [above, 33 n.], which has also influenced 3. 11. 21 'quin et Ixion . . .'.

Prometheus : Horace's Prometheus is punished not on the Caucasus but in Tartarus (so 2. 18. 34 ff., *epod.* 17. 67); his sufferings seem to be eternal (cf. Hes. *th.* 616 and the hyperbole at Prop. 2. 1. 69 f. 'idem Caucasia solvet de rupe Promethei / bracchia'). There was an old form of the legend by which Prometheus was sent to the underworld like the other Titans; cf. Aesch. *Prom.* 1016, 1029, 1050 f., Th. Zielinski, *Tragodumenon libri tres*, 1925, pp. 34 ff., *RE* 23. 679. This version might have commended itself to Hellenistic court-poets (cf. the unfavourable view in 1. 3. 27 f.); if it was followed by Maecenas in his *Prometheus*, that would explain the cluster of Horatian allusions.

Pelopis parens : Tantalus is a regular participant in underworld scenes (Hom. *Od.* 11. 582 ff., etc.); he is paired with Prometheus in the two Horatian parallels cited above. The periphrasis *Pelopis parens* is heroic, but is also a reminder of his crimes (cf. *epod.* 17. 65): he served up Pelops to the gods to see if they could distinguish him from animal meat (Pind. *O.* 1. 46 ff.). The alliteration with *Promethei* is unusually obvious for Horace, and gives the archaic colouring of Roman tragedy.

38. laborem decipitur : for music as a relief for care cf. 1. 32. 15 n. For *decipere* in the sense of 'to beguile' (*fallere*) cf. Ov. *trist.* 4. 1. 14 'fallitur ancillae decipiturque labor' (with de Jonge's parallels), Housman 2. 521 (= *CR* 14, 1900, 259) and on Manil. 1. 240, Meleager, *anth. P.* 7. 195. 1 ἀκρίς, ἐμῶν ἀπάτημα πόθων, Lucian, *Nigr.* 7 ἐξαπατῶσι τὴν νόσον, Milton, *P.L.* 2. 460 ff. 'if there be care or charm To respite, or deceive, or slack the pain Of this ill mansion'. There may be a special point in our passage as Prometheus and Tantalus were normally deceivers of others.

laborem is a litotes for the sufferings of the damned; cf. 2. 14. 20, Pind. *O.* 1. 60 πόνον (of Tantalus), 2. 67. The juxtaposition with *dulci* is pointed, and the retained accusative a poeticism on the Greek model. *laborum*, which is also well-attested, has been defended as a Greek genitive of relation (Plaut. *Epid.* 239 'nec sermonis fallebar tamen', K.–S. 1. 474); but the word would more naturally be taken with *sono* (which is absurd), and the plural suggests a series of torments rather than the agony of the moment (Heinze).

39. Orion : here included among the sinners (cf. 3. 4. 72, *RE* 18. 1. 1072, Roscher 3. 1. 1023 ff.). He was a mighty hunter in the under-world because this was his occupation in life; cf. Hom. *Od.* 11. 572 f. τὸν δὲ μετ' Ὠρίωνα πελώριον εἰσενόησα / θῆρας ὁμοῦ εἰλεῦντα κατ' ἀσφοδελὸν λειμῶνα, Pl. *resp.* 619, Tib. 1. 3. 63 f. (lovers love), Virg. *Aen.* 6. 485, 6. 654 f. 'quae cura nitentis / pascere equos, eadem sequitur tellure repostos', Ov. *met.* 4. 445, Pope, *Rape of the Lock* 1. 55 f. 'Her Joy in gilded Chariots, when alive, And Love of *Ombre*, after Death survive'.

40. timidos . . . lyncas : for the timidity of the poets' 'lynx' (prob-ably the African caracal) cf. 4. 6. 33 'fugacis', Stat. *Ach.* 2. 122, *RE* 13. 2474 f. The noun makes an alliterative pair with *leones* : lions were a difficult quarry because of their bravery (here one must understand *fortes*), lynxes because their sharp eyes allowed them to run in time. Perhaps there was a legend that Orion had exceptional sight; the notion would suit the bright constellation. *lynx* is normally feminine (Prisc. *gramm.* 2. 218. 3 ff. comments on our passage); but the vowel-sounds of *timidas agitare lyncas* might have seemed to lack variety (in spite of the changes of quantity). The poem ends in harmony and peace, a marvellous contrast to the boisterous humour of the opening stanzas.

14. EHEV FVGACES

[W. S. Anderson, *Californian Studies in Classical Antiquity* 1, 1968, 45 ff.; P. J. Connor, *Latomus* 29, 1970, 756 ff.; Pasquali 643 ff.; Quinn 99 ff.; N. Rudd, *AJPh* 81, 1960, 376 ff.; Williams 584 ff.; A. J. Woodman, *Latomus* 26, 1967, 377 ff.]

1–12. *The years glide away, Postumus, and piety will provide no bulwark against death, however much you propitiate Pluto, who pens in even the strongest with the waters that all who live on earth must sail, rich and poor alike.* 13–24. *Even if we avoid war and sea-faring and fevers, Cocytus and the Danaids and Sisyphus must be faced; land and house and wife must be left, and of the trees you cultivate none will go with you but the sad cypresses.* 25–8. *A more deserving heir will use*

*up the hoarded Caecuban, and stain the floor with a superior vintage
that is worthy of a pontiffs' dinner.*

Postumus cannot be certainly identified. Some have supposed
that he is fictitious, which would be contrary to Horace's practice
in the *Odes* (except where Greek names like Thaliarchus are concerned); by another view he is the poet Rabirius (L. Herrmann,
Latomus 25, 1966, 769 ff.), who wrote about the death of Antony
(Sen. *ben.* 6. 3. 1, Schanz–Hosius 2. 267 f.). A more plausible candidate
is the Postumus of Propertius 3. 12, who in 21 B.C. was preparing to
join Augustus's Parthian expedition; on this hypothesis the *placens
uxor* of the ode (21 f.) is the Aelia Galla of the elegy, who is described
as a lady of exemplary fidelity (for one speculative argument for the
identification cf. 22 n.). Propertius develops in considerable detail
a comparison of the married couple with Ulysses and Penelope, and
among the epic hero's other adventures he records the visit to the
shades (3. 12. 33 'nigrantisque domos animarum intrasse silentum');
it is a curious coincidence that the ode shows a number of similarities
with the *Odyssey*, particularly in its representation of the underworld
(see notes on 8, 10, 18, 20, 21), but these are hardly specific enough
to demonstrate that Postumus was already being associated with
Ulysses. It is an objection to the identification that Propertius's
friend seems younger and livelier than Horace's, but this could be
due to a difference of genre: if he were a man in his forties he might
be old enough to listen to lyric admonitions on death and young
enough to receive a romantic elegy on his perhaps younger wife (in
the ode the *uxor* is expected to survive the husband).

Propertius's Postumus has plausibly been identified with a successful relative of his own: cf. *ILS* 914 'C. Propertius Q.f. T.n. Fab.
Postumus / IIIvir cap. et insequenti anno pro / IIIvir., q., pr. desig.
ex s.c. viar. cur., pr. ex s.c. pro aed. cur. ius dixit, procos.', *PIR* P
754, *RE* 22. 1. 986 f. The prosperous magistrate of the inscription is
of the right status to offer ostentatious sacrifices, own salubrious
parkland, and hoard vintage Caecuban; if he came from Etruria
(over the border from Propertius's Assisi), that might give extra
point to Horace's gloomy reference to the monster Geryon (8 n.).
As for Aelia Galla, she may have been the daughter or perhaps
rather the sister of Aelius Gallus, the second prefect of Egypt (vol. i,
p. 338). The affairs of Aelius Gallus were almost fraternally intertwined with those of Seius Strabo, who was prefect of the praetorian
guard at the end of Augustus's reign, and thereafter of Egypt: the
former was father by adoption of Sejanus, the latter by blood (cf.
G. V. Sumner, *Phoenix* 19, 1965, 140 ff.); the former was patron of
Strabo the geographer, the latter may have given him his name

(Bowersock 128 f.). Now Seius on his mother's side was nephew of Terentia, the childless wife of Maecenas; his own equestrian family came from Volsinii in the south of Etruria just as Maecenas came from Arezzo in the north. Here we have a nexus of relationships that makes it possible that Propertius Postumus, and in particular Aelia Galla, should be celebrated by two writers in Maecenas's circle.

Melancholy reflections on death were a commonplace of Greek poetry from the earliest times. Already Alcaeus contrasted the gaiety of the symposium with the doom to come (38 A. 1 ff.):

> πῶνε [καὶ μέθυ' ὦ] Μελάνιππ' ἄμ' ἔμοι· τί [φαῖς
> †ὅταμε[....] δίνναεντ' Ἀχέροντα μεγ[
> ζάβαι[ς ἀ]ελίω κόθαρον φάος [ἄψερον
> ὄψεσθ'· ἀλλ' ἄγι μὴ μεγάλων ἐπ[ιβάλλεο·
> καὶ γὰρ Σίσυφος Αἰολίδαις βασίλευς [ἔφα
> ἄνδρων πλεῖστα νοησάμενος [θανάτω κρέτην·
> ἀλλὰ καὶ πολύιδρις ἔων ὑπὰ κᾶρι [δὶς
> δίνναεντ' Ἀχέροντ' ἐπέραισε . . .

Here as in Horace we have 'Sisyphus Aeolides' and a river of the underworld; whatever evasive action one takes, death is inevitable. Variations on the same theme are common in elegy and tragedy (6 n., 13 n.), in sepulchral epigram and the Hellenistic poets (10 n., I. 4. 18 n.). The Epicureans were particularly obsessed by death (Pease on Cic. *nat. deor.* I. 86), and if Lucretius seems to protest his indifference too much, he is only following the traditions of his school (Sen. *epist.* 24. 18). The subject was handled by Philodemus in his περὶ θανάτου (D. Bassi, *Herculanensium Voluminum quae supersunt collectio tertia* I, 1914, 19 ff., T. Kuiper, *Philodemus over den Dood*, Diss. Amsterdam, 1925, Gigante 63 ff.), and by Cicero in the first book of his *Tusculan Disputations*. Among the Augustan poets Varius wrote an unexplained work *de morte*, Virgil an underworld scene modernized by mystical speculation, while the elegiac poets shared an interest in death-beds and funeral pyres. Some have explained these preoccupations by the poets' own morbidity, others by the *Angst* of an age of leisure and civil war (cf. Boucher 18, 65 ff., 484 ff.); yet where literary convention plays so important a part, speculation is unfruitful. In the next century a skeleton of silver was produced at Trimalchio's dinner (Petron. 34. 8) and engraved on two of the flagons of Boscoreale.

As suits his subject Horace's imagery is largely Greek, and his description of the underworld follows a well-established convention (above, pp. 203 f.). Tityos and Sisyphus can be traced to the eleventh book of the *Odyssey*, the Danaids to the painting of Polygnotus at Delphi (18 n.); Styx and Cocytus are Homeric rivers, though their

sluggish character belongs to a later tradition (17 n.). Yet as so
often Horace introduces original notes that are relevant to Roman
society and his friend's particular status and ethos. Postumus seems
to have been a man of great possessions, who was conspicuously
scrupulous about his religious observances (2 n.), the management of
his estates (22 n.), and his household expenditure (26 n.); the gravity
and reticence of Horace's style may also reflect something about
the ode's recipient. The storms of the Adriatic (14) and the malarial
Sirocco (15 n.) are not illustrations that would have occurred to
a Hellenistic poet; even the punishments of the underworld are given
a Latin ring (19 nn.). Postumus's devotion to his wife is a Roman
rather than a Greek poetical theme; she makes a change from the
conventional hetaera of sympotic epigram. The property rights of
the dead (24 n.) and the privileged position of the single *heres* (25 n.)
may be illuminated by the legal arrangements of the poet's own
society. Other modern elements are the vintage Caecuban (25), the
presumably elaborate *pavimentum* (27), and the ceremonial dinners
of the priestly college (28), to which Postumus himself may have
belonged.

The ode is a masterpiece of construction. The first three stanzas
constitute a rolling period that seems designed to imitate the flood
of time (5 n.); after stating his thesis on the inevitability of death
(1–4), Horace proceeds to the uselessness of evasive action (5–8) and
the necessity to cross the river of the underworld (9–12). The next
three stanzas repeat to some extent the same movement (there should
be a colon rather than a full-stop at 16 *austrum*); once again we have
the uselessness of evasion (13–16), the necessity of death (again
expressed by an emphatic gerundive), and the river of the underworld. Finally the second section is capped by a single stanza wryly
predicting the extravagant behaviour of Postumus's heir (25–28).
Horace balances his words with classical regularity: cf. the polar
expressions 'land and water' (10 n.), 'kings and peasants' (11 f.), the
anaphora of *frustra* (13 ff.), the contrasts at 17 ff. *visendus . . .
linquenda . . . sequetur*, 25 f. *absumet . . . servata*. There is a repeated
use of 'tricolon' (3 f. *rugis, senectae, morti*, 13 ff. *Marte, Hadriae,
Austrum*, 18 ff. *Cocytos, Danai genus, Sisyphus*, 21 ff. *tellus, domus,
uxor*); sometimes the 'law of increasing clauses' is observed (1. 21.
1 n.). But Horace's skill at organization achieves more than rhetorical
emphasis. By his subtle variations of person (6 *places*, 10 *vescimur*,
etc.) and his ambiguous gerundives (11, 17, 21) he seems to be addressing both his friend Postumus and all mankind (Williams, loc.
cit.); the application of the poem is at the same time particular and
universal.

The date of the ode to Postumus is impossible to determine, but it is likely to have been written before the Ode to Dellius (above, p. 53); on the other hand the sombre and constricting rivers of the underworld seem to be derived from the Fourth *Georgic* (9 n.), which had given a new impetus to poetical eschatology. Certainly Bücheler was wrong to put the poem early on grounds of immaturity (*RhM* 37, 1882, 234 = *Kl. Schr.* 2. 438 f.); he mistakenly criticized it for its conventional mythology, its tendency towards hyperbole (see 5 n., 26 n.), and certain stylistic idiosyncrasies which he failed to explain (6 *inlacrimabilem*, 11 *enaviganda*, 13 *carebimus*, 26 ff. *mero . . . potiore cenis*). It would be juster to commend its formal perfection and authoritative tone (cf. the late 4. 7), its thought-provoking economy (17 *flumine languido*, 19 f. *longi . . . laboris*, 21 f. *placens uxor*, 23 *invisas cupressos*), its Roman realism in facing the inevitable (5 ff., 13 ff., cf. 1. 24. 19 f.). Yet in comparison with the ode to Dellius, Horace seems to be turning his back on life: the dear wife is loved only to be lost, the adjuration to enjoyment has an un-Epicurean bitterness (25 ff.), the underworld is dominated by those symbols of futility, Sisyphus and the Danaids. To that extent this justly celebrated poem is uncharacteristic.

Metre: Alcaic.

1. eheu . . . anni: the opening word strikes a melancholy note that is maintained through the rest of the poem. Horace's *sententia* was already a familiar quotation in the ancient world (Hier. *in Am.* 3. 6, *in Ezech.* 1. 1, Diom. *gramm.* 1. 445. 27 f., Serv. *gramm.* 4. 470. 25). For similar references to the flight of time cf. 1. 11. 7, 2. 5. 13 n., 2. 11. 5 ff., 3. 29. 48, 3. 30. 5, *serm.* 2. 6. 40, Theoc. 2. 52, Sen. *epist.* 108. 24–5, Otto 112 f. (with *Nachträge*, p. 154).

fugaces: time has a continuing propensity to give us the slip (cf. Sen. *epist.* 1. 3 'rei . . . fugacis et lubricae', Prud. *cath.* 11. 5 f., *Thes.l.L.* 6. 1. 1474. 52 ff.). The adjective suits running water (2. 3. 12 'lympha fugax'), and so coheres with *labuntur* below; the image seems to be sustained by 2 *moram* and 3 *instanti*, and may be continued even in 4 *indomitae* (see note). Some prefer to see a military metaphor (Quinn 102, D. West ap. Costa 33), appropriate in addressing a soldier, but though this suits *moram*, *instanti*, and *indomitae*, it is unlikely to be primary; it is incompatible with *labuntur* (which sets the tone of the stanza), and would involve the assumption that the years and old age are fighting on different sides, the former dissolving in rout and the latter pressing in pursuit. Quinn also suggests the analogy of a fugitive slave (cf. Palladas, *anth. P.* 10. 87. 1 τὸν βίον τὸν δραπέτην) but this idea finds no support in the rest of the stanza.

Postume Postume : the repetition gives a sad and serious tone; cf. Sappho 114. 1 παρθενία παρθενία, ποῖ με λίποισ' ἀποίχῃ;, Herodas 10. 1 f. ἐπὴν τὸν ἑξηκοστὸν ἥλιον κάμψῃς / ὦ Γρύλλε Γρύλλε, θνῆσκε καὶ τέφρη γίνευ (with Headlam's parallels), ev. Luc. 10. 41 Μάρθα Μάρθα, Wölfflin 289 f., J. B. Hofmann, *Lateinische Umgangssprache*, 1936, p. 59. For other instances of *geminatio* in Horace cf. 2. 17. 10, 3. 3. 18, 4. 4. 70, *epod*. 6. 11, 7. 1, 17. 7.

2. labuntur : the verb suggests the continuous and deceptively silent gliding of a river; cf. 1. 2. 19, *epod*. 2. 25, *epist*. 1. 2. 43 'labetur in omne volubilis aevum', *Thes.l.L*. 7. 2. 786. 83 ff. For the application of the verb to the lapse of time cf. Ov. *am*. 1. 8. 49 f. 'labitur occulte fallitque volatilis aetas, / ut celer admissis labitur amnis aquis' (for the text see G. P. Goold, *HSCPh* 69, 1965, 22), *met*. 15. 179 f. 'adsiduo labuntur tempora motu / non secus ac flumen', *fast*. 1. 65 with Bömer's note, *Thes.l.L*. 7. 788. 8 ff. In our stanza the stream of time becomes an uncontrollable Italian torrent; cf. 3. 29. 33 ff., Sen. *epist*. 23. 8, Marc. Aur. 4. 43 ῥεῦμα βίαιον ὁ αἰών, Pohlenz 2. 170.

nec pietas : the futility of our efforts to avoid death becomes a dominating idea of the poem; cf. 4 *indomitae*, 5 *non si*, 6 *inlacrimabilem*, 13 and 15 *frustra*. The land-owning Postumus may have paid more than average attention to traditional observances; cf. 5 *trecenis*, 28 *pontificum*, 4. 7. 23 f. (to the patrician Torquatus) 'non te facundia, non te / restituet pietas'. For the uselessness of piety see 1. 24. 11 n., Virg. *Aen*. 2. 429 f., Ov. *am*. 3. 9. 37 f., Stat. *silv*. 5. 1. 154 f., Fitzgerald, *Omar Khayyam* 71 'nor all your Piety and Wit . . .'; cf. also the epic commonplace 'his augury could not save him' (Hom. *Il*. 2. 859, Ap. Rhod. 2. 815 ff., 4. 1502 ff., Virg. *Aen*. 9. 328). For the *quid profuit?* motif in general cf. 1. 28. 4 n., Esteve-Forriol 137.

moram : the word can be used of a barrier against floods; cf. Stat. *Theb*. 1. 358 f. 'flumina nullae / aggeribus tenuere morae'. However, in our passage *adferet* suggests a less concrete usage; the same collocation is found eight times in Cicero's speeches.

3. rugis : conventionally a sign of advancing years (cf. ῥυτίδες).

instanti senectae : the participle suggests relentless pressure (stronger than Solon 24. 10 W. γῆρας ἐπερχόμενον) and a towering threat (but not overhead as in Mimnermus 5. 6 W. γῆρας . . . ὑπερκρέμαται). Both aspects of the word suit a river in flood; cf. Stat. *Theb*. 9. 487 f. (Hippomedon fights the Ismenus) 'instant undae sequiturque labantem / amnis ovans'. Horace's expressions are growing progressively stronger, to suit time's apparent acceleration; at first the years simply slip away, but soon the viewpoint changes and age comes bearing down (this does not involve the oddity of a continuous military metaphor, cf. 1 n.).

4. indomitaeque morti: not just 'unsubdued' but 'impossible to subdue' (like *invictus*, ἀήττητος). For such descriptions of death cf. Hom. *Il.* 9. 158 Ἀΐδης τοι ἀμείλιχος ἠδ' ἀδάμαστος, Philodemus, περὶ θεῶν 1. 18. 24 Diels τὸν δ' Ἀΐδην ἄμαχον καὶ ἀδάμαστον, Paul, 1 *Cor.* 15. 55 ποῦ σου, θάνατε, τὸ νῖκος; Some have thought that Admetus was originally a deity of the underworld.

The adjective literally means 'untamed', of animals. It suits the military metaphor of the stanza, so far as this is present (see 1 n. on *fugaces*). But it might also suggest an uncontrollable river (for the familiar comparison with bulls cf. 4. 14. 25 'tauriformis . . . Aufidus'); for similar expressions see 3. 29. 40 'fera diluvies', 4. 14. 20 'indomitas . . . undas' (of the sea), *epist.* 1. 14. 30 'multa mole docendus aprico parcere prato' (to be trained), Prop. 1. 20. 16 'indomito fleverat Ascanio' (evidently a standing epithet, perhaps Hellenistic in origin), Liv. 21. 30. 5 'domita . . . fluminis vi', Plin. *nat.* 36. 1 'ad fluminum impetus domandos', *Thes.l.L.* 5. 1. 1947. 64 ff., 7. 1. 1225. 33 ff., T. S. Eliot, *The Dry Salvages* 1 f. 'I do not know much about gods; but I think that the river Is a strong brown god—sullen, untamed and intractable' (an image that suggests time; cf. H. Gardner, *The Art of T. S. Eliot*, 1949, pp. 170 f.). Of course if *indomitaeque morti* had appeared in isolation nobody would think of rivers, but the adjective may be adequate to sustain an image that has already been established (cf. above, 2. 9. 1 ff.).

5. non si . . .: Horace picks up the idea of *pietas* mentioned above. The thought seemed complete at the end of the first stanza, but the sentence flows on with a whole series of continuing developments (7 *qui . . .*, 9 *scilicet . . .*, 11 *sive . . .*). The rolling period suits the passage of the years and in particular the image of a river; cf. 3. 29. 33 ff. (the torrent of time), 4. 2. 5 ff. (Pindar's poetry). The editors who print a semicolon at *morti* are over-punctuating.

trecenis: an indefinite large number (3. 4. 79, *serm.* 1. 5. 12, E. Wölfflin, *ALL* 9. 188 ff.); the multiple of three suits a sacred context (Pease on Virg. *Aen.* 4. 510). For hecatombs cf. *epod.* 17. 39, Mayor on Juv. 12. 101, *RE* 7. 2786 f.; for a triple hecatomb cf. Liv. 22. 10. 7 (a state offering after Trasimene). Here the long hyperbaton (*trecenis . . . tauris*) throws emphasis on the numeral. The fantastic hyperbole lightens for a moment the poem's sombre tone; Horace hints that there is something absurd about Postumus's religious scrupulosity. For doubts about the efficacy of sacrifice cf. Aesch. *Ag.* 1168 ff., Pers. 2. 44 ff.

quotquot eunt dies: 'every day that passes'; for *eunt* cf. 4. 5. 7, Ov. *ars* 2. 663, *Thes.l.L.* 5. 2. 645. 16 ff. Ps.-Acro comments 'dixit autem *eunt* pro mortalitatis dolore, quasi *fluunt et pereunt*', but this is to give the word too much emotional connotation. *dies* formally balances 2 *anni*; both words are in conspicuous positions in the opening clauses of their stanzas.

6. amice : the word sustains the sympathetic note of the opening stanza; its position heightens the affectionately teasing tone of the hyperbole (cf. 2. 9. 5 'amice Valgi'). Peerlkamp found the vocative strange after *Postume*, and proposed the fatuous *annique*; yet cf. *epod*. 1. 2 'amice' . . . 4 'Maecenas', *epist*. 1. 7. 5 'Maecenas' . . . 12 'dulcis amice'.

places : the verb need not imply that the propitiation is successful (cf. Juv. 12. 89). The juxtaposition with *inlacrimabilem* is pointed.

inlacrimabilem : the adjective, which is perhaps a coinage of Horace's own, can be either active (as here) or passive (as at 4. 9. 26); cf. ἀδάκρυτος, *miserabilis* (1. 33. 2 n.), *flebilis* (2. 9. 8 n.). For similar descriptions of Hades cf. 2. 3. 24, Hom. *Il*. 9. 158 ἀμείλιχος, Manil. 5. 327 f. (on Orpheus) 'et silvis addidit aures / et Diti lacrimas'. For the idea that Death cannot be bribed cf. *epist*. 2. 2. 178 f. 'Orcus . . . non exorabilis auro', Solon 24. 9 f. W. (= Theognis 727 f.) οὐδ' ἂν ἄποινα διδοὺς θάνατον φύγοι οὐδὲ βαρειὰς / νούσους, οὐδὲ κακὸν γῆρας ἐπερχόμενον, Theognis 1187 ff., Aesch. fr. 279 Mette (= 161 N.) μόνος θεῶν γὰρ Θάνατος οὐ δώρων ἐρᾷ, / οὔτ' ἄν τι θύων οὔτ' ἐπισπένδων ἄνοις. / οὐ βωμός ἐστιν οὐδὲ παιωνίζεται, / μόνου δὲ Πειθὼ δαιμόνων ἀποστατεῖ, Soph. fr. 770 P. (= 703 N.), Orph. *h*. 87. 9; contrast Tiberian. *anth. Lat.* 719[b]. 3 'aurum quo pretio reserantur limina Ditis'.

7. ter amplum : the expression must be taken with three-bodied Geryon (see next note) rather than with the much vaster Tityos. *amplus* is a dry euphemism for 'huge'; cf. Varro, *rust*. 2. 4. 4 'amplae' (of pigs), Suet. *Tib*. 68. 1 'corpore . . . amplo'. There is also a hint at the dignity and wealth of Geryon, which were of no avail to him.

8. Geryonen : more poetical than the variant *Geryonem*; both forms are attested in Martial, but there too -*en* is correct (Housman 2. 830 = *JPh* 31, 1910, 253 f.). Geryon was killed in Spain by Hercules, who drove away his cattle (Hes. *th*. 287 ff.); the legend was popularized by the *Geryoneis* of Stesichorus, and was particularly influential in Italy (Roscher 1. 2. 1630 ff., *RE* 7. 1286 ff., Suppl. 3. 1061 ff., M. Robertson, *CQ* 19 N.S., 1969, 207 ff., D. Page, *JHS* 93, 1973, 138 ff.). His triple body is often portrayed in literature and art; cf. Aesch. *Ag*. 870 τρισώματος, Lucr. 5. 28 'tripectora tergemini vis Geryonai', Virg. *Aen*. 6. 289 'forma tricorporis umbrae', *CIL* 4. 2440 'Geryones trimembres' (of three Pompeian *scortatores*). Though not included in the Homeric νέκυια, he had associations with the underworld long before Horace and Virgil (J. H. Croon, *The Herdsman of the Dead*,

1952, pp. 27, 32, 67 ff., J. Fontenrose, *Python*, 1959, pp. 334 ff.) ; his dog was a brother of Cerberus (Hes. *th.* 309 ff.), his cattle were pastured with those of Hades (Apollod. 2. 5. 10), he appears as Cerun with Hades and Persephone in a third-century wall-painting from the Tomba dell'Orco at Tarquinia (*RE* 7. 1295, L. Banti, *The Etruscan Cities and their Culture*, 1973, pl. 37a, R. Herbig, *Götter und Dämonen der Etrusker*, 1965, Taf. 37). Perhaps Postumus had Etruscan associations (above, p. 223) ; cf. 2. 17. 13 n. for Maecenas and the Chimaera.

Geryon is mentioned in our passage as a terrifying monster who with his three lives was difficult to kill (Sil. 1. 280 ff.) ; for a similar point cf. Philodemus, *de morte* 4. 37. 22 ff. (p. 79 Gigante) τοὺς πλείστους ἀγνοοῦντας ὅτι πᾶς ἄνθρωπος, κἂν ἰσχυρότερος ᾖ τῶν Γιγάντων, ἐφήμερός ἐστι πρὸς ζωὴν καὶ τελευτήν. It may also be relevant that he was a cattle-owner (Anderson, op. cit., p. 57), and therefore in a strong position to offer hecatombs to Pluto.

Tityonque : a gigantic monster, much vaster than Geryon, and therefore particularly difficult to confine ; cf. Hom. *Od.* 11. 577 ὁ δ' ἐπ' ἐννέα κεῖτο πέλεθρα. Unlike Geryon, he was regularly found since Homer in descriptions of the underworld ; cf. 3. 4. 77, 3. 11. 21, Lucr. 3. 984, Virg. *Aen.* 6. 595 f., Diog. Oen. 14. 1. 5 ff., Roscher 5. 1037 ff. In *diatribe* he may have been used to point a particular moral to landowners ; cf. Phaedr. *app.* 5. 13 ff. 'novem porrectus Tityos est per iugera / tristi renatum suggerens poenae iecur ; / quo quis maiorem possidet terrae locum, / hoc demonstratur cura graviore adfici'.

9. compescit unda : for the restraining rivers of the underworld cf. 2. 20. 8, Virg. *georg.* 4. 478 ff. 'quos circum limus niger et deformis harundo / Cocyti tardaque palus inamabilis unda / alligat et novies Styx interfusa coercet', *Aen.* 6. 438 f. 'tristisque palus inamabilis undae / alligat et . . . Styx . . . coercet', Prop. 4. 11. 16. The motif is un-Homeric and perhaps derived from the *Georgics* ; Virgil may have returned the compliment in the *Aeneid* (at least if the attractive variant *tristi . . . unda* is accepted). *compescere* usually refers to physical constraints, and there may be a conscious paradox (derived from Virgil) in 'bonds of water'. Horace may even have been aware that *compescere* meant by origin *con-pascere* (though the derivation of the word is usually ignored) ; it would certainly be appropriate that the rancher Geryon should himself be penned in.

omnibus : for the commonplace cf. 1. 28. 15 n. and 16 n., 2. 3. 28 n.

10. terrae munere : *terrae* balances *unda*; the contrast is sustained by 11 f. *enaviganda . . . coloni*, 17 ff. *flumine . . . tellus*. Horace appropriately applies to a landowner the conventional poetic periphrasis for all mortals ; cf. Hom. *Il.* 6. 142 βροτῶν οἳ ἀρούρης καρπὸν ἔδουσιν, 13. 322, 21. 465, *Od.* 8. 222, Simonides 542. 24 f. εὐρυεδέος ὅσοι / καρπὸν

αἰνύμεθα χθονός, Phanocles 2 Powell ἀλλὰ τὸ Μοιράων νῆμ᾽ ἄλλυτον, οὐδέ
τῳ ἔστιν | ἐκφυγέειν ὁπόσοι γῆν ἐπιφερβόμεθα (a context similar to our
own), Sen. *Phoen.* 221 f. Some compare *epist.* 1. 2. 27 'fruges consumere
nati', but that refers rather to the wastefulness of Penelope's suitors.

vescimur : Horace makes his admonitions more palatable by
turning from the second to the first person (cf. 2. 16. 17 n.). *vescor*
is more general than *edo* (Cic. *nat. deor.*2. 59 'nec iis escis aut potionibus vescuntur') and also grander (note the frequency in Cicero's
philosophica). Some comparative statistics are given in *Thes.l.L.*
5. 2. 100. 16 ff., but further discrimination is necessary.

11. enaviganda : the voyage must be seen through (cf. ἐκπερᾶν); the
verb is found in a different sense at Cic. *Tusc.* 4. 33. The prosaic
compound sums up the situation with brevity and emphasis (note
its delayed position); for similar gerundives cf. 17 and 21, 1. 28. 16,
Prop. 3. 18. 22 ff.

sive reges : for the conventional polar expression cf. 1. 4. 13 f.
(with notes), Simonides 520. 5 f., Prop. 3. 5. 17, Marc. Aur. 6. 24
Ἀλέξανδρος ὁ Μακεδὼν καὶ ὁ ὀρεωκόμος αὐτοῦ ἀποθανόντες εἰς ταὐτὸ
κατέστησαν, Job 3. 19 'The small and great are there; and the servant
is free from his master'. A Pompeian mosaic shows a king's sceptre
and diadem and a beggar's stick and knapsack on either side of a
skull (O. Brendel, *MDAI(R)* 49, 1934, 163 ff. with Taf. 10). Kings
were naturally rich, as is implied by *inopes coloni*.

13. frustra . . . : cf. 3. 2. 14 'mors et fugacem persequitur virum',
Callinus 1. 14 f. πολλάκι δηϊοτῆτα φυγὼν καὶ δοῦπον ἀκόντων | ἔρχεται,
ἐν δ᾽ οἴκῳ μοῖρα κίχεν θανάτου, Simonides 524 ὁ δ᾽ αὖ θάνατος κίχε καὶ
τὸν φυγόμαχον, Aesch. fr. 708. 3 f. Mette (= 362. 3 f. N.), Eur. fr.
10 N., Dem. 18. 97, Sall. *hist.* fr. 1. 55. 15, Prop. 3. 18. 25 f., Koran,
Sura 4 'Wherever ye be death will overtake you, although ye be in
lofty towers'.

carebimus : the verb can be used of bad things as well as good
(2. 10. 6 f., Cic. *Tusc.* 1. 88, Petron. 89. 15 'bello carens', *Thes.l.L.*
3. 449. 34 ff.), and of voluntary abstention as well as objective lack
(ibid. 452. 30 ff.). For the combination of both usages cf. *epist.* 1. 1.
41 f. 'sapientia prima / stultitia caruisse', Cic. *Cael.* 42 '(iuventus) ne
intersit insidiis, scelere careat'.

14. fractis . . . Hadriae : warfare and navigation often provide parallel *exempla* (2. 13. 15 n.). For the storms of the Adriatic cf. 1. 16. 4 n.;
here the danger is accentuated by *fractis*, which suggests dangerous
reefs. More indirectly the participle hints at a hoarse voice, like
rauci; note the alliteration in this couplet of *f*, *c*, and *r*, the last of
which was rolled by the Romans.

15. per autumnos . . . austrum : not 'throughout autumns', but 'each succeeding autumn' (2. 3. 6 n.). For the unhealthiness of the season cf. Hippocr. *aph.* 3. 9 ἐν φθινοπώρῳ ὀξύταται αἱ νοῦσοι καὶ θανατωδέσταται τοὐπίπαν, Bion 2. 13, Waszink on Tert. *anim.* 48. 1, *Thes.l.L.* 2. 1603. 63 ff.; the sultry Sirocco blew (Arist. *sign.* 973ᵇ8 f. νοτὸς . . . διὰ τὸ νοσώδη εἶναι, Nissen 1. 386 ff.), and malaria was rife in Italy (Brunt 611 ff.). The propertied classes fled to the hills or the sea (cf. *serm.* 2. 6. 18 f. 'nec plumbeus Auster [me perdit] / autumnus- que gravis, Libitinae quaestus acerbae', *epist.* 1. 7. 1 ff., 1. 16. 16); for Horace's theme cf. especially Mart. 4. 60. 5 f. 'nullo fata loco possis excludere; cum mors / venerit, in medio Tibure Sardinia est'. The alliteration of *au* and *m* in the stanza sounds a more sombre note than the raucous consonants above.

16. metuemus : like *carebimus* an urbane understatement for 'avoid' (*Thes.l.L.* 8. 905. 18 ff., cf. 2. 2. 7 n.). *corporibus* should be taken with *metuemus* as well as with *nocentem* (for the double duty of the case cf. 2. 11. 11 n.); for the dative cf. 2. 8. 21, *serm.* 1. 2. 131, Afran. *com.* 40 f.

17. visendus : Horace turns now from the negative 'you cannot escape death' to the affirmative 'you must die'. *visere* suggests view- ing rather than visiting (cf. 1. 4. 8), and is here a sinister euphemism; for the similar use of *videre* cf. 2. 13. 22 n. There may be a conscious paradox in the idea of inspecting blackness (cf. Virg. *Aen.* 6. 134 f. 'bis nigra videre / Tartara', Milton, *P.L.* 1. 63 'darkness visible'); see also 18 n.

ater : the strongly emotive adjective is elsewhere used of dark water (3. 27. 18, Virg. *Aen.* 5. 2), and is often associated with death and the underworld (André 51); cf. especially Pind. fr. 130 ἔνθεν τὸν ἄπειρον ἐρεύγονται σκότον / βληχροὶ (= *languidi*) δνοφερᾶς νυκτὸς ποταμοί, Virg. *Aen.* 6. 132 'Cocytusque sinu labens circumvenit atro'.

flumine languido : we avoid the turbulent *fluctus* of the Adriatic only to face the sluggish *flumen* of Cocytus. *flumine* means ρεύματι, 'stream' (Ov. *trist.* 5. 3. 23), and is to be taken closely with *errans*. The rivers of the underworld are sometimes portrayed as eddying (Alcaeus 38 A. 2, 8 δινάεντα), sometimes as torpid (cf. 9 n., Pind. loc. cit., Prop. 4. 11. 15 'vada lenta paludes', Sen. *Herc. f.* 554 'langui- dum', 686); for mud and swamps cf. Ar. *ran.* 145 f. εἶτα βόρβορον πολὺν / καὶ σκῶρ ἀείνων, Pl. *Phaedo* 113 a–b, Dieterich 81 ff., F. Graf, *Eleusis und die orphische Dichtung Athens in vorhellenistischer Zeit*, 1974, pp. 103 ff. Virgil followed Plato in combining turbulence and filth (*Aen.* 6. 296 'turbidus hic caeno vastaque voragine gurges').

18. Cocytus : a regular feature of the underworld since Homer (cf. *Od.* 10. 513 f., Pease on Cic. *nat. deor.* 3. 43). An ancient reader would

remember that it was the river 'named of lamentation loud' (Milton,
P.L. 2. 579); there are tears in the underworld though Pluto sheds
none (7). The combination of a word of sound with a word of sight
(*visendus*) seems deliberately pointed (2. 13. 24 n.); cf. Hermesianax
7. 9 f. Powell Κωκυτόν τ' ἀθέμιστον . . . / εἶδε (Hermann: ἠδὲ cod.).

Danai genus: the fifty daughters of Danaus, except for Hypermestra, killed their husbands on their wedding-night. Their punishment in the underworld was to carry water in leaky vessels (Rohde,
Psyche, app. 3, Frazer on Paus. 10. 31. 9, Dodds on Pl. *Gorg.* 492 d,
E. Keuls, *The Water Carriers in Hades*, 1974); it is characteristic of
the restraint of the ode that the reader has to supply the details for
himself. The story was not Homeric, but was portrayed by Polygnotus at Delphi and described in the pseudo-Platonic *Axiochus*
(371 e); it was represented also in the portico of Augustus's Palatine temple, a fact which helps to explain the many contemporary
references (3. 11. 25 ff., Tib. 1. 3. 79 f., Prop. 2. 31. 4, 4. 11. 27 f., Ov.
am. 2. 2. 4, *epist.* 14, *ars* 1. 73 f., *trist.* 3. 1. 59 ff.).

19. infame: the very Roman word, here emphatically placed, is used
with sinister economy (cf. 3. 11. 25 f. 'notas / virginum poenas'). It
balances *damnatus* below.

longi . . . laboris: the legal genitive again suggests the world of
Roman public life (cf. *Thes.l.L.* 5. 1. 15. 54 ff., H.–Sz. 76). The litotes
longi (= *aeterni*) maintains the reticence of the passage; cf. 2. 16. 30,
3. 11. 38 'longus . . . somnus', 4. 9. 27, Asclepiades, *anth. P.* 12. 50. 8
τὴν μακρὰν νύκτ' ἀναπαυσόμεθα, *Ecclesiastes* 12. 5 'because man goeth
to his long home'.

20. Sisyphus Aeolides: Sisyphus regularly appeared in the underworld since Homer (*Od.* 11. 593 ff.); it is relevant for our poem that
in the post-Homeric tradition he escaped but was recaptured (Alcaeus 38 A. 7 f., Theognis 702 ff., Soph. *Phil.* 448 f., 625). For the
heroic patronymic cf. Hom. *Il.* 6. 154, Hes. fr. 43 (a). 75, Alcaeus
38 A. 5, Theognis 702, Pind. fr. 5. 1; for the use of both name and
patronymic in Latin poetry cf. E. J. Kenney, *CR* N.S. 16, 1966, 271.
Aeolides increases the suggestion of shiftiness (cf. Pearson on Soph.
fr. 912 μηδ' αἰόλιζε ταῦτα); so Virg. *Aen.* 6. 529 (of Ulysses).

21. linquenda . . .: Horace's philosophic acceptance of death has
some affinities with the gibes of *diatribe*, where men's reluctance to
leave their possessions was ridiculed; cf. especially Lucian, *cat.* 20
(perhaps from Menippus) οἴμοι τῶν κτημάτων. — οἴμοι τῶν ἀγρῶν. —
ὀττοτοῖ, τὴν οἰκίαν οἵαν ἀπέλιπον. — ὅσα τάλαντα ὁ κληρονόμος σπαθήσει
παραλαβών. — αἰαῖ τῶν νεογνῶν μοι παιδίων. — τίς ἄρα τὰς ἀμπέλους
τρυγήσει ἃς πέρυσιν ἐφυτευσάμην; For other references to the abandon-

ment of property cf. Solon 24. 7 f. W. (= Theognis 725 f.) τὰ γὰρ
περιώσια πάντα / χρήματ' ἔχων οὐδεὶς ἔρχεται εἰς Ἀίδεω, Phoenix 1. 22 f.
Powell ἐγὼ δ' ἐς Ἀίδην οὔτε χρυσὸν οὔθ' ἵππον / οὔτ' ἀργυρῆν ἅμαξαν
ᾠχόμην ἕλκων, Prop. 3. 5. 13 'haud ullas portabis opes Acherontis ad
undas', Ov. trist. 5. 14. 12, Petron. 43. 8 'hoc solum enim secum tulit',
Sil. 5. 265 ff., Job 1. 21, 1 Tim. 6. 7 οὐδὲν γὰρ εἰσηνέγκαμεν εἰς τὸν
κόσμον ὅτι οὐδὲ ἐξενεγκεῖν τι δυνάμεθα (see J. N. D. Kelly, A Commentary on the Pastoral Epistles, 1963, p. 136), Philo, spec. leg. 1. 295,
Lucian, dial. mort. 20 (10). 1, Char. 14, Mart. 8. 44. 9 'rape conger
aufer posside: relinquendum est', Palladas, anth. P. 10. 58. 1 γῆς
ἐπέβην γυμνὸς γυμνός θ' ὑπὸ γαῖαν ἄπειμι, anon. ibid. 9. 145. 5 f.

tellus : primarily the word refers to the earth as opposed to the
underworld (cf. Ov. epist. 18. 169 'digna quidem caelo es, sed adhuc
tellure morare', met. 15. 448). It also suits the contrast between land
and water that has been found in the previous stanzas (10 n.). It
further suggests Postumus's fertile estate (Horace is not now thinking of himself, as uxor shows); for the collocation with domus and
uxor cf. 2. 3. 17 f. 'cedes coemptis saltibus et domo / villaque' (a close
parallel), epist. 1. 2. 47 'domus et fundus', Hom. Od. 14. 64 (Eumaeus)
οἰκόν τε κλῆρόν τε πολυμνήστην τε γυναῖκα, Lucian, Char. 20 ἀλλ'
ἀνάγκη τὸν μὲν γυμνὸν οἴχεσθαι, τὴν οἰκίαν δὲ καὶ τὸν ἀγρὸν καὶ τὸ
χρυσίον ἀεὶ ἄλλων εἶναι καὶ μεταβάλλειν τοὺς δεσπότας, cat. 20 (see
previous note), Gerhard 115 f. Yet tellus by itself can hardly mean
'estate'; at serm. 2. 2. 129 'propriae telluris erum' the adjective makes
a difference ('a bit of land of his own').

domus : the emotive word most naturally refers to a town-house;
cf. 2. 3. 17 (cited above), where the domus is distinguished from the villa.

placens : the word is more reticent than amata; cf. Hom. Il. 9. 336
ἄλοχον θυμαρέα, Od. 23. 232, Suet. Tib. 7. 2 '(uxorem) bene convenien-
tem'. Postumus's wife makes an agreeable contrast with the notorious
Danaids.

22. uxor : with great economy Horace recalls Lucretius's famous
lines 'iam iam non domus accipiet te laeta neque uxor / optima,
nec dulces occurrent oscula nati / praeripere . . .' (3. 894 ff.). Possibly
a commonplace lay behind this passage; cf. Peek, GV 1827. 1 f.
οὐκέτι δὴ μάτηρ σε, Φιλόξενε, δέξατο χερσὶν / σὰν ἐρατὰν χρονίως ἀμφι-
βαλοῦσα δέρην. On the other hand Horace's uxor seems Roman
rather than Greek, and is presumably directly influenced by Lucretius himself. It is sometimes forgotten that Lucretius is rejecting the
attitude that he describes; he adds the dry comment 'nec tibi earum /
iam desiderium rerum super insidet ullum' (3. 900 f.). Horace ignores
this derisive element, and unlike Lucretius he says nothing about
children; Postumus had only a remote heres.

It may be significant that Propertius writes to his Postumus
'pendebit collo Galla pudica tuo' (3. 12. 22). That passage has a
general resemblance to Virg. *georg.* 2. 523 f. 'interea dulces pendent
circum oscula nati, / casta pudicitiam servat domus'; Virgil in turn
is certainly imitating Lucretius, loc. cit. (note the collocation *dulces
. . . oscula nati*). If Propertius was writing about the same lady as
Horace, he might have been moved, consciously or subconsciously,
to recall the same range of ideas. There may be a literary allusion to
the couple in Juvenal's sixth satire, where the hero is perhaps called
Postumus because he thinks he is marrying a good woman (6. 28 f.) :
'uxorem, Postume, ducis? / dic qua Tisiphone, quibus exagitate
colubris' (exagitate *Hadr. Valesius*: -are *vel* -ere *codd., edd.*).

harum : deictic. The scene is Postumus's country estate or suburban *horti*; cf. 2. 3. 9 ff., 2. 11. 13 f., 'cur non sub alta vel platano vel
hac / pinu iacentes . . .?' (with the parallels there quoted), Cic. *leg.*
1. 15 citing Pl. *leg.* 625 b (walking in the cypress-groves). Quinn
(106) thinks that the picture is of a man looking out from the *triclinium* into the garden of Postumus's town-house; this suits the
multiplicity of trees less well, especially if the interpretation of
sequetur given below is correct (24 n.). He relies on Lucretius's mention of melancholy talk at a banquet (3. 912 ff.), but is wrong to link
that passage with the lines on the *uxor* that Horace has already
imitated (cf. Woodman, Anderson, opp. citt.). He attaches significance to the fact that the end of the ode describes a drinking-party,
but in a poem on mortality Horace could draw on the traditional
imagery of sympotic verse without actually setting his scene at
a symposium.

colis : the verb suggests careful tending; Roman landowners gave
much thought to their trees (2. 13. 2 n., 2. 15. 4 n., Sen. *epist.* 12. 2,
Tac. *ann.* 11. 3. 2). The planter must take long views (2. 13. 3 n.), as
if he expected to live for ever; cf. Philodemus, *de morte* 4. 38. 34 ff. (=
p. 80 Gigante) οὐδὲ τὴν ἀθανασίαν ἀπελπίζει καθάπερ ἐστὶ δῆλος ἄρτι
κυπαρίττους φυτεύων (for the slow-growing cypress cf. Varro, *rust.*
1. 41. 5), Sen. *epist.* 101. 4 (citing Virg. *ecl.* 1. 73 'insere nunc, Meliboee,
piros, pone ordine vites'), Lucian, *cat.* 20 (above, 21 n.). Horace may
have recalled Philodemus's remark, but if so he has given it an extra
point; the funereal associations of the cypress, though attested in
Greece (*RE* 4. 1933 f.), were characteristically Roman (below, 23 n.,
Pasquali 647).

23. invisas : the adjective is naturally used in contexts referring to
death (1. 34. 10 n.). Here it makes a contrast alike with *placens* above
and with the implied *amoenitas* of the other trees.

cupressos : the cypress was cultivated both for use and amenity

(Hehn 286 ff., *RE* 4. 1909 ff.); it was highly profitable to landowners who could wait for their return (Plin. *nat.* 16. 141 'vulgoque dotem filiae antiqui plantaria ea appellabant'). It was associated by the Romans with death (*epod.* 5. 18 'cupressus funebris'), particularly in the case of rich and important men (Lucan 3. 442 'et non plebeios luctus testata cypressus'). Its branches were placed at the door of the mourning house (Plin. *nat.* 16. 139, Paul. Fest. 63 M. = 56 L., Serv. auct. *Aen.* 4. 507), on the funeral altar and the pyre itself (Virg. *Aen.* 3. 63 f., Ov. *trist.* 3. 13. 21, Serv. *Aen.* 6. 216); our passage is associated with these customs by Porphyrio ('quia funeribus cupressi adhibebantur') and by Servius (*Aen.* 3. 64). Yet it seems more picturesque to think of the cypresses planted round graves (Claud. *rapt. Pros.* 2. 108 'tumulos tectura cypressus', Prob. *georg.* 2. 84); this gives the most pointed meaning to *sequetur* (see below), and also suits the plural better (at *Aen.* 6. 216 f. 'feralis ante cupressos / constituunt' Virgil is referring to a heroic funeral, where whole trees are used instead of the normal branches). For the widespread association of the cypress with death see further F. Lajard, *Recherches sur le culte du cyprès pyramidal chez les peuples civilisés de l'antiquité*, 1854, pp. 293 ff.

24. brevem : 'short-term' (i.e. in respect of *dominium*); cf. 1. 36. 16 'breve lilium', 2. 3. 13. There is a contrast with 19 *longi*, perhaps also at a more formal level with the conventionally tall cypresses; cf. Catull. 64. 291 'aerea cupressu', Serv. *ecl.* 1. 25 'viburnum brevissimum est, cupressus vero arbor est maxima'.

dominum : 'proprietor', suggesting the legalistic Roman's pride in *dominium soli*. Horace suggests that ownership is only temporary; cf. *serm.* 2. 2. 129 ff. (Ofellus) 'nam propriae telluris erum natura neque illum / nec me nec quemquam statuit; nos expulit ille, / illum aut nequities aut vafri inscitia iuris, / postremum expellet certe vivacior heres' (with Lejay's note), *epist.* 2. 2. 171 ff. 'tamquam / sit proprium quicquam, puncto quod mobilis horae / nunc prece, nunc pretio, nunc vi, nunc morte suprema / permutet dominos et cedat in altera iura'. See further Eur. *Phoen.* 555 οὔτοι τὰ χρήματ' ἴδια κέκτηνται βροτοί, *suppl.* 534 f., Lucil. 550 f. with Marx's note, Sen. *ben.* 6. 3. 2 'quid tamquam tuo parcis? procurator es', anon. *anth. P.* 9. 74. 1 f. ἀγρὸς Ἀχαιμενίδου γενόμην ποτέ, νῦν δὲ Μενίππου / καὶ πάλιν ἐξ ἑτέρου βήσομαι εἰς ἕτερον (presumably with an allusion to the Cynic Menippus), Lucian, *Nigr.* 26 τούτων φύσει μὲν οὐδενός ἐσμεν κύριοι, νόμῳ δὲ καὶ διαδοχῇ τὴν χρῆσιν αὐτῶν εἰς ἀόριστον παραλαμβάνοντες ὀλιγοχρόνιοι δεσπόται νομιζόμεθα (*breves domini*), Marc. Aur. 12. 26. Editors sometimes quote Lucr. 3. 971 (life is given for *usus* not *mancipium*), but the point there is different.

sequetur : the primary meaning, we suggest, is 'go with' or 'pertain to' in a semi-legal sense (*Vocabularium Iurisprudentiae Romanae* 5. 371). Cf. especially the common formula 'H.M.H.N.S.' (*hoc monumentum heredem non sequitur*), designed to prevent the alienation of a tomb to extraneous heirs; cf. *serm.* 1. 8. 13 'heredes monumentum ne sequeretur', Petron. 71. 7, *ILS* 3. 2, p. 772, C. C. Mierow, *TAPhA* 65, 1934, 163 ff., F. de Visscher, *Le Droit des tombeaux romains*, 1963, pp. 101 f. From some aspects a tomb could be regarded as actually belonging to the dead; cf. Gaius, *inst.* 2. 4 '(res) religiosae quae diis manibus relictae sunt', Ulp. *dig.* 11. 7. 4 'naturaliter enim videtur ad mortuum pertinere locus in quem infertur, praesertim si in eum locum inferatur in quem ipse destinavit', E. Breccia, *Iscrizioni greche e latine*, 1911, no. 401 Ἀχιλλᾶς καὶ Ἄπις καταλίποσιν τὸν ἑατῶν τάφον τοῖς ἑατῶν νεκροῖς, P. M. Fraser and B. Nicholas, *JRS* 48, 1958, 117 ff. (inscription from Alexandria) τὸ δ[ὲ μνημεῖον] μενεῖ τοῖς ἐνκ[ειμέν]οις σώμασιν ἀκαταχρημά[τιστον ἀεί, F. Schulz, *Classical Roman Law*, 1951, pp. 342 f., de Visscher, op. cit., pp. 199 ff., J. A. Crook, *Law and Life of Rome*, 1967, pp. 133 ff. Cf. also Mart. 1. 116. 5 f. (on a funerary garden) 'si cupit hunc aliquis, moneo, ne speret agellum : / perpetuo dominis serviet iste suis', *ILS* 8342 'hi horti ita uti o. m. que sunt cineribus servite meis . . .'.

It may be objected that the suggested use of *sequi*, though common with *heredem* (note *heres* below) does not seem to be attested with *dominum*; and it must be conceded that Horace's writing here is less than fully technical. It may further be argued that *sequetur* must be a literal verb of motion to make the required contrast with *linquenda*; but a Roman reader would not distinguish too sharply the various meanings of *sequi*, and indeed a measure of ambiguity may be deliberate. If *sequetur* is simply a verb of motion, as commentators assume, then *cupressos* must refer to branches round the pyre. In that case they do not follow their owner very far or very long; when he leaves for Cocytus they are consumed on the *tellus* not far from where they grew.

25. heres : distaste at leaving one's property to an heir is naturally found in many societies; cf. the Egyptian Petosiris 'Your heir will satisfy his desires' (P. Gilbert, *Latomus* 5, 1946, 69), *Ecclesiastes* 2. 18 'Yea I hated all my labour which I had taken under the sun : because I should leave it unto the man that shall be after me . . .', *Sirach* 14. 4–5 'He that withholdeth from himself gathereth for another, And a stranger shall satiate himself with his goods. He that harmeth his own soul, to whom will he do good? For he hath no delight in his own goods' (cf. M. L. West, *HSCPh* 73, 1969, 129 ff.). For Greek parallels cf. Theognis 918 χρήματα δ' ἀνθρώπων οὑπιτυχὼν ἔλαβεν, Pind.

O. 10. 88 ff. ἐπεὶ πλοῦτος ὁ λαχὼν ποιμένα | ἐπακτὸν ἀλλότριον | θνᾴσκοντι στυγερώτατος, Theoc. 16. 59, Lucian, *cat.* 8, 20, *Char.* 17. But criticisms of the heir are particularly common among the Romans; cf. 2. 3. 20, 3. 24. 62, 4. 7. 19 f., *serm.* 2. 3. 122 f. 'filius aut etiam libertus ut ebibat heres, | dis inimice senex, custodis?', *epist.* 1. 5. 13 f., 2. 2. 175 f., 2. 2. 191 f. 'nec metuam quid de me iudicet heres | quod non plura datis invenerit', Catull. 68. 123 f., Phaedr. 4. 21. 18, Pers. 6. 33 f., 6. 65 ff., Mart. 8. 44. 12 ff., 13. 126 'unguentum heredi numquam nec vina relinquas, | ille habeat nummos, haec tibi tota dato'.

There were several reasons for the prominence of the alien heir (N. Rudd, *The Satires of Horace*, 1966, pp. 224 ff.). Roman law insisted on a named *heres*, who by the *lex Falcidia* of 40 B.C. was guaranteed at least a quarter of the estate; he was not necessarily a close relative since by the *lex Voconia* of 169 B.C. a member of the top property-class could not institute a woman as his heir (cf. Brunt 563 f., J. Crook, *PCPhS* 19, 1973, 43 f.). At the same time there was a sharp decline in the birth-rate of the rich because of the increased status of women (F. Schulz, *Classical Roman Law*, 1951, pp. 106 ff., K. Hopkins, 'Contraception in the Roman Empire', *Comparative Studies in Society and History* 8, 1965/6, 124 ff.). Horace twice addresses reflections on the *heres* to Manlius Torquatus, the last of his line (4. 7. 19 f., *epist.* 1. 5. 13 f.); Postumus may have been in the same position. Horace himself as a freedman's son seems to have had no legal relatives (cf. *epist.* 1. 1. 102 f.); after the death of Maecenas he suddenly had to make new arrangements, and left his property to Augustus (Suet. *vit.* 76 f. Rostagni).

dignior : worthier to own Postumus's property inasmuch as he used up the Caecuban. The ancients were concerned that the recipients of their benefactions should be deserving (*serm.* 1. 6. 51, 2. 2. 103, *epist.* 1. 7. 22 ff., A. R. Hands, op. cit. [p. 34], pp. 74 ff.); for similar remarks about heirs cf. Philodemus, *de morte* 4. 24. 10 ff. χωρὶς τοῦ μηδὲ φαύλους εἶναι μηδ' ἀναξίους ἐνίοτε τοὺς κληρονομήσοντας ... (to meet the objection τοῖς κληρονόμοις ἔσται τὰ πονηθέντα). Horace's sentence contains a criticism, not too seriously intended, of Postumus's frugal habits; cf. Porphyrio 'haec cum invectione dicuntur, corripientia eum quod ad nimiam parsimoniam se constringat, adservans quod heres prodige sit abusurus'. Here as often the poet combines his reflections on death with advice to drink and be merry; but he makes the point on this occasion not by direct exhortations but by unwelcome predictions.

It is argued against *dignior* that the spendthrift who spills the wine is going much further than Horace would recommend (A. Y. Campbell, Woodman, loc. cit.). Yet at this point he is simply talking of using up the wine (*absumet*), and for the purposes of the poem even conspicuous consumption is better than uneconomical prudence. Campbell proposed *degener* (cf. 3. 24. 61 f. 'indignoque pecuniam / heredi properet', *epod.* 1. 34 'discinctus aut perdam nepos', Paul. Nol. *carm.* 26. 284 f. 'tanti non degener heres / seminis'); but if the heir is to be criticized so severely, the poem loses a very characteristic paraenesis (which is supported by Porphyrio's comment). It is true that heirs are conventionally unworthy, but when Horace says *dignior* to the impeccable Postumus he is fully aware of the paradox.

It may be noted finally that at Lucr. 3. 962 'aequo animoque agedum †magnis concede: necesse est' M. L. Clarke proposes *mage dignis cede* (*dignis* already Lachmann) and compares our passage (*C.R.* N.S. 20, 1970, 9). The thought would be somewhat similar to Horace's: the old no longer deserve life because they have lost the capacity to use it (3. 961 'nunc aliena tua tamen aetate omnia mitte'). Editors compare Epictetus 4. 1. 107 εἶτα οὐκ ἐκστήσῃ τῶν ἀλλοτρίων; οὐ παραχωρήσεις τῷ κρείσσονι; (cf. also 110 ἐπὶ τί οὖν εἴληφα ταῦτα; — χρησόμενος).

26. servata centum clavibus : *servata* makes a contrast with the emphatic *absumet*. The hyperbole underlines the absurdity of Postumus's carefulness; the alliteration may be meant to suggest jangling. The main danger to a household's stores in a slave society is not burglary from outside but pilfering at home; hence the careful use of keys (*serm.* 2. 3. 145 ff.), which goes back to the *Odyssey* (21. 46 ff.). Cicero's prudent mother sealed even the empty jars 'ne dicerentur inanes aliquae fuisse quae furtim essent exsiccatae' (*epist.* 16. 26. 2); Pliny complains 'claves quoque ipsas signasse non est satis' (*nat.* 33. 27); see further Fraenkel and Headlam–Thomson on Aesch. *Ag.* 609, Mayor on Juv. 14. 132.

mero : 'unmixed wine' implies heavy drinking (1. 18. 8 n.).

27. tinguet pavimentum : such a floor might be of marble or mosaic as well as of humbler materials (Blümner 95); for the *pavimentum* as a symbol of luxury cf. Sen. *contr.* 2. 1. 12, Sen. *epist.* 114. 9, Suet. *Aug.* 72. 1 'insigni pavimento conclavia'. For the spilling of wine at symposia cf. Cic. or. fr. VI. 1, *Pis. 22, Phil.* 2. 105 'natabant pavimenta vino, madebant parietes', Vitr. 7. 4. 5 'ita conviviis eorum et quod poculis et pytismatis [Mayor on Juv. 11. 175] effunditur simul cadit siccescitque', Petron. 38. 15, Salv. *eccl.* 4. 33 'natant tricliniorum redundantium pavimenta, [vino] Falerno nobili lutum faciunt ...' (a rich but frugal man justifies himself to God by contrasting himself with his heirs). In view of the absence of carpets the ancients could be careless about what they dropped; Pliny tells of the artist Sosus

'qui Pergami stravit quem vocant ἀσάρωτον οἶκον, quoniam purga-
menta cenae in pavimentis quaeque everri solent velut relicta fecerat
parvis e tessellis tinctisque in varios colores' (*nat.* 36. 184). This last
phrase shows that *tinguere pavimentum* might naturally be used of
ornamentation by mosaics; Horace derisively applies the expression
to the stain of wine.

superbo : the wine is proud because it is a select Caecuban; for
similar connoisseurs' personifications cf. 2. 6. 15 n., *epist.* 1. 15. 18
'generosum', Lucil. 1131 Χίός τε δυνάστης, Salv. loc. cit. 'nobili'
(apparently modelled on our passage). Horace is making a contrast
between the superior wine (*superbus* is connected with *super*) and
the lowly pavement. It is a difficulty that *mero* is qualified by both
superbo and *potiore*; editors compare 1. 18. 16 'arcanique fides prodiga
perlucidior vitro', but there the two adjectives are clearly of different categories (*arcanique fides prodiga = perfidia*). Yet the phrase
pontificum potiore cenis might possibly be regarded as a new explana-
tory colon (in Greek there would be an ὄντι); the change to a comparative may make such a construction easier.

Several conjectures have been proposed (cf. C. O. Brink, *PCPhS*
17, 1971, 29). *superbus* (second hand in Fea's cod. Vat. A) balances
dignior well; for such arrogance cf. Mart. 8. 44. 12 ff. 'heres . . .
superbus', Hom. *Od.* 14. 95 (of the suitors) οἶνον δὲ φθινύθουσιν ὑπέρβιον ἐξαφύοντες (though Horace might subconsciously have taken
ὑπέρβιον as an adjective). On the other hand *superbo* provides a
characteristic hypallage (cf. 1. 37. 31 f. 'superbo . . . triumpho',
4. 15. 7 f.); moreover it is supported by the admittedly imprecise
notes of the ancient commentators (Porph. 'superbo autem [pavi-
mento] pro *ipse superbus*', ps.-Acro 'pro *ipse superbus*; hypallage
figura'). *superbum* (codd. Lambini) seems to be paralleled by Varro,
rust. 3. 1. 10 'pavimentis nobilibus', Lucr. 4. 1178 'postesque super-
bos'; yet the suggestion of height does not suit the floor even by
way of paradox, while the rhyme *pavimentum superbum* is unconvincing in this position. Lynford conjectured *superbis* (cf. Sidon.
epist. 9. 13. 5. 56 'epulas superbiores'), which has won support from
Brink and Woodman, op. cit.; but even if change were thought
desirable, this is less vivid than *superbus* (there is more reason to
picture the *heres* than the *cenae*), uneconomically repeats what is
sufficiently expressed by *pontificum*, and makes a much less pointed
contrast with *pavimentum*.

28. pontificum potiore cenis : 'as desirable as a dinner . . .'; in such
circumstances Latin often uses a comparative (1. 19. 6 n.) and a plural
(1. 9. 24 n.). The poem has moved from the scenes of Greek poetry to
the prosaic world of Roman society (for priestly dinners cf. 1. 37.

2 n., Varro, *rust.* 3. 2. 16 'collegiorum cenae, quae nunc innumerabiles excandefaciunt annonam macelli'); *cena* (also found at 3. 29. 15) is avoided by the epic poets, Tibullus, and Propertius (Axelson 107). The Caecuban is being compared not with a whole dinner but with the wine served on such an occasion (cf. 2. 6. 14 n. on compendious comparison). The brachylogy is not clumsy (Bücheler), but adds concentration and distinction to the style.

15. IAM PAVCA ARATRO

[Commager 85 ff.; Grimal 395 f.]

1–10. *Great villas, fishponds, and gardens will soon drive out the useful cultivation of grain, vines, and olives.* 10–20. *Our ancestors' standards were different: personal poverty and public wealth, not private porticos but turf huts, with the public money spent on fortifications and temples.*

Denunciations of luxury building were a theme of Greek *diatribe* that had a conspicuous relevance for Roman moralists of the first century B.C. (below, p. 288). At the beginning of his poem Horace concentrates on a particular aspect of the problem, the effect of such constructions on Italian agriculture. It was no doubt already a commonplace that the countryside was being drained of wealth to suit the megalomania of the *aedificatores*; cf. especially Sen. *exc. contr.* 5. 5 'scilicet ut domus ad caelum omne conversae brumales aestus habeant, aestiva frigora, et non suis vicibus intra istorum penates agatur annus, ut sint in summis culminibus mentita nemora et navigabilium piscinarum freta, arata quondam populis rura singulorum nunc ergastulorum sunt latiusque vilici quam reges imperant' (this declamation has several themes in common with our ode, though it is surely not derived from it). Horace deals with what might seem a less likely consequence, the virtual disappearance of agricultural land under the palaces of the rich; the extravagant hyperbole is appropriately stated not in the present tense but in the form of a dire prophecy (cf. 5 n., Hes. *op.* 176 ff.). It is easy to point out that Horace's fears are illusory, but this is to miss the feeling of the poem: these alien mountains of stone are symbolic of a plutocratic system that seems to be crushing the idealized countryside of the past.

Horace's predictions next turn to artificial ponds, which will soon stretch on all sides larger than the Lucrine Lake. Such *stagna* were

often constructed for the beneficent purpose of fish-farming (Varro,
rust. 3. 17, Colum. 8. 16, J. M. C. Toynbee, *Animals in Roman Life
and Art*, 1973, pp. 209 ff., *RE* 20. 2. 1783 ff.); but the Romans dif-
fered from the Greeks in regarding fish as a gluttonous taste (cf.
Val. Max. 9. 1. 1), and the construction of fish-ponds could be represented as interference with the natural distinctions ordained for
the elements (2. 18. 21 n.). It is even more important that some of the
so-called *piscinarii* (Cic. *Att.* 1. 19. 6) regarded their ponds as a source
of amusement rather than profit (Varro, *rust.* 3. 17. 5 says that Hortensius would not eat his fish, but sent to Puteoli instead). By his
use of the word *visentur* (3 n.) Horace categorizes these ponds as
an amenity of the rich. Similarly eighteenth-century improvers destroyed agricultural land to 'polish a prospect'.

The poet next turns to *horti*, which had achieved great magnificence in the first century B.C. (Grimal 101 ff.); one has only to think
of the parks of Cicero and his friends, and in Horace's own day of
Maecenas and Sallustius (for favourable mention cf. also 2. 3. 9 ff.,
2. 11. 13 ff., 2. 14. 22). But even Cicero in some moods could criticize
the Epicurean *otium* encouraged by such places (*de orat.* 3. 63, cf.
Sen. *ben.* 4. 13. 1), and their artificiality was attacked in the Augustan
period by the Stoic Papirius Fabianus (Sen. *contr.* 2. 1. 13), in agreement with an attitude expressed by Chrysippus himself (Plut. *Stoic.
repugn.* 1044 d = *SVF* 3. 714). In accordance with the theme of his
poem Horace makes no overt allusion to such criticisms but concentrates on the loss to viticulture and olive-growing caused by
shade-trees and aromatic plants. In real life some at least of the
cultivation he reprehends made more economic sense at this date
than arable farming; cf. Cato, *agr.* 1. 7 'vinea est prima . . . secundo
loco hortus inriguus . . . sexto campus frumentarius', 8. 2 'sub urbe
hortum omne genus, coronamenta omne genus . . . murtum coniu-
gulum et album et nigrum, loream delphicam et cypriam et silvati-
cam . . . haec facito uti serantur', 133. 2, Varro, *rust.* 1. 23. 4 'nec
minus ea discriminanda in conserendo quae sunt fructuosa propter
voluptatem, ut quae pomaria ac floralia appellantur'. But just as
with the *piscinae* Horace ignores this aspect and concentrates on the
rich man's pleasure; for a similar attitude cf. Quint. *inst.* 8. 3. 8
(though he is talking of artificial ornament) 'an ego fundum cul-
tiorem putem in quo mihi quis ostenderit lilia et violas et anemonas
sponte surgentes quam ubi plena messis aut graves fructu vites
erunt? sterilem platanum tonsasque myrtos quam maritam ulmum
et uberes oleas praeoptaverim?' This passage has close affinities with
our ode, but makes the points about the vines (4 n.) and the clipped
myrtle (11 n.) more obviously; it may therefore be derived not
from Horace but from a common store. Perhaps Horace has taken

themes from a *diatribe* against horticultural elaboration and linked
it with the Roman anxiety at the decline of arable land and a free
peasantry (cf. Brunt 345 ff.); the result is that a rather theoretical
ethical standpoint is presented as if it were a conclusive social argument.

In the second half of the ode (10 ff.) Horace turns to the manners of
earlier Italy; for this sort of contrast cf. 3. 6. 33 f. 'non his iuventus
orta parentibus / infecit aequor sanguine Punico', Cic. *parad.* 13
(a comparison of owners of marble halls with Fabricius 'qui nihil
habuit eorum, nihil habere voluit'). He now widens the issue from
the destruction of agricultural land to private self-seeking in general;
in the last two stanzas he returns to the theme of building with which
the poem began. He idealizes the past in a traditional Roman way;
he invokes Romulus and Cato in the interests of old-fashioned farming, though nothing is known of the former and too much of the
latter (11 n.). By implication he favours Augustan ideology by denouncing the magnificence of independent noblemen and by recommending the public construction of fortifications and temples.

The manner of the ode is well designed to suit its subject. There is
nothing so personal as an individual recipient, not even the shadowy
tu to whom such allocutions are sometimes addressed (2. 18. 7 n.);
though there is feeling in the poem, it is expressed in austere statements about the future and the past. The nouns of the opening stanzas
need little elaboration as they are carefully chosen for their good or
bad associations, on the one hand *aratro, iugera, ulmos, olivetis*, on
the other *moles, stagna, platanusque caelebs, narium*. In the second
half (10 ff.) the diction becomes appropriately more official and
prosaic; cf. *praescriptum, auspiciis, norma, census, commune, decempedis*. Like the monumental stonework that Horace admires, this
compact poem derives its ornament from the solidity of its construction.

Horace gives a sharp criticism of a degenerate society where, in
spite of all the growth of wealth and taste, there is a loss of the frugal
virtue and public spirit of former days. He was effectively imitated
in Goldsmith's *The Deserted Village* (275 ff.):

> The man of wealth and pride
> Takes up a space that many poor supplied;
> Space for his lake, his park's extended bounds,
> Space for his horses, equipage and hounds;
> The robe that wraps his limbs in silken sloth
> Hath robbed the neighbouring fields of half their growth;
> His seat, where solitary sports are seen,
> Indignant spurns the cottage from the green.

But the Latin poet makes his point with greater concentration and authority; here as nowhere else in the second book he seems to be foreshadowing the Roman Odes.

Metre: Alcaic.

1. iam: 'soon' (1. 4. 16, 2. 5. 10); the adverb underlines the hyperbole of the prophecy.

aratro: ploughing was thought meritorious as traditional hard work that provided food for the people; cf. Sen. *exc. contr.* 5. 5 [above, p. 241], Plin. *nat.* 18. 32 'censoria castigatio erat minus arare quam verrere', 18. 35. But it was more economical to import grain in bulk from Africa; not surprisingly, Cato had put ploughland low in his list of priorities [above, p. 242].

iugera: the word had emotive associations of frugal peasants, allotments to veterans, etc.

regiae moles: the adjective suggests the gigantic constructions of an Eastern king (cf. *ars* 65 'regis opus'), so different in spirit from the ideals of the old Roman Republic; there may be a suggestion of the pyramids (cf. 3. 30. 2 'regalique situ pyramidum', Frontin. *aq.* 1. 16 'tot aquarum tam multis necessariis molibus pyramidas videlicet otiosas compares aut cetera inertia sed fama celebrata opera Graecorum'). *moles* belongs to the topic (Cic. *Mil.* 85 'substructionum insanis molibus', cf. also *carm.* 3. 29. 10 'molem propinquam nubibus arduis'). Here the noun suggests the inert bulk of the piles; cf. Goldsmith, *The Deserted Village* 65 f. 'Along the lawn, where scattered hamlets rose, Unwieldy wealth and cumbrous pomp repose'.

2. latius: to be taken with *extenta*, not with *visentur* (as Porphyrio suggests). The first three words of the clause emphasize the extent of the ponds. The adverb balances *pauca*; Horace's second hyperbole is put in a more positive form than his first.

3. visentur: an emphatic word for 'see', here with a hint of wonder (1. 2. 8, *carm. saec.* 12). It was part of the commonplace to emphasize the prospect from the villa; cf. Sen. *epist.* 89. 21 'nullus erit lacus cui non villarum vestrarum fastigia immineant', D. Fehling, *Ethologische Überlegungen auf den Gebiet der Altertumskunde* (*Zetemata* 61), 1974, pp. 54 f. *undique* therefore seems to refer to the multiplicity of views, not of observation points. This interpretation gives more point than a reference to the admiration of passing strangers.

Lucrino ... lacu: ablative of comparison (apparently misunderstood by Porphyrio). The Lucrine Lake near Puteoli was a shallow lagoon cut off from the sea by a causeway (the *semita Herculea*); it is now smaller than in antiquity because of the eruption that produced Monte Nuovo in 1538. It was famous for its shellfish and particularly its oysters, thanks to the enterprise of Sergius Orata at the beginning of the first century B.C.; cf. *epod*. 2. 49, Varro, *Men*. 501, Str. 5. 4. 6, Val. Max. 9. 1. 1 (reporting L. Crassus's strictures on Orata), Juv. 4. 140 f. with Mayor's note. It had recently been linked with the deeper Lake Avernus to form a first-class naval harbour, the *portus Iulius* built by Agrippa.

4. **stagna** : the word can be used neutrally of standing water (it is derived from *stare*) or fishponds. Here it easily bears a pejorative implication of stagnation.

platanusque . . . : the clause is closely linked by *-que* to its predecessor (both are under *undique*); the spreading *platanus* (derived from πλατύς) balances the broad extent of the ponds. Because of its shade the plane was a conventional part of the *amoenus locus* (2. 11. 13 n.), and in Greece was often associated with public places like the Agora, the Academy, and the Lyceum. In Italy it belonged essentially to the parks of the rich: it was lovingly fed with wine by Hortensius (Ov. *rem*. 141, Plin. *nat*. 12. 8, Macr. *sat*. 3. 13. 3), it shaded the speakers of the *de oratore* at L. Crassus's Tusculan villa (Cic. *de orat*. 1. 28), it was planted by Seneca (*epist*. 12. 2) and the younger Pliny (*epist*. 5. 6. 20, cf. 1. 3. 1), and the roots of a plane plantation can be seen in one of the luxurious villas recently excavated at Castellammare di Stabia (Grimal 225). See further Mayor on Juv. 1. 12, Hehn 294 ff., Grimal, index s.v. Platane.

caelebs : of a tree round which no vine is trained (contrast *ulmos* below); cf. Ov. *met*. 14. 663, Plin. *nat*. 17. 204 'iuxta suam arborem aut circa proximam caelibem' (which shows that the usage was not merely poetical), Mart. 3. 58. 2 ff. '(villa) non otiosis ordinata myrtetis / viduaque platano tonsilique buxeto / ingrata lati spatia detinet campi'. In the moral climate of Augustan Rome *caelebs* has associations of uselessness and self-indulgence; these are transferred to the plane, which is unproductive (Virg. *georg*. 2. 70 'steriles platani') and supports no vines (Antip. Thess. *anth. P.* 9. 231 is exceptional). For similar censures cf. ps.-Ov. *nux* 17 ff., Sen. *dial*. 7. 17. 2 'cur arbores nihil praeter umbram daturae conseruntur?', Plin. *nat*. 12. 6, Quint. *inst*. 8. 3. 8 [above, p. 242].

5. **evincet** : the verb can be used in agricultural contexts for 'overrun'; cf. Plin. *nat*. 18. 147 'si evicerint herbae, remedium unicum in aratro', 18. 185.

ulmos : the elm was particularly used for supporting vines (*RE* 9 A. 1. 552 f., K. D. White, *Roman Farming*, 1970, p. 236); in agricultural writers and elsewhere it often has the epithet *marita* (*Thes.l.L.* 8. 403. 83 ff.), which must be understood here. For its other virtues cf. especially Varro, *rust*. 1. 15, *RE* 9 A. 1. 548 ff.

tum : the stop after *ulmos* should probably be a semicolon rather
than a period. Horace seems to be suggesting the language of prophecies, where a prediction is followed by a list of concomitants
(here undesirable) ; cf. Virg. *Aen.* 1. 291 'aspera tum positis mitescent
saecula bellis' (so καὶ τότε in Greek oracles). It would be wrong to
interpret the adverb as *postea* (*ecl. 8. 27* f. 'aevoque sequenti / cum
canibus timidi venient ad pocula dammae'); the *violaria* do not
make a climax after the plane.

violaria : *violae* are a standard element in natural and artificial
paradises; cf. Petron. 127. 9, Plin. *epist.* 2. 17. 17, Longus 4. 2, Grimal
279, D.–S. 3. 293. Varro found practical difficulties in growing them
(*rust.* 1. 35. 1), but had no moral objection; indeed he recommended
violaria if the flowers could be sold to a near-by city (*rust.* 1. 16. 3,
1. 23. 5).

6. myrtus : paired with violets already by Ibycus 315. 1 (the bay
comes in the next line); for the conjunction of one set of plants
(*myrtus*) with the places where others grew cf. Cic. *nat. deor.* 2. 156
'vitibus olivetisque' (with Pease's note), Mart. 3. 58. 2 f. (cited above
on 4 *caelebs*). The myrtle was serviceable for garlands and comparatively cheap (1. 38. 5 n., Teles, p. 13. 9 H.); but its cultivation had
been similarly censured by Chrysippus (above, p. 242). As the present context shows, its offence was its agreeable smell; cf. Theophr.
hist. plant. 6. 8. 5, Virg. *ecl.* 2. 54 f., Plin. *nat.* 15. 123, Cornutus, *nat.
deor.* 24 (cited vol. i, p. 422), D.–S. 3. 291.

omnis copia narium : *copia* might naturally suggest a supply of
corn or similar produce (1. 17. 14) ; here the abundance is represented
as less wholesome. *omnis* means 'every sort of'; cf. *epist.* 1. 5. 2
'holus omne', Cic. *epist.* 7. 26. 2 'fungos helvellas herbas omnis'.
narium strikes a derisive note; cf. Varro, *Men.* 511 'hic narium
Seplasiae, hic ἡδύχους Neapolis'. In our passage the genitive is possessive, as if the nostrils owned the abundance; for a similar extravagance cf. Ael. *var. hist.* 3. 1 ὁρᾶται δὲ τὸ χλοάζον πᾶν καί ἐστιν
ὀφθαλμῶν πανήγυρις.

7. spargent : the verb is naturally applied to the sowing of seed
(σπείρειν) ; corn was grown in olive-groves. But soon nothing will
be scattered but a smell; *odorem* like *narium* gives a contemptuous
anticlimax.

olivetis : the word is used bitterly of places from which the olive-
trees had been removed. Bücheler suggested that nothing is lost
but the corn that grew in the *oliveta* (*RhM* 37, 1882, 234 f. = *Kl.
Schr.* 2. 439) ; but the olive and vine were twins in beneficence (Plin.
nat. 14. 150 'liquores humanis corporibus gratissimi, intus vini, foris
olei'), and it would spoil the rhetoric if the olive-trees remain when

the vines by implication are destroyed (4 n.). The olive had whole-some associations with frugality (1. 31. 15), utility, and the Italian countryside (2. 6. 16 n., Cic. *rep.* 3. 16, Plin. *nat.* 15. 8 'principatum in hoc quoque bono obtinuit Italia e toto orbe').

8. fertilibus : 'productive', as opposed to *caelebs* above. *priori* under-lines the sad contrast with former days: it suggests with great economy that the olive groves have been expropriated to form a rich man's garden (ps.-Quint. *decl. mai.* 13. 2 'quod cives pascebat nunc divitis unius hortus est').

9. spissa ramis : like a Greek compound in πυκνο-; *ramis* can include twigs as well as branches. For the shade of the bay cf. Virg. *georg.* 2. 18 f. 'etiam Parnasia laurus / parva sub ingenti matris se subi-cit umbra', Plin. *nat.* 17. 88 'umbrae ... enormes ... lauris', Plin. *epist.* 5. 6. 32; contrast the elm, which was pruned to let sun in on the vines. Here there may be a suggestion that the bay will be made unnaturally dense by clipping (see below on 11 *intonsi*); otherwise the last of Horace's prophecies seems a truism, particularly when compared with its predecessors.

laurea : common in Latium (cf. *Laurentes*) like the myrtle; cf. Theophr. *hist. plant.* 5. 8. 3 ἡ μὲν πεδεινὴ δάφνην ἔχει καὶ μυρρίνους. It was a constant feature of elegant gardens (Plin. *nat.* 15. 130 ff., Grimal, index s.v. Laurier), and as an aromatic plant it follows well after *violaria* and *myrtus*. Yet at first sight it makes a curious climax, not just because it had some practical uses (*RE* 13. 1438 f.) but because it was a prize in athletics and war. There is a paradox in its providing the dense shade that typifies the inactive life (1. 7. 19 n.).

10. excludet : cf. Sen. *nat.* 1. 3. 1, Stat. *silv.* 1. 2. 154 f. 'excludunt radios silvis demissa vetustis / frigora', Auson. *Mos.* 15 'exclusum viridi caligine caelum'. Here the verb balances *spargent*; it par-ticularly suits *ictus*, which are penetrating thrusts.

ictus : cf. Soph. *Ai.* 877 ἡλίου βολῶν, Eur. *Ba.* 458, *Ion* 1134, *Or.* 1259. In Latin as in Greek a genitive is normally added to show the source (so *solis, Phoebi, luminis, radiorum*; cf. *Thes.l.L.* 7. 1. 166. 28 ff.); yet for Horace's bold poeticism cf. perhaps Eur. *Phoen.* 169 ἑῴοις ὅμοια φλεγέθων βολαῖς ἀελίου, where the genitive is plausibly deleted by Wecklein for metrical reasons. Here the ambiguous ex-pression may recall the apotropaic qualities of the bay, which was used as a defence against lightning (*RE* 13. 1440).

Romuli : though he was originally regarded as a pastoralist, Varro attributes to him the introduction of two-*iugera* allotments (*rust.* 1. 10. 2, cf. also Cic. *rep.* 2. 26); the elder Pliny likewise contrasts these with the gardens and fishponds of his own day (*nat.* 18. 7

'bina tunc iugera p. R. satis erant nullique maiorem modum ad-
tribuit, quo servorum paulo ante principis Neronis contento huius
spatii viridiariis? piscinas iuvat maiores habere, gratumque si non
aliquem culinas'). For the simplicity of his life cf. Virg. *georg.* 2.
532 f. 'hanc olim veteres vitam coluere Sabini, / hanc Remus et
frater'. It was thought to be attested by the *casae Romuli*, two pre-
historic huts carefully preserved on the Palatine and Capitoline;
cf. Virg. *Aen.* 8. 654, Prop. 4. 1. 9 f., Ogilvie on Livy 5. 53. 8, Bömer on
Ov. *fast.* 1. 199, Platner–Ashby, *s.v.*, *RE* 18. 3. 26 f.

11. **intonsi** : cf. 1. 12. 41 n. Bücheler, loc. cit. (7 n.), followed by both
Kiessling and Heinze, plausibly saw a contrast with the clipped
shrubs of ornamental gardens; for these cf. Plin. *nat.* 16. 140, Plin.
epist. 5. 6. 17, 5. 6. 35, and especially Quint. *inst.* 8. 3. 8, a passage
which has affinities with our own (above, p. 242).

Catonis : M. Porcius Cato, *cos.* 195, *cens.* 184 B.C. He himself
boasted of his hard upbringing in the Sabine hills (*or. fr.* 128) and
of his *abstinentia* (*or. fr.* 132 f., 173); later ages saw in him an exem-
plar of old Roman virtue, a reputation that does less than justice
to his sharp intelligence. For his denunciations of luxurious villas
cf. *or. fr.* 174, 185 'dicere possum, quibus villae atque aedes aedificatae
atque expolitae maximo opere citro atque ebore atque pavimentis
Poenicis sient', Plut. *Cat. mai.* 4. 4 [cf. 1. 12. 43 n.]. Horace's words suit
the censor rather than the author of the *De Agricultura*, whose precepts show less respect for ancient norms than his preface would
suggest; the champion of progressive and profitable agriculture
would have been surprised to find his views coupled with those of
Romulus.

12. **auspiciis** : the word suggests the authority of a Roman magistrate. It particularly suits Romulus, whose career was punctuated
by auguries (cf. also Cic. *rep.* 2. 16).

norma : the word is found elsewhere in poetry only at *ars* 72 and
Lucr. 4. 514 (Axelson 102). As it literally means a set square it
coheres with the subject of building that dominates the poem (cf.
14 *decempedis*). In its metaphorical sense it suits the rigid standards
of a censor (such as Cato); for censorial action against luxury cf.
Val. Max. 8. 1 damn. 7, Vell. 2. 10. 1.

13. **†privatus** : the contrast with *commune* seems in itself highly
appropriate (ἴδιος as opposed to δημόσιον or κοινόν), but the following
antithesis 15 *privatis* . . . 18 *publico* is then disconcerting; either the
original pattern should be repeated or it should be completely
abandoned. At 15 the adjective is necessary to exclude public
colonnades (for another argument see 20 *novo* n.); on the other hand

census needs no qualification to describe a private fortune. We have considered *probatus*, as part of a pluperfect (to translate 'the approved census' would destroy the balance between the two clauses) ; for the interchange of *b* and *v* cf. 1. 25. 20 n., for the corruption of an opening iambus in Alcaics cf. 2. 1. 21 n. *probare* is a natural word for the censorial approval of senators and *equites*; cf. *CGL* 7. 132 (it renders δοκιμάζειν), Mommsen, *Staatsrecht* 3, 1887, 493 n. 3 (instances in late antiquity). One would have to understand *probatum erat* in a less technical sense with *commune magnum*: 'they had laid the seal of their approval on a small capital assessment—and a large public treasury' (the verb's shift of meaning would be pointed rather than clumsy).

census : strictly the censors' valuation of property, notably to determine equestrian status; the word therefore follows well after the mention of the elder Cato. It was generally avoided by the poets, but is often found in Ovid and Manilius.

14. commune : public property, here the national treasury (τὸ κοινόν) ; cf. *Thes.l.L.* 3. 1977. 51 ff.

decempedis : the ten-foot rules of the surveyor and architect (Dilke 67, 73). The prosaic word, here balancing *brevis*, can have a suggestion of aggrandizement and expropriation ; cf. Cic. *Mil.* 74 'cum architectis et decempedis villas multorum hortosque peragrabat'.

15. metata : here passive, cf. *serm.* 2. 2. 114 'metato in agello', *Thes.l.L.* 8. 891. 83 ff. Horace is imitated by Jerome, *epist.* 14. 6 ' "Filius hominis non habet ubi caput reclinet" ; et tu amplas porticus et ingentia tectorum spatia metaris?'

privatis : whereas colonnades used to be public works; the adjective is in antithesis with 18 *publico* (see also above, 13 n.). The Greek orators taught the Romans to contrast the private and the public, whether in respect of wealth, buildings, or expenditure; cf. Dem. 3. 25 δημοσίᾳ μὲν τοίνυν οἰκοδομήματα καὶ κάλλη τοιαῦτα καὶ τοσαῦτα κατεσκεύασαν ἡμῖν ἱερῶν καὶ τῶν ἐν τούτοις ἀναθημάτων, ὥστε μηδενὶ τῶν ἐπιγιγνομένων ὑπερβολὴν λελεῖφθαι· ἰδίᾳ δὲ οὕτω σώφρονες ἦσαν καὶ σφόδρ' ἐν τῷ τῆς πολιτείας ἤθει μένοντες ὥστε τὴν Ἀριστείδου καὶ τὴν Μιλτιάδου καὶ τῶν τότε λαμπρῶν οἰκίαν εἴ τις ἄρ' οἶδεν ὑμῶν ὁποία ποτ' ἐστίν, ὁρᾷ τῆς τοῦ γείτονος οὐδὲν σεμνοτέραν οὖσαν· οὐ γὰρ εἰς περιουσίαν ἐπράττετ' αὐτοῖς τὰ τῆς πόλεως, ἀλλὰ τὸ κοινὸν αὔξειν ἕκαστος ᾤετο δεῖν, 23. 206 ff., Musonius 19, p. 109 Hense τί δ' ἂν ὄναιτό τις τηλικοῦτον ἀπ' οἰκίας μεγέθους τε καὶ κάλλους ἡλίκον ἀπὸ τοῦ χαρίζεσθαι πόλει καὶ πολίταις ἐκ τῶν ἑαυτοῦ;, Cic. *Mur.* 76 'odit populus Romanus privatam luxuriam, publicam magnificentiam diligit', *Flacc.* 28, Sall. *Cat.* 9. 2, 52. 22 'pro his nos habemus ... publice egestatem

privatim opulentiam', Val. Max. 4. 4. 9, Plin. *paneg.* 51. 1 ff. 'parcus
in aedificando . . . at quam magnificus in publicum es', P. Perrochat,
Les Modèles grecs de Salluste, 1949, pp. 73 ff., Vischer 151 f. Other
writers were reluctant to accept the merits of public extravagance; cf.
Cic. *off.* 2. 60 'theatra porticus nova templa verecundius reprehendo
propter Pompeium; sed doctissimi non probant, ut et hic ipse
Panaetius . . . et Phalereus Demetrius, qui Periclem principem
Graeciae vituperat quod tantam pecuniam in praeclara illa pro-
pylaea coniecerit', Plin. *nat.* 36. 5 'qua magis via inrepunt vitia quam
publica?'

opacam : 'shady'; for the transference of the epithet cf. Virg.
ecl. 1. 52 'frigus captabis opacum'. The adjective could hardly be
used literally of a shaggy bear (*arcton*) in spite of Catull. 37. 19
'opaca . . . barba'. Yet Horace may be using a calque for a Greek
word like δασύς which could be used both of woolly animals and of
shady places; see below on 16 *excipiebat*.

16. porticus : a private colonnade was a symbol of luxury; cf. below,
p. 288, Mayor on Juv. 7. 178, Hier. *epist.* 14. 6 [above, 15 *metata* n.].
For a contrast cf. Suet. *Aug.* 72. 1 'porticus breves'.

excipiebat Arcton : in Mediterranean countries it is as important
to 'catch' coolness as the sun. For the use of the verb cf. Sen. *epist.*
55. 7 'esse illam (villam) totius anni credo: occurrit enim Favonio
et illum adeo excipit ut Bais neget', Pallad. 1. 8. 3; cf. also Juv.
7. 182 f. 'longis Numidarum fulta columnis / surgat ut algentem
rapiat cenatio solem'. *excipere*, here used of trapping the sun,
literally suggests lying in wait for an animal (L. P. Wilkinson, *CQ*
N.S. 9, 1959, 188). This suits *Arcton*, which means a real bear as well
as the northern constellation (the two words were perhaps originally
distinct, cf. H. Usener, *RhM* 23, 1868, 334 f. = *Kl. Schr.* 4, 1913, 28);
Horace perhaps remembered Hom. *Il.* 18. 488 where it is the Bear
who lies in wait (ἥ τ' αὐτοῦ στρέφεται καί τ' Ὠρίωνα δοκεύει).

For similar complaints about careful orientation cf. Varro, *rust.*
1. 13. 7 'hi laborant ut spectent sua aestiva triclinaria ad frigus
orientis, hiberna ad solem occidentem potius quam ut antiqui in
quam partem cella vinaria aut olearia fenestras haberet', Sen. *exc.*
contr. 5. 5 [above, p. 241]. Yet other writers recommend the practice
(Vitr. 6. 1. 2, 6. 4, Colum. 1. 6. 2, Plin. *nat.* 18. 33), and the younger
Pliny delights in its success at his Tuscan and Laurentine villas
(*epist.* 2. 17. 7, 5. 6. 28, 5. 6. 31); so also Sidon. *carm.* 22. 179 'porticus
ad gelidos patet hinc aestiva Triones'.

17. fortuitum spernere caespitem : turf that is there for the collecting;
cf. Sen. *epist.* 90. 8 'philosophia haec cum tanto habitantium periculo
inminentia tecta suspendit? parum enim erat fortuitis tegi', Petron.

135. 8 v. 9 'fortuitoque luto', Pind. *P.* 4. 34 f. ἁρπάξαις ἀρούρας /
δεξιτερᾷ προτυχόν. For the prosody *fortũĩto* cf. *Thes.l.L.* 6. 1. 1172. 67 ff. ;
dactylic poets were of course compelled to treat the -*u*- as consonan-
tal (as also *pituita*).

Bonded turves can be a useful though simple building material;
cf. Caes. *civ.* 3. 96. 1, Virg. *ecl.* 1. 68, Sen. *epist.* 8. 5 'domus munimen-
tum sit adversus infesta temporis. hanc utrum caespes erexerit an
varius lapis gentis alienae, nihil interest: scitote tam bene hominem
culmo quam auro tegi', Rut. Nam. 1. 555, Bömer on Ov. *fast.* 6. 265.
There may be an allusion to the *casae Romuli* (10 n.). *spernere* suits
a literal kicking of the turf; cf. perhaps Goldsmith's 'spurns the
cottage from the green' (above, p. 243).

18. **leges sinebant** : *non sinere* is an austere synonym for 'to forbid',
naturally applied to the laws, like οὐκ ἐᾶν (Aeschin. 3. 21). Horace's
statement is not literally true; cf. Plin. *nat.* 36. 4 'marmora invehi,
maria huius rei causa transiri quae vetaret, lex nulla lata est'.

oppida : fortified towns (cf. Varro, *ling.* 5. 141, *RE* 18. 1. 709 ff.);
city walls were the most conspicuous monumental constructions of
primitive Italy (Virg. *georg.* 2. 156 'tot congesta manu praeruptis
oppida saxis'). Porphyrio was therefore wrong to take *oppida et templa*
as a hendiadys for *oppidorum templa*; Italy had little enough to set
beside the wide range of public constructions that the Greek orators
mention in similar contexts, and Horace is unlikely to have under-
played the most obvious.

publico sumptu : an official phrase; Cicero's order is *sumptu publico*
(four times in the *Verrines*), but here the adjective is emphatic. The
phrase should be taken with both *oppida* and *templa*; the same is
true of *novo . . . saxo* below. *iubentes* is also a *vox propria* with
leges (*Thes.l.L.* 7. 2. 1255. 59 ff.).

20. **novo decorare saxo** : adorn with newly quarried stone; through
the ages it was the normal Roman practice to reuse old materials
('non redivivo lapide' Lambinus). The phrase balances 17 *fortuitum
. . . caespitem*, just as 18 *publico* balances 15 *privatis*; for the kind of
tricolon where the third clause contains an antithesis to both previous clauses cf. 2. 12. 4 n., 2. 12. 19 n.

decorare emphasizes that in a frugal age plain stone was regarded
as an ornament. Moralists more normally contrast the luxury of
private buildings with the modesty of Republican temples (Sall.
Cat. 12. 3 f., Plin. *nat.* 36. 6 'tantas moles in privatam domum trahi
praeter fictilia deorum fastigia'), and Augustus for other reasons also
overstated the prevalence of mud-brick in earlier Rome (Suet.
Aug. 28. 3 'urbem . . . marmoream se relinquere quam latericiam
accepisset', Dio 56. 30); Horace's sober statement is nearer fact (cf.

Pease on Cic. *div.* 2. 99). His words are obviously relevant to the Augustan building programme (cf. 3. 6. 1 ff.); the poem would naturally fit a date about 28 B.C. (yet for an earlier hint cf. *serm.* 2. 2. 101 ff.).

16. OTIVM DIVOS

[J.-M. André, *L'Otium dans la vie morale et intellectuelle romaine*, 1966; K. Barwick, *RhM* 93, 1950, 249 ff.; K. Büchner, *Humanitas Romana*, 1957, pp. 176 ff.; M. Hubbard ap. Costa 1 ff.; K. Latte, *Philologus* 90, 1935, 294 ff. 294 ff. (= *Kl. Schr.*, pp. 876 ff.); W.-L. Liebermann, *Latomus* 30, 1971, 294 ff.; V. Pöschl, *Horazische Lyrik*, 1970, pp. 118 ff. (= *Hermes* 84, 1956, 74 ff.); H. Womble, *AJPh* 88, 1967, 385 ff.]

1–8. Tranquillity is the prayer of the restless merchant, as soon as he is caught in a storm, and of the gorgeous Persian warrior; but it cannot be bought, Grosphus, by Eastern riches. 9–16. Neither Eastern riches nor Roman authority can move off mental agitations, and the anxieties that flit round gilded ceilings; but the man with a small income and a modest home sleeps free from anxiety. 17–24. There is no point in the many targets of our short lives, none in our restless journeyings, as nobody can escape from himself. The speed and strength of schooners and cavalry give no protection against anxiety. 25–32. One should enjoy good moments as they come without anxiety for the future, and make little of trouble, seeing that happiness is never complete. Achilles did great things, but Tithonus lived longer, and perhaps I may be vouchsafed something that you have been denied. 33–40. You receive the plaudits of your cattle and your mares, you are clad in double-dyed sheep's wool; but I have been granted a small estate, an uninflated inspiration, and indifference to the crowd.

Horace's *Ode on Tranquillity* is addressed to Pompeius Grosphus, a prosperous Sicilian landowner (33 ff.); other instances of the name all reveal a Sicilian connection, apart from two duumvirs at Pompeii in 59 A.D. (*RE* 21. 2. 2273). In the *Epistles* Grosphus is commended to Iccius, who is collecting the revenues from Agrippa's Sicilian property (and so worth befriending): 'utere Pompeio Grospho, et si quid petet ultro / defer; nil Grosphus nisi verum orabit et aequum' (1. 12. 22 f.). For another Sicilian Grosphus half a century earlier cf. *Verr.* 3. 56 'Eubulidas est Grospus Centuripinus, homo cum virtute et nobilitate domi suae tum etiam pecunia princeps'; the context shows that he derived his money from arable land. Silius mentions a Grosphus of Agrigentum as early as the Second Punic War (14.

208 ff. 'altus equorum / mille rapit turmam atque hinnitibus aera flammat / pulveream volvens Acragas ad inania nubem. / ductor Grosphus erat, cuius caelata gerebat / taurum parma trucem, poenae monimenta vetustae'); both here and in our poem there are references to cavalry squadrons, neighing horses, and cattle (real or bronze). Silius seems to have taken *hinnitibus* from Horace (34), and so perhaps his other material; but it also seems possible that the Grosphi had well-known associations with cattle and cavalry. Perhaps they were a long-established Sicilian family which won distinction first in war (γρόσφος means a spear) and later in ranching; they could have acquired their *nomen* from the patronage of Pompey. Horace's friend is described by Porphyrio as an *eques Romanus*, a plausible piece of information that is probably not simply derived from the ode, though it would suit 22 *turmas*. His equestrian status coheres with his many schemes (cf. 17 n. for a disregarded pun on his name); these may have extended beyond landowning to include Eastern commercial ventures (cf. 1 ff., 7 *venale*, 19 n.), though a large-scale operator would not expect to be literally caught in a storm. It is true that the Epicureanism of the ode might suggest that Grosphus was an Epicurean (cf. the Stoic 2. 2 and the Peripatetic 2. 10), but to the Romans an interest in the school was not incompatible with strenuous activity.

otium was a word capable of many implications, both good and bad (see J.-M. André, op. cit.). To the man of affairs, like Grosphus, it was often just the opposite of *negotium* (cf. 1 n.); it is strange that the energetic Romans should have modelled their word for business on the negative Greek ἀσχολία. To antique moralists *otium* suggested indolence, luxury, and the downfall of cities; this pejorative sense is absent from Horace's poem, and may indeed be implicitly rejected (5 n.). To the statesman the word meant 'peace' whether at home or abroad; it was not bracing enough for Augustan political writing (André, op. cit., pp. 389 ff.), but in the second stanza it is used of foreign nations without scandal. To rich Romans *otium* was the leisure needed for innocent enjoyment, particularly in the country; perhaps Grosphus thought that he had already attained it. To literary men like Horace it had the more positive qualities of Greek σχολή, and suggested the peace and quiet necessary for creative activity; cf. *epist.* 1. 7. 35 f. 'nec / otia divitiis Arabum liberrima muto', Virg. *georg.* 4. 563 'studiis florentem ignobilis oti', Ov. *trist.* 1. 1. 41. To the philosopher, and in particular the Epicurean, *otium* signified the withdrawal from the crowd that was thought desirable for spiritual felicity; cf. Sen. *epist.* 68. 10 '"otium," inquis "Seneca, commendas mihi? ad Epicureas voces delaberis?"', Epicurus, frr. 426, 551 (εὐημερία), Leo, *anth. P.* 15. 12. 1 ff.

In our poem yet another idea is apparent, something like 'calm of mind'; the ode only hangs together if the second stanza introduces an ideal inward tranquillity that is opposed to the short-term aspirations of the merchant and soldier. This is not a natural meaning of *otium*, and Horace does not employ it very directly; yet ἡσυχία and *tranquillitas* are regularly used of mental as well as climatic or political quietude. The nautical *exemplum* of the first stanza recalls Pindar's εὐδία, 'a blessed state whose serenity and brightness are caught in the image of fine weather after a storm' (C. M. Bowra, *Pindar*, 1964, p. 250, citing *O*. 1. 98, *P*. 5. 10 f. [above, 2. 9. 1 n.], *I*. 7. 37 ff.); cf. further Eur. *Ba*. 389 ff. ὁ δὲ τᾶς ἡσυχίας / βίοτος καὶ τὸ φρονεῖν / ἀσάλευτόν τε μένει . . . , Péron 290 ff., Taillardat 179 f. Similar metaphors occurred in the philosophers, notably Epicurus, who contrasted the tumult of the storm with the calm of the spiritual haven; cf. fr. 425 (Heinze cites *epist*. 3. 128 λύεται πᾶς ὁ τῆς ψυχῆς χειμών, but there the meaning seems to be 'winter', cf. Σ Alcaeus 286. 2 τὰ τοῦ χειμῶνος διαλύεται, Philodemus, *anth.P*. 10. 21. 4 τὸν χιόσι ψυχὴν Κελτίσι νειφόμενον), Plut. *maxime cum princip*. 778 c Ἐπίκουρος τἀγαθὸν ἐν τῷ βαθυτάτῳ τῆς ἡσυχίας ὥσπερ ἐν ἀκλύστῳ λιμένι καὶ κωφῷ τιθέμενος, H. Fuchs, *Augustin und der antike Friedensgedanke*, 1926, pp. 179 ff., Marx on Lucil. 626, J.-M. André, op. cit., p. 231 n. 4. This coheres with the Epicurean character of the poem in general (cf. Syndikus 1. 439 ff.): simplicity of life is approved (14 n.), fear and desire reprehended (15 n.), living for the moment recommended (25 n.), the vicissitudes of fortune accepted (27 f.), the censure of the mob scorned (39 n.).

The ode owes a more particular debt to Lucretius (Pöschl, op. cit., pp. 131 ff., Syndikus 1. 440 ff.). Already the opening lines imitate a passage from the fifth book describing the supplications of a commander-in-chief in a storm (1 n.), while the picture of the anxious man running away from himself is influenced by the end of the third book (20 n.). But the main borrowing is from the great proem of the second book, 'suave mari magno'; there as in our ode the tumult of seafaring and war is contrasted with the tranquillity of the wise. Lucretius, like Horace, alludes to the shortness and anxiety of life (2. 16 ff.) and the fewness of nature's needs (2. 20 f.); he criticizes the luxury of gilded ceilings (2. 28), purple textiles (2. 35), and oriental treasure-chambers (2. 37 *gazae*), and recommends the simplicity of the country (2. 29 ff.). Like Horace, too, he proceeds from wealth to a display of power (21 n.), which he regards as equally incapable of repelling anxiety (2. 40 ff.):

> si non forte tuas legiones per loca campi
> fervere cum videas belli simulacra cientis,
> subsidiis magnis et ecum vi constabilitas,

ornatas armis †itastuas pariterque animatas,
his tibi tum rebus timefactae religiones
effugiunt animo pavidae, mortisque timores
tum vacuum pectus linquunt curaque solutum.
quod si ridicula haec ludibriaque esse videmus,
re veraque metus hominum curaeque sequaces
nec metuunt sonitus armorum nec fera tela
audacterque inter reges rerumque potentis
versantur neque fulgorem reverentur ab auro
nec clarum vestis splendorem purpureai,
quid dubitas quin omnis sit haec rationis potestas?

Yet in spite of all these imitations Horace has largely redistributed
the themes of his model; one may note for instance how his references
to *purpura* (7, 36) and *gazae* (9) are given new settings.

Horace's ode has in fact an intricate organization that owes
nothing to any predecessor. It breaks up into five groups of two
stanzas each (Barwick, op. cit., against Heinze), the first pair making
a characteristically indirect introduction. The argument proceeds
with schematic antitheses and fertile reiteration: the first two stanzas
support each other by anaphora, the next two are contrasted (so 5
and 6, 9 and 10), while stanzas 7 and 8 both contain internal opposi-
tions. The transitions from one pair to the next are smoothed over
by the development of ideas that have already been adumbrated:
thus the third stanza is linked to its predecessors by *gazae* (9 n.) and
tumultus (10 n.), *cura* in the sixth stanza points both backwards and
forwards (21 n.), the contrast between Grosphus and Horace in the
ninth and tenth stanzas grows with apparent naturalness out of the
eighth. Other dominating themes help to unify the seemingly
isolated stanzas, notably sailing, warfare, commerce, luxury, simplicity, speed. The Sapphic metre does not allow much room for
manœuvre, but Horace achieves remarkable compression without
loss of limpidity. At the same time his sharp verbal wit shows itself
in pointed contrasts and double meanings; see notes on 5 *otium*,
10 *miseros tumultus*, 11 *laqueata*, 13 *parvo bene*, 14 *tenui*, 15 *levis
somnos*, 16 *sordidus*, 17 *brevi fortes, iaculamur*, 19 *mutamus*, 20 *fugit*,
21 *vitiosa*, 26 *lento*, 29 *abstulit clarum*, 31 *et mihi . . .* , 38 *tenuem*,
39 *Parca non mendax*.

But these are merely externals; Horace achieves more than a con-
catenation of *sententiae* in the manner of the Silver Age. The moralizing is naturally traditional, but should not disconcert anybody who
understands the presuppositions of the ancient world, which was
more interested in the objective and universal aspects of behaviour
than in morbid introspection and egotistical self-revelation. The
abstract truisms are related in the Roman way to credible particu-

lars, and Grosphus's properties and ambitions are convincingly set against Horace's *parva rura* and *tenuis Camena*. Yet the poet treats his prosperous friend as a sympathetic person (so *epist.* 1. 12. 23), and shows none of the asperity or moral superiority of the *diatribe* or Lucretius; he jokes about Grosphus's self-assertive name (17 n.) and admiring cows (34 n.), insinuates his paraenesis tactfully and obliquely, and attributes any felicity of his own to the Muses and the Fates. In spite of its superficial air of conventionality the Ode on *Otium* turns out to be most original in spirit as well as in form: it is distinguished not only by organization and wit but by the rarer qualities of humanity and serenity.

Metre: Sapphic.

1. **otium** : the emphatic first word declares the subject of the poem. In the first instance 'tranquillity' is opposed to the toils of the storm-tossed merchant; cf. 1. 1. 15 ff. 'luctantem Icariis fluctibus Africum / mercator metuens otium et oppidi / laudat rura sui', *serm.* 1. 1. 31 (though these passages refer to ultimate retirement rather than immediate deliverance). *otium* cannot mean 'calm weather' without further elaboration, yet it helps the atmosphere of the poem that the word sometimes bears such associations; cf. 1. 15. 3, Sen. *nat.* 1. 2. 8 'quies aeris et otium et tranquillitas'.

divos rogat : even the *negotiator* (whose name shows his restlessness) is driven in a crisis to seek for *otium*. Even the richest man finds that money cannot buy everything (some general proposition of this kind may be derived from 7–8, though there the illustrations are determined by the immediate context). Even the most worldly materialist resorts to prayer; for this ridiculous spectacle cf. 3. 29. 57 ff., Lucr. 5. 1229 ff. '(induperator) non divum pacem votis adit ac prece quaesit / ventorum pavidus paces animasque secundas / nequiquam ... ?', D. Wachsmuth, ΠΟΜΠΙΜΟΣ Ο ΔΑΙΜΩΝ, 1967, pp. 435 f. Horace on the other hand recommends an inner *otium* that depends neither on wealth nor supplications; for this last point cf. Porph. *ad loc.* 'dicit omnes stulte sibi a dis otium optare cum ipsi illud sibi praestare possint, quippe cum nullis praemiis ematur', *epist.* 1. 18. 111 f. 'sed satis est orare Iovem quae ponit et aufert; / det vitam, det opes: aequum mi animum ipse parabo', Epicurus, *sent. Vat.* 65 μάταιόν ἐστι παρὰ θεῶν αἰτεῖσθαι ἅ τις ἑαυτῷ χορηγῆσαι ἱκανός ἐστι.

in patenti ... Aegaeo : in an exposed sea (Virg. *georg.* 2. 41), far from the coast; there is a formal contrast with the hidden moon. The Aegean was connected by some with αἰγίς, 'a storm'; cf. also 3. 29. 63 'Aegaeos tumultus', Artemidorus, *oneir.* 2. 12, p. 120 Pack.

2. prensus : for the substantival use of the singular participle cf.
3. 20. 16, *serm.* 1. 2. 131, K.–S. 1. 224. *deprehensus* is the prosaic expression for 'caught in a storm'; cf. Lucr. 6. 429, Catull. 25. 13, Serv.
auct. *georg.* 4. 420 'et *deprensis* verbum proprie nauticum cum tempestate occupantur'. Cf. also *comprehendere* (Cic. ap. Macr. *sat.* 2. 3. 5
'volui in consulatu tuo venire, sed nox me comprehendit'), καταλαμ-
βάνειν (Ap. Rhod. 2. 1086, Chariton 3. 2. 6).

simul : at the first signs of storm the merchant is quick enough
to cry for *otium*; cf. 3. 29. 58 f. 'ad miseras preces / decurrere'.

3. neque certa . . . : Horace characteristically balances a positive
with a negative and an accusative with a nominative. *certa* refers to
the reliability of clearly visible stars (Tib. 1. 9. 10 'ducunt instabiles
sidera certa rates'); contrast *dubius* (Juv. 5. 22).

5. otium : for similar anaphora in moralizing cf. 1. 16. 17 n.; Horace
recalls the triple denunciation of *otium* at Catull. 51. 13 ff. (Fraenkel
211 ff.), but he rejects the rueful viewpoint there represented. This
change of attitude is to be explained by the poetical contexts, and
not (as is sometimes said) by the intervention of the Civil Wars;
Sallust was defensive about *otium* but Cicero was favourable (cf.
leg. agr. 2. 9). In our passage the word makes a contrast with *furiosa* (cf. 4. 15. 17 f.) and especially with the juxtaposed *bello* (Caes.
civ. 2. 36. 1, Liv. 3. 30. 2, Manil. 3. 24 'tot bella atque otia', J.-M.
André, op. cit., pp. 79 ff.). Even the most warlike nations pray for
peace (ps.-Acro), and *otium* is the goal of all restlessness; cf. *serm.*
1. 1. 29 ff., Arist. *Nic. eth.* 1177^{b}4 ff. δοκεῖ τε ἡ εὐδαιμονία ἐν τῇ
σχολῇ εἶναι· ἀσχολούμεθα γὰρ ἵνα σχολάζωμεν καὶ πολεμοῦμεν ἵνα
εἰρήνην ἄγωμεν, *pol.* 1334^{a}14 ff., Epicurus, *epist.* 3. 128, ps.-Sall.
epist. 1. 6. 2 'postremo sapientes pacis causa bellum gerunt, laborem
spe otii sustentant' (with Vretska's note), Aug. *civ.* 19. 12 'pacis
igitur intentione geruntur et bella' (with Fuchs, op. cit. [p. 254],
pp. 17 ff.).

bello furiosa : the word-order emphasizes *bello* (Darnley Naylor)
and suggests a reminiscence of δοριμανής, Ἀρειμανής; for Horatian
methods of representing Greek compounds cf. Norden, *Agnostos
Theos*, p. 161 n. 4. Thrace was associated with Ares and manic behaviour generally (Lycurgus, Bacchanals, etc.), but the reference
would have a special topicality after Crassus's campaign (about
29 B.C.). For the conventional combination 'sailor and soldier' cf.
2. 13. 15 n.

6. Medi pharetra decori : the phrase balances *bello furiosa Thrace*.
The grandiose *Medi* links the Parthians with their Persian predecessors, likewise redoubtable archers (cf. Virg. *georg.* 4. 290 'pharetratae

... Persidis'). For ornamental quivers cf. Ov. *met.* 2. 421 (with Bömer's note), Sen. *Ag.* 217, Stat. *Theb.* 7. 661, *RE* 19. 2. 1823; by this conventional picture Horace combines the notions of war and wealth.

7. non gemmis . . . : these precious adornments develop the idea of *decori.* 'Purple and gold' go closely together (a little less closely with *gemmis*) ; for the combination cf. Lucr. 2. 51 f., 5. 1423, Pease on Virg. *Aen.* 4. 134. Horace is thinking primarily of Persian warriors, certainly not of Thracians, and therefore no longer of the merchant of the first stanza.

venale . . . : by this pejorative word Horace links the warrior with the merchant : the one is as materialistic as the other. He also seems to be pointing at Grosphus (note the placing of the vocative), who was evidently a rich man. He does not mean that the Parthians thought literally of buying peace; already his argument is beginning to shift, and he is referring to a true, more spiritual tranquillity. For similar metaphors cf. Isoc. 2. 32 δόξα δὲ χρημάτων οὐκ ὠνητή, Sen. *epist.* 27. 8, Clem. *paed.* 2. 3. 39. 4 σοφία δὲ οὐκ ὠνητὴ νομίσματι γηΐνῳ οὐδ' ἐν ἀγορᾷ, *Job* 28. 15 ff. 'It cannot be gotten for gold, neither shall silver be weighed for the price thereof . . . No mention shall be made of coral or of pearls : for the price of wisdom is above rubies'.

The run-over into the adonius is very rare ; cf. 1. 2. 19 f. 'uxorius amnis' (the Tiber out of control), 1. 25. 11 f. 'interlunia' (an intractable word divided after the preposition). There is no obvious explanation in our passage ; one might suspect an imitation of Greek if the feature were attested in Alcaeus as well as Sappho (cf. Page, *Sappho and Alcaeus*, p. 318). *nec auro* is to be preferred to *neque auro* ; the former is the reading of the paradosis, avoids an unparalleled elision, and underlines that the connective is not on all fours with *neque* above.

9. enim : Barwick (op. cit., p. 252) regards this as an instance of the common transitional use of *enim* ('for I need hardly mention that internal as well as external peace is beyond the power of wealth to secure'). However, on this interpretation one would expect the contrast between the two sorts of *otium* to be brought out at the beginning of the sentence. *enim* needs no special explanation if we recognize that *otium* has begun to have a spiritual reference in 7–8.

gazae : the exotic Persian word (1. 29. 2 n.) picks up *Medi*. Presumably *gazae* corresponds to *gemmis* as *lictor* to *purpura* and *laqueata* to *auro* (see notes below). Some see a chiasmus in *purpura, auro, gazae, lictor*, but this leaves the conspicuous *gemmis* without a balancing noun. For the commonplace cf. Varro, *Men.* 36 'non fit thensauris, non auro pectus solutum ; / non demunt animis curas ac

religiones / Persarum montes, non atria divitis Crassi', Lucr. 2. 37 ff.
'quapropter quoniam nil nostro in corpore gazae / proficiunt neque
nobilitas nec gloria regni, / quod superest, animo quoque nil prodesse
putandum'. Yet Horace goes further: riches do not simply fail to
banish anxiety, but positively increase it.

consularis submovet lictor : after wealth Horace turns to power,
following a traditional pattern; cf. 2. 10. 5–12, Lucr. 2. 38 (cited
above), Epicurus, *sent. Vat.* 81 οὐ λύει τὴν τῆς ψυχῆς ταραχὴν . . .
οὔτε πλοῦτος ὑπάρχων ὁ μέγιστος οὔθ' ἡ παρὰ τοῖς πολλοῖς τιμὴ καὶ
περίβλεψις . . . , fr. 548 τὸ εὔδαιμον καὶ μακάριον οὐ χρημάτων πλῆθος
οὐδὲ πραγμάτων ὄγκος οὐδ' ἀρχαί τινες ἔχουσιν οὐδὲ δυνάμεις, Plut.
tranq. anim. 477a οὔτ' οἰκία πολυτελὴς . . . οὔτε μέγεθος ἀρχῆς . . .
εὐδίαν παρέχει βίῳ καὶ γαλήνην τοσαύτην ὅσην ψυχὴ καθαρεύουσα πραγμάτων καὶ βουλευμάτων πονηρῶν, Diog. Oen. 24. 2. 3 ff. Chilton.

submovet is determined by *lictor* rather than by *gazae*; it is the *vox
propria* for 'moving on' a crowd from the path of a magistrate (Liv.
3. 48. 3 '⟨i⟩. . . lictor, submove turbam', Mayor on Juv. 1. 37). For
a similar moralizing illustration cf. Sen. *epist.* 94. 60 'non est quod
tibi tranquillitatis tuae fastidium faciat ille sub illis fascibus purpura
cultus, non est quod feliciorem eum iudices cui summovetur quam te
quem lictor semita deicit. si vis exercere tibi utile, nulli autem grave
imperium, summove vitia'. Editors there refer *purpura cultus* to the
magistrate, but *sub fascibus* must point to the lictor; this implies
that lictors wore purple even in the city (not mentioned at *RE* 13.
508). Therefore Horace's *consularis lictor* picks up 7 *purpura* just
as *gazae* picks up *gemmis*; but the reference to Roman *imperium*
is a new development that balances the treasuries of the East.

10. miseros tumultus mentis : *tumultus* (opposed to *otium* at Sen.
Thy. 560) is well chosen to suit both civil commotions and psychological disturbances (cf. Sen. *epist.* 56. 5); it is also applicable to the
storm of the first stanza (cf. Stat. *silv.* 2. 2. 28) and the wars of the
second, and so gives unity to the imagery of the poem. The genitive
mentis comes not just after adjective and noun (thus 3. 30. 2) but in
the next line; this doubly emphatic position, apparently unparalleled
in the *Odes*, suits the shift of meaning (the hubbub of the *mind* rather
than the populace). *miseros* suits the metaphor rather than the
street-scene; cf. Lucr. 2. 14 'o miseras hominum mentes' (the usage
is familiar in moralizing).

11. curas . . . volantis : the participle suggests a persistent agitation
that is difficult to pin down; cf. Theognis 729 f. φροντίδες ἀνθρώπων
ἔλαχον πτερὰ ποικίλ' ἔχουσαι / μυρόμενοι ψυχῆς εἵνεκα καὶ βιότου (so
already Hom. *Od.* 19. 516 f. πυκιναὶ δέ μοι ἀμφ' ἀδινὸν κῆρ / ὀξεῖαι
μελεδῶναι ὀδυρομένην ἐρέθουσιν). In our passage the anxieties are

clearly external to the human body, like the winged κῆρες or the
troubles from Pandora's jar (Hes. *op.* 100 ff.); cf. Lucian, *Charon* 15
(of a swarm over the earth) ἐλπίδες ... καὶ δείματα καὶ ἄγνοιαι καὶ
ἡδοναὶ καὶ φιλαργυρίαι καὶ ὀργαὶ καὶ μίση καὶ τὰ τοιαῦτα ... ὁ φόβος δὲ
καὶ αἱ ἐλπίδες ὑπεράνω πετόμενοι, ὁ μὲν ἐμπίπτων ἐκπλήττει ἐνίοτε καὶ
ὑποπτήσσειν ποιεῖ, αἱ δ᾽ ἐλπίδες ὑπὲρ κεφαλῆς αἰωρούμεναι ... ἀναπτά-
μεναι οἴχονται, Headlam–Thomson on Aesch. *Ag.* 427 f., Onians 86 f.
and 404. Horace's image suggests not harpies or obscene birds (which
are too large and solid), but rather bats (compared to dreams by
Virg. *Aen.* 6. 284, Stat. *Theb.* 10. 114); the rich's man's glittering
house has no such filthy intruders, but his own *curae* are far worse
(for similar points cf. 16 n., 21 n.).

laqueata ... tecta: the panelled ceiling (*laquear* or *lacunar*) was
a symbol of luxury in Roman poetry; cf. 2. 18. 1 n., Enn. *scaen.*
94 ff. V. = 89 ff. J. 'vidi ego te adstante ope barbarica / tectis caelatis
laqueatis / auro ebore instructam regifice' (with Jocelyn's note),
Lucr. 2. 28 'nec citharae reboant laqueata aurataque templa',
Blümner 94 f., *RE* 12. 369 ff., C. W. Mendell, *YClS* 11, 1950, 285 ff. As
such ceilings were often gilded, the theme of 8 *auro* is sustained.
laqueata can mean 'noosed' as well as 'coffered', and Horace perhaps
means us to remember the sword of Damocles (3. 1. 17 f., Pers. 3. 40
'auratis pendens laquearibus ensis'). In fact the Romans may have
confused *lacuar* ('coffered ceiling') with *laquear* ('lamp-chain'); cf.
H. Nettleship, *Contributions to Latin Lexicography*, 1889, pp. 513 f.

13. vivitur parvo bene: the impersonal *vivitur* suits the sententious-
ness (like *on* in French); cf. Plaut. *trin.* 65 'ut diu vivitur, bene
vivitur'. *bene* is well juxtaposed with *parvo*; the 'good life' is not what
the *bon viveur* supposes (cf. *epist.* 1. 6. 56 'si bene qui cenat bene vivit').
For the commonplace cf. *serm.* 2. 2. 1 'quae virtus et quanta, boni,
sit vivere parvo' (the precepts of Ofellus), Epicurus, *epist.* 3. 131,
frr. 459–77, *sent. Vat.* 25, Lucr. 5. 1118 f. 'divitiae grandes homini sunt
vivere parce / aequo animo; neque enim est umquam penuria parvi',
Tib. 1. 1. 25, Sen. *Med.* 333, Lucan 4. 377, Claud. 3. 215 'vivitur
exiguo melius', Kier, *passim*, Vischer, *passim*.

cui: a rather formal, old-fashioned equivalent for *si cui*; cf. 3. 16.
43 'bene est, cui deus obtulit ...', Cic. *leg.* 2. 19 'qui secus faxit, deus
ipse vindex erit', K.–S. 2. 281 ff. The indefinite pronoun well suits
the impersonal verb (cf. Wackernagel, *Vorlesungen* 1. 148). Therefore
Peerlkamp's *ubi* (which gives an unattractive elision) is unnecessary.

paternum: the adjective suggests *pietas*, antique frugality, and
the absence of personal acquisitiveness; cf. Sen. *dial.* 9. 1. 7 'placet
... argentum grave rustici patris sine ullo nomine artificis'.

14. splendet: the salt-cellar was proverbially *purus* (Catull. 23. 19,

Pers. 3. 25), and in a properly run house was naturally a piece of polished silver. Its solitary resplendence provides a healthy contrast with the ceiling of the previous stanza. For more dazzling displays of plate cf. 4. 11. 6, *serm.* 2. 2. 4 f., *epist.* 1. 5. 7, 1. 5. 23 f.

tenui : the adjective reinforces *parvo* and makes a contrast with *splendet*; as salt was both literally and metaphorically *tenue* (see next note), it is well juxtaposed with *salinum*. The implication is simplicity rather than indigence; cf. *serm.* 2. 2. 53 f. 'sordidus a tenui victu distabit, Ofello / iudice' (see Lejay, p. 316), 2. 2. 70, Cic. *Tusc.* 5. 89 (on Epicurus) 'hic vero ipse quam parvo est contentus. nemo de tenui victu plura dixit', *Lael.* 86, Eur. fr. 893. 1 f. N. ἀρκεῖ μετρία βιοτά μοι / σώφρονος τραπέζης.

salinum : as salt was the poor man's condiment it suggested frugality; cf. *serm.* 1. 3. 14 'concha salis', 2. 2. 17 'cum sale panis', Plin. *nat.* 31. 89, Call. *ep.* 47. 1 (with Gow–Page, *HE* 1175). Nevertheless the salt-cellar derived religious associations from its importance (Porph. ad loc., Arnob. *nat.* 2. 67), and came to symbolize an ordered domestic existence (Pers. 3. 24 f. 'sed rure paterno / est tibi far modicum, purum et sine labe salinum'). Hence even an old-fashioned moralist might permit a silver *salinum*; cf. Val. Max. 4. 4. 3 (Aemilius Papus has one as heirloom), Liv. 26. 36. 6 (Laevinus exempts it from his ban), Plin. *nat.* 33. 153.

15. levis somnos : the adjective picks up *parvo* and *tenui*, though Horace is now turning to more intangible things. There seems to be a paradoxical point with *auferre* (for which cf. *epod.* 5. 96, *Thes.l.L.* 2. 1333. 24 ff.) : the poor man's sleep is 'too light' to carry off. There may also be a contrast with the rich man's possessions which might be 'lifted' more literally by *sordidus cupido*. Of course Horace is not thinking of a 'light sleeper' in a critical sense, but of healthy and refreshing slumbers; cf. *epod.* 2. 28 'somnos quod invitet levis', *culex* 206, Milton, *P.L.* 5. 3 f. 'for his sleep Was Aerie light, from pure digestion bred' (for *gravis* cf. Lucr. 4. 956, *Thes.l.L.* 6. 2. 2288. 11 ff.). The sleep of the poor is often contrasted with the insomnia of the rich; cf. 3. 1. 21 f., *epist.* 1. 10. 18, Epicurus, fr. 207 κρεῖττον δέ σοι θαρρεῖν ἐπὶ στιβάδος κατακειμένῳ ἢ ταράττεσθαι χρυσῆν ἔχοντι κλίνην καὶ πολυτελῆ τράπεζαν, Sen. *epist.* 90. 41 with Summers's note, *Herc. O.* 644 ff., Lucan 5. 505 f. 'in quorum pectora somno / dat vires fortuna minor', Clem. *paed.* 2. 9.

timor aut cupido : desire and fear are often combined in ancient psychology as irrational attitudes towards good and bad things in the future; cf. Zeno ap. Cic. *Tusc.* 4. 11, Epicurus, fr. 485, Lucr. 6. 25 'finem statuit cuppedinis atque timoris'. *cupido* is not here lust but avarice (3. 16. 39, 3. 24. 51, *Thes.l.L.* 4. 1423. 45 ff.). Porphyrio regards the masculine gender as strange, but this is the older usage (cf. the sex of the god), and invariable in Horace.

16. sordidus : the adjective should be taken only with *cupido* (*pace* Müller) ; cf. the common *sordes* for meanness. There is a contrast with *splendet* (also at the beginning of an even line) ; the dirt that really matters is not found in the cottages of the just (Aesch. *Ag.* 772 ff. Δίκα δὲ λάμπει μὲν ἐν / δυσκάπνοις δώμασιν, / τὸν δ' ἐναίσιμον τίει· / τὰ χρυσόπαστα δ' ἔδεθλα σὺν / πίνῳ χερῶν παλιντρόποις / ὄμμασι λιποῦσ' . . .). There seems also to be a suggestion that this shabby *cupido* is quite unlike the golden boy of Hellenistic epigram.

17. quid brevi fortes . . . : our vigorous attitudes are at variance with the feebleness of our condition. Cf. 2. 11. 11 n., Simonides 520. 1 ff. ἀνθρώπων ὀλίγον μὲν / κάρτος, ἄπρακτοι δὲ μεληδόνες, / αἰῶνι δ' ἐν παύρῳ πόνος ἀμφὶ πόνῳ, Pind. *N.* 11. 43 ff. τὸ δ' ἐκ Διὸς ἀνθρώποις σαφὲς οὐχ ἕπεται / τέκμαρ· ἀλλ' ἔμπαν μεγαλανορίαις ἐμβαίνομεν, / ἔργα τε πολλὰ μενοινῶντες, Eur. *Ba.* 397 ff. βραχὺς αἰών· ἐπὶ τούτῳ / δὲ τίς ἂν μεγάλα διώκων / τὰ παρόντ' οὐχὶ φέροι;, *epitaph*. Bion. 102 ff. ἄμμες δ' οἱ μεγάλοι καὶ καρτεροί, οἱ σοφοὶ ἄνδρες / . . . εὕδομεν εὖ μάλα μακρὸν ἀτέρμονα νήγρετον ὕπνον, Cic. *Arch.* 28, Petron. 115. 14 (on the merchant Lichas) 'ite nunc mortales et magnis cogitationibus pectora implete'.

brevi aevo means 'within our short life-span'; cf. anon. ap. Sen. *nat.* 3 praef. 3 'tollimus ingentes animos et maxima parvo / tempore molimur'. The emphatic *brevi* is pointedly juxtaposed with *fortes*, but it would be too sarcastic to interpret 'deriving confidence from our short lives'. Editors take *brevi aevo* as ablative absolute, but such a hyperbaton only seems natural with a participle (as at 2. 7. 27 f. 'recepto / dulce mihi furere est amico').

iaculamur : the ambitions of life are conventionally expressed in terms of aims and target (cf. τοξεύειν, στοχάζεσθαι) ; in spite of the allusions to war in this poem (5, 21), the image here seems to be derived rather from athletics (cf. Pind. *N.* 9. 55, *I.* 2. 35 ff.). There is a pun on the name 'Grosphus' (ignored by editors except for Tescari, who is too tentative): γρόσφος is the Greek for a throwing-spear or *iaculum* (Plb. 6. 22. 4, Str. 4. 4. 3, Plut. *Sulla* 18. 6, D.–S. 3. 39; for γροσφομάχοι = *velites* cf. Plb. 1. 33. 9, 6. 21. 7). By his choice of verb Horace implies that Grosphus is engaged in ambitious schemes, but the tactful first person avoids any objectionable criticism; for the bedside plural ('how are we today?') cf. Wackernagel, *Vorlesungen* I. 42 ff. There may be another play on Grosphus's name at *epist.* I. 12. 22 'petet' [cited above, p. 252].

18. multa : the word is placed with unusual emphasis at the beginning of the line and the end of the sentence (thus providing a

strong contrast with *brevi*) ; for a similar rhythm cf. Lucr. 4. 1011 f.
'porro hominum mentes, magnis quae motibus edunt / magna, . . .'.
There is a suggestion of hyper-activity (πολυπραγμοσύνη) ; cf. Democritus, fr. 3 τὸν εὐθυμεῖσθαι μέλλοντα χρὴ μὴ πολλὰ πρήσσειν μήτε
ἰδίῃ μήτε ξυνῇ (from the beginning of the περὶ εὐθυμίης, as is shown
by Sen. *dial.* 9. 13. 1), Pind. loc. cit. [17 n.], Patrocles, fr. 1. 3 N.
τί δῆτα θνητοὶ πόλλ' ἀπειλοῦμεν μάτην;

terras alio calentis sole : the sun is common to all (Menander,
fr. 416 a. 4 Koerte), yet paradoxically seems different in other
countries; cf. 2. 7. 4 n., Lucian, *patr. enc.* 6 καὶ γὰρ εἶδε τὸν ἥλιον
πρῶτον ἕκαστος ἀπὸ τῆς πατρίδος, ὡς καὶ τοῦτον τὸν θεόν, εἰ καὶ κοινός
ἐστιν, ἀλλ' οὖν ἑκάστῳ νομίζεσθαι πατρῷον διὰ τὴν πρώτην ἀπὸ τοῦ τόπου
θέαν. Horace's words imply regions farther afield than Sicily ; perhaps
Grosphus was involved at a high level in eastern trade. There is
a conscious imitation of Virg. *georg.* 2. 512 'atque alio patriam quaerunt sub sole iacentem' ; as that passage refers to literal exiles, Horace
provides a connection of thought with the following clause.

19. mutamus : 'take in exchange for home'; cf. ἀλλάττειν, 1. 17. 2 n.,
1. 37. 24 n. Some interpret 'exchange one country for another' (Sen.
epist. 104. 8 'quid prodest mare traicere et urbes mutare? si vis ista
quibus urgeris effugere, non aliubi sis oportet sed alius') ; but this
makes *alio sole* less poignant. If Grosphus was engaged in trade
the commercial tone of *mutamus* might be pointed, but this cannot
be used as a positive argument that he was so engaged; cf. *epist.*
1. 11. 27 'caelum . . . mutant' of the Grand Tour.

patriae quis exul : the three clauses of this impassioned tricolon
are arranged to begin at different places in the line (cf. 1. 35. 34 ff.).
For the Graecizing genitive cf. Theoc. 24. 129 φυγὰς Ἄργεος, Ov.
met. 6. 189, *Thes.l.L.* 5. 2. 2100. 84 ff. *exul* is pejorative ; the traveller
suffers the equivalent of exile, which is none the better for being self-
imposed.

20. fugit : the perfect is not gnomic but means 'is in the position
of having escaped' ; as *fugere* can mean 'to go into exile' (Virg. *ecl.*
1. 4, cf. φεύγειν), se fugit balances *patriae exul*. Though the clause is
formally parallel to its two predecessors, Horace is now insinuating
an explanation for our restlessness, namely that we are trying to
escape from ourselves; for this commonplace cf. *serm.* 2. 7. 111 ff.
(with Lejay, p. 555), *epist.* 1. 14. 13 'in culpa est animus qui se non
effugit umquam', Lucr. 3. 1068 f. 'hoc se quisque modo fugitat, quem
scilicet ut fit / effugere haud potis est', Sen. *epist.* 28. 2 'quaeris quare
te fuga ista non adiuvet? tecum fugis', *dial.* 9. 2. 14, Arist. *Nic. eth.*
1166ᵇ13 f. ζητοῦσί τε οἱ μοχθηροὶ μεθ' ὧν συνημερεύσουσιν, ἑαυτοὺς δὲ
φεύγουσιν.

21. scandit . . . : cf. the unusually close parallel at 3. 1. 37 ff. 'sed timor et minae / scandunt eodem quo dominus, neque / decedit aerata triremi et / post equitem sedet atra cura'. Our stanza was deleted by C. Prien (*RhM* 13, 1858, 353 ff.), followed by Lehrs (1869), Kiessling, Heinze, Klingner, K. Büchner, *JAW* 267, 1939, 135 f., H. Fuchs, *MH* 4, 1947, 164 ff. (= Oppermann 33 ff.), U. Knoche (ed. G. Maurach), *AClass* 13, 1970, 35 ff. It has been rightly defended by Friedrich 188 ff., Latte, op. cit., P. J. Enk, *Mnemosyne*, 4, 1936/7, 166 f., Barwick, op. cit., Pöschl, op. cit., Syndikus 1. 451.

Some scholars complain that the stanza interrupts the sequence of thought, but in fact this is perfectly coherent: 17 ff. 'the restless schemer for the future cannot escape himself', 21 ff. 'however fast he travels, anxiety always keeps up' (for the same progression cf. *serm.* 2. 7. 112, 115), 25 f. 'let the mind that is happy for the moment avoid anxiety for the future'. The idea that anxiety always keeps up is found in the proem of Lucretius's second book (48 'curaeque sequaces'), the very area that provides so many other themes for our poem (above, pp. 254 f.); it is therefore most unlikely to be an inter- polation from *carm.* 3. 1. 37 ff. (see Pöschl, op. cit., p. 134). Lucretius says in the same context that armed power cannot avert anxiety, another observation that is likely to have directly influenced our stanza (though the citation from Nonius at 2. 43a 'fervere cum videas classem lateque vagari' is very difficult to fit into Lucretius's trans- mitted text). Admittedly Horace seems to be describing not the commander of an army (as Lucretius is), but the private owner of a bronze-plated schooner (see *aeratas* n. below) and a charging *eques* at a glittering parade; but these are simply modifications of the Lucretian prototype, designed to suit the status and interests of Grosphus (as at 3. 1. 39 f. of Maecenas). Finally one can argue that the whole ode breaks up into five pairs of stanzas (above, p. 255); lines 9–16 and 25–32 make coherent sections, but if our stanza is deleted the pattern is disrupted.

scandit : in conjunction with *aeratas* the verb hints at a hostile boarding-party. This is more pointed than in 3. 1. 38 (cited above), and suggests again that our passage has priority.

aeratas : the word is normally used of the bronze prows of war- ships, which were used for ramming (Plin. *nat.* 32. 3 'rostra illa aere ferroque ad ictus armata', C. Torr, *Ancient Ships*, 1894, p. 63 n. 143, *Thes.l.L.* 1. 1059. 23 ff.); here the reference is rather to a private schooner (cf. 3. 1. 39, *epist.* 1. 1. 93 'locuples quem ducit priva triremis'), which might presumably be armour-plated against pirates, and also to cut the waves more effectively. Horace is combining the ideas of strength and speed; he thus sustains the idea of rapidity which pervades this part of the poem (cf. *fugit, nec turmas relinquit, ocior*).

vitiosa : anxiety could be regarded as an unhealthy mental condition, especially as it was linked with such deficiencies as *timor*, *cupido* etc. (cf. Cic. *Tusc.* 4. 14 'perturbationes . . . vitiosae'). There might also be the suggestion that it nullifies the most splendid enterprises; cf. *epist.* 1. 1. 85 ff. 'cui si vitiosa libido / fecerit auspicium, cras ferramenta Teanum / tolletis, fabri' (where *auspicium* makes the implication clear). Finally, in collocation with *scandit aeratas* the adjective suggests a corrosion in the metal (not just a tarnishing as proposed by D. West ap. Costa 38) that creeps up the prow from the water; significantly *aerugo* is used of corrosive emotions like envy (*serm.* 1. 4. 101 with Lejay, Ov. *met.* 2. 798, cf. Aesch. *Ag.* 834 ἰός) and avarice (*ars* 330 with Brink).

22. nec . . . relinquit : Cura does not let go of her quarry; cf. 3. 4. 77 f. 'incontinentem nec Tityi iecur / reliquit ales' (though there no pursuit is implied), 3. 2. 31 f. 'raro . . . deseruit'. She is regarded as something external (cf. 3. 1. 40, *serm.* 2. 7. 115), rather like a hounding Fury; cf. Aesch. *Eum.* 250 f. ὑπέρ τε πόντον ἀπτέροις ποτήμασιν / ἦλθον διώκουσ' οὐδὲν ὑστέρα νεώς, Pease on Virg. *Aen.* 4. 384 and 386.

turmas : 'per hoc ostendit neque mari neque terra quemquam curas suas effugere' (Porph.); for the polar expression cf. 1. 6. 3 'navibus aut equis' with note. The contrast echoes that of the first two stanzas, but Horace is now talking not of Thrace but of the Roman army; the *eques* Grosphus may have taken part in glittering parades. Some regard the plural squadrons as less vivid than the single horseman of 3. 1. 40; yet Horace here comes closer to the army manoeuvres in Lucretius's proem (Syndikus 1. 450 n. 54), again an indication of priority.

23. ocior cervis : for the commonplace cf. Plaut. *Poen.* 530, Catull. 64. 341, *Thes.l.L.* 3. 954. 25 ff.

agente nimbos : the picture of a wind driving clouds is Homeric (*Il.* 5. 525 f., 11. 305 f., 12. 157). Yet here the clouds (heavy *nimbi*) may be heaped up rather than scattered; cf. Hom. *Il.* 1. 511 νεφεληγερέτα Ζεύς (Cook 3. 1. 30 ff.), Ov. *am.* 1. 8. 9, Sen. *Phaedr.* 737 'ocior nubes glomerante coro' (if this is modelled on our passage it is further evidence for authenticity). It is relevant that clouds in poetry often symbolize trouble (1. 7. 15, 2. 9. 1 n.). The wind is a pursuer (cf. *agente* of hunting animals); this provides a climax after the deer, which are naturally pursued.

24. ocior Euro : for this and similar epic phrases cf. Virg. *Aen.* 8. 223, 12. 733, Otto 366, Bömer on Ov. *met.* 1. 502; the double comparison is also conventional (Hom. *Od.* 7. 36 ὠκεῖαι ὡς εἰ πτερὸν ἠὲ

νόημα, Virg. *Aen.* 5. 319, Lucan 5. 405). Heinze and Büchner regard
the expression as un-Horatian; they are rightly contradicted by
Barwick, op. cit., pp. 257 f. and Pöschl, op. cit., p. 126.

25. laetus in praesens . . . : the tone is Epicurean; cf. 1. 11. 8 n.,
1. 31. 17 n., 3. 8. 27 'dona praesentis cape laetus horae', 3. 29. 32 'quod
adest', Lucr. 3. 957 'semper aves quod abest, praesentia temnis'.
But the contrast between the 'near, present, possible' and the 'far,
absent, future, impossible' is much older than the philosophers; cf.
D. C. Young, *Three Odes of Pindar*, 1968, pp. 116 ff.

26. oderit curare : 'let the mind refuse to worry about'; for the weak
sense of *odisse* cf. 1. 38. 1 n., *epist.* 1. 16. 52. *curare* makes a contrast
with *laetus* and picks up *cura* in the previous stanza.

amara : the neuter plural suggests the generalizations of Greek
moral philosophy; cf. 1. 29. 16 n., 3. 3. 2 'prava iubentium'.

lento . . . risu : the adjective applies both to a physical smile (the
mouth 'gives') and to mental tolerance; cf. Cic. *de orat.* 2. 279 'ridiculi
genus patientis ac lenti', E. Zinn, *Gymnasium* 67, 1960, 51 f. Bentley
proposed *leni* (cf. Cic. *rep.* 6. 12 'leniter adridens'); as *lenis* can be
applied to wine, it makes a contrast with *amara* and suits the metaphor of *temperet*. On the other hand one can argue in favour of *lento*
that the required attitude is not geniality, but tolerance and acceptance (for the Epicurean element cf. 1. 11. 3 n.). Wade's *amarulenta*
may be recorded as a warning against excessive reliance on the
ductus litterarum.

27. temperet : 'assuage'; the verb suggests not just mixing but
'toning down' (1. 20. 11 n.), and so suits *amara*. For a similar metaphor cf. anon. *anth. P.* 7. 155. 1 f. (on a comic actor) ὁ τὸν πολυστένακτον
ἀνθρώπων βίον / γέλωτι κεράσας Νικαεὺς Φιλιστίων. For a stronger
claim cf. 4. 12. 19 f. 'amaraque / curarum eluere efficax'.

nihil est ab omni parte beatum : perfect and permanent felicity
is impossible (for *ab omni parte* cf. Bömer on Ov. *met.* 3. 70); but this
is a positive encouragement to snatch happiness for the moment
(*laetus* is contrasted with the more other-worldly *beatum*). Usually
the aphorism is more pessimistic; cf. Theognis 441 οὐδεὶς γὰρ πάντ'
ἐστὶ πανόλβιος, Pind. *O.* 7. 94 f., *P.* 3. 86 ff., 5. 54, *N.* 7. 55 f., *I.* 3. 18,
Bacch. 5. 53 ff. οὐ γάρ τις ἐπιχθονίων / πάντα γ' εὐδαίμων ἔφυ, fr. 54,
Hdt. 1. 32. 8, Eur. frr. 45 N., 661 οὐκ ἔστιν ὅστις πάντ' ἀνὴρ εὐδαι-
μονεῖ· / ἢ γὰρ πεφυκὼς ἐσθλὸς οὐκ ἔχει βίον / ἢ δυσγενὴς ὢν πλουσίαν ἀροῖ
πλάκα, Headlam on Herodas 9 b. 1.

29. abstulit clarum . . . : the *exempla* illustrate the maxim that
nobody's happiness is complete, but again they must not be interpreted too pessimistically; in that case the blessings at the end of the

stanza (32 *porriget hora*) would show an incoherent change of direction. Therefore *clarum* is at least as emphatic as *abstulit* (pointedly juxtaposed): Achilles had a short life, but a glorious one (cf. Hom. *Il.* 9. 412 ff.). For *cita mors* cf. *serm.* 1. 1. 8, Hom. *Il.* 1. 417 ὠκύμορος (of Achilles); the adjective may also suggest that the fleet-footed warrior was not quick enough to escape death.

30. longa Tithonum . . . : men's lots have credits and debits which are different in every case. Tithonus's credit is expressed by the emphatic *longa*, which almost means 'eternal' (2. 14. 19 n.); from this point of view it balances *clarum*, which described the credit of Achilles (the variation in the formulation is characteristic of Horace). One might suppose at first sight that *longa* simply reinforced the misery of *minuit senectus*; but if there is to be a coherent transition to the next clause Tithonus's compensation must be explicitly stated (it is not enough to infer *formosum* or *immortalem*).

Tithonus is proverbially a representative of old age; cf. Aristo of Chios ap. Cic. *senec.* 3, Plaut. *Men.* 854, Varro, *Men.* 544–8, Headlam on Herodas 10, pp. 411 f., Otto 349, *RE* 6 A. 1518 f. He is well chosen as a foil to Achilles, and his own story showed the kind of contrast that Horace is trying to evoke. He was given immortality but not youth, and a voice but not strength; cf. 1. 28. 8 n., *h. Aphr.* 237 f. τοῦ δ' ἦ τοι φωνὴ ῥεῖ ἄσπετος οὐδέ τι κῖκυς / ἔσθ' οἵη πάρος ἔσκεν ἐνὶ γναμπτοῖσι μέλεσσι. He should not be regarded in this context as merely contemptible; the cicada into which he was turned could be an object of congratulation (*Anacreontea* 32. 1 μακαρίζομέν σε, τέττιξ).

minuit : the verb (which makes a formal contrast with *longa*) suggests Greek μινύθειν, which is used of the wasting of the body.

31. et mihi . . . : after the grand *exempla* Horace humorously turns to himself (cf. 1. 16. 22 n., 1. 22. 9); he may be 'handed on a plate' (*porriget*) what Grosphus cannot achieve by his many exertions. He is thinking not of old age (ps.-Acro) nor of riches, but of the tranquil felicity of a poet; he makes his point tactfully with *forsan*, the future *porriget*, the indefinite *hora*. There seems to be a whimsical comparison of the two men with Achilles and Tithonus: Grosphus has horses and perhaps ships, but his material splendour is vulnerable, Horace is unglamorous and growing old, but he has the gift of song like the cicada (34 n., Pl. *Phaedr.* 259 b–c, Posidippus, *anth. P.* 12. 98. 1 τὸν Μουσῶν τέττιγα with Gow–Page, *HE* 3074 f.), and perhaps also a poet's qualified immortality. *abstulit* and *porriget* seem to balance one another (even though the object of the former is Achilles himself and not some advantage he possessed); this suggests a contrast between Achilles and Horace, and an analogy between Achilles and Grosphus.

33. **greges centum Siculaeque vaccae** : probably a grandiose hendiadys for *greges* of cattle, the most conspicuous manifestation of
agricultural wealth (1. 31. 5 n.). For the construction cf. Ov. *met.*
15. 645 'concilium Graecosque patres'. For this rare sense of *grex* cf.
epod. 2. 11 f. 'mugientium . . . greges', *serm.* 1. 3. 110, Cic. *Phil.* 3. 31,
Virg. *Aen.* 6. 38 with Servius, ps.-Quint. *decl. mai.* 13. 13.

Some understand *greges* of sheep as opposed to cattle; cf. Virg.
Aen. 7. 538 f. 'quinque greges illi balantum, quina redibant / ar-
menta', Ov. *met.* 4. 635, Stat. *silv.* 4. 5. 17 f. 'non mille balant lanigeri
greges / nec vacca dulci mugit adultero' (an imitation of our passage,
but that is not decisive). On this latter interpretation *balant* would
have to be understood from *mugiunt*, but the zeugma is made more
difficult by the balancing *tollit hinnitum* below (why should the sheep
alone have their noise unspecified?). The formal correspondence of
centum, *quadrigis*, *bis* (West ap. Costa 54) also suggests that only
one kind of animal is meant in the first clause. It can be added that
the repeated *u* sounds (*centum, Siculaeque, circum, mugiunt*) seem
to evoke the mooing of cattle (see also the note on 34 *mugiunt*), just
as *hinnitum* represents the neighing of a horse. Finally, if *greges* refers
to sheep the mention of *lanae* in 37 is uncharacteristically repetitive.

circum : the postponement of the preposition is a sign of heightened style; for the construction in hexameters see Norden on Virg.
Aen. 6. 329.

34. **mugiunt** : cf. Theoc. 16. 36 f. πολλοὶ δὲ Σκοπάδαισιν ἐλαυνόμενοι
ποτὶ σακοὺς / μόσχοι σὺν κεραῇσιν ἐμυκήσαντο βόεσσι, 90 ff., Stat. loc.
cit. [33 n.], ps.-Quint. *decl. mai.* 13. 13 'tibi omne armentis mugiet
nemus'. Yet in our passage the farmyard noises seem agreeably
humorous: the cows stand round the great Grosphus in a *corona* and
pay tribute in their noisy way. The rarefied breath of the Greek Muse
(38) is more to Horace's taste, much as Callimachus preferred the
cicada's chirp to the donkey's bray (fr. 1. 29 ff.) : ἐνὶ τοῖς γὰρ ἀείδομεν
οἳ λιγὺν ἦχον / [τέττιγος, θ]όρυβον δ' οὐχ ἐφίλησαν ὄνων. / θηρὶ μὲν οὐα-
τόεντι πανείκελον ὀγκήσαιτο / [ἄλλος, ἐγ]ὼ δ' εἴην οὐλαχὺς ὁ πτερόεις . . .

tibi : the anaphora is a sign of the grand style (like the hendiadys
and postponed *circum* of 33); it suits panegyrics just as much as
hymns. Horace himself is content with a single *mihi* (37).

tollit hinnitum : the verb combines the idea of lifting the head
and raising a cry. The onomatopoeia of the noun (cf. Quint. *inst.*
1. 5. 72) is helped by the elision; for the synaloepha cf. 2. 2. 18 f.,
4. 2. 22 f., H. Mörland, *SO* 41, 1966, 108 ff., and for hexameters Virg.
Aen. 6. 602 with Norden's note.

35. **apta quadrigis equa** : mares were particularly prized in the
chariot-race; cf. Virg. *georg.* 1. 59 'Eliadum palmas Epiros equarum',

Pind. *P.* 2. 8, 4. 17, Bacch. 3. 3 with Jebb's note, Soph. *El.* 734. Sicilian horses are still mentioned in the Roman period; cf. Cic. *Verr.* 2. 2. 20, Veg. *mulom.* 3. 6. 4. *quadrigis* suggests the ostentation of the Olympic victor as well as the restless speed that Horace deprecates (*epist.* 1. 11. 28 f. 'navibus atque / quadrigis petimus bene vivere'). *apta* means *idonea* (rather than *iuncta*); cf. Ov. *Pont.* 1. 2. 84.

bis Afro murice tinctae : for double-dye (which implies magnificence) cf. *epod.* 12. 21, Cic. *Att.* 2. 9. 2, Plin. *nat.* 9. 135 'at Tyrius pelagio primum satiatur inmatura viridique cortina, mox permutatur in bucino' . . . 137 'dibapha tunc [in the late Republic] dicebatur quae bis tincta esset, veluti magnifico impendio, qualiter nunc omnes paene commodiores purpurae tinguntur'. For African purple cf. *epist.* 2. 2. 181, Tib. 2. 3. 58, Ov. *fast.* 2. 319 (with Bömer's note), *RE* 2 A. 609 (s.v. Girba) ; for purple in general cf. Mayor on Juv. 1. 27, *RE* 23.2.2000 ff., Pease on Virg. *Aen.* 4. 134, M. Reinhold, *History of Purple as a Status Symbol in Antiquity* (*Collection Latomus* 116), 1970. Grosphus was entitled to the *angustus clavus* of an *eques*, but Horace seems to be suggesting something more than that, possibly a commercial interest in luxury textiles (cf. Cic. *Verr.* 4. 59 for this Sicilian product).

There is something ironic about *murice* no less than about *mugiunt*; Horace is making a delicate cross-reference to line 7 where it was stated that purple cannot buy *otium*. It should further be observed that though *murex* can be used for purple by serious poets, it literally refers to a malodorous shellfish, and so easily takes on a satiric note; cf. Pers. 2. 65 'coxit vitiato murice vellus', Mart. 4. 4. 6 (of a bad smell) 'quod bis murice vellus inquinatum', 9. 62. 1 ff. Similarly Horace's *tinctae*, which could obviously be neutral in tone, is capable of bearing a suggestion of contamination.

37. lanae : wool suggests luxury (cf. Taillardat 319 f. on εὔερος) ; for the grandiose plural cf. 3. 15. 13. But in conjunction with *murice* there seems to be an ironic note (cf. *epist.* 2. 1. 207) ; so more obviously *gnom. Vat.* no. 177 Sternbach (on Diogenes) ὁ αὐτὸς κατανοήσας μειράκιον ἐπὶ τῇ πολυτελείᾳ τῆς χλαμύδος σεμνυνόμενον, Οὐ παύσῃ, μειράκιον, ἐπὶ προβάτου σεμνυνόμενον ἀρετῇ;, Lucian, *Demonax* 41 ἰδὼν δέ τινα τῶν εὐπαρύφων ἐπὶ τῷ πλάτει τῆς πορφύρας μέγα φρονοῦντα, κύψας αὐτοῦ πρὸς τὸ οὖς καὶ τῆς ἐσθῆτος λαβόμενος καὶ δείξας, Τοῦτο μέντοι πρὸ σοῦ πρόβατον ἐφόρει καὶ ἦν πρόβατον, Marc. Aur. 6. 13 (of a purple robe) τρίχια προβατίου αἱματίῳ κόγχης δεδευμένα, 9. 36.

mihi . . . : the last two stanzas are closely bound together not just by the contrast of the emphatic pronouns but by the enjambement at 36 f. (unparalleled in our poem) ; the build-up of Grosphus has overrun the stanza. Horace now reveals his own blessings, which are three in number to match those of Grosphus. His odes sometimes end on a personal note (1. 1. 29 ff., 1. 31. 15 ff., 2. 1. 37 ff., 3. 1. 45 ff.), especially with a contrast between the poet and a grander friend (1. 20. 9 ff., 2. 17. 22 ff., 4. 2. 53 ff.); this feature is already found in Philodemus, *anth. P.* 11. 44 (to Piso).

parva rura : the adjective picks up 13 *parvo* (just as 38 *tenuem* picks up 14 *tenui*); Horace thus delicately suggests that he *vivit bene*. The stable countryside seems to make a contrast with the sea of the first stanza; for praises of rustic simplicity cf. Kier 21 ff. Horace relates these commonplaces to his own Sabinum (*serm.* 2. 6. 1 'modus agri non ita magnus'); what is general in the fourth stanza is particular in the tenth.

38. spiritum : words for breath can be applied to the sound of a wind-instrument (2. 13. 24 n.), to the emanation of poetry (Hermesianax 7. 36 Powell), to the voice of the Muse (Pind. *O.* 13. 22 Μοῖσ' ἀδύπνοος), or as here of the poet himself; cf. Alcaeus, *anth. P.* 7. 55. 5 (on Hesiod) τοίην γὰρ καὶ γῆρυν ἀπέπνεεν, Dioscorides, ibid. 7. 407. 3 (on Sappho and the Muses) ἴσα πνειοῦσαν ἐκείναις. The grandiose *spiritus* (πνεῦμα) normally suggests something inflated and inspired; cf. 4. 6. 29 'spiritum Phoebus mihi, Phoebus artem' (the conventional contrast between *ingenium* and *ars*), Virg. *ecl.* 4. 54, Prop. 3. 17. 40 'qualis Pindarico spiritus ore tonat', Petron. 83. 8 'poeta sum et ut spero non humillimi spiritus', Longin. 8. 4, Philostr. *vit. soph.* 492 (on Gorgias) ὁρμῆς τε γὰρ τοῖς σοφισταῖς ἦρξε . . . καὶ πνεύματος. In our passage the idea of inspiration is supported by *Camenae* but undercut by *tenuem* (E. R. Schwinge, *Philologus* 107, 1963, 95 f.): the Muse may breathe on Horace (cf. Virg. *Aen.* 9. 525 'aspirate canenti'), but he does not claim to be *plenus dea*.

Graiae . . . Camenae : Latin poetry in the classical Greek manner is contrasted with the pretentious African purple; the poetical *Graiae* is naturally preferred to *Graecae* in such a context. The Camenae had been chosen as patrons by Livius Andronicus and Naevius, whereas the Muses were Ennian (O. Skutsch, *CQ* 38, 1944, 79 ff. = *Studia Enniana*, 1968, pp. 18 ff., J. H. Waszink, *C & M* 17, 1956, 139 ff., Suerbaum 347 ff.). The paradoxical collocation with *Graiae* underlines the fusion of elements in Horace's lyrics; cf. vol. i, p. 3 (add 4. 8. 20 'Calabrae Pierides' of Ennius).

tenuem : the adjective balances 37 *parva*. Breath is literally insubstantial compared with the grossness of material riches, while metaphorical *tenuis* might be modestly used of a speaker's voice. Yet rarefied air also goes with intellectual subtlety (cf. *epist.* 2. 1. 241 ff., Ar. *nub.* 230, Onians 78 n. 2); in particular Horace is claiming the λεπτότης of the Callimacheans (1. 6. 9 n., *laus Pis.* 242 'Ausoniamque chelyn gracilis patefecit Horati', M. Campbell, *Hermes* 102, 1974, 44 ff.). Moreover *spiritum tenuem* endorses 14 *mensa tenui*; Horace thus connects his life-style with his poetic style (H. J. Mette, *MH* 18, 1961, 136 ff. = Oppermann 220 ff., Syndikus 1. 454, Bramble 156 ff.).

39. Parca non mendax : in this Callimachean context (cf. above on 34 *mugiunt*, 38 *tenuem*) Horace must be thinking of fr. 1. 37 f. Μοῦσαι γὰρ ὅσους ἴδον ὄθματι παῖδας / μὴ λοξῷ πολίους οὐκ ἀπέθεντο φίλους (cf. 4. 3. 1 ff.). But he goes one better than his model by combining once again references to his poetry and his life: his fairy godmother is not just the Muse but the Fate herself. *non mendax* would naturally apply to the Fate's utterances (*carm. saec.* 25 'veraces', Pers. 5. 48 'tenax veri'), but here it refers to her actions; cf. Pind. *N.* 4. 41 ff. ἐμοὶ δ' ὁποίαν ἀρετὰν / ἔδωκε Πότμος ἄναξ, / εὖ οἶδ' ὅτι χρόνος ἕρπων πεπρωμέναν τελέσει. The litotes of *non mendax* is modest ; so too the idea that Horace owes his felicity to fate rather than merit. *Parca* suggests 'sparing' and seems to be in formal tension with *non mendax* (which implies openhandedness) ; *malignum*, with its hint of meanness, provides another correspondence.

malignum spernere volgas : Horace's *parva rura* have given him a material *otium* that allows him to live as independently as the great landowner. More important he is spiritually tranquil, and can disregard the trumpeting of cows and men ; cf. Epicurus, fr. 187 οὐδέποτε ὠρέχθην τοῖς πολλοῖς ἀρέσκειν, Lucr. 5. 1127 ff., Oltramare 265. In the present context, where he is linking his life with his poetry, there must also be a Callimachean disdain for popular taste and criticism (1. 1. 32 n., 2. 20. 4 n.) ; the concluding phrase is couched in the form of a social judgement, but in reality it refers to philosophy and literature.

17. CVR ME QVERELLIS

[F. Boll, *Kleine Schriften zur Sternkunde des Altertums*, 1950, pp. 115 ff. (= *Sokrates* 5, 1917, 1 ff. = Oppermann 1 ff.) ; A. Bouché-Leclercq, *L'Astrologie grecque*, 1889 ; Cairns 73 ff., 222 ff. ; D. R. Dicks, *Hermes* 91, 1963, 70 ff. ; Fraenkel 216 ff. ; Housman 3. 905 ff. (= *CQ* 9, 1915, 31 ff.) ; H. Mörland, *SO* 40, 1965, 75 ff. ; F. Olivier, *Mélanges Charles Gilliard*, 1944, pp. 24 ff. (= *Essais*, 1963, pp. 267 ff.) ; Th. Plüss, *ZG* 65, 1911, 549 ff.]

1–4. Your anxiety is groundless, Maecenas; the fates do not wish you to predecease me, nor do I. 5–16. But if you are snatched away first, I am sworn to follow, and shall not be torn from my other half by the monsters of the underworld. 17–30. No matter what the destructive part

*of my horoscope, our stars are marvellously sympathetic. You were
snatched from death by Jupiter, to the applause of the Roman people:
I should have been brained by a tree-trunk but for Faunus, the
protector of Mercury's men.* 30–2. *It is your part to make grandiose
thank-offerings: I shall sacrifice a modest lamb.*

The background to this poem presents a number of problems.
Horace implies that Maecenas recovered from illness at the same
time that he himself escaped from a falling tree: *pace* Mörland, loc.
cit., this is the only thing that explains the astrological sympathy
of the two men's stars (21 f.) and the fact that neither has yet made
his thank-offering (30 ff.). The celebration of Maecenas's recovery is
also mentioned in 1. 20 (apparently written some years after our
ode), Horace's misadventure in 2. 13 and 3. 8 (for the chronology see
above, p. 201). At first sight it seems puzzling that in 1. 20 the poet
is silent about his own escape and in 3. 8 about Maecenas's, even
though that ode is addressed to him (cf. E. Ensor, *CR* 16, 1902, 209 ff.,
Mörland, loc. cit.). But Horace no doubt exaggerates the temporal
coincidence to suit the astrological fancies of the present poem;
elsewhere he can deal with either of the events in isolation without
feeling bound to mention the other.

Illness had made a subject for poetry since Euripides's *Hippolytus*
and Callimachus's story of Acontius and Cydippe (fr. 75, cf. Aristaenetus, *epist.* 1. 10); the theme was taken over by the Roman
love-poets (Tib. 1. 5. 9 ff. with K. F. Smith's note, 3. 10, Prop. 2. 28,
Ov. *am.* 2. 13, *ars* 2. 315 ff., *epist.* 20 and 21, J. C. Yardley, *Phoenix* 27,
1973, 283 ff.), and later Greek novelists and rhetoricians found in it
welcome opportunities for sentiment (Himerius, *orat.* 45 Λαλιὰ εἰς
τὸ ὑγιαίνειν τὸν ἑταῖρον). When Horace calls Maecenas part of his soul
and describes his resolve to share his death, some attention should
be paid to the literary proprieties; cf. Prop. 2. 28. 41 f. 'si non unius,
quaeso, miserere duorum; / vivam si vivet, si cadet illa cadam',
[Tib.] 3. 10. 19 f. 'Phoebe fave; laus magna tibi tribuetur in uno / corpore servato restituisse duos', Ov. *am.* 2. 13. 15 'in una parce duobus',
epist. 20. 233 f., Himerius 45. 2 μετεῖχον γάρ, ὦ φίλοι, τοῦ πάθους καὶ
πρὸς τὴν νόσον ἐμεριζόμην τῷ πόθῳ ... Also important for our poem
is the congratulatory address on a public man's recovery (on the
prerequisite prayers cf. *RE* 8 A. 266 f., Weinstock 219); no prose
specimen has survived of what must have been a common type, but
Statius's *Soteria* to Rutilius Gallicus (*silv.* 1. 4) provides an effusive
poetical substitute. In a similar spirit to Horace he refers to the
applause of the people (13 f. 'nosterque ex ordine collis / confremat'),
expresses his gratitude to the gods (1 f.), and contrasts his humble
thank-offering with the sacrifice of bulls (127 ff.):

> qua nunc tibi pauper acerra
> digna litem ? nec si vacuet Mevania valles
> aut praestent niveos Clitumna novalia tauros
> sufficiam. sed saepe deis hos inter honores
> caespes et exiguo placuerunt farra salino.

Our poem should be seen in part as an original formulation of the *soteria* (Cairns, locc. citt., citing Dr. A. Hardie) ; this type of thanksgiving was religious in origin (cf. *RE* 3 A. 1221 ff. for the relevant festivals), but later tended to eulogize not the god (cf. Liban. *orat.* 5) but the man. Horace adds a new dimension to the situation by linking Maecenas's recovery with his own escape, and he remoulds the literary form by starting with his sympathetic friendship and only proceeding at the end of the poem to the theme of deliverance.

He achieves his aim by an ingenious use of the topical science of astrology (1. 11. 2 n.) ; for technical colouring see the notes on 17 *adspicit*, 18 *pars violentior*, 19 *natalis horae, tyrannus*, 20 *Hesperiae . . . undae*, 22 *consentit astrum*, 23 *tutela*, 29 *Mercurialium*. Yet he aims at general effects rather than professional precision ; one may compare the rodomontade of Horos in Propertius 4. 1. It is clear that Horace did not himself take astrology seriously (cf. 1. 11. 1 f.) ; if he had known his own horoscope he would not have offered us three alternatives (17 ff.) with such indifference. On the other hand, in view of his skill elsewhere in evoking an addressee's ethos, it is likely that Maecenas was interested in the subject and knew his own horoscope ; such a blend of erudition and fantasy would suit the modish Etruscan (note perhaps also the grandiloquent astronomy at 3. 29. 17 ff., Virg. *georg.* 1. 5 ff.), and though he had some Epicurean propensities (cf. 3. 29. 13 ff., 32 ff.), he does not seem to have been a committed rationalist (J.-M. André, *Mécène: Essai de biographie spirituelle*, 1967, pp. 15 ff.). Yet there is no need to exaggerate the strength of his devotion to astrology ; Horace's affected magniloquence of manner together with his insouciance about the actual details suggests that badinage on the subject was not unacceptable.

If interpreted with discretion the ode may reveal a little more about Maecenas's temperament (André, op. cit., pp. 33 ff.) as well as his friendship with Horace. We hear elsewhere that he suffered from *perpetua febris* (Plin. *nat.* 7. 172, cf. 22 *impio Saturno* n.), and that his insomnia could be relieved only by music and waterfalls (Sen. *dial.* 1. 3. 10) ; in an obscure prose fragment he contemplated his own obsequies (Quint. 9. 4. 28), and in an admittedly not over-serious poem he prayed for life under whatever physical handicaps (*carm.* fr. 4 = Sen. *epist.* 101. 11 'debilem facito manu, debilem pede coxo . . .'). Our ode tends to confirm his hypochondria even in the days of his power ; though there is a conventional element in his *querellae*

(1 n.), the coherence with the later portrait cannot be entirely explained away. Horace plays round his patron's emotions with deft sensitivity (cf. Pers. 1. 116 f.); he professes to share his anxieties in the manner of *consolatio* (vol. i, pp. 280 f.), reminds him of the ovation that set the seal on his recovery, by recounting his own escape suggests that Maecenas's danger is also over, and recalls him at the end from his fiery Etruscan demonology (13 n.) and his even more terrifying astrological dynamics to the reassuring and life-giving ritual of a modest country sacrifice (32 'humilem... agnam'). But though the ode seems to show an unusually sympathetic relationship, it has been seen that such demonstrations were almost *de rigueur* in the *soteria*. The impassioned declarations of loyalty (13 ff.) show a conscious extravagance that is not always recognized; and though Horace did not long survive Maecenas, he was too sensible to die of a broken heart. The tone of the poem is subtler than is allowed by Romantic scholars, and the whimsical contrast between Jove and Faunus (22–30) is a warning not to take the rest too solemnly. If Horace's friendship with Maecenas was less intense than is sometimes supposed, that does not make it less creditable. The poet was not afraid to overplay his genuine esteem, and the patron accepted the semi-serious irony without misunderstanding.

Metre: Alcaic.

1. **cur** ... : a reproach rather than a genuine question; cf. 1. 8. 2 f. 'Sybarin cur properes amando / perdere'. But though Maecenas seems to have been a hypochondriac (see above), we do not need to believe that he literally distressed Horace in this way (cf. Cairns 223 f.). Ancient writers often suggest that their work has been sparked off by some observation of the recipient; cf. 3. 8. 3 'miraris', *epod.* 14. 1 ff. (see below), *epist.* 1. 1. 2 f., Catull. 7. 1 f. 'quaeris quot mihi basiationes ...', Prop. 1. 22. 1 f., 2. 1. 1, 2. 31. 1, 3. 11. 1, 3. 13. 1, 3. 19. 1 'obicitur totiens a te mihi nostra libido', W. Abel, *Die Anredeform bei den römischen Elegikern*, Diss. Berlin, 1930, pp. 31 ff., A. Ramminger, *Motivgeschichtliche Studien zu Catulls Basiagedichten*, Diss. Tübingen, 1937, pp. 7 ff., A. N. Sherwin-White, *The Letters of Pliny*, 1966, pp. 6 f.

exanimas : cf. Cic. *Mil.* 93 'me quidem, iudices, exanimant et interimunt hae voces Milonis quas audio adsidue'. For similar protests cf. *epod.* 14. 5 'occidis saepe rogando' (see Grassmann 128), Plaut. *Men.* 922 'occidis fabulans', Ter. *Andr.* 660 'quor me enicas?', Eur. *Hipp.* 1064 οἴμοι, τὸ σεμνὸν ὥς μ' ἀποκτενεῖ τὸ σόν, Menander, *Sam.* 528. But in our passage *exanimas* also points forward to 5 f. 'partem animae ...'; there Horace suggests that the loss of Maecenas would literally be the death of him.

2. nec dis amicum est nec mihi : the adjective is a poeticism; cf. Hom. *Il.* 2. 116 οὕτω που Διὶ μέλλει ὑπερμενέϊ φίλον εἶναι, *Od.* 13. 145 ἔρξον ὅπως ἐθέλεις καί τοι φίλον ἔπλετο θυμῷ. *nec mihi* produces an unexpected climax; *amicum* is now seen to be warmer than the Homeric φίλον. *mihi* (here emphatic) is pointedly juxtaposed with *te* (cf. 1 *me... tuis*) ; the two names are further intertwined at 3 *Maecenas mearum*, where the possessive gains emphasis from the hyperbaton.

3. obire : a solemn but prosaic word (2. 20. 7 n.) that suits the theme of death as a journey (10 ff.). As it can be applied to the setting of heavenly bodies it may even provide a lead-in to the astronomical tone of the later stanzas.

4. grande decus : for similar phrases applied to patrons cf. 1. 1. 2 n., Firm. *math.* prooem. 1 'Mavorti decus nostrum'. The noun has sacral associations (K. Eckert, *WS* 74, 1961, 77 ff.); so also the grandiloquent apposition (Norden, *Agnostos Theos*, pp. 173). For the collocation with *columen* (corresponding to 1. 1. 2 *praesidium*) cf. Auson. 418. 56, Sidon. *epist.* 8. 5. 1, *carm.* 23. 2, 23. 70 f. (no doubt all influenced by our passage).

columenque : the horizontal ridge-pole that supported the roof, hence the person who was the 'key-stone' or 'corner-stone' of his group; cf. Plaut. *Epid.* 189 (obviously grandiloquent) 'senati qui columen cluent', F. Leo, *Ausgewählte Kl. Schr.* 1. 29, E. Vetter, *Glotta* 2, 1910, 248 ff., E. Fantham, *Comparative Studies in Republican Latin Imagery*, 1972, pp. 45 f. *columen* was associated with *columna* 'a pillar', which is used much less commonly in a similar metaphor; cf. 1. 35. 14 n., Lucil. 580 'Lucili columella hic situs Metrophanes'. For similar expressions in ancient and modern Greek cf. also Alexiou 193 ff.

5. a : the regretful interjection has an emotional tone rare in Horace; cf. 1. 27. 18 'a miser', Virg. *ecl.* 6. 47, 10. 47 ff. In our passage the poet seems to be pulling himself up, as if he had suddenly realized that Maecenas's fears might be justified; cf. *epod.* 5. 71, Ter. *heaut.* 94 'habeo. ah quid dixi? habere me? immo habui, Chremes' (for similar nuances see P. Richter in W. Studemund, *Studien* 1, 1873, pp. 399 f.), Pers. 1. 8 'nam Romae quis non—a, si fas dicere'.

partem animae : cf. 1. 3. 8 'animae dimidium meae' with bibliography ad loc.; add *anth. Lat.* 445. 4 ff. (= [Sen.] *epig.* 53. 4 ff. Prato) 'nunc pars optima me mei reliquit, / Crispus, praesidium meum, voluptas, / . . . consumptus male debilisque vivam : / plus quam dimidium mei recessit', Aug. *conf.* 4. 6. 11 'nam ego sensi animam meam et animam illius unam fuisse animam in duobus corporibus, et ideo mihi horrori erat vita, quia nolebam dimidius vivere, et ideo forte mori metuebam, ne totus ille moreretur quem multum amaveram', *gnom. Vat.* ed. Sternbach 137 and 296, Otto, *Nachträge*, pp. 133 f. For the use of *pars*, which suggests a substantial share, cf. Luck on Ov. *trist.* 1. 2. 43 f.; μέρος does not seem to be found in the Greek parallels. In the next line Horace gives new life to the trite expression by pretending to take it literally.

6. maturior vis : *maturior* means 'earlier than in my case' rather than 'premature' or 'somewhat early' (in spite of 1. 2. 48 'ocior aura') ; a comparison between the two men suits the mood of the preceding lines (2 n.). As the euphemistic adjective suggests ripeness, there seems to be an oxymoron in its use with *vis*; contrast Milton, *Lycidas* 4 f. 'And with forc't fingers rude Shatter your leaves before the mellowing year'. For *vis rapit* cf. 2. 13. 20 n.; the present tense actualizes the alarming possibility.

alteram : the MSS. read nominative *altera*; for *moror* 'I linger' cf. 2. 20. 3 n., Pease on Virg. *Aen.* 4. 325, *carm. epig.* 493. 3 'amissa est coniunx, cur ego et ipse moror?' Yet it is clumsy and complicated for Horace to identify himself so explicitly with one part of his own soul. Burmann (on Val. Fl. 6. 733) proposed *alteram*, a conjecture that has received insufficient attention ; he is strongly supported by Porph. 'partem quae apud me est non retinebo', ps.-Acro 'hic autem dicit sine dubio alteram partem non retinendam una pereunte', Sen. *Herc. f.* 1258 f. 'cur animam in ista luce detineam amplius / morerque nihil est' (the balance of the sentence requires that *morer* should be transitive). *non moror* has sometimes the dismissive tone of 'I'm not keeping you' ; hence the colloquial *nil moror* 'I don't care about'.

It is conventional for friends and lovers to maintain a lack of interest in their own survival compared with that of the other party. Cf. *epod.* 1. 5 f. 'quid nos, quibus te vita si superstite / iucunda, si contra, gravis', Plaut. *merc.* 472 f. 'certumst, ibo ad medicum atque ibi me toxico morti dabo, / quando id mi adimitur qua caussa vitam cupio vivere', Lucan 5. 775, Otto 374 f. with *Nachträge*, pp. 227 f., Lattimore 203 ff. For the motif *vivam si vivet* cf. above, p. 272, F. Olivier, *Essais*, 1963, pp. 155 ff.

7. nec carus aeque : understand *cuiquam* (cf. Porph. 'nec carus, inquit, alii futurus sicuti tibi sum'). Editors generally understand *mihi* ; but that pronoun is too particularizing to be left unexpressed, and the idea of self-love is irrelevant to the context. *aeque* means 'as much as before' ; for the ellipse cf. *Thes.l.L.* 1. 1044. 72 ff.

nec superstes integer : 'it will not be my whole self that will outlive you' ; *integer* ('unimpaired') continues the metaphor of 5 *partem animae* (cf. the parallels there cited). Horace turns from others' attitudes (*carus*) to his own psychological condition.

8. ille dies : the day of death; cf. Prop. 2. 20. 18 'ambos una fides auferet, una dies' (with Enk's note), *Thes.l.L.* 5. 1. 1032. 32 ff. For other instances of the day as agent cf. Headlam on Herodas 5. 22.

utramque ducet ruinam : 'will drag down both of us' (rather than 'will bring our dissolution with it'); cf. Sen. *Herc. O.* 1629 f. '(quercus) cadens latam sui / duxit ruinam', Virg. *Aen.* 2. 465 f. 'ea lapsa repente ruinam / cum sonitu trahit', 9. 712 f. (in every case the enjambement reinforces the sense). *ruinam* continues the metaphor of *columen*; *ducet* suggests that there is a chain reaction when the support is withdrawn (for metaphorical *ruinae* cf. D. West, *The Imagery and Poetry of Lucretius*, 1969, pp. 64 ff.). *utramque* is used by the common poetical hypallage for *utriusque*.

10. sacramentum : after the despondency of the second stanza Horace shows new resolution, and at the same time justifies his assurance that Maecenas will not predecease him (2). The *sacramentum* is the soldier's oath to his commander; in 32 B.C. a similar oath was taken throughout Italy by the civilian supporters of Octavian (A. von Premerstein, *Vom Werden und Wesen des Prinzipäts*, *ABAW* N.F. 15, 1937, 40 ff., P. Herrmann, *Der römische Kaisereid*, *Hypomnemata* 20, 1969, pp. 78 ff., Weinstock 223 ff. and *MDAI(A)* 77, 1962, 306 ff.). For *sacramentum dicere* cf. Caes. *civ.* 1. 23. 5, 2. 28. 2 ; for Horace's metaphor cf. Cic. *Att.* 9. 10. 2 'quod non . . . Pompeium tamquam unus manipularis secutus sim', Petron. 80. 4 'ego mori debeo qui amicitiae sacramentum delevi'.

As an alternative explanation F. Olivier, op. cit. [p. 271], pointed to the episode in 27 B.C. when the tribune Apudius swore to share Augustus's death (Dio 53. 20); for similar acts of devotion by Gauls and Spaniards cf. Caes. *Gall.* 3. 22. 1 ff., Sall. *hist.* 1. 125, Nic. Dam. *FGrH* 90 F 80, Val. Max. 2. 6. 11, Plut. *Sert.* 14. 4–5, Premerstein, op. cit., p. 54. Olivier argued that the ordinary military oath did not oblige a soldier to share his commander's death; but surely Horace is exaggerating for rhetorical purposes the requirements of the *sacramentum*. In particular he is extending the topic of shared journeys (2. 6. 1 n.) to apply to the underworld (cf. Dom. Mars. *carm.* fr. 7. 1 'Vergilio comitem . . . Tibulle' with M. J. McGann, *Latomus* 29, 1970, 779 f., *Thes.l.L.* 3. 1774. 57 ff.); perhaps he is recalling the joint expedition of Theseus and Pirithous. One may compare especially *epod.* 1. 11 ff. 'te vel per Alpium iuga / inhospitalem et Caucasum / vel Occidentis usque ad ultimum sinum / forti sequemur pectore'; as this poem belongs to the time of Actium it is likely to have been coloured by the *coniuratio Italiae* of 32 B.C. (cf. E. Wistrand 305 ff. = *Horace's Ninth Epode*, 1958, pp. 17 ff.).

ibimus ibimus : for the heroic tone cf. 1. 7. 26 'ibimus, o socii

comitesque'; for the emotional *geminatio* cf. 2. 14. 1 n. The plural
refers to Horace and Maecenas; though the future suggests the
language of a *sacramentum* (see also next note), a real soldier would
have said *ibo* in the singular. But Horace is combining the ideas of
equality and deference (cf. *praecedes*) to suit his ambivalent relationship with his patron. Some refer the future only to Horace (for the
change of number cf. Tib. 2. 4. 5 'seu quid merui seu nil peccavimus') ;
but it is unreasonable to regard *comites parati* as singular in sense.
Others refer to the collective oath of a *coniuratio* (cf. Serv. *Aen.* 8. 1),
but Horace should not emphasize that his relationship with Maecenas
is shared by others.

At first sight the free-will implied in *ibimus* seems at variance
with the predestination of so much of the poem. But a Stoic at any
rate would have seen no inconsistency; cf. Cleanthes, fr. 2 Powell
(= *SVF* 1. 527) ἄγου δέ μ᾽ ὦ Ζεῦ καὶ σύ γ᾽ ἡ πεπρωμένη / ὅποι ποθ᾽
ὑμῖν εἰμὶ διατεταγμένος, / ὡς ἕψομαί γ᾽ ἄοκνος· ἢν δὲ μὴ θέλω / κακὸς
γενόμενος οὐδὲν ἧττον ἕψομαι, Virg. *Aen.* 8. 133 'fatis egere volentem',
Sen. *epist.* 107. 11 (after translating Cleanthes) 'ducunt volentem fata,
nolentem trahunt'.

11. utcumque praecedes : the conjunction means 'whensoever' (1.
17. 10, H.–Sz. 635) ; this is a variation of the indefinite 'wherever'
common in oaths of this kind. Elsewhere in Horace the word implies
'on every occasion when', but here he is talking only of the journey
of death. *praecedes* also reflects the formulae of oaths and similar
declarations of loyalty; cf. *epist.* 1. 3. 27 'quo te caelestis sapientia
duceret, ires', Hdt. 6. 74. 1 ἄλλους τε ὅρκους προσάγων σφι ἡ μὲν
ἕψεσθαί σφεας αὐτῷ τῇ ἂν ἐξηγῆται, Dion. Hal. *ant. Rom.* 10. 18. 2,
11. 43. 2, Sen. *dial.* 8. 1. 5, Headlam on Herodas 5. 43.

supremum carpere iter : cf. Soph. *Ant.* 807 f. τὰν νεάταν ὁδὸν /
στείχουσαν, Eur. *Alc.* 610, Simmias, *anth. P.* 7. 203. 4, Auson. 212. 16.
For the *via leti* cf. 1. 28. 16 n. *carpere* suggests plodding persistence ;
cf. Lejay on *serm.* 1. 5. 95, *Thes.l.L.* 3. 493. 74 ff.

13. Chimaerae : here a monster of the underworld (cf. Virg. *Aen.*
6. 288, Lucian, *dial. mort.* 24 (30). 1, *nec.* 14) ; for similar hazards in the
path cf. also Ar. *ran.* 143 f., 288 ff. In this hyperbolical stanza Horace
is evoking implausible fantasies: the Chimaera was proverbially
chimerical (Lucr. 2. 705 ff., Pease on Cic. *nat. deor.* 1. 108). It had a
significant place in Etruscan art (W. L. Brown, *The Etruscan Lion*,
1960, see index) ; Horace seems to be teasing his patron for his an-
cestral superstitions. One may note in particular the unforgettable
bronze from Arezzo, Maecenas's home town (could it have been conspicuous there in antiquity?) ; cf. *CAH*, plates, vol. i. 336 f., Brown,
op. cit., pp. 155 ff., L. Banti, *Etruscan Cities and their Culture*, 1973,

pp. 272 f. and pl. 85 b (on p. 173 she points out that Arezzo was a centre of metal-work in the third century B.C.).

igneae refers to the Chimaera's fiery breath (4. 2. 16, Hom. *Il.* 6. 182, Hes. *th.* 319, Pind. *O.* 13. 90, Lucr. loc. cit., Virg. *Aen.* 7. 786). The two elements of air and fire are pointedly juxtaposed; cf. Enn. *ann.* 522 (on Paluda) 'cui par imber et ignis, spiritus et gravis terra'.

14. nec si resurgat : for 'Hundred-Handers' in the underworld cf. West on Hes. *th.* 734–5, Virg. *Aen.* 6. 287 f. 'centumgeminus Briareus . . . / . . . flammisque armata Chimaera'; in view of the collocation one suspects that Horace and Virgil may be drawing on a common source in a lost Greek νέκυια. *si resurgat* cannot refer to a resurrection as the scene is set in Hades; Gyges must be prostrate like the notorious sinners (cf. 3. 4. 73 f., Pind. *P.* 1. 27 f., Claud. *rapt. Pros.* 2. 338 'et Tityos tandem spatiosos erigit artus'). For Horace's boldness cf. Manil. 5. 576 'altera si Gorgo veniat, non territus illa'. The conditional clauses may seem over-cautious, but the ancients sometimes hedged their fancies with such provisos (Aesch. *Ag.* 37 f.); Horace is underlining the remoteness of the contingency (cf. Lucil. 31 'non Carneaden si ipsum Orcus remittat', Sen. *Phaedr.* 121).

Gyges : *gigas* is read by the MSS. here and at 3. 4. 69, by Prisc. *gramm.* 2. 268, 3. 182 (who cites our passage for another purpose), and at Sen. *Herc. O.* 167, 1139, 1168; but this was not a proper name in either Greek or Latin (the oblique cases would be protected by the metre). *gigas* as a common noun deserves more consideration, as by some accounts there was only one Hundred-Hander (Hom. *Il.* 1. 402, West on Hes. *th.* 147); *centimanus gigas* might be combined with *Chimaerae* just as *belua centiceps* with *Eumenidum* (2. 13. 34 ff.). Yet Muretus's *Gyges* is very plausible, as this was actually the name of one of the Hundred-Handers (cf. West on Hes. *th.* 149, citing Herodian 2. 678. 27 L. Γύγης Γύγου καὶ Γύγητος ἐπὶ τοῦ γίγαντος· ὅτε δὲ ἐπὶ τοῦ βασιλέως τῆς Λυδίας λέγεται, σπονδειακόν ἐστι καὶ ἰσοσυλλάβως κλίνεται); in Latin MSS. the form is well attested at Ov. *am.* 2. 1. 12, *fast.* 4. 593, *trist.* 4. 7. 18, Serv. auct. *Aen.* 10. 565 (it was particularly exposed to corruption because of the unfamiliar scansion). In the Latin poets many editors favour *Gyas*, but the name is never applied to the Hundred-Hander except as a variant (West, loc. cit.); admittedly *Gyas* (perhaps connected with γύης) is a big man at Virg. *Aen.* 10. 318 (cf. also 5. 118).

15. divellet : the verb suits the Hundred-Hander better than the remoter Chimaera; for the zeugma cf. 1. 9. 18 ff., 3. 24. 45 ff., 4. 4. 43 f.

16. Iustitiae : for the personification cf. 1. 24. 6 n. Δίκη, as one of the Horae, was a goddess of fate (Roscher 1. 2. 2738 ff.), who was

to be given an astrological significance by the neo-Platonists
(Bouché-Leclercq, op. cit., pp. 601 f.); here *potenti* suits such an
implication. At this point Horace turns back from his personal re-
solves to the scheme of Providence (cf. 2 'nec dis amicum').

placitumque Parcis: the Μοῖραι were sisters of Δίκη (Hes. *th.*
901 ff.); they were associated with birth, and make a natural introduction to the astrology of the next two stanzas. For the formal and
authoritative *sic placitum* cf. Virg. *Aen.* 1. 283 (Jupiter's speech),
1. 33. 10 n. ('sic visum'). The grandiloquence is helped by the alliteration and the position of *-que* (2. 19. 24 n.).

17. seu . . . : 'whether Libra or dire Scorpio influences me as the
more destructive part of my horoscope'. The long and turgid sentence
suits the extravagance of the subject-matter; contrast the simplicity
of the ending (30 ff.).

Libra: for this sign of the zodiac see *RE* 13. 116 ff., Bouché-
Leclercq, op. cit., pp. 141 f., J. Bayet, *Mélanges de littérature latine*,
1967, pp. 377 ff. (= *REL* 17, 1939, 141 ff.).

Scorpios: the sign after Libra, which was often regarded as
Scorpio's *chelae* or *bracchia* (Serv. *georg.* 1. 33, J. Bayet, op. cit.,
pp. 382 ff.); the Greek spelling is common in astrological contexts
(Garrod on Manil. 2. 365). Scorpio was associated with warfare (Manil.
4. 217 ff.) through its lord, Mars, and *formidolosus* may suggest danger
in battle; for the use of the signs (as opposed to the planets) as the
fundamental determinants of the cause of death Professor Pingree
calls our attention to Dorotheus 4. 1. 144–5, Hephaestio 2. 25. 15. In
our passage the adjective also alludes to the frightening qualities
of a real scorpion; for the same ambiguity cf. Manil. 2. 213 'acri
Scorpios ictu', 2. 236 f., 4. 217, Lucan 1. 658 ff. 'tu qui flagrante mina-
cem / Scorpion incendis cauda chelasque peruris, / quid tantum,
Gradive, paras?' See further *RE* 3 A. 588 ff., Bouché-Leclercq, op. cit.,
pp. 142 f., Pease on Cic. *nat. deor.* 2. 113, W. Deonna, *Mercure et le
Scorpion* (*Collection Latomus* 37), 1959, pp. 12 ff.

adspicit: a technical word of astrology, here used in a non-
technical sense. Properly it should refer to the 'aspect' or geometrical
relationship of one sign to another, but here the object is the individual Horace; cf. perhaps Sen. *nat.* 2. 32. 7 'summissiora (sidera)
forsitan propius in nos vim suam dirigunt, et ea quae frequentius
mota aliter nos aliterque prospiciunt' (below in the crux at 8 one
should perhaps read 'aliud nos aliter aspicit' as Dr. H. M. Hine
suggests to us). Kiessling saw in the conjunction of *adspicit* and *horae*
a reference to the technical ὡροσκοπεῖν; the *horoscopos* in the ancient
sense of the word is the sign that observes the hour of birth as it
comes up over the eastern horizon (ὁ τὴν ὥραν σκοπῶν). But in our

passage *adspicit* and *horae* are used in a different way, and any
association with ὡροσκοπεῖν can only be verbal.

18. pars violentior : to be taken predicatively with *adspicit* as referring to all three signs (as the balance of the sentence requires).
Ps.-Acro (not cod. A) and many editors apply the phrase only to
Scorpios; but Scorpio is not the *pars violentior* of all horoscopes, and
Horace disclaims certainty about his own (cf. Boll, op. cit., p. 122).
pars here means that the sign is a part (μόριον) of the total *genitura*
(for which see 19 n.); in technical writers the word represents μοῖρα,
a degree of the zodiac.

violentior describes not simply power (δύναμις) but violent force
(βία); cf. Boll, op. cit., p. 122. Horace seems to be referring to the
part of the *genitura* that determines death. Professor Pingree suggests
that he means the 8th place on the zodiac from the *horoscopos* (counting inclusively); cf. Bouché-Leclercq, op. cit., pp. 280 ff.

19. natalis horae : here the *genitura* or 'horoscope' in the loose
modern sense, i.e. the relevant celestial phenomena at the moment
of birth; cf. perhaps Tac. *ann.* 6. 21. 2 (Thrasyllus and Tiberius) 'in-
terrogatur an suam quoque genitalem horam comperisset, quem tum
annum, qualem diem haberet'. *hora* more normally means the *horoscopos* in the strict ancient sense (17 n.); cf. *Thes.l.L.* 6. 3. 2963. 20 ff.

tyrannus : such personifications are common in astrological contexts; here the note of *formidolosus* and *violentior* is sustained.

20. Hesperiae Capricornus undae : for Capricorn (αἰγόκερως) cf.
RE 3. 1550 f., Bouché-Leclercq, op. cit., pp. 144 ff. The sign had a fish-
tail and was associated with the water; cf. Prop. 4. 1. 86 'lotus in
Hesperia quid Capricornus aqua', Manil. 4. 569 'militiam in ponto
dictat', ps.-Manetho, *apotelesm.* 4. 23 γαίης τε καὶ ὕδατος ἀμφίβιος
θήρ, Bouché-Leclercq, op. cit., p. 144 n. 2. One of the crises of
Horace's life was his escape from shipwreck off Capo Palinuro, presumably in the naval disaster of 36 B.C. (3. 4. 28, cited below). He
seems to have been accompanying his new patron Maecenas at the
time; cf. App. *civ.* 5. 99. 414 (after the disaster Octavian sent Maecenas to Rome), Wistrand 304 f. (= *Horace's Ninth Epode*, 1958,
pp. 16 f.). The episode must have been unforgettable to the partici-
pants, and may be reflected in Virgil's story of Palinurus (*Aen.* 5.
833 ff., 6. 337 ff.); certainly it is very much to Horace's purpose to remind Maecenas of the dangers they had shared and survived.

Signs of the zodiac were sometimes assigned influence over particular areas (Manil. 4. 696 ff. with Housman, vol. iv, pp. xii ff.,
Bouché-Leclercq, op. cit., pp. 328 ff.). By some accounts Capricorn
prevailed in the far west; cf. Manil. 4. 791 ff. 'tu, Capricorne, regis

quidquid sub sole cadente / est positum gelidamque Helicen quod
tangit ab illo, / Hispanas gentes et quot fert Gallia dives' (with
Housman's note). It is true that Italy was under the dominion of
other signs, but by the ambiguous *Hesperiae* (1. 28. 26 n.) Horace
may have deliberately confused the issue.

The stanza as a whole could possibly be connected with 3. 4. 26 ff.,
where Horace talks of the three crises of his life: 'non me Philippis
versa acies retro, / devota non exstinxit arbor, / nec Sicula Palinurus
unda'. As has been seen, Scorpio suits warfare and Capricorn the
sea. The parallelism would be complete if Libra could be linked with
danger from falling objects; it is natural enough by astrological
standards that a balance should have such implications, but positive
evidence is so far lacking.

21. utrumque nostrum : the emphatic *utrumque* (note the long
hyperbaton) underlines once more the two men's community of
interest (cf. 8 f. 'utramque ... ruinam'), and leads in to the contrasting sentences that occupy the rest of the poem. *nostrum* is presumably the neuter of *noster* (for the use of the possessive in astrology
cf. Plin. *nat.* 2. 23 'astroque suo eventus adsignat et nascendi legibus',
carm. epig. 1536. 4 'voluit hoc astrum meum') ; the collocation with
utrumque seems unusual, but Horace may be suggesting that each
sign in some way belongs to both men. Shorey and Tescari regard
nostrum as the genitive plural of *nos* ; but the partitive genitive would
be impossible (contrast *serm.* 2. 1. 29 'nostrum melioris utroque'),
and though non-partitive *nostrum* is occasionally found (K.–S. 1.
598) its use here would be pointlessly confusing. A. Y. Campbell
proposed *utcumque* 'in either event' (used in a different sense in
line 11), but *nostrum astrum* could not then refer to two signs ; the
MSS. are supported by 8 *utramque*, by Porphyrio on 22, and by Pers.
5. 45 *amborum* [22 n.]. One might consider *utrique* as a possessive
dative (with *nostrum* as partitive genitive).

incredibili modo : a strong expression ('miraculously') though a
prosaic one. For the lack of a word-break after *in-* (made easier by
the previous elision) cf. vol. i, p. xli.

22. consentit astrum : in this obscure passage *astrum* seems to refer
to the *horoscopos*, not to the *pars violentior* (though one might expect
the word to pick up *Libra*, etc.), nor yet to the *genitura* as a whole
(an interpretation that gives good sense but is not easy to parallel
satisfactorily). The first explanation is supported by Persius's imitation, 5. 45 ff.: 'non equidem hoc dubites, amborum foedere certo /
consentire dies et ab uno sidere duci. / nostra vel aequali suspendit
tempora Libra / Parca tenax veri, seu nata fidelibus hora / dividit in
Geminos concordia fata duorum, / Saturnumque gravem nostro Iove

frangimus una, / nescio quod certe est quod me tibi temperat astrum'
(see Housman 2. 852 ff. = *CQ* 7, 1913, 18 ff.). In Persius (and he at
any rate must have understood astrology) *sidere* means 'a sign of the
zodiac', and so presumably does his *astrum* (cf. the prototype at *epist.*
2. 2. 187 'scit Genius, natale comes qui temperat astrum'); *ab uno
sidere duci* seems to refer to an identity of *horoscopi* (not of course of
whole *geniturae*; the position of the planets would vary except for
people born at the same time, which was not the case with Persius
and Cornutus). Horace on the other hand says simply that the two
men's signs are in a sympathetic relationship; cf. possibly Manil.
2. 633 ff. 'Scorpios et Cancer fraterna in nomina ducent / ex semet
genitos, nec non et Piscibus orti / concordant illis' with Housman,
vol. ii, p. xxi (however, Horace is referring not to friendship but to
shared crises). Boll, op. cit., connects our stanza with the astrological concept of συναστρία, though the illustrations he cites belong to
a later age.

Iovis: 'a man's natal sign determines his character and pursuits,
but for accidents or escape from accidents he must thank the planets'
(Housman 3. 908, though for exceptions cf. above, 17 n.). Jupiter
was the saviour star *par excellence*; cf. Cic. *rep.* 6. 17 'hominum
generi prosperus et salutaris ille fulgor, qui dicitur Iovis' (with
Macr. *somn.* 1. 19. 20), *div.* 1. 85 (with Pease's note), Prop. 4. 1. 83,
Ov. *Ib.* 211 (with La Penna's note), Firm. *math.* 2. 13. 6 [below, 23 n.],
Bouché-Leclercq, op. cit., pp. 97 f., Housman 3. 909. The use of simple
Iuppiter for the planet (rather than *stella Iovis*) develops with the
growth of astral mysticism (F. Cumont, *AC* 4, 1935, 5 ff., Pease on
Cic. *nat. deor.* 2. 52, *RE* 20. 2. 2031); as Horace is mixing astrology
with conventional religion (cf. 30 ff.), the personification suits his
purpose well.

impio . . . Saturno: the adjective points to the Kronos of legend
who castrated his father and ate his children; the interlacing with
Iovis . . . tutela is pointed. For the hostility of the two planets, which
corresponds to the antagonisms of myth, cf. Pers. 5. 50 [above,
17 n.], *cat. cod. astr.* 5. 3. 101. 2 ὁ Ζεὺς ἀναλύει τὰ ὑπὸ τοῦ Κρόνου δεσμού-
μενα, Housman 3. 909. Saturn was the malefic planet; for literary
references cf. Prop. 4. 1. 84 'et grave Saturni sidus in omne caput',
Ov. *Ib.* 215 f., Lucan 1. 652, *Aetna* 243, Juv. 6. 569 f., Nicarchus,
anth. P. 11. 114. 3 f., Serv. auct. *Aen.* 4. 92 (on *Saturnia* as an epithet
for Juno) 'scit enim Saturni stellam nocendi facultatem habere',
Roscher 2. 1. 1475 f. It is particularly relevant to Maecenas's case
that Saturn caused fevers and other diseases; cf. Ptol. *tetr.* 2. 83
νόσους μακρὰς καὶ φθίσεις καὶ συντήξεις καὶ ὑγρῶν ὀχλήσεις καὶ ῥευματι-
σμοὺς καὶ τεταρταϊκὰς ἐπισημασίας . . . ἐμποιεῖ, *cat. cod. astr.* 7. 215. 28
Κρόνος τὴν κυρείαν τοῦ θανάτου λαβὼν ποιεῖ διὰ νόσων πολυχρονίων ἢ

284 HORACE: ODES II

φθίσεων καὶ ῥευματισμῶν καὶ ῥιγοπυρέτων, Firm. math. 3. 2. 8, 3. 2. 26, 4. 19. 8.

23. tutela : the word is naturally used of a god (Tib. 2. 5. 113), and is particularly suited to Jupiter the protector; cf. ILS 3069 'Iovis tutelae', Firm. math. 2. 13. 6 'detento Iove per quem vitae confertur hominibus salutare praesidium', Roscher 6. 661, 694. tutela is also found in astrological contexts (Manil. 2. 434, 4. 698); though the protectorate in our passage is of a different kind, the word retains a technical colouring. It may also be significant that Horace uses tutela of his patron's protection (epist. 1. 1. 103); Jupiter is to Maecenas as Maecenas is to himself (cf. 1. 12. 50 n.).

refulgens : appropriate to the bright planet; cf. Cic. rep. 6. 17 'ille fulgor qui dicitur Iovis', Macr. somn. 1. 19. 19 'fulget Iovis, rutilat Martis'. The bad effect of Saturn is reversed by Jupiter 'in trine aspect' (i.e. five signs away, counting inclusively); cf. Firm. math. 4. 19. 8 (on Saturn) 'quodsi eum benivolae stellae habentem dominium sic sicut diximus positum bona radiatione conveniant, istas valitudines vel praesidium dei alicuius vel sollers medicina curabit', 6. 29. 8 f. For such radiatio (ἀκτινοβολία) see further Bouché-Leclercq, op. cit., pp. 247 ff.

24. eripuit : earlier in the poem it is Death who snatches (5 rapit), but here it is the deliverer; cf. Hom. Il. 3. 380 ἐξήρπαξε, Tib. 1. 5. 10 'te dicor votis eripuisse meis', Stat. silv. 1. 4. 94. Astrology deals with narrow escapes as well as with death.

volucrisque Fati : the adjective is probably genitive, meaning 'winged'. Fatum is not normally given so picturesque an adjective, but Horace is perhaps alluding to the winged demons of Etruscan mythology; cf. J. D. Beazley, Etruscan Vase-Painting, 1947, pp. 8 f., 133 f. (Alcsti or Alcestis), 166 f. (with pls. 30. 1, 37. 1), R. Herbig, Götter und Dämonen der Etrusker, 1965, p. 22 (on Vanth) with Taf. 42. 1. Death has wings in artistic representations of Memnon and Sarpedon and later of ordinary dead people (Roscher 5. 508 ff.). For other allusions cf. serm. 2. 1. 58 'seu mors atris circumvolat alis', Eur. Alc. 262 πτερωτὸς Ἅιδας (see Dale's note), 843 ἄνακτα τὸν μελάμπεπλον νεκρῶν (μέλανας πτέρυγας ἔχων Σ, μελάμπτερον Musgrave), Peek, GV 632. 4 (= Kaibel, EG 89. 4) Ἅιδης οἱ σκοτίας ἀμφέβαλεν πτέρυγας, Gratt. 348 (of Orcus), Sen. Oed. 165, John Bright, Speech, 23 Feb. 1855 'The angel of death has been abroad throughout the land; you may almost hear the beating of his wings'.

Some take volucris as accusative with alas (thus already ps.-Acro); the meaning would then not be 'winged' (which would be tautological) but 'swift' (cf. 3. 29. 53 f. 'celeris . . . pennas'). This would make a good contrast with tardavit, but is less vivid; if an Etruscan allusion is intended the wings must be emphasized as much as possible.

25. tardavit : Servius comments 'et bene *tardavit* quia necessitas fati impediri potest, non penitus eludi' (*Aen.* 4. 610). For the postponement of destiny cf. 1. 28. 20 n., Pease on Virg. *Aen.* 4. 696, Lucan 6. 607 ff.

cum populus frequens . . . : cf. 1. 20. 3 f. 'datus in theatro / cum tibi plausus' (with note ad loc.); as in that passage Horace concentrates his attention on the demonstration (normally reserved for magistrates) that greeted Maecenas's recovery. It is therefore wrong to emend to *cui* (Lachmann), or to interpret *cum* as a continuative 'whereat' (which suits the end of a straggling period better than a μέν clause). The official *populus* emphasizes the political significance of the demonstration; for *frequens* cf. 1. 35. 14 n.

26. theatris : the plural refers to theatrical performances (the prosaic *spectacula*); cf. *serm.* 1. 10. 39, Prob. *app. gramm.* 4. 201 'inter theatrum et theatra hoc interest quod theatrum moenia ipsa significat, theatra vero ludos scenicos esse demonstrat' (cited by A. Magariños, *Emerita* 22, 1954, 220 f.).

ter crepuit sonum : for 'three claps' cf. 1. 1. 8 n., Prop. 3. 10. 4 'manibus faustos ter crepuere sonos'. *ter* makes alliteration with *theatris* (2. 1. 10 n.), *sonum* a contrast (*theatris* implies seeing).

27. me : for such comparisons between Horace and his addressee, particularly at the end of an ode, cf. 2. 16. 37 n.

cerebro : the word is used informally for the top of the head; cf. Juv. 3. 269 f. 'unde cerebrum / testa ferit', *Thes.l.L.* 3. 860. 71 ff. Yet there may also be a reminder of the gruesome injuries of epic poetry; cf. Hom. *Il.* 8. 85 etc., Virg. *Aen.* 9. 419, 12. 537. Horace describes his accident with the same vigorous humour at 2. 13. 1 ff.

28. sustulerat : 'had carried me off'; yet as *tollere* normally means 'to lift up', there is a verbal contrast with *inlapsus* (cf. 3. 4. 44 'fulmine sustulerit caduco'). The actualizing indicative emphasizes the closeness of Horace's escape (the apodosis comes first, as commonly with this construction); cf. 3. 16. 3 f., K.-S. 2. 403 f., H.-Sz. 328.

nisi : Horace is imitating the 'unless' that introduces divine intervention in Homer (*Il.* 3. 374, 5. 312, 20. 291, etc.). For the sudden diversion of weapons in epic cf. Hom. *Il.* 8. 311, 13. 562 f., 15. 464 f., 20. 438 f., 21. 593 f., Virg. *Aen.* 9. 745 f., 10. 331 f., Sil. 9. 455 f., Claud. *rapt. Pros.* 2. 228 ff. Silius, in his account of the Sardinian campaign of 215, describes how Apollo diverted a weapon from Ennius (12. 406); if the account of the incident went back to Ennius himself (*RE* 3 A. 83), Horace might have recalled it here. Yet the fact that Silius describes Ennius's adventures as *nota parum* suggests that they were his own invention (F. Leo, *Geschichte der röm. Literatur*, 1913, p. 151 n. 1).

Faunus : for Faunus as protector of the Sabinum cf. 1. 17. 2 n.; elsewhere Horace ascribes his escape to the Muses (3. 4. 27) or to Liber (3. 8. 7). The Greek Pan was the son of Hermes, so the Latin Faunus naturally saves a *vir Mercurialis*; the poet whimsically contrasts his own protector with Maecenas's. At this point of the poem Horace is moving to ideas more general than those of astrology (*pace* F. Boll, *Philologus* 69, 1910, 167).

ictum : cf. 3. 8. 8 ' arboris ictu'. The word suggests a directed blow, as if the tree had an evil intent. The idea suits the mock-epic tone (see above on *nisi*).

29. dextra levasset : Faunus 'lightened the blow' in the sense of making it less forceful; cf. Liv. 34. 39. 2 'alii leves admodum ictus erant'. The verb also means 'to raise', so there is a paradoxical point in saying *sustulerat nisi levasset*; there may even be a verbal play on the idea of 'raising by the hand'. There is perhaps also an astrological allusion (as Professor Pingree suggests to us): in ἀκτινοβολία (23 n.) the right aspect was stronger than the left.

Mercurialium : Horace humorously calls himself a *vir Mercurialis* because he is a poet; perhaps he professed a special attachment to the god (vol. i, pp. 127 f.). Properly speaking the *Mercuriales* were a *collegium* that took Mercury for its patron; cf. Cic. *Q.f.* 2. 6(5). 2 'Furium . . . Capitolini et Mercuriales de conlegio eiecerunt', *ILS* 2676 (Augustan) 'mag. colleg. Lupercor. et Capitolinor. et Mercurial. et paganor. Aventin.', *RE* 15. 974, Wissowa 305. Livy connects a guild of corn-merchants with the foundation of the Aventine temple of Mercury (2. 27. 5, *RE* 4. 384). It has been suggested that Horace's father, as a *coactor*, would naturally worship at the Aventine temple (A. Oxé, *WS* 48, 1930, 52 ff.); but though such circumstances might give an ultimate explanation for Horace's devotion to Mercury, they can form no part of the public meaning of the poem.

Horace also seems to be using *Mercurialis* for somebody born under the star of Mercury (the original meaning of the English 'mercurial'); the word represents the Greek Ἑρμαϊκός. Such persons were supposed to be interested in literature; cf. Valens, p. 4. 11 Kroll (= *cat. cod. astr.* 2. 91. 19 ff.) κυρίως δὲ ποιεῖ . . . ῥήτορας φιλοσόφους ἀρχιτέκτονας μουσικούς, Ptol. *tetr.* 4. 178, Firm. *math.* 3. 7. 4 'si vero in diurna genitura sic fuerit inventus, facit philologos aut laboriosarum litterarum peritos', 4. 19. 24. Horace seems to have been unaware of his own horoscope (17 ff.), but an astrological allusion (here humorous) can hardly be denied; see further F. Boll, *Philologus* 69, 1910, 164 ff., Wissowa 306.

30. custos virorum : Pan was normally the guardian of flocks (1. 17. 3 n.). *virorum* adds a touch of mock-solemnity (cf. 3. 1. 22).

reddere victimas : the noun suggests the cattle appropriate to Jupiter (whereas *hostia* is used of *minores pecudes* like lambs); cf. Plaut. *Pseud.* 329 (Ballio has been compared with Jupiter) 'nolo victumas: agninis me extis placari volo'. For the payment of vows after lucky escapes cf. above, p. 273, Hdt. I. 118. 2 σῶστρα γὰρ τοῦ παιδὸς μέλλω θύειν τοῖσι θεῶν τιμὴ αὕτη προσκεῖται, Tib. I. 5. 10, 3. 10. 23, Prop. 2. 9. 25, 2. 28. 61 f., Ov. *am.* 2. 13. 23 f.

31. aedemque votivam memento : Horace is teasing his patron; for a private citizen to build a temple to Jupiter would be absurdly ostentatious. The pomposity is sustained by the formal *memento* (2. 3. 1 n.).

32. humilem . . . agnam : the lamb suits alike the shepherd's god and the modest worshipper (cf. Tib. I. 1. 22, Ov. *trist.* 1. 10. 43 f.); for the sacrifice of a female animal to the male Faunus cf. 1. 4. 12 n. The contrasted offerings symbolize the life-style of the two men; for this motif cf. 3. 23. 17 ff., 4. 2. 53 ff., Virg. *ecl.* 3. 85 ff., Juv. 12. 3 ff., Headlam on Herodas 4. 16.

18. NON EBVR NEQVE AVREVM

[Commager 79 ff.; W. Kroll, *WS* 37, 1915, 228 f.; C. W. Mendell, *YCIS* 11, 1950, 281 ff.; N. Rudd, *Hermathena* 118, 1974, 99 ff.; H. Womble, *TAPhA* 92, 1961, 537 ff.]

1–8. *My house does not glitter with ivory and gold, marble and purple;* 9–14 *but I have been granted a vein of talent by the gods, and a Sabine estate by my rich patron.* 15–22. *You build a mansion, forgetful of your mortality, and extend your villa into the sea;* 23–8 *you uproot your neighbour's boundary-stones and evict your own clients.* 29–40. *Yet the rich man has no more certain habitation than the underworld; the earth opens impartially to the poor and the sons of kings. Mercury pens in the cunning and the proud, and relieves the poor man whether summoned or not.*

The poem begins with an imitation of Bacchylides (fr. 21) in the manner of the 'mottoes' of the first book (vol. i, p. xii):

> οὐ βοῶν πάρεστι σώματ᾽ οὔτε χρυσός,
> οὔτε πορφύρεοι τάπητες,
> ἀλλὰ θυμὸς εὐμενής,
> Μοῦσά τε γλυκεῖα καὶ Βοιωτίοισιν
> ἐν σκύφοισιν οἶνος ἡδύς.

Horace follows in part the pure trochees of his model, and shows a similar variation in the length of his lines. He proceeds from what he lacks to what he has, again like Bacchylides; he deploys his clauses in a paratactic series (*non* . . . *non* . . . *neque* . . . *nec*), and introduces his list of advantages at line 9 with the conjunction *at* (= ἀλλά). He takes over the reference to gold and purple and ingeniously conflates it with another Bacchylidean line, χρυσῷ δ' ἐλέφαντί τε μαρμαίρουσιν οἶκοι (fr. 20 B. 13). He claims the same combination of goodwill and literary interests, though he expresses himself in modern and Roman terms. And there perhaps the resemblance ends. Bacchylides was inviting the Dioscuri to a banquet (Athen. 11. 500 b), making excuses for the simplicity of his arrangements, and offering something more worth while in compensation (for this theme cf. vol. i, pp. 244 ff.). Horace, on the other hand, is denouncing contemporary materialism, and his ethical commonplaces owe less to the maxims of early Greek poetry than to the prose philosophizing of a later age.

The ψόγος of luxury, originating in major thinkers like Plato and Epicurus, was vulgarized in the *diatribae* of the Hellenistic period. For a later specimen with some resemblance to Horace's poem see Musonius, fr. 19, p. 108 H. (περὶ σκέπης) τί δ' αἱ περίστυλοι αὐλαί; τί δ' αἱ ποικίλαι χρίσεις; τί δ' αἱ χρυσόροφοι στέγαι; τί δ' αἱ πολυτέλειαι τῶν λίθων, τῶν μὲν χάμαι συνηρμοσμένων, τῶν δ' εἰς τοίχους ἐγκειμένων; (for further material cf. Plut. *cup. div.* 523 e–f, Clem. *paed.* 2. 3. 35 ff., 2. 12. 118 ff., van Geytenbeek 111 ff., *RLAC* 3. 1002). Cynic moralizing was extended to verse in the compositions of Cercidas (D. R. Dudley, *A History of Cynicism*, 1937, pp. 74 ff.) ; for his influence on Horace through Philodemus cf. Gigante 123 ff. For a more straightforward denunciation of extravagance cf. Phoenix 6. 9 ff. Powell ἀλλ' οἰκίας μὲν ἐγ λίθου σμαραγδίτου / . . . ἐχούσας καὶ στοὰς τετραστύλους / πολλῶν ταλάντων ἀξίας κατακτῶνται (see Gerhard 117 ff., and for such gnomic poetry in general 228 ff.). But Phoenix is unsophisticated and Cercidas eccentric as well; their dominating interest is moral rather than literary, and this is sufficient to differentiate them from Horace.

The Roman orators were fond of denouncing extravagance, particularly in building (cf. already Cato, cited 2. 15. 11 n.) ; they thus rationalized their mortification at the prosperity of their enemies (cf. Cic. *Sest.* 93 for Gabinius on Lucullus and Cicero on Gabinius). The same themes were taken up by Sallust to explain the loss of the antique national unity (Earl 13 ff., 46 ff.). Similar ideas became part of the mainstream of poetry (Williams 578 ff.), notably in Lucretius, Horace's *Sermones* (cf. Lejay's commentary), and Virgil's *Georgics*; they were particularly suited to Augustan ideology, and provide the subject for several of Horace's odes (2. 15, 3. 1, 3. 24, Kroll, loc. cit.

with *Studien*, pp. 242 ff.). *convicium saeculi* was congenial to the
sardonic Romans (Sen. *contr.* 2. 1, especially Papirius Fabianus at
2. 1. 10, ps.-Quint. *decl. mai.* 13. 2, Vretska on ps.-Sall. *epist.* 1. 8. 1,
Oltramare, *passim*); they were not in the least deterred by their
private riches (Sen. *epist.* 86, 89. 20–21, etc.). The commonplaces about
building were still exploited in late antiquity, sometimes with little
reference to contemporary social conditions; cf. Hier. *epist.* 14. 6
[above, 2. 15. 15 n.], 46. 11 'ubi sunt latae porticus? ubi aurata
laquearia? ubi domus miserorum poenis et damnatorum labore
vestitae? ubi ad instar palatii opibus privatorum extructae basilicae,
ut vile corpusculum hominis pretiosius inambulet . . .?', *in Is.* 8. 24
(24. 284 B Migne) 'tunc domus quarum nunc sunt aurata laquearia,
et pauperibus absque tecto et tugurio frigore morientibus, parietes
earum vestiuntur marmorum crustis, et secti eboris nitore resplen-
dent, remanebunt vacuae', D. S. Wiesen, *St. Jerome as a Satirist*,
1964, pp. 20 ff. Similarly Horace's denunciation of an eviction may be
paralleled in Ambrose's essay on Naboth (below, 26 n.).

Horace sometimes gives immediacy to his moralizing by contrasting his own simplicity with the luxury of his friends (cf. 2. 16, 3. 16,
3. 29, etc.); editors do not observe that though our poem has no
addressee, it seems to some extent to be hinting at Maecenas (the
recipient of the previous ode). When the poet refers to his Sabinum
with the words 'nec potentem amicum / largiora flagito' (12 f.), he
can only be talking of his patron; this means that the *dives* of the
previous sentence is also Maecenas, to whom Horace properly asserts
his *fides* and his literary talent (9 ff.). This makes it easy in retrospect
to associate the opening lines with Maecenas's notorious grandeur:
the Etruscans were traditionally famous for their ivory-work (cf.
also Augustus, *epist. ad Maecen.* fr. 32 M. 'ebur ex Etruria'), Maecenas may have been humorously connected with the Attalids of
Asia Minor (5 n.), he was certainly notorious for the numbers of his
dependants (8 *clientae*, Petron. 71. 12 *Maecenatianus*, RE 14. 1. 207),
indeed line 8 ('trahunt honestae purpuras clientae') only seems to
make sense if it alludes to the gorgeous retinue of an old-style
Etruscan (this is the decisive argument, cf. note ad loc.). In the next
section of the poem (15 ff.) the theme of luxury building fits the
owner of the *turris Maecenatiana* (3. 29. 10, *RE* 14. 1. 216), which already existed in 31 B.C. (*epod.* 9. 3 'alta . . . domo'); though nothing
is directly attested, Maecenas may also have had a *villa maritima*
at Baiae (cf. 3. 1. 33–40). The repeated allusions to death and the
underworld (18, 29 ff., 34 ff.), though easily paralleled in poems of
this kind, suit Maecenas's own morbid obsessions (above, p. 273).
The contrast between poor and rich, which began with Horace and
his patron, is sustained throughout the poem; the reference to the

sons of kings, though natural in such contexts, is particularly applicable to Maecenas (1. 1. 1, 3. 29. 1). Prometheus is set in the underworld (35), just as at 2. 13. 37; without observing the other possible allusions, Kiessling conjectured that this unusual form of the legend was derived from the *Prometheus* of Maecenas. If that is so, the parallel mention of Tantalus, again exactly as in 2. 13. 37, may come from the same source; the Lydian king whose riches brought nothing but torment might have seemed a potent symbol to the Etruscan Maecenas, *Tantali genus* by temperament if not by heredity.

It will immediately be objected that Horace's censure of the *dives* does not suit his patron; in particular the sketch of the treacherous eviction (26 ff.) is offensive if addressed to a landowner. The difficulty is one about social discretion rather than historical truth, for confiscated estates are likely to have contributed significantly to Maecenas's vast wealth. Horace cannot be rebuking his patron, but after all he is not directly addressing him; he exploits the ambiguity of *tu* (17) to shift from the real Maecenas to the conventional plutocrats of *diatribe* (perhaps with an element of affectionate mockery). One might compare *epist.* 1. 1, which is dedicated to Maecenas at the beginning and reverts to him at the end (94 ff., 103 ff.), but in between moves from self-criticism (27 ff.) to clichés on materialism; cf. especially 45 f. 'impiger extremos curris mercator ad Indos, / per mare pauperiem fugiens, per saxa, per ignis'. In our poem Horace's criticisms of luxury may seem nearer the mark, but he must have seen the irony of denouncing the magnificence on which he himself depended; similarly in *serm.* 2. 6 (clearly directed at Maecenas) he sets the town-mouse amid ivory and crimson (102 f.), in *carm.* 3. 1 his comments on the insomnia of the rich and the anxieties of *equites* have a particular application to his patron, in 3. 16. 41 ff. (addressed to Maecenas by name) he contrasts his own modest revenues with the domains of the Lydian Alyattes, surely a friendly thrust at the descendant of Etruscan kings, in 3. 29 he extols the advantages of simplicity in a context that begins with the *turris Maecenatiana*. He says these things not by way of reproach but rather as a kind of *eucharisticon* (cf. Cairns 74 f.), expressing thanks without fulsomeness for benefits received (2. 18. 14 'satis beatus', 3. 1. 47 f., 3. 16. 37 ff., *epod.* 1. 31 ff., *serm.* 2. 6. 1 ff.); similarly in his programmatic first satire his censure of meanness and commendation of contentment have particular force when addressed to his patron.

The date of the ode cannot be proved, but some questions are raised by Virgil's similar eulogy of rustic simplicity (*georg.* 2. 461 ff.):

> si non ingentem foribus domus alta superbis
> mane salutantum totis vomit aedibus undam,
> nec varios inhiant pulchra testudine postis

inlusasque auro vestis Ephyreiaque aera,
alba nec Assyrio fucatur lana veneno
nec casia liquidi corrumpitur usus olivi;
at secura quies et nescia fallere vita,
dives opum variarum, at latis otia fundis ...
non absunt.

There as in our poem we find respectful dependants (a Roman feature) and glistening fittings, as well as an over-all similarity of structure; it is evident that the poet who wrote later must have been familiar with the prior passage. In addition, Virgil and Horace are both indebted to Lucretius 2. 20 ff.:

ergo corpoream ad naturam pauca videmus
esse opus omnino, quae demant cumque dolorem,
delicias quoque uti multas substernere possint.
gratius interdum neque natura ipsa requirit,
si non aurea sunt iuvenum simulacra per aedes
lampadas igniferas manibus retinentia dextris,
lumina nocturnis epulis ut suppeditentur,
nec domus argento fulget auroque renidet,
nec citharae reboant laqueata aurataque templa,
cum tamen inter se prostrati in gramine molli
propter aquae rivum sub ramis arboris altae
non magnis opibus iucunde corpora curant ...

Prima facie Horace derives his *at* from Bacchylides, and in turn influences Virgil, who finds no *at* in Lucretius; but nothing is certain, especially in view of the imbalance and apparent corruption presented by Lucretius's transmitted text. Similarly Horace's mention of Attalus, which seems to be closely integrated with the context (5 n., 6 n.), might have suggested to Virgil 'cloth-of-gold' (464), which was named after this king (Plin. *nat.* 8. 196). It may also be noted that Virgil's *dives opum variarum* (468) looks back to *varios postis* (463), while his *latis otia fundis* are implicitly contrasted with the mere acreage of rich landowners; in the same way Horace's non-material advantages are described in terms appropriate to wealth (9 *fides*, 10 *benigna vena*). In theory this feature could have been borrowed either way, but as Horace seems to be ingeniously alluding to the Bacchylidean θυμὸς εὐμενής (see notes ad loc.) it is perhaps too much to believe that he managed to imitate Virgil at the same time. If Horace has priority, the poem must be assigned to the triumviral period soon after the acquisition of the Sabinum (12 ff.).

Other arguments are inconclusive. The lack of an addressee proves nothing about the date, as the same feature is found in other denunciations of luxury (2. 15, 3. 1, 3. 6, 3. 24, the last written perhaps about 28 B.C.). The ode has affinities with the satires in subject-matter and with the epodes in metre, but much the same could be said of 3. 24 (though there the more lyrical Asclepiads and the political commitment make some difference). The style seems relatively jejune with its paratactic constructions (cf. Bacchylides) and simple antitheses (Syndikus 1. 465); the reader misses the charm and humanity of 1. 31 and 2. 16. Yet even here Horace should not be underestimated; the writing is denser and wittier than might immediately be apparent, the structure turns out to be much more intricate than anything in Bacchylides (29 n.), and behind the commonplaces of *diatribe* and declamation something may still be detected of genuine human relationships.

Metre: Hipponactean, i.e. a trochaic dimeter catalectic alternating with an iambic trimeter catalectic (vol. i, p. xlvi); the combination was used by Alcaeus (Bass. *gramm*. 6. 270. 21 'ab illo tractatum frequenter'), and also by Prudentius in his *epilogus*. The trochees are pure (i.e. the fourth syllable is always short); in this Horace imitates Bacchylides and is imitated in turn by Prudentius (*epil*. 8 'rotatiles trochaeos'). There is only one hiatus after the dimeter (5); there are two in Prudentius (25, 29). The trimeter begins 18 times with an iambus and only once with a spondee, in Prudentius 16 times with an iambus and once with a spondee; Horace again is imitating the lightness of Bacchylides (contrast the even lines of *carm*. 1. 4 where there is one iambus against 9 spondees). The fourth syllable of the trimeter is resolved at 34 *regumque pueris* (see note). The second metron of the trimeter begins 4 times with an iambus (2, 14, 38, 40), 16 times with a spondee; Prudentius has 8 iambi and 9 spondees, *carm*. 1. 4 has no iambi and 10 spondees. There is no attempt to organize the sense in four-line stanzas (there is enjambement after 4, 12, 20, 24, 32, 36); instead we have a structure of 14 +14 +12, an organizing principle attested e.g. in the single triad odes of Pindar.

1. non . . . : ancient discourse often proceeds by combining positive with negative propositions (cf. P. H. Schrijvers, *Horror ac Divina Voluptas*, 1970, pp. 209 ff.). For rejections of luxury with a similar movement cf. 1. 31. 3 ff. (see vol. i, p. 348), 3. 16. 33 ff., *epod*. 1. 25 ff., 2. 49 ff., Archilochus 19. 1 W. οὔ μοι τὰ Γύγεω τοῦ πολυχρύσου μέλει, Bacch. fr. 21 [above, p. 287], Lucr. 2. 24 ff., Virg. *georg*. 2. 461 ff. [above, pp. 290 f.], Maecen. *carm*. fr. 2 Morel 'lucentes, mea vita, nec smaragdos, / beryllos mihi, Flacce, nec nitentes, / nec percandida margarita quaero, / nec quos Thynica lima perpolivit / anellos neque iaspios lapillos' (the name of the author is lost, but for Maecenas's Etruscan interest in jewels cf. Augustus, *epist. ad Maecen*. fr. 32 M., *eleg. in Maecen*. 1. 19; the poem might even be a rejoinder to our

own), Prop. 3. 2. 9 ff. 'quod non Taenariis domus est mihi fulta columnis, / nec camera auratas inter eburna trabes / . . . at Musae comites et carmina cara legenti . . .', Ov. *am.* 1. 3. 7 ff. 'si me non veterum commendant magna parentum / nomina . . . / at Phoebus comitesque novem vitisque repertor / hac faciunt et me qui tibi donat Amor, / et nulli cessura fides . . .' (both elegists are partly influenced by Horace, cf. especially *trabes* and *fides*), Petron. 135. 8, Stat. *silv.* 4. 5. 17 ff.

ebur : for the Bacchylidean prototype cf. p. 288. Ivory was a conventional symbol of regal magnificence, often combined with gold or marble; cf. 1. 31. 6 n., Cato, *or.* fr. 185 M. [above, 2. 15. 11 n.], Enn. *scaen.* 95 f. V. = 90 f. J. [above, 2. 16. 11 n.], *RE* 5. 2356 ff., *Thes.l.L.* 5. 2. 20. 75 ff. It was inlaid in walls and furniture, and perhaps significantly for our passage in ceilings (Prop. 3. 2. 10, Sen. *nat.* 1 praef. 8 'lacunaria ebore fulgentia', *Thy.* 457), but ps.-Acro goes too far with his comment 'pro derivativo ut sit *eburneum*'.

aureum . . . lacunar : for coffered ceilings cf. 2. 16. 11 n.; Horace characteristically introduces a contemporary Roman feature into his Bacchylidean 'motto'. Such ceilings were sometimes decked with gold leaf or ornaments; cf. Austin on Virg. *Aen.* 1. 726, Sen. *epist.* 90. 9 'lacunaria auro gravia', Prud. *perist.* 12. 49 'bratteolas trabibus sublevit'. For the protests of moralists cf. Lucr. 2. 28 [above, p. 291], Philo, *somn.* 2. 8. 55, Sen. *dial.* 12. 10. 7, Plin. *nat.* 33. 57 'laquearia quae nunc et in privatis domibus auro teguntur post Carthaginem eversam primo in Capitolio inaurata sunt censura L. Mummi', Musonius, fr. 19, p. 108 H. [above, p. 288], ps.-Lucian, *cyn.* 9, Mendell, op. cit., pp. 285 ff.

2. mea : emphatic, as is shown by the position; cf. 7 *mihi* (ἐμοί, 'for *me*'), 11 *me*.

renidet : Horace is influenced by Lucr. 2. 27 [above, p. 291]; he is imitated in turn by Arnob. *nat.* 6. 3 'laquearibus aut renideant aureis'. The word suits the reflection on the ceiling of the light from the hanging chandeliers. Verbs of shining are often applied to ivory as well as to gold (cf. Bacch. fr. 20 B. 13 μαρμαίρουσιν); *renidere* is warmer than the Greek original as it implies a smiling welcome (2. 5. 20 n., *epod.* 2. 66 'renidentis lares').

3. trabes : *trabs* properly describes a wooden beam, but the word can be extended by way of metaphor to other materials; Plin. *nat.* 36. 64 applies it to an obelisk. Horace is referring to the stone ἐπι-στύλιον or architrave (the English word is derived from *trabs*) that rests on the capitals of the columns.

Hymettiae : for the grey-blue marble of Hymettus cf. Str. 9. 1. 23, Val. Max. 9. 1. 4, Plin. *nat.* 17. 6, 36. 7 'iam L. Crassum oratorem [cos.

95 B.C.], illum qui primus peregrini marmoris columnas habuit in eodem Palatio, Hymettias tamen nec plures sex aut longiores duodenum pedum, M. Brutus in iurgiis ob id Venerem Palatinam appellaverat', J. B. Ward Perkins in *Enciclopedia dell'arte antica* 4, 1961, 861. Pliny's *tamen* implies that by his time Hymettian marble was relatively modest; even in our passage the climax is marked by the Numidian marble of the columns.

4. premunt columnas : marble columns were another conventional symbol of luxury; cf. 2. 15. 16 n., *epist.* 1. 10. 22, Ar. *nub.* 815 ἀλλ' ἔσθι' ἐλθὼν τοὺς Μεγακλέους κίονας, Prato on [Sen.] *epig.* 51. 1, Blümner 92. The verb emphasizes the crushing load.

ultima : the word naturally suggests that the marble came from deep in the heart of Africa; in fact the quarries were at Simitthus near Ghardimaou in the north-west of modern Tunisia. The import of distant luxuries was conventionally deplored by moralists; cf. Philo, *somn.* 2. 8. 54 τί δὲ Ἀσίαν καὶ Λιβύην καὶ πᾶσαν Εὐρώπην καὶ τὰς νήσους ἐπερχόμεθα, κίονας ἀριστίνδην ἐπιλελεγμένους καὶ ἐπιστυλίδας ἐρευνῶντες;, Sen. *epist.* 114. 9, 115. 8 'ingentium maculae columnarum, sive ex Aegyptiis harenis sive ex Africae solitudinibus advectae', Musonius, fr. 19, p. 108 H., Bramble 110 n. 1. They were esteemed precisely because of their remote origin; cf. Hdt. 3. 106. 1 αἱ δ' ἐσχατιαί κως τῆς οἰκεομένης τὰ κάλλιστα ἔλαχον, R. Gnoli, *Marmora Romana*, 1971, p. 10.

recisas : 'cut away'; 'the only way to obtain a block was to isolate it laboriously from the parent rock by cutting narrow trenches all round it' (J. B. Ward Perkins, *Proceedings of British Academy* 57, 1971, 139, cf. plate 5). The verb suggests the lopping of branches from a tree (Virg. *Aen.* 12. 208); the metaphor of *trabes* is thus sustained.

5. Africa : in conjunction with the stereotyped *ultima* the name primarily suggests the continent rather than the Roman province (3. 16. 31, *serm.* 2. 3. 87). It is true that the quarries of Simitthus belonged to the province between 46 and 30 B.C. and again after 25 (*RE* 1. 714, 17. 2. 1384 ff.), but at the most this gives the word an extra association; one could not use such circumstances to support a pre-Actium dating of the poem (above, p. 291). For Numidian marble (*giallo antico*) cf. Prop. 2. 31. 3 'Poenis . . . columnis', Plin. *nat.* 36. 49 'M. Lepidus [cos. 78 B.C.] . . . primus omnium limina ex Numidico marmore in domo posuit magna reprensione', Stat. *silv.* 1. 5. 36, Juv. 7. 182, *RE* 3 A. 2268 f., J. B. Ward Perkins, *JRS* 41, 1951, 96 f., R. Gnoli, op. cit. [4 n.], pp. 139 ff. and figs. 123–5. The Romans, like Italians of later periods, combined different varieties of variegated marble; cf. Stat. *silv.* 1. 2. 148 f., 1. 5. 36 ff., 2. 2. 85 ff., 4. 2. 26 ff., Mart. 6. 42. 11 ff., Lucian, *Hipp.* 5.

Attali : in 133 B.C. Attalus III of Pergamum left the Roman people his kingdom (D. Magie, *Roman Rule in Asia Minor*, 1950, 2. 780 f.) ; the new territory became *Asia provincia*, so there is a contrast with *Africa* at the beginning of the line (even though that word seems to refer principally to the continent). The episode was important in a discussion of *luxuria* as 133 was one of the many dates that could be assigned to the onset of the decadence.

6. **ignotus heres** : a long-lost cousin, such as might inherit an estate in New Comedy; for the phrase cf. *cod. Just.* 6. 24. 11 'extraneum etiam penitus ignotum heredem quis constituere potest'. There must be a reference to the historical fact that Attalus unexpectedly bequeathed his kingdom to the distant *populus Romanus*; for his lack of relatives cf. Magie, op. cit. 2. 778 f. Porphyrio wrongly comments 'suspicionem dat qua existimemus falso testamento Romanos hanc sibi hereditatem vindicasse' (cf. Sall. *hist.* 4. 69. 8) ; it is equally irrelevant to see a reference to Aristonicus, the pretender to Attalus's throne.

Conceivably there was a sophisticated joke connecting the magnificence of Maecenas with that of the Attalids; their territory included Lydia, the reputed mother-country of the Etruscans (cf. *serm.* 1. 6. 1). Telephus appears on the Great Frieze of Pergamum as the Attalids' ancestor (cf. E. V. Hansen, *The Attalids of Pergamum*[2], 1971, pp. 340 ff., 408 f., 468 f., *RE* 2. 2305 f.) ; by some accounts he was also the father of the Tyrrhenus who migrated to Etruria (Lycophron 1245 ff., Dion. Hal. *ant. Rom.* 1. 28. 1, Roscher 5. 291 and for Etruscan art 5. 306 ff., F. Schachermeyr, *WS* 47, 1929, 154 ff.). Such a piece of antiquarianism would have appealed to Maecenas's Etruscan pride and erudite tastes (3. 8. 4). One may note the reference to *Attalicis condicionibus* in an ode addressed to Maecenas (1. 1. 12).

regiam occupavi : *regiam* balances 2 *domo*. The emphatic *Attali* is to be taken primarily with *regiam* and only secondarily with *heres*. *occupavi* has a semi-legal tinge; such a take-over would be contrary to all reasonable expectation.

7. **Laconicas** : for Laconian purple (from Gythium) cf. Alcman 1. 64 f., Ov. *rem.* 707, *carm.* fr. 5 Morel 'at si contuleris eam Lacaenae' (Housman : *etiam lacernae* codd.), Plin. *nat.* 9. 127 (the best in Europe), 21. 45, Juv. 8. 101, Paus. 3. 21. 6 (second only to Tyre), Clem. *paed.* 2. 10. 115, D'Arcy Thompson, *Fishes*, p. 212, *RE* 23. 2. 2007. The adjective balances 3 *Hymettiae*: Athens and Sparta make a frame round Africa and Asia.

8. **trahunt . . . purpuras** : this is naturally interpreted 'trail purple robes' (Rudd, op. cit., p. 100) ; cf. *ars* 214 f. 'sic priscae motumque et

luxuriem addidit arti / tibicen traxitque vagus per pulpita vestem',
Varro, *Men.* 311 'quod tum erant in Graecia, coma promissa, rasa
barba, pallia trahentes', Ov. *fast.* 1. 409, *epist.* 21. 162, Val. Max. 7. 8.
1, Hom. *Il.* 6. 442 Τρωάδας ἑλκεσιπέπλους, Archippus 45, Ephippus
19. 4 σεμνὸς σεμνῶς χλανίδ᾽ ἕλκων. Commentators are deterred because
such luxury does not seem to suit *honestae . . . clientae*, but if Horace
is alluding to Maecenas's retinue (above, p. 289) a reference to Etruscan magnificence would be appropriate; cf. Posidonius, fr. 53 Edelstein and Kidd (= *FGrH* 87 F 1) παρὰ δὲ Τυρρηνοῖς δὶς τῆς ἡμέρας
τράπεζαι πολυτελεῖς παρασκευάζονται ἄνθινά τε στρωμναὶ καὶ ἐκπώματα
ἀργυρᾶ παντοδαπά, καὶ δούλων πλῆθος εὐπρεπῶν παρέστηκεν ἐσθήσεσιν
πολυτελέσι κεκοσμημένων, Diod. Sic. 5. 40. 3 (clearly also derived from
Posidonius [87 F 119], though he is not actually cited) οἱ μὲν εὐπρεπείᾳ
διαφέροντές εἰσιν, οἱ δ᾽ ἐσθῆσι πολυτελεστέραις ἢ κατὰ δουλικὴν ἀξίαν
κεκόσμηνται. The women of old Etruria, as represented on the tomb-
paintings, wore brightly coloured robes, which if not trailing were
sometimes voluminous (cf. Heurgon 213 ff. with fig. 46). Maecenas
himself was criticized for his loose tunics and exotic cloaks (*eleg. in
Maecen.* 1. 25 f., Sen. *epist.* 92. 35, 114. 4–6, *RE* 14. 1. 214); for his association with purple cf. Juv. 12. 38 f. 'vestem / purpuream teneris
quoque Maecenatibus aptam', perhaps *eleg. in Maecen.* 59 f. (apostro-
phizing Bacchus) 'et tibi securo tunicae fluxere solutae, / te puto purpureas tunc habuisse tuas' (as *solutae* recalls Maecenas's own dress, so
presumably does *purpureas*). It seems likely that he affected the
customs of his ancestors, and that this was misrepresented by his
critics (Heurgon 318 ff.). If some Etruscans kept up their magnificent
retinues till the time of Posidonius or Diodorus, one might reasonably expect Maecenas to follow suit; it is true that Dio speaks of
restrictions on purple in 36 B.C. (49. 16. 1), but he should not be taken
too seriously (Reinhold, op. cit. [2. 16. 35 n.], pp. 46 f.).

Commentators generally assume that Horace is referring to the
manufacture of purple fabrics; already Porphyrio observes 'hoc illo
pertinet quod praetextas togas cum sibi nobiles conficiunt ad spem
magistratuum gerendorum, votum sit uxoribus clientum ad matro-
nam conficientis convenire et purpuram cum ipsa carpere'. But the
toga praetexta of magistrates had only a purple border, so if this line
of thought is to be pursued one would rather look for a reference to
stragula vestis (*RE* 4 A. 2. 2251 ff.); cf. Bacch. loc. cit. πορφύρεοι
τάπητες (Horace's fourth instance of luxury, like his first, is clearly
influenced by his Greek model), 3. 29. 15 (to Maecenas) 'sine aulaeis et
ostro'. For the contribution by dependants of luxury textiles cf. Cic.
Verr. 4. 58–9 'nulla domus in Sicilia locuples fuit ubi iste non tex-
trinum instituerit. mulier est Segestana perdives et nobilis, Lamia
nomine; per triennium isti plena domo telarum stragulam vestem

confecit, nihil nisi conchylio tinctam', Petron. 30. 11 'vestimenta mea cubitoria perdidit, quae mihi natali meo cliens quidam donaverat, Tyria sine dubio'. Yet it seems more vivid for Horace to picture a throng in the *atrium* (Virg. *georg*. 2. 461 f.) rather than a thriving cottage-industry.

A greater difficulty arises with the verb *trahere*, which in such contexts normally means 'to tease wool', i.e. to smooth it out with the fingers before spinning; cf. Porph. loc. cit. *carpere*, Lucr. 4. 376 'quasi in ignem lana trahatur' (Pl. *leg*. 780 c εἰς πῦρ ξαίνειν, *corp. paroem. gr.* 2. 27), Ov. *met*. 2. 411 'lanam mollire trahendo', Juv. 2. 54 f. 'vos lanam trahitis calathisque peracta refertis / vellera', Blümner, *Technologie* I². 109 n. 5, C. E. Bennett, *CQ* 8, 1914, 148 ff. (both these writers reject any such interpretation in our passage). It was obviously more economical to do this process before dyeing (Varro, *Men*. 325 'denique etiam suis manibus lanea tracta ministrasset infectori'), and *purpuras* naturally refers not to the raw wool but the finished material (3. 1. 42 f. 'nec purpurarum sidere clarior / delenit usus', 4. 13. 13). Moreover the menial task of preparing wool for spinning was performed by *ancillae* rather than *honestae clientae*.

Elsewhere *trahere* is used of drawing the threads from the spindle (= *deducere*); cf. Ov. *epist*. 3. 75 f. 'nos humiles famulaeque tuae data pensa trahemus, / et minuent plenos stamina nostra colos', Mart. 6. 3. 5, Metrodorus, *anth. P*. 14. 134. 4, Blümner, *Technologie* I². 127 n. 1. At this stage the wool was already dyed (Hom. *Od*. 6. 53 ἠλάκατα στρωφῶσ' ἀλιπόρφυρα, Blümner, op. cit., p. 230), but Horace's use of *purpuras* does not really suit spinning any more than it does 'teasing'. It would be better to see a reference to the more ladylike occupation of weaving; *trama*, 'the woof', may be derived from *trahere*, like *spuma* from *spuere* (J. Marquardt, *Das Privatleben der Römer*, ed. 2, 1886, p. 525 n. 1, F. Bücheler, *RhM* 60, 1905, 319 = *Kl. Schr*. 3. 331), and one may also compare Hom. *Il*. 23. 762 πηνίον ἐξέλκουσα παρὲκ μίτον (cf. Blümner, op. cit., pp. 148 ff.). But even if *trahere* could be used of weaving, the object should refer to the woof-thread, whereas *purpuras* (it must be insisted) naturally implies the finished material.

honestae ... clientae : the adjective is complimentary, but can be a little patronizing ('worthy'); cf. Cic. *Verr*. 3. 27 (*aratores*), 3. 183 (*scribae*). The feminine noun is attested in Plautus and Afranius, but apart from our passage not again till Fronto. The Etruscan *etera* (masculine) seems to have been the equivalent of a Roman client (Heurgon 93 f.); some of these people enjoyed a privileged position (Th. Frankfort, *Latomus* 18, 1959, 17 ff.).

9. at fides : for the sequence of thought cf. the passages cited from Bacchylides (p. 287), Virgil (pp. 290 f.), Propertius, and Ovid (note on 1 *non*). *fides* is a characteristically Roman adaptation of θυμὸς εὐμενής; the word follows naturally after *clientae* (clients had a right to expect this quality), and also suits Horace's relations with Maecenas. He is playing on the financial meaning of the word, 'creditworthiness' (Plaut. *Most.* 144 'res fides'); cf. *epist.* 1. 6. 36 f. 'scilicet uxorem cum dote fidemque et amicos / et genus et formam regina Pecunia donat' (though there the pun is ironic). Some see a reference to *fides* 'a lyre' (cf. Bacch. μοῦσά τε γλυκεῖα); this cannot be the primary meaning (cf. *epist.* 1. 1. 57 'est animus tibi, sunt mores, est lingua fidesque', Ov. *am.* 1. 3. 13 [above, 1 n.]), and even as a pun is quite unconvincing (the Bacchylidean Muse is represented by *ingeni*).

ingeni benigna vena est : cf. *ars* 408 ff. 'natura fieret laudabile carmen an arte / quaesitum est. ego nec studium sine divite vena / nec rude quid possit video ingenium'. For the 'native genius' (φύσις) of the creative writer cf. Brink on *ars* 408–18; for Horace's combination of moral and literary qualities cf. 1. 17. 13 f. 'dis pietas mea / et Musa cordi est', Bacch. loc. cit., Ov. *am.* 1. 3. 11 ff. *benigna* primarily means 'lavish' (*epod.* 17. 66 'benignae . . . dapis'), and is a word appropriate to patrons (14 n.); it also glances in a purely formal sense at the Bacchylidean εὐμενής. *ingeni* should be taken directly with *vena* (Quint. *inst.* 6. 2. 3 'tenuis quoque et angusta ingeni vena'), not with *benigna* (Horace does not lavish his *ingenium*); for the genitive form in -*i* cf. 1. 17. 21 n., Bo 223.

vena (like φλέψ) can describe either a gushing spring or a seam of ore. For the former image cf. Lucr. 1. 412 f., Ov. *am.* 3. 9. 25 f., *trist.* 3. 7. 15 f., 3. 14. 33 f. 'ingenium fregere meum mala, cuius et ante / fons infecundus parvaque vena fuit', *Pont.* 2. 5. 21 'ingenioque meo, vena quod paupere manat', 4. 2. 20, Juv. 10. 119 'largus et exundans . . . ingenii fons', Onians 64 f. *benigna* suits a free-flowing gush a little better than an inert seam (in spite of Plin. *nat.* 34. 149 'metallorum omnium vena ferri largissima est Cantabriae') ; the adjective suggests more profuseness than Aesch. *Pers.* 487 Σπερχειὸς ἄρδει πεδίον εὐμενεῖ ποτῷ (cited by A. J. Woodman, *Latomus* 26, 1967, 400).

Horace has wittily combined this image with a reference to veins of metal; this suits his comparison of material and spiritual riches (cf. the play on *fides*). The mining metaphor prevails at *ars* 409 f. (Brink calls attention to *rude*); that passage is imitated in turn by Juv. 7. 53 ff. 'sed vatem egregium cui non sit publica vena, / qui nil expositum soleat deducere, nec qui / communi feriat carmen triviale moneta' (by an ambiguity similar to Horace's, *nil expositum deducere* suggests the Callimachean image of the common well). The metaphorical senses of English 'vein' seem to be derived from seams of metal (*OED* s.v. III).

10. pauperemque : the word suggests modest circumstances rather than squalor (1. 12. 43 n.). A poet was conventionally poor, whether as a client, a lover, or a moralist; cf. 3. 29. 14, *epist.* 2. 2. 51 f., Leonidas, *anth. P.* 6. 302, Call. fr. 193. 17, Theoc. 16, Tib. 1. 1. 5 (though he was an *eques Romanus*), Prop. 1. 8. 39 f., Ov. *trist.* 4. 10. 22 'Maeonides nullas ipse reliquit opes', Petron. 83. 9 'amor ingenii neminem umquam divitem fecit', Juv. 7. 8 ff., Palladas, *anth. P.* 9. 169 ff., Archipoeta (Manitius, 1913, p. 30, 61 f.) 'poeta pauperior omnibus poetis / nichil prorsus habeo nisi quod videtis', Stroh 214 f.

dives me petit : normally the rich man is courted; cf. Cic. *epist. ad Nepotem* fr. 3 (p. 152 Watt) 'qui habet ultro appetitur, qui est pauper aspernatur', *Thes.l.L.* 2. 284. 16 ff. (*appetere*). Here *dives* points to Maecenas (p. 289); one may contrast the more modest tone of 2. 20. 6 'ego quem vocas'.

11. nihil supra deos lacesso : ' I do not provoke the gods any further' (i.e. by asking for greater happiness); they have done enough by granting *fides et ingeni benigna vena* (the stanza refers turn about to divine and human benefactions). For the view that prayers should be limited cf. *serm.* 2. 6. 4 'nil amplius oro', Sil. 16. 83 f., Mart. 4. 77. 1 f. 'numquam divitias deos rogavi, / contentus modicis meoque laetus', Fraenkel on Aesch. *Ag.* 350. *lacesso* cannot simply mean 'demand' (an unparalleled sense that would be otiose before *flagito*). *nihil* is the ordinary internal accusative (a stronger equivalent of *non*); it is wrong to say with some editors that *lacesso* takes the double accusative of verbs of asking.

12. nec potentem amicum : cf. *epist.* 1. 18. 86 'dulcis inexpertis cultura potentis amici', 1. 18. 44. In our passage Maecenas is implied (as is shown by *Sabinis* below), but the reference is unobtrusive and the awed tones slightly humorous: though Maecenas enjoyed *potentia* he might not wish to claim it.

13. largiora flagito : it would be a mark of ingratitude to keep clamouring; for a typical ancient attitude to benefactions cf. *epist.* 1. 17. 44 f. 'distat sumasne pudenter / an rapias'. Horace is not afraid of Maecenas's response (3. 16. 38 'nec si plura velim tu dare deneges').

14. satis beatus : cf. *epod.* 1. 31 f. 'satis superque me benignitas tua / ditavit', Catull. 23. 27 'sat es beatus', Prud. *cath.* 7. 216; here the adverb echoes the philosophic ἀρκεῖν (G. C. Fiske, *Lucilius and Horace*, 1920 and 1966, p. 352). *beatus* suggests partly riches (keeping up the theme of the poem), partly spiritual happiness; there is a paradox in the idea that the latter can admit less than perfection. But Horace will not provoke the gods by rivalling them in felicity;

beatus answers to *deos* as *Sabinis* to *amicum* (i.e. after alternate references to divine and human benefactors this fifth clause combines
hints of both).

unicis Sabinis : this is supposed to mean 'my single Sabine estate'
(Porphyrio comments 'donando me uno fundo Sabino'); this coheres admirably with *satis* and gives a contrast with *supra* and
largiora. The trouble is that *Sabini* means 'the Sabine people' and
hence 'the Sabine countryside', but not unambiguously anything
so limited as 'a Sabine estate' (L. Müller, endorsed by Housman
2. 613 = *CR* 17, 1903, 466). Cf. 3. 4. 21 f. 'vester in arduos /　tollor
Sabinos' (correlated with the place-names *Praeneste, Tibur, Baiae*),
Ov. *fast.* 4. 685 'hac ego Paelignos, natalia rura, petebam' (so *am.*
2. 16. 37 f.), Mart. 7. 31. 11, 10. 44. 9, Plin. *epist.* 3. 4. 2 'cum . . . in
Tuscos excucurrissem', 4. 1. 3, 4. 6. 1 'Tusci grandine excussi, in
regione Transpadana summa abundantia', 5. 6. 1, 5. 6. 45 'cur ego
Tuscos meos Tusculanis . . . praeponam', 9. 15. 1, 9. 36. 1, 9. 40. 1,
Juv. 8. 180 'in Lucanos aut Tusca ergastula mittas'.

If that is so, Horace could have talked of visiting the Sabines, or
even of being contented with the Sabines (meaning those in his immediate neighbourhood); but the addition of *unicis* gives the false
impression that the Sabine country was a single entity all of which
brought him benefit (to put the point in other words, he might have
said *Sabina regione contentus sum* even if he owned only a small part,
but not *una Sabina regione contentus sum* unless he owned the lot).
This difficulty might encourage us to take *unicis* as 'one and only'
in the sense of 'unparalleled' (3. 14. 5); such an interpretation suits
the plural better, and the paradoxical combination with *satis* gives
quite a Horatian point. Unfortunately in the context (after *supra*,
largiora, satis) 'only' ought to be the primary meaning. If the text is
sound one would have to say that Horace has combined two meanings of *unicis* neither of which in isolation is completely coherent; for
the sacrifice of precision for point cf. the note on 30 *fine*.

Müller proposed *unico Sabino*, which gives impeccable sense, but
the corruption is not a plausible one. *unciis* could mean 'roods', i.e.
small units of square measure (Colum. 5. 1. 10, *RE* 9 A. 1. 658 ff.);
the prosaic tone of the word might be tolerated in a poem of this
kind (cf. 2. 15. 14 *decempedis*), but the disparagement of the Sabinum
seems excessive even by way of humour. (Alternatively *unciis* might
mean 'percentages', but this would be a very odd way of referring to
rents.) Madvig understood *satis* as 'crops'; but the word cannot be
separated from *beatus*, and the collocation of three ablatives would be
extremely infelicitous. *iugeris* would give the right sense; however,
the form of the ablative is rare, though attested in Cato and Varro
(Neue–Wagener 1. 841 f., *Thes.l.L.* 7. 2. 627. 33 ff.).

The Sabine country was near-at-hand and unfashionable (Catull. 44. 1 ff.), and the very name had associations of frugality. There is therefore a contrast not only with *beatus* but with the previous references to Africa and Asia (5).

15. truditur dies die : the theme of luxury is not interrupted as the sentence is subordinate in sense to what follows: the flight of time makes hyperactivity pointless (cf. 2. 11. 9 ff., 2. 16. 17 ff.). For the succession of the days cf. *epod.* 17. 25 'urget diem nox et dies noctem' (so *carm.* 4. 7. 9 ff. of the seasons), Sen. *epist.* 24. 26 'diem nox premit, dies noctem' (on the topic *quousque eadem?*), Ammianus, *anth. P.* 11. 13. 1 f. ἠὼς ἐξ ἠοῦς παραπέμπεται, εἶτ' ἀμελούντων / ἡμῶν ἐξαίφνης ἥξει ὁ πορφύρεος. *truditur* suggests a mechanical sequence; cf. Alcaeus 346. 5 f. ἁ δ' ἀτέρα τὰν ἀτέραν κύλιξ / ὠθήτω, Petron. 45. 2 'quod hodie non est cras erit: sic vita truditur', Paul. Nol. *carm.* 16. 2 (imitating Horace), Yeats, *The Countess Cathleen*, Act 4, 'The years like great black oxen tread the world And God the herdsman goads them on behind'. The repetition of *dies* increases the impression of unvarying regularity.

16. novaeque . . . lunae : the noun means both 'moons' and 'months' (to balance *dies*); for the moon as a symbol of immutable mutability cf. 2. 11. 10 n. *pergunt* is not just a fairly weak auxiliary (Ellis on Catull. 61. 27), but suggests unremitting persistence (thus balancing the passive *truditur*); the moons paradoxically keep on fading away (instead of the normal *pergunt ire*). *interire* here means 'to wane', φθίνειν; it also suggests human death (cf. 18 *funus*). A progression is formed by the three juxtaposed words *novae, pergunt, interire*; in particular the emphatic *novae* makes a contrast with *interire* (unlike mankind the moon waxes again).

17. tu : the emphatic pronoun marks a contrast with the first person of 1–14. In *diatribe* the preacher turns to the offending individual; cf. 3. 24. 4, *epist.* 1. 1. 48 'discere et audire et meliori credere non vis?', Pers. 5. 91, Epictetus, *passim*. We suggest that Horace's sentence should perhaps be regarded as an indignant question.

secanda marmora : Horace picks up the theme of marble (3 f.); here he is speaking not of quarrying (though *cod. Theod.* 10. 19. 1 uses the word in this sense) but of cutting into thin ornamental *crustae* (for which *secare* is the *vox propria*). Cf. Sen. *ben.* 4. 6. 2 'tenues crustas et ipsa qua secantur lamna graciliores', Plin. *nat.* 36. 47–8 (the practice was introduced at Rome by Mamurra 'ne quid indignitati desit'), 36. 51 'sed quisquis primus invenit secare luxuriamque dividere importuni ingenii fuit', Blümner 91 f., *Technologie* 3. 183 ff.

18. locas : the verb is used of placing contracts; cf. 3. 1. 35 (the *villa maritima* is built by a *redemptor*), *epist.* 2. 2. 72. There is a satirical implication that the rich man should be inviting tenders from funeral-undertakers; for this use of *locare* cf. *serm.* 1. 8. 9, Val. Ant. fr. 62 'funere locato', Cic. *Verr.* 5. 120, Plin. *nat.* 7. 176, Juv. 3. 32, *Thes.l.L.* 6. 1. 1603. 38 ff. There is a verbal point in the collocation of *locas* and *sub* (here 'just before'), and a formal contrast with *struis* below. The rich man is treated as if he were on the point of death because he is subject to the normal hazards of life; cf. ps.-Quint. *decl. mai.* 9. 17 'non me aurata laquearia nec radiantes marmore columnae nec graves crustae fecerint immemorem fragilitatis', Hier. *epist.* 46. 11 [cited above, p. 289].

sepulcri immemor struis domos : for the theme cf. Philodemus, *de morte* 4. 38 (Gigante 80) θεμέλια καταβαλλόμενος οἰκήσεων οὐδ' εἰς χιλιοστὸν ἔτος ἐπιτελεσθῆναι δυνησομένων, Lucian, *Char.* 17 ἢ τί γὰρ οὐκ ἂν ποιήσειεν ἐκεῖνος ὁ τὴν οἰκίαν σπουδῇ οἰκοδομούμενος καὶ τοὺς ἐργάτας ἐπισπέρχων εἰ μάθοι ὅτι ἡ μὲν ἕξει τέλος αὐτῷ, ὁ δὲ ἄρτι ἐπιθεὶς τὸν ὄροφον ἄπεισι τῷ κληρονόμῳ καταλιπὼν ἀπολαύειν αὐτῆς, αὐτὸς μηδὲ δειπνήσας ὁ ἄθλιος ἐν αὐτῇ. The tomb might be a large structure, like that of Plancus or Caecilia Metella, prepared years in advance (the ancient Romans showed even greater forethought than Browning's bishop). *struis* ('pile') is a more vigorous word than its compounds, and suits the rich man's ill-timed energy. *domos* (picking up 2 *domo*) refers not to Baian villas but to town-houses (rhetorical plural); the rich man thinks that he will soon be possessor of an attractive *domicilium* but his real destination is a *sepulcrum haud pulcrum* (note the chiasmus).

20. Bais : after three lines on the *domus* (17–19) come three on the *villa maritima*. The place-name keeps up the excessively luxurious note of *marmora*. For the attractions of the area cf. 3. 4. 24, *epist.* 1. 1. 83, Varro, *Men.* 44, Cic. *Cael.* 35, Prop. 1. 11, Str. 5. 4. 7, Sen. *epist.* 51, J. H. D'Arms, *Romans on the Bay of Naples*, 1970.

obstrepentis : the sea is pictured as an obstreperous crowd (cf. 4. 14. 48); this suits the image of *summovere* in the next line. Angry or volatile mobs are often compared with the waves; cf. 1. 1. 7 n., Hom. *Il.* 2. 144 ff., Plb. 11. 29. 9–11 (with Walbank's note), 21. 31. 10–11, Cic. *Cluent.* 138, Virg. *Aen.* 7. 586 ff. (Latinus), Liv. 38. 10. 5 ('vulgata similitudine'). For the reverse comparison (as in our passage) cf. Virg. *Aen.* 1. 148 ff.

urges : 'press'; the verb implies both urgency and the physical force needed to shove off the sea. The infinitive is analogous to the one found with *instare* (Cic. *Verr.* 3. 136, etc.); the construction is different at Tac. *ann.* 11. 26. 1 'abrumpi dissimulationem ... urgebat'. It would be wrong to understand *ministros*, as the rich man is described as personally occupied in piling and pushing.

21. **submovere** : the rich man is portrayed as an arrogant authoritarian driving the sea away with his lictors (cf. 2. 16. 10). Because of the absence of tides the Romans were able to extend their villas into the sea whether for fish-farming or amenity or both ; for illustrations cf. M. Rostovtzeff, *Social and Economic History of the Roman Empire*, 1957, vol. i, pls. viii, ix, J. P. V. D. Balsdon, *Life and Leisure in Ancient Rome*, 1969, pl. 5. Moralists conventionally censured such constructions as the mark of a tyrant or madman (like Xerxes or the flatterers of Canute) who showed an impious disregard for the boundaries of nature (cf. Philo, *somn.* 2. 17. 117 ff.). See 3. 1. 33 ff. 'contracta pisces aequora sentiunt . . .', 3. 24. 3 f., *epist.* 1. 1. 83 ff., Sall. *Cat.* 13. 1, 20. 11 'divitias quas profundant in extruendo mari', Varro, *rust.* 3. 17. 9 (L. Lucullus's *piscinae*), Tib. 2. 3. 45 with K. F. Smith's parallels, Sen. *contr.* 2. 1. 13 'adversum naturam', Manil. 4. 263 'litoribusque novis per luxum inludere ponto', Vell. 2. 33. 4 (Pompey calls Lucullus *Xerxes togatus*), Petron. 120. 89 'permutata rerum statione'.

litora : one can say 'maria summovere' (cf. Sen. *contr. exc.* 5. 5. 2, Sen. *dial.* 9. 3. 7), but at first sight it seems strange to talk of pushing aside the shore (which by the modern way of thinking is part of the land). Peerlkamp considered *promovere* (*grom.* p. 350 'possessionem promovendo suam', Cassiod. *var.* 9. 6. 4 'quantis spatiis in visceribus aequoris terra promota est'); but this spoils the image of a lictor thrusting aside a fluid mob. E. Wistrand meets the difficulty by taking *litora* as 'inshore waters' (*Nach Innen oder Nach Aussen?*, 1946, p. 40); for further instances of this usage cf. E. Löfstedt, *Coniectanea*, 1950, pp. 84 ff. (though in our passage he interprets 'the line of the shore', V. Skånland, *SO* 42, 1968, 93 ff.). Without going so far as to refer *litora* to inshore waters, one may find help in Wistrand's general thesis that the ancients often looked at the shore from the viewpoint of the sea ; thus he cites (p. 24) Sen. *epist.* 89. 21 'nec contenti solo nisi quod manu feceritis mare agetis introrsus' (i.e. 'outwards' by modern feeling). Similarly Horace's *litora* refers to the limit of the water (not the land), which is pushed away (not forward).

22. **parum locuples** : the adjective is used in its etymological sense of 'rich in landed property' (*loco*) ; cf. Cic. *rep.* 2. 16, Nigid. ap. Gell. 10. 5. 2. The phrase balances 14 'satis beatus'.

continente ripa : ablative with *locuples*; the phrase balances *unicis Sabinis. continens* means 'continuous', 'uninterrupted' (and so is particularly applied to mainlands or continents) ; cf. Liv. 44. 28. 12

'qui propiores continenti litori erant' (as opposed to Chios), Paul. Nol. *carm.* 24. 31, *Thes.l.L.* 4. 710. 1 ff. There is a play of words on the idea of 'confining' or 'restricting' (*continentia* = 'moderation'); cf. Shakespeare, *Midsummer Night's Dream* 2. 1. 92 'Have every pelting river made so proud / That they have overborne their continents'. *ripa* is seldom applied to the sea and suggests a bank of earth rather than simply the water's edge (*litora* above); cf. 3. 27. 23 f. 'trementis / verbere ripas' (*litus* would imply less of a physical obstacle), Colum. 1. 5. 5 (on the siting of a seaside villa) 'numquam ex ripa sed haud paulum summota a litore'.

23. quid quod . . . : the transitional formula (K.–S. 2. 277) is too prosaic as a rule for the highest poetry; it is found at *epod.* 8. 15, Pacuv. *trag.* 143, Ov. *am.* 2. 8. 9, Sen. *Ag.* 265 (see Tarrant's note). Here it makes a progression from vanity to something worse.

usque : cf. Apul. *met.* 9. 38. 3 'licet privato suis possessionibus paupere fines usque et usque proterminaveris, habiturum te tamen vicinum aliquem'. The adverb is spatial rather than temporal, and describes a steady advance rather than just a repeated action ('progressively', not 'continually'). It is in tension with *proximos* ('farther' and 'nearest' point in different directions), but syntactically it belongs to *revellis*. Wickham interprets τοὺς ἀεὶ ὁμόρους, but even if *usque* referred to time it could not mean 'at any given moment'.

proximos : 'belonging to your neighbour'; cf. Plaut. *rud.* 404 'aquam hinc de proxumo rogabo'. *Latifundia* were naturally extended by adding contiguous properties (*agros continuare*); cf. 2. 2. 10 f., 3. 16. 41 f., *serm.* 2. 6. 8 f. 'o si angulus ille / proximus accedat qui nunc denormat agellum', *epist.* 2. 2. 177 f., Sen. *epist.* 90. 39, ps.-Quint. *decl. mai.* 13. 2 'postquam proximos quosque revellendo terminos ager locupletis latius inundavit' (imitating our passage), 13. 11 'parum est proximos aequare terminos'. The elder Pliny commends Pompey 'qui numquam agrum mercatus est conterminum' (*nat.* 18. 35).

24. revellis : 'uproot'; the prefix balances that of 21 *submovere*. The *dives* shows no more regard for the *termini* than if they were obstructions in a field; cf. Ov. *rem.* 87 (of a tree), *met.* 12. 341 (of a rock), Pers. 5. 92 'dum veteres avias tibi de pulmone revello' (a pun on 'grandmothers' and 'groundsel'). The word suggests a vigorous action (Virg. *Aen.* 4. 427) rather than a difficult one: the object comes away.

agri : at first sight the word may seem otiose, but *proximos agri terminos* almost means *proximi agri terminos*; by a hypallage natural in poetry the adjective is assigned to the more picturesque word. At the same time unqualified *agri* produces a clearer antithesis with 20 *maris*. Heinze supplied *tui*, which would mean that the rich man pulled up his own boundary-stones; this is rhetorically wrong even if in practice the *termini* could be looked at from the viewpoint of either neighbour.

terminos : for the sanctity of boundary-marks cf. Paul. Fest. 368 M. = 505 L. 'denique Numa Pompilius statuit eum qui terminum exarasset et ipsum et boves sacros esse', Riccobono, *Fontes* I². 12. 5 (*lex Iulia Agraria*) 'quique termini hac lege statuti erunt, ne quis eorum quem eicito neve loco moveto sciens dolo malo', Ogilvie on Liv. I. 55. 3, Bömer on Ov. *fast.* 2. 639 ff., Dion. Hal. *ant. Rom.* 2. 74, Mayor on Juv. 16. 38, *grom.* pp. 350 f., *dig.* 47. 21 'DE TERMINO MOTO', Pl. *leg.* 842 e, *deut.* 27. 17 'maledictus qui transfert terminos proximi sui', *prov.* 22. 28, 23. 10 'ne attingas parvulorum terminos et agrum pupillorum ne introeas', *RE* 5 A. 784 f., Dilke 98 ff.

ultra limites clientium : *ultra* makes a formal contrast with *proximos* at the end of the previous line. *clientium* echoes 8 *clientae*; Horace had no clients, but that is better than maltreating them. Like the removal of boundary-stones such behaviour was subject to antique sanctions and poetic damnation; cf. *lex XII tab.* 8. 21 (Riccobono, *Fontes* I². 62) 'patronus si clienti fraudem fecerit, sacer esto', Virg. *Aen.* 6. 609 'aut fraus innexa clienti' (Servius cites 26 f. 'pellitur . . . deos'). When Horace says 'falle clientem' to Torquatus (*epist.* I. 5. 31), though he means 'give your client the slip', he humorously uses a verb that suggests fraud.

26. salis : the verb suggests light-hearted transgression (ὑπερβασία); cf. I. 3. 24 'transiliunt vada', I. 18. 7. At the same time something of the literal meaning of the word remains: Remus jumped over his brother's wall to show his disregard for its sanctity (cf. Pease on Cic. *nat. deor.* 3. 94, Ogilvie on Liv. I. 6. 3–7. 3, Plut. *quaest. Rom.* 271 a). Horace is using forceful words to express the rich man's energy (19 *struis*, 24 *revellis*). There may even be a touch of paradox in the idea of so athletic an *avarus*; usually such people are old misers crouching over crocks of gold (*epod.* I. 33, Virg. *georg.* 2. 507).

pellitur . . . : this clause is still influenced by *quid quod*; otherwise it disrupts the sequence too much and obscures the extent of the contrast implied by 29 *tamen*. The asyndeton points an antithesis between the action of the rich man (*revellis et salis*) and the sufferings of the peasant (*pellitur*); for similar asyndeton with antithesis in subordinate clauses cf. F. Leo, *Plautinische Forschungen*, 1912, p. 272 n. 4. A colon should be printed after *avarus* (a mere comma would weaken the climax), and the question-mark not till 28 *natos*.

Once again *pellitur* is a strong word, more physical than the technical *expellere*, and placed emphatically at the beginning of the clause; for the singular verb preceding a plural subject cf. K.–S. I. 45 f. The Romans with their feeling for property often describe the pathos of expropriation; sometimes force or fraud was used, but there need be no formal breach of the law. Cf. especially *serm.* 2. 2. 127 ff. (Ofellus), Sall. *Jug.* 41. 8 'interea parentes aut parvi liberi militum, uti quisque potentiori confinis erat, sedibus pellebantur', Virg. *ecl.* 1 and 9, ps.-Virg. *dirae*, Plin. *nat.* 2. 175 'haec (terra) in qua conterminos pellimus furtoque vicini caespitem nostro solo adfodimus ut qui latissime rura metatus fuerit . . . quam tandem portionem eius defunctus obtineat?', ps.-Quint. *decl. mai.* 13. 2 'aequatae solo villae et excisa pagorum sacra et cum coniugibus parvisque liberis respectantes patrium larem migraverunt veteres coloni', Juv. 14. 141 ff., Ambr. *Nab.* 1. 1–2 = 2. 469 Schenkl: 'quis opulentissimorum non exturbare contendit agellulo suo pauperem atque inopem aviti ruris eliminare finibus? . . . hoc metu percitum humanum genus cedit iam suis terris, migrat cum parvulis pauper onustus pignore suo, uxor sequitur inlacrimans, tamquam ad bustum prosequatur maritum. . . . quousque extenditis, divites, insanas cupiditates?' (see also below, 32 n.), Brunt 551 ff. For a Greek specimen of the topic cf. *orac. Sib.* 8. 30 ff.

   paternos . . . deos : the Penates (2. 7. 4 n.). The noun makes a climax (one expects 'heirlooms') and is paradoxically combined with *ferens* (so more pointedly Plin. *nat.* 2. 21 'digitis deos gestant') ; for *deus* of a god's image cf. 3. 23. 16, K. F. Smith on Tib. 2. 5. 22. *sinu* literally means the fold in the robe, but also implies solicitude; cf. Tac. *ann.* 1. 40. 4 'profuga ducis uxor parvulum sinu filium gerens'.

28. et uxor et vir : the woman is mentioned first (contrary to Latin usage) because her maltreatment is particularly objectionable. Some argue that the images are carried by the wife, the heavier children by the husband (cf. Ambr. loc. cit. 'onustus pignore suo'), but no such discrimination is intended (cf. Petron. 123. 226 f. 'ille manu pavida natos tenet, ille penates / occultat gremio'). The husband is a village Aeneas who rescues his household gods and his children (not his father in this case) with a piety that is set against the *mala fides* of his patron.

   sordidosque natos : there is a chiasmus in the progression *paternos, uxor, vir, natos.* There may be an implication that the images were shiny; *epod.* 2. 66 'renidentis Lares' is not simply metaphorical (cf. Juv. 12. 88 'fragili simulacra nitentia cera', Prud. *Symm.* 1. 203 f.). The grubbiness of the children should not be exaggerated; *sordes* are attributed to respectable people like mourners and *rei*, and in particular to the unsophisticated country and its inhabitants. Cf. Virg. *ecl.* 2. 28 'sordida rura', Mart. 1. 49. 28 'infante . . . sordido' (with Friedlaender's parallels), 12. 57. 2 'laremque villae sordidum' (an oxymoron), Tac. *Germ.* 20. 1, Claud. 26. 357 f.

29. nulla . . . : in the last part of the poem (29–40) Horace proceeds
to admonish the *dives*. This section is shorter than its two predecessors (1–14, 15–28), but unlike them it is organized as a unity, without
a break after the first eight lines (as at 8 and 22); the persistent enjambement gives an urgency to the style that makes a contrast with
the structural simplicity of the Bacchylidean opening (1–8). Lines
29–31 are very difficult, partly because of uncertainties about the
text and construction, partly also because of the poet's deliberate
double-meanings. We suggest as a working translation: 'All the
same, no palace awaits the rich man more surely than the rapacious
underworld, that fixed terminus'. For the complications see the following notes.

certior : i.e. more certainly in prospect; cf. such expressions as
certa mors (*Thes.l.L.* 3. 927. 37 ff.). The adjective also suggests the
'fixed abode' of respectable citizens (*epist.* 1. 7. 58 'lare certo',
Thes.l.L. 3. 901. 15 ff.) ; the evicted client has lost his cottage, but his
patron may not live to see his palace built.

tamen : the contrast is with lines 15–28 as a whole. The rich man
builds palaces but has none to go to except that of Orcus. He en-
croaches unnaturally on the sea, but the land will open up for him
without any difficulty. He oversteps the boundaries imposed by
nature and morality, but he himself will soon reach his limits.

30. rapacis Orci : *Orcus* sometimes refers to the ruler of the underworld, sometimes (like Ἀίδης) to the underworld itself; cf. *RE*
18. 1. 908 ff., Wagenvoort 102 ff. Both meanings seem established in
Horace (2. 3. 24, 3. 27. 50 against 3. 11. 29), and both seem to be
combined here; for such ambiguities cf. *RE* 18. 1. 915 ff. (pointing
out that *ad Orcum* and *Orco* are used rather than *in Orcum*). The
meaning 'underworld' provides mention of an area to balance *aula*;
the genitive is 'appositional' like *fons Timavi* (2. 6. 10 n.). On the
other hand personal Orcus produces a contrast with 25 'limites
clientium' and leads more naturally to 34 'satelles Orci'. *rapacis*
primarily suits the king (*h. Dem.* 2 f. ἦν Ἀιδωνεὺς / ἥρπαξεν, Call. *ep.*
2. 5 f. ᾗσιν ὁ πάντων / ἁρπακτὴς Ἀίδης οὐκ ἐπὶ χεῖρα βαλεῖ, Sen. *Phaedr.*
1152 'patruo rapaci'), but it is also compatible with the place; cf.
Virg. *georg.* 2. 492 'strepitumque Acherontis avari', though that passage may partly suggest the river (so perhaps Lucr. 3. 37–40).

Bentley proposed *capacis* (cf. Sen. *Herc. f.* 658 f. 'dominantem . . . /
regno capaci'), but this destroys the point that the grasping landowner is himself the victim of rapacity. *capacis* would suggest that
there is room for everybody, even the most demanding; but Horace
is saying that the *avarus* will have to limit his territorial ambitions
(cf. 38 *coercet*). A. Y. Campbell proposed *capaciorve*, which is open to

the same objections; in addition it leaves the reference to the underworld too inexplicit.

fine destinata: it seems best to take these words together as ablative of comparison after *certior*; admittedly *finis* is not directly
comparable with *aula*, but this difficulty is lessened if *Orci* is taken
partly in a spatial sense (see previous note). For feminine *finis* cf.
epod. 17. 36 'quae finis aut quod me manet stipendium?' (note *manet*
as in our passage), Lucr. *passim* (he seldom uses the masculine),
Virg. *Aen.* 2. 554, 5. 327 f., 384, 12. 793, Prop. 1. 16. 21, *Thes.l.L.*
6. 1. 787. 6 ff., H. Bauer, *Glotta* 10, 1920, 122 ff.; some editors object
that in Virgil euphony plays a part (cf. Gell. 13. 21. 12), but such considerations are secondary at best. *destinare finem* is a natural expression in various senses; cf. Fronto, p. 204 N. = p. 193 van den Hout
'nullo itineris destinato fine', ps.-Hil. *libell.* 8 'cum certum sit Dei
iudicium post finem huius aevi destinatum'. *finis* contains the idea
both of a temporal end (Cic. *Mil.* 101, Dem. 18. 97) and a territorial
limit; for something of the same ambiguity cf. Eur. fr. 916. 4 ff. N.
κοὐκ ἔστιν ὄρος κείμενος οὐδεὶς / εἰς ὄντινα χρὴ κέλσαι θνητοῖς, / πλὴν ὅταν
ἔλθῃ κρυερὰ Διόθεν / θανάτου πεμφθεῖσα τελευτή.

Some take *destinata* to agree not with *fine* but with *aulā* (understood from *aula* below); the meaning would presumably be 'than the
palace marked out by the boundary of Hades'. But it is inelegant to
have an ablative dependent on an ablative, particularly where the
two juxtaposed words might agree; the compression seems too obscure even for the epodic style (cf. *epod.* 1. 5 f., 1. 19 ff.). *destinare*
properly means 'to fasten down', and hence 'to fix on' or 'earmark'
for a particular purpose; cf. 2. 7. 20 n., Liv. 7. 28. 5 'locus in arce
destinatus'. In our passage *destinata aula* would naturally suggest
a palace that has been destined for the rich man; and this idea is not
easily compatible with the ablative *fine*. The verb does not normally
mean 'to mark out' (which would be compatible with *fine*); there
is an apparent exception at *culex* 391 f. 'hunc (locum) et in orbem /
destinat', but this imprecise poet is perhaps conflating *in orbem
designat* and *in tumulum destinat*.

Servius quotes the line in the form 'rapacis Orci sede destinata'
(*Aen.* 6. 152). This is not just a trivial case of misquotation as he is
demonstrating that *sedes* can be used for *sepulcrum* (cf. also Tac.
ann. 1. 8. 5 'in campo Martis sede destinata'); the loss of *de* before
destinata might have led to interpolation. *sede destinata* provides
a perfect balance to *certior . . . aula*; *sede* refers to a spatial area
in a way that *fine* does not. Moreover *sedem destinare* would normally
mean 'to plan to acquire an abode', and so has particular point when
addressed to an ambitious *aedificator* (cf. *Thes.l.L.* 5. 1. 758. 73 ff.).
On the other hand *fine* keeps up the idea of boundaries that is so

important in the context; note particularly the contrast with 24 f. 'ultra limites' and 32 'quid ultra tendis?'

Other suggested interpretations may be more briefly dismissed. If *destinata* were taken as nominative one might try to translate 'An equally uncertain palace awaits the rich man, being marked out as it is by the limit of grasping Orcus'. But though *nullus* is sometimes used with a verb for *non* (Catull. 8. 14 'rogaberis nulla'), *nulla certior domus* cannot mean *domus haudquaquam certior*; *fine* still seems an inappropriate ablative with *destinare*; and if the rich man's *aula* is being contrasted with the client's cottage, then we lose the comparison with the Hall of Hades. Alternatively one might take *fine destinata* as ablative absolute and interpret 'No palace that awaits the rich man has more secure tenure than the poor man's cottage, seeing that the end of death has been fixed'. This avoids the difficulty of treating *rapacis Orci* as spatial; on the other hand the pun on *aula* is again spoiled, and the sentence is poorly integrated if *certior* is dissociated from *fine destinata* (*certus* and *destinatus* make a natural pair). W. A. Camps suggests that *aulā* should be understood with *rapacis Orci* and then *fine destinata* interpreted as 'at his fated end' (*AJPh* 94, 1973, 142 f.); but though the ellipse of the ablative can be paralleled (he cites Lucan 1. 446), it is surely impossible to have a loosely attached ablative of a different category in the same context.

31. aula : the Greek word for a palace suits both a rich man's house (2. 10. 8) and the underworld; cf. 3. 11. 16, Eur. *Alc.* 259 f. ἄγει μέ τις . . . νεκύων ἐς αὐλάν, Fedeli on Prop. 4. 11. 5, *CIL* 5. 6128 'praecipitem memet superi mersere sub aulas'. On the other hand the evicted client would only have a *casa*.

manet : the verb is particularly appropriate to the underworld; cf. 1. 28. 15, Aesch. *cho.* 103 f. τὸ μόρσιμον γὰρ τόν τ' ἐλεύθερον μένει . . . , Norden, *Kl. Schr.*, pp. 27 f., *Thes.l.L.* 8. 291. 35 ff. There is a contrast between the feverish striving of the verbs in the second person and the sinister patience of death (Syndikus 1. 469).

32. erum quid ultra tendis? : 'why do you strain proprietorship farther?'; we propose that *erum* should be taken with *tendis* and not with *manet* (the latter is supported by the comment of ps.-Acro and by a citation at Serv. *Aen.* 6. 152). For the use of 'concrete for abstract' cf. 1. 35. 22 (with bibliography there cited), Sen. *Phaedr.* 925 'ordiri virum', Petron. 97. 9 'ut saltem ostenderet fratrem', Housman 3. 1178 (= *Hermes* 66, 1931, 405 f.), Goodyear on Tac. *ann.* 1. 4. 4, pp. 122 f., R. D. Williams on Stat. *Theb.* 11. 659. If taken with the previous sentence *erum* seems otiose after *divitem*; the difficulty is accentuated by the word's emphatic position at the beginning of a line and followed by a full-stop (for which there is no parallel in this or similar poems). The prosaic *erus* describes a man's relation to his servants or as here to his property; cf. *serm.* 2. 2. 129 'propriae telluris erum' (similarly in our passage *erum* is in tension with *tellus* at the end of the line), *epist.* 1. 16. 2, Catull. 31. 12. On the other hand if the word is taken with the previous sentence it seems uncharacteristically imprecise: *Orcus*, the logical subject, suits *divitem manet* but not *erum*, and the same can be said even of *nulla aula*, which means 'no palace anywhere' (not 'none of his palaces'). If one looks for a point of reference in 26–8, *erus* cannot mean *patronus*; one is driven back to 19 *domos*, which is too remote.

   aequa tellus : normally the earth is said to be just because it pays back what is put into it by the farmer (Virg. *georg.* 2. 460 'iustissima tellus', *RE* 9 A. 2. 1847). Here the idea is extended to impartiality between rich and poor; cf. 1. 4. 13 f. 'aequo pulsat pede pauperum tabernas / regumque turris', 3. 1. 14, Otto 228 f. Horace also seems to be saying with poetic brevity that rich and poor receive an equal allotment in the grave (ps.-Acro 'dum par sit omnibus sepulcri mensura'). This interpretation produces an antithesis, which otherwise would be lacking, between *ultra* and *aequa*; in a context that refers so much to territorial aggrandizement it is desirable that *aequa* should mean 'equal in extent' as well as 'impartial'. For the theme cf. Simonides 520. 4 ff. ὁ δ' ἄφυκτος ὁμῶς ἐπικρέμαται θάνατος· / κείνου γὰρ ἴσον λάχον μέρος οἵ τ' ἀγαθοί / ὅστις τε κακός, Ambros. *Nab.* 1. 2 = 2. 470 Schenkl 'nudos recipit terra quos edidit, nescit fines possessionum sepulchro includere. caespes angustus aeque et pauperi abundat et diviti, et terra quae viventis non cepit affectum totum iam divitem capit'.

33. pauperi : in the underworld all doors are flung open to the poor, whereas in life they are too often turned away.

   recluditur : Horace is partly thinking of a literal opening of the ground to receive the ashes of the dead. But the verb he uses better suits the opening of the underworld (cf. Virg. *Aen.* 8. 244 f., Sil. 13. 523 f., Val. Fl. 4. 231 'reclusaque ianua leti'); he thus sustains the image of the *aula* (31 n.).

34. regumque pueris : *regum* echoes 5 f. 'Attali . . . regiam'; for the polarism with *pauperi* cf. 2. 14. 11 n. *pueris* is grandiose for *filiis* (Porph. ad loc., 1. 19. 2 n., Brink on *ars* 83); one suspects a hint at Maecenas's Etruscan ancestry (above, p. 290). The emphasis is different at Pers. 3. 17 f. 'et similis regum pueris pappare minutum / poscis'; there *pueris* describes an age as well as a relationship. For the metrical resolution cf. *epod.* 2. 61 'has inter epulas'.

   satelles Orci : *satelles* describes a courtier at an Eastern palace (cf. 31 *aula*, 33 *recluditur*); one may compare the semi-humorous anthro-

pomorphism of Lucian's underworld scenes, a feature presumably
derived from Menippus. Probably Mercury is meant (cf. below on 36
revinxit, 38 *hic*); this view, though now generally abandoned, was
already propounded in the seventeenth century (cf. Stanley on Aesch.
cho. 1). He is often described as ψυχοπομπός (1. 10. 17 n.) and an intermediary between heaven and the underworld (1. 10. 19 n.); in this
capacity he could reasonably be regarded as an equerry of Hades
(Kaibel, *EG* 575. 1 = Peek, *GV* 1883. 1 ἄγγελε Φερσεφόνης, Claud.
rapt. Pros. 1. 76 ff.). *satelles* well suggests his gentle and noiseless
efficiency; the word's hint of corruptibility (3. 16. 9) suits his general
reputation, even though the bribe failed on this occasion.

Editors generally assume that Charon is meant (cf. Leonidas,
anth. P. 7. 67. 1 Ἀίδεω λυπηρὲ διήκονε, Virg. *georg.* 4. 502 'portitor
Orci'); this interpretation is supported by the reading *revexit* (36 n.).
satelles seems an unsuitable word for so rough a retainer, but it might
be defended as an instance of sardonic humour. It is more serious
that the theory runs into difficulties at 36 *hic* (see note).

35. callidum Promethea : for a possible allusion to Maecenas's *Prometheus* see above, p. 290. For the cleverness implied by the name cf.
Hes. *th.* 511 ποικίλον αἰολόμητιν (with West's parallels), Aesch. *Prom.*
944 σοφιστήν, Catull. 64. 294 'sollerti corde Prometheus'. Such qualities
were insufficient to get him out of Hades; cf. Alcaeus 38 A. 7 ἀλλὰ καὶ
πολύιδρις ἔων (of Sisyphus's failure to escape his destiny).

36. revinxit : the other reading *revexit* is accepted by all modern
editors; it suits Charon well, but not Mercury (*vehere* implies more
than πέμπειν). *revinxit* would have to mean 'untied' (not 'tied fast',
the normal meaning); cf. Colum. 1. 8. 16 'num vilicus aut alligaverit
quempiam domino nesciente aut revinxerit', surely not a novel use
of the word (note also Catull. 63. 84 'religatque iuga manu'). There
is no evidence elsewhere that Hermes was invited to free Prometheus
(he offers no encouragement in the Aeschylean play), but Horace is
using an unfamiliar form of the legend. *revinxit* well suits the unbinding of Prometheus Bound, Προμηθεὺς δεσμώτης (the title of the
play is probably Alexandrian, cf. O. Taplin, *JHS* 95, 1975, 184 ff.);
it also makes a characteristic epigram when combined with *captus*
(in so pointed a poem this is a significant argument). *nec revinxit*
balances 38 *coercet*; the ode is contrasting the territorial expansion
of the acquisitive man (26 'salis avarus') with the constraints of the
underworld.

auro captus : cf. Lucan 4. 820 'Gallorum captus spoliis et Caesaris
auro', *Thes.l.L.* 3. 337. 46 ff. *auro* picks up the notion of wealth that
runs through the poem (cf. 1 *aureum*). Though Orcus himself was
incorruptible (2. 14. 5 n.), some had tried to bribe their way out of

death; the doctor Asclepius was seduced by χρυσὸς ἐν χεροὶν φανείς (Pind. *P.* 3. 55). If Charon were the *satelles*, then *auro* would be contrasted with the modest fare on the outward journey.

Housman proposed *aure captus*, 'impaired in hearing', which he preferred to join to the next sentence (1. 98 f. = *JPh* 17, 1888, 310 ff.); he thus attempted to mitigate the difficulty of *hic* (see next note), and in so doing produced an antithesis with 40 *audit*. But *aure captus* implies a permanent disability, and can hardly be used like *surdus* of 'turning a deaf ear'; if the phrase is joined to the next sentence it weakens the effect of the sacral *hic . . . hic* (see below).

hic . . . hic: for the repetition of the demonstrative in religious language (Norden's 'Er-Stil') cf. 1. 21. 13 n. The pronoun naturally refers to 34 *satelles*, and suits Mercury admirably; the god is at the same time gentle and inexorable (1. 10. 17 ff., 1. 24. 16 ff.) and brings both constraint (38 n.) and relief. On the other hand if the *satelles* is Charon, then 38 *levare* and 40 *vocatus audit* (as well as the sacral *hic*) seem unsuitable; nobody called to Charon until he was on the bank of the Styx. One might attempt to meet this argument by pointing to the Etruscan Charun, who is portrayed in art as a ψυχο-πομπός who separates the dying from their dearest (F. de Ruyt, *Charun, démon étrusque de la mort,* 1934); one might even speculate that Maecenas in his *Prometheus* had represented Charon in such a guise. But it is most unlikely that in a passage full of conventional literary patterns Horace is using an eccentric legend of purely personal application.

Most editors refer *hic* to *Orci*, which must then be given some emphasis. But if *Orci* is stressed, one looks in vain for a meaningful relationship with 30 *rapacis Orci*; on the other hand if the emphasis is put on *satelles* (as the word-order suggests), there is a natural progression from Orcus to the equerry of Orcus. One's impression that *satelles* is dominant is reinforced by the last words of the previous sentence, *auro captus* (Housman felt this difficulty, cf. previous note). It is true that Orcus may be summoned by those in distress (Lucr. 5. 996 'horriferis accibant vocibus Orcum', Aesop 60, cited 38 n., Ov. *met.* 7. 605), but this does not outweigh the formal argument given above.

superbum Tantalum : one of the traditional sinners of the underworld; he is appropriately mentioned in this context as he stole the gods' ambrosia to make his friends immortal (Pind. *O.* 1. 60 ff.). He was notorious for pride (Pind. *O.* 1. 55) and wealth (*corp. paroem. gr.* 2. 660 τὰ Ταντάλου τάλαντα τανταλίζεται); he thus makes a good contrast with 39 *pauperem*. For later moralists he sometimes represents the superstitious man (Lucr. 3. 980 f.), sometimes the miser (Lejay on *serm.* 1. 1. 68, Hense on Teles, p. 34), sometimes insatiable greed (cf. Max. Tyr. 33. 4 d δίψα διηνεκὴς ἀνδρὸς φιληδόνου, Macr. somn. 1. 10. 13, Otto 349, Buffière 486 ff.).

38. genus : at a literal level this refers to Pelops, etc. (cf. epod. 17. 65 'Pelopis infidi pater'). In a moralizing poem it is more pointed to underline the allusion to Tantalus's spiritual descendants; for an apparent reference to Maecenas see above, p. 290.

coercet : for the constraints of the underworld cf. 2. 14. 9 n., carm. epig. 1504. 10 'fabulas Manes ubi rex coercet' (the writer may have interpreted Horace's hic as Orcus, but his views are not necessarily reliable, cf. 1. 4. 16 n.). The verb is particularly pointed in our poem where the theme of boundaries keeps recurring. It also suits the picture of Mercury shepherding the dead ; cf. the striking parallel at 1. 10. 18 f. 'virgaque levem coerces / aurea turbam'.

levare : the verb makes a contrast with coercet (note the chiasmus), but in spite of its gentleness has a sinister note (like vocatus atque non vocatus below). For the metaphor cf. Aesop 60 Hausrath γέρων ποτὲ ξύλα κόψας καὶ ταῦτα φέρων πολλὴν ὁδὸν ἐβάδιζε. διὰ δὲ τὸν κόπον τῆς ὁδοῦ ἀποθέμενος τὸ φορτίον τὸν Θάνατον ἐπεκαλεῖτο. τοῦ δὲ Θανάτου φανέντος καὶ πυθομένου δι' ἣν αἰτίαν ἐπεκαλεῖτο, ἔφη "ἵνα τὸ φορτίον ἄρῃς". It might be argued that this parallel supports the view that hic in our poem is Orcus; for the equivalence of Orcus and Thanatos cf. Macr. sat. 5. 19. 4 (referring to Euripides's Alcestis), RE 18. 1. 919 f. But Horace is not directly imitating this particular fable (ἄρῃς involves a variation of the expected commonplace), but rather the general way of talking that the fable presupposes; similar things could have been said of any chthonic deity.

functum pauperem laboribus : pauperem picks up 33 pauperi (once again note the chiastic order 'poor, rich, rich, poor'). functum laboribus combines the idea of defunctum and κεκμηκότα; cf. also Eur. fr. 449. 3 N. τὸν δ' αὖ θανόντα καὶ πόνων πεπαυμένον (Cic. Tusc. 1. 115 'at qui labores morte finisset graves').

40. vocatus atque non vocatus : the collocation was semi-proverbial; cf. Thuc. 1. 118. 3 (on Apollo and the Spartans) καὶ αὐτὸς ἔφη ξυλλήψεσθαι καὶ παρακαλούμενος καὶ ἄκλητος, Jul. or. 8. 250 c, Suidas 1. 83. Normally to come unbidden is a helpful act (Heliodorus 4. 16. 3 τὸ θεῖον . . . ἐπίκουρον γίνεται καὶ ἄκλητον εὐμενείᾳ πολλάκις φθάνον τὴν αἴτησιν); but here the words make a sinister climax (the emphasis is different at Sen. dial. 6. 20. 1 '[mors] omnibus finis, multis remedium, quisbusdam votum, de nullis melius merita quam de eis ad quos venit antequam invocaretur'). non vocatus makes an obvious oxymoron with the juxtaposed audit (cf. 3. 7. 21 f. 'scopulis surdior Icari / voces audit', Hdt. 1. 47. 3 καὶ οὐ φωνεῦντος ἀκούω). Polar expressions lend

themselves to such paradoxes; cf. Eur. *Her.* 1106 ὠή, τίς ἐγγὺς ἢ πρόσω φίλων ἐμῶν; (with Wilamowitz's note).

audit : a *vox propria* for a god (1. 2. 27 n., Virg. *georg.* 4. 7 'auditque vocatus Apollo'); a *satelles* appropriately answers a summons. A. Ruppersberg proposed *audet* with the sense of *vult* (*Philologus* 68, 1909, 526 ff.); but this spoils the paradox of *non vocatus audit*. Lambinus took *levare audit* closely together ('consents to relieve'); but the construction is unparalleled, and it is perhaps too difficult to dissociate the infinitive from *vocatus atque non vocatus*. The closing cadence leaves behind the asperities of *diatribe*, and recalls the ending of a hymn, particularly Horace's own hymn to Mercury (1. 10. 17 ff.). If Mercury is meant also here, Horace's association with the god (vol. i, pp. 127 ff.) gives these lines a personal dimension; we are surely not meant to forget that the poet regards himself as a *pauper*.

19. BACCHVM IN REMOTIS

[V. De Falco, *RF* 14 N.S., 1936, 371 ff.; Fraenkel 199 ff.; Pasquali 11 ff.; V. Pöschl, *Hermes* 101, 1973, 208 ff.; Th. Sinko, *Eos* 32, 1929, 1 ff.; Troxler-Keller 56 ff.]

1–8. I have had a vision of Bacchus teaching song in the mountains, and I am still beside myself with a fearful joy. 9–16. I am permitted to sing of Bacchanals and miraculous streams, of Ariadne's crown and the doom of Pentheus and Lycurgus. 17–32. Thou canst divert rivers and seas, and bind the Maenads' hair with a snood of vipers; thou didst wrestle with the bestial Rhoetus, and show thyself as fit for war as for peace; Cerberus did thee no hurt in the underworld, but rubbed his tail and licked thy feet.

Horace had no lack of models for an Ode to Bacchus. The seventh Homeric Hymn described in archaic narrative the god's adventure with the pirates. Anacreon invoked Dionysus with old-world simplicity, but introduced a personal love-interest that had nothing to do with cult (357). A grander note must have been sounded in innumerable dithyrambs, while a fragment of Pratinas gives an impression of breathless excitement (*PMG* 708. 3 ἐμὸς ἐμὸς ὁ Βρόμιος, ἐμὲ δεῖ κελαδεῖν, ἐμὲ δεῖ παταγεῖν). There was an abundance of material in Attic drama, not only in such plays as the *Lycurgeia* of Aeschylus and the supremely influential *Bacchae* of Euripides, but in many incidental choral odes (cf. Soph. *Ant.* 1115 ff., Ar. *ran.* 324 ff.). In the Hellenistic age traditional cult poems continued (cf. Philo-damus, pp. 165 ff. Powell), but there must also have been a growing tendency to mysticism (cf. *Orph. h.* 53 of the imperial period). The celebration of Bacchus was a favourite topic in the Augustan poets (cf. 1. 18. 13 n., 3. 25, Prop. 3. 17, Ov. *met.* 4. 17 ff., *trist.* 5. 3). But though no subject could be more trite, Horace makes out of it an original and striking poem.

The literary Hellenistic hymn had sometimes postponed the tra-ditional opening invocation; Callimachus describes Apollo's ap-proach before he turns to praise him (*h.* 2. 1 ff.), and so here, by a characteristic procedure of Augustan poetry, Horace relates his subject-matter to an alleged personal experience (cf. 1. 22, 1. 34, 2. 13, Prop. 2. 31, 3. 8). The poet's vision is itself a literary topic, though it derives from genres other than the hymn (Stemplinger 236, O. Falter, *Die Dichter und sein Gott bei den Griechen und Römern*, Diss. Würzburg, 1934, pp. 79 ff.). The Muses appeared to Hesiod on Helicon and taught him song (*th.* 22–34 with West's note); the theme of the mountain epiphany was adapted in various ways by Calli-machus (cf. anon. *anth. P.* 7. 42, Kambylis 70 ff.), Ennius (cf. Kambylis 196 ff., O. Skutsch, *Enniana*, 1968, pp. 126 ff.), Virgil (*ecl.* 6. 65, per-haps following Gallus), and Propertius (3. 3). Archilochus met the Muses when driving a cow to market and received from them a lyre in exchange (p. 5. 22 ff. Tarditi); Alcman describes an epiphany of Apollo (47 ἦρα τὸν Φοῖβον ὄνειρον εἶδον); Pindar saw the Mother of the Gods in a vision and Demeter in a dream (C. M. Bowra, *Pindar*, pp. 50 ff.), and honoured at least the latter with a poem (fr. 37); he also told how Pan had been seen singing one of his paeans between Helicon and Cithaeron (*vit. A*, p. 2 Dr., J. A. Haldane, *Phoenix* 22, 1968, 18 ff.). Socrates wrote a prelude to Apollo, who had appeared to him in a dream (Pl. *Phaed.* 60 e), and in the Roman Empire the elder Pliny (Plin. *epist.* 3. 5. 4), John the Divine (*apoc.* 1. 11), and Cassius Dio (73. 23. 2 ff.) were given supernatural encouragement for their varied literary activities. Aelius Aristides was turned to poetry by Asclepius, Athene, and Dionysus himself; in the last case the god dictated the disappointing refrain χαῖρ' ὦ ἄνα κισσεῦ (50. 39, C. A. Behr, *Aelius Aristides and the Sacred Tales*, 1968, pp. 116 ff.). For epiphanies cf. further *RE* Suppl. 4. 277 ff., *RLAC* 5. 832 ff.

After the matter-of-fact detachment of the first stanza, appro-priate in describing miracles, Horace breaks into the eerie *euhoe* of the possessed (5 ff.); similarly in the fourth Roman ode (3. 4. 1 ff.) a classically serene invocation is followed by a mysterious vision (Syndikus). At the same time the clear-cut vignette of Bacchus the music-master gives place to the ill-defined terror of the thyrsus; in Dionysiac worship pleasure and pain were inextricably mixed (cf.

3. 25. 18 'dulce periculum'), and the god's double aspect makes an organizing principle in Horace's poem (cf. especially 27 n., Syndikus 1. 477, Pöschl, op. cit., pp. 222 ff.). In the third stanza Horace pulls himself together (9 n.) and lists Bacchus's achievements with the summary allusiveness of sophisticated poetry (cf. vol. i, p. 126, Prop. 3. 17. 21 ff., Ov. *fast.* 3. 715 ff., Boucher 273 ff., 301 ff.); the hysterical Thyiads are combined with the god's delicious bounty, the immortality of Ariadne contrasted with the doom of Pentheus and Lycurgus. In the fifth and sixth stanzas (where the hymn proper begins) the tone is heightened by the 'Du-Stil' of genuine cult (17 n.); the god's daemonic power is illustrated by his subjugation of natural forces and his overthrow of mythological monsters. The tension slackens somewhat in the penultimate stanza (25 n.) where Bacchus's peaceful qualities are emphasized, and the poem ends with an underworld scene of grotesque charm that matches the vivid opening stanza. Horace has listed the god's multifarious aspects not only with brilliant concentration but with subtle fluctuations of tone.

But has the ode any profounder purpose than a display of stylistic virtuosity? It is clearly relevant that in the Augustan age Bacchus was treated by the poets as a source of inspiration. Already in classical Greece he was the patron of dithyramb, tragedy, and comedy, his rites were accompanied by the *aulos* and the drum, as a god of Delphi he was associated with Apollo and as a mountain god with the Muses (Soph. *Ant.* 965, Paus. 9. 30. 1, etc.), he was given such titles as Μουσαγέτης (*IG* 12. 5. 46, *RE* 5. 1031) and Μελπόμενος (*RE* 15. 589 f.), his wine was not only a subject for poetry but an aid to composition (Archilochus 120 W., Ar. *ran.* 354 ff.). It is more important for our purposes that philosophers connected the inspiration of the poet with the frenzy of the possessed; cf. Democritus, fr. 21 Ὅμηρος φύσεως λαχὼν θεαζούσης, Pl. *Ion.* 533 e οὕτω δὲ καὶ ἡ Μοῦσα ἐνθέους μὲν ποιεῖ αὐτή, *Phaedr.* 245 a, Kroll 24 ff., Dodds 80 ff., R. Harriott, *Poetry and Criticism before Plato*, 1969, pp. 78 ff., Pease on Cic. *div.* 1. 80, Russell on Longinus 13. 2, Brink on *ars* 295–8. In the Hellenistic age the actors' guild ('Technitae of Dionysus') concerned themselves not only with drama but with all forms of music and poetry displayed at the public festivals (*RE* 5 A. 2484 ff.). Callimachus not only associates Dionysus with Apollo and the Muses (fr. 191. 7 f.), but regards him as responsible for poetical inspiration (*ep.* 8. 3 f. ᾧ δὲ σὺ μὴ πνεύσῃς ἐνδέξιος, ἤν τις ἔρηται / "πῶς ἔβαλες;" φησί "σκληρὰ τὰ γιγνόμενα"). The currency of the theme in Hellenistic poetry may be inferred from a passage in Lucretius (8 n.) as well as repeated allusions by later Romans; cf. 3. 25, Prop. 2. 30. 37 ff., 3. 2. 9 'nobis et Baccho et Apolline dextro', 4. 1. 62 etc., Ov. *am.* 1. 3. 11 f., *trist.* 5. 3. 1 ff., Lygd. 4. 43 ff., Lucan 1. 64 f., Stat. *silv.* 1. 5. 3, 5. 3. 6. See further E. Maass, *Hermes* 31, 1896, 375 ff., Kroll 30 ff., De Falco, loc. cit., P. Boyancé in *Fondation Hardt, Entretiens* 2, 1953, 196 ff. (over-speculative), Wille 530 ff. (with references to art), Troxler-Keller 56 ff.

All this explains why Horace chose Bacchus as a subject, but it does not give the poem the kind of seriousness that some critics suggest. Few will suppose that he is recounting a paranormal psychological experience such as is plausible in the case of Aelius Aristides and perhaps even of Hesiod (though the recurrence of such visions in the early poets is an argument for incredulity). When Fraenkel says that Horace did see Dionysus (p. 200), this only means that he could visualize legend; even if that is true (and Horace had a less pictorial imagination than Catullus or Ovid), it is not what is usually meant by an epiphany. Horace's vision seems as literary as those of other Roman poets; even if he describes his experience more dramatically, his essential detachment is demonstrated by the dry aside 'credite posteri' (Williams 69). He may have had more insight into classical Greek literature than some of his contemporaries, but a re-creation of archaic cult was not his main purpose, and the Indian miracles (17 f.) and contorted Gigantomachy (21 ff.) are un-deniably Hellenistic. The concluding catabasis implies no deeper involvement, and the frescoes of the Villa of the Mysteries and Villa Farnesina reveal nothing of the poet's attitudes. We cannot even say that Horace is saying something profound about the subconscious processes of his own poetic composition; the inspiration of Bacchus, which elsewhere moves him to irony (*epist.* 1. 19. 3 f., 2. 2. 78), is here mentioned only in the second stanza, and even in 3. 25 tends to be interpreted far too solemnly. Since the Romantic movement it has become difficult to understand the literary preconceptions of the ancient world, when form might matter more than self-expression and a poet could assume a mantle without having a message to preach. The craftsman who moulded the Ode to Bacchus was an Apollonian not a Dionysiac, a Gray not a Schiller; his controlled ecstasy implied no commitment but was contrived with calculating deliberation; unlike the fasting Bacchae, when he shouted 'Euhoe' he was well fed (Juv. 7. 62) and in his right mind.

Metre: Alcaic.

1. **remotis . . . rupibus** : the landscape is hinted at, not drawn in de-tail. *rupibus* may be suggested by art; Orpheus and his animals are sometimes portrayed among the rocks. Bacchus was a mountain god (Anacreon 357. 4 f., Soph. *OT* 1105 f., etc.), described by such adjectives as ὀρειφοίτης (Bruchmann 90) and φιλοσκόπελος (ibid. 94);

hence the ὀρειβασία of his devotees. Epiphanies commonly took place in the mountains (p. 315 and 2 n.), and the Bacchic landscape was traditionally wild and isolated (3. 25. 12 *devio*), but Horace's fantasy may have been partly designed to suit his own Sabine retreat.

2. vidi : in describing visions the ancients spoke in a matter-of-fact way of 'seeing a god'. For epiphanies to literary men see above, p. 315. In view of the remote scene of Horace's experience, manifestations of Pan (or Faunus) are particularly relevant; cf. Hdt. 6. 105. 1 (Philippides sees the god in the mountains), Virg. *ecl.* 10. 26 'Pan . . . quem vidimus ipsi', Pease on Cic. *nat. deor.* 2. 6 (p. 560) and *div.* 1. 101.

docentem : Bacchus is depicted as χοροδιδάσκαλος (cf. 3 'discentis', 4. 6. 43 'docilis modorum'). No exact parallel presents itself, though he is portrayed on a Berlin vase listening to music (O. Jahn, *Arch. Zeit.* 13, 1855, 151 ff., Beazley, *ARV²* 1336. 2); similarly Pan played to the nymphs (Pl. *anth. P.* 9. 823, *RE* Suppl. 8. 1006), and Orpheus was often the centre of an admiring audience. Sometimes a god is said to teach or dictate his songs to a poet (cf. 1. 24. 2 n., Hes. *th.* 22 καλὴν ἐδίδαξαν ἀοιδήν); here Horace more modestly eavesdrops on a lesson taught to others (cf. Virg. *ecl.* 6. 82 ff.).

credite posteri : the brusque parenthetic apostrophe is reminiscent of Callimachus (*RE* Suppl. 13. 246, Newman 46) or his Roman imitators (Catull. 66. 71, Prop. 4. 8. 6). The implication is that future generations will naturally tend to incredulity; cf. Ov. *fast.* 3. 370 'credite dicenti, mira sed acta loquor'. Miracles become harder to believe with the lapse of time; cf. *epod.* 9. 11 ff. 'Romanus eheu— posteri negabitis— / emancipatus feminae / fert vallum et arma miles', Sen. *Thy.* 753 'o nullo scelus / credibile in aevo quodque posteritas neget', *Octavia* 358 ff. 'ferro es nati moritura tui / cuius facinus vix posteritas, / tarde semper saecula credent' (with Hosius's note), Plin. *paneg.* 9. 2 'credentne posteri . . .?', *paneg. lat.* 2. (12). 12. 3, *Claud.* 26. 423. Some editors interpret 'future generations will believe me even if my contemporaries do not'; but the former explanation is supported by the parallels, including one from Horace himself.

3. nymphasque : the nymphs suckled the infant Dionysus and with the satyrs were permanent members of his thiasus. For their musical tastes cf. *Orph. h.* 53. 6 εἰς ὕμνον τρέπεται σὺν ἐυζώνοισι τιθήναις, Roscher 3. 1. 518 f.

4. capripedum : Pan was αἰγιπόδης (*h. Hom.* 19. 2) or τραγόπους, and his attributes were gradually extended to the satyrs (Roscher 4. 488 f., *RE* 3 A. 51 ff.). The compound adjective (also at Prop. 3. 17. 34) suggests the language of old poetry; it is no doubt influenced by Lucr. 4. 580 ff. 'haec loca capripedes Satyros Nymphasque tenere / finitimi fingunt et Faunos esse locuntur / . . . chordarumque sonos fieri'. By juxtaposing the feet and the ears Horace produces a vivid and slightly bizarre conceit (cf. D. West ap. Costa 56).

acutas : Horace visualizes the satyrs' attentiveness (cf. 1. 12. 11 n.); the adjective balances *discentis*. It is also applicable in general to the goat-like ears of satyrs; cf. Porph. ad loc. 'nam sic videmus Satyros fingi oblongis auribus acutisque', ps.-Acro 'et ad audiendum et ad ipsarum aurium figuram', Sil. 13. 333, Nemes. *ecl. 3*. 32 (of the infant Bacchus and Silenus) 'aut digitis aures astringit acutas', Lucian, *deor. conc. 4* οἱ δὲ Σάτυροι ὀξεῖς τὰ ὦτα, Bacch. 2, Nonnus 14. 138 ff.

5. metu : here not the normal respect of a god-fearing man (1. 35. 37) but excitement at the epiphany, which is supposed to have happened a few minutes before (*recenti*). Cf. Hom. *Il.* 20. 131 χαλεποὶ δὲ θεοὶ φαίνεσθαι ἐναργεῖς, Richardson on *h. Dem.* 188–90, Naev. *trag.* 43 (*Lucurgus*) 'iam ibi nos duplicat advenientis . . . timos pavos', Pease on Virg. *Aen.* 4. 279, *ev. Luc.* 1. 29 διεταράχθη (Mary, on being greeted by Gabriel), *RE* Suppl. 4. 317 f. Similarly the sight of Pan induces panic (*RE* Suppl. 8. 969 f., 987), and all nature shudders at the *adventus* of a god (F. Adami, *JKPh* Suppl. 26, 1901, 231, *RLAC* 5. 841 f.).

6. plenoque . . . pectore : a phrase properly used of prophets (cf. ἔνθεος) and by extension of 'inspired' poets; cf. 3. 25. 1 f. 'quo me, Bacche, rapis tui / plenum?', Sen. *suas.* 3. 5–7, who attributes *plena deo* to Virgil (cf. E. K. Borthwick, *Mnemosyne* 25, 1972, 408 ff.), Ov. *trag.* 2 (*Medea*) 'feror huc illuc ut plena deo', *fast.* 6. 538 with Bömer's note, Leo on Sen. *trag.* vol. i, p. 166 n. 8, Lucan 1. 675, 5. 166, *ev. Luc.* 1. 67 καὶ Ζαχαρίας ὁ πατὴρ αὐτοῦ ἐπλήσθη Πνεύματος Ἁγίου καὶ ἐπροφήτευσεν. Sometimes a metaphor from conception is apparent; cf. Longinus 13. 2 ἐγκύμονα τῆς δαιμονίου καθισταμένην δυνάμεως (with Russell's note), Gray, *Elegy* 46 'Some heart, once pregnant with celestial fire', Onians 489 f. See further Norden on Virg. *Aen.* 6. 77–80, H. Hanse, *Gott Haben*, 1939, p. 135, Onians 50 ff., Dodds 64 ff.

turbidum laetatur : the topic of high Greek poetry is supported by a Graecizing accusative (cf. 2. 12. 14 f. 'lucidum fulgentis'). *laetatur* provides an unexpected climax (Darnley Naylor); for joy at an epiphany cf. *ev. Luc.* 24. 52 (the end of the book) ὑπέστρεψαν εἰς Ἰερουσαλὴμ μετὰ χαρᾶς μεγάλης, Adami, loc. cit. [5 n.], pp. 232 ff., K. Buchholz, *de Horatio hymnographo*, Diss. Königsberg, 1912, pp. 46 f., *RE* Suppl. 4. 318. *laetitia* is most often used of a serene gladness, but *turbidum* suggests the muddy eddies of a mind in a whirl (cf. Pherecrates 115 γελῶντα καὶ χαίροντα καὶ τεθολωμένον); oxymoron is often found in expressions referring to pain and pleasure. For the double aspect of psychic experience cf. Porph. ad loc. 'viso enim deo quis non perturbetur, licet gaudeat?', Lucr. 3. 28 f. 'his ibi me rebus quaedam divina voluptas / percipit atque horror' (this must be the travesty of a religious motif), Calp. 1. 90 'mixtus subit inter gaudia terror'.

7. parce Liber : for Horace's deprecation cf. 1. 18. 13 f. 'saeva tene ... / ... tympana'. *parce* is a ritual word (still used in the Catholic Church) = φείδεο; cf. G. Appel, *de Romanorum precationibus*, 1909, p. 120, Fraenkel 411 n. 1. For the sacral *geminatio* (as with *euhoe*) cf. *epod*. 17. 7 'solve solve turbinem', C. Prato on [Sen.] *epig*. 2. 7 (on *parce*), Norden on Virg. *Aen*. 6. 46, Dodds on Eur. *Ba*. 107, Barrett on Eur. *Hipp*. 58–60.

Horace's Alcaic enneasyllables only end 11 times with a quadri-syllable or double disyllable, but 3 of the instances occur in this ode (cf. 11 *atque truncis*, 19 *viperino*). The usage is found only in Books I and II, but is not enough to prove exceptional earliness (thus Pasquali 14). The anaphora of *parce* seems to mitigate the eccentricity (vol. i, p. xlii), for some reason that is difficult to explain.

8. gravi ... thyrso : for the ablative cf. 1. 12. 23 f. 'metuende certa / Phoebe sagitta', 3. 2. 4, anon. *anth*. *Pl*. 185. 2 θύρσῳ δεινός. *metuende* picks up 5 *metu* and makes specific the cause of Horace's fear. The vocative gerundive is a mark of high poetry rather than of genuine cult, but it hints at the sacral use of detached vocative adjectives or participles; cf. 1. 12. 21 f. 'proeliis audax, neque te silebo, / Liber' (this corrects note ad loc.), 2. 7. 2 n., Virg. *Aen*. 11. 557 'alma, tibi hanc, nemorum cultrix ...', 11. 789 f. 'da, pater, hoc nostris aboleri dedecus armis, / omnipotens', Ov. *fast*. 3. 1 f. 'bellice, depositis clipeo paulisper et hasta, / Mars ades', 4. 319 f.

The thyrsus was the ivy-tipped wand of Bacchus whose touch induced frenzy (Dodds on Eur. *Ba*. 113, Palmer on Ov. *epist*. 13. 33, F. J. M. de Waele, *The Magic Staff or Rod in Graeco-Roman Antiquity*, 1927, pp. 84 ff.). Later it was regarded as an instrument of poetic inspiration; cf. Lucr. 1. 922 f. 'sed acri / percussit thyrso laudis spes magna meum cor' (one must posit a less secular prototype where Dionysus touched the poet), Prop. 2. 30. 38 'docta cuspide', Ov. *am*. 3. 15. 17 'corniger increpuit thyrso graviore Lyaeus' (echoing ibid. 3. 1. 23), *trist*. 4. 1. 43, *Pont*. 2. 5. 67, Juv. 7. 60. The emphatic *gravi* implies supernatural potency rather than physical force.

9. fas ... est : it was *nefas* to reveal the mysteries of Bacchus (1. 18. 13 n.), and often even to see a god; cf. Liv. 1. 16. 6, Virg. *Aen*. 6. 266 'sit mihi fas audita loqui', Ov. *epist*. 16. 63, Sen. *epist*. 115. 4

'nonne velut numinis occursu obstupefactus resistat et ut fas sit vidisse tacitus precetur?', Hosius on Auson. *Mos.* 186, Wagenvoort 184 ff. Bentley proposed *sit* for *est* in our passage: he thought a confident statement incompatible with the terror of the previous stanza. But the indicative shows that the prayer for mercy has been answered: Horace gains in coherence like Cassandra (Aesch. *Ag.* 1178 ff.) and the Sibyl (Virg. *Aen.* 6. 102). For similar assertions cf. Soph. fr. 941. 14 P. = 855. 14 N. εἴ μοι θέμις, θέμις δὲ τἀληθῆ λέγειν, Ov. *fast.* 6. 7 f. (following 'est deus in nobis') 'fas mihi praecipue vultus vidisse deorum / vel quia sum vates vel quia sacra cano', Sil. 1. 17 ff.

pervicacis : persons under Bacchic possession were unnaturally strong and tireless; cf. 3. 25. 9 'exsomnis', Eur. *Ba.* 187 ὡς οὐ κάμοιμ' ἄν (with Dodds on 194 ἀμοχθί and 1090–3), Ar. *ran.* 401 ἄνευ πόνου, Nonnus 24. 348 ἀκοιμήτοιο χορείης. With its suggestion of austere persistence, the adjective makes something of an oxymoron with the giddy *Thyiadas.*

Thyiadas : i.e. *Bacchas*; cf. 3. 15. 10, Soph. *Ant.* 1151, Catull. 64. 391, Pease on Virg. *Aen.* 4. 302, *RE* 6 A. 684 ff., M. P. Nilsson, *The Dionysiac Mysteries of the Hellenistic and Roman Age,* 1957, pp. 4 f. The name was particularly associated with Delphi (cf. Paus. 10. 6. 4 for Thyia, the mother of Delphos), and was still given to a *collegium* in Plutarch's time: cf. *quaest. Gr.* 293 f (12) τῶν Θυιάδων ἀρχηγός (with Halliday's note), *Is. et Osir.* 364 e (with Griffiths's note). The word is derived from θυίειν or θύειν 'to rush'; *pace* Bentley, it was sometimes spelt *Thyades* (*etym. M.* s.v. Θυάδες αἱ Βάκχαι παρὰ τὸ θύω τὸ ὁρμῶ καὶ πλεονασμῷ τοῦ ι Θυιάδες). In our passage the name follows naturally after the mention of *thyrsus.*

10. vinique fontem . . . : a miraculous reaction of nature (*RE* Suppl. 4. 319) to the epiphany of the god; cf. *h. Hom.* 7. 35 f., Soph. fr. 5 P., Eur. *Hyps.* fr. 57 Bond, *Ba.* 142 f. ῥεῖ δὲ γάλακτι πέδον, ῥεῖ δ' οἴνῳ, ῥεῖ δὲ μελισσᾶν / νέκταρι, 706 ff. ἄλλη δὲ νάρθηκ' ἐς πέδον καθῆκε γῆς, / καὶ τῇδε κρήνην ἐξανῆκ' οἴνου θεός· / ὅσαις δὲ λευκοῦ πώματος πόθος παρῆν, / ἄκροισι δακτύλοισι διαμῶσαι χθόνα / γάλακτος ἑσμοὺς εἶχον· ἐκ δὲ κισσίνων / θύρσων γλυκεῖαι μέλιτος ἔσταζον ῥοαί (with Dodds's note on 704–11), Pl. *Ion* 534 a αἱ βάκχαι ἀρύονται ἐκ τῶν ποταμῶν μέλι καὶ γάλα κατεχόμεναι, ἔμφρονες δὲ οὖσαι οὔ, Callixeinos, *FGrH* 627 F 2. 31 (Athen. 5. 200 c), Sen. *Oed.* 491 ff., Philostr. *imag.* 1. 14, Nonnus 22. 16 ff., 45. 148. For similar exuberance in the Golden Age cf. Virg. *georg.* 1. 131 f., Tib. 1. 3. 45 (with K. F. Smith's note), Ov. *met.* 1. 111 ff., *Aetna* 13 f., Gatz 229; so of the Promised Land *exod.* 3. 8 γῆν ῥέουσαν γάλα καὶ μέλι (milk was more significant to the Jews than to the Greeks, and the concept may have originated from the East). Milk and honey were potent substances, the food of the gods, offerings

to the dead, Christian sacraments in second-century Alexandria and
in the Coptic Church till modern times. For many interesting details
see H. Usener, 'Milch und Honig', *RhM* 57, 1902, 177 ff. (= *Kl. Schr.*
4. 398 ff.), K. Wyss, *Die Milch im Kultus der Griechen und Römer*,
1914 (*RGVV* 15. 2), pp. 40 ff., Pease on Virg. *Aen.* 4. 486, W. F. Otto,
Dionysos: Mythos und Kultus, 1933, pp. 91 f. (the wine-miracle), *RE*
15. 379 ff., 1576 ff.

uberes : for the adjective cf. A. Ernout, *Aspects du vocabulaire latin*,
1954, p. 133; it suits streams of milk particularly well.

11. atque : the instances of *atque* in the four books of the *Odes* total
11, 4, 1, 2; the corresponding figures for *ac* are 7, 1, 1 (or 2), 0 (for
the chronological implications see p. 4). Horace elides *atque* only
twice (in the first book); on the other hand the elegists virtually
never use *atque* before a consonant, and the epic poets show a considerable reluctance. Horace's practice suits his masculine style,
which values solidity more than smoothness (cf. the frequency of
unelided *atque* in the elder Cato); metrical convenience is a bonus
rather than an explanation. See further Axelson 82 ff., Ross 26 ff.

truncis . . . cavis : tree-trunks, not thyrsi; cf. *epod.* 16. 47 'mella
cava manant ex ilice', Virg. *georg.* 2. 452 f., Ov. *am.* 3. 8. 40, *RE* 15.
367. *lapsa* means not just 'falling' but 'flowing'; cf. ῥεῖ in Eur. loc. cit.,
fontem and *rivos* above.

12. iterare : 'ex integro cantare ac repetere' (Porph.); the poet repeats the lesson he has learned. The verb in this sense may simply be
a solemn archaism; cf. Plaut. *Cas.* 879 'operam date dum mea facta
itero', Asell. *hist.* 2, *Thes.l.L.* 7. 2. 549. 9 ff. But the strangeness of the
usage makes one suspect a technical term of bee-keeping (cf. 1. 7.
32 n. of ploughing); after the best honey had been strained from the
combs a second yield was squeezed out (Colum. 9. 15. 13). In any case
Horace is making an elegant apology for his derivative theme.

13. beatae : 'beatified' (a participle); cf. 4. 8. 29 'caelo Musa beat'.
When Ariadne was deserted by Theseus on Naxos, she was rescued
by Dionysus, married, and made immortal (see West on Hes. *th.*
949). According to later versions her bridal crown was set among the
stars as the Corona Borealis; cf. Epimenides, fr. 25, Pherecydes,
FGrH 3 F 148, perhaps *Ox. pap.* 2452 fr. 2. 18 (with Turner's note).
The theme was popularized by the astronomically-minded Hellenistic
scholars and poets, who in turn influenced the Romans; cf. Eratosthenes, pp. 66 ff. Robert, Aratus, *phaen.* 71 f., Ap. Rhod. 3. 1003,
Catull. 66. 59 ff., Virg. *georg.* 1. 222, Ov. *fast.* 3. 459 ff., *met.* 8. 177 ff.,
Nonnus 47. 446 ff. By some later accounts Ariadne herself was turned
into a star (Prop. 3. 17. 7 f., etc.); catasterism was a popular belief

in Horace's day, as is shown by Caesar's comet. See further Roscher 6. 892 ff., *RE* 2. 805 f., 4. 1643, Pease on Cic. *nat. deor.* 2. 108, Bömer on Ov. *fast.* 3. 459 ff., Weinstock 370 ff.

additum stellis honorem : for curiously similar expressions cf. Germ. 72 'hunc illi Bacchus thalami memor addit honorem', Avien. *Arat.* 198 'haec Ariadnei capitis testatur honorem', Prud. *c. Symm.* 1. 142 ff. 'mox Ariadneus stellis caelestibus ignis / additur: hoc pretium noctis persolvit honore / Liber, ut aetherium meretrix illuminet axem'. Though *honorem* is used more concretely in our passage (1. 17. 16 n.), one is tempted to posit a common source, perhaps the *Aratea* of Cicero; cf. Aratus, *phaen.* 71 f. Στέφανος τὸν ἀγανὸς ἔθηκεν / σῆμ' ἐμέναι Διόνυσος ἀποιχομένης Ἀριάδνης, Cic. *Arat.* fr. 13 T. 'hic illa eximio posita est fulgore Corona' (we do not know how the passage developed). For similar uses of *addere* cf. further Virg. *Aen.* 8. 301 'decus addite divis', Auson. *Mos.* 149.

14. tectaque Penthei disiecta : the deeds of Dionysus included the punishment of disbelievers, among whom Pentheus and Lycurgus are often paired (Prop. 3. 17. 23, Ellis on Ov. *Ibis*, p. 187). The former was famous above all from the *Bacchae* of Euripides, which was imitated by both Pacuvius and Accius; the plural *tecta* (cf. *Ba.* 595 δώματα Πενθέος) and the litotes *non leni ruina* both have a flavour of tragic diction. His story was often represented in art, notably in the house of the Vettii at Pompeii (Roscher 3. 2. 1931 ff., *RE* 19. 1. 549). Here Horace does not describe the grisly σπαραγμός, but by the use of *disiecta* he may intend a delicate reminder (cf. the hint at Orpheus's fate at *serm.* 1. 4. 62 'invenias etiam disiecti membra poetae'). Rather he concentrates on the god's miraculous power that made fetters drop, doors open, and walls collapse; for the escape from Pentheus's palace cf. *epist.* 1. 16. 78, Eur. *Ba.* 587 f. τάχα τὰ Πενθέως μέλαθρα διατινάξεται πεσήμασιν, 591 f. εἴδετε λαΐνα κίοσιν ἔμβολα / διάδρομα τάδε, 633 (with Dodds², pp. xxxii f.), Nonnus 44. 35 ff. See further O. Weinreich, *Gebet und Wunder, Tübinger Beiträge zur Altertumswissenschaft*, Heft 5, 1929, 280 ff. (= *Religionsgeschichtliche Studien*, 1968, pp. 118 ff.); he compares *act. apost.* 16. 26 (on the escape of Paul and Silas at Philippi) ἄφνω δὲ σεισμὸς ἐγένετο μέγας ὥστε σαλευθῆναι τὰ θεμέλια τοῦ δεσμωτηρίου.

16. exitium Lycurgi : as a punishment for harassing Dionysus or his followers the Thracian Lycurgus was blinded (Hom. *Il.* 6. 130 ff., Nonnus 21. 166), immured in a cave (Soph. *Ant.* 955), driven to madness, self-mutilation, wife-murder, or suicide, rended by horses or eaten by panthers (*RE* 13. 2433 ff.). He was the subject of an Aeschylean tetralogy, and of a play by Naevius (*Lucurgus*). *Thracis* not

only recalls the Thracian associations of Dionysus, but also underlines the king's barbarity (like the name 'Lycurgus'). For a more
favourable view cf. Firm. Mat. *error.* 6. 7–9, who compares him with
Sp. Postumius, cos. 186 B.C. and author of the salutary legislation
de Bacchanalibus.

17. tu . . . : as if overcome by sudden emotion, Horace breaks into
the hymn of praise which he has claimed the right to sing. The structure is a sophisticated development of the Homeric type where the
narrative ends with a salutation; for anaphora of *tu* in religious
contexts cf. 1. 10. 9 n. Here one stanza is devoted to the earth, two
to heaven, and one to the underworld; the first of these stanzas consists of a tricolon with an expanded third member (17–20), the last
to some extent dies away (29–32). The pattern of alternate rising and
falling repeats on a larger scale a movement that can already be
sensed in 9–16.

The present tenses deserve note: though the ability to divert
rivers and twine snakes can be regarded as permanent attributes of
the god, *mare barbarum* seems to refer to a more definite occasion.
But it should be observed that similar presents are found in aretalogies even when particular exploits are in question; cf. Virg. *Aen.*
8. 293 ff. 'tu nubigenas, invicte, bimembris / Hylaeumque Pholumque manu, tu Cresia mactas / prodigia, et vastum Nemeae sub rupe
leonem', Sen. *Ag.* 384 ff., Claud. *rapt. Pros.* 2 praef. 37 ff. 'solvis
Amazonios cinctus, Stymphalidas arcu / adpetis, occiduo ducis ab
orbe greges . . .'.

flectis amnis : *flectis* must mean 'divert' (though less appropriate
with *mare*), and not simply 'subdue'; cf. Naev. *trag.* 42 'se quasi
amnis celeris rapit sed tamen inflexu flectitur'. The grandiloquent
amnis (with *barbaros* presumably understood) suggests the large
rivers of the East crossed by Bacchus on his journey to India; this
expedition became a literary theme, particularly after the conquests of Alexander (Eur. *Ba.* 13 ff., Norden on Virg. *Aen.* 6. 804 f.,
Frazer on Apollod. 3. 5. 1, Nock 1. 134 ff. = *JHS* 48, 1928, 21 ff.). For
spectacular river-crossings cf. Eur. *Ba.* 568 f. τόν τ' ὠκυρόαν διαβὰς
Ἄξιον (which might allude to a miracle), Nonnus 12. 124 ff. (Hermus
and Pactolus stop flowing), 23. 126 f. (the panthers cross the Hydaspes
dry-hoofed in an amphibious chariot), Xen. *anab.* 1. 4. 17–18 (the
Euphrates had sunk for Cyrus), Plut. *Lucull.* 24. 4 ff., *Josh.* 3. 13 ff.
(the Israelites cross the Jordan). For the stopping of rivers in other
contexts cf. 1. 29. 10 n.

mare : there seems to be an allusion to the same obscure episode
at Sen. *Herc. f.* 903 f. 'adsit Lycurgi domitor et rubri maris'; the *mare*
rubrum included the Indian Ocean as well as the Red Sea, but even

so this makes a notable parallel to the exploit of Moses (*exod.* 14. 21, cf. the aretalogies at *exod.* 15. 4, *psalm.* 78. 14). The legend about Bacchus may lie behind the story that the Pamphylian sea retreated before Alexander; cf. Callisthenes, *FGrH* 124 F 31 (with Jacoby's commentary, vol. ii D, pp. 427 f.), Menander, fr. 751 K., Sen. *suas.* 1. 11 (Alexander at Ocean) οὐδ' ἐπὶ τῷ Παμφυλίῳ πελάγει τὴν ἐμπρόθεσμον καραδοκοῦμεν ἄμπωσιν· οὐδὲ Εὐφράτης τοῦτ' ἔστιν οὐδὲ 'Ινδός . . . , Josephus, *ant. Jud.* 2. 339–48 (a comparison of Moses and Alexander), Plut. *Alex.* 17. 3 f. (with Hamilton's commentary), W. W. Tarn, *Alexander the Great,* 1948, 2. 357 f., 373 f., E. Mederer, *Die Alexanderlegenden bei den ältesten Alexanderhistorikern,* 1936, pp. 6 ff. For the supernatural calming of waters cf. also 1. 12. 29 n.; as early as Homer, Dionysus found refuge in the sea by a parting of the waves (*Il.* 6. 135 f., cf. Nonnus 20. 353).

barbarum: the adjective suggests the exotic tales of the East, perhaps also that Bacchus could tame the savage waters.

18. **separatis . . . iugis**: editors accept Porphyrio's explanation 'secretis ac remotis', but then *separatis* would need a point of reference (separated from what?). Rather one might suggest an allusion to the 'two peaks' traditionally assigned to Parnassus (to be distinguished from the much lower Phaedriades at Delphi). They are often mentioned in Dionysiac contexts, and one was particularly sacred to the god; cf. Soph. *Ant.* 1126 (hymn to Dionysus) διλόφου πέτρας (with Jebb's note), Eur. *Ion* 1126 f., *Ba.* 307 δικόρυφον πλάκα, *Phoen.* 226 ff. with schol., Bömer on Ov. *met.* 1. 316, Lucan 3. 173 'Parnasosque iugo . . . desertus utroque', 5. 72 f., 78 'unoque iugo, Parnase, latebas', *RE* 18. 4. 1595 ff. (with abundant parallels). It may be argued that the Thracian Bistonides had no business on Parnassus, but such considerations would not have deterred an Augustan poet.

A *iugum* is something that joins (*iungit*); so there is a characteristic verbal play in qualifying the word with *separatis*. There may also be a contrast between *separatis* and 19 *coerces* ('hold together').

uvidus: i.e. with wine; cf. 1. 7. 22 n. (*uda*), 4. 5. 39 'dicimus uvidi', Eur. *El.* 326 μέθῃ δὲ βρεχθείς. But the word is less trivial than *madidus*, with which Porphyrio equates it (cf. Stat. *silv.* 4. 8. 8 f. 'madenti . . . deo').

19. **nodo**: a headband (3. 14. 22); *coercere* is naturally used of the hair (Ov. *met.* 1. 477, etc.). The frenzied Maenads are often portrayed with hair flying loose; cf. Dodds on Eur. *Ba.* 831–3, 862–5, Nonnus 20. 342 ἀνάμπυκας. But sometimes they wore a snake (in art, if not in life); cf. Eur. *Ba.* 101 f. στεφάνωσέν τε δρακόντων / στεφάνοις, Nonnus 14. 341 ἡ μὲν ἐχιδναίῳ (*viperino*) κεφαλὴν ἐζώσατο δεσμῷ. For an animated illustration cf. the cup by the Brygos painter reproduced

by Martin Robertson, *Greek Painting*, 1959, p. 107 (= Beazley, *ARV*²
371. 15). In our passage the emphatic *viperino*, with its suggestion
of writhing, both balances *flectis* and makes a contrast with *coerces*.

20. Bistonidum : female Bistones. The name of this tribe is used by
Roman poets for 'Thracian' (*RE* 3. 504 f., *Thes.l.L.* 2. 2016. 11 ff.),
presumably following Hellenistic models. It was associated with
Orpheus, so suits Bacchanals (cf. *ciris* 165 ff.).

sine fraude : 'without damage' (cf. *carm. saec.* 41); the phrase is
often used in legal writers for 'without penalty'. Horace is describing
the immunity not just of the god (cf. 29 *insons*) but of the Bacchae
(*Bistonidum* seems to go partly with *fraude*); they had acquired the
invulnerability of the possessed (Dodds on Eur. *Ba.* 695–8, 761–4).

21. parentis : not just 'our common father' (1. 12. 13 f. 'solitis
parentis / laudibus') but 'thy parent'. The ambiguous word suits
the story that Dionysus was born a second time from Zeus's thigh; cf.
Eur. *Ba.* 524 Ζεὺς ὁ τεκών, Aristides, *orat.* 4. 52 ὁ πατὴρ ἑκατέρας τῆς
φύσεως μετέσχεν εἰς αὐτόν.

per arduum : cf. 1. 3. 37 f. 'nil mortalibus ardui est : / caelum ipsum
petimus' (invading heaven is uphill work), Virg. *georg.* 1. 324 'ruit
arduus aether'.

22. Gigantum : Dionysus is occasionally mentioned in literature as
one of the victors in the Gigantomachia; cf. Eur. *Ion* 216 ff., *Cycl.*
5 ff., Apollod. 1. 6. 2 Εὔρυτον δὲ θυρσῷ Διόνυσος ἔκτεινε, Nonnus 25.
87 ff. (defeats Porphyrion, Enceladus, Alcyoneus), 25. 206 (more
sensationally) μοῦνος ἀποτμήξας ὀφιώδεας υἶας Ἀρούρης, 48. 43 ff. Art
is a better source (as usual with this subject), and Dionysus appears
alike in vase-painting and sculpture, notably the Parthenon metopes
and the frieze of the Pergamum Altar. Cf. *RE* Suppl. 3. 669 ff.,
Vian 83 ff., 138 ff., 206 f., and *Répertoire des gigantomachies*, 1951,
pp. 18 ff., 71, 80 ff., 85 ff., Beazley, *ARV*² 1724, *ABV* 724, *Parali-
pomena*, 1971, p. 532.

scanderet : presumably by 'piling Pelion on Ossa'; this stratagem
was originally devised by the Aloadae (Hom. *Od.* 11. 315 f.), but in the
Roman period was imputed repeatedly to Giants (3. 4. 51 f., *RE* 18. 1.
305 f., 1595, Suppl. 3. 735). Horace pictures not a heavenly ladder
(Pind. fr. 162, Cook 2. 114 ff.), but a siege-ramp such as was used by
the Roman army; cf. *ciris* 33 f., *Aetna* 48 'construitur magnis ad
proelia montibus agger' (with Sudhaus's note), Gratt. *cyn.* 63 f., I. A.
Richmond, *JRS* 52, 1962, 154 (on the works at Masada) 'it is a huge
agger some 675 ft. long, and climbs 225 ft. at an incline of 1 in 3'.

impia : predicative and emphatic: the impiety consisted in the
climbing (cf. 1. 3. 38).

23. Rhoetum : for this giant cf. 3. 4. 55, Sidon. *carm.* 6. 24 (presumably from Horace) ; the name is applied to a centaur at Virg. *georg.* 2. 456 (*Rhoecum* P), Ov. *met.* 12. 271, Lucan 6. 390 (*Rhoece* Housman), Val. Fl. 1. 141, 3. 65, Claud. 9. 13, and to a drunken warrior with a large *crater* at Virg. *Aen.* 9. 344 and 345. Some have emended to *Rhoecum* (ῥοικός = 'bow-legged'), the name of a centaur at Call. *h.* 3. 221, Ael. *var. hist.* 13. 1 ; cf. also Naev. *carm.* fr. 19. 3 'Runcus ac Purpureus filii Terras' (where ῥύγχος may play a part). Housman comments (3. 1103) 'the Centaur's true name . . . is to be learnt, not from Latin MSS, where *c* and *t* are much confused, but from Greek, where κ and τ are not' ; but one feels some hesitation about admitting a conjecture in so many places. For similar names to Rhoetus cf. *RE* Suppl. 3. 757 (Eurytus, Erytus, etc.) ; one cannot distinguish the giant from the centaur as proper names are shared elsewhere (Eurytus, Mimas, Ophion). In our passage the rolled *r* makes alliteration with *retorsisti* and *horribilis* to suggest a lion's roar.

24. horribilisque : the proposal of Bochart and independently of Bentley for *horribilique*; cf. ps.-Acro 'maxilla metuendus'. The nominative underlines the attribute of the god and makes an excellent antithesis with 30 'cornu decorum' (for such contrasts cf. above, p. 316). In this dithyrambic context there are great attractions in the mannered ἀπὸ κοινοῦ construction (= *unguibus malaque horribilis*) ; the same word-order is found in exactly the same place in the two following stanzas (28 n., 32). On the other hand *horribilique* does not seem to underline quite enough that the god has actually become a lion (ps.-Acro 'in leonem versus') ; the instrumental ablative suggests that he has simply equipped himself with artificial claws and a false face.

For the metamorphosis of Dionysus cf. *h. Hom.* 7. 44 ὁ δ' ἄρα σφι λέων γένετ' ἔνδοθι νηός, Eur. *Ba.* 1017 f. φάνηθι ταῦρος ἢ πολύκρανος ἰδεῖν / δράκων ἢ πυριφλέγων ὁρᾶσθαι λέων, Euphorion, fr. 19 Powell = Ael. *nat. anim.* 7. 48 (the temple at Samos κεχηνότος Διονύσου, cf. Plin. *nat.* 8. 57), Ant. Lib. 10. 2, Nonnus 6. 182 ff., 36. 300 ff., 36. 329, 40. 44, Roscher 1. 1. 1152, A. B. Cook, *JHS* 14, 1894, 108 f., M. Ninck, *Die Bedeutung des Wassers im Kult und Leben der Alten*, 1921, pp. 142 f., 162 f. Dionysus is sometimes helped by lions in gigantomachies (Vian 83 f., 139, N. Alfieri–P. E. Arias, *Spina*, 1958, Taf. 66) ; they are believed by some originally to have symbolized the god's metamorphosis (Vian 206 f.). Pöschl (who keeps *horribili*) thinks that Horace is referring to a lion in the god's retinue (the ambiguity is already felt by Bentley) ; but though he seems to see the slight difficulty of the conventional interpretation, the ablative could not be read in the sense he desires.

horribilemque was proposed by Trendelenburg (*Arch. Anz.* 13, 1898, 127 f.) ; cf. Porphyrio (who must have read the ablative) 'non leonis unguibus et horribili mala retorsisti, sed retorsisti Rhoetum qui est leonis unguibus et horribili mala'. Trendelenburg points to the Gigantomachy on the Pergamum altar (which Horace had probably seen), where a giant in lion's form (described simply as Leon) has his head held in a wrestler's grip by an unidentified god (not Dionysus, who appears elsewhere on the frieze); cf. E. Schmidt, *Der Grosse Altar zu Pergamon*, 1961, pp. 30, 93, pl. 18, *RE* Suppl. 3. 748 f. (on Leon the giant of Miletus). The verb *retorsisti* suits a wrestling-match with a lion, such as is associated with Cyrene (Pind. *P.* 9. 26 f.) and above all with Hercules, who is sometimes portrayed gripping the lion in a τραχηλισμός or neck-hold; cf. E. N. Gardiner, *JHS* 25, 1905, 273, W. L. Brown, *The Etruscan Lion*, 1960, pp. 141 f. and pl. 51, Headlam on Herodas 2. 77. *horribilem* suits a barbarous giant (3. 4. 50 'fidens iuventus horrida bracchiis', Eur. *Phoen.* 127 ff., Nonnus 1. 18 φρικτὰ . . . φῦλα Γιγάντων, J. Fontenrose, *Python*, 1959, pp. 58, 83) ; it would reflect the contorted realism of Hellenistic sculpture, and provide a contrast with the amiable Cerberus below. On the other hand *horribilis* concentrates the attention on Bacchus, where it belongs; *unguibus* suits the victorious god better than the tightly gripped victim, and if Trendelenburg had watched kittens at play he might not have thought *retorquere* inappropriate to lions.

mala : lions' claws and jaws are vividly portrayed in art; cf. T. J. Dunbabin, *The Greeks and their Eastern Neighbours*, 1957, pp. 46 ff., W. L. Brown, op. cit. For claws cf. further *RE* 13. 971, for jaws Manil. 4. 536, Stat. *Theb.* 2. 680, Hom. *Il.* 16. 489 ὑπὸ γαμφηλῇσι λέοντος.

25. quamquam . . . ferebaris : it seems best to join this clause to the previous sentence (thus Kiessling, Heinze); for such a postponed concessive clause cf. 3. 11. 15 ff. 'cessit immanis tibi blandienti / ianitor aulae / Cerberus, quamvis furiale centum / muniant angues caput . . .'. At first sight the sentence seems flat and otiose (Peerlkamp characteristically deleted), but one suspects a subtle imitation of the straggling manner of Greek choral lyric (cf. 2. 4. 9 ff.).

Some editors begin a new sentence at *quamquam*. On this hypothesis *quamquam . . . dictus* would be the protasis (cf. K.–S. 2. 444 f.), *non . . . ferebaris* the apodosis; but there is a lack of connection with the previous sentence, and the series of *tu*'s is unconvincingly interrupted. Some alternatively interpret *quamquam* as 'and yet'; as 27 *sed* also means 'and yet', this makes the thought see-saw too much.

choreis . . . : cf. Eur. *Ba.* 378 ff. ὃς τάδ' ἔχει, θιασεύειν τε χοροῖς / μετά τ' αὐλοῦ γελάσαι. Words like χορεύειν are repeatedly used of Bacchic rites, but *choreis* may give a more frivolous impression. *iocis* refers to fun and games (1. 2. 34 n.) rather than humour; the word should be taken closely with *ludo*, with which it is often combined (cf. 2. 12. 18 f., Lucil. 111). Dionysus was traditionally πολυγηθής, φιλοπαίσμων, etc., but 'Jolly Bacchus' was over-emphasized in the Roman and Renaissance tradition.

26. idoneus : a word with a prosaic flavour (Axelson 105 f.), often used of fitness for war (cf. 3. 26. 1 'vixi puellis nuper idoneus'). For Bacchus's unmilitary nature cf. Ov. *met.* 3. 553 f.

27. ferebaris : 'you were *reported* to be'; some think the word repetitive after *dictus*, but it is more emphatic and points to a contrast between gossip and facts (*eras* = 'you were all along'). Horace is rebutting alternative legends in the Hellenistic manner; cf. Stemplinger 98. *esse* is not necessary with *fertur* (*Thes.l.L.* 6. 1. 551. 22 ff.), though usual in classical prose.

sed idem pacis eras mediusque belli : 'but you were not only a mediator of peace but midmost in the fight' (with the emphasis on *belli*). *medius* is here used with pointed compression in two different senses. For the latter cf. Virg. *Aen.* 10. 379 'medius densos prorumpit in hostis'; for the former and more difficult use cf. *Aen.* 7. 536 'dum paci medium se offert' (though there the intervention is also physical), Sil. 16. 220 f. 'vobis ad foedera versis / pacator mediusque Syphax', Heges. 4. 6. 10 'pacis medius bellum incendit', *Thes.l.L.* 8. 590. 47 ff., Heinsius ap. J. Willis, *Latin Textual Criticism*, 1972, p. 140 (comparing μεσίτης). *medius* is usually taken as 'half-way' (or 'neutral'), but no satisfactory parallel is adduced; and on this theory *idem* becomes unintelligible.

idem refers to a combination of diverse attributes; for polar expressions describing divine omnipotence cf. H. S. Versnel, *Mnemosyne* 27, 1974, 380. For the double aspect of Dionysus cf. above, p. 316; for the combination of peace and war cf. Eur. *Ba.* 861 δεινότατος, ἀνθρώποισι δ' ἠπιώτατος, Plut. *Dem.* 2. 3 μάλιστα τῶν θεῶν ἐζήλου τὸν Διόνυσον ὡς πολέμῳ τε χρῆσθαι δεινότατον, εἰρήνην τ' αὖθις ἐκ πολέμου τρέψαι πρὸς εὐφροσύνην καὶ χάριν ἐμμελέστατον, Diod. Sic. 4. 4. 4, *eleg. in Maecen.* 1. 57 ff., Lucian, *dial. deor.* 22 (18). 1, Aristides, *orat.* 4. 53, *anth. Pl.* 183. For the god's association with peace cf. the first stasimon of Euripides's *Bacchae*, especially 419 f. φιλεῖ δ' ὀλβοδότειραν Εἰρήναν; for war cf. ibid. 302 Ἄρεώς τε μοῖραν μεταλαβὼν ἔχει τινά (Horace's age would think of the Indian expedition as well as the Gigantomachy).

The position of *-que* also deserves note: *pacis eras mediusque belli* = *pacis eras bellique medius*. This stylized mannerism is common enough in the *Odes* (1. 30. 6 n.), but in our poem it is repeated at the end of successive stanzas (24 *horribilisque* if the conjecture is accepted, 28 *mediusque*, 32 *tetigitque*). Horace seems to be imitating a feature which he had noticed in Greek choral lyric; cf. Pind. *O*. 6. 41 f. τᾷ μὲν ὁ Χρυσοκόμας / πραΰμητίν τ' Ἐλείθυιαν παρέστασέν τε Μοίρας (cf. schol. Α τοὺς συνδέσμους μεταθετέον· ὁ γὰρ λόγος οὕτως ἀπαιτεῖ).

29. te vidit: such phrases are naturally used in describing remote exploits; cf. 4. 4. 17, Sen. *Oed*. 424 ff. (the Indian saw Bacchus). Here the verb formally balances 2 *vidi*, though this time it is the subject of the sentence that is vividly described.

insons: 'without hurting thee'; Porphyrio comments 'non *semper insons* sed *tibi insons*, id est *qui tibi nocere non potuit*'. The explanation of this strange usage seems to be that *insons* means the same as *innocens* (Paul. Fest. 296 M. = 383 L., *CGL* 6. 587), which can also mean *innocuus, innoxius*, ἀβλαβής (1. 17. 21). Poets sometimes act on the principle that words that are equal to the same word are equal to one another (*Bedeutungslehnwörter* or *calques sémantiques*). Pöschl (op. cit., p. 221) refers *insons* to Cerberus's change of heart ('without the will to hurt'); but one feels that the emphasis should be on the dog's overt behaviour.

Cerberus: Dionysus descended to the underworld to bring back his mother Semele (Frazer on Apollod. 3. 5. 3, *RE* 10. 2397); his catabasis was familiar enough to be satirized in the Aristophanic *Frogs* (cf. also Diod. Sic. 4. 25. 4). For a more profound connection with the underworld cf. Heraclitus, fr. 15 ὠυτὸς δὲ Ἀίδης καὶ Διόνυσος, W. F. Otto, *Dionysos*, 1933, pp. 106 ff., M. P. Nilsson, *Dionysiac Mysteries* [9 n.], pp. 116 ff. It is a noteworthy coincidence that the Ode to Mercury also ended with the underworld (1. 10. 17 ff.), and one suspects that the pattern was set by the mystical hymns of Horace's own day.

aureo cornu: as a god of animal vitality, Dionysus was often represented as a bull (Nilsson, *GGR* 1³. 215, 571). He was worshipped in this guise at Elis and elsewhere; cf. Eur. *Ba*. 1017 φάνηθι ταῦρος, *PMG carm. pop*. 871 ἐλθεῖν ἥρω Διόνυσε / Ἀλείων ἐς ναὸν / ἁγνὸν σὺν Χαρίτεσσιν / ἐς ναὸν / τῷ βοέῳ ποδὶ δύων, / ἄξιε ταῦρε, / ἄξιε ταῦρε, Plut. *quaest. Gr*. 299 a–b (36) with Halliday's note, *Is. et Osir*. 364 f (35) with Hopfner's note. He was given appropriate epithets, βούκερως (Pearson on Soph. fr. 959. 2), ταυρόκερως, δίκερως (Bruchmann 83 ff.), *cornifer, bicorniger*. In early Greece the ὠμοφαγία of cattle brought communion with the god (cf. Dodds² on Eur. *Ba*., pp. xvii ff.); even in the Roman period he had attendants called βουκόλοι (M. P. Nilsson, *Dionysiac Mysteries* [9 n.], pp. 58 ff.). He was portrayed with a bull's horns in art (Philostr. *imag*. 1. 15. 2, Roscher 1. 1149 ff.) and by the poets; for the Augustans cf. Tib. 2. 1. 3 (with K. F. Smith's

note), Ov. *am.* 3. 15. 17, *ars* 1. 232, 3. 348 'insignis cornu', *fast.*
3. 789.

The horns of sacrificial victims were sometimes gilded (Hom. *Il.*
10. 294, A. B. Cook, *JHS* 14, 1894, 122), and Dionysus, like other
gods, was given golden attributes (Soph. *OT* 209, Eur. *Ba.* 553). For
his golden horns cf. anon. *anth. P.* 9. 524. 23 χρυσόκερων (a word used
of Pan as early as Cratinus 321. 1); Horace's singular *cornu*, which
has puzzled some, seems to have been influenced by the ambiguous
Greek compound. Gold was conveniently available in the rivers of
Lydia; cf. Stat. *silv.* 3. 3. 62 'aurato reficit sua cornua limo' (with
Vollmer's note). Bücheler refers *cornu* to a drinking-horn (*RhM* 37,
1882, 236 ff. = *Kl. Schr.* 2. 440 ff.), but this is incompatible with
decorum.

30. decorum : for the sometimes effeminate beauty of Dionysus
cf. 1. 18. 11 n., Roscher 1. 1126 ff., Dodds² on Eur. *Ba.*, p. xxxi.

leniter atterens caudam : for Cerberus's amiability cf. 2. 13. 34 n.,
3. 11. 15 ff., Hes. *th.* 770 ff. ἐς μὲν ἰόντας / σαίνει ὁμῶς οὐρῇ τε καὶ
οὔασιν ἀμφοτέροισι, / ἐξελθεῖν δ' οὐκ αὖτις ἐᾷ πάλιν, Soph. fr. 687 P. =
625 N., Lucian, *luct.* 4. Cerberus must be rubbing his tail against
Bacchus, though this action is more characteristic of a cat than
a dog. Some interpret 'against his own body' (cf. Sen. *Herc. f.* 812),
but *atterens* must mean more than tail-wags. 'Smooth friction' makes
an oxymoron, as *atterens* normally suggests something more abrasive.

31. et recedentis : Cerberus was not usually friendly to a departing
guest (Hes. loc. cit.), but here defers to the divinity of Bacchus.
Upton transferred *et* to precede *leniter*, so that both gestures can be
made at the departure; but the transmitted text is closer to Hesiod.

trilingui : Cerberus had usually three heads, and therefore three
mouths, three tongues, and three barks (*RE* 11. 271 ff., H. Usener,
RhM 58, 1903, 168 ff., Norden on Virg. *Aen.* 6. 417–25).

32. pedes : the sixth word in the stanza to refer to a part of the body.
Cerberus licks the god's feet as a sign of submission; cf. Claud.
1. 189 f. 'tunc insula notos / lambit amica pedes', Paul. Nol. *carm.*
26. 259 (on *Daniel* 14) 'sic aliquando ferae circum iacuere prophetam /
orantisque pedes linguis mulsere benignis', Nonnus 22. 29 f. μηκεδανοὶ
δὲ δράκοντες ἐβακχεύοντο χορείῃ / ἴχνια λιχμώοντες ἐχιδνοκόμου Διονύσου. Our passage hints at a religious tradition (cf. *RLAC* 8. 743 ff.
for foot-washing) as well as at the behaviour of real dogs.

20. NON VSITATA

[K. Abel, *RhM* 104, 1961, 81 ff.; Fraenkel 299 ff.; K. Gantar, *Živa Antika* (Skopje), 1971, pp. 135 ff.; Pasquali 551 ff.; Plüss 179 ff.; R. Reitzenstein, *NJA* 21, 1908, 98 ff. = *Aufsätze zu Horaz*, 1963, pp. 18 ff.; E.-R. Schwinge, *Hermes* 93, 1965, 438 ff.; Suerbaum 167 ff.; J. Tatum, *AJPh* 94, 1973, 4 ff.; Williams 570 ff.]

1–8. *I shall soar through the air superior to the jealousies of men; in spite of my humble life I shall not be confined by the waters of the Styx. 9–12. Even now I am being metamorphosed into a swan. 13–20. Now I shall fly to the ends of the earth and be studied by barbarian peoples. 21–4. Let there be no mourning at my funeral; monuments are superfluous.*

Poets might be compared with birds for reasons other than mere tunefulness (cf. Schwinge, loc. cit., Syndikus 1. 481 f.). Pindar was associated with the eagle for majesty, speed, and force (cf. *O.* 2. 88, *N.* 3. 80 ff., 5. 21, C. M. Bowra, *Pindar*, 1964, pp. 9 ff.), and Bacchylides for his range of flight (5. 31 ff. τὼς νῦν καὶ ἐμοὶ μυρία πάντᾳ κέλευθος / ὑμετέραν ἀρετὰν / ὑμνεῖν, cf. M. R. Lefkowitz, *HSCPh* 73, 1969, 53 ff.); though recent expositors refer some of these passages to the victor rather than the poet, what matters here is the general interpretation of antiquity, as represented by the Pindaric scholia. Such themes are satirized by Aristophanes, who develops a line from Anacreon (378. 1) to suggest a remoteness from reality and loss of direction (*av.* 1372 ff.): ἀναπέτομαι δὴ πρὸς "Ολυμπον πτερύγεσσι κούφαις. / πέτομαι δ' ὁδὸν ἄλλοτ' ἐπ' ἄλλαν μελέων / . . . τότε μὲν νοτίαν στείχων πρὸς ὁδόν, τοτὲ δ' αὖ βορέᾳ σῶμα πελάζων / ἀλίμενον αἰθέρος αὔλακα τέμνων (cf. D. J. Stewart, *CJ* 62, 1967, 357 ff.). Horace himself compares Pindar's sublimity with the spectacular flight of the swan (4. 2. 25 ff. 'multa Dircaeum levat aura cycnum, / tendit, Antoni, quotiens in altos / nubium tractus'), and in the present poem by a similar metaphor he more indirectly hints at his own literary qualities (see notes on 1 *non usitata nec tenui*).

But his main point in using the image of the swan is to suggest the extent of his future fame; for this motif cf. Σ Pind. *P.* 8. 46 (on 33 ποτανόν) πετόμενον, ἐπεὶ τὰ ποιήματα εἰς πᾶσαν δικνεῖται πόλιν. A similar claim is attested as early as Alcman 148 (= Aristides, *orat.* 28. 54) ἑτέρωθι τοίνυν καλλωπιζόμενος παρ' ὅσοις εὐδοκιμεῖ, τοσαῦτα καὶ τοιαῦτα ἔθνη καταλέγει ὥστ' ἔτι νῦν τοὺς ἀθλίους γραμματιστὰς ζητεῖν οὗ γῆς ταῦτ' εἶναι, λυσιτελεῖν δ' αὐτοῖς καὶ μακράν, ὡς ἔοικεν, ἀπελθεῖν ὁδὸν μᾶλλον ἢ περὶ τῶν Σκιαπόδων ἀνήνυτα πραγματεύεσθαι. Though there is nothing at least in this summary about flying, Alcman might have

derived such an idea from the mysterious *Arimaspea* (for which see
J. D. P. Bolton, *Aristeas of Proconnesus*, 1962); cf. especially Max.
Tyr. 10. 2 (on Aristeas) ἡ δὲ ψυχὴ ἐκδῦσα τοῦ σώματος ἐπλανᾶτο ἐν τῷ
αἰθέρι, ὄρνιθος δίκην, πάντα ὕποπτα θεωμένη, γῆν καὶ θάλατταν καὶ ποταμοὺς καὶ πόλεις καὶ ἔθνη ἀνδρῶν . . . (for such supernatural experiences
cf. 1. 28. 5 n., *RLAC* 8. 29 ff.). It is noteworthy that the *Arimaspea*
gave prominence to the Issedones, who are mentioned in another
fragment of Alcman (156), and the Hyperboreans, who figure in our
ode (16 n.); if Horace's fantastic conception had an archaic antecedent, this might have been provided by Alcman. Theognis at
any rate uses the motif of flight to describe the celebrity his poems
have given Cyrnus, though unlike Horace he makes little attempt to
actualize his metaphor (237 ff.) :

> σοὶ μὲν ἐγὼ πτέρ' ἔδωκα, σὺν οἷς ἐπ' ἀπείρονα πόντον
> πωτήσῃ, κατὰ γῆν πᾶσαν ἀειρόμενος
> ῥηιδίως. θοίνῃς δὲ καὶ εἰλαπίνῃσι παρέσσῃ
> ἐν πάσαις, πολλῶν κείμενος ἐν στόμασιν . . .
> οὐδέποτ' οὐδὲ θανὼν ἀπολεῖς κλέος, ἀλλὰ μελήσεις
> ἄφθιτον ἀνθρώποις αἰὲν ἔχων ὄνομα,
> Κύρνε, καθ' Ἑλλάδα γῆν στρωφώμενος, ἠδ' ἀνὰ νήσους
> ἰχθυόεντα περῶν πόντον ἐπ' ἀτρύγετον,
> οὐχ ἵππων νώτοισιν ἐφήμενος· ἀλλά σε πέμψει
> ἀγλαὰ Μουσάων δῶρα ἰοστεφάνων·
> πᾶσι δ' ὅσοισι μέμηλε καὶ ἐσσομένοισιν ἀοιδὴ
> ἔσσῃ ὁμῶς ὄφρ' ἂν γῆ τε καὶ ἠέλιος.

Hellenistic and Roman poets similarly laid claim to an international
reputation (14 n.), but the comparison with migrating birds belongs
to an earlier world, and does not seem to be attested in the later
period outside Horace's poem.

The supernatural aspects of the swan are also relevant. The bird
was thought to sing melodiously before its death (10 n.); its splendour
and its music connected it with Apollo, and its distant northern
flight with the felicity of the Hyperboreans (16 n.). Elderly poets
were compared with it because of its swan-song and its white plumage (10 n.), other-worldly philosophers because of its conspicuousness
and its air of mystery (Gantar, op. cit.): cf. Olympiodorus, *in Alc.*
2. 83 ff. Westerink φασὶ δὲ ὅτι ἡνίκα ὁ Σωκράτης ἤμελλεν δέχεσθαι, ὄναρ
εἶδεν ὅτι κύκνος ἄπτερος ἐν τοῖς γόνασιν αὐτοῦ καθῆστο καὶ παραχρῆμα
πτεροφυήσας ἀνέπτη εἰς τὸν ἀέρα καὶ ἔκλαγξέ τι λιγυρόν, ὡς πάντας
θέλξαι τοὺς ἀκούοντας· τοῦτο δὲ ἐδήλου τὴν μέλλουσαν δόξαν τοῦ ἀνδρός,
ibid. 2. 156 ff. μέλλων τελευτᾶν ἐνύπνιον εἶδεν ὡς κύκνος γενόμενος ἀπὸ
δένδρου εἰς δένδρον μετέρχεται, καὶ ταύτῃ πόνον πλεῖστον παρεῖχε τοῖς
ἰξευταῖς. The swan's miraculous death and perhaps also its feathers

(12 n.) made it a symbol of immortality on the lines of the phoenix; Horace may be influenced by the kind of myth satirized by Lucian, *Peregr.* 39 γὺψ ἀναπτάμενος ἐκ μέσης τῆς φλογὸς οἴχοιτο εἰς τὸν οὐρανὸν [ἀνθρωπίνῃ] μεγάλῃ τῇ φωνῇ λέγων· "Ἔλιπον γᾶν βαίνω δ᾽ ἐς "Ὄλυμπον. The strangest part of the ode is Horace's actual transformation into a swan (9 ff.), but this is also made easier for him by the tradition. Metamorphoses were an ancient theme of folk-tale (cf. Proteus, Circe, etc.), and in the Hellenistic age became a minor category of literature; it is enough to refer to the prose *Alloioseis* of Antigonus of Carystus, the verse *Heteroeumena* of Nicander (Gow, pp. 142 ff., 205 ff.), the *Metamorphoses* of Parthenius, Theodorus, Ovid, and Apuleius, the Μεταμορφώσεων συναγωγή of Antoninus Liberalis (ed. I. Cazzaniga), the brief mention of the subject by the rhetorician Menander (3. 393 Sp.). Transformations into birds were notably favoured, as may be seen from the ὀρνιθογονία attributed to Boeus or Boeo (24 f. Powell, *RE* 3. 633 f.) and imitated by Aemilius Macer (Ov. *trist.* 4. 10. 43 f., Schanz–Hosius 2. 164 f.); in Latin literature one may also compare Virg. *Aen.* 10. 192 f., Ov. *met.* 2. 373 ff. (on Cycnus) 'cum vox est tenuata viro canaeque capillos / dissimulant plumae, collumque a pectore longe / porrigitur digitosque ligat iunctura rubentis, / penna latus velat, tenet os sine acumine rostrum', 2. 580 ff., 5. 543 ff., 559 f., 670 ff., 7. 379, 12. 144 f., 14. 498 ff., *ciris* 496 ff., Apul. *met.* 3. 21. 5 'promicant molles plumulae, crescunt et fortes pinnulae, duratur nasus incurvus, coguntur ungues adunci', W. Quirin, *Die Kunst Ovids in der Darstellung des Verwandlungsaktes*, Diss. Giessen, 1930, pp. 18 ff. In particular one may point to Eur. fr. 911 N. χρύσεαι δή μοι πτέρυγες περὶ νώτῳ / καὶ τὰ Σειρήνων πτερόεντα πέδιλ᾽ ἁρμόζεται· / βάσομαι τ᾽ εἰς αἰθέρα πουλὺν ἀερθεὶς / Ζηνὶ προσμίξων (text by von Arnim, *suppl. Eur.* p. 8); Satyrus thought that this passage referred to Euripides's own departure from Athens, and a similar misunderstanding could have encouraged Horace in his first-person fantasy. It should further be observed that whereas in Homer metamorphosis took place instantaneously, later writers tried to catch a half-way stage (so already Eur. fr. 930 N. οἴμοι δράκων μου γίγνεται τὸ ἥμισυ· / τέκνον, περιπλάκηθι τῷ λοιπῷ πατρί); such an approach suited the ultra-realism of Hellenistic art and literature, and Horace's treatment (9 n., 11 n., 12 n.) descends from a well-established convention (cf. L. P. Wilkinson, *Ovid Recalled*, 1955, pp. 160 ff., E. J. Bernbeck, *Beobachtungen zur Darstellungsart in Ovids Metamorphosen*, Zetemata 43, 1967, pp. 100 ff.). For further details see G. Lafaye, *Les Métamorphoses d'Ovide et leurs modèles grecs*, 1904 and 1971, pp. 24 ff., S. Viarre, *L'Image et la pensée dans les Métamorphoses d'Ovide*, 1964, pp. 36 ff., A. S. Hollis's commentary on Ovid, *met.* 8, pp. xv ff.

It is no accident that Horace's claims to fame are made at the
end of a book, where a poet sometimes talked of himself and his work.
The pattern was already established in early Greece, where there
was a real danger of the poet's identity being forgotten; cf. *h. Ap.*
172 ff. *"τυφλὸς ἀνήρ, οἰκεῖ δὲ Χίῳ ἔνι παιπαλοέσσῃ, | τοῦ πᾶσαι μετό-
πισθεν ἀριστεύουσιν ἀοιδαί." | ἡμεῖς δ' ὑμέτερον κλέος οἴσομεν, ὅσσον ἐπ'
αἶαν | ἀνθρώπων στρεφόμεσθα πόλεις εὖ ναιετάωσας.* The name *sphragis*,
which is sometimes given to the motif, is derived from Theognis
19 ff. :

> Κύρνε, σοφιζομένῳ μὲν ἐμοὶ σφρηγὶς ἐπικείσθω
> τοῖσδ' ἔπεσιν, λήσει δ' οὔποτε κλεπτόμενα,
> οὐδέ τις ἀλλάξει κάκιον τοὐσθλοῦ παρεόντος·
> ὧδε δὲ πᾶς τις ἐρεῖ· Θεύγνιδός ἐστιν ἔπη
> τοῦ Μεγαρέως· πάντας δὲ κατ' ἀνθρώπους ὀνομαστός.

The convention was continued by more literary ages when the poet's
identity no longer needed the same protection; cf. Timotheus 791.
229 ff. (including a mention of his native Miletus), Call. fr. 203 (the
epilogue to the *Iambi*), Eratosthenes, fr. 35. 18 Powell τοῦ Κυρηναίου
τοῦτ' 'Ερατοσθένεος, Nicander, *ther.* 957 f. καί κεν 'Ομηρείοιο καὶ εἰσέτι
Νικάνδροιο | μνῆσιν ἔχοις τὸν ἔθρεψε Κλάρου νιφόεσσα πολίχνη, *alex.*
629 f., Meleager, *anth. P.* 12. 257. The Romans followed the Hellenistic
poets: cf. Virg. *georg.* 4. 563 ff. 'illo Vergilium me tempore dulcis
alebat | Parthenope . . .', Prop. 1. 22 (his Umbrian origin), 2. 34 b.
93 f., Hor. *carm.* 3. 30 (his Apulian origin and lasting fame), *epist.*
1. 20 (more whimsical, as suits the genre), Ov. *am.* 1. 15. 35 ff., 3. 15
(origin and fame), *ars* 2. 744, 3. 812, *met.* 15. 871 ff., *trist.* 4. 10, *Pont.*
4. 16. See further Stemplinger 172 ff., Wilamowitz, *Sappho und
Simonides*, pp. 296 ff., H. Thesleff, *Eranos* 47, 1949, 116 ff., Fraenkel
362 f. (with literature there cited), W. Kranz, *RhM* 104, 1961, 3 ff.,
97 ff. (= *Studien zur antiken Literatur und ihrem Fortwirken*, 1967,
pp. 27 ff.), H. Lloyd-Jones, *JHS* 83, 1963, 96 ff. (Posidippus), A. H.
Griffiths, *BICS* 17, 1970, 37 ff. (Philodemus, *anth. P.* 11. 41), Curtius
515 ff., Suerbaum 23, 134 ff.; for similar declarations at the beginning
of a poem or book cf. vol. i, p. 1, Kranz, op. cit., Gow on Theoc. 1. 65.

Particularly important for Horace's ode were the epitaphs written
for poets by themselves or more commonly by others; cf. especially
Call. *ep.* 35, Leonidas, *anth. P.* 7. 715, Meleager, ibid. 7. 417–
19, W. Crönert in *XAPITEΣ Friedrich Leo . . . dargebracht*, 1911,
pp. 123 ff., M. Gabathuler, *Hellenistische Epigramme auf Dichter*,
Diss. Basel, 1937. Such epitaphs contain the name of the poet, perhaps a mention of his city and parentage, sometimes a declaration of
achievement and a claim to future fame; they may on occasion have
acted as a *sphragis* at the end of a collected book (Gabathuler,

pp. 48 f.). Similar epitaphs were written by, or attributed to, Naevius, Plautus, Pacuvius (Gell. 1. 24), Ennius (see below), and Virgil; for discussion and bibliography cf. H. Dahlmann, *Studien zu Varro De Poetis, Abh. der Akad. der Wissenschaften in Mainz* 10, 1962, 617 ff., Suerbaum 333 ff. One may also compare the poems where a dying person gives last instructions; cf. Prop. 1. 21, 2. 13. 17 ff., 4. 11, Stat. *silv.* 5. 1. 177 ff., Esteve-Forriol 142 f., Cairns 90 f. (he labels the type *mandata morituri*). Poems of these different kinds might contain an exhortation to mourn; cf. Solon 21. 1 f. W. μηδέ μοι ἄκλαυτος θάνατος μόλοι, ἀλλὰ φίλοισι / καλλείποιμι θανὼν ἄλγεα καὶ στοναχάς (rendered by Cic. *Tusc.* 1. 117 'mors mea ne careat lacrimis, linquamus amicis / maerorem ut celebrent funera cum gemitu', cf. *senec.* 73). Horace on the other hand forbids mourning; for this motif see Posidippus's *sphragis* 21 f. μηδέ τις οὖν χεύαι δάκρυον· αὐτὰρ ἐγὼ / γήραϊ μυστικὸν οἶμον ἐπὶ 'Ραδάμανθυν ἱκοίμην (for text and parallels see H. Lloyd-Jones, op. cit.), and especially Enn. (?) *var.* 17 f. 'nemo me dacrumis decoret, nec funera fletu / faxit. cur? volito vivos per ora virum' (cf. Suerbaum 169 ff.). Propertius similarly finds literary achievement a substitute for funereal pomp: cf. 2. 13. 19 ff. 'nec mea tunc longa spatietur imagine pompa, / nec tuba sit fati vana querella mei. / . . . sat mea sic magna est, si tres sint pompa libelli . . .'.

Horace follows the Ennian epigram by combining a rejection of mourning with a claim to immortality through his writings. Such assertions were made by the Greeks of loved ones (as by Theognis of Cyrnus) or of patrons (as in Pindar, or Horace's fourth book); but when applied to the poet himself they seem characteristically Roman (Stroh 235 ff.). Yet a late Greek analogy to Horace's ode can be found in the so-called epistles of Phalaris (54, p. 421 Hercher): ἅμα δὲ μηδὲ οἴεσθε ἕνα τῶν νεκρῶν Στησίχορον ἀλλ' ἐν τοῖς ποιήμασιν εἶναι, ἃ κοινὰ πάντων ἀνθρώπων πεποίηται . . . παρὰ δὲ Καταναίοις . . . εἰς ἄλλο τι τῆς φύσεως μεταβαλούσης τελευτῆσαι . . . τὸν δ' ἄνδρα μὴ στένετε μηδ' ὀλοφύρεσθε . . . τέθνηκε μὲν γὰρ τὸ σῶμα τὸ Στησιχόρου, τοὔνομα δὲ παραλαβὼν ὁ ἀνήνυτος αἰὼν εὐκλεὲς μὲν ἐν βίῳ μακάριον δ' ἐν μνήμαις ἀναθήσει . . . εἴς τε τοὺς ἄλλους ἀνθρώπους διαπέμψασθε (τὰ μέλη) ἐπιμελῶς. Parts of the passage quoted look like the pastiche of some poetical source, presumably not Stesichorus himself (the personal element seems too great), but an epigram about him or purporting to be by him; for a poem of this kind cf. Antip. Thess. (or Sid.) *anth. P.* 7. 75 Στασίχορον ζαπληθὲς ἀμέτρητον στόμα Μούσας / ἐκτέρισεν Κατάνας αἰθαλόεν δάπεδον, / οὗ κατὰ Πυθαγόρεω φυσικὰν φάτιν ἁ πρὶν 'Ομήρου / ψυχὰ ἐνὶ στέρνοις δεύτερον ᾠκίσατο (probably this has the same Hellenistic source as Homer's metempsychosis into Ennius; cf. H. Fuchs, *MH* 12, 1955, 201 f., C. O. Brink, *AJPh* 93, 1972, 557 ff.). A part may also have been played by the Simonidean elegy on the

Spartan dead at Thermopylae (531), which bears a general resemblance both to the penultimate sentence quoted above from 'Phalaris' and to the last stanza of Horace's ode: εὐκλεὴς μὲν ἁ τύχα, καλὸς δ' ὁ πότμος, / βωμὸς δ' ὁ τάφος, πρὸ γόων δὲ μνᾶστις, ὁ δ' οἶκτος ἔπαινος. It is well known that in the parallel ode at the end of the third book Horace imitated this same elegy (εὐρὼς οὔθ' ὁ πανδαμάτωρ ἀμαυρώσει χρόνος); when he transfers this encomium of the Spartan dead to himself, an apparently arrogant procedure, he could have been influenced by first-person epigrams on the classical Greek poets, in which the predictions of fame would have been fulfilled by the time of writing.

Apart from speculations about antecedents, Horace's tone of voice seems unusually difficult to recapture (cf. Williams, loc. cit.). The claim to poetic immortality is bold and confident, as suits the end of a collection; contrast the similar pretensions of 3. 30 with the comparative diffidence of 1. 1. The swan's soaring flight over seas and continents suggests boundless hopes of future fame, the peoples who will read Horace extend to the potential limits of the Roman empire (18 n.), like the most glorious patriots of history he will need no physical monument (24 n.). But at the same time there is an undercurrent of self-disparagement: he is aware of his humble origins and inferior social position (6 n.), and still seems to sense (as he no longer does in 3. 30) the hazard of his ambition (see note on 13 *notior Icaro*). The fantasy of the metamorphosis in the third stanza seems part of the same ironic whimsicality; though such grotesqueness was traditional, one is reluctant to believe that the poet saw no oddity in its application to himself. From the shrivelling of his earthly body the *biformis vates* hopes to be transformed to new splendour; of course he is thinking not of the mystical immortality of the phoenix but of the enduring reputation of a true poet. In choosing bizarre symbols to express this thought, he shows an agreeable detachment from a deeply felt aspiration.

Metre: Alcaic.

1. **non usitata** : when the metaphor is interpreted, Horace is primarily talking of his own future fame (for the litotes cf. *epod.* 5. 73 'non usitatis . . . potionibus'). But we are meant to see that his extraordinary renown is the counterpart of his extraordinary talent ('nec enim volgaria scribit' Porph.); cf. 3. 1. 2 f. (the next poem in the collection) 'carmina non prius / audita', 4. 9. 3 'non ante vulgatas per artis', 1. 26. 10 n. (add *epist.* 1. 19. 32 f., Enn. *ann.* 217), Milton, *P.L.* 1. 13 ff. 'my advent'rous song, That with no middle flight intends to soar Above the Aonian mount, while it pursues Things

unattempted yet in prose or rhyme'. Horace is not simply alluding
to the novelty of a metamorphosis; that idea does not cohere with
tenui.

nec tenui : a wing is normally thin (*ciris* 50 'tenui conscendens
aethera penna'), but Horace's will be out of the ordinary; once again
he alludes to the extent and endurance of his fame (cf. 2. 2. 7 f.
'illum aget penna metuente solvi / fama superstes'). He is also hinting
at a literary judgement parallel to that of *non usitata*; in this sense he
is retracting the irony of such phrases as 1. 6. 9 'tenues grandia' (see
note ad loc.), 2. 1. 40 'leviore plectro' (significantly at the end of the
first poem in the book). When Gray imitates Horace he is referring
exclusively to style (*Progress of Poesy* 113 ff.) : 'Tho' he inherit   Nor
the pride, nor ample pinion,   That the Theban eagle bear,   Sailing
with supreme dominion,   Thro' the azure deep of air' (*per liquidum
aethera*).

2. penna : the singular emphasizes the means of locomotion rather
than the anatomical parts.

biformis : both man and bird; such words are often used of hybrids
(Cic. *carm*. fr. 30. 13 f. T. 'biformato impetu / Centaurus', Virg. *Aen*.
6. 25, Bömer on Ov. *met*. 2. 664). Horace is not yet visualizing a half-
finished metamorphosis (the process would be complete before take-
off), though it remains true that the third stanza develops in concrete form the potentialities of the adjective. At this stage *biformis*
suggests in a more abstract way the two facets of the poet's nature
(L. Müller compared 3. 22. 4 'diva triformis', where Hecate does not
reveal all her shapes simultaneously). Horace sees a piquant contrast
between the 'immortality' of his poetry and his mundane corporeal
existence (cf. Reitzenstein, loc. cit., though some of his phraseology
is too mystical).

liquidum : 'clear' (the primary meaning of the word); cf. 3. 4. 24
'liquidae . . . Baiae', Plaut. *most*. 751, Enn. *sat*. 4 'liquidas . . . aetheris
oras', Virg. *georg*. 1. 404, *Aen*. 7. 65, *paneg. in Mess*. 209. For the 'sea
of air' cf. Taillardat 431; Horace no doubt also remembers Pind.
N. 8. 41 f. ὑγρὸν αἰθέρα (though there the adjective rather suggests
'yielding'). *aethera* is not just the equivalent of *caelum*, but gives
a hint of immortality (1. 28. 5 n.).

3. vates : the grandiose word has an emphatic position at the end of
a colon and the beginning of a line; it makes a surprising climax after
biformis.

neque in terris morabor : such expressions are used of deities
leaving mankind in disgust; cf. Hes. *op*. 197 ff. καὶ τότε δὴ πρὸς
Ὄλυμπον ἀπὸ χθονὸς εὐρυοδείης / . . . ἀθανάτων μετὰ φῦλον ἴτον προ-
λιπόντ' ἀνθρώπους / Αἰδὼς καὶ Νέμεσις, Theognis 1135 ff. ἐλπὶς ἐν

ἀνθρώποισι μονὴ θεὸς ἐσθλὴ ἔνεστιν, / ἄλλοι δ' Οὐλυμπόνδ' ἐκπρολιπόντες ἔβαν. / ᾤχετο μὲν Πίστις, μεγάλη θεός, ᾤχετο δ' ἀνδρῶν / Σωφροσύνη, Χάριτές τ', ὦ φίλε, γῆν ἔλιπον, Eur. Med. 439 f., Aratus, phaen. 133 f. καὶ τότε μισήσασα Δίκη κείνων γένος ἀνδρῶν / ἔπταθ' ὑπουρανίη, Virg. georg. 2. 473 f., Ov. met. 1. 150 'terras Astraea reliquit' (with Bömer's note), Pont. 1. 6. 29, Juv. 6. 1 f. 'credo Pudicitiam Saturno rege moratam / in terris'. Similar phrases are also applied to great and good men departing for a more celestial sphere; cf. Pl. Phaed. 115 d οὐκέτι ὑμῖν παραμενῶ ἀλλ' οἰχήσομαι ἀπιὼν εἰς μακάρων δή τινας εὐδαιμονίας, Cic. rep. 6. 15 'quid moror in terris? quin huc ad vos venire propero?', Prop. 2. 2. 3 'cur haec in terris facies humana moratur?', Ov. epist. 18. 169 'digna quidem caelo es, sed adhuc tellure morare', Suet. Ner. 33. 1 'nam et morari eum desisse inter homines producta prima syllaba iocabatur'.

4. longius : Horace imagines that he is at his last hour (cf. 9 iam iam). The literal-minded Peerlkamp thought that he had first been prostrated by the news of Maecenas's death (8 B.C.): 'tandem, consilii certus, ingenti animo hoc composuit, composito venenum hausit' (a reductio ad absurdum of the view that the Odes describe events directly).

invidiaque maior : 'superior to envy' (maior balances longius in a purely formal sense); Horace is imitating both the thought and the construction of Call. ep. 21. 4 ὁ δ' ἤεισεν κρέσσονα βασκανίης (the poet's own epitaph). For the traditional jealousies of literary men cf. further Hes. op. 26 καὶ πτωχὸς πτωχῷ φθονέει καὶ ἀοιδὸς ἀοιδῷ, Call. h. 2. 107 τὸν Φθόνον ὡπόλλων ποδί τ' ἤλασεν, fr. 1. 17 ἔλλετε Βασκανίης ὀλοὸν γένος. Horace says that he himself was envied and abused for his material advantages (serm. 1. 6. 46 ff., 2. 1. 75 ff., 2. 6. 47 f., epist. 1. 14. 37 f.), and in particular because of his poetry; cf. serm. 1. 10. 78 ff., 2. 3. 13, epist. 1. 19. 35 f., 2. 1. 89, carm. 4. 3. 16. For the idea (implicit in our passage) that great men are less envied after their deaths cf. 3. 24. 31 f. 'virtutem incolumem odimus, / sublatam ex oculis quaerimus invidi', epist. 2. 1. 12 'comperit invidiam supremo fine domari', Pind. pae. 2. 55 f. ἤδη φθόνος οἴχεται / τῶν πάλαι προθανόντων, Soph. Ai. 964 f., Thuc. 2. 45. 1, Arist. rhet. 1388ª10 f. πρὸς δὲ τοὺς μυριοστὸν ἔτος ὄντας ἢ πρὸς τοὺς ἐσομένους ἢ τεθνεῶτας (φιλοτιμεῖται) οὐδείς, Cic. Balb. 16, Marc. 29, ps.-Sall. epist. 2. 13. 7 (with Vretska's note), Prop. 3. 1. 21 f. 'at mihi quod vivo detraxerit invida turba / post obitum duplici faenore reddet honos', Ov. am. 1. 15. 39 'pascitur in vivis Livor, post fata quiescit' (also a sphragis), trist. 4. 10. 121 ff., Vell. 2. 92. 5, Stat. Theb. 12. 818 f. (to his epic) 'mox tibi si quis adhuc praetendit nubila livor / occidet, et merito post me referentur honores', Mart. 1. 1. 4 ff., 3. 95. 8, Gudeman on Tac. dial.

15. 1 and 23. 11, *carm. epig.* 618. 2 f., 922. 2, 1030. 4, Hobbes, *Leviathan* 'the praise of ancient authors proceeds not from the reverence of the dead but from the competition and mutual envy of the living'. For other references to envy or carping criticism of poets cf. Leonidas, *anth. P.* 9. 356. 3 f., Virg. *ecl.* 7. 26, Ov. *am.* 1. 15. 1, *Pont.* 4. 16. 1, Phaedr. 2. 9. 10, 3 prol. 60, 4 prol. 15 f., Philippus, *anth. P.* 11. 321, Mart. 9. 97, Sidon. *epist.* 9. 16 vers. 9 f., Kroll 124 ff.

5. **urbis** : the civilized habitations of men (Virg. *georg.* 1. 25 'urbisne invisere, Caesar'), where envy and injustice are rife; the Dike of Aratus took to the hills before leaving the earth (118 ff., cf. Virg. *georg.* 2. 473 f.). There is a contrast with the wide open spaces of 2 and the barbarian peoples of 13 ff. For *relinquam* see some of the passages cited on 3.

pauperum sanguis parentum : it was conventional in the *sphragis* to mention one's antecedents, and epigrams on Greek poets often do the same. Horace makes a virtue of necessity by drawing a contrast between his origin and achievement; cf. 3. 30. 12 'ex humili potens', *epist.* 1. 20. 20 ff. 'me libertino natum patre et in tenui re . . .'. For *sanguis* (= 'scion') cf. 3. 27. 65, Pind. *N.* 6. 35, Gow on Theoc. 24. 73, Sil. 11. 177; the grandiloquence makes a piquant contrast with *pauperum*.

6. **quem vocas** : 'whom you send for'; cf. *serm.* 1. 6. 61 'abeo et revocas nono post mense', 2. 7. 29 f. 'si nusquam es forte vocatus / ad cenam', Plaut. *Stich.* 182 'negare nulli soleo si quis me essum vocat', Cic. *Mur.* 71, Catull. 44. 21, 47. 7 'quaerunt in trivio vocationes', Nep. *Att.* 14. 2 'namque eos vocabat quorum mores a suis non abhorrerent', Nicarchus, *anth. P.* 11. 330. 1 f. ἐκλήθην ἐχθὲς, Δημήτριε· σήμερον ἦλθον / δειπνεῖν· μὴ μέμψῃ, κλίμακ' ἔχεις μεγάλην (this suggests that καλεῖν and *vocare* refer to urgent summonses). *vocas* implies a social inferiority; for more humorous ways of making the same point cf. 4. 12. 15 (of Virgil) 'iuvenum nobilium cliens' (*cluere* is the correlative of *vocare*, cf. F. Bücheler, *RhM* 37, 1882, 238 = *Kl. Schr.* 2. 442), Augustus, fr. 33 M. (to Maecenas about Horace) 'veniet ergo ab ista parasitica mensa ad hanc regiam'. Bentley exaggerates when he says 'haec interpretatio parasiti potius gulam quam gratum clientis animum exprimit'; *dilecte* is designed to remove any such embarrassing impression. On the other hand Fraenkel goes too much the other way (300) when he compares *serm.* 1. 6. 47 'tibi, Maecenas, convictor'; it is part of Horace's purpose to emphasize the unimportance of his worldly status (cf. *pauperum* above).

Some editors (following ps.-Acro) explain 'whom you call *dilecte*'; but *dilecte* could not conceivably be separated from *Maecenas* (cf. 1. 20. 5 n., Pind. *P.* 1. 92 ὦ φίλε, Stat. *silv.* 2. 4. 32 'Melior dilecte').

Plüss understands that Maecenas is summoning the dead Horace back to life (23 n.); but this destroys the balance with *pauperum sanguis parentum* (both clauses must be in some degree pejorative). Bentley explains 'whom you call *pauperum sanguis parentum'* (he preferred *vocant*); but this makes the repetition of *non ego* incoherent.

7. obibo : Horace uses the language of real death to describe the deathlessness of his poems (cf. 2. 2. 5 *vivet* n.); so 3. 30. 6 f. 'non omnis moriar, multaque pars mei / vitabit Libitinam'. The verb makes a contrast with *parentum*, perhaps also with the soaring flight of the swan; it is relatively rare in grand poetry (Axelson 104 f.), though found elsewhere in the *Odes* (2. 17. 3, 3. 9. 24). There is an apparent discrepancy between our passage and the first of these parallels ('nec dis amicum est nec mihi te prius / obire'); but the purpose of the two poems is different, and Horace is not consciously revising his earlier attitude to Maecenas.

8. Stygia . . . unda : the dark river of the underworld is opposed to the clear upper air. As the Greek name implies 'hateful', there is also a contrast with *dilecte*.

cohibebor : for the restraint of the grave cf. 1. 28. 2 n., 3. 4. 80, for watery barriers 2. 14. 9 n., *carm. epig.* 1109. 24 'nec cohibebor aquis'.

9. iam iam : doubled *iam* is sometimes used to describe things that are going to happen 'any minute now'; cf. *epod.* 2. 68 'iam iam futurus rusticus', Cic. *Att.* 7. 20. 1, Virg. *Aen.* 2. 530 (with Austin's note), 8. 707 f. 'ipsa videbatur ventis regina vocatis / vela dare et laxos iam iamque immittere funes' (the engraver has caught the critical moment), Wölfflin 314, *Thes.l.L.* 7. 1119. 16 ff. G. L. Hendrickson suggests that as *iam iam* refers to future events, the metamorphosis is less grotesque than if it were described as actually happening (*CPh* 44, 1949, 30 ff.); this argument amounts to little as the future event is visualized in excited anticipation as already present.

residunt . . . : the flesh on Horace's legs is shrinking, and so the skin becomes loose and rough like a bird's. *cruribus* might be dative rather than ablative (Virg. *Aen.* 8. 467 f. 'mediisque residunt / aedibus' is more clearly local); yet there is some unreality about such debates (cf. Housman on Lucan 9. 715). *pellis* is not normally applied to human beings, and seems to be used proleptically of the tough new skin; cf. *epod.* 17. 21 f. 'fugit iuventas et verecundus color / reliquit ora pelle amicta lurida', Lucr. 6. 1194 f. (of the victims of the plague), Juv. 10. 192 'deformem pro cute pellem' (of an old man). In view of this last parallel Horace may also be hinting at his own physical deterioration (see next note); there is a touch of humour in the noun's emphatic position (cf. 3 *vates* n., 11 *superne*).

10. album : a conventional epithet of swans (Gow on Theoc. 25. 129,

Bömer on Ov. *met.* 2. 539); the adjective identifies the bird for the first time in the poem. It seems relevant that Horace was *canus* (2. 11. 5 n.); white hair, particularly poets', is sometimes compared with swans' plumage. Cf. Ar. *vesp.* 1064 f. κύκνου τε πολιώτεραί δὴ / αἴδ' ἐπανθοῦσιν τρίχες, Eur. *Her.* 110, 691 ff. παιᾶνας δ' ἐπὶ σοῖς μελά/θροις κύκνος ὡς γέρων ἀοι/δὸς πολιᾶν ἐκ γενύων / κελαδήσω, *Ba.* 1365, Ov. *met.* 2.373 f. (with Bömer's note), *trist.* 4. 8. 1 'iam mea cycneas imitantur tempora plumas', Horap. 2. 39 (of the Egyptians) γέροντα μουσικὸν βουλόμενοι σημῆναι κύκνον ζωγραφοῦσιν. οὗτος γὰρ ἡδύτατον μέλος ᾄδει γηράσκων.

mutor : a very common word in metamorphoses; cf. Virg. *ecl.* 8. 70 'carminibus Circe socios mutavit Ulixi', Bömer on Ov. *met.* 1. 1.

alitem : a grandiose word for a large bird, which emphasizes the all-important wings. Horace is not thinking of the mute swan but of the noisy 'whooper', still an occasional winter migrant to the Mediterranean area. This was associated with Oceanus and the rivers of the north; cf. Hes. *scut.* 316 κύκνοι ἀερσιπόται μεγάλ' ἤπυον (near Oceanus), Alcman 1. 100 f. (with Page's note), Eur. *Phaethon* 77 f. (Diggle) παγαῖς τ' ἐπ' Ὠκεάνου / μελιβόας κύκνος ἀχεῖ, Ar. *av.* 769 ff., Sen. *Ag.* 679, *RE* 2 A. 783. The whoop was extended in imagination to a beautiful song, particularly before the bird's death; cf. Aesch. *Ag.* 1444 ff. ἡ δέ τοι κύκνου δίκην / τὸν ὕστατον μέλψασα θανάσιμον γόον / κεῖται (with Fraenkel's note), Pl. *Phaed.* 84 e, Arist. *hist. an.* 615ᵇ2 ᾠδικοὶ δὲ καὶ περὶ τὰς τελευτὰς μάλιστα ᾄδουσιν . . . 5 φωνῇ γοώδει, Call. fr. 194. 46 ff. Yet some were sceptical even in the ancient world; cf. Ael. *var. hist.* 1. 14, Plin. *nat.* 10. 63 'olorum morte narratur flebilis cantus, falso, ut arbitror aliquot experimentis', Lucian, *electr.* 5 κρώζουσιν οὗτοι πάνυ ἄμουσον καὶ ἀσθενές, ὡς τοὺς κόρακας ἢ τοὺς κολοιοὺς Σειρῆνας εἶναι πρὸς αὐτούς. Cf. further 4. 3. 19 f., D'Arcy Thompson, *Birds*, pp. 179 ff., *RE* 2 A. 785 ff., Otto 104 f., Wilamowitz on Eur. *Her.* 110, Palmer on Ov. *epist.* 7. 2, Bömer on Ov. *fast.* 2. 110, W. G. Arnott, *G & R* 24, 1977. 149 ff. (the dirge of the whoopers).

The story of the singing swan was encouraged by the bird's connection with Apollo (16 n., D'Arcy Thompson, op. cit., p. 184), the Muses (Eur. *IT* 1104, Call. *h.* 4. 252), and perhaps Orpheus (Pl. *resp.* 620 a). Hence poets and other literary men are often compared or identified with swans; cf. 1. 6. 2 'Maeonii carminis alite', 4. 2. 25 ff. [above, p. 332], Leonidas, *anth. P.* 7. 19 (on Alcman), Virg. *ecl.* 9. 36 'argutos inter strepere anser olores', Antip. Sid. *anth. P.* 7. 30. 1 f. (on Anacreon), Eugenes, *anth. Pl.* 308. 2, Sidon. *epist.* 8. 11. 7, 9. 15. 1 vers. 32 (of Horace) 'Iapygisque verna cycnus Aufidi', Christodorus, *anth. P.* 2. 382 ff. Θήβης δ' Ὠγυγίης Ἑλικώνιος ἵστατο κύκνος / Πίνδαρος ἱμερόφωνος, ὃν ἀργυρότοξος Ἀπόλλων / ἔτρεφε, above, *album* n.

11. **superne** : for the short last syllable cf. Leo, *ALL* 10. 435 ff. The word (here contrasted with *cruribus*) is naturally used in accounts of hybrids, etc.; cf. *ars* 3 f. 'ut turpiter atrum / desinat in piscem mulier formosa superne', Hom. *Il.* 6. 181 πρόσθε λέων, ὄπιθεν δὲ δράκων, Praxilla 754. 2 παρθένε τὰν κεφαλάν, τὰ δ' ἔνερθε νύμφα, Lucr. 5. 905, Virg. *Aen.* 3. 426, Lucian, *ver. hist.* 1. 8 τὸ δὲ ἄνω γυναῖκες ἦσαν, Milton, *PL* 1. 462 f. 'upward man And downward fish'.

nascunturque : the verb is used of the sprouting of feathers or wings; cf. Ov. *met.* 5. 548 'vixque movet natas per inertia bracchia pennas', 11. 732. The Greek is πτεροφυῶ; cf. especially Pl. *Phaedr.* 251 c, Lucian, *Icar.* 10, Liban. *ep.* 109. 2 καὶ γὰρ εἰ πέτεσθαί με ἐθέλεις, πτερὰ μὲν οὐ φύσω, τῷ μὴ δύνασθαι δὲ ἀνιάσομαι καὶ μέμψομαί γε τὸν παρόντα χρόνον, ὅτι με μὴ δείκνυσιν ἕτερον Δαίδαλον, Milton, letter to Diodati, Sept. 1637 'πτεροφυῶ, et volare meditor: sed tenellis admodum adhuc pennis evehit se noster Pegasus'. Of course *nascuntur* is more poetical than 'sprout'; the word balances 7 *obibo* and has a hint of regeneration.

leves : contrasted with 9 *asperae*, also at the end of a line.

12. **per digitos umerosque** : Peerlkamp, who absurdly deleted the stanza, protested that the shoulders should come before the fingers. But elsewhere metamorphosis begins at the extremities (just as here the legs are mentioned first); cf. Lucian, *ver. hist.* 1. 8 ἀπὸ δὲ τῶν δακτύλων ἄκρων ἐξεφύοντο αὐταῖς οἱ κλάδοι καὶ μεστοὶ ἦσαν βοτρύων. H. Fuchs also objected that there should be a mention of the important *bracchia*, which turned into wings (*ANTIΔΩPON, Festschrift E. Salin*, 1962, pp. 155 f.). But *digitos umerosque* comprises *bracchia* (Bell 9), and for the shoulders cf. Ov. *met.* 11. 789 'utque novas umeris adsumpserat alas'.

plumae : the noun is reserved for the climax at the end of the sentence and the stanza. The feathers need not strike an entirely frivolous note, however grotesque their appearance here; cf. Pl. *Phaedr.* 246 d (on the wings of the soul) πέφυκεν ἡ πτεροῦ δύναμις τὸ ἐμβριθὲς ἄγειν ἄνω μετεωρίζουσα ᾗ τὸ τῶν θεῶν γένος οἰκεῖ, κεκοινώνηκε δέ πῃ μάλιστα τῶν περὶ τὸ σῶμα τοῦ θείου . . ., Plut. *Plat. quaest.* 1004 d ἦν (τὴν διαλογιστικὴν δύναμιν) οὐκ ἀπὸ τρόπου πτερὸν προσηγόρευσεν ὡς τὴν ψυχὴν ἀπὸ τῶν ταπεινῶν καὶ θνητῶν ἀναφέρουσαν, K. Thraede, *Grundzuge griechisch-römischer Brieftopik*, 1970, pp. 174 ff.

13. **Daedaleo** : the emphatic adjective implies a comparison with Horace's own felicitous craftsmanship, and mitigates the derogatory effect of *Icaro*. *daedalus* had already been naturalized in Roman poetry; cf. especially Lucr. 2. 505 f. 'Phoebeaque carmina chordis / daedala'.

notior : this reading suits the fame that is the subject of the poem;

cf. 19 'noscent Geloni', Bacch. 5. 29 f. (αἰετός) ἀρίγνω-/τος μετ' ἀνθρώποις ἰδεῖν. For the dry *notus* cf. 2. 2. 6, 3. 4. 70, etc.; for the comparative cf. Prop. 2. 13. 8 (in a similar context) 'tunc ego sim Inachio notior arte Lino', 3. 34. 88, Mart. 12. 52. 12. Yet it is an awkward circumstance that Icarus was famous for his fall rather than his flight (Bentley); cf. 4. 2. 2 ff. 'ceratis ope Daedalea / nititur pennis vitreo daturus / nomina ponto', Ov. *trist.* 1. 1. 89 f., 3. 4. 22, Sen. *Herc. O.* 689 f., *RE* 9. 985 ff. As the first of these passages refers to the dangers of imitating Pindar, one would naturally suppose that a similar point was being made here (the topic may have been traditional of poets); it is a further embarrassment that *notus* can mean not just 'famous' but 'notorious'. The general drift of the stanza (as of the poem) must be serious: one recalls that Icarus gave his name to a sea, and Ovid tells how fishermen and ploughmen looked up in wonder at his flight (*met.* 8. 217 ff.). But at the same time there seems to be an ironic undercurrent: Horace is wryly aware of the danger of appealing to the general judgement of mankind.

Other proposals are unsatisfactory. The well-supported variant *ocior* gives an impossible hiatus, and the speed of flight is immaterial. For Bentley's *tutior* cf. 3. 4. 36 'inviolatus' (see next note), Ov. *trist.* 3. 4. 21; yet in high poetry the ablative of comparison would more naturally suggest that Icarus himself was *tutus* (cf. 1. 19. 6 'marmore purius' with note, 1. 24. 13, 3. 9. 8, 3. 12. 8, 3. 13. 1). Peerlkamp's *audacior* gives an unparalleled elision (vol. i, p. xli); though the adjective suits poets well (Brink on *ars* 10), it is not directly relevant in a discussion of posthumous fame. Withof proposed *cautior*, but we do not expect a poet with such grandiose ambitions to play safe (a point that can be used to some extent also against *tutior*).

14. **visam . . . :** for dangerous journeys to the ends of the earth cf. 3. 4. 30 ff. 'insanientem navita Bosphorum / temptabo et urentis harenas / litoris Assyrii viator. / . . . visam pharetratos Gelonos / et Scythicum inviolatus amnem', 1. 22. 5 n. The verb suggests the wonder of the explorer.

The ambition for world-wide fame is attested as early as Alcman (above, p. 332), and becomes a commonplace with Hellenistic and Roman poets. Ovid assigns such glory to Callimachus (*am.* 1. 15. 13 'Battiades semper toto cantabitur orbe'); as the other writers in this elegy are characterized by references to their works, it looks as if the claim originated with Callimachus himself. Aratus may be reversing the topic when he teases a fellow poet for his use as a text-book in barbarian schools (*anth. P.* 11. 437 αἰάζω Διότιμον ὃς ἐν πέτρῃσι κάθηται / Γαργαρέων, παισὶν βῆτα καὶ ἄλφα λέγων); this epigram is adapted by Horace himself when he mocks his book of epistles for its provincial readership (*epist.* 1. 20. 13 and 18, significantly in the *sphragis*). For other Roman instances of the commonplace cf. Enn. *ann.* 3 f. 'latos per populos res atque poemata nostra / . . . cluebunt', Catull. 95. 5 'Zmyrna †canas [suas?] Satrachi penitus mittetur ad undas', Tullius Laurea 9 Morel, Ov. *am.* 1. 15. 29 f. 'Gallus et Hesperiis et Gallus notus Eois / et sua cum Gallo nota Lycoris erit' (with *ars* 3. 537 perhaps a reminiscence of Gallus's own sonorous elegies), Virg. *ecl.* 8. 9, Prop. 2. 7. 17 f. 'hinc etenim tantum meruit mea gloria nomen, / gloria ad hibernos lata Borysthenidas', Ov. *am.* 1. 3. 25 f., *trist.* 4. 9. 19 ff., 4. 10. 128, Mart. 1. 1. 2, 5. 13. 3, 7. 88. 5 (he would rather be sung in Gaul than by those who drink the Nile), 8. 61. 3 ff., 9. 84. 5 f., 10. 9. 3 f., 11. 3. 3 ff., 12. 2 (3). 1.

gementis : cf. Hom. *Il.* 23. 230 Θρηίκιον κατὰ πόντον· ὁ δ' ἔστενεν οἴδματι θύων, Soph. *Aj.* 675, *Ant.* 592, Virg. *Aen.* 3. 555. The participle would remind an ancient reader of the supposed derivation of *Bosphorus* (cf. Virg. *georg.* 3. 223 for the *gemitus* of bulls); for a similar point cf. Stat. *silv.* 4. 3. 57 'maestum pelagus gementis Helles'.

15. Syrtisque : the southern boundary of Mediterranean civilization, balancing the Bosphorus in the north; they are mentioned elsewhere in the commonplace about dangerous journeys (1. 22. 5, 2. 6. 3, Ov. *am.* 2. 16. 21). The Gaetuli lived south-west of Carthage, but their name is sometimes applied to the Syrtes; cf. Virg. *Aen.* 4. 40 f. with Pease, 5. 192 with Servius.

canorus ales : *ales* must be a noun when combined with an adjective; therefore Horace is still referring to a bird and not just to a winged man. There is elegance rather than awkwardness in the repetition of 10 *alitem*; now the case is nominative and the emphasis is put on *canorus* (Horace's music, like the swan's, is appreciated at his death). The adjective suits a swan well (10 n., Prop. 2. 34. 83 f. 'canorus . . . olor', Virg. *Aen.* 7. 700); it also suggests melodious verses (*epist.* 2. 2. 76, *ars* 322). There seems to be a contrast between the tuneful cry of the high-flying swan and the deep boom of the sea below (14 *gementis*).

16. Hyperboreosque campos : the Hyperboreans are mentioned in this emphatic position because of their remote and inaccessible situation; cf. *h. Hom.* 7. 29 ἢ ἐς Ὑπερβόρεους ἢ ἑκαστέρω, Pind. *I.* 6. 23 καὶ πέραν Νείλοιο παγᾶν καὶ δι' Ὑπερβορέους, Catull. 115. 6, Juv. 6. 470, Cook 2. 1. 493 ff. In particular one may compare Pind. *P.* 10. 29 f. ναυσὶ δ' οὔτε πεζὸς ἰών κεν εὕροις / ἐς Ὑπερβορέων ἀγῶνα θαυμαστὰν ὁδόν, followed by a description of Perseus's journey there (presumably by flying); the point of the myth might be that the victor can metaphorically reach this fortunate land if he is carried there, like Theognis's Cyrnus, on the wings of poetry (A. Köhnken, *Die Funktion des*

Mythos bei Pindar, 1971, pp. 158 ff.). The country is often regarded as a resting-place for the dead, but in view of the further travels in the next stanza Horace cannot be emphasizing this aspect. It is more important that the Hyperboreans are associated with Apollo and his swans; cf. Alcaeus 307 c (a prose paraphrase from Himerius) ὁ δὲ ἐπιβὰς ἐπὶ τῶν ἁρμάτων ἐφῆκε τοὺς κύκνους ἐς Ὑπερβορέους πέτεσθαι . . ., Hecataeus of Abdera, *FGrH* 264 F 12, Ael. *nat. anim.* 11. 1 (a scene at the Hyperborean temple of Apollo) ἐνταῦθά τοι καὶ οἱ κύκνοι συναναμέλπουσιν ὁμορροθοῦντες καὶ οὐδαμῶς οὐδαμῇ ἀπηχὲς καὶ ἀπῳδὸν ἐκεῖνοι μελῳδοῦντες, ἀλλ' ὥσπερ οὖν ἐκ τοῦ χορολέκτου τὸ ἐνδόσιμον λαβόντες καὶ τοῖς σοφισταῖς τῶν ἱερῶν μελῶν τοῖς ἐπιχωρίοις συνᾴσαντες, Mart. Cap. 9. 927 'unde enim . . . cycnos Hyperboreos citharae cantus adducit?', *RE* 9. 275.

17. me . . . me: the two emphatic pronouns in the penultimate stanza balance *non ego . . . non ego* in the second stanza.

Colchus: the Colchian Phasis was often regarded as the eastern extremity of the known world; cf. Pind. *I.* 2. 41, Eur. *Andr.* 651, *trag. adesp.* 559 N. εἰς Φᾶσιν ἔνθα ναυσὶν ἔσχατος δρόμος, Pl. *Phaed.* 109 b μέχρι Ἡρακλειῶν στηλῶν ἀπὸ Φάσιδος, Prop. 3. 22. 11, Housman on Manil. 5. 45. Here the conventional association of the country is maintained though Horace is talking of flying and not of sailing.

qui dissimulat metum . . .: for Dacian wars cf. vol. i, p. xxxiii; for the fearfulness of Rome's enemies (a commonplace of patriotic discourse) cf. 2. 13. 18 f., *epist.* 2. 1. 256; for the toughness of Marsian soldiers (associated with Mars) cf. 1. 2. 39 f. Horace is concentrating on the north, where the swans come from; for his motif of fame among barbarian peoples see above, pp. 332 f., Pind. *I.* 6. 24 f. (after mentioning the Hyperboreans) οὐδ' ἔστιν οὕτω βάρβαρος οὔτε παλίγγλωσσος πόλις, / ἅτις οὐ Πηλέος ἀΐει κλέος ἥρωος. He adds a modern note by associating the extent of his fame with the limits, actual or potential, of the Roman empire (for such themes see F. Christ, op. cit. [2. 9. 22 n.], pp. 29 ff.) ; cf. especially Cic. *Arch.* 23 'cupere debemus quo hominum nostrorum tela pervenerint, eodem gloriam famamque penetrare', Ov. *met.* 15. 877 f. (also a *sphragis*) 'quaque patet domitis Romana potentia terris / ore legar populi' (cf. also the reference to Octavian's wars in the *sphragis* at Virg. *georg.* 4. 560 ff.). On the other hand, in the last poem of the third book Horace concentrates on the extent of the empire in time rather than in space (3. 30. 7 ff.).

19. noscent: note the characteristic variation of construction after *visam*. The inchoative verb does not suit the swan well (13 *notior* is much easier), and *discent* below confirms that *me* refers to the poet rather than the bird. It should also be observed that *noscent* suggests less detailed study than *discent* (applied to the Roman west); cf. Stat. *Theb.* 12. 814 f. (of the epic itself) 'iam te magnanimus dignatur noscere Caesar; / Itala iam studio discit memoratque iuventus'.

Geloni : the name is semi-legendary at this date (2. 9. 23 n.); like *Colchus* it gives a romantic association to contemporary frontier-policy. For genuine Roman interest in the Scythians cf. vol. i, p. xxxiv.

peritus : the adjective goes further than *discet* and implies specialist knowledge. It is a prosaic word found only once in Virgil and Ovid, never in Lucretius, Catullus, Tibullus, Valerius, Silius (Axelson 102). It is here used proleptically and humorously not of the Roman settlers but of the native inhabitants.

20. Hiber : the Spaniards and Gauls as western peoples complete the boxing of the compass. The Greek name is used as a poeticism for *Hiberus*; as *Hiber* also suggests the River Ebro, it makes a good pair with *Rhodanique potor*.

Rhodanique potor : the phrase is modelled on Greek compounds in -πότης (*epist.* 1. 19. 3 'quae scribuntur aquae potoribus'); here the vigorous noun suggests that the barbarians took great swigs of the Rhone (hence there is a piquant contrast with *peritus*). It was an old poetic way of identifying the inhabitants of a country to mention the river that they drank; cf. 3. 10. 1, 4. 15. 21, Hom. *Il.* 2. 825 πίνοντες ὕδωρ μέλαν Αἰσήποιο, Pind. *O.* 6. 85 f., Call. *h.* 1. 40 f., Virg. *ecl.* 1. 62, Ov. *fast.* 4. 68 with Bömer's note, Crinagoras, *anth. P.* 9. 430. 2, *anth. Pl.* 61. 6, Sidon. *epist.* 1. 8. 1 'bibitor Araricus', 4. 17. 1 'potor Mosellae Tiberim ructas', *carm.* 5. 479, Norden, *Kl. Schr.*, pp. 184 ff., *Thes.l.L.* 2. 1964. 39 ff.

21. inani funere : the phrase is intended to suggest κενοτάφιον (as if that meant a burying rather than a place of burial). Here it is not the body that is missing but something more essential (ps.-Pl. *Axioch.* 365 e τὸ ὑπολειφθὲν σῶμα ... οὐκ ἔστιν ὁ ἄνθρωπος, Cic. *rep.* 6. 26); Horace is using the language of mystical philosophers to describe the 'immortality' of a poet (cf. Stat. *silv.* 2. 7. 110 'terras despicis et sepulcra rides'). The meaning 'useless' is also present to balance *supervacuos* below (see note); cf. *Anacreontea* 30. 12 τί δὲ γῇ χέειν μάταια;, Virg. *Aen.* 6. 885 f., Ov. *met.* 2. 340 f. with Bömer's note, *carm. epig.* 474. 10, 475. 2, 6. But this implication is merely secondary; when Peerlkamp proposed *inanes* (cf. Prud. *cath.* 11. 34 'venerans inanes nenias') he destroyed Horace's central point, that his real self would be found not in the grave but in his poems.

neniae : cf. 2. 1. 38 n.; possibly the repetition of the word is intended to link the end of the book with the beginning. Horace is thinking of the excessive lamentations of hired mourners (*praeficae*);

cf. Brink on *ars* 431 ff., M. Durry, *Éloge funèbre d'une matrone romaine*, 1950, p. xii.

22. turpes : both 'unseemly' and 'unsightly'; cf. Ov. *ars* 1. 534 'nec facta est lacrimis turpior illa suis', *XII tab.* ap. Cic. *leg.* 2. 59 'mulieres genas ne radunto neve lessum funeris ergo habento', Pease on Virg. *Aen.* 4. 673.

querimoniae : an archaic word used several times in Horace (Brink on *ars* 75). Note the alliteration of whimpering nasals in 21 f.

23. compesce clamorem : Horace once more addresses Maecenas directly. He is alluding to the *conclamatio*; cf. Prop. 1. 17. 23, 2. 13. 28, 4. 7. 24, Virg. *Aen.* 4. 674, Serv. *Aen.* 6. 218 'post ultimam conclamationem comburebantur', *RE* 3. 347 f., Blümner 483, Bömer on Ov. *fast.* 3. 560. The peremptory adjurations to restraint are derived from the end of the ritual lament; cf. Lucr. 3. 955 'compesce querellas', Prop. 4. 11. 1 with Fedeli's note, Sen. *Herc. O.* 1427 'compesce voces', 1674, 1832, Stat. *silv.* 2. 6. 103, 5. 1. 179, Lucianus, *anth. P.* 7. 308. 3, anon. ibid. 7. 667. 3, Lattimore 217 ff., Alexiou 226.

24. supervacuos honores : the adjective is first found here and in Livy as an equivalent of the metrically intractable *supervacaneos*. Horace is referring to the monument itself (cf. Aesch. *cho.* 511 τίμημα τύμβου, Virg. *Aen.* 10. 493 'honos tumuli'), not to the honours paid to it; he is giving a new direction to a commonplace that would normally be applied to the pointlessness or extravagance of burial in general (Epicurus, fr. 578, Maecen. ap. Sen. *epist.* 92. 35 'nec tumulum curo: sepelit natura relictos', Tac. *Germ.* 27. 2 'monumentorum arduum et operosum honorem'). For his thought cf. Porph. ad loc. 'supervacua est enim sepultura ei qui immortalitatem videtur per carmina consequi', Simonides cited above (p. 337), Thuc. 2. 43. 2 τὸν ἀγήρων ἔπαινον ἐλάμβανον καὶ τὸν τάφον ἐπισημότατον οὐκ ἐν ᾧ κεῖνται μᾶλλον ἀλλ' ἐν ᾧ ἡ δόξα αὐτῶν ἀείμνηστος καταλείπεται, Sen. *Herc. O.* 1826 f., Lucan 8. 798 f., Plin. *epist.* 9. 19. 6 'impensa monumenti supervacua est: memoria enim nostri durabit si vita meruimus'. He appropriately ends the book with the moral maxim that the things men strive for are largely unnecessary (cf. 1. 38. 1 ff., 3. 1. 45 ff.); yet as suits a *sphragis*, his modesty about material reward is the result of a just pride in his literary achievement.

INDEX NOMINVM

INDEX VERBORVM

INDEX RERVM